10,000
GARDEN QUESTIONS
Answered by 20 Experts

10,000
Garden Questions

ANSWERED BY 20 EXPERTS

THIRD EDITION

MARJORIE J. DIETZ
EDITOR

•

Originally edited by F. F. Rockwell

*New drawings for the third edition
by Reisie Lonette*

VOLUME I

An American Garden Guild Book
DOUBLEDAY & COMPANY, INC.   GARDEN CITY, NEW YORK

Contents

Introduction
To the Third Edition

IT IS with satisfaction and pride that the publishers and editors present this new, completely revised third edition of *10,000 Garden Questions Answered*. For three decades, *10,000 Garden Questions Answered* has served hundreds of thousands of home gardeners as the "family Bible" of garden information. Young gardeners in household upon household and in every section of the country have relied on it as a primary source of gardening knowledge and inspiration. Now with this completely up-dated edition, containing numerous new illustrations, it is hoped that another generation of gardeners as well as former friends and devotees of previous editions will find it even more pertinent and helpful than in the past.

As with previous editions of *10,000 Garden Questions Answered*, the mountains of diversified gardening queries and their answers have been separated into 16 general sections, as follows:

The botanical names of plants, in this revised third edition, have been up-dated to conform as nearly as possible to the International Code for the Nomenclature of Cultivated Plants. Beginners who balk at the use of botanical plant names can take comfort from the prevalence of common names of plants which also appear. Unfortunately, there is no recognized authority for common plant names, but the Editors have been as consistent as is possible in an area where such confusion abounds.

F. F. Rockwell, the dean of American garden writers and home gardener *par exellence,* was the first editor of *10,000 Garden Questions Answered.* The following excerpts, which are from his original Introduction, are as relevant today as when he first wrote them and require no further embellishment or explanation:

"The preparation of *10,000 Garden Questions Answered* was originally undertaken in response to numerous requests from readers of *The Home Garden Magazine.* It seemed worthwhile to present, in some organized and permanent form, the wealth of information which the answers to these questions convey. Our purpose was to make this data available to the reader in a form that would enable him to refer to it quickly, and find readily, all the information on any particular subject. The most practical method of obtaining this objective, it seemed to us, was to arrange this material in general categories or sections.

"For each of these sections an introduction which gives general information on the subject covered has been prepared. The introductions are *based upon the questions most generally asked* concerning the subject discussed. In other words, these questions, instead of being answered individually, have been answered in a composite reply that presents the general principles involved and provides a background for the more specific questions which follow.

"This treatment has two distinct advantages. In the first place, it enables the reader to get much more from the answers to the individual questions; in the second, it has saved a great amount of space.

Actually, the *answers* to more than 13,000 questions are contained in the present volume.

"The advantages of having questions answered by experts widely experienced in many lines are obvious. Too often such answers are compiled from outdated reference books. The answers in this volume are by persons who are actually *doing* the things they write about. Many of them are recognized internationally as authorities in their respective fields. At the same time, with few exceptions, their daily work brings them into direct contact with the problems of home gardeners the country over.

"With some fifty different persons contributing information of one sort or another, it is inevitable that many differences of opinion have arisen. In so far as possible, the recommendations and suggestions made on any specific subject have been brought into harmony by correspondence or discussion. There are cases where this has not been possible. The result is honest differences of opinion such as would be forthcoming on almost any garden question that might be asked of any group of experts—differences similar to those that would be found in every field of human endeavor, in any science or art, and horticulture partakes of both.

"Our aim has been to present the home gardener with *practical* information in readily available form, concerning his own personal problems. To the extent that this has been accomplished, we will have succeeded in making the kind of book we set out to create."

Marjorie J. Dietz

What Is YOUR Question?

(Suggestions as to how to use this book most effectively)

To get from these pages the information you wish, most completely and in the shortest time, read carefully the following paragraphs. They explain, first, how this book is put together; and, second, the definite steps to take in finding the answer to a specific problem, or to one so general in character that it might not be possible to locate it through the Index.

Organization Plan

There are 16 main divisions or sections, covering Soils and Fertilizers; Planning and Landscaping; Ornamental Plants and Their Culture; Trees, Shrubs, and Vines; Bulbs, Tubers, and Corms; Roses; Perennials; Annuals and Biennials; Lawns and Turf Areas; The Home Vegetable Garden; Home-grown Fruits; House Plants; Plant Troubles and Their Control; Weeds; Regional Garden Problems and Sources for Further Information. The sources section covers Books, State Agricultural Experiment Stations, Horticultural and Special Plant Societies, Botanical Gardens, Arboreta and Public Gardens and Sources for Plants and Seeds.

Each of these sections is organized along the following lines:

1. A general introduction, giving basic information about the subject concerned. (The introduction for Soils and Fertilizers, for instance, describes the function of the soil in connection with plant growth, different types of soil, soil acidity, the various nutrients essential to plant growth, the part which humus plays in the soil, and so on.)

2. Following the introduction, the questions, in most sections, are arranged in the following order:

What to Grow   Winter Protection
Soils and Fertilizers   Propagation
Culture   Specific Plants
                           (*In Alphabetical Order*)

Use of Index

In most instances any specific question can be located through the use of the Index.

1. Formulate your question in your own mind as definitely as possible. (It will be helpful to write it down on paper.)
2. Pick out the KEY WORD in the question. (For instance, it might be "How should I train *tomatoes?*" "How can I *graft* a good variety of apple on a wild tree?" or "What is a good *perennial* to grow in the *shade?*"
3. Then look up the key word ("tomato," "graft," "perennial" or "shade") in the Index. Under this item, in the Index, you will probably find several references. One of these (example: "tomato, staking") may indicate exactly what you are looking for, and you can then turn at once to the specific question you have in mind.

More General Questions

The question in your mind may, however, be of such a nature that you do not know what to look for in the Index to locate it. Suppose, for example, that you have seen somewhere, growing high on a wall, a vine-like plant with hydrangea-like flowers, and you would like to know what it is. A search through the section on "Vines—Perennial" should reveal that it is the climbing hydrangea (*Hydrangea petiolaris*).

It is recommended that, in looking up questions on any general subject—such as fertilizers, lawns, vegetables, fruits—*the introduction be read in full first*. Here you will find in text form the answers to many questions, some of which may not reappear in the questions and answers. Familiarity with the introduction will also help materially in augmenting the information to be gained from the answers to specific questions.

In the answers to some questions the reader is referred to his State Experiment Station. A list of these stations is given on page 723, and a list of Botanical Gardens and other public gardens to visit is given on page 728.

The list of books and bulletins (page 711) will guide the reader to full and detailed information on many different garden subjects. All of these page references are in Volume II.

THE EDITORS OF
10,000 Garden Questions Answered

MARJORIE J. DIETZ, a graduate of the Ambler School of Horticulture, was associated with *Flower Grower* and *The Home Garden* magazines, first as Managing Editor, then as Editor. She is the author of many gardening articles and several books, including *The Concise Encyclopedia of Favorite Wild Flowers* and *Landscaping and the Small Garden.* She is Associate Editor of *Plants & Gardens,* a quarterly of the Brooklyn Botanic Garden.

MARCUS BAINRIDGE, JR. has traveled extensively in this country and abroad in pursuit of his nursery vocation and gardening hobby. Flowering shrubs are his favorites but there is hardly a plant he does not enjoy growing.

R. MILTON CARLETON has written on both the popular and technical aspects of horticulture. His books include *Vegetables for Today's Garden* and *The Small Garden.* He is Research Director for *Growth Systems, Inc.* and is Garden Editor for *Chicago Today.*

ELIZABETH C. HALL, Senior Librarian of The Horticultural Society of New York, is a graduate of Radcliffe College and of the Ambler School of Horticulture. She was a member of the staff of The New York Botanical Garden, serving as Librarian, Associate Curator of Education and Instructor in the children's gardencraft program.

BEBE MILES has contributed many articles to garden magazines on varied aspects of home gardening, with the major emphasis being on her favorite subjects: bulbs and native plants. She is the author of *The Wonderful World of Bulbs.*

MARGARET C. OHLANDER, garden editor and writer, is a graduate of Cornell University. For several years she was the managing editor of *Flower Grower* magazine, and continued in the same position when it became *The Home Garden* magazine. Her special interests include annual and perennial plants, shrubs and house plants.

ROBERT W. SCHERY, Director of The Lawn Institute, is a nationally recognized authority on turf. Major research projects have included tropical floristics and economic botany as well as subjects of interest to home gardeners. He is the author of *A Perfect Lawn*.

GEORGE L. SLATE, Professor of Pomology Emeritus, New York State Agricultural Experiment Station (Cornell University), Geneva, New York, is a small fruit breeder and originator of important raspberries, blackberries and strawberries. He is the author of many articles in horticultural publications.

HELEN VAN PELT WILSON is the author of numerous garden books and a respected writer on many phases of home gardening. African-violets and geraniums are two of her favorite plants. One of her most recent books is *House Plants Are for Pleasure*.

CYNTHIA WESTCOTT is a plant pathologist who is well known for her interest in roses. She has written many articles for major gardening publications and is the author of several reference manuals, including *The Gardener's Bug Book* and *Plant Disease Handbook*. One of her most popular books is *Anyone Can Grow Roses*.

Other horticultural authorities who helped in the preparation of the first edition and its subsequent revision are the following: F. F. Rockwell, Montague Free, T. H. Everett, R. C. Allen, Robert S. Lemmon, P. J. McKenna, W. E. Thwing, Alex Laurie, C. H. Connors, T. A. Weston, Esther C. Grayson, Helen S. Hull, Louis Pyenson, O. Wesley Davidson, Francis C. Coulter, Alex Cumming, Henry E. Downer, Kathleen N. Marriage, John Melady, H. Dewey Mohr, H. Stuart Ortloff, Hildegard Schneider, P. J. Van Melle, Thomas A. Williams, Paul Work, and J. H. Clark.

Also John H. Beale, George A. Buchanan, George E. Burkhardt, L. C. Chadwick, A. S. Colby, Charles F. Doney, E. V. Hardenburg, D. C. Kiplinger, Stuart Longmuir, Harriet K. Morse, George D. Oberle, E. L. Reber, Roy P. Rogers, Kenneth D. Smith, Nancy Ruzicka Smith, John V. Watkins, Robert E. Weidner, Natalie Gomez and John Wingert.

ARTISTS who have prepared illustrations for the first and second editions are: George L. Hollrock, Pauline W. Kreutzfeldt, Helen Reddy, Carl Sigman, William Ward, Eva Melady, Tabea Hofmann, H. B. Raymore, Natalie Harlan Davis, Frederick Rockwell, Esther C. Grayson, and Katherine Burton. New drawings for the third edition were made by Reisie Lonette.

10,000
GARDEN QUESTIONS
Answered by 20 Experts

1
Soils and Fertilizers

BEFORE TRYING to understand soil, stop thinking in such outmoded terms as "the dirt under your feet" or "common as dirt." Far from being common, soil is perhaps the most complex substance with which man must work to stay alive. Without it, there would be no plants—his only source of the starches and sugars that are the fuels on which all living animals run.

The homeowner interested in gardening, unlike the farmer, does not make selection of soil his first concern, and few homes are purchased because they happen to have good soil under them. This vital substance for growing plants is not even considered until long after the purchase contract has been signed. It becomes of concern only when the owner becomes interested in gardening.

As a result, millions of prospective gardeners find themselves with stubborn clay or dry, porous sands rather than an ideal garden soil—a mellow loam rich in organic matter. One British authority described that ideal soil as one so loose and friable that an arm could be thrust into it up to the elbow. Most American gardeners would be happy with a soil into which they could thrust a hand up to the wrist!

A Test That Determines Soil Type

All too often, gardeners try to guess what is in their soil and—guess wrong. The only way to be sure is to make a wash test. Light sandy soils that contain little clay are easy to test. Heavier soils with a high clay content are difficult because of the strong electrical attraction of acid clay particles for lime. (There are alkaline clays but most are acid.) The bond between clay and lime can be broken by adding 2 tablespoons of a common fertilizer—nitrate of soda—to the test.

To make the test: Begin with a clean half-gallon Mason jar or other round glass container. Add half a cup of soil to the jar and pour in enough water to half fill it. Screw the lid on tightly and swirl the water around rapidly for about a minute. Let it settle. Repeat this swirling several times. Next, allow the water to stand until it is clear. Clay particles are extremely fine and may take a week to settle.

When the water has cleared, the various-sized particles will be in layers. On top will be the clay particles and on the bottom the larger bits of mineral matter such as sand and fine gravel. Between them, there is a layer of silt.

Importance of Organic Material

Since organic matter makes up less than 5 per cent of the volume of most soils, it is not conspicuous in wash tests, yet in comparison with the pure mineral components, it is far more important. Actually, no mixture of clay, sand, and silt can be called a true soil unless it contains some organic matter. In soils, organic matter has two important roles. The first of these is mechanical—as an absorbent and adsorbent agent to soak up solutions of plant nutrients such as nitrogen, phosphorus, and potash. It also serves as a reservoir for moisture, freeing the passageways between soil grains so air can enter freely.

By separating soil particles, organic matter helps form the desirable "crumb" structure that makes soil friable and easy to work. It also has an electrical attraction for the microscopically fine particles of clay, attracting them like flies to honey. This effect helps loosen heavy clay loam so it is more workable and able to contain the air vital to plant growth.

The second role of organic matter is to provide a home for the billions of microorganisms that exist in any true soil. Pick up a handful of loam from a garden and you will hold in your hand more living organisms than there are human beings on earth. Until the gardener understands that soil is alive, he cannot appreciate why he must add organic matter, why these tiny bits of matter are vital to proper feeding of plants, and why without them, the addition of fertilizer to soils would be all but wasted.

The most important function of these microorganisms is to attack the remains of plants such as roots and buried trash, as well as added organic substances, and break them down into simpler forms that living plants can use for food. Plants are no more capable of dining off the dead residues of last year's crop than they are of eating a hamburger. Without teeth or a digestive system similar to that of animals, they can only absorb nutrients in the form of a soup—a solution of nutrients that have been predigested for them by bacteria.

This process of predigestion may take place in stages, with one species of soil organism doing the preliminary breaking down of plant protein, for example, into amino acids, with a third reducing them to ammonia. Since only acid-soil plants are able to use ammonia directly, this must be attacked by a fourth group which produces nitrate nitrogen, a compound most plants can absorb directly through their roots.

There is another way in which bacteria and other soil organisms enter into the nutritional aspect of growing plants. Most gardeners feel that when they add fertilizers to soil, these materials directly enter plant roots and are consumed completely. This might be true if root hairs filled practically every minute chink in the soil, but such is not the case. The roots of many plants are in contact with a small fraction of 1 per cent of the volume of soil through which they penetrate. If there is any free water between the grains of soil, fertilizers dissolved in this water are pulled downward by the force of gravity and are lost in drainage channels.

Bacteria, fungi, and other soil organisms, however, are plants that need the same food elements as do higher plants with green leaves. Instead of allowing excess fertilizer to escape, they absorb it and use it for their own growth. Since these soil organisms do not live long— at the most a few days—when they die the food they absorbed is released to feed plants that have already used up the fertilizer the gardener applied days before.

A gardener—faced with the problem of soil unsuited to growing most plants—has two alternatives. Both will call for the use of organic matter. The first solution is the more simple—adapt the plants to the soil by choosing those that can survive under existing conditions. For example, he may want to garden at a summer home where sandy soil makes certain plants impossible to grow. Yet there are hundreds of species that thrive near salt water, both in tropical and temperate climates. Away from the spray there are shrubs, trees, and vines that can grow in sandy soil. His one problem will be the constant addition of organic matter which disappears rapidly in sandy soils. Even these tolerant species of plants must somehow be provided with the elements it provides.

A second alternative is to adapt the soil to the plants that he really wants to grow; in short—produce topsoil. A great deal of nonsense is written about the aeons needed to build an inch or two of black loam. True, in nature this is a slow process in which decaying leaves and plant wastes must work downward, with a slow accumulation of microorganisms, all modified by weather and other phenomena.

When, however, a gardener must work over a relatively small area, he can modify a heavy clay loam into an acceptable garden soil in a single year. Again, the solution is the incorporation of that magic ingredient of all good soils—organic matter. What can he use?

Provided it contains some fibrous material that has relative permanence in contact with soil, any form of organic matter will produce results. A substance such as dried blood, valuable as it is as the best organic fertilizer available, is worthless as a producer of the type of fibrous residue needed to build soil. Some substance such as lignin or cellulose is necessary to provide the long-lasting, porous remains that soil needs for aeration.

When the material applied is already partially decayed, then not only is time saved, but the chance of plant injury is reduced. When fresh plant wastes and green manures are turned under in the soil or added to the compost pile, there is a period when active fermentation takes place, releasing more carbon dioxide than roots can use if growing at the time, or than bacteria can tolerate in the compost pile. This is an important reason for composting, of which more later.

Even when it has gone through a preliminary decomposition, an application of organic matter can be improved by fertilizer additions in twice the amount recommended for the crops to be grown. Bacteria, working on plant wastes in soil, demand so much nitrogen, for example, that they often cause plants to turn yellow because of the lack of this vital growth element. Fertilizing prevents this.

A compost pile is little more than a huge culture of microorganisms. They begin the process by which organic wastes are converted to a long-lasting form that will improve soil for periods as long as half a century. Since these organisms are plants, they require the same foods as plants with green leaves. In addition, they must have an outside source of starches and sugars for energy, since they cannot make their own. Instead, they extract these from plant wastes.

Available Composting Materials

Peat moss: Peat moss derived from sphagnum bogs is perhaps the most universally available source of humus today. It is an excellent amendment for a variety of soils and kinds of plants and gardens. A neglected yet valid use for peat moss is adding it to the compost pile, not for further breakdown, which it doesn't need, but for the purpose of picking up soil organisms not present in peat bogs. At the same time, it helps aerate the compost pile. Peat moss has a low nutritive value, but it improves both clay and sandy soils and also serves as a home for soil organisms. Sphagnum peat, usually sold in 6-ft. cubic bales, is an attractive brown in color, of a crumbly texture, and easy to handle. It is acid. Many domestic peats are derived from decayed reeds and sedges. They are fine-textured and dark to reddish-brown in color. For home gardeners who can buy it in bulk, sedge peat, while not as valuable as sphagnum peat moss, is useful as a soil amendment.

Sewage sludge: As a soil amendment, air-dried sewage sludge can be had for the hauling from most local treatment plants. Processed sludge has distinct disadvantages as a lawn fertilizer, for which purpose it is widely sold. Composting improves the processed form for lawn use. Raw sludge has one bad quality if used on the vegetable garden. It can carry the organisms of amoebic dysentery unless exposed to freezing for an entire winter. Composting also kills these organisms.

Ground corn cobs: These are higher in sugars than most composting materials, which means they will need extra nitrogen to use up this excess. Otherwise, corn cobs can cause a build-up of fungi, some of which can be harmful.

Spent mushroom manure: Near some cities, mushroom growers will sell the worn-out mushroom soil which contains more than half of decayed manure. Like peat moss, it is low in nutrients, since the mushrooms have used these as food, but otherwise it is an ideal soil amendment. An advantage is that composting for use in mushroom beds has destroyed weed seeds.

Fallen leaves: Although highly touted as a source of plant food, leaves are generally a poor source of nutrients but they do become a source of humus. (Before a leaf is shed by a tree, all the available plant food it contains is withdrawn into the woody trunk and twigs.) Leaves are largely fiber, and for this reason improve soil. Leafmold, which results from the slow decay of fallen leaves, becomes more nutritive in the process because it contains the remains of dead microorganisms and other accumulated substances.

Weeds: Until they have set seeds, weeds are a good source of composting material. If you must compost weeds of high seed content, you had best make a separate pile and leave it for a year before using.

Lawn clippings: Lawn clippings are unusually rich in nutrients compared with other green matter because only the most active part, the growing tip of the blade, is removed in mowing. The clippings decay quite fast in the compost pile.

Animal manures: They were once the only source of fertility for gardens. This type of fertilizer has its advantages in that in addition to supplying some plant nutrients, humus and desirable bacteria are also added to the soil. The humus-forming value of manure is increased when it is combined with straw or a coarse grade of peat moss, often found with poultry manures.

The availability of animal manures today differs from region to region. In rural areas which often border suburban developments, there can be ample supplies of both cow and horse manures. Numerous riding stables exist today in both urban and suburban areas. One caution: Some riding stable proprietors, mostly in cities, heavily treat the manure with disinfectants and deodorizing chemicals, which are toxic to plants. Such treated manure should be composted in a separate pile before being applied to the soil. Test the composted manure before spreading by planting tomato seeds in it. If it is still toxic, the seeds may germinate, but will die quickly.

Green manure: The use of cover crops to be plowed under as green manure is often recommended, but it generally is impractical except in the vegetable plot. There, winter rye (the grain, not rye grass) can be sown whenever an area becomes empty of crops. It will grow in fall and even in winter when temperatures are above freezing. After it has been tilled into the soil in spring (using additional fertilizer) a month must elapse. This limits green manuring to areas where late crops are to be sown, or the areas that will lie fallow for a season.

Sawdust and wood chips: Not all that is written about the use of wood products as soil amendments can be taken as gospel. For example, soft woods such as pine, spruce, and fir are claimed to be unsuitable because they contain resins. Although their presence will slow up the process of reducing woody products to decayed organic matter, it will also mean that the resultant substance will last much longer once in the soil.

Sawdust and wood shavings in particular need treatment with added fertilizer (about a pint of a mixed fertilizer to a bushel of sawdust) and also about the same amount of lime added to the soil under the layer of sawdust or wood chips for each bushel spread out for tilling.

The Techniques of Composting

Although many homeowners find composting a nuisance, there are reasons why practicing this method of treating wastes is part of being a good citizen. In this age of consideration for the environment, a major problem is that of disposing of the millions of tons of solid waste engendered by the processes of living.

Plant wastes, table scraps, dust from the vacuum cleaner, and many other materials discarded into the garbage can can go onto the compost pile, where they will serve a useful purpose instead of contributing to the community's problem. The number of different materials that can be disposed of in this way is amazing. They include dead rats, bones, table wastes, lawn clippings, leaves, weeds, plants pulled from the garden, hair, wood shavings and sawdust, spoiled grain, clippings from woolen cloth, as well as countless other substances that came originally from a living organism.

Starchy and sugary products—spoiled cereals, jellies, potato peelings, and similar materials—do supply bacteria with the energy foods they need to do their work, but they lack nitrogen, which is also essential. Added fertilizer will make up for this.

A traditional prohibition has been against the addition to the pile of fats, greases, and waxes. The reason given was that these materials prevented the decay of organic matter. While it is true that large amounts of fatty materials could prevent breakdown of the entire mass of organic matter, smaller amounts only slow up the process slightly. Actually, waxes and fats are needed in a finished compost because they are essential to the formation of humus, perhaps the most valuable form of organic matter in gardening.

A soggy compost pile will not work. Choose a well-drained, level location in light shade. If located in a sunny spot, the heat in summer can go so high as to kill bacteria near the surface. As it is, the heat generated in decay can go as high as 150° F. inside the pile, so added sun heat is not needed. In arid regions, the pile can sit in a slight depression to save water, but should not be so deep that the bottom layer will drown.

Sprinkle the area where the compost is to be built with finely ground limestone, the grade used for topping driveways. Build the pile like a super "poor boy" sandwich out of alternate layers of organic materials and good garden soil, each about 4 ins. thick. Sprinkle every other layer with a commercial fertilizer such as 5–10–5, about as thick as sugaring strawberries. The layer that doesn't get fertilizer should be sprinkled with finely ground limestone.

Purely organic fertilizers are not as useful for this purpose because they must themselves be broken down before they will provide the necessary nutrients. However, those who wish to use organic materials exclusively can use dried blood, fish emulsion, or urine.

If the amount of organic matter available is small, the area covered by the pile should be reduced, so several layers can be built up in a short period. A depth of 2 or 3 ft. is necessary if the interior of the pile is to heat up properly. As each layer is placed, it should be sprinkled so that it will be moist but not soggy.

A month after it has been started (if the temperature is not below freezing) the pile should be turned over and over to mix thoroughly all the layers. This will release excess carbon dioxide that slows up bacterial action and will provide extra oxygen for the use of microorganisms. If the pile seems dry, moisten it. Turn again every month. Under ideal conditions, with outdoor temperatures above 70° F., the compost might be ready in three months, but over winter, may take eight to ten.

What Is Humus?

The need for constantly replacing organic matter in soil lies in its vital role in building up the humus content. But what is humus?

Actually, nobody really knows. It is somehow tied up with lignin (a substance from wood), with protein and a colloidal complex—that about states what we know about it. The three or four lignin chemists who know more about it than anyone else differ and argue about its composition.

But what humus does is far from mysterious. It is so thirsty that it will absorb between 80 per cent and 90 per cent of the water in a saturated atmosphere. In comparison, the best clay can do is to absorb 20 per cent. It makes soil nutrients much more available. It breaks down slowly, releasing its protein in the form of nitrogen over a period of from five to fifty years. Thus it is a "built-in" source of plant nutrients available even when other sources fail.

An important function of humus is to pull tiny soil particles such as clay into clumps or "crumbs," which make a heavy clay more porous, easier to work, and a better place in which to grow plants.

The breakdown of organic matter into humus is slower when fats and waxes are present, but the final release of the desirable elements in humus is correspondingly slowed up. Because of the more rapid destruction of humus in tropical and subtropical climates, it has little chance to accumulate. This means that organic matter is used up faster in such climates and must be replaced more often. Humus in warm climates is lighter in color; in northern soils it is often a deep blackish-brown.

Why pH Is Important

The term pH often confuses gardeners. Although the technical physics and chemistry behind the pH theory call for a college course or two, actually in use, this scale is no more difficult to understand than a thermometer. It measures the hydrogen-ion concentration in a given substance on a scale of from 0 to 14. Since the hydrogen-ion concentration has a direct relation to the acidity or alkalinity of a substance, with a device for measuring that concentration, we can tell how "sour" or "sweet" a given soil may be. This measuring can be done in two ways: First, an electric bridge can measure this directly. Such a device is too expensive for the home gardener but most county agents have one, as do state experiment stations that make soil tests. Secondly, although not quite as hairline accurate, the small pH test kits sold in garden centers are adequate and usually give a reading within a tenth of a point or two. They are chemical and indicate pH by a change in color of test papers. For a small price, the gardener can determine one of the most important factors in gardening.

But why is pH important? First, it tells us what chemical nutrients can be available to a plant *if they are present.* A pH test does *not* tell you, for example, that phosphorus is present, but only if the soil is not too acid or too alkaline to allow phosphate to be released.

The point at which all elements are available to plants that do not require highly acid soil has its center at pH 6.5. On the pH scale, 7.0 is considered as neutral, where acidity and alkalinity balance out each other. Thus somewhere between 6.0 and 7.0 is perhaps the best point to strive for in altering soil acidity.

Acid-soil plants such as rhododendron, blueberry, mountain-laurel, and others are able to thrive in acid soil because they do not use nitrogen from the soil directly, but depend on a special type of fungus on their roots, called mycorrhiza, which is able to change ammonium nitrate into nitrate nitrogen. These plants also tolerate some free aluminum at their roots, an element which is released at a pH of 5.5 or lower.

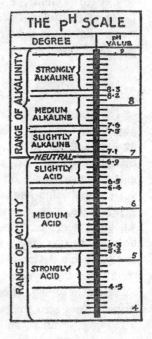

The degree of acidity or alkalinity of the soil is indicated by the pH scale, which ranges from 1 to 10, with 7 as the neutral point. Practically all vegetables, and the great majority of other plants, thrive in neutral to moderately acid soil, with a pH of 6 to 7.

Not only does acidity decrease the availability of elements directly, but also it reduces the activity of soil bacteria until at 5.0 such activity might cease entirely. Since organic matter is available to plants only after bacteria have digested it first, the effect on growth is obvious. Another effect of pH is the release of toxic elements such as aluminum, which is released at a low pH (below 5.5) and also at a high pH (8.5). The prevalence of disease is also affected by pH, both by acid and alkaline soils.

The physical condition of the soil can also be involved with pH, since liming to increase alkalinity improves the "crumb" structure of soils containing large amounts of clay.

Modifying pH

To increase the pH reading of light sandy loams one full point (e.g., from 5.5 to 6.5) apply 35 lbs. of ground limestone (agricultural limestone) to 1,000 sq. ft.; on medium loam, 50 lbs.; and on heavy clay loam, 70 lbs.

To reduce the pH of a light sandy loam one full point (e.g., from 6.0 to 5.0) apply 10 lbs. of dusting sulfur to 1,000 sq. ft.; on medium loam, 15 lbs. will be needed, and on heavy clay loam, 20 lbs.

A word of caution is needed on a common recommendation—the use of aluminum sulfate for acidifying soils. This chemical is widely used in greenhouses for acidity for azaleas. However, as a pot plant, an azalea is only intended to live through the flowering period for which it was forced and then can be discarded. The permanent effect of aluminum on its roots means nothing. In garden soils, however, aluminum is a bad actor if a pH of 5.5 or lower is to be maintained, damaging roots and stunting plants. Ammonium sulfate can be used instead. Although not nearly as effective pound for pound as dusting sulfur, it has the added advantage of supplying nitrogen in ammonium form which acid-loving plants can use. Use double the amount recommended for sulfur, but be sure to dissolve ammonium sulfate in water for applying.

Nutrient Elements

The "big three" in nutrient elements are nitrogen, phosphorus, and potash. They are the ones that must be declared on the bag of fertilizer you buy. The three figures, such as in a combination of 5–10–5, mean that the bag contains 5 per cent nitrogen, 10 per cent phosphorus, and 5 per cent potash.

These elements do not occur in pure form but as compounds with other materials. When they are elements in an organic fertilizer, they can be highly complex and are unavailable to plants until they have been digested or broken down into simpler forms by soil organisms. These organisms are partially dormant at temperatures below 60° F. and grow progressively more active up to about 90° F. Thus organic fertilizers are not too effective in early spring on hardy crops. However, because they add organic matter, they have one value not possessed by pure chemical or mineral fertilizers.

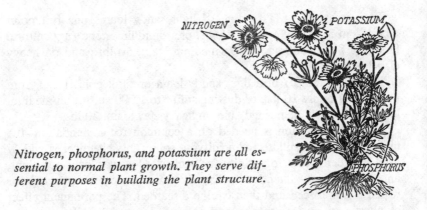

Nitrogen, phosphorus, and potassium are all essential to normal plant growth. They serve different purposes in building the plant structure.

One argument used against chemical fertilizers is that they "burn" foliage. This is true, but only when they are misapplied. If used in excess—if not watered in—many fertilizer salts are so "thirsty" that they will actually suck water out of leaves and roots. Water is a vital element in plant nutrition. In fact, some plants are 90 per cent water. The answer to burning is to water in any chemical fertilizer as soon as applied. Fertilizers in solution simply do not burn.

Whether applied in organic or chemical form, all plant nutrients must be broken down into near-elemental form before they can be taken up by roots. Plants cannot distinguish between nitrogen, phosphorus, or potash from the breakdown of organic matter and the same elements from a chemical source.

Nitrogen

Nitrogen is vital to the formation of all proteins. It is an essential element of chlorophyll, the green chemical that permits plants (and plants alone) to manufacture starches and sugars. Many of the compounds in plants—amino acids, aromatic compounds, etc.—must have nitrogen. It is the "grow" element, forcing soft, lush growth when used in excess. Because of the importance of nitrogen in plant growth, it is essential to have an available supply. Since nature cannot provide nitrogen in sufficient quantities, other sources are essential, namely, commercial fertilizers and manures. Nitrate of soda, sulfate of ammonia, dried blood, cottonseed meal, and the various manures are some of the materials used for supplying extra nitrogen when it is needed in greater amounts than the soil seems able to provide.

Phosphorus

Phosphorus also enters into the composition of proteins and amino acids. It is associated with cell division. It contributes to stiff stems that hold foliage to the sunlight. Flowering and seed formation must have this element. It is a difficult element to manage, since it locks up rapidly as soon as it touches soil and so must be applied in excess of actual use by plants. Many gardens that have been fertilized for years are practically low-grade phosphate mines, but this phosphorus is in an insoluble form that plants cannot use.

Superphosphate, mistakenly called acid phosphate—it is alkaline in reaction—is processed to delay this "fixing" process as long as possible. Phosphate rock, often recommended by organic garden enthusiasts, becomes slowly available as it is dissolved by soil acids. It is seldom of much use the first year it is applied and, weight for weight, is far less effective than superphosphate.

Perhaps one of the most sacred cows in gardening is bone meal. True, in Victorian England, bone meal *was* one of the few good fertilizers available, but it was a far different product than the dehydrated, devitalized product of today. Every dedicated gardener of that day had a bone grinder in his potting shed or garden house. Fresh, raw bone, with scraps of meat clinging to it, was ground and used immediately as a fertilizer. It included the marrow, blood, meat scraps, and valuable minor elements in addition to uncooked phosphorus. Today's bone is all but worthless.

Although recommended for use on bulbs (which are actually injured in many cases by fertilizers), it is useful largely because it has no effect and gives the gardener something he thinks is doing good.

Potassium

Potassium—in the form of potassium hydroxide (potash)—has been neglected in plant nutrition. This is due to the fact that it is abundant in most American soils and when analyses are made for total nutrients, seems to be in adequate supply. Unfortunately, soil-bound potash is in a form that is difficult for plants to use. As a result, annual applications of potash in soluble form are essential, particularly if root crops are being grown. Potassium is an important catalyst in photosynthesis, is essential for starch formation and the movement of sugars in the plant, and is important to seed formation. It helps form stiff stems and is essential in formation of tubers and roots. It is a vital element in protein synthesis and in the utilization of nitrogen by plants.

Wood ashes, which also supply lime, are a convenient source of potassium. One point often overlooked in using wood ashes is that until the potash they contain has been dissolved and absorbed by the soil, a free lye solution is present. This can cause injury to roots for two or three days following application.

Muriate of potash and sulfate of potash are chemical salts that also need to be used carefully to avoid injury to plants.

The Minor Elements

Actually, these are minor in amounts used by the plants, not in their effects on growth. Of these, iron is the one most commonly in short supply. The rest are practically always present from decaying organic matter when this material is used freely, and when pH is held between 6.0 and 6.9.

A convenient way to apply iron is in the form of ferrous ammonium sulfate, applied in solution. Four oz. of ferrous sulfate and 4 oz. of ammonium sulfate, dissolved in 3 gals. of water, form a solution that can be applied to soil directly, or even to a lawn if applied with a sprinkling can while walking at a moderate pace across the grass. If applied too liberally, it can turn grass a blackish-green for two or three weeks.

Iron deficiency shows up as a yellowing of the foliage and is particularly conspicuous on pin oaks.

Water and Plant Growth

Over vast areas of the United States, the growing of vegetables, for example, is practically impossible without some means of supplying water artificially. Elsewhere, the incorporation of large amounts of organic matter improves the water-holding capacity of soils to tide plants over periods when water is scarce.

Water is particularly important when mineral or chemical fertilizers are used. Since they are usually salts, they are hygroscopic and will actually pull water out of plant tissues unless they are in dilute solutions. Either they should be applied before soil is dug or tilled, or should be applied with a hose ready to water them in thoroughly as soon as applied.

Water in excess can cause problems. What is not commonly known is that roots are incapable of absorbing water and nutrients unless oxygen is also present in soil. A plant top can actually wilt for lack of water while its roots are completely submerged. The ideal soil is one that can absorb abundant water in its organic substances, but one in which the passages between the organic and mineral particles are filled with air.

On heavy soils, which are easy to overwater, the common recommendation of allowing plants to dry out between watering has some validity, but on most soils fit for growing plants, a much sounder policy is to keep the soil constantly moist to the root depth, without applying so much water that air passages are drowned out.

—*R. Milton Carleton*

Types of Soil

How do you recognize the value of natural soil? How do you improve it?   The nutritional value of soil is hard to determine by casual inspection. A test must be made to determine it. However, dark soils usually have organic matter. A wash test as described in the Introduction will tell a great deal about a soil.

Are there special kinds of soil for different plants?   Root crops require friable, light soils for best development. Crops with fine roots do better in coarse open soil, while coarse-rooted plants grow better in more dense soils composed of finer particles.

SANDY SOIL

We have a sandy lot and wish to enjoy good results. Should we put black topsoil on?   Yes. Extremely sandy soil needs loam but also plenty of organic matter.

What depth of topsoil should we use on sandy ground?   Add 3 ins. loam and spade to a depth of 6 ins. However, without additional organic matter, on very sandy soil, loam is usually lost by being washed down into the sand.

My front yard is mostly sand. What flowers would be best to plant?   Portulaca, California-poppy, annual phlox, calliopsis, cockscomb, morning-glory, anthemis, milkweed, aster, baby's-breath, liatris, yucca. To remedy situation, add manure and fertilizer.

How can we make a vegetable garden on pure sand?   The only way this is possible is in raised beds made out of 2 × 12 planks for sides. Lay plastic and set the beds, usually 3 ft. by 12 ft., on this base. Fill with a good loam. If soil is heavy, punch holes in the plastic.

Our soil is sandy. How can we grow good roses?   Add manure or peat moss. Keep soil fertilized and water heavily when necessary. Plenty of organic matter will be needed or roses will do poorly.

Our soil (on river front) is solid sand. Would surfacing it with black dirt be sufficient for planting fruit trees?   No. A very large hole should be dug for each tree, and filled with good soil in which to plant.

What would you suggest for a home garden at the seashore where there is a lot of sand? Additions of organic matter, such as manures, seaweed, peat moss, will help, although it would be better to mix some loam with the sand. Also dig under green-cover crops.

I have a piece of very sandy land and wish to grow excellent corn. Can it be done? Yes, manure heavily or apply organic materials as recommended above; also apply a complete fertilizer several times during growing season.

Our soil is all gravel. How can I adjust this for growing vegetables? Add mixture of loam and manure to a depth of 3 ins. and spade to a depth of 6 ins.

What is the best way of keeping land in shape for vegetables? The soil is light and sandy but well drained. Spade in manure every fall. Keep well fertilized and properly cultivated.

Our soil is very sandy and is acid. What can we do so we can grow a vegetable garden? Increase the organic content of the soil by incorporating green-manure crops, farm manures, or other non-acid materials such as leaves, straw, plant refuse, or non-acid peat. Apply lime as needed to modify the acidity.

Our Long Island soil is very sandy; my vegetables are never much of a success. Is this because of the soil? No matter how much topsoil we put on, it sinks in. Add loam and plenty of organic matter. A 3-in. layer should be spaded to a depth of 6 ins. Any vegetable can be grown if well watered and fertilized.

Our soil is sandy; fertilizer seems to cause worms in the underground vegetables. Is this due to the soil? The soil is infested with wireworms. Apply 2 lbs. of a 5 per cent chlordane dust per 1,000 sq. ft. of soil surface. Work well into upper 6 ins. of the soil. If there is objection to chlordane, Morraw Meal, a toxic organic plant product, can be used instead.

My ground is sandy. What is the best vegetable to plant? Any vegetable will grow in sandy soil if fertilized frequently. Apply fertilizer high in phosphorus and potash.

For sandy soil plant material see also Section III.

CLAY SOIL

What makes clay so sticky? Clay is composed of very minute particles which have a large surface to absorb water. High water content causes the stickiness.

Should clay soil be worked when wet? No; never. It puddles and makes a poor environment for roots. Digging too soon in spring may make it practically useless for the season.

How much wood ashes is it safe to use on heavy clay soil? At least 10 lbs. per 100 sq. ft.

My garden plot is heavy clay soil and produces well, but it is hard to work up. Would well-rotted manure and wood ashes be of benefit? Yes. Fine cinders would also be beneficial.

Can coal ashes be used to loosen clay soil? Only if they have been exposed to weather to leach out harmful substances. So few homes burn coal today that supply is limited. Steam cinders from high-temperature boilers in electric-generating plants are plentiful. They can be used up to one third the volume of clay to be treated. Break up or discard cinders more than $1/4$ in. in diameter.

What proportion of steam cinders should be mixed with clay to make it good for flowers? A 2-in. layer spaded in will be safe.

Are steam cinders in clay soil better than sand? Yes; they are of more help in opening it up and admitting air.

Does it make any difference what kind of sand is mixed with clay soil to lighten it? To what depth should the sand be spread on before spading in? Yes. Coarse or ungraded sands, containing a large proportion of $1/16$- to $1/8$-in. particles, will bring about the greatest improvement when added to a clay soil. Incorporate a 3-in. layer of such sand.

What shall I do to keep ground loosened? It gets sticky and lumpy. I mixed in sand and ashes but they did not help. Probably too little sand was used. Manure and/or peat moss should improve such a soil.

My ground gets hard and dry on the surface, so that it is difficult for the young shoots to break through. It is soft enough beneath the surface. What can I do? Incorporate sand, and, if possible, well-rotted compost or peat moss, in the upper surface.

My garden soil is mostly clay. I dug under quite a few leaves in an effort to add humus to the soil. Will leaves tend to make the soil acid? Usually not; but it would be advisable, in any case, to test the soil for acidity, which see.

Is chemical fertilizer harmful to clay soil? No. Often necessary to furnish mineral elements so plants will grow. Ground limestone, a 2-in. layer, spaded into clay, will make it more workable. Gypsum is also recommended; consult your county agent concerning its use.

What can be added to a clay soil to increase root growth? It is slightly acid, and in partial shade. If wet, soil must be drained by use of tile. Add organic matter or peat moss. Slight acidity is all right for vegetables and for most ornamental plants. (See Acidity, this section.)

What kind of fertilizer is best for inert clay soil? Incorporation of organic matter and ground limestone will probably benefit such a soil. The fertilizer to apply will depend upon the crop to be grown.

How may I improve a heavy, extremely wet clay soil? Pine trees thrive on it. The physical condition of an extremely wet clay soil can be improved by using 4-in. agricultural drain tile (see Drainage) and the incorporation of liberal amounts of screened cinders or sand. Add ground limestone, as necessary, to lower the acidity.

Will adding ashes and dry leaves to thin clay soil bring it to the consistency of loam? Yes, if you add enough, and wait long enough. Apply compost, peat moss, or both, to hasten the process.

The soil in the garden is very clayey and needs conditioning. How can I do that with all the shrubbery and perennials in? Remove perennials after hard frost and spade in 3 ins. of compost or peat moss and 2–3 ins. of steam cinders or ground limestone. Replant perennials at once.

What are the best materials to mix with a heavy soil of blue clay? Peat moss, compost, and fine cinders.

What crops would help to break up soil of blue clay? Shallow-rooted ones, such as rye and oats.

Is lime helpful to soil of blue clay? Have soil tested to determine if lime is needed; usually it is helpful. (See Lime, this section.)

How does gray clay differ from red clay? Depends on kinds of minerals the clay is composed of and amount of air present when clay was formed. Red clay usually contains iron.

Is gray clay fertile? Yes, but probably would be better for plants if it is fertilized.

What can be done with gray clay soil to make it produce? Add compost or peat moss first, then apply fertilizers as crop growth may indicate the need for them.

Is it best to grow a green-manure crop in gray clay soil over winter, or dig it up in the fall and leave it so? Fertilize soil, grow a winter cover crop, and plow under in spring.

What will darken light-colored (gray) clay soil? How many years will it take to make such soil black in color? Organic matter—manure, etc. It would require several years of constant applications, but it is not at all necessary to make the soil black in order to have it productive.

Is pipe-clay soil acid? Clay soils vary in their degree of acidity. To determine the reaction of the particular soil in mind, test it or send a sample to your State Agricultural College. (See Acidity, this section.)

I have a patch of heavy red clay soil to condition. Is there an easy way to do it? I've used peat moss, sand, leafmold, and well-rotted manure. Use more of the same. Sorry; no easy way.

My tract of land has heavy, tough red clay base, with only light topsoil covering. What is best treatment? Grow cover crops of soybeans plowed under before beans are ripe. Follow with crop of rye to be plowed under the following spring.

Will peat moss make a red clay soil heavier? No. It loosens it up and makes it easier to handle.

What green-manure crop is best for rocky clay soil, and when should it be sown? Grow soybeans planted in spring, and turn under before beans are ripe. Follow with rye or oats, to be plowed under the following spring.

I have a rocky clay soil that has never been used except to grow grass. Should it be exposed to the winter, or put to cover crop? For a small area, remove surface rocks, add 3 ins. of peat moss with some sand or ashes, and plow under. Do not disk or harrow until spring.

What does a white clay soil need, when it becomes baked hard after a rain? In the early spring it is loose and mellow. Needs organic matter in the form of peat moss, compost, or leafmold. Apply a 3-in. layer and spade in.

How can a very heavy yellow clay soil around the foundation of a house be improved so that plants will grow in it? Incorporate 2 ins. of steam cinders screened through ¼-in. mesh, and 2 ins. of compost, straw, or peat, preferably in the fall.

What is the best way to prepare heavy clay for fruit trees? Drainage must be good for fruit trees in heavy soils. Spade or plow under a liberal quantity of compost or peat moss. Sod spaded under is likewise good.

The soil of my garden consists mostly of clay. Would it be suitable for planting trees such as apples, pears, and cherries? Yes, if well drained.

How can I prepare clay soil in full sun for growing lilies? All varieties will grow in moderately heavy soil. Add 3 ins. of well-rotted compost or peat moss and spade to a depth of 6 ins. Soil must be well drained for satisfactory results with lilies.

What ornamental plants will grow in clay soil? If well prepared—organic matter added, well drained, fertilized—clay soils will support growth of almost all plants.

What shrubs, flowers, and trees grow best in red clay soil? If soil is well drained, most shrubs and trees will grow. For flowers, add compost or peat moss along with fine cinders.

We have clay ground and must prepare it inexpensively. What vegetables will be successful? Spade in a 3-in. layer of organic matter, and expect any vegetable to grow. However, root crops will do better in lighter soils.

Is it practical to begin a vegetable garden on a rocky clay soil of poor color and texture? Probably not, unless no other soil is available. Remove surface rocks and add large quantities of compost or peat moss each year. Fertilizer will also be needed.

Soil Problems

What kind of soil is most adaptable for general gardening?   Any well-conditioned soil which would grow a crop of corn.

Is there any way to change the condition of a poor soil?   Unless the soil condition is extremely unfavorable, it can be improved to the extent that it will produce good crops. The addition of plenty of organic matter is a basic need.

I am planning my first garden. How do I go about preparing the land for it?   Add manure (600 lbs. per 1,000 sq. ft.); or 5 bales peat moss (50 bushels) per 1,000 sq. ft.; fertilize it with a good complete garden fertilizer, 30 lbs. per 1,000 sq. ft.; lime it (if test shows need). (See also Handling of Soil.)

Is it advisable to apply lime and commercial fertilizer through the winter on the snows for early melting and absorption?   Lime and commercial fertilizers, for some crops, can be applied in the fall, but in most cases they are more economically applied in the spring. Chemical fertilizers leach out and are lost over winter.

Are wood ashes as good or better than coal ashes for the garden? Under what conditions should each be used?   Wood ashes and coal ashes serve two distinct purposes—the former adds potash, the latter improves mechanical condition of soil.

If annuals are cut off at the ground in fall, instead of being pulled out, will the soil benefit by decomposition of the roots?   Yes.

In clearing off my vegetable plot, I burned the old tomato vines. Does this in any way injure the soil for next year's crop?   No. It really should be of benefit.

What can I do to improve tough, gummy black virgin soil? I have added sand.   Not enough added. Apply a 3-in. layer of compost or peat moss. Fertilizer will also help.

What is best treatment for a soil that does not produce root crops?   It probably is too heavy; lighten with organic materials and cinders. It can lack phosphorus and potassium, which can be added in the form of superphosphate and potassium chloride. (See Introduction.)

Our soil is a heavy black gumbo and bakes badly. Should I use manure, sand, sawdust, or peat moss? For long-lasting improvement, incorporate 2 to 3 ins. of peat moss, a mixture of half peat moss and half coarse sawdust, plus 2 ins. of coarse sand, many of whose particles are $\frac{1}{16}$- to $\frac{1}{8}$-in. in diameter.

How can I make a hard-packed, black alkali soil friable and productive? (Nevada.) Sulfur must be added to neutralize the alkali. If not, soil must be drained by use of tile. Add compost or peat moss to loosen soil.

DEPLETED SOIL

What is the quickest way to bring an old used garden spot back into quick production? Spade in organic matter in the fall. In the spring, apply superphosphate, hoe, rake, and plant. Add complete fertilizer just before planting, and again during summer.

I have been raising flowers on the same ground for some time. What can I use to keep it in shape? Incorporate organic matter such as leaves or peat moss in the soil between the plants. Apply a good complete fertilizer as needed.

I have planted flowers in the same spot for the last 15 years, using only a commercial fertilizer. My flowers do not have as large blossoms as they used to, but bloom very well. Should I add anything more, or do as I am doing? Unless the soil is very rich, it would be beneficial to add compost or peat moss, or some other form of organic matter.

ERODED SOIL

What causes erosion? Erosion—the washing away of soil on slopes by the runoff of surface water—results when the soil is left more or less bare and is so handled that it lacks humus to absorb moisture.

Please tell me how to handle a lot that is very sandy and slopes. The water washes the soil off as fast as it is replaced. I had thought of making about 3 different elevations (terraces). Is this too many for a garden about 50 ft. deep? If the slope is not too steep, the trouble may be overcome by increasing the organic content of the soil through the use of green manures, strawy manure (if you can get it), compost, or peat moss. On steep slopes handle the situation by strip-working the lot, or by terracing with railroad ties or stonework. Two terraces should be sufficient on a 50-ft. lot unless the grade is very steep.

How do you keep sharp slopes from opening and washing out? Avoid cultivation near and in these areas. If practical, plant black locust trees (small) to hold soil. If possible, build walls to form terraces on steep slopes.

What suggestions do you have for hillside soil that is mostly decomposed granite? Prepare small pockets or local areas of good soil by using compost or peat moss, and use plants which root as they spread. Crown vetch will hold such a hillside once it is established.

How can one improve clay soil on a hillside to make it good garden soil? Add compost, spade under, and plant ground covers (ornamental) to hold soil in place. If wanted for vegetables, arrange the slope in terraces.

FOR FLOWERS

What type of soil is best for a mixed flower border? A sandy loam, slightly acid (pH 6.5) in reaction, with manure, compost, or peat moss worked in.

My annuals and perennials grow tall and spindly. Could this be due to overfertilization, lack of sun, or lack of some fertilizer element? The garden site receives sunlight half the day. The spindling growth of annuals and perennials may be due to lack of sunlight, improper fertilization, or other factors; or to any combination of them. Give as much sunlight as possible; improve the drainage and aeration of the soil; increase the phosphorus and potash in relation to nitrogen in the fertilizer used. A fertilizer low in nitrogen may be best for a few years.

Why do plants grow thin and scraggly? What is lacking in soils that produce such growth? Lack of balanced nutrition. Usually an addition of complete fertilizer will help. Drainage should be good. Calcium (lime or gypsum) may be needed to make good roots. Test your soil.

My flowers grow very poorly, and usually die before long. What causes this? The chances are your soil lacks fertility, moisture-holding capacity, and aeration. Additions of humus and fertilizers should correct these handicaps.

How can you keep soil in good condition in the grimy atmosphere of big cities? Adequate drainage should be provided. A periodic soil test will determine the amount of lime necessary to maintain the correct soil reaction.

Do soil conditions cause double-flowered cosmos to be single? Doubling of flowers is a hereditary tendency. Soil conditions rarely have any effect. Improper selection of seed is the usual cause. Many flowers never come 100 per cent double from seed.

Are earthworms harmful or beneficial in the garden? I find in a short time they eat all humus in the soil the same as they do when they get into flower pots. Earthworms are not harmful in outdoor soils, unless present in very unusual numbers. In the greenhouse or in pot plants they are a nuisance. If too numerous, apply 5 lbs. of arsenate of lead to 1,000 sq. ft. and water in.

Would a garden plot laid out on the edge of a lake be satisfactory? And how would one get it in condition? Yes. Add compost or peat moss at rate of 300 lbs. per 1,000 sq. ft. Humus content is likely to be low.

NEGLECTED SOIL

Why is soil that has lain idle for years so deficient in plant food? When grass, weeds, leaves, etc., are continually decaying on it, wouldn't natural compost be made? The weeds which grow on poor soils may not require the same proportions of elements for growth as cultivated plants. When these weeds die down, they fail to change these proportions. Besides, insufficient aeration, due to lack of turning the land, may cause trouble.

How can I restore the fertility of an old garden? Soil is sand, with a clay subsoil. I've tried manure, lime, and commercial fertilizer. The

predominance of sand seems the difficulty. Try heavy applications of organic matter, such as compost, manure, peat moss, straw, alfalfa, hay, or the use of green manure.

Last year was the first time my garden was plowed in 30 years. I think I need lime, as the ground showed green moss. How much should I use? The best way to tell lime need is to test soil. Green moss is not an indication of acidity. More likely drainage is poor, or nutrients are lacking.

I had a ½-acre vegetable garden last year; plot had been uncultivated for 15 years. Applied a ton of lime after plowing and 2 truckloads of manure direct to plants. Seeded the plot to rye and perennial rye grass last fall, and it looks all right. What, if anything, would you suggest adding this season before and after plowing? Apply 40 to 50 lbs. of 20 per cent superphosphate per 1,000 sq. ft.

I recently bought a 171-acre farm which has not been worked for about 9 years. How can I determine what to plant? Have your soil tested. Insure proper drainage. Consult your county agent.

Have just bought a 3-acre place which has not been worked for 4 years, but annual crop of hay has been cut. Can I bring this into cultivation in a year? Yes. Plow in the fall. Fertilize heavily in the spring. Consult your county agent.

The plot I expect to use as a vegetable garden is a vacant lot infested with weeds. Will turning the weeds under be sufficient preparation of the soil? The turning under of weeds will add organic matter to the soil. However, it may be too acid or alkaline: test for this. It may be poorly drained. It may need fertilization.

Our back yard is full of wild grass and weeds. Will soil be suitable for anything after condition is changed? Modern weed killers, which destroy all vegetation but do not sterilize the soil, can be used to kill all weeds and are available from garden shops. Usually, a short wait is necessary before seed can be sown. By fertilizing heavily before spraying, soft growth is stimulated and kill is improved. As soon as vegetation is dead, it can be dug or tilled. The chances are good that the soil can be modified to produce the common vegetables and garden flowers satisfactorily.

If the soil produces a vigorous crop of weeds, is it a sign that it will grow desirable things well? Usually, yes. If the desired crops are adapted to the soil type supporting the weed growth, they should do well.

What is the best way to handle soil which has been allowed to grow with bracken and creeping berry vines and has lain idle for years? Mow or cut off and remove all undesired plants. (They may be put into compost heap.) Remove undesired woody material such as limbs and small trees. Plow or dig and leave in rough condition through winter. In spring, redig, fertilize heavily, and plant.

POOR SOIL

How can subsoil fill be converted so that vegetables can be grown? If organic matter can be worked in heavily, any subsoil other than pure clay can be made fit to grow crops. Allow 6 weeks to elapse, then test for fertility and pH. Many subsoils are rich in minerals but lack organic matter.

How can I build up soil that is mostly cinders? In the upper 8 to 10 ins. incorporate compost and haul in soil. The final proportion of cinders should be not more than ¼ of the total volume in top 6 ins.

My garden plot is mostly brown soil and not too fertile. How can I make it fertile? Apply compost and a complete fertilizer.

My soil is very poor. How can I improve it? Add 3 ins. compost or peat moss; spade to a depth of 6 ins. Before raking add a good complete garden fertilizer at 4 lbs. per 100 sq. ft.

Are flowers or vegetables likely to grow in soil from which the top 18 ins. have been removed? Usually not. By manuring the subsoil and planting green-manure crops, the soil may be made fairly good after 2 or 3 years.

How much topsoil do you advise using over fill in order to grow flowers and vegetables? At least 6 ins.; preferably more.

I am planning to make a garden where the sod is rather heavy. How can I destroy this? Till or spade in the fall or spring. Apply complete fertilizer before spading to hasten decomposition. Sod land makes the finest of soils. If infested with quackgrass, kill this with Dalapon (sold by dealers in farm supplies) before turning the sod under.

I have a brand-new home; the builder put in very little loam, and the soil itself is very poor. How can I improve it? Without adding topsoil, the process of improvement will be very slow. Heavy additions of manure would have to be substituted. This should be worked in in the fall or spring. Soil should be tested for acidity and proper corrections made. Fertilizers should be added, and green-manure crops planted—rye in the fall (2 to 3 lbs. per 1,000 sq. ft.), followed by soybeans next spring (after plowing rye under). After plowing the soybeans under, soil should be in fair shape.

I used topsoil from the farm to enrich my soil, but results were poor. How can I determine what is wrong? Topsoil, often sold as "from a farm," can be from a worn-out, abandoned one and worthless. See answer to above question.

What is the quickest, cheapest, and best way to rebuild "stripped" land, where loam was scraped off? See answer to above.

Will it be necessary to add extra fertilizer to the topsoil we have just put on? Add a fertilizer high in phosphorus and potash.

STONY SOIL

To produce a good crop of the common vegetables, what fertilizer is best for shale ground that has not been farmed for several years? Any complete fertilizer, such as 4–12–4 or 5–10–5, applied at 4 lbs. per 100 sq. ft., twice or three times a year.

Do stones continually work to the surface? If so, why? Yes, small ones do. Alternate freezing and thawing in winter, digging and cultivation, and also wetting and drying in spring, summer, and fall, bring stones to surface.

What shall I do for stony land? I continually rake stones off, but more appear. There is no remedy other than to keep on removing surface rocks.

WET SOIL

Will you explain the terms "well-drained soil" and "waterlogged soil"? A well-drained soil is one in which surplus water runs off quickly and which dries out readily after a rain or watering. A waterlogged soil is the opposite and contains too much water and little air.

Can a low, wet area be used for general gardening? Only if it can be drained.

What vegetables will stand a wet, soggy soil best? Beets seem to like wet sour spots, but carrots won't even come up in these spots. No vegetables will grow in soggy soil. If no other soil is available, raised beds made with 12-in. boards can be built and filled with a soil that drains well.

Our soil is in the shade and has too much moisture. What can we do for it? Improve the drainage by the installation of 3- or 4-in. agricultural tile, 12 to 15 ins. deep, with lines 12 to 15 ft. apart, and incorporate liberal amounts of organic matter. Only shade-tolerant plants will grow, no matter how you improve the soil.

What can be done to eliminate excess water at the foot of a terraced hill? The water always stands in the garden at the foot of the hill. Provide a shallow grass-covered or stone-paved ditch to carry off the excess water, or install a tile drain.

The earth in back of my home is wet and mossy. Is there anything I can do about fertilizing it for a garden? At present nothing will grow. Soil must be drained by use of agricultural tile. Apply 4–12–4 or 5–10–5 fertilizer at 4 lbs. per 100 sq. ft.

My garden is on a slope and the lower end is wet, with heavy soil. Is there any simple way to drain this ground and loosen the soil? Incorporate steam cinders and organic matter. If this does not rectify the situation, tile drain.

My garden plot is low and level, the soil moist and heavy in the spring. Will leaves and grass cuttings help, or should I use sand? Soil should be drained by use of tile. The addition of humus will help the soil but will not correct poor drainage. Unless you can afford to apply one third as much sand as the amount of soil you treat, sand may only make the soil less workable, e.g., a 2-in. layer to treat soil to a depth of 6 ins.

How much lime should be used to correct soil in wet condition? Lime is not a corrective for wet soils. Add lime only if the soil is too acid for crops to be grown. Improve drainage first.

A sewer pipe backed up last fall and overflowed in a small plot where vegetables were planted. What can I do to purify the ground? Dig it up, and leave in rough, open condition. In a very short time the ground will "purify" itself.

Will waste water from a sand-washing plant damage land where it settles? (Texas.) Since sand-washing plants differ greatly in their practices, this is a difficult question to answer. Have the soil tested for acidity, nitrogen, phosphorus, potash, soluble salts, and organic matter. Consult your county agent.

MOSSY SOIL

The soil turns green in one of my perennial garden beds. What is the best way to remedy this condition? As it is probably caused by poor drainage and lack of aeration, improve the drainage by one of the methods previously suggested. Moss usually means a soil low in fertility. Add organic matter and fertilizer.

What kind of fertilizer should be used when the soil is heavy and has a green top coating? See answer to above question.

What is the cause, and what the remedy, for soil that has a green mosslike formation over the top? See answer to above question.

Does green moss growing on the soil in the borders indicate an acid condition of the ground? No. It usually indicates poor drainage or lack of fertility. If it is a green scum (algae), excess nitrogen (especially if from organic sources) and poor aeration may be responsible.

How can I overcome excessive moss on slope? Usual reasons for the excessive growth of moss are poor underdrainage and infertile soil. Rake out as much moss as possible, apply compost or organic matter, and maintain fertility by applying fertilizer rich in nitrogen in spring and fall.

What is the best type of fertilizer for soil which has not had previous nourishment and which contains a large percentage of clay? Although sunny it tends to become mossy. Tile drain the garden plot; incorporate compost or organic matter; add commercial fertilizer suitable to the crop to be grown.

I have a strip of soil a few feet wide where everything dies that is planted. Why? May be due to packing of soil by constant walking. Try aerating by adding screened cinders or coarse sand. The trouble may also be caused by the application of some toxic weed killer.

WOODLAND AND SHADED SOIL

What is the quickest, cheapest, and best way to convert a former wood lot into usable land? Remove stumps by hand, tractor, or dynamite, then work under compost or organic matter and fertilizer.

Does a garden of vegetables and flowers do well in soil which has just been cleared of hickory, oak, and wild cherry trees? There is a great deal of leafmold in the soil. It will do better in subsequent years, when aeration changes the structure of the soil. When well rotted, leafmold is a good soil conditioner.

Is acid woodland soil in any way beneficial as fertilizer? Woodland soil is not a fertilizer but may serve as a soil conditioner. It can be used as a satisfactory mulch, containing a high percentage of organic matter, and later worked into the soil.

In red virgin soil under and near red-cedar, would oak leafmold and chicken fertilizer, mixed with sand, produce good vegetables? Only if the trees do not shade the garden spot. Check pH and lime if reading is less than 6.0.

What can I do with soil surrounded by fir trees to make it suitable for flowers? Deep spading and incorporation of a 2-in. layer of finely screened cinders should help.

What attention must be given soil from which oak trees have been cleared? Through the years many layers of oak leaves have rotted and naturally form a part of this soil. Such a soil may be somewhat acid. It should be tested and, if necessary, lime applied. For most plants a pH of 6.0 to 6.9 is best.

What is the best treatment of soil under pine trees for the growth of roses and old-fashioned annuals? If the shade is dense, despite soil preparation, neither will grow.

A willow tree shades my yard; the roots mat the soil for yards around. Is there any way to make flowers grow beneath it? Not satisfactorily.

My soil receives sun from noon on. The few things which grow taste like wood (tomatoes, strawberries, etc.). Why? Soil tested poor, but 5–10–5 was added, plus sheep manure. Not enough sun. No fertilizer can substitute for sunlight.

How should I treat the ground where no sun ever shines? The ground packs. Outside of ferns and shade-loving plants, nothing should be grown under such conditions. The packing of the ground may be reduced by working in leafmold or peat moss.

How can damp, cold, shady soil be fertilized to substitute for sunshine? There is no substitute for sunshine. Additions of nitrogen are helpful if trees take all the nourishment. Flowering plants and vegetables should not be planted in such localities.

What is deficient in soil when plants run to slender stems instead of branching? May not have enough sun. Add a fertilizer low in nitrogen (2–10–10 or 0–12–12), 5 lbs. per 100 sq. ft.

Soil Preparation

PLOWING AND DIGGING

When should soil be tilled or plowed? Any time of year when not so wet as to roll in large clods, or so dry as to be a powdery dust.

Does it harm soil to work it while wet? Yes, especially if the soil is heavy. Plowing compacts such soils, and clods and unbreakable lumps will result. Heavy soils will puddle and bake and will be difficult to work into a friable state.

What makes soil break up into large, hard lumps after it is plowed? The structure is bad—too clayey. Add compost, peat moss, and other organic materials, and cinders, or sand. Do not till or dig while soil is wet.

Is it better to plow gardens in the fall or spring? Fall plowing is better, especially when there is sod to be turned under. It reduces erosion, exposes heavy soils to frost, kills exposed insects, brings about decay of organic matter, and makes for earlier planting. In the South, however, where little or no freezing occurs, fall plowing is apt to cause leaching.

I have a field that hasn't been plowed for years. I would like to have a vegetable garden. Is it best to plow in fall? Fall plowing is best in such cases.

We had land plowed which has not been cultivated for about 40 years. What is the best time to put lime and fertilizer on soil? Plow early in the fall. Add lime at 2 lbs. or more per 100 sq. ft. (as test indicates) and a complete fertilizer at the same rate (or preferably a week or two later) and cultivate in. In the spring, hoe, apply fertilizer, rake, and seed.

Last year I made a new garden by filling in about 10 to 18 ins. deep with loam. What should be done with this ground to put in proper shape for this year's home garden? Add manure or compost and till or dig, preferably in the fall.

We plan to make a garden on a city lot infested with poison-ivy, wild honeysuckle, and blackberry vines. Can you make any suggestions as to how we can rid soil of these? Will the roots from these vines ruin such root crops as potatoes? Kill woody plants with a chemical brush killer. Poison-ivy is dangerous, even when dead, so handle with care. Plant vegetables and remove, by frequent hand hoeing, shoots of weeds that appear. Roots of the vines will decompose and not injure vegetables.

Should ground be tilled or loosened up each year before planting, or only a little hole dug to put in bulbs or seeds? It is better to plow or spade soil before planting each crop and easier in the long run.

Is it undesirable to leave soil barren after plowing, or after crops have been harvested? It should either be kept cultivated, or mulched. If there is time (before the plot will be needed for future use) grow a green-manure crop.

Does burning weeds on vacant lots in any way harm the soil for growing vegetables? The lots have lain idle for a great many years. No. A certain amount of minerals is added and weed seeds are killed. Where there is a choice in the fall, between burning or digging, it is better to dig or till.

Should I burn off the garden in the fall, or should stalks be plowed under? If your old stalks are disease free, it is better to plow under than burn. Diseased material should be burned.

In plowing cleared ground that had a growth of wild berries and brush, what should the procedure be? Spray with a brush killer. Burn off dead brush, fertilize, and dig or till.

How can I loosen up hardpan soil on 40-acre field? Use a sub-soil plow.

How do you prepare soil in the fall for spring flower beds? Apply compost or peat moss. Dig and allow soil to weather over winter. In spring apply a garden fertilizer at recommended rate, then rake or till before planting.

Will you please define spading and trenching?   See Section V.

After spading in fall, how does one proceed in spring? If manure is dug in at time of spring spading, can lime also be used? How? See above. Add lime only if a pH test reads less than 6.0.

CULTIVATING

What is meant by the term "in good tilth"?   Soil which has suitable crumbly structure, sufficient humus, and is well drained. To help secure good tilth, use compost or peat moss or grow a green-manure crop; tile if necessary.

Soil is ready to be dug when a handful, firmly compressed, crumbles apart readily. If it remains in a sticky mass, with moisture on the surface, it is still too wet.

How fine should soil be prepared for planting?   For seed beds fine enough so that few lumps remain, else seed covering will be difficult. For large plants, coarse soil is better than fine.

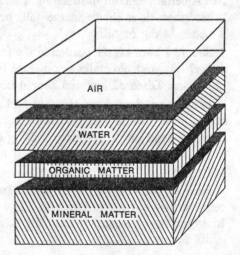

Relative composition of soil with good structure.

How can I know that my soil is right for growing vegetables and flowers? If the structure is crumbly, the soil is dark; if compost, peat moss, and a complete fertilizer are added, good crops will grow. To make sure, have a soil test made.

Is cultivating—stirring the soil—necessary except to control weeds and grass in such crops as corn and potatoes? Usually, mulching substitutes for cultivation. In some soils, a fine dust mulch cuts off air movement between soil and the atmosphere, hardly a desirable situation.

What is the best way to tell if soil is in condition to cultivate? Put a *clean trowel* or spade into your soil. If, when you pull the tool out of the soil, many particles cling to the clean surface, the soil is too wet to be cultivated.

What is meant by "fallow"? Fallow means plowing the land and allowing it to stand idle with no crop. It may be spaded or tilled while fallow.

What is the purpose of fallowing? For the control of weeds by plowing them under. Soil standing idle one year stores moisture for next year's crop. For this reason, the practice is used mostly in arid regions.

DRAINAGE

How can I properly drain a garden that stays wet too long? If the situation cannot be corrected by incorporation of 3 to 4 ins. of

Wet soils are improved by laying tiles to increase drainage—a very simple operation.

sand or cinders, install 3- or 4-in. agricultural drain tile. Set the tile 15 to 18 ins. deep, with the lines 15 to 18 ft. apart. Carry the lines to an open ditch or storm sewer.

What is best way to drain off a 1-acre garden that is too wet? Would some kind of furrow arrangement be sufficient? Would it be better tiled, or drained to storm-water sewer?   Installation of tile drains would be the more satisfactory and in the end more economical on such a large plot.

We have so much subsoil water that in winter our ground in spots is continually water-soaked. What can I do to counteract this in spring?   Tile drain the lot. (See previous questions.)

How can we provide drainage economically at low end of lot? Water forms in pool during heavy rains.   If the situation cannot be corrected by slight modification of the grade, or shallow ditching, install 3- to 4-in. agricultural drain tile.

Our lot is wide, but slopes. At this spot (at the end of the lot) we have "soggy" soil for days after a rain. Is there anything we can do about it?   Tile drain the lower end of the lot. Carry the tile to an open ditch or storm sewer if possible. Drain into sump holes if the water cannot be carried off.

I plan a combination vegetable garden and orchard on a very poor site. Since drainage would be expensive to install, would you advise against the project?   Vegetables can be raised in beds above ground level made with 12-in. sides. No orchard trees will thrive with wet feet.

COAL ASHES

Can hard-coal stoker cinders be plowed into heavy soil to lighten it without bad effect?   If weathered over winter and broken down to ¼ in. or finer. Clinkers make good subdrains if buried deeply.

Soil in home vegetable garden packs hard when dry. Would coal ashes benefit this condition?   Yes, use 1 in. incorporated into top 6 ins. of soil. Screen through a ¼-in. mesh before applying. Be sure they have been exposed outdoors over winter before using.

What are the benefits from the fine siftings of coal ashes applied to a vegetable garden and mixed with the soil?   The mechanical condition is improved, more air is admitted, bacteria work more efficiently, and roots grow faster.

Can coal ashes be used in the garden at the same time bone meal

is worked into the soil? Yes, they can be used at the same time, but they should be fine enough to lighten soil.

Are coal ashes of any use as a chemical fertilizer? Coal ashes have very little, if any, fertilizer value. They do improve the mechanical condition of most soils.

Do coal ashes help prevent cutworms? To a degree. If a 1-in. layer is placed about bases of plants, cutworms will have difficulty in attacking them.

A couple of years ago I noticed that an acquaintance had dumped his winter's coke ashes in a low spot in back of his yard. In spring he smoothed them out and set his tomato plants there, and they bore a heavy crop of fruit. Is there any plant food in coke ashes that is good for tomatoes? Or was that just an accident that the plants did so well in the ashes? The coke ashes improved the soil aeration, and thus helped produce better growth.

Are briquette ashes good for entire garden? I burn briquettes in the fireplace. Yes; for mechanical betterment of the soil, improving its texture.

Will ashes from fireplace, in which some cannel coal has been used, be harmful in garden use? Cannel-coal ashes contain a harmful oil unless completely burned.

Can the fine white ash of cannel coal be used to lighten a heavy soil? Yes. (See previous question.)

I understand cannel-coal ashes are strong in phosphorus and potash. Are they suitable to be added to the flowers and vegetable garden? As mechanical aids mostly; they have but little nutrient value.

Soil Acidity

pH

What is the meaning of the symbol pH? See Introduction.

I have several books on flower growing, but none gives the types of soils (acid or alkaline) in which all plants thrive best. Can you give me this information? No *complete* list has ever been worked out. Of the vast number of plants grown, comparatively few show marked preferences for decidedly acid or alkaline soils. The vast majority exhibit a wide tolerance. (See following questions.)

What plants grow well on acid soils of fair to good fertility (pH 5.0 to 5.5)?

Andromeda	Fir	Pumpkin
Arbutus, Trailing	Hemlock	Radish
Azalea	Huckleberry	Raspberry
Beans	Hydrangea (Blue)	Red-cedar
Bent Grasses	Lily	Red Top
Birch, White	Lupine	Rhododendron
Blackberry	Millet	Rye
Blueberry	Mountain-laurel	Skimmia
Buckwheat	Oak, Scrub	Soybean
Camellia	Oak, Red	Spruce
Cedar, White	Oats	Strawberry
Cineraria	Orchard Grass	Sweet Potato
Cowpea	Orchid	Tobacco
Corn	Parsley	Turnip
Cranberry	Pea	Vetch, Hairy
Cucumber	Peanut	Violet
Cyclamen	Pepper	Watermelon
Daffodil	Pine	Wintergreen
Dewberry	Plantain	Wheat
Endive	Potato	Zinnia
Ferns		

What plants grow better on slightly acid or neutral soils (pH 5.6 to 6.5)?

Beans	Endive	Rye
Blackberry	Oats	Soybean
Brussels Sprouts	Orchard Grass	Squash
Buckwheat	Parsley	Strawberry
Carrot	Pea	Sweet Potato
Cabbage	Pepper	Tobacco
Clover, Crimson	Pumpkin	Tomato
Corn	Radish	Turnip
Cowpea	Red Top	Wintergreen
Cucumber	Rhubarb	Wheat

What plants do not grow well on strongly acid soils, but prefer slightly acid or slightly alkaline soils (pH 6.5 to 7.0)?

Alfalfa	Currant	Muskmelon
Apple	Dahlia	Nasturtium
Asparagus	Delphinium	Oak, White
Aster	Eggplant	Onion
Avens	Elm, American	Pansy
Baby's-breath	Everlasting Pea	Parsnip
Barley	Fescue, Sheep's	Peach
Balsam	Fescue, Tall	Pear
Beets	Flax	Peppermint
Beggar Weed	Foxglove	Petunia
Berseem	Foxtail	Phlox
Blue Grass	Gladiolus	Plum
Bokhara	Gooseberry	Poppy
Broccoli	Grape	Quince, Orange
Brome Grass	Helianthus	Rape
Camomile	Hemp	Salsify
Candytuft	Horseradish	Sorghum
Carnation	Hops	Spearmint
Cauliflower	Hydrangea (Pink)	Speltz
Celery	Iris	Spinach
Chard	Kale	Stock
Cherry	Kohlrabi	Sunflower
Chicory	Lady's Finger	Sweet-alyssum
Chrysanthemum	Larkspur	Sweet pea
Clover, Alsike	Leek	Sweet Vernal
Clover, Hungarian	Lentil	Sweet William
Clover, Japanese	Lettuce	Timothy
Clover, Mammoth	Linden, American	Vetch
Clover, Red	Lobelia	Walnut
Clover, White	Mangel Wurzels	Watercress
Clover, Yellow	Maple	Willow
Collards	Marigold	Wisteria
Columbine	Meadow Grass	Witch-hazel
Cosmos	Meadow Oat	Woodbine
Cotton	Mignonette	

What makes the soil acid? Soil acidity is common in many regions where rainfall is sufficient to leach large proportions of calcium and magnesium out of the soil. Decay of organic matter releases carbon dioxide. Combined with soil water, this forms carbonic acid.

Soils also become acid due to the use of acid-forming fertilizers, such as sulfate of ammonia and ammonium phosphates. The following table shows the relative acidifying or alkalinizing power of various fertilizing, liming, or acidifying materials, rated in terms of commercial limestone (calcium carbonate) as 1.0:

Material	Acidifying	Alkalinizing
Dolomitic Limestone	– –	1.1
Hydrated Lime (Calcite)	– –	1.4
Hydrated Lime (Dolomitic)	– –	1.7
Sodium Nitrate	– –	0.3
Calcium Nitrate	– –	0.2
Potassium Nitrate	– –	0.2
Ammonium Nitrate	0.6	– –
Ammonium Sulfate	1.1	– –
Monoammonium Phosphate	0.6	– –
Diammonium Phosphate	1.1	– –
Urea	0.8	– –
Sulfur	3.1	– –
Ferrous Sulfate	0.4	– –
Aluminum Sulfate	0.5	– –

Where can soil be sent to have its acidity determined? To your State Agricultural Experiment Station, college or university. (See list of Stations in Section 16.)

What simple means can be used to detect acid soil? Soil-test kits for testing pH are available at most garden shops. They test both alkalinity or acidity.

Testing the soil for acidity is an easy job which any home gardener can do with a test kit. Testing for nutrients is more complicated.

Is moss an indication of acidity? No. Moss grows on either acid or alkaline soil. Usually it means low fertility and high moisture.

Are toadstools an indication of soil acidity? No, they are not.

What will an acid soil produce? Notable among the plants that do best in an acid soil are those of the Ericaceae, which includes such plants as azalea, rhododendron, leucothoe, pieris, mountain-laurel, and others. (See previous question under pH.)

How can an acid soil be neutralized? An acid soil can be neutralized by adding ground limestone. The amount required can be determined by a soil analysis. (See Introduction.)

What is "sour" soil? A "sour" soil is a term sometimes used to denote the condition that develops in a poorly drained soil. More often, as the term is used, it is synonymous with an acid soil. If by "sour" soil is meant an acid soil, it can be sweetened by adding agricultural ground limestone or other forms of lime.

What can I do to counteract sour soil in seed boxes? The "sour" soil condition in seed flats can be prevented or corrected by providing sufficient drainage. Separate the boards on the bottom of the flat ¼ in., or bore a few holes in the bottom. Raise the flats on bricks or wood strips. "Sourness," in these cases, generally does not mean acidity.

How can I improve a dry, acid, heavy clay soil? Incorporate a liberal amount of peat moss, but first mix 10 to 15 lbs. of pulverized limestone with each bale of peat before the latter is worked into the soil. Apply additional limestone to the soil if needed. Always test for pH after soil settles following treatment.

I am making a vegetable garden on a piece of lawn; the soil is very acid. Will it be worth trying? Since most vegetables will do well on a slightly acid soil, this very acid soil could be changed without undue expense to grow vegetables by adding ground limestone.

What type of fertilizer is used in planting vegetables in acid soil? If the soil is too acid to produce the vegetable crop in mind, apply lime. In addition apply a fertilizer best suited to the particular crop.

My soil is neutral. Is there any chemical I can add to the soil to make it acid? I wish to try acorns from red oaks, and other things. Finely ground sulfur or ammonium sulfate can be used to make the soil more acid. Red oaks, however, will do well on a neutral soil.

Can the soil in a garden in a limestone country be made permanently acid? No. An acid soil made under such conditions can be maintained only by periodic treatment.

What use is sulfur for soil? How do you use it? Sulfur is used to increase the acidity of the soil. See Introduction for amounts.

What materials should be used in maintaining an acid-soil garden in a limestone country? Acid peat moss or oak leafmold, flowers of sulfur and ammonium sulfate.

How should acidifying materials be handled in the development and maintenance of an acid-soil garden in a limestone country? Make provision for perfect drainage of the area. Incorporate a liberal application of peat moss. Add dusting sulfur in the quantity, and as often, as soil tests (made at least once a year) indicate that it is necessary.

What are the best kinds of leaves for producing an acid condition in the soil? Leafmold from oak leaves has long been considered the ideal acidifying material for plants requiring an acid soil, such as rhododendrons, azaleas, and mountain-laurel. Recent experiments, however, indicate that this assumption is incorrect. Oak-leaf compost increased the pH temporarily, but after 45 days the pH value was higher (*less acid*) than before the application. However, there is no doubt that oak leafmold is beneficial to the growth of the acid-loving plants. In soils high in humus, acid-soil plants can tolerate higher pH readings.

Will you please tell me how to prepare a soil mixture using oak leafmold for growing blueberries? Dig a hole 3 to 4 ft. wide for each plant; incorporate 3 ins. of leafmold in the bottom; mix the soil for filling with ⅓ its bulk of leafmold, and pack tightly around the roots. Keep the surface over the roots mulched heavily with the oak leafmold, or with sawdust. Use ammonium sulfate to further acidify.

ALKALINITY

What is the best method for soil reconstruction? Our soil is of a lime structure (moderately alkaline). Our water is hard and slightly chlorinated. Compost at the rate of 1 lb. to a sq. ft. and 2½ lbs. of superphosphate for each 100 sq. ft. This should be thoroughly mixed with the soil. Sow green-manure crops in the fall. Use an acid commercial fertilizer for plants.

What is the best way to counteract highly alkaline soil? Sulfur or ammonium sulfate is used for the purpose. A soil with pH 8.0 (alkaline) will require 4 lbs. of sulfur to 100 sq. ft. to make it slightly acid (pH 6.0), or 8 lbs. of ammonium sulfate for the same area. Ammonium sulfate acts much more quickly than sulfur.

Would like to know what grows best in alkaline soil. What will counteract too much alkali? Very few plants do well in strongly alkaline soil. Use sulfur or ammonium sulfate for acidification.

We have alkaline soil. I succeed with most flowers but not with gladiolus. The bulbs rot. What is the reason? (Washington.) Gladiolus plants do better in slightly acid soil—acidify it with sulfur and use acid-forming fertilizer.

Our soil has considerable alkali in it. For that reason I have hesitated about trying to raise lady's-slippers. What can I do to grow these? Leafmold acidified with sulfur will produce satisfactory growth. Acid peat moss mixed with leafmold will also do. It is doubtful, however, that an alkaline soil will remain fit for native orchids, if they are meant by "lady's-slipper." If you mean impatiens (a garden balsam) it will grow in slightly alkaline soil.

What vegetables will grow in alkali ground? No vegetables grow well in highly alkaline soil. The most tolerant of alkalinity are asparagus, beet, lima bean, cauliflower, muskmelon, parsnip, and spinach.

Can any chemical be used to correct alkali in soil? My soil is heavy and moist. The best methods of control for such conditions consist of (1) providing a soil mulch to retard evaporation, and (2) applications of gypsum if the soil needs calcium; or sulfur, if it needs to be acidified. True western alkali soils are almost impossible to fit for garden use.

I have had much difficulty in growing flowers and plants, as many turn yellow. (Soil has been diagnosed by county agent as highly alkaline.) Why? Poor drainage may cause accumulation of alkaline salts. Apply iron sulfate at 1 to 2 lbs. per 100 sq. ft. More than 1 application may be necessary. Or use dusting sulfur (see Introduction).

What can one add to alkali water to make it suitable for irrigation on a small garden plot? (Kansas.) Water may be acidified by sulfuric, phosphoric acid, or other acids. This should be done, however, only on the advice of your Agricultural Experiment Station. Treating alkali water would probably be too costly for garden use.

LIME

What are the functions of lime in soil improvement?   Lime furnishes calcium which is needed for root development, strengthening of cell walls, and for formation of protoplasm and proteins; counteracts acidity; hastens decomposition of organic matter; aids in development of nitrogen-fixing bacteria; reduces toxicity of certain compounds.

What type of lime should be used in the garden?   Agricultural lime is the slowest but the most lasting. Several weeks may pass before its effect on soil is noticed. Hydrated and burned lime are much quicker in action, but tend to destroy humus. One hundred lbs. of ground limestone is equivalent in action to 74 lbs. of hydrated lime, or 56 lbs. of burned lime. The amounts to use will vary with the acidity of the soil. Usually 2 lbs. of agricultural limestone per 100 sq. ft. is sufficient, unless soils are extremely acid.

What is raw ground limestone?   Raw ground limestone is calcium carbonate, and is the material most commonly used for counteracting acidity. In urban areas, use fine crushed limestone for drives. Agricultural lime is identical.

What is hydrated lime?   Hydrated or slaked lime is formed from burned or quicklime (calcium oxide) and water. Hydrated and burned or quicklime are quicker acting than ground limestone (calcium carbonate). It is sometimes called slaked lime or quicklime.

Is lime the only material with which to sweeten an acid soil?   Some form of lime is usually used to correct soil acidity. The most commonly used forms are ground limestone, dolomitic limestone, and hydrated lime. Other materials that may be used are calcium cyanamide and wood ashes.

Can dry lime, left over from plastering a room, be used in any way as a fertilizer?   It may be used to alkalize acid soil, but is apt to be too coarse and lumpy. If lime is needed, apply it in the fall.

Would lime, such as I can purchase at the hardware store, be good for acid soil?   If it is hydrated lime, it can injure roots.

Can marl be used in the place of lime, with the same, or as good, results?   Marl (a natural deposit of calcium-bearing clay) is coarse, and its effect is very gradual and slow. Ordinarily, ground limestone is both less expensive and much more satisfactory.

What is "overliming" injury? Too much calcium (lime) in the soil causes the soil to become alkaline. Some elements as boron, manganese, iron, zinc, etc., are not soluble in an alkaline solution, and because they are needed in small amounts by plants, poor growth develops. Usually the growth is chlorotic (yellow). Overliming can be corrected by applying sulfur to the soil at 1 lb. per 100 sq. ft. More than one application may be necessary to bring about the desired acidity. Pin oaks are especially sensitive to overliming.

When and under what conditions should lime be added to the soil? Only when the soil is too acid for plants, and when calcium is low.

When, and when not, should lime be used around flowers and shrubs? Use lime only if the soil is so acid as to require correction. Use lime if calcium is lacking and the soil is acid. Use gypsum (calcium sulfate) when calcium is lacking and the soil is alkaline.

What is gypsum? A mineral composed of calcium sulfate which contains 2 molecules of water. Used in horticulture to add needed calcium to the soil when it is not necessary to decrease acidity. It is also used to improve the physical condition of soils and, under some conditions, to improve drainage and soil aeration.

Is gypsum (plaster of Paris) a useful soil amendment? Gypsum is valuable as a source of calcium where the soil is already alkaline and a change in the pH of the soil is not desirable. Called land plaster in England, it has been used for over a century. It is not as effective in breaking up clay soils as ground limestone, however.

Is lime needed to improve a gravelly soil? Have soil tested; it may not need it.

How can lime benefit clay soil, if the soil is originally composed of disintegrated limestone? As stated by some authorities, benefit is obtained by cementing finer particles into larger ones. The flocculation (cementing of particles) of clay soils as a result of liming has been questioned. For cementing soil particles, humus is better than lime.

Should a garden be treated with lime in the fall or spring? If ground limestone is used, it is best applied in the fall, but may be applied in spring.

How much lime should be used (for one application)? See Introduction under pH.

Is it necessary to put lime on the garden every year? Lime should be used only on acid soils. If needed, apply agricultural lime in the fall. Usually 2 lbs. per 100 sq. ft. is sufficient.

Can lime be strewn over the ground in winter with the snow? Yes, although it is better to apply early in the fall.

Why is it harmful to put commercial fertilizer and lime into the soil at the same time? What chemical reaction takes place? If lime is allowed to come into contact with superphosphate or fertilizer, the solubility, and hence the availability, of the latter may be reduced, especially in a non-acid or slightly acid soil. In soils that are acid, there is no objection to the application of fertilizer and lime at the same time, providing they are well incorporated into the soil and pH is not lower than 5.5.

When leaves are spaded in, in the fall, should lime be used in the spring? Most leaves do not produce an acid reaction, so that liming is not necessary unless your soil is naturally acid.

What crops need lime in the soil, and which do better without it? *Legumes* do better in neutral or slightly alkaline soils, hence lime additions are often necessary. *Acid-tolerant plants* like azaleas, rhododendrons, etc., need no lime although they need calcium. (See questions under pH.) For most plants lime should be applied only when the soil is very acid, since they do best in *slightly* acid soil (6.0 to 6.9 pH).

Instead of sand, I put very fine limestone on my soil, which has a preponderance of gumbo. It has made soil nice to work with. Will this small amount be apt to affect garden annuals and perennials? I have also added a great deal of barnyard fertilizer. Small amounts of lime can do no harm. The change in the soil structure was probably due to the manure rather than to the lime.

In foundation planting, I assume it is possible that lime coming loose from building and washing into soil may have disastrous effect on such acid-loving plants as azaleas and rhododendrons. Is this so? There is rarely much lime in the soil from this source. However, any chunks of plaster should be removed. If soil seems alkaline, apply dusting sulfur at 2 to 4 lbs. per 100 sq. ft. Sulfur is an acidifying agent.

Should I sprinkle my lawn with lime in the fall? If soil needs lime, it will be most effective when applied in the fall. In acid soil areas, periodic applications of limestone are recommended.

Will lime put on lawn on which oak and dogwood trees are growing injuriously affect such trees? Not unless excessive amounts are used. Have the soil tested and apply limestone only when needed.

My soil is covered with white-pine needles from adjacent trees. Should this make additional liming or other treatment advisable? Pine needles produce acidity, hence constant use of lime may be required to counteract this condition.

Sewage sludge is very acid from aluminum sulfate. Is lime the proper neutralizer, or does it leave the valuable plant and soil bacterial elements in a non-desirable form? Sewage sludge does not necessarily contain aluminum sulfate. If it does, lime is a good corrective; or superphosphate may be used.

When vegetable soil is too acid, as ascertained by laboratory test, how much lime should be applied to overcome a state of hyperacidity? See Introduction under pH.

I am planning to plant a small vegetable plot. Can one add too much lime? Lime should not be added, unless a test shows it is needed. Decidedly it can be overdone.

SOIL TESTING

What is the best method of determining the treatment a given soil requires? Test your soil; or have it tested. Your county agent or State Agricultural or Experiment Station will do this for you.

What is the approximate cost of having soil analyzed? It varies. A few states make no charge.

Are the chemistry sets on the market practical? They are rough tests only, worth very little unless interpreted by a trained technician.

Can I learn the true nature of the soil from a test? Yes. A good soil-testing kit will give acidity, nitrates, phosphates, potassium, calcium, etc., but note answer to above question.

What size of soil sample is desired? If your soil varies in nature from place to place, don't mix soil for tests, as is often recommended. It can vary as much as 3 to 4 points in pH and nutrients in a few feet. A general mixture test is worthless. In such cases, send separate samples. Write your Experiment Station for directions before sending sample.

How can I obtain information on soil analysis without the necessity of taking a course in chemistry?   Write to your Agricultural Experiment Station for information on soil testing. Several stations have published bulletins on this subject.

After testing, how can I know what to add to soil, in what quantities, and when?   Without experience in testing, one cannot tell from a soil test just what kinds of quantities of fertilizers to use. Send your sample to your Agricultural Experiment Station. All fertilizers contain analysis on each bag.

Which soil should I send for analysis? Soil screened last fall and stored in cellar, or fresh soil as soon as frost is out of it?   Tests of cold soils are inaccurate. Wait until mid-June before taking samples in cool climates.

How can we determine what vegetable or fruit a soil is best suited to produce?   The best procedure is to consult your local county agricultural agent.

Should untilled soil be analyzed to determine its fertility?   Such tests are meaningless if you intend to use soil in tilled condition. Work soil and allow organic matter to decompose before testing.

Should I have my soil tested to determine its acidity?   If plants grown do well, it is not necessary. It is desirable to have periodic tests of soils which are used to grow plants that require specific soil reactions, such as rhododendrons and azaleas. Home test kits will tell pH accurately enough and usually cost no more than a laboratory test. They can make many future tests without additional cost.

Can soil condition be determined by what is found growing on it, such as wild blueberries and sour-grass? Can soil with fine shell stone be good?   Yes. For example, blueberries indicate acid soil; dandelions alkaline soil. Too much lime from shells may be detrimental to some plants.

Plant Nutrients

What are the various elements of plant nutrition; and their uses? The three essential elements and their effect on plant growth are: *Nitrogen:* this element enters into the structure of protoplasm, chlorophyll, and various plant foods; it is needed for both the vegetative and reproductive stages of growth; its use is usually manifested by an increase in vegetative growth. *Phosphorus:* it is essential to cell division and for the formation of nucleoproteins; it aids root development; hastens maturity, or stiffens tissues; and stimulates flower and seed production. *Potash:* necessary for the manufacture and translocation of starches and sugar; it is a general conditioner, overcoming succulence and brittleness, hastening maturity and seed production, and aiding in root development.

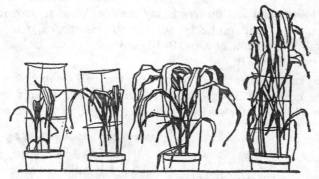

Nitrogen, phosphorus, and potassium are all needed for normal plant growth. Of the four pots of corn above, the first (left) lacked nitrogen; the second, phosphorus; the third, potassium. The one on the right was supplied with all three.

NITROGEN

How can I recognize nitrogen deficiency? The whole plant is dwarfed and the older leaves turn from green to yellow, and then to brown, and remain attached to the plant. Stalks are slender, and few new stalks develop.

How can nitrogen deficiency be corrected? Apply ammonium sulfate at ¾ lb. or sodium nitrate at 1 lb. per 100 sq. ft. Ammonium sulfate tends to make soil more acid; sodium nitrate makes it more alkaline. A complete fertilizer (as 4–12–4, or 5–10–5) will correct the deficiency of nitrogen as well as supply phosphorus and potash.

What is lacking in my garden soil, since the carrots I raise, though of good size, are almost tasteless and colorless? Nitrogen is lacking; a complete fertilizer (4–12–4, or 5–10–5) at 4 lbs. per 100 sq. ft. will correct this.

What causes yellowing of foliage? It may be due to poor drainage, or to lack of nitrogen.

What shall I do for soil that grows annuals and perennials too large and weedy, but weak-stemmed? Probably too much nitrogen in the soil and not enough phosphorus and potassium. Use a 0–10–10 fertilizer, or something similar, 2 lbs. per 100 sq. ft. for one or two applications. Excess nitrogen usually disappears rapidly.

All foliage and few flowers is my trouble. What is wrong? Too much nitrogen and probably not enough phosphorus and potash; add both in the form of a 0–10–10 fertilizer (or similar) at rate of 2 lbs. per 100 sq. ft.

What causes an excess of nitrogen in the soil? Have added 10 lbs. of bone meal in a 35-sq.-ft. bed for annuals, and some dehydrated manure (100 lbs.) for spring. Excess nitrogen, or the symptoms of

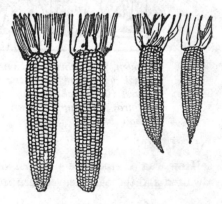

Potash is especially important for fruit and grain crops. The two ears of corn at the right show the result of potash (potassium) deficiency.

excess nitrogen, may be brought about through the excessive use of nitrogenous fertilizers, high-nitrogen complete fertilizers, or a deficiency of phosphorus and potash. The amount of manure you have applied constitutes overfertilization. Bone meal usually is locked up in an insoluble form and has little effect on growth.

PHOSPHORUS

How can I recognize phosphorus deficiency? The whole plant is dwarfed, but the foliage is a dark, dull green; leaf stem (petiole) often turns purple. Areas between veins on leaf sometimes turn purple, and leaf margins often turn yellow. Loss of lower foliage follows.

How can phosphorus deficiency be corrected? Apply treble superphosphate or superphosphate, at 5 lbs. per 100 sq. ft.

POTASH

How can I recognize potash (potassium) deficiency? Lower foliage begins to turn yellow at leaf margin; leaf often mottled yellow and green in between veins; margins of leaves turn brown and foliage drops from plant; plant generally stunted.

How can potash (potassium) deficiency be corrected? Apply muriate of potash or sulfate of potash, 1 lb. per 100 sq. ft.

What fertilizer should I use to encourage fruits and vegetable roots? Plants grow all to tops. Withhold nitrogen and increase the proportion of phosphorus and potash in the mixture. Use a 2–10–10 fertilizer for a few years, adding additional nitrogen only where, and as, needed.

Some soils tend to develop barren vines. What is lacking? This is usually the result of too little phosphorus and potash.

What does soil lack that produces an abundant crop of any vegetable above ground, but no root vegetables such as potatoes, beets, turnips, or salsify? Phosphorus and potassium are probably deficient in this soil. (See previous questions.)

My garden is made of filled earth and has a large amount of street sweepings in it, high in leafmold. All root crops fail; beans and corn are only crops that succeed. Why? Lack of phosphorus and potassium may cause the trouble. However, all fertilizer elements are lacking in leafmold. Try a complete fertilizer.

TRACE ELEMENTS

What are "trace" elements? Elements (present in most soils) which are needed in very small amounts, for plant nutrition. Some of these are present in such small quantities that they are known as trace elements (see discussion below).

What are the principal trace elements? Boron, chlorine, copper, iron, manganese, zinc, and molybdenum.

Is boron a necessary ingredient in all types of soils? A small amount of boron is essential for plant growth, and to prevent various physiological disorders. It is present in most soils in sufficient quantity. It is most apt to be deficient in soils low in organic matter. If overused, it can be toxic to plants.

How should boron be used in the soil? Boron is commonly applied in the form of borax, at the rate of 10 to 15 lbs. *per acre.* This is only 4 to 5 ozs. per 1,000 sq. ft.

How can I be sure that my soil will have enough sodium for good growth of beets? Use ½ to 1 lb. nitrate of soda, or ½ lb. table salt, per 100 sq. ft. Most mixed fertilizers contain enough sodium for beets, however.

My garden soil turns a red color on top when dry; why? The red color probably is due to a surface growth of red algae. These minute plants do no harm and are often found on moist soils. They go unnoticed until the soil surface dries and their red color is then apparent by contrast.

Are iron or steel filings beneficial in darkening colors of perennials, especially roses and lilacs? No. Iron sulfate (copperas) is beneficial where iron in soil is low; chiefly useful in greening foliage, not darkening flower color.

HUMUS

What is humus? For practical purposes, humus may be defined as the resultant brown or dark-brown substance that develops following the breakdown of organic materials by various soil organisms. Actually, no one knows the exact chemical composition but a soil gel with lignin, a component, is as good a definition as any.

How does one recognize the different types of humus, such as peat, leafmold, muck, etc? *Peat:* soft, brown, spongy, semigranular material; domestic peats, unless kiln dried, contain more water than the imported type. *Muck:* black, represents further state of decay than peat—not so useful. *Bacterized Peat:* supposedly treated; usually no better than muck. *Leafmold:* brownish-black material with some undecomposed leaves and twigs present; useful soil conditioner. *Wood Soil:* usually leafmold, but further decomposed; useless without additions of fertilizer.

In what forms is potential humus available to the average home gardener? See previous question. Manure, straw, peat moss, kitchen waste, seaweed, sawdust, decayed wood chips, pine needles, hay—all these must decompose before becoming humus. The compost pile (which see) is probably the best of all sources of humus for the home garden.

What is the function of humus in the soil? Among the important functions of humus are to effect granulation of the soil, thereby improving drainage and soil aeration; to increase its water-holding capacity; to increase the bacterial activity; to increase the percentage of such essential elements as nitrogen and sulfur; and to help in transforming essential elements from non-available to available forms.

Is humus important to soil fertility? Yes; by increasing moisture absorption and the activity of several of the essential elements, especially nitrogen.

How is humus incorporated into the soil? By spading or plowing.

Is spring or fall the best time to add humus to soil? Any time the soil can be worked. Humus does not injure growing plants.

Our soil is rich but hard to work. What is the best source of humus? Manure, peat moss, or a compost heap.

What method do you recommend to maintain humus and bacteria in soils? Keep soils aerated by the addition of compost and/or peat moss. Use green-manure crops (which see) wherever possible.

What is to be done when humus keeps the earth too moist? Incorporate sand or weathered steam cinders.

What would you recommend to keep a very rich black soil from caking? It forms a hard crust about an inch deep. Add humus—manure, peat, alfalfa hay. Incorporate fine steam cinders in the top 6 ins.

What causes soil to become very hard? Lack of organic matter.

A bog was dug up to make a lake; stuff removed looks like excellent humus. How can this material be converted to garden use? The material should make an excellent mulch, or to mix with soil. Unless soil on which this is used is very acid, the acidity of the humus will have no detrimental effect. If the material is lumpy, place in small piles to dry; pulverize before applying.

Do commercial fertilizers supply humus? The application of organic fertilizers such as soybean and cottonseed meals supplies a very small amount of humus. The inorganic fertilizers do not supply humus.

PEAT MOSS

What is the difference in value between peat moss and peat? Between domestic and imported peat? Peat moss is moss (usually sphagnum) in an advanced state of disintegration; peat is a product of some kind of vegetation (not necessarily moss) largely decomposed. Domestic peat is usually of sedge origin, although we have some sphagnum peat in this country. Imported peat is usually sphagnum peat. Unfortunately, the terms peat and peat moss are used interchangeably in garden shops. Sedge peat is of less value than that from sphagnum.

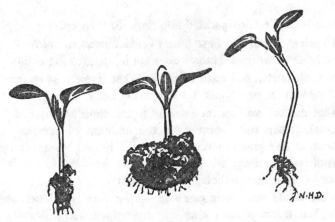

Humus in the soil absorbs and holds moisture, encouraging fibrous root growth. Center seedling above was grown in a half-soil, half-peat moss mixture; the other two in very sandy and very clay soil lacking humus.

Does peat have any value as a fertilizer? Yes, but it is very slowly available. Domestic sedge peat contains up to 3 per cent nitrogen. Sphagnum peat ("peat moss") contains less than 1 per cent nitrogen. It is slower in availability than the sedge peat. Do not rely on peat or peat moss for fertility. Use in conjunction with fertilizer.

Is peat moss good for flower gardens in general? Yes. When dug into the soil, it helps retain moisture, and in other ways increases productiveness.

When is the best time to use peat moss—spring or autumn? Apply any time that soil is being worked if humus is needed.

Is it true that peat moss worked into the soil will make a heavy soil lighter and will cause a light soil to hold more moisture? Yes. In this respect its action is similar to that of compost or manure.

As a winter protection is peat moss considered as good as straw or leaves? No. Peat moss as a mulch can blow away, or at the opposite extreme, it can mat together, forming an impenetrable barrier against water. It is better used as a soil additive.

What is the best way to use peat moss in flower gardens? Work it into the bed.

I use peat moss as litter in my hen coop. Will I have to add anything to it for use in the vegetable garden? Yes. It is desirable to add superphosphate at the rate of 5 lbs. per 100 sq. ft. of ground.

What plants can tolerate peat moss? All acid-tolerant plants (azaleas, hydrangeas, oaks, coniferous and broad-leaved evergreens, etc.). Most other plants benefit through its use. Alkaline-loving plants are the exception. But adding lime (about a quart to a bushel) offsets acidity.

Why doesn't peat moss freeze? If sufficient moisture is present, peat moss freezes. If perfectly dry, its fluffiness provides an air cushion.

In the propagation of certain plants on a large scale, I need to have about ¼ of my soil mixture consist of peat moss. Is there any suitable substitute that could be found in the South Carolina low country? Well-rotted compost is best or you can use shredded sugarcane, shredded redwood bark, or decomposed pine needles.

What is the best substitute for peat moss? Sedge peat, bagasse (sugarcane pulp), leafmold, pine needles, shredded redwood bark, ground barks of most trees, compost, and sawdust used in smaller amounts than peat.

Manures

A local riding stable gives away manure for the hauling. How can it be used in the garden? Although manure is a valuable soil amendment when composted, most riding stables spray their stalls with disinfectants, fly repellents, and other toxic chemicals. See Introduction for ways to handle this material.

Is cow manure a good fertilizer for a vegetable garden? Not if maximum production is wanted. It is not too rich in food elements, but is a valuable soil amendment. Allowing it to rot in a compost heap over winter is the best way to prepare it for use.

Is manure worked into the garden this year of any value in future years? Yes. Like all organic matter, manure becomes humus eventually and will continue to affect soil for years.

How does poultry manure differ from other types? We are in a broiler-producing area and can get it for nothing. Unless it is mixed with litter, it does not add much to the organic content of soil: it is of use largely as a source of nitrogen for immediate effect. Mixing it with superphosphate and wood ashes will not only make it more pleasant to handle, but will kill odors and increase its fertilizer value.

Is it necessary to use commercial fertilizer if I use the manure from our 200 hens? Yes, if you want maximum production. A farm fertilizer such as a 2–10–10 would balance its high nitrogen. Or mix poultry manure with superphosphate and wood ashes; or use muriate of potash instead of wood ashes. The poultry manure should be aged until a strong odor of ammonia disappears before mixing with wood ashes.

We have a kennel and accumulate dog manure. Does it have any value as a fertilizer? Dog manure, like poultry manure, is high in nitrogen. It should be mixed with litter, compost, and superphosphate before using.

Would dumping cat litter and its manure on the compost pile hurt

the compost? On the contrary, it would improve the finished compost if allowed to age for a few weeks.

Can the contents of a privy be used as compost? Although there are aesthetic prejudices against such use, one of the famous English fertilizers, Clays, was nothing but artificially dried privy scrapings, used almost with reverence by gardeners up to the time of World War II. If aged for a year and perhaps applied only to soil in which ornamental plants grow, it would be a good use for material which is otherwise a nuisance.

I planted a small vegetable garden of about 2,000 sq. ft. I plan to enrich soil with a compost and dried cow manure this year. How much should be used? At least 100 lbs. of dried cow manure should be used to 1,000 sq. ft. If you can afford it, triple the amount.

I am no longer able to get barnyard fertilizer for my garden plot. Is there a substitute fertilizer that I can procure? "Commercial" (dried and ground) cow manure and sheep manure are available in most garden centers. Incorporate green manures, and, in addition, apply a fertilizer recommended for garden use.

Under what conditions can dried manure be used in place of rotted manure? It is useful as an ingredient in the compost heap or it can be mixed with soil in a flower or vegetable garden.

Can a garden have too much goat manure? Goat manure is reasonably strong in nitrogen. It should be used in about the same way as described for sheep manure.

Should goat manure and straw be put on frozen ground, or put in compost heap until spring? Better in compost heap, if mixed with other materials, otherwise, it would be better to spread the manure and straw on the ground. If left in a pile, some leaching will take place, and not on the spot where wanted.

I procured fresh horse manure but find it difficult to keep it from "burning." Can leaves be mixed with it? When horse manure is "burned," it loses most of its nitrogen, but it is still good as a soil conditioner. Mixing peat or leaves or chopped straw with horse manure and keeping it wet will reduce burning.

Will wood shavings harm horse manure? No. Apply to soil in the fall.

Is horse stable manure harmful to roses and delphiniums? Much stable manure is treated to control flies and odors. Well-composted manure *may* be safe but test on tomato seedlings first.

LIQUID MANURE

Is there any fertilizer than can be used as a liquid for the small home garden?   Five teaspoons of a regular 5–10–5, 5–10–10, 7–7–7, or similar grade of complete fertilizer per gallon of water will make a satisfactory liquid fertilizer. Such fertilizers are about 75 per cent soluble. Do not use premium grades of fertilizers containing much organic materials. Apply 1 gal. to 5 sq. ft.

How can you make liquid fertilizer, using chemical ingredients which are cheap to buy?   A liquid fertilizer containing 1 teaspoonful each of saltpeter (potassium nitrate), superphosphate (monocalcium phosphate), and Epsom salts (magnesium sulfate) is satisfactory.

Green-Manure Crops

What is a green-manure crop? A cover crop?   The term "green-manure crop" refers to any crop that may be turned into the soil in an undecomposed, green-tissue stage. In contrast, a cover crop refers to a more or less permanent crop used for the purpose of preventing erosion.

How are green-manure crops planted?   For small areas, seeds of the green-manure crops can be broadcast. For large areas a drill is used. Seeds should not be covered too deeply—approximately twice their diameter is sufficient.

Legumes—such as clover, vetch, and soybeans—help to increase the soil's nitrogen supply.

What are several good summer green-manure crops? The crops most commonly used for summer green manure are alfalfa, cowpeas, crimson clover, red clover, sweet clover, crotalaria, lespedeza, soybeans, and Sudan grass.

What green-manure crop can be left growing in the ground over winter, to be turned under in spring? The most common winter green-manure crops are rye, perennial rye grass, and oats.

What quantity of seed should be sown, per 1,000 sq. ft., of green-manure crops? Alfalfa, ½ lb.; cowpeas, 2½ to 3 lbs.; crimson clover and red clover, ½ lb.; sweet clover, ½ to ¾ lb.; crotalaria, ½ to ¾ lb.; lespedeza, ½ lb.; soybeans, 2–3 lbs.; Sudan grass, ½ to ¾ lb.; rye, 2 to 3 lbs.; rye grass, 1 to 2 lbs.; buckwheat, 1½ lbs. These are approximate amounts. For thick and quick coverage, on small areas, they can be increased up to double these quantities.

I cannot obtain cow manure. What do you suggest as a substitute? Old, partly rotted straw, or alfalfa hay, together with a complete fertilizer, can be used as substitutes. Plow in early in the fall and add fertilizer at time of plowing. Or use a green-manure crop.

How tall should a green-manure crop be before it is turned under? In general, it is best to turn under green crops when their succulence is near the maximum, yet at a time when abundant tops have been produced. This stage occurs when they are about, or a little beyond, half mature. Always allow at least three weeks to elapse between plowing under a green-manure crop and planting.

Are clover and buckwheat good for soil? Clover and buckwheat are good green-manure crops, but soybeans and rye are better and quicker. Sow soybeans in the spring and plow under in early fall. Sow rye in September and plow under in the spring. Use 2 lbs. per 1,000 sq. ft.

Where a green-manure crop is plowed under in fall, is it advisable to follow with a winter crop? Only where there is possibility of soil erosion.

What winter green-manure crops can be used following the turning under of red clover? Rye, rye grass, or oats.

How soon after the summer green-manure crop is turned under can the fall crop be sown? It is advisable to delay the sowing of the second crop three weeks, if possible; but follow the specific planting dates recommended for the winter crop used.

When should winter green-manure crops be sown? Late August or early September. Rye can be sown as late as first week of October. If soil areas are available, sow at any time if space is not needed for planting the same season.

If soil is respaded in spring, following turning under of green manure (clover) in fall, will the crop come to the top? If the green-manure crop is turned under at the proper time, it will be sufficiently decomposed by spring so that respading can be done.

When land is cleared, and winter rye sown, what should be done in spring to prepare for vegetables? Plow the rye under in April. Apply a fertilizer recommended for vegetables at twice the recommended rate.

How can organics and nitrogen be supplied in city gardens without compost or chemical fertilizer? Peat moss and dried manures may be used. Soybean meal and cottonseed meal will add nitrogen.

Should turf and large roots be removed from virgin soil or turned under to make humus? It is advisable to turn under as much organic matter as possible in preparing soil for planting. Turf and roots of annual and herbaceous plants should be turned under. Remove the large roots of woody plants.

Can a green-manure crop be planted which will raise the pH and sweeten the soil? No, green-manure crops in themselves exert very little influence on the degree of acidity of the soil.

When there is a shortage of animal fertilizer, what kind and proportion of other fertilizer are suggested for garden use? Incorporate green manures. Apply fertilizers made for vegetable gardens at twice the recommended rate.

Do any plants, other than legumes and green-manure crops, supply any nutrients to soil? Any plant which is turned under supplies a certain amount of nutrients. The proportions vary with the type of plant.

Does planting rye in fall and plowing under in spring keep up fertility of the soil? The use of rye as a green-manure crop will do little toward increasing the nitrogen content of the soil; in fact, it may even decrease it temporarily. It does, however, add humus, and thus helps to increase crop production.

Should green-manure crops such as rye be used every year? In gardens devoted to the production of vegetables or annual flowers, it is advisable to sow a winter green-manure crop each autumn.

At what stage should rye be turned under? As late as possible to produce more green growth, and up to within 3 weeks of planting time.

Should rye be completely covered when it is turned under? Yes, but the green-manure crop should be incorporated with the upper 8 to 12 ins. of soil instead of being plowed or dug under in a layer. If a few of the stems are not covered, it is all right.

What is a legume? All leguminous plants belong to the pea family, recognizable by the formation of their flowers. Peas, beans, and clovers are legumes. They all attract bacteria which collect nitrogen and store it on the roots. The small nodules on the roots, when they decay, add nitrogen to the soil.

What is the special advantage of using a leguminous green-manure crop? The advantage of a legume (as compared to a non-legume) is that the nitrogen content of the soil will be increased by the root-nodule organisms. However, the legume crops take longer to grow. For a small garden, rye or perennial rye grass is usually more practical.

Are inoculant powders for use on legumes really helpful? Yes. These inoculant powders are listed under various trade names (such as Nitragen, Legume Aid) and are obtainable in local garden stores. They are used to assist in the development of nitrogen-fixing bacteria on the roots of leguminous plants. They are applied when seeds are planted. The mixtures vary with the crop to be planted, so the crop should always be mentioned when buying these products.

Is it advisable to try to grow alfalfa for soil improvement in southern part of Maine? Yes. But plant early (mid-August) to avoid heaving out and winter killing. Sow 12 to 15 lbs. per acre.

How is the land prepared for growing alfalfa? Same as for any other crop. It may be necessary to add lime.

When is it best to plant crimson clover and expect results from it in improving the soil for a garden? Crimson clover is usually seeded in July or August, or at least 6 weeks before normal date of the first killing frost in fall. It may be turned under the following spring or early summer.

Do you plow crimson clover under when it is in bloom? It is best to turn it under when in bloom, or shortly after this stage. It can, however, be turned under at any stage; but the less growth has been made, the less humus will be produced.

Are Austrian peas good to use as a green-manure crop? Yes, they are a good winter crop. Use soybeans as a summer crop. Plow both under to add organic matter to the soil.

At what rate should soybeans be sown for a green-manure crop? Three lbs. per 1,000 sq. ft.

Compost

What is "compost"? Compost is the term applied to organic matter—such as leaves, weeds, grass clippings, and the like—which has been sufficiently decayed to form a light, crumbly mold. In making compost in a compost heap, soil and manure are often mixed with the vegetable matter.

Should the average home gardener have a compost heap? Yes, by all means. It is about the only adequate substitute for the "well-rotted" manure which is less available than it used to be.

BUILDING

What materials are used in making a compost heap? Plant refuse: cornstalks, cabbage stems, dead foliage, and discarded vegetables; leaves, grass cuttings, garbage, soil, manure (in fact, any vegetable matter that will decay), plus lime and complete fertilizers. Weeds, even when seeding, may be used if the heap is to be remade at the end of each 3 months, turning it inside out so that every part of the heap is completely decomposed before use. A heap treated in this way is so well rotted that most seeds and insect eggs are destroyed.

How is a compost heap constructed? Heaps 4 ft. wide and 6 ft. long are a convenient size for the small place. Dig out this area to a depth of from 12 to 18 ins. and throw the soil to one side. The bottom layer should be cornstalks, cabbage stems, and other coarse material, tamped down. Over this lay 2 or 3 ins. of soil, and then

2 or 3 ins. of manure, if available. Peat moss can be used if manure cannot be had. Sprinkle raw ground limestone over every other layer at the rate of a quart to a wheelbarrowload of compost material. On alternate layers apply a complete chemical fertilizer, about a quart to each alternate layer. Add layers of leaves, cuttings, weeds, etc., with a layer of soil, manure, or peat moss every 12 to 18 ins. Keep sides even but sloping very gradually inward toward top. When all material has been placed in layers, soak thoroughly with hose and cover entirely with 3 ins. soil, well firmed down. The top is left saucer-shaped to receive and absorb rainfall. Do not let heap dry out at any time. At end of 3 months remake entire heap, turning inside out, if rapid decomposition is desired.

What length of time is required for a well-made compost heap to rot? Four months to a year, depending on its composition and whether or not ingredients have been added to hasten decay; usually about 9 months.

What is a good formula for making a compost pile break down quickly? I understand lime should not be used as it causes loss of nitrogen. Lime should be used, but should not come in immediate contact with added fertilizer.

Is the use of a compost starter advisable? Most of those sold are only fertilizers plus limestone. Your own fertilizer will be much cheaper. Others are bacterial cultures. Bacteria can be added for nothing with garden soil.

How often should a new compost heap be started? To maintain a constant supply of compost, a new heap should be started every 6 months.

How is rotted compost used in gardening? It should be sieved through a coarse (1-in.) screen and then diluted with 3 or 4 parts of garden soil. It can be worked into the garden by applying a 1½ in. layer and cultivating it into the upper 6 ins. of soil. For a lawn dressing, apply the sieved compost without dilution with soil.

How should decomposed compost be removed from the heap? Cut sections down vertically with a spade, leaving straight, clean sides where it has been removed. Sift through a 1-in. sifter and save coarse siftings for a new compost heap.

Must I use compost in my garden? I have no space for a compost pile. Unless you can afford to buy peat moss in large amounts, compost is the only way to supply organic matter. For those with limited space, composting in the plastic bags used for disposing of lawn clippings and other wastes will solve the problem. Mix leaves, lawn clippings, or even garbage with about a handful of a good mixed fertilizer, plus a pint or two of good garden soil to each bushel. Dried leaves should be sprinkled enough to moisten them through, but not make them soggy. Clippings and garbage will not need additional moisture. Seal the materials in a plastic bag and tie shut. Stack the bags in any convenient place (I have used a garage and a root cellar). At temperatures above 70° F., material will be ready for use in three to four months.

GARBAGE

Are these any good for the compost heap: orange peels, banana peels, and green corn shucks? Yes, any vegetable refuse free of disease is all right. Even weeds with seeds are all right if properly fermented. Do not, however, use coffee grounds. Tests at the U.S.D.A. show they are slightly toxic to plants.

Can fresh table refuse and garbage be applied to the garden? I have been putting everything through a meat chopper and this makes a fine lot of refuse. The problem is how to apply it. Are orange skins of much fertilizing value? The materials mentioned, by themselves, do not constitute fertilizers, but when rotted in a compost pile they are valuable.

The refuse from my incinerator consists mostly of ashes and unburned garbage, such as grapefruit, orange peels, etc. Is this O.K. to bury in soil having a large clay content? Yes; but better to make a compost heap with 6-in. alternate layers of soil, garbage, grass cuttings, etc. It would take a year to make a good compost, but it's worth the trouble.

After apples have been crushed and squeezed for cider, would it be advisable to use the apple pomace in the compost pile? Yes, apple pomace is all right to add to compost; cover with soil.

What is the case for, and against, adding garbage to the compost heap? Garbage is a most desirable source of compost. Each layer of garbage must, however, be immediately covered with soil to prevent odors. If dogs run loose in your community, unsorted table garbage will attract them unless the heap is fenced in. Garbage also attracts rodents. Garbage can be placed in a pit, at a distance from house, each layer being sprinkled with a layer of soil and of raw ground limestone. When the contents of the pit are decomposed, it can be added in layers to a new compost heap when one is being built. In this way rodents are kept out of the compost heap and garbage is decomposed underground without odor.

GRASS CLIPPINGS

What good are grass cuttings? How fast do they decay? Clippings make satisfactory compost. If layered with soil in thin layers (4 ins. of soil and 2 ins. of clippings), or added to a mixed heap, a compost will be ready in less than a year.

HICKORY HULLS

Do the hulls (not shells) from hickory nuts cause soil acidity? We have 3 hickory trees on a double lot and don't know whether to put the hulls into the compost pile or burn them. Hickory and walnut hulls contain a chemical that is toxic to plants, so should not be added to the compost pile.

LEAVES

Should the leaves for compost be rotted? It is best to have them at least partly rotted before placing them in compost heap. If not, it is likely to take a full year for them to decompose, unless manure or peat moss is also used in the compost pile.

Are elm leaves good to use on the compost heap? Yes.

How do you make fertilizer out of maple leaves? Add to compost heap in the same way as other leaves.

Should anything be used with leaves for compost? Compost or peat moss, lime, and complete fertilizers. Leaves are low in plant nutrients and must have added fertilizer to be of much use.

What can be added to accumulated leaves in the fall to hasten decomposition? Make a pile 4 ft. wide and any desired length. Each layer of leaves 12 ins. deep should be sprinkled with a complete commercial fertilizer at the rate of a pint per bushel of leaves.

Is soil put on the compost pile (made largely of leaves) to help decomposition? Yes.

Will this fall's leaves be fertilizer by next spring? Can anything be

done to hurry the process?   Not that soon. It will take about a year. Leaves saved from fall and composted in the spring may make good leafmold by fall.

Much has been said about the value of a compost of rotted leaves. I understand that some leaves, due to high acid content, have practically no value as manure. Which should be burned and which should be saved?   Leafmold from most trees is only slightly, if at all, acid. This reference is to leaves of deciduous trees. Evergreens, however, will produce acid leafmold. The use of lime is an easy way to correct any such acidity.

Are the ashes from burned leaves and grass cuttings of any benefit, or of as much benefit, as those same leaves and cuttings if they were permitted to decay?   No. If leaves and clippings are made into a compost, they serve a much better purpose than when burned.

SPECIAL PROBLEMS

What can the home gardener make from refuse, etc., to take the place of 5–10–5 and nitrate of soda?   Make a compost pile of straw, weeds, grass clippings, leaves, and other plant parts. (See Compost, Introduction, this section.)

All the refuse from our lawns and vegetables and flower gardens has gone into our compost pile. This includes corn and dahlia stalks, peonies, etc. The entire pile has been covered with clay subsoil (topsoil being scarce). A little fertilizer has been added and some leaves. It is our intention to use this pile, accumulated during summer and fall, by digging it into the vegetable gardens. Is this good practice? A better method would have been to make alternate layers of soil and refuse together, with a definite amount of commercial fertilizer and lime. The only thing to do now is to turn the pile several times, mixing all the ingredients together.

Will you give me an idea of the fertilizer value of compost, with inorganic chemicals added, as compared to that made of organic matter only?   Organic fertilizers are less satisfactory to add to composts than inorganic, largely because of their slower action. Once decomposed, there should be little difference between the two. Inorganic fertilizers and lime are added to the compost heap both to hasten decomposition and to supply nutrients otherwise low or lacking.

In making a compost pile, is it more advisable to pile up on top

of ground, or to dig pit and gradually fill in? In dry climates, a slight depression is best, but elsewhere, pile should be on level ground.

How do you keep a compost pile from smelling? If smelly ingredients are used (e.g., raw sewage sludge), using superphosphate on alternate layers instead of lime will kill odors.

What is a good substitute for city dwellers for the objectionable compost pile? Try making compost in plastic bags. Mix organic materials with fertilizers (1 qt. to a bushel). Mixture should be slightly damp. Seal and store at 70° F. or higher. Don't use lime until compost is ready to use in 3 to 6 months.

Does the compost lose any of its elements when kept in the house all winter and dried up? The mechanical structure of such soils is affected more than its nutritional value. If stored inside, storing in plastic bags will keep it moist. Drying kills soil organisms vital to plant life.

Compost pits are sometimes thickly inhabited by very large, fat earthworms. Are these harmful, or should they be left in the decomposing material? Worms do no damage in the compost; in fact, they assist in the decomposition of vegetable matter. When compost is sifted for use, they will be eliminated.

PESTS AND DISEASES

In making a compost heap, how can we avoid carrying over diseases of previous year, as tomato and potato blight, etc.? Do not use diseased tops, vines, or fruits for composting, unless special care is taken in "turning" heap. (See next question.)

Some of the waste vegetable matter I put in my compost heap had a lot of aphids or similar insects on it. I put lime and superphosphate with the compost. Will the aphids be killed during the winter? The adults will probably die, but the eggs may carry over. At the time of making the compost the vegetable matter should have been sprayed with malathion. However, if the heap is turned "inside out" every 3 months and if every part is thus thoroughly fermented, most insects and diseases will be destroyed.

Does it do any harm to put moldy fruit, vegetables, or mildewed shrubs and leaves into the compost? Any vegetable matter which is not infected with disease or infested with insects may be used safely for composting. Molds resulting from decay do no harm.

Explain the chemistry of the compost heap. Would the pests it might harbor outweigh the advantages for a small (50 × 100 ft.) garden?   A compost heap is a mixture of soil, fertilizer, and organic matter. In decomposing, the combination does not always get rid of all diseases and pests. To save organic matter, a compost pile is worth having.

Organic Fertilizers

What is organic fertilizer?   An organic fertilizer is one which is derived from organic materials—plant or animal substances. All are compounds of carbon. Some of these materials, such as cottonseed meal, bone meal, tankage, and castor pomace, may add small amounts of humus as well as nutrients to the soil. Others, such as urea or ureaform, may not add humus.

What is best for a vegetable garden, compost or chemicals?   Use both. They complement each other. Compost is organic but is not a balanced fertilizer, while a chemical fertilizer contains no organic matter to supply humus.

What fertilizers are best for loose soil?   Loose soil will be benefited by the incorporation of organic matter, to increase the humus. The use of commercial fertilizer does not depend upon the soil structure.

What causes soil to crack in dry weather?   Heavy soils will crack unless sufficient organic matter is present to prevent cohesion of the fine particles.

Is bone meal a good fertilizer for all plants?   No. Bone meal is a safe fertilizer to use, but it contains no potash and only a small amount of nitrogen. Although high in phosphorus, this element is released very slowly. Based on amount of essential ingredients contained, it is more expensive than some chemical fertilizers. However, gardeners use it for many purposes.

COTTONSEED MEAL

What nutrients does cottonseed meal contain?   Cottonseed meal contains approximately 7 per cent nitrogen, 2.5 per cent phosphoric acid, and 1.5 per cent potash.

How long does it take for cottonseed meal to mix with soil? Part of the nitrogen and other essential elements of cottonseed meal are readily available; the remainder becomes available more slowly.

On what plants can cottonseed meal be used, and in combination with what other fertilizer? It can be used on nearly all plants as it contains about 7 per cent nitrogen, which becomes available slowly; also 3 per cent phosphorus, and 2 per cent potash. It can be used with superphosphate. Cottonseed meal is especially recommended for use on rhododendrons and other ericaceous plants.

DRIED BLOOD

Is blood meal a fertilizer? Dried blood is high in nitrogen but low in both phosphorus and potash. Its greatest value is as a source of minor elements in soluble form. Unfortunately, it is too valuable an industrial material to be economical as a fertilizer.

LEAFMOLD

In using leafmold as a fertilizer should it be used liberally or sparingly? Leafmold is not a very high-grade fertilizer. It is a good soil conditioner, and as such can be used liberally—a covering 4 ins. deep is all right.

What effect do pine needles have on soil? They acidify it, and help improve condition. They eventually add humus.

When should fallen leaves be used? After decomposition; apply to soil at any time of the year.

Last fall I spaded my garden a foot deep and on the bottom I put a heavy layer of maple leaves. This was covered over with a foot of earth. Was this worth while? It would be better to spade leaves into the soil in the fall; or let them decay first and add to soil later.

How do hard maple tree leaves affect the soil if left where they fall over winter? It is better to compost them. Little value if left on top of soil.

Do large quantities of mixed leaves (elm, maple, oak, beech) make good fertilizer when rotted? They make a good soil conditioner but are of comparatively little fertilizer value; not nearly so effective as manures unless a heavy dosage of fertilizer is added in rotting them.

Is it true that the leaves of silver leaf and other poplars, spaded into the soil, are toxic to the growth of flowers?   No.

Will oak leaves make the ground sour?   No. When decomposed, they make an excellent soil conditioner. Used in quantity, they will make the ground acid but only temporarily. They are frequently employed for this purpose.

SLUDGE

The dried and pulverized sludge from sewage-disposal plants is used as a fertilizer not only for lawns and flowers but vegetables as well. Therefore, would not the liquid and sludge from septic tanks, after it has passed from the first compartment and just before it passes into the third or final compartment, be a good fertilizer? How would it compare with the liquid manure used by farmers?   Such sludge should be satisfactory as a fertilizer. It should compare favorably with liquid manure. The one danger is that liquid raw sludge can carry the organism of amoebic dysentery, as well as other diseases.

The local sewage disposal sells sewage settlings. Nothing has been added to this. How does this compare in value with barnyard manure and with other commercial fertilizers, for use on lawn and garden? (I have sandy soil.)   Sewage sludge is actually an expensive fertilizer when fertilizer efficiency is considered. See health hazard mentioned above.

What is the value of sludge from sanitary district beds? At what rate should it be applied for flower or vegetable gardens?   Recent reports from the Ohio Agricultural Experiment Station indicate that the analysis of sewage sludge from 10 different cities varied as follows: nitrogen, 0.88 to 2.98 per cent; phosphoric acid, 0.42 to 2.10 per cent; potash, 0.05 to 1.6 per cent. The report further showed that the nitrogen in sewage sludge was not more than 10 to 15 per cent as effective as the nitrogen in nitrate of soda. In raw sludge practically all soluble nitrogen has been washed away with runoff water.

TANKAGE

What is tankage?   Tankage is a by-product of slaughterhouses, which contains such refuse as lungs, intestines, bones, etc. These are processed, dried, and ground to produce a material used in stock feeds and for fertilizer.

What is the value of tankage? It contains about 4 to 10 per cent nitrogen and 7 to 14 per cent phosphoric acid. It is lacking in potash content.

How is tankage applied? About 4 lbs. per 100 sq. ft.; usually as a top- or side-dressing to growing plants, hoed or cultivated into the soil. It is often employed in place of nitrate of soda, which is quicker acting. It must be kept *perfectly dry* in storage, or it will quickly decay.

WOOD ASHES

Are wood or leaf ashes good for the garden? Yes. They contain potash and lime.

How do wood ashes affect manures? Wood ashes containing lime have a tendency to hasten the decomposition of manure.

Where can I use wood ashes and chicken manure to the best advantage? Do *not* use together, if chicken manure is fresh. Otherwise the combination is good. Mix ashes and chicken manure at 3 to 1 ratio.

What is the best way to apply wood ashes to lilies and roses? Since the majority of lilies do better in somewhat acid soils, wood ashes should not be used. Apply wood ashes to roses in the spring; about ½ to 1 lb. around each plant.

What is the best way to use wood ashes in acid soil? Wood ashes tend to reduce acidity because of lime content. Apply to the soil in fall or spring; 4 to 6 lbs. per 100 sq. ft. Fresh wood ashes will form lye when first applied. Do not use on plants in active growth.

What plants and trees benefit by an application of wood ashes? Almost all plants. Those that need potash—fruit trees, vegetable root crops, hydrangeas, carnations, roses, peonies, etc.—are especially benefited.

Will the action of wood ashes and cinders destroy alkali on irrigated land? (Washington.) Neither wood ashes nor cinders would have any effect. If the soil is alkaline, sulfur is needed.

Every year I burn a considerable amount of brush. Are the ashes

good fertilizer? Wood ashes are especially good for their potash content.

Do oak wood ashes have any value as fertilizer for flowers or vegetables? Yes. They contain potash, and are always safe to use.

If I put wood ashes from our fireplace on the vegetable and flower beds, will the oil from the coal ashes mixed with them harm the plants? Burned coal ashes do not contain oil. They do contain toxic substances that must be leached out by weathering over winter before being applied. Cannel coal, if incompletely consumed, contains oil.

Is there any value in wood coke from bonfires if applied to garden in fall? Applied in fall, it would be partly wasted. Better to save it under cover and apply in the spring.

Should I spread the wood ashes from my fireplace around as they are available during the winter; or must I store and use during the growing season? Store your ashes under cover to prevent leaching of potash. Leached wood ashes contain little potash, though still of some value.

Are the ashes of burned leaves, twigs, and winterkilled dry stalks of vegetation of any material value if burned on the garden plot? Yes; but the ashes would have more value if stored under cover and scattered in the spring.

MISCELLANEOUS MATERIALS

Is crab meal a good fertilizer? Fresh crab contains 2 to 3 per cent nitrogen and 2 to 3 per cent phosphoric acid. Its immediate efficiency is relatively low. Mixed fertilizer made with dried and ground king crab may contain 9 to 12 per cent nitrogen.

Can crab meal be used on most garden plants with benefit? Yes. Its cost will govern the extent of its use.

Is charcoal good to add to soil to help plants? Yes, it adds a small amount of phosphorus and considerable potash and lime. These materials, however, as found in charcoal, become available very slowly.

Are rotted cranberries good as a fertilizer? They would add a small amount of organic matter, but very small quantities of the essential elements for plant growth.

What effect is caused on soil by a daily application of coffee

grounds? Tests at the U.S.D.A. indicate that coffee grounds are slightly toxic to plant growth. Small amounts added to compost are harmless but of little value.

Some people say that soapy water is beneficial to soil and growth of vegetation. Is this so? Soapy water is not beneficial, and sometimes injurious if large amounts are poured in one spot, particularly where soap contains naphtha.

What fertilizer value is there in eggshells? Eggshells contain a considerable quantity of calcium, and a very small amount of nitrogen. Crush or grind them.

What about burying fish trimmings deep in the earth? Fish remains make an excellent fertilizer. Bury them just deep enough to avoid objectionable odors.

I'm burying all my garbage around the plants. Do you think this will be sufficient fertilizer? No; garbage at its best is a very low-grade fertilizer; it is excellent to add humus, but should be supplemented by a complete fertilizer.

Can leather dust be used as a garden fertilizer? Leather dust contains some nitrogen, but it decomposes *very* slowly, so that quick results should not be expected.

Is sawdust good to put on a garden? It can be used to lighten soil and as a mulch. If applied at a rate of more than 1 in., sawdust must have added nitrogen to decay.

I have some very fine sawdust, of white pine. What would be its effect if worked into soil in which vegetables or flowers are planted? It should help lighten your soil if it's heavy. Do not use thicker than 1 in.

How does one prepare kelp and other common seaweeds (which wash up on beaches along Long Island Sound) for fertilizer? If conditions are such that it can be done, the kelp can be handled as a green manure or plowed or spaded under. Otherwise, it can be composted and applied at an opportune time.

What value is sea kelp as a fertilizer? Sea kelp is high in potash, will compare favorably with farm manure in nitrogen, but is low in phosphorus.

Where can I buy sea kelp in Iowa for fertilizer? Most of the sea kelp is processed for liquid fertilizer on the West or East coasts. In its natural state, it is too bulky to be shipped any distance.

Can sea kelp be used immediately, or must it be stored? Sea kelp is used fresh as a green manure by farmers and gardeners near the seashore. For shipping, it is dried, then burned to an ash. In this state it can be used at once, or stored. The ash contains about 30 per cent potash.

Are other seaweeds as valuable as a fertilizer as sea kelp? Seaweeds vary considerably in nutritive value. They are worth using if readily available.

Will you please tell me if seaweed is any good to use as a fertilizer. If so, how can I use it for best results, as I live on the seashore? I can get all the seaweed I need. Seaweed is a good fertilizer. For one who can get the material fresh it is best used as a green manure spread on the land and turned under. It need not be washed.

What soil-conditioning property has chimney soot? When is it applied? Scotch soot from the peat-burning fireplaces was a reasonably good source of nitrogen. Soot from stokers, etc., contains toxic substances. Oil-burner soot can be harmful.

Inorganic Fertilizers

What is inorganic fertilizer? An inorganic fertilizer is one derived from mineral or chemical substances, such as phosphate rock, potash salts, nitrate salts (nitrate of soda).

What is a chemical fertilizer? A chemical fertilizer is one derived from chemically processed or manufactured materials, rather than from natural organic substances. The term is somewhat misleading in that organic fertilizers also may be treated with chemicals to increase their rate of availability. Many fertilizers contain both types of materials.

Are chemicals injurious to future plant growth? Not if they are used correctly. They do not, however, add humus to the soil.

Why don't we use stone dust as a natural fertilizer, which it really is? Pulverized granite (granite meal) is used as a source of potash in some areas. It contains about 5 to 10 per cent potash, along with a wide assortment of other elements. It is applied at rates of ½ to 2 tons per acre, and lasts for a long time. On acid soils pulverized phosphate rock is usually a satisfactory source of phosphate when used liberally. Some rocks are nearly devoid of fertilizer elements.

When preparing the soil in the spring for a garden of either flowers or vegetables, is it necessary to apply a chemical for better results? Usually additions of chemical fertilizers decidedly help production. They go to work at once, while organic fertilizers do not begin to feed plants until warm weather starts their decay.

What is the fertilizer value of calcium carbonate? Calcium carbonate in itself is of no value as a fertilizer, since it is insoluble in water. It must be converted into the bicarbonate form, or some other soluble calcium salt, before calcium becomes available to the plant. It may also beneficially modify the structure of the soil.

NITRATE OF SODA

For what purpose is nitrate of soda used? Nitrate of soda furnishes a readily available source of nitrogen. Nitrogen stimulates the vegetative growth of the plant and is also essential for the reproductive phases. If used in large amounts, it can cause greasy or pasty soils that are hard to work.

What can we use in place of nitrate of soda? Ammonium sulfate, ammo-phos, cottonseed, soybean meal, or tankage.

SULFATE OF AMMONIA

What is sulfate of ammonia used for? This is used as a source of nitrogen. It contains about 20 per cent nitrogen.

When should sulfate of ammonia be used? How much? This is a good fertilizer to use when nitrogen is required. Apply about 5 to 10 lbs. per 1,000 sq. ft.

Is ammonium sulfate best spread on ground when soil is being dug, or later, and raked in? Ammonium sulfate is best applied after the soil is spaded and raked into the upper 2 to 4 ins. of the surface soil.

UREA

What is urea? Urea is a water-soluble organic compound containing 45 to 46 per cent nitrogen. It is a natural chemical found in urine. In soil, urea almost immediately decomposes to ammonium nitrogen and carbon dioxide.

Does urea leave an acid residue? Yes, but only a slight amount of acidity is left—about a third as much as would be left from a similar amount of nitrogen from sulfate of ammonia.

SUPERPHOSPHATE

Is there any way to add phosphorus to soil without using commercial fertilizer? Yes, in the form of pulverized phosphate rock, bone meal, or basic slag. All may take a year or more to become available.

Are the effects of superphosphate somewhat similar to those of bone meal? Yes, the effects are similar. Bone meal contains a low percentage of nitrogen not found in superphosphate. The phosphorus in bone meal, however, is only available over a long period of time. It can "lock up" in completely insoluble form.

How should one use agricultural lime and superphosphate? They should not be mixed. If so, the phosphates are made unavailable.

Is there any advantage in applying superphosphate to perennial border or rock gardens? Many soils are deficient in phosphorus. If perennials or rock plants are planted in such a soil, they will be benefited by applications of superphosphate.

How should phosphate be used? I have some and do not know how to apply it to flowers. Phosphate is best applied when the flower beds are first prepared, by working it into the upper 4 to 6 ins. of soil. If plants are already in the bed, apply the phosphate between the plants and work it into the soil as deep as possible (down 6 to 8 ins.) without disturbing or injuring the roots. Apply 30 to 40 lbs. per 1,000 sq. ft.

When and how often should superphosphate be applied to perennials and rock plants? In addition to the use of superphosphate at the time the beds are prepared, yearly applications of phosphorus are advisable, especially in soils tending to be deficient in this element, by an application of a complete fertilizer in the spring.

MURIATE OF POTASH

What is the best time and method to apply muriate of potash to a

vegetable garden? If the amount of potash applied in the complete fertilizer recommended for vegetable gardens is not sufficient, apply an additional quantity (1 lb. per 100 sq. ft.) and incorporate it in the surface 2 to 3 ins.

How often should muriate of potash be applied? Usually one application a year is sufficient. Soil tests will show if additional quantities are needed.

My soil is deficient in phosphorus and potash. What shall I apply to correct this condition? Apply commercial fertilizers such as 2–10–10 or 0–10–10; or superphosphate and muriate of potash.

Complete Commercial Fertilizers

What are the principles of fertilization? Stated briefly, fertilization is practiced to supply the necessary essential elements to secure a normal growth of the plant.

What is commercial fertilizer? The term "commercial fertilizer" applies to any carrier of essential nutrient elements, that is sold (by itself or mixed with other such carriers) commercially.

How can an amateur tell what formulas—such as 10–6–4 and 8–5–3—mean? Formulas such as 10–6–4, 8–5–3, etc., are used to express the percentages of the major ingredients in fertilizers; namely, nitrogen, phosphorus, and potash. A 10–6–4 fertilizer denotes 10 per cent nitrogen, 6 per cent phosphorus, and 4 per cent potash.

Do commercial fertilizers aid or destroy existing bacteria and humus in the soil? Commercial fertilizers aid the beneficial bacteria of the soil. At the same time they may hasten the decomposition of humus.

Does commercial fertilizer burn the minerals out of the ground? No; it adds essential minerals to the soil.

Will commercial fertilizer restore a worn-out soil? Commercial fertilizers will furnish the necessary essential elements and can restore the soil in this respect. To restore humus and to improve the physical condition of the soil organic matter must be added.

What are some substitutes for fertilizer? There are no substitutes for fertilizer. Compost is used for its organic value, but there is little fertilizer value in it, unless applied in very heavy quantities (at least 20 tons per acre).

Is there a fertilizer generally good as an all-plant fertilizer, for shrubs, perennials, vegetables, rhododendrons, trees, and grass lawns? There is no one fertilizer that would be considered best for all these groups of plants. Most garden shops offer several types of fertilizers for special plants.

How can one tell just what kind of fertilizer is best to use? Soil tests will give a partial answer; the habit of growth of the plant is also a determining factor. Ornamental plants normally showing vigorous top growth respond best to a low-nitrogen fertilizer, and vice versa. Fleshy-rooted plants respond best to a fertilizer low in nitrogen, high in phosphorus and potash.

Can one add certain chemicals to the soil of the garden vegetable patch, in order to get bigger and better crop yields? A 2–10–10 or similar analysis, is listed for use on root crops. Use a general vegetable fertilizer for other vegetables. Side dressings of a nitrogen fertilizer may be advisable for the leafy vegetables.

How long does it take for organic or inorganic fertilizers to become available to plants? Inorganic nitrogenous fertilizers are readily available. The insoluble organic nitrogenous fertilizers are slowly available. Phosphorus from superphosphate penetrates the soil slowly, but is readily available in the monocalcium form. Potash is readily available. Slowly available forms of nitrogen are ureaform and IBDU.

What is the best fertilizer for a new vegetable garden? In general, a 4–12–4 or 5–10–5 fertilizer. For root or tuber crops a 2–10–10 is satisfactory. Exact analysis is not important, so long as the proportions are approximately the same.

What fertilizers should be added to the soil to make vegetables yield bountifully? See previous question. For leafy vegetables, follow the spring application with a side dressing of ammonium sulfate when the tops are half grown.

What is the best fertilizer to use in midsummer? For leafy crops, ammonium sulfate or nitrate of soda. For other common crops, use a product specifically labeled for use on vegetables.

Is it possible to mix one's own fertilizer for a successful home garden? To make your own fertilizer, several separate ingredients are needed. It is usually much more satisfactory to buy a ready-mixed fertilizer.

Are there garden fertilizers that are good, and more reasonable in price than the highly advertised brands? In general the regular 4–12–4, 5–10–5, and 7–7–7 farm fertilizers are the least expensive. They are good fertilizers.

Is a commercial fertilizer enough to use for the garden? Or should something be used in the fall and left through the winter? A complete fertilizer should be sufficient in itself. Additional nitrogen may be required for some crops; if so, it should be applied in the spring or when its need is obvious. Green manures or compost are needed in addition.

I have on hand a 100-lb. bag of lawn fertilizer; also 100-lb. bag of bone meal. Can these be used? In what proportions? Rather than attempt to mix these fertilizers, use the lawn fertilizer for the lawn and most flower and vegetable crops. Use the bone meal for plants with fleshy and tuberous roots.

Is commercial 5–10–5 fertilizer comparable to fertilizers with special trade names? Trade-name fertilizers are usually somewhat better than commercial grades of similar analysis, due to the use of better materials, better mixing, and sometimes the addition of trace elements. The standard formula fertilizers, however, are used with success by both amateur and commercial growers.

Can a garden fertilizer recommended for vegetables, and hydrated lime, nitrate of soda, etc., be kept several seasons? Which should be used the season it is bought? Practically all garden fertilizers can be kept for several years *if* they are kept dry. Some, such as ammonium sulfate, cake on standing and should be crushed before applying.

Are fertilizers in tablet form recommended? They are satisfactory for use on house plants. Liquid house-plant foods are more readily available and usually cheaper.

I have a plot 20 × 20 ft., just covered with 6 ins. of sandy loam. What kind of fertilizer could I use to make good soil for raising flowers of various kinds? Incorporate 12 to 16 lbs. of a good mixed garden fertilizer in the upper 3 to 5 ins. of the soil.

What formula, in a commercial-type fertilizer, gives best results for growth of annuals, perennials, and shrubs in a mixed border? Exact formulae are not too important so long as the product is balanced. Read the bag.

What type of fertilizer should be used on plants in winter to have blooms and good color in foliage? The liquid house-plant foods, made by mixing a dry complete fertilizer with water, used at half the rate recommended, will do well.

What commercial fertilizers are suitable for fruit trees? Complete fertilizers; also ammonium sulfate, cyanamide, nitrate of soda, superphosphate, muriate of potash, and several others.

Applying Fertilizers

When should one fertilize the garden—fall or spring? For lawns, permanent plantings of shrubs, evergreens, and flowers, fertilizers may be applied in the fall or spring with equal success. It is best to apply fertilizers to annual crops at, or just previous to, planting time.

Is it better to place fertilizer on the garden in the fall and turn it over in the spring? Or turn the soil first, and then apply the fertilizer? Commercial fertilizers for the most part are best applied after spading or plowing, a week or 10 days before planting, and raked into the upper 2 to 3 ins. of the soil. Superphosphate may be spaded in in either fall or spring.

Should I plant first, and then fertilize? Or vice versa? Fertilizer can be applied and worked into the soil just before planting, or at planting time. One or more subsequent applications may be necessary during the growing season.

For a new garden, do I have to fertilize the ground before I plant? Usually it is necessary to fertilize. A soil analysis will indicate what is needed.

Are better blooms obtained when fertilizer is used at time of setting out plants, or at time buds form? For best results apply the fertilizer at the time the plants are set. Make a subsequent application at or previous to bud formation.

Do you advocate putting fertilizer in the rows under the seeds; or between the rows? Recent experiments show that it is best to apply the fertilizer 2 to 3 ins. to the side and 1 to 2 ins. below the seed.

My soil is very rich but no fertilizer has been added since last fall. Is it necessary to apply any when ground is so good? No. Except to make sure the soil is maintained in that condition.

What is the best fertilizer to use for soil that has been cleared of trees and in which it is desired to make a vegetable garden? Any good mixed, complete fertilizer designed for vegetables.

How do you fertilize plants that remain in the same spot in the garden? Apply the fertilizer between the plants and hoe it into the upper few inches of soil without disturbing or injuring the roots of the plants. If soil is dry, water thoroughly.

How often during the season should the flower garden be fertilized? When? Once or twice a season. Apply fertilizer in the spring as growth starts, and again in midsummer if growth is not satisfactory.

What kind of fertilizer is best for peat soil which is turning acid? Peat soils usually become *less* acid as they are cultivated. A soil test would be advisable. If soil is acid, use a non-acid fertilizer. (See Introduction.)

Is it good practice to use a commercial fertilizer on acid-loving plants? Yes, if it is needed. Use a fertilizer specifically recommended for acid-loving plants.

Am draining cedar swamp for garden. Soil is black swamp muck, highly nitrogenous, about 2 ft. thick; white sand subsoil. What fertilizer should be used? The fertilizer to apply will depend upon the nutrient test of the soil and the crops to be grown. A cedar swamp would be acid. For most crops lime would be necessary.

How much water should be applied to garden after fertilizing? Soil is sandy and both commercial and fresh manures are used. Water garden when needed as indicated by tendency of plants to wilt.

Soil Sterilization

What are the different ways to sterilize soil for seeds? Steam, very hot water, and chemicals, such as tear gas (chloropicrin), methyl bromide and Vapam.

How does the gardener sterilize soil with steam? Make a soil pile 12 ins. deep. Place 4 ins. agricultural tile 2 ft. apart in center of pile and running full length. Plug tile at one end. Insert steam pipe or hose in the other end. Cover entire pile with building paper or canvas. Inject steam for 2 hours; remove cloth; allow to cool. Remove tile, and continue the process. Steam sterilization makes structure better. Its effects are entirely beneficial. This is usually impractical for a gardener to do. Small quantities of soil for pot plants may be sterilized in a pressure cooker, without closing the steam valve.

What is an easy and efficient method of sterilizing soil for growing seedlings in small greenhouse where steam is not used? Boiling hot water should be poured over the soil and, in addition, the seeds should be dusted with Captan, Thiram Terrachlor (PCNB) or similar compounds.

What is Larvacide? It is a gas which is packaged in bottles or cylinders as a liquid (chloropicrin, or tear gas) and is applied to the soil with a special applicator. The soil should be 60° F. or warmer, and medium moist. Three c.c. of liquid (a small teaspoonful) is injected about 3 to 6 ins. deep, spaced 10 ins. each way. A heavy watering is applied immediately. Follow with two other applications on successive days. The treatment controls soil diseases, insects, and weeds.

What chemicals can be used to sterilize small amounts of soil? The most practical is Vapam, which requires no special equipment. Follow the simple directions.

How do you sterilize soil with formaldehyde? Where steam is not available, formaldehyde may be used. Use commercial formalin —1 gal. to 50 gals. of water. One gal. of the solution is used to 1 sq.

ft. of soil 6 ins. deep. Pour solution on, cover for 24 hours, then uncover and permit to dry for 2 weeks before using.

How do you sterilize soil for potted plants? Use steam, hot water, or chemicals. A pressure cooker may be used satisfactorily.

How is sand, used as a rooting medium, best sterilized? If small quantities are wanted, place sand in shallow flat or box, and pour boiling water through it.

How do you sterilize soil in a perennial bed? This cannot be done satisfactorily unless chemicals are used—formaldehyde, chloropicrin, Vapam or mercuric compounds. Beds must be free of plants before chemicals are applied.

Plant Stimulants

How is Vitamin B$_1$ used in garden? Don't waste your time with Vitamin B$_1$; it has proved a failure under most conditions.

What is gibberellic acid? How does it affect plants? Gibberellic acid is a growth-stimulating substance produced by a fungus that attacks rice plants and causes them to grow rapidly for some time before the fungus finally injures too much of the tissue. When applied to some plants, a 10 part per million solution of gibberellic acid in water will stimulate a marked increase in rate of growth—especially in the length of stems and petioles. This stimulated growth is sometimes attractive and sometimes not. Gibberellic acid often hastens flower maturity and, in some instances, it increases flower size. Dwarf varieties of a given species usually respond most markedly to gibberellic acid. Standard sorts respond less, and giants are generally unresponsive. One of the interesting and perhaps most valuable properties of gibberellic acid is that of overcoming the dormancy effect in some plants and seeds. Except for its use as a seed stimulant, gibberellic acid is a research tool rather than an everyday useful chemical.

What is colchicine, and how is it used? An alkaloid from colchicum is used by plant breeders in attempts to change inherited characteristics of plants by doubling the chromosomes.

Where can I acquire colchicine?   From drugstore or local chemical supply house. It is a very poisonous substance; must be used with caution. Comes in paste or solution, which is applied to top buds of shoots of plants. Of some use to plant breeders, not to average gardener.

I desire information concerning "hormones."   Hormones (more properly called plant-growth regulators) are useful for reducing the time required for some cuttings to root. Most all of them are dusts in which the cutting is dipped. Some are sprayed on developing fruits to prevent drop. Some are sprayed on flowers and thus produce fruits without pollination (tomatoes, holly, etc.). Some are used to increase keeping quality of fruits and vegetables in storage.

Is there anything to the theory of enrichment of the soil with chemicals to include all those needed by the body?   If your entire food supply comes from a given plot of ground, this is important, but the varied diet of the average American means it has little significance.

Soil Detriments

Have soapsuds or soapy water from washing clothes any value as fertilizer?   The amount of material added in washing water will have very little effect on the nutrient content of the soil. Grease tends to clog the soil, and is objectionable. Naphtha is detrimental.

Is baking powder (double-action) of any use as fertilizer? If so, how is it used?   Under the usual soil conditions it has no fertilizer value, and it might even be detrimental.

Is castor oil good for soil around plants?   No.

Artificial Soils

What is "Cornell Mix"—used for starting seedlings?   It is mostly horticultural-grade vermiculite plus nutrients. To make a peck of the mix, use 4 qts. of vermiculite, 4 qts. shredded peat moss, 1 teaspoon-ful of 20 per cent superphosphate, 1 tablespoonful of ground lime-stone plus 4 tablespoonfuls of a 5–10–5 or similar fertilizer. The limestone should be dolomite lime, not high calcium. If this is not available (it is found only in limited areas) add a level tablespoonful of finishing lime to a quart of water and wet the mix with this. Finish-ing lime is about 50 per cent magnesium. You can substitute 2 tea-spoonfuls of Epsom salts for the lime.

A local greenhouse is growing plants in nothing but a 50-50 mix-ture of peat moss and sand. Is this feasible for garden use? Only under special conditions: liquid fertilizer in a weak solution must be used in place of water for irrigation. In a raised bed on desert sand, this mixture has been used for a vegetable garden in Arizona. Ex-pensive, but better than no garden!

What is gravel culture? The commercial name, "slop culture," defines it. Plants are grown in gravel with slow drains. Nutrients are dissolved in water and slopped over the plants whenever they seem needed. Although not too scientific, it is easier to use than the prac-tice of true hydroponics, which calls for highly accurate analyses of the nutrient solutions.

A gardening friend uses a mixture of half pet litter and half peat moss for house plants, starting seedlings, and rooting cuttings. I tried it, but it was a flop. What was wrong? Probably the type of pet lit-ter you used. One type is nothing more than dried clay without any treatment. Mixed with peat moss, it forms a worthless, greasy mess. The type that really works (and highly effectively) is made of burned clay that forms grainy, porous particles. To test a given brand, soak in water for an hour. Swirl it around and if all the litter goes into sus-pension, it is plain clay and worthless. If still gritty, use it.

This mixture is good for seedlings up to the time they form the third leaf, but after that they need feeding. For house plants, use a house-plant fertilizer at one fourth the recommended rate, dissolved in water and used for watering plants every time they need moisture.

What is vermiculite? It is a form of mica that, when heated, ex-plodes like popcorn. Treated to 2,500° F. in the process, it is then sterile, holds moisture, and if not overwatered, allows air to reach the roots of plants. It contains a small percentage of potash, but no other plant food. It can be used as a mulch, as an artificial soil base, and is used commercially as a filler in fertilizers. Most lightweight fertilizers have a vermiculite base.

I have used vermiculite for rooting cuttings and starting seeds, but it gets soggy. What am I doing wrong?   Watering too often. Vermiculite sops up about three to four times its volume in water, but then can't hold much more. Use a flat with a window-screen wire bottom and it will drain better.

How is ground sphagnum moss used? Is it mixed with soil?   No, it is used as a bed in which to sow seeds so they can be exposed to light without drying out. It contains a natural biotic which prevents damping-off of seedlings. It is a highly valuable material. (It is especially recommended for the fine seeds of azaleas and rhododendrons and other ericaceous plants. It contains no nutrients so the seedlings must be fertilized or soon transplanted.)

Is cod-liver oil a good plant food for flowers?   No.

Do castor beans and sumac sap the soil much?   Yes, the very luxuriant foliage depletes soils of nitrogen in particular.

SOILLESS CULTURE

What is water culture?   Growth of plants in a watertight container filled with a weak solution of fertilizer salts.

What is sand culture?   Growth of plants in a container of sand through which a weak fertilizer solution either drips continually, or is poured on at intervals.

What house plants can be grown in sand culture?   With care, almost any house plants.

What is gravel culture?   Growth of plants in a watertight container filled with some inert medium, preferably slightly acid, which is flooded, manually or mechanically, from below with a weak fertilizer solution.

What flowering crops may be grown in gravel culture if a greenhouse is available?   Any crop which can be grown in soil. Roses, carnations, chrysanthemums, snapdragons, calendula, annuals, orchids, are all successfully grown.

What vegetable crops may be grown by an amateur in gravel or water culture?   It is not practical to attempt to grow vegetables unless a greenhouse is available. Tomatoes, lettuce, cucumbers, radishes, spinach, kale, etc., can be grown.

What type of soilless culture is best suited for the home? Sand culture; it requires less equipment than gravel culture, and is more foolproof than water culture.

What type of soilless culture is best suited for commercial use? Gravel culture. Less troublesome than water culture; requires less labor than sand culture. No type will accomplish any more than will normal soil culture, and will require greater skill and equipment.

Will chemical gardening (soilless culture) succeed commercially? Probably not. Good soil has many advantages over soilless culture, not the least of which is the former's adaptation to the use of large-scale equipment. When people realize that good soil is clean and very responsive to proper enrichment with all necessary nutrient elements, soilless culture will become a by-gone fad, except where it is used as a valuable research method.

Has the experiment with tank farming contributed much to general practices and knowledge in general gardening? Tank farming (which is water culture) has not contributed much; but gravel and sand culture have been very helpful in the study of general garden problems, particularly from the standpoint of plant nutrition. However, much has been learned about the needs of minor elements from studies in water culture.

What is a "nutrient solution," for soilless gardens? It is composed of fertilizer elements completely soluble in water. Obtain chemicals from your druggist and use the following formula for water, sand, or gravel cultures:

Potassium nitrate	1.0 oz.
Monocalcium phosphate	0.5 "
Magnesium sulfate	0.75 "
Water	5 gals.
Iron sulfate	1 tsp.

2
Planning and Landscaping

GARDENS are for people—the people who own them. A beautiful garden does not just spring up overnight! This is especially true in the small gardens of today where space is so limiting. New materials and techniques have broadened our horizons in garden making. People today expect things of their gardens that their parents did not consider important at all.

Outdoor living has become a pleasurable way of life for most modern families. Planning for a patio or terrace, where one can have cookouts and entertain in the out-of-doors, is a "must" in almost every garden plan. Westerners have had a great influence on garden design all over the nation. Patios were seldom heard of (in the East at least) fifty years ago, but with the Spanish influence in Southern California, their popularity has swept the country from west to east. There are few homes being built today where a patio is not considered an important part of the over-all plan.

The Japanese have also had an influence on our gardens, first on the Pacific coast, where thousands of Japanese have made their homes since the turn of the century. The deceptively simple gardens they prefer, often with small plants, and their techniques, such as those followed in the art of bonsai, have all influenced modern gardens from the West Coast to the East. During the past three quarters of a century, the plants native to Japan have become so popular in American gardens that today nearly half the plants in every garden are native to Japan.

You the homeowner must decide whether you should do your own landscaping or engage a landscape architect or designer. These men are trained to observe the potentialities inherent in a property. They generally know from experience what can be done and will look well, and at the same time be functional. Often it pays in the long run to consult a reputable firm and let them study the situation and then present various possibilities to you.

On the other hand, you, in common with many of us, may be inhibited by a budget or just like to do things yourself. If you are in this group, you will enjoy landscaping your own property. Even so, you might consider going to a large local nursery that has landscape planners on its staff and ask them to draw up a rough plan of what they think might be best for you. The costs for such services vary, but are usually quite reasonable. Then, with that plan as a guide, you can start.

Planning the Outdoors

If you have just bought a place that is already landscaped, many of your problems are solved, but some problems remain. Is everything you want and need in a garden present? If not, which of the plants and features don't you like?

To start your plans, list the things you want of your garden. Are there small children who need an enclosed play area easily seen from the house? Do you want a vegetable garden, tennis court, swimming pool, general game area? Do you want flower beds to work in as a hobby, do you need hedges for protection or some kind of screening for privacy? Is your land on a slope where you might build a rock garden? Do you already have sufficient shade at the right places or should you plan for more?

The mood of the garden should reflect the taste and preference of its owners. The garden's outstanding features should dominate but not at the expense of the entire (landscape) scheme. The garden should be beautiful. This results partially from proper basic design, but also depends on the kinds of plant materials you select and how they are used. You should not be able to see all the garden at once, from the front, or from the patio, or even from the rear of the house. Some of the areas can be artfully hidden by shrubs, by trees, or by correctly placed screening of some kind, such as fences.

Space for bulbs, annuals, and perennials should be planned for if these are to be enjoyed and cut for arranging indoors. However, the flower beds should not be extensive unless this aspect of gardening is a major interest. Weeds do grow even though you can keep them in check pretty well with the right kind of mulching materials. Plan to use them liberally, for they save much work and are beneficial to most plants.

The Plan on Paper

On a large piece of graph paper, draw to scale (1 in. equaling 20 ft. is a good one) the basic components of your property: house, driveway, garage, existing features such as trees, patio, walks, etc. Then indicate additions or changes you wish to make. Remember that in placing trees and flower beds about the area, one should always leave space for garden equipment to move about.

Proper screening in the garden is essential. The utility area, the children's sandbox, the vegetable garden, the street, objectionable views are all omnipresent in most gardens. Consider hedges of the proper kinds of trees or shrubs, which grow just high enough but no higher and do not take monthly shearing. Or there are woven-sapling or board fences that are long-lasting and on which vines can be trained. In fact, there is a varied assortment of wood arbors, fencing, and walls that landscape architects are using the country over to provide privacy and shelter without detracting from beauty.

Selecting Trees and Shrubs

Pick out the right kinds of shrubs and trees. Elms are not considered dependable any more and in addition they take a lot of care and space. Try smaller trees, like crab apples and magnolias. These and many others go well with the smaller modern houses and require little attention. Take the same care with shrubs. Lilacs, for instance, need spraying and much pruning and even then are colorfully ornamental for a short two-week period during the entire year, whereas viburnums usually need no attention, have interesting flowers in the spring, colorful fruits in the fall, and autumn foliage color—some even have interesting trunk and branch formations which are of interest every season of the year.

In selecting shrubs, you might also think of those like leucothoe, mahonia, forsythia, cornelian-cherry (*Cornus mas*), and like plants, which have merit in cut arrangements indoors. There is nothing

quite like the visual promise of spring when one forces a few branches of forsythia or cornelian-cherry into bloom in early February,
when outside everything is cold and seemingly lifeless.

A beautiful garden is an interesting one in which hidden areas
suddenly come into view as one walks around. Try an espaliered
yew on the monotonous piece of fencing around the utility area in
such a way that it cannot be seen from the house. Or a few evergreens off in a corner somewhere, hidden from the major viewing
points but definitely evident as one comes upon them from the garden
path.

Planting Near the House

Foundation plantings need careful thought. However, the new
homeowner as well as those who are faced with the renovation of
an overgrown planting can be heartened by the trend toward fewer
shrubs being set out around the house foundation. The object is not
to have the house in a "sea" of shrubbery—whether evergreen or
deciduous—but to use a few plants for accent and connect them
with ground-covering plants such as pachysandra, myrtle, or English
ivy. It's true that some houses, both old and new, need special
treatment to hide architectural defects. In such cases, bold, imagina-
tive solutions are needed, and this can well be the time to seek
professional help. (However, it should be kept in mind that not all
nurserymen are landscaping authorities and often their sole objective
is to sell as many plants as possible.) Sometimes the solution to a
problem house does not solely lie in plantings anyway; the right
color house paint and minor architectural renovations should be considered first.

It is difficult for beginners, sometimes, to pass up the inviting
young coniferous evergreens advertised for foundation plantings and
at such attractive prices. Most of these will actually grow into tall
trees that will take a major amount of annual pruning to keep them
in proper perspective. This does not help aesthetically or with the
low-maintenance idea. Rather, select plants like leucothoe, the new
dwarf forms of mahonia, and truly dwarf needle evergreens that
never grow above eye level in height. In this last group are many
junipers and yews—and they are hardy over most of the country.
There are deciduous shrubs in this category, too. Select a good

reference book on shrubs and there will be found lists of the proper plants to use. When you know what you want, then start trying to find them in local nurseries or through mail-order sources.

The front entrance of your house should be given special thought. It should never be hidden, nor appear small and cramped because of inappropriate plantings. It should have grace and beauty achieved by planting soft-textured shrubs which seem to extend a gracious invitation to enter. An expansive lawn, unadorned with specimens or flower beds in its center, sets off the house to good advantage. Trees can be planted to the side or to frame the house. Unfortunately, many of us must use hedges for privacy in front, but even here, with a bit of careful planning, you should be able to come up with an interesting shrub border that might fit the situation better.

The Patio or Terrace

The patio (or terrace) is one of the most important adjuncts of houses today. Chances are, especially if you buy a new house, it already exists. If not, you will want to make the addition. Located next to the house, preferably outside the living room or dining area where sliding glass doors lead out to it, it is the transition between house and garden. The patio can be paved (there are many kinds of surfaces you can build) and sheltered from view of the neighbors or the street if necessary by a planting of evergreens or hedge, or sometimes by arbor-fence combinations (preferably of wood rather than plastic). Take advantage of any attractive views of your garden or distant hills—if you are fortunate enough to have them.

It should be furnished with table and reclining chairs that are in keeping with the architecture of the house. There might be planters or containers with interesting plants (or herbs) in them, a hanging basket or two if you are prepared to keep them properly watered, and even a surrounding bed or two of flowers or herbs. These beds might be raised 2–3 ft. above the ground level, for easier viewing and weeding and—if herbs are planted—appreciation of their various scents.

There should be some shade on the patio, either from a large tree just outside its boundaries, or from a small dogwood (which has horizontal branches) planted within the patio itself. A pool might be provided for, or even a small fountain, and of course there should be a few discreetly placed lights for nighttime. If executed with thought and care, the patio is of interest throughout the entire year, always there to lure people to your out-of-doors.

The Sun Deck

In hilly areas, where houses are built on steep banks or hills, and in dunes and along the seashore—anywhere there is no room for a paved patio as such, the sun deck is an excellent substitute. It is not an innovation from California, but rather a modern extension of the mid-Victorian porch which was so firmly attached to the house and used extensively three quarters of a century ago. The modern deck starts at the house, but extends outward in all sorts of forms and heights—sometimes only a few feet above the rocky ground, in other places high above the bank below.

In other situations, it is on the roof or the top of the garage. It is usually built of wood boards with about a ¼-in. distance between them. Lounging chairs and a table or two are necessary, and in places where it is substituting for the patio, large tubs or pots of plants can be included. Of course, the larger the tubs the less frequently they have to be watered.

Recreation Areas

So your family wants a swimming pool! It is probably the most popular property improvement in America today. There should be the proper place with planned screening, and most town ordinances call for fences around pools to prevent accidents. The pool should be a minimum of 34 × 14 ft. (the larger the better), with a minimum of 8 ft. under the diving board. But get a professional to build it for you, since amateurish mistakes in this area can prove costly and most discouraging.

The interests of some run to tennis, croquet, swings, ladder-trapezes, a basketball backboard, or volleyball, and if yours is one of these, plan for them rather than providing for them any old place on your property.

Lighting the garden at night can be a most desirable asset. Only a few spotlights are needed, and your electric company can tell you where to obtain them and how to install the underground weatherproof wiring system. With a few spare outlets, the lights can be moved from place to place in the garden as different plants come into bloom; or direct spotlights to trees, or for safety to steps along the garden walk. An arrangement of a few lights, most of which might be seen from the patio or living-room window, lengthens the time the out-of-doors can be enjoyed.

Growing plants need water, and fortunately with the easily laid plastic pipe available now, underground sprinkler systems and water outlets do not have to be the first things put in the garden. Admittedly, an 8-in. trench must be dug for the pipe, but this can often be done without too much disturbance to existing plants and turf. So it can be left until time and money are available, if necessary. Installing the system is one of the things you can do yourself, unless your property is very extensive.

These then are a few of the things to consider and plan for in your garden. It is for your pleasure and relaxation. Think of the low-maintenance angle. Buy trees and shrubs that do not require spraying or constant pruning. Use mulches on the flower beds and about trees and shrubs to reduce weeding and watering. Proper planning at the start can result in a beautiful garden.

—Donald Wyman

 Planning the Landscape

DESIGN PRINCIPLES

What are the principles to consider in the design of a garden? Balance, scale and proportion, contrast, rhythm, and dominance. With these principles in mind the planner uses space, lines, forms, colors, patterns, and textures to create orderly beauty.

What are the essential things to keep in mind in planning the planting of a property? What you want most from your garden. List the items: play space for the children; an area in which to entertain such as a terrace or patio; space for family recreation; special gardens such as a rock or rose garden. One should also keep in mind the need for shade, for screening out objectionable views, movement of equip-

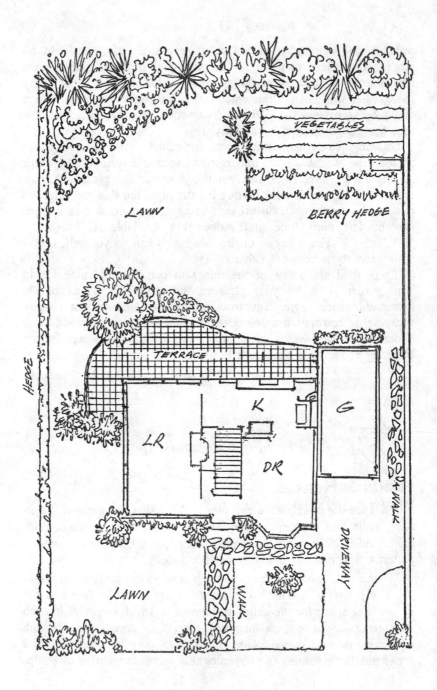

VEGETABLES

LAWN

BERRY HEDGE

HEDGE

TERRACE

K

G

LR

DR

DRIVEWAY

POOL + WALK

WALK

LAWN

ment over the area, and especially the need of beauty and interest in plants during every season of the year. The resulting plan should satisfy most of your needs as you now visualize them.

We have just bought a large suburban house, but the grounds have not been cared for properly and are overgrown. What is the best way to plan a renovation so we will not make mistakes?   See a landscape architect. Tell him what you would like to have in the way of flowering trees, flower gardens, recreation area, etc. and ask his advice. He will submit a plan and give approximate costs of providing some or all of the things you want.

We only have a small garden and do not want to hire a landscape architect, but we need help. What should we do?   Make a plan on graph paper of what you have, with trees, house, drive, and shrubs located. Possibly take a few pictures. Then go to a nurseryman who offers planning service. Some of the larger nurseries have skilled landscape people on their payroll and they can give you much expert advice on the spot from your plan and pictures for a reasonable fee. Also, they might plant the garden for you when you order plants from them.

Is it necessary to make a plan of a garden?   For any but the very simplest of gardens a plan will be found to be a great help in carrying out your intentions. Changes and rearrangements are more easily made on paper than in the garden itself. A plan is also most useful in estimating quantities; if the planting is not to be done all at once, it is essential.

Why should a garden be "balanced"?   Balance, whether symmetrical or irregular, gives a garden picture a feeling of stability and restfulness. A garden that lacks it will be less pleasing, although it may not be immediately apparent what the trouble is, particularly in a naturalistic composition.

Our new house was erected on an overgrown lot. We spent so much money on the house we will have to do the landscaping ourselves. How do we go about it?   Make a list of all the shrubs and

A suburban property planned for privacy and outdoor living comfort. It is enclosed on both sides by a hedge and fence and a mixed shrub border at the rear which includes some coniferous evergreens. The berry hedge which screens the vegetable garden could be of blueberry plants.

trees you have. Then on a piece of graph paper plot in one color those that you want to keep for one reason or another. Also plot what you would like to have in another color—trees for shade, flowers, or screening purposes; shrubs for beauty or screening; a flower garden; utility and game area, etc. Incorporate these with the plants you want to keep.

What is meant by the term "focal point"?   A focal point is a point of highest interest in the development of the design, such as a garden pool, or a group of particularly striking plants. It serves as a center around which the design can be built.

In a square garden, where should the focal point be?   In the center, usually. In a square design the important lines lead to or from the center.

What is a vista?   A vista is a narrow view framed between masses of foliage. It tends to concentrate the observer's attention, rather than allowing it to spread over a wide panorama.

Must a garden be level?   A geometrical garden need not be level, but the slope should be away from the principal point from which the garden is seen, rather than from side to side. A naturalistic garden should have, if possible, a natural grade, irregular rather than level or smoothly sloping.

How do you decide on the size of a garden?   How large a garden can you take care of? Don't lay out more plantations than you can properly care for. A garden should be in scale with its surroundings, not too big for the house; nor so small as to seem insignificant. If the size of the property is limited, it is well to have the garden occupy the whole space instead of leaving a fringe of unusable space around it.

What is the rule for good proportion in the size of a garden?   There is no hard-and-fast rule. Oblong areas are most effective when they are about one and a half times as long as they are wide; but the method of treating them and the surrounding foliage masses affect this considerably. Generally an oblong is better than a square; and an oval (on account of perspective) more effective than a circle.

How can you accent a planting?   Plantings made up of all one kind of plant, or of a few similar varieties, are likely to be monotonous and uninteresting. By using an occasional plant of a different sort an accent is created that makes the planting more interesting.

What is the difference between a formal and a naturalistic garden? Formal design uses straight lines and circular curves or arcs. Informal design uses long, free-flowing curves. Formality emphasizes *lines;* informality emphasizes *space,* a concept necessary today in low-maintenance landscaping.

What is required in a formal garden? A formal garden is essentially a composition in geometric lines—squares, oblongs, circles, or parts thereof. It need not be large, elaborate, or filled with architectural embellishment.

Which is the better suited to a small place, a formal or an informal garden? Topography controls the type of design. On flat ground in proximity to buildings the rectangular (formal) type of design is easier to adapt. On rough land greater informality is desirable, particularly on slopes and in wooded areas.

What are the steps necessary to develop a small property? Rough

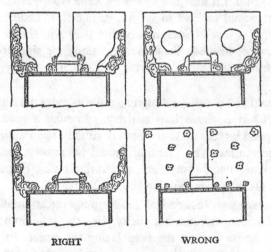

RIGHT   WRONG

Some mistakes to avoid in planting: (Top) Leave lawn areas open, free from beds or scattered borders in center of grass plots. (Below) Shrubs planted in unconnected polka-dot pattern increase maintenance and impede mowing operations. Better to mass them in borders or "islands" where they can be mulched together and increase their landscape effects.

grading; staking out walks, drives, and garden area; installation of utilities (water, gas, sewage, etc.); preparation of planting areas; planting trees, shrubs, and perennials; making the lawn, are all of importance.

Is there anything that can be done in advance of building on a lot that would improve the land or save time later on? The lot is 100 × 100 ft., with trees, bushes, weeds, etc. Clear out undesirable wild growths and trees where they are too thick. Confer with the builder to avoid destroying attractive native shrub masses in locations near the property lines where they may be valuable as part of future shrub borders.

We have a new home to landscape completely, and very little money to put into it. What do you advise concerning first plantings in our garden, to take away the bare, new look? Shade trees come first. Then important screen and background plantings of shrubs, flowering trees, and evergreens. These are the framework of the landscape picture. Add details later.

I have just built a new home, with a large front yard, in a country town. What would be best to set out or plant? Shade trees are important. Plant a few in such a way that they will throw their shade where it is most needed. Shrub borders along the side property lines will help frame the picture. Avoid too much planting against the house.

How would you go about designing a town-house garden area about 18 × 25 ft.? It is shady half the day. In such a garden you will have to depend largely upon the pattern of the design and upon architectural accessories. The planting should be mostly specimen evergreens, perhaps dwarf evergreens, and spring bulbs. For the summer, a few annuals, either in pots or beds, will give color.

Can you suggest economical landscaping for a small temporary home? Maintain extreme simplicity. Use the minimum of planting next to the house and in the area facing the street. In the rear, if possible, have a compact vegetable garden bordered with annual and perennial flowers.

What sort of garden would you plant in a plot 60 × 30 ft.? An area of this sort is usually most effectively developed by having an open grass or gravel panel in the center, with flower borders along the sides backed by shrub borders, or hedges, and a strong terminal feature at the end. This last could be a lily pool or patio.

I have read that a garden should not "compete with a view." Why? How is it prevented? The intimate detail of a garden suffers by comparison with a wide view into the surrounding landscape. It is usually wiser to surround the garden with an enclosure to shut off outside views, but if these are worth-while, provision should be made to take advantage of them from some point within the garden.

My house is surrounded by trees, but there is a fine view now obscured by foliage. What should I do? Do not hesitate to cut out trees or trim them to form a vista so the view can be seen from some vantage point in the house or on the terrace. Often this can be achieved by removing lower branches rather than whole trees.

Foundation Plantings and Entrances

(See also Foundation Material—Sections 3 and 4.)

What kind of shrubbery would you plant in front of a new house with a 30-ft. frontage? Use tall, upright-growing plants at the corners and low-growing, rounded masses between. Avoid too much planting. If the house foundation is low enough, leave some spaces bare to give the house the effect of standing solidly on the ground. Either deciduous or evergreen material is suitable.

We have large trees (oak, gray birch, maple, and ironwood). What should be planted near the house? The yard slopes toward the south and the house is new, so we are starting from scratch. Let the trees constitute the principal landscape feature. Use a minimum of planting near the house—ground covers along the foundation, a few shade-loving shrubs at the corners or either side of the entrance.

What is the best method of foundation planting for an "unbalanced" house—one with the door not in the center? An unbalanced composition for a foundation planting can be made extremely attractive. The fact that the door is not in the center will make it even more interesting. Naturally the doorway should be the point of interest, and your maximum height should begin on either side, tapering irregularly to the corners of the house where a specimen shrub or evergreen may go a little higher in order to break the sharp lines of the house corner. These corner accents need not be so tall as the main planting on either side of the doorway.

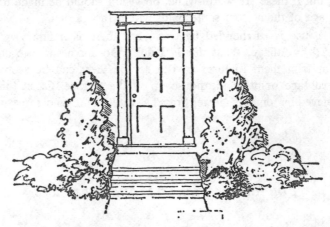

A symmetrically balanced entrance planting, especially suitable for a house of formal colonial design. Often the plantings at the door are all that are needed near the house.

What is best for planting around a small house on a small acreage? Everyone has evergreens. Can't we have simplicity and still be different?   Deciduous shrubs can be just as interesting throughout much of the year although it is the evergreens which lend interest in the winter. Why not use deciduous shrubs with a few evergreens as a background?

Can I plant flowers along the base of our house?   Unless the house is an architectural jewel which should not be hidden, shrubs and ground covers with flowers planted in front of them give a better effect than flowers alone, which are apt to look too small and inadequate near a house foundation.

How shall I landscape the front of our Cape Cod house? It was built about 1810 and during the 6½ years we have owned it every minute has been spent in restoring the old pine paneling inside and

The Cape Cod type of home calls for a low foundation planting, in keeping with its architectural lines.

developing the flower and vegetable gardens outside. **There is the main house with front door in the center, an ell, and a long shed-garage combination. What treatment all along the front would you suggest?** Planting for a Cape Cod house should be very simple, perhaps a boxwood, privet (pruned to a rounded form), or Japanese holly on each side of the door, and a clump of lilacs at one corner of the house. Shade trees are important and should be carefully placed. A small dooryard enclosed by a low picket fence often adds to the charm if the house sets far enough back from the highway to permit its being used.

What can be done with a narrow front lawn between an old-fashioned house with a high porch and the street—which is lined with large old maples? Instead of grass, which will not thrive in shade or under maples, try to establish a ground cover such as myrtle or pachysandra. However, the most practical solution may be gravel. Hide the porch foundation with a low hedge or informal grouping of yews or Japanese holly (*Ilex crenata*). Improve the soil with peat moss and fertilizer applications and water often during the growing season.

Could you tell me what kind of foundation planting I could use for an English-type home? The English style, being informal, calls for informal planting. Avoid symmetrically balanced groups of planting, or too much planting. Accent the doorways, the corners, and leave the rest open. Vines are important to soften brickwork or stone.

Do you suggest landscaping around a farmhouse? Of course, a farm home needs planting. The same rules and options apply here. Use a few shrubs and small-flowering trees at the sides.

What sort of foundation planting is appropriate to a French chateau-type house? Avoid rigid balance, and hold the planting down to the minimum. Use a few choice things rather than many ordinary plants. A few clumps of broad-leaved evergreens are particularly effective.

A small home calls for simplicity of design in landscaping.

The doorway of my house is a reproduction of an old colonial door, with leaded side lights and fanlight. How should I plant this so as to enhance rather than detract from its beauty? For an elaborate doorway, which is sufficiently interesting in itself, elaborate planting is unnecessary. Possibly the most effective thing would be to plant a big old lilac on either side of the door or for a more formal effect, plant an Irish or cone-shaped yew on each side.

Should planting either side of the front door always be alike on both sides? Generally yes. But if the house is in an informal or picturesque architectural style, the planting should also be informal and picturesque. Use a tall, dark plant on one side, with a few smaller things around its base, and on the other side use something lighter, more graceful and spreading. Don't use too many kinds of plants and too many sorts of foliage. (See following question.)

A balanced, but not symmetrical, planting at the front door.

My colonial house seems to me to have a very plain doorway. How can I plant it to make it seem more important? Where the doorway is formal, but very plain, interest must be created through the planting. Use identical groups on either side, but select the various plants carefully for form, texture, and foliage color. Evergreens give great dignity and are less likely to get too large in a short time. Tall masses to accent the lines of the doorway, with more spreading plants around them, usually make the most effective arrangement.

What plants should be used around a modern ranch-type house in front of a large rock outcrop? Make use of the natural rock by all means, planting rock plants and creeping junipers around it. Low yews and azaleas might be in the foundation planting with a dogwood or crab apples at the sides.

We have a cabin among trees and woodland. We would like to make the immediate grounds look much nicer than they now are. How could we go about it? Underplant the area with various kinds of native ferns and woodland wildflowers. Take a walk through your woodlands and select a few shrubs for transplanting. Avoid using exotic material.

How could a rather steep hillside, partly wooded, be planted to make it more attractive? Such a wooded hillside could be underplanted with native shrubs, evergreens, ferns, mountain-laurel, azaleas, rhododendrons, and woodland wildflowers. A system of trails leading through the area would add to its interest.

Screening

How can I disguise my chicken house and yard so that they will not injure the appearance of my property? If the wire of the chicken run is strong enough, you might plant a vine such as honeysuckle on it. The house itself can be made less conspicuous by planting a group of pines and hemlocks around it. Or the whole thing can be hidden behind a dense hedge.

Would a mixture of plants with various colored leaves or blossoms be satisfactory in an informal screening for enclosing a yard? Usually a suitable boundary screen consists of one variety of shrub. Too varied a planting competes with the interest inside the garden instead of merely framing it. Variety in leaf, flower, and fruit may be inside the boundary screen or in foundation plantings of buildings.

What are some fast growing vines that would make good screens? Bower actinidia, Dutchman's-pipe, Virginia-creeper, Kudzu vine and grape vines.

What type of shrubs make good informal screening for enclosing yard? Choice is determined by size of area to be enclosed and height of objects to be "screened out." Persian lilac is excellent for areas of a quarter acre and larger. Smaller gardens may use *Rosa hugonis, Rosa rubrifolia,* truehedge columnberry, or privet, untrimmed. A taller plant growing up to 12 ft. high but excellent for a narrow screening hedge is *Rhamnus frangula* 'Columnaris' or 'tallhedge', as it is often called.

Trees and Shrubs

Should trees be removed from gardens? Not necessarily. If the trees are fine old specimens, they should be left, and the garden designed around them using plants that will withstand shade; otherwise they should be taken out. Often trees form an important part of the garden's design.

Many American elms are being removed in our town because they have succumbed to the Dutch elm disease. What are some good large shade trees to use as substitutes? Maples, hackberry, yellow-wood, beech, ash, honey locust, especially the 'Moraine' and the yellow-leaved 'Sunburst' locusts, sweet-gum, cucumber tree, Amur cork tree, buttonball, Sargent cherry, various oaks, sophora, lindens and zelkova.

Many builders today try to retain a tree or two next to the house. Such trees provide some shade and can become an important part of the landscape design.

Can shrubs and small trees be used in a flower garden? Yes, an occasional compact-growing tree or shrub in the garden relieves the monotony of perennial and annual plantings. Especially suitable is the tree rose.

We plan to landscape a 3-acre tract. Will you name flowering shrubs that give a succession of bloom throughout the year? For spring: azalea, forsythia, rhododendron, *Viburnum carlesii.* For summer: honeysuckle, hydrangea, buddleia, roses, abelia, heather, rose-of-Sharon. For fall: abelia, witch-hazel. For autumn color: *Euonymus alatus,* dogwood, viburnum, Japanese barberry, sumac, spice-bush, and blueberry.

Can you suggest hardy shrubbery for a small country home? Standard varieties of deciduous shrubs, such as spirea, lilac, deutzia, philadelphus, and weigela, can always be relied upon to thrive with the minimum amount of care. Interest can be added to the planting by using some of the rarer varieties, such as *Philadelphus virginalis,* hybrid lilacs, and a few of the small-flowering trees, such as flowering crab, dogwood, and redbud.

Shade

(*See also Shade—Section 3.*)

There is no sun in my garden from September until May. What is the best way to treat a garden of this kind? Since the floral display in this garden will be effective only from late spring to early fall, make sure the garden background is interesting enough to make the garden attractive during the rest of the year. Use evergreen, berry-bearing shrubs and ones that have good fall color. Then for flowers select only those plants that bloom during the time when sunlight is available.

Will you suggest perennial flowering plants for a garden in shade? Aconitum, ajuga, aquilegia, campanula, cimicifuga, dicentra, digitalis, ferns, hosta, hemerocallis, hesperis, lily-of-the-valley, thalictrum, tradescantia, trillium, valeriana, and viola are the principal shade-tolerant kinds of garden flowers. There are many varieties of most.

Which flowers are best for part shade? Perennials for part shade: *Achillea filipendulina,* aconite, cimicifuga, digitalis, *Anemone japonica, Lobelia cardinalis,* mertensia, hosta, helleborus, day-lily, trollius, primrose, Virginia-cowslip, May-apple, and showy lady's-slipper.

What plants, tall, medium, low, may I use in a garden shaded by oak trees? What soil improvements should be made to overcome acidity from oaks? Your location should be ideal without treatment for all of your native wildflowers, such as cypripediums, ferns, May-apple, and Jack-in-the-pulpit. (See Woodland Wildflowers.) For taller plants you have a wide choice from such things as holly, mountain-laurel, azalea, blueberries, and rhododendron. The combination of these should be an attractive planting.

Name a few evergreen shrubs doing well in the shade. Abelia, barberries, fothergilla, mountain-laurel, leucothoe, privets, andromedas (*Pieris*), rhododendrons, evergreen azaleas, yews, arborvitaes, and certain viburnums.

Please name a few plants that will grow in dense shade, around base of large tree. Must I put them in pots on account of roots of tree? Few plants will subsist on what's left in the soil after the roots of a large tree have filled the surface and used all available food. Try digging out pockets, filling them with good loam, and planting one of the following: *Viola canadensis, Mahonia repens, Vinca minor,* Kenilworth-ivy, pachysandra. Potted plants would be of only temporary value. If these fail you would be better off to spread crushed stone over the area and to leave it bare of plants.

Which flower is the best to plant under a big maple tree where there are lots of roots and practically no sun? Altitude is 6,600 ft. Norway maple (*Acer platanoides*) foliage is so dense that few plants can survive both shade and the fight for root space and food. Deep watering of all maples encourages the development of deeper rooting, thus freeing the surface from this strangling network. Ground covers that accept the challenge of most maples are *Vinca minor, Mahonia repens,* pachysandra, *Sedum stoloniferum.*

Which plants would grow well along a shady wall? *Euonymus fortunei vegetus,* aquilegia, lady's-slipper, hepatica, *Epimedium niveum,* dicentra, digitalis, sanguinaria, ferns, mertensia, anemone, primula, pulmonaria, aconitum, dodecatheon, thalictrum, *Anchusa myosotidiflora,* and day-lilies. Trees which provide shade for plants in nature also supply abundant humus in the soil by their decayed leaves. Shade plants in the garden appreciate humus, too.

Banks

(*See also Section 3.*)

Will you suggest some shrubs for the rocky bank in front of our house? Junipers are always good, both the shrubby types and the trailing types for over the rocks. The memorial rose (*Rosa wichuraiana*), *Stephanandra incisa* 'Crispa' and 'Arnold Dwarf' forsythia all root wherever their branches touch moist soil and are ideal for such

When a bank is too steep for good grass growth and its maintenance, plant a ground cover such as English ivy for year-long greenery.

situations. If vines would qualify, try the climbing hydrangea or the Virginia-creeper.

How should a sloping area (15 × 3 ft.) along a driveway be planted? Fence or wall would be unsuitable. The location is sunny. Such a place is best treated by planting the slope with some easy-to-take-care-of, low, trailing shrub or perennial. *Phlox subulata, Teucrium chamaedrys, Juniperus chinensis sargentii,* or *Euonymus fortunei* 'Colorata' would be suitable.

How fast does the memorial rose grow? And how far apart should it be planted? This is one of the best shrubs for bank planting, rooting all along its stems which can grow 4 ft. a year. A new planting should have the plants spaced about 4 ft. apart.

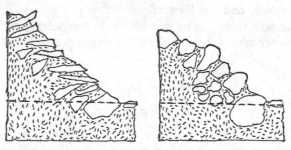

Method of placing stones to hold a slope or a terrace without a formal wall. (Left) Using flat field stones. (Right) Using boulders. Either method can become the basis for a future rock garden.

Surface Drainage

What is a dry well, and what is it used for?   A dry well is a pit dug 5 or 6 ft. deep, filled with stones and gravel. A pipe or sewer leading either from the house or from a poorly drained area leads into this, and provides drainage for difficult situations.

What can be done to prevent rain water from draining off the highway onto a sloping property, causing erosion?   A low bank along the highway should be constructed, and at the lowest point in the gutter so created a catch basin can be installed to gather the water and lead it, through a pipe, to a place where it will do no harm. Such a catch basin can be simply two 18-in. sewer tiles, one on top of the other, with a grating fitted into the top and a 4-in. side outlet about 1 ft. below the top. If there is a great deal of water, it may have to be a brick, concrete, or stone basin.

How can I construct a catch basin to take off surplus rain water from the drive?   Two pieces of 18-in. sewer tile, set one on top of the other, and with an iron grating fitted into the top, make a good, cheap catch basin. Smaller tile are too difficult to clean; larger are seldom needed. If the amount of water to be taken care of is large, a 4-in. or 6-in. tile pipe can be taken from the top catch-basin tile (which can be obtained with a side outlet) and carried some distance away to a low point where the water will do no harm, or to the storm sewer.

Lawns in the Landscape Scheme

Should a garden have a lawn space in the middle?   Not all gardens should be so designed, but there are many advantages to this type of layout. A grass panel serves as a foreground to the floral displays in the beds and as a space for chairs and tables. Such a garden is easier to maintain than one made up of many small beds.

A lawn can provide background for the house and the trees, shrubs, and other features that make up the landscape.

How would you grade a front lawn where the house is small and is several feet below the highway level? A gradual slope from the house up to the street is usually more pleasing than abrupt terraces. To prevent water draining toward the house, however, the grade should be carried down from the house slightly, to a low point from which the water can drain off to the sides before the slope up to the street begins. (See Section 4, Lawn and Turf Areas.)

Fences, Gates, and Walls

Is a wattle fence appropriate for the home garden? Yes, they are excellent for screening of the small garden utility area to give privacy. They are made of thin split saplings and are quite durable.

I have a horizontal clapboard fence but it looks rather monotonous in design. What can I do to make it more interesting? Since it is of wood, clinging vines would not prove satisfactory. Why not espalier a pyracantha, yew, or fruit tree against it?

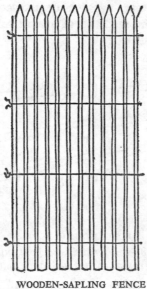

WOODEN-SAPLING FENCE

Where can I get a design for a picket fence? There are many designs for the old-fashioned picket fence. To select the right one, consult a general garden book.

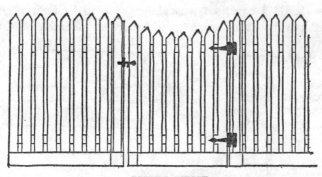

PICKET FENCE

What sort of fence is best for use along the road in front of a modified colonial house where something elaborate would be out-of-place? A simple post-and-rail fence, such as the one in the accompanying sketch, has proved very satisfactory. It can be painted white, or, if made of chestnut, cypress, or redwood, left unpainted to weather. If it has to be made proof against small animals, wire can be attached to the inside.

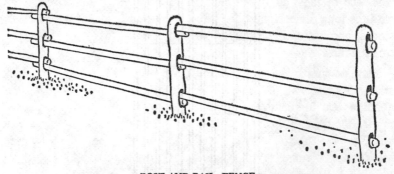

POST-AND-RAIL FENCE

A post-and-rail fence is excellent support for climbing roses or vines such as clematis.

I need a moderate-priced fence to shut out the view of the street from my front lawn. What shall I use? A fence of palings made of 1 × 4 in. redwood, 5 ft. 6 in. high, will answer your purpose. Or a stockade-type fence which comes already built in sections of varying heights.

How should I construct a retaining wall, to be built of stones? Since it may be called upon to withstand considerable pressure, a

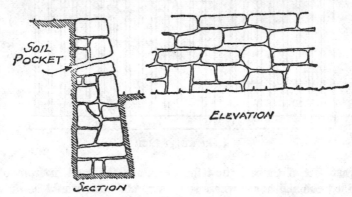

Side view and cross section of a dry stone wall with soil pockets for plants.

dry wall must have an adequate foundation, and the stones must be firmly bedded. The accompanying sketch shows that the foundation is as wide or wider than the wall and goes down below frost level. The face of the wall slopes back slightly, and all the stones are set with the long dimension horizontal. Use squarish rather than rounded stones, and use as large ones as you can get. Avoid "chinking" with small stones.

How do you make soil pockets in which to grow plants in a dry wall? As the wall is being laid, leave gaps all the way through it, about 4 ins. in diameter. Be sure these openings slope downward toward the back of the wall to keep soil and plants from being washed out. See that the soil is continuous from the face of the wall to the soil back of the wall to permit moisture to penetrate to it constantly. Fill the holes thus made with rich soil. Be sure the stones above them make solid bridges over the holes. (See Wall Gardens, this section.)

What kind of gate is best to use with a clipped privet hedge? A well-designed gate of stained, weathered, or painted wood, or wrought iron.

Do you recommend wire gates for gardens? Wire gates are not usually so decorative as wooden or iron gates. They are suitable for vegetable areas or dog runs.

To be correct, must the planting either side of a garden gate or entrance be the same? A symmetrically balanced arrangement is the usual thing, but it is often less interesting than an unsymmetrical treatment such as the one in the following sketch. Here a ceramic container planted with a shrub is balanced by the tall, dark evergreen on the other side. Such a treatment is easier to arrange when the position of the entrance, or conditions of shade, etc., make a symmetrical arrangement difficult. It is more lively and striking.

We have a picket fence but have difficulty with visitors not thinking to close the gate. How do you construct one of those self-closing affairs? The old method used in colonial times was simple enough. Merely place a heavy metal ball on a chain. Attach one end of the chain to a sturdy post about 4 ft. high, the other end to the gate. In this way the weight of the ball closes the open gate.

A board-on-board fence is not difficult for the home gardener to construct, once the necessary upright posts are securely positioned and the horizontal boards, top and bottom, have been fastened to them. Such a fence makes an attractive background for temporary or more permanent plantings.

Espalier Plant Forms

What is an espalier?   Popularly it is a plant that has been trained by special pruning to grow all in one plane, against a wall or fence. This old-world practice is now returning as a popular hobby and is an easy way of making dull, monotonous walls look most interesting.

What are some plants that can be espaliered?   Pyracantha, forsythia, *Cotoneaster horizontalis,* fruit trees, crab apples, yews, mockoranges, Japanese quince, *Jasminum* species, magnolias, and *Tamarix* species.

Is training espaliers time-consuming?   Not necessarily. A shearing or clipping to the right form at the start, then about twice a year, is all that is necessary. Bending and tying young twigs in place should be done when they are young and pliable—in the spring. They should be tied to wires firmly, but not so tight the wires will girdle the twigs. Such wires should be loosened or changed periodically.

What are some of the forms used in training espaliers?   Fan shapes with 3–7 main leaders from the base; horizontal branches on either side of one central-leader; curved fan types; horizontal cordon, oblique cordon, U-shaped forms, and gridirons of various shapes.

What is more important in pruning espaliers, the time of pruning or the shape? Always the shape must be kept in mind. Even taking off a single wrong bud may retard the final shaping for a year or more. Never prune off any buds or twigs without having a mental picture of the final shape desired.

Driveways

What material do you recommend for the building of a driveway? Many materials make satisfactory driveways, but much depends on whether the drive is straight or curved, flat or sloping, in cold country or warm. A good, cheap driveway for a level drive in the New York area can be made of either cinders mixed with loam and sand or bank-run gravel. Either can be finished with grits or bluestone screenings. If there are curves or grades, crushed stone with a tar binder is practically mandatory.

How would you build a driveway on a steep slope to prevent washing? What material should be used? For a short driveway on a steep slope, granite paving blocks set in sand make an ideal material. They are rough enough to give good traction in icy weather, they need no maintenance, they are good-looking. For a long driveway, they may be too uneven for comfortable riding, and concrete, heavily scored to provide traction, may be better. But it is a hard, uncompromising-looking material.

I am building a driveway for my home. What sort of parking space for visiting cars do you recommend, and where should it be located? Parking space for at least one guest car should be provided right at the front door or the path leading to it, so arranged that the use of the driveway by other cars is not prevented. (See next question.) Parking for a larger number of cars should be located at a distance from the front entrance of the house. It should be constructed of the same material as the driveway.

When guests come to the house and leave their cars before the front door, it is impossible for anyone else to use the driveway from the garage to the street. How can I avoid this situation?   Construct a pass court in front of the door wide enough so that a car can stand at the door and another pass it on the outside. The court should be about 30 ft. long and 16 ft. wide. Any interesting shape can be given it to make it a pleasing part of the landscape picture.

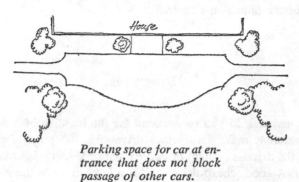

Parking space for car at en-
trance that does not block
passage of other cars.

What is the most practical shape for a turn court at the garage on a small property?   The so-called Y-turn takes up the least space and yet provides for easy turning, either for your own car coming out of the garage, or for other cars using the driveway. The radius of the curves in the accompanying sketch should be 15 ft. to 20 ft., and it is important that the space into which the cars back be at least 14 ft. wide.

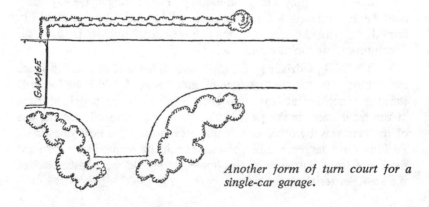

Another form of turn court for a
single-car garage.

How large should a turn-around in front of the house be? The largest cars require a turning space about 60 ft. in diameter for making a complete turn without backing. An area of bluestone or gravel that large is often out of proportion to the house. It can be broken up with a grass island (but this should not have anything else planted in it). To make arrival at the house door easy, it is wise to distort the shape of the turn-around somewhat, making it more of an apple shape instead of a true circle.

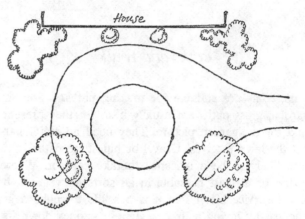

Turn-around for car.

Would you recommend brick or stone edging for a driveway or path? For a driveway, brick edging is somewhat too fragile unless the bricks are set in a heavy foundation of concrete. Then they are likely to be ugly. Granite paving blocks (Belgian blocks) are better because they are heavy enough to stay put without cement. For pathways, brick is ideal. Small rounded stones are useless for either purpose and never are aesthetically pleasing.

What sort of edging should I use for a brick walk or driveway? There are three standard patterns of edging: sawtooth, rowlock, and stretcher. For garden paths where there are no grass edges, sawtooth looks well, and it uses less brick than does rowlock. Against a lawn or grass edge rowlock is better because the mower can be run up on it and there is less hand clipping. Stretcher edging uses the least brick of all, but, since the bricks do not go down into the ground any farther than the bricks of the walk itself, it provides less stability for the walk.

What can I use to edge a driveway that will look well, but also make a strong, permanent edge?   Granite paving blocks are ideal for this. They are so heavy they will stay in place without concrete to hold them. Do not let them stick up above the lawn area. Set them on end, with the short dimension parallel to the line of the driveway.

Paths and Walks

What materials are suitable for making paths?   For an average flower garden, grass paths are usually best, for they present a green foreground for the garden picture. They need no maintenance other than what the lawn receives. Gravel or bluestone paths in the flower garden are likely to be a nuisance to take care of. Where a path must be dry, or at least passable in all sorts of weather, brick and flagstone are serviceable. Often it is possible to make a grass path more practical by laying a line of stepping-stones down its middle, or along either edge.

Should a path be laid out in a straight line or with a curve?   Generally speaking, a path should be as direct as possible, because the purpose of it is to provide a passage between two points. However, a natural-looking path should follow the contour of the garden, curving around trees or shrubs that are in a direct line. Sharp curves are to be avoided, and all unnecessary turns. When a curve is to be made, it should have a long, gentle sweep. For very small paths, a straight line, with no curves at all, is advisable.

How should I construct a brick walk?   Brick walks look best when laid in sand rather than cement mortar. Provide a gravel or cinder bed about 6 ins. thick, then put down a layer of fine sand, set the edge courses, and fill in the field brick in whatever pattern you wish. Fill the cracks between the bricks with fine sand, wash it well, and tamp thoroughly. In tamping, lay a heavy board on the walk and pound that rather than the bricks themselves. The walk will be smoother if you do this and you will break fewer bricks.

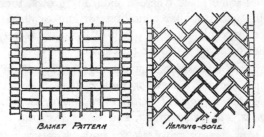

BASKET PATTERN   HERRING-BONE

Two "patterns" for laying bricks for a walk.

What pattern should be used in laying a brick walk? There are two standard patterns, basket and herringbone. Either may be varied somewhat according to taste. The basket pattern is more economical, since there is no cutting of brick. The accompanying sketch shows basket pattern with a rowlock edge and herringbone with a sawtooth edge. In laying out the walk, set only one edge course first. Lay out a section of the field to see how the pattern is working out, then set the other edge. Do not decide on a predetermined width for the walk and then try to fit the pattern into it.

I have been thinking of putting in a gravel path. Is it commonly used in the garden? Gravel paths are often used. They are inclined to look a bit formal and cold, however, and they are not so comfortable to walk upon as grass. Also in the winter the stones and snow stick to the soles of shoes and so can be brought into the house.

What sort of stones are suitable for a path of stepping stones? Water-washed flat stones with rounded edges are the most effective. If these are unobtainable, other flat stones or random slates or flagstones can be used, which are thick enough to bear the weight of traffic. Discarded, broken-up sections of concrete paving can also be used.

Are sections of tree trunks practical and long lasting as stepping stones? Yes, the chain saw has made it simple and inexpensive to cut flat cross sections of any sized tree trunk, 4–6 ins. thick. These can be treated with some wood preservative or used in their natural state as stepping stones in the garden and be expected to have a long life.

Is it possible to encourage the growth of moss? I want to put some between stepping stones. Moss can be started only by transplanting sods of it from some place where it naturally grows. Find a variety that is growing under similar conditions of sun or shade. Probably you will get better results by using plants of *Arenaria verna caespitosa,* the moss sandwort, which can be purchased.

Will you suggest some plants for placing between stepping stones? Various thymes, sedums, *Cerastium tomentosum, Euonymus fortunei* 'Kewensis', *Mazus reptans, Potentilla tridentata, Sagina subulata, Veronica repens, Tunica saxifraga,* and *Viola arenaria.*

Can you recommend a substitute for tanbark to use on our woodland garden path? Wood chips should be suitable, if you live in an area where they are available. They are often available for a slight charge from utility companies and should last for three or four years before they decay. Another substance—if your path is not too extensive—is pine bark, usually available from garden centers. A third material, but of much finer texture than the others, is sawdust, a practical solution if you live in a lumbering region.

Garden steps should be comfortable and safe for the user as well as attractive. These steps combine bricks and railroad ties.

Of what shall I build my garden steps? Steps of stone with brick or flagstone treads harmonize well in many gardens. All-brick steps often look too harsh and formal. Field stone is all right if you can find enough flat ones. Concrete is much too unyielding. Grass steps held in place by steel bands imbedded in the turf are beautiful but hard to make and to maintain. For very informal situations, sod, gravel, or tanbark steps held up by field stone or log risers are most effective. Sometimes the steps themselves are made of squared sections of cypress, black locust logs, or railroad ties.

Patios and Terraces

(See also Roof Gardens, Container Gardening and Window-Box Gardens, this Section.)

What is the difference between a patio and a terrace?   In popular thinking, not much. The terms are used interchangeably. Actually, the patio originated with the Spanish and we have come to associate terra cotta pottery and tiles with it. Usually a patio is partly enclosed, with shrubbery, or glass, or ornamental wooden screening. A terrace is more open without so much shelter.

Where should the patio be located?   Immediately outside the living room or dining room, where it is easily accessible and can be seen from indoors. Be sure to plan it and plant it so that it is most attractive from indoors. The use of sliding glass doors adds a picture-window effect.

What is the best material for paving a patio?   Depends on your likes and dislikes. It should go well with the house, or its foundation, or the chimney. Tile, gravel, paving stones, bricks, even redwood planks are all possibilities.

I want to build a partially enclosed patio. What do you suggest to enclose it with?   If there is a view of merit, be certain to take full advantage of it. Shield it from prevailing winds. A low brick or stone wall with small openings, louvered redwood or redwood to form a "board-on-board" arrangement, glass or plastic, or a hedge or border of shrubbery. There are many possibilities. Consult your lumber-yard salesmen. Principal purpose is to give some privacy and shelter from winds.

I would like to have some flower beds on my patio. Do they belong? Certainly, and you might consider raised beds, using walls of brick or stone to raise the planting surface 2 ft. above the ground. If herbs are planted they would be much closer to smell and touch. Weeding

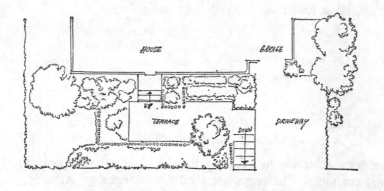

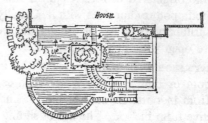

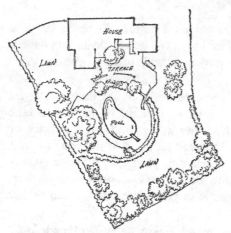

A terrace can be constructed in a variety of shapes and forms, as shown by the 3 examples here. They should harmonize with the house and not appear as tacked-on additions, lacking landscaping or privacy plantings. The plan at left shows how terrace area can be extended to include swimming pool.

TERRACE AND PATIO SHAPES

such beds is not a backbreaking chore as it might be if the beds were at ground level.

How do I provide shade for the patio?   If a large tree is not already there, plant a dogwood, crab apple, magnolia, or some other small tree. Dogwood is ideal because it has horizontal branching and one can sit under it. A larger tree, like a hemlock, pine, oak, or maple, just outside the patio walls, would do the same trick, but place it where one can take fullest advantage of its shade at the right time of day.

Patio or terrace furniture should be in harmony with its surroundings.

Is there any special furniture for the patio that is best?   It certainly should be weatherproof. Chairs and tables might be of metal and heavy enough so they would not be blown around. Lounging chairs should be of a type to go well with the architecture of the house and type of patio constructed.

Should pots for plants on the patio be large or small?   The larger pots are more decorative and usually in keeping with the patio idea. What is even more important, they do not dry out as fast. Don't eliminate large wooden tubs as possibilities on the patio. Some of these, well planted, make excellent ornaments for display.

Is there any reason why a sandbox for our two small children should not be placed in one corner of our patio? If it is in the shade, and easily seen from the house, it would be an excellent place for the sandbox—if you really want it there!

Which flowers will grow on a very windy terrace? Dwarf phlox, astilbe, dianthus, *Gypsophila repens,* hemerocallis (day-lilies), evergreen candytuft, lavender, marigolds, geraniums, low-growing zinnias.

How should I construct a flag terrace, and the steps down from it to the lawn? The flagstone, 2 ins. or so thick, can be laid on a bed of cinders or gravel covered with a thin layer of fine sand. No mortar is needed if the flags are heavy enough to stay in place. Slate cannot be used so easily. Brick can be substituted for flag. Steps should have treads with at least 1 in. overhang, and there should be a solid concrete foundation under them. Ramps, parapets, or wing walls should be substantial and have copings with the same overhang as the step treads. Steps and walls should be laid in cement mortar.

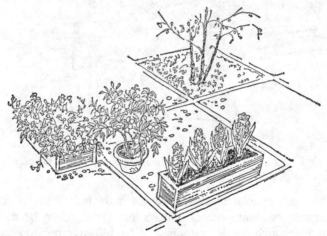

A terrace area can become a garden by leaving soil pockets among the pavement for trees and other plants. Seasonal color accents can be provided by plants in pots or containers.

Will you suggest a plant giving a long period of bloom for the narrow border around my flagged terrace? Lantana. Purchase young blossoming plants from a florist or garden center and plant 18 ins. apart. They will grow into sturdy shrubs by midsummer; not winter hardy. Try an edging of lobelia on the inside. A more economical substitute for the lantana would be dwarf marigolds.

Which plants are suitable for a patio?   In the northeast or north a patio might include a permanent planting of broad-leaved evergreens, an espaliered fruit tree (if there is a sunny wall), and a wisteria vine. Potted foliage plants (monstera, *Nephthytis afzellii,* dracaena, dieffenbachia, etc.) and potted geraniums, fuchsias, lantanas, begonias, and caladiums; crown-of-thorns and other succulents (such as crassulas) could be set out in warm weather. Patios in warm climates have a wider choice of plants, including such shrubs as oleanders, camellias, and gardenias; also bougainvillea and vines and other semitropical plant material.

I would like to have a patio garden. Would this be suitable with a colonial house?   Patio gardens are usually made within a courtyard or similar enclosure. Although they are of Spanish origin and suited to this type of dwelling, the idea can be adapted to any style of architecture today. If you have or can arrange a suitable protected terrace or courtyard adjacent to your colonial house, you can use flat stones or flagging to pave the area, put potted plants in white containers instead of Spanish pottery ones and, by using colonial ornaments and furniture, arrange a fitting outdoor living area which would serve the same purpose as a patio.

Are sun decks recent additions to outdoor living?   Actually no, they are adapted from the mid-Victorian porch of the last century, which was firmly attached to the house. They now are built over slopes, in the trees, over the garage, and many other places, giving opportunity for the sun-loving people of today to enjoy outdoor relaxation. Building a redwood sun deck over the edge of a steep bank makes it possible to have outdoor living where there is no room for the standard patio or terrace. Usually more exposed to the elements, there is opportunity for outdoor entertainment and gardening by growing plants in tubs.

I want to screen one side of our patio from the view of the road, but I don't like the idea of a wall. What do you suggest?   Landscape architects have come up with all sorts of beautiful screening ideas— actually walls made of wood but with the boards cut and put together in interesting ways so that the "wall" is actually a thing of beauty when viewed from either side. Cedar, redwood, translucent glass or plastic, louvered slats of redwood, etc.–all have been used effectively. The salesmen in your local lumber yard will have suggestions. Look through general gardening books for specific suggestions.

Garden Lighting

Is garden lighting costly to maintain?   No. The lights are turned on for such a short time the cost of electricity is negligible. Initially the installation of weatherproof lights, wiring, and sockets might seem expensive, but the results of being able to illuminate parts of the garden and its paths at night adds a new appreciation of the garden.

Should lights be directed up to or down on foliage in the garden at night?   Both. Varying this direction brings about diversification of interest–a few flowers in bloom by the walk and at another place a spotlight on tree branches from below.

Are garden lights set out permanently in one situation?   Not necessarily. The initial installation of underground wiring would include a series of weatherproof plugs so that lights of various types could be changed from place to place as different plants come into bloom.

Are there special lamps for garden lighting?   Yes. Your electrical contractors can recommend fixtures of different types and will do the initial installation. A diversified series of lights, illuminating plants to show both flowers and form as well as steps and walks, brings a new enjoyment to the garden at night.

Garden Pools

(See also Water Gardens)

How should a small pool be constructed?   The accompanying sketch shows a simple concrete pool and the necessary plumbing connections. For the successful growing of aquatics the deep part of the pool should be 1½ ft., and if it is to be used at all by birds, some part of it should be shallow enough for them. They do not like water more than 2 ins. deep.

How shall I go about building a small pool? Excavate the ground about 6 ins. deeper on bottom and wider at the sides than you wish the pool to be. Insert drainage if pool is to be large enough to require it (see accompanying sketch); if it is very small, this will not be necessary. Fill hole with gravel layer, tamp down firm, or line with chicken wire. Pour cement, 1 part cement to 3 parts mixed sand and gravel. Add water enough so that mixture will spread evenly. Layer should be about 4 or 5 ins. thick. Next day finish with a coat of cement mortar, 1 part cement to 2 parts sand, applied with a trowel.

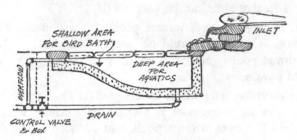

Cross section detail of inflow and overflow for small pool.

How thick should the concrete walls of a garden pool be? The thickness of the walls of a pool depends on its size. A large pool naturally has to have thicker walls. For the average small pool (6 ft. or so in diameter) walls 6 ins. thick are sufficient. Some reinforcement in the form of wire or steel rods should be used.

How soon after finishing the construction of a small pool can plants be put in? Leave the pool filled with water for about 2 weeks, flushing occasionally, before planting or putting in fish.

Are plastic pools feasible? I do not want to go to the expense of putting in a concrete pool, but would like to have a small pool for a few years' trial. Plastic molded pools are available in small sizes and are quite inexpensive when compared with concrete pools. Various types are frequently advertised in the garden magazines. They can be easily installed by any gardener.

I want to paint my pool blue. What kind of paint shall I use?

There is a special paint available from seed or department stores for just this purpose.

What shape should a small pool be?   It depends on your location and general garden design. If your garden is informal, an informally shaped pool would be best. This should be basically circular or "egg-shaped" with gently curving, irregular contours. By using the garden hose to lay out the shape of the pool, good curves may be attained. Avoid sharp curves and too many irregularities. Simplicity is the keynote.

I want to build a small informal pool. About what size should I make it?   A good-looking small pool might be about 25 sq. ft. in size but smaller sizes can be successful.

I want to build a small formal pool with a fountain and statue at the back. What shape would be best for the pool?   A round or oblong formal pool is always good. If your garden is very formal, you could have a rectangular pool.

Will goldfish live over winter in my pool?   That depends on how deep and how large the pool is and on your winter temperatures. Goldfish can live over in large pools that do not freeze solid in the winter, but will not live over winter in small pools that either freeze solid, or have only a few inches of water under the ice in winter. Under such conditions the fish actually smother to death.

I understand pools take time to clean and it may be too much for me but I'd like to try one for a while without going to the labor and expense of constructing a concrete pool. What do you suggest?   By all means, try a pool temporarily. Line it with heavy polyethylene film, the edges tucked in the soil at the sides, rocks at the edges as for other pools. You can even purchase a small circulating pump and install a fountain—these are available. In this way, with little expense, you can have your pool for trial. It will last longer than you think!

For plants in and about pools, see Water Gardens, this section.

Do you recommend putting a fountain into a small home garden?   Elaborate fountains throwing large streams of water are rather expensive to maintain and too impressive for a small garden. A small fountain which drips water slowly over a shallow basin or a wall fountain that runs a tiny stream into a bowl are pleasing and in scale.

Are electric pumps for small fountains difficult to maintain? No, there are excellent long-lasting ones available today that recirculate the water. They are easy to care for. Be sure you buy a good one and install it where it is easily accessible.

I want water at various places in my garden for a pool, for sprinklers, for a fountain, and for just watering plants during dry spells. Can I put in a simple water system myself? Yes—use plastic pipe. It is easily laid in a V-shaped trench in lawn or garden about 8 ins. deep. Outlets and connections are all available, as are drain plugs so the system can be easily drained before winter. The expense is only a fraction of what metal pipe would be—and it is much easier to install.

Game Areas

How can I lay out a badminton court? Allow about 30 by 60 ft. of level lawn space for a badminton court.

I want to make part of my garden into an area for a bowling green and for horseshoe pitching. How much room is necessary? For a bowling grccn you should have a smooth grass area at least 60 ft. long. A gutter of sand 1½ ft. wide and about 6 ins. deep should surround this strip. For horseshoes, you will need an area 10 × 50 ft. The sand pit at either end should be 6 ft. sq., with a stout wooden or iron stake in the center.

How much room does a croquet lawn require? About 30 × 60 ft. A level, well-mowed area is essential for this game. (See Lawns.)

What games or equipment would be suitable for a children's game area? A wading pool, sandbox or sand pit, swings, seesaw, sliding board, ball court.

My children want a tennis court. What is the most practical type? The surface choices are clay, grass, asphalt, or all-weather. It depends on your individual preferences, local conditions, and budget. It should not be a do-it-yourself project, but one for the contractors, who have had experience in building them.

What is the simplest means of fencing in a pool to keep out animals

and small children? Probably a simple wire fence, 4 ft. high. This could be augmented by a shrub planting on the outside to hide the pool as well as to give protection from winds. A yew hedge would be ideal, and eliminate the leaf problem in the fall.

What are the things to keep in mind in planning for a swimming pool? Situation, size, and shape. But also plan for the necessary maintenance, and for a flat area around the pool, usually paved, for sun-bathing and relaxing in general. Also the fencing in of the pool, to keep out animals and small children. Have a small camouflaged space for the filtering equipment. Drainage of the pool is also very important.

Would a rectangular or informally shaped swimming pool be best? Depends on your wishes and your budget. Usually the latter are more expensive to build.

Where should I locate a swimming pool? Preferably on flat land, in the sun, and away from overhanging tree branches, but nevertheless in a protected area if possible, out of windy areas.

What is the minimum size of a swimming pool if one wants to really swim? Probably 34 ft. × 14 ft., and if there is a diving board, a depth of at least 8 ft. where the diver hits the water. Of course, the larger the pool the more room to swim!

We want to provide a play area for two very small children. What do you suggest? First a sandbox, at least 6 × 6 ft., with arrangements for covering it with canvas to keep out rain and prevent dogs and cats from digging in it. This should be located where there is some shade and preferably screened with shrubs to prevent youngsters from wandering too much. Second, a swing-ladder-trapeze affair of either steel or wood, easily seen from the house. Several types are readily available from department stores. A shallow wading pool might be included.

Tool Houses and Utility Areas

I want to fix up some space in my garage as a tool house and potting shed. How can I arrange this? Build a long bench, at convenient height for standing, to be used for potting plants, mixing sprays, etc. Under this have drawers or shelves for pots, labels, and baskets, and bins for fertilizers and mulching materials. Over the bench, racks may be built for holding vases, and a peg board will be a convenient holder for small tools such as trowels, dibbers, and hand cultivators. A space against one wall should be left for the wheelbarrow and lawn mower. Wooden racks for rakes, hoes, and other long-handled tools (which are hung handle down) can be made by nailing a strip of wood on the wall, about 6 ft. above the floor. Pairs of tenpenny nails protruding from this hold the tools. The garden hose needs a special rack where it will not be damaged by sharp tools. A stout 2-ft. bracket jutting out from the wall will be convenient for this purpose.

Where and how can I provide a convenient storage place for my vegetable garden tools and equipment?   A small addition to the garage, opening out into the vegetable garden, makes an ideal tool house. If the garden is fairly large and the garage not conveniently near, a small separate building, disguised as a garden house, will serve. On a sloping lot, enclosed space under a rear deck often makes a good place for this equipment. Also the large mail-order houses have available small prefabricated tool houses that are easily erected in a concealed part of the garden.

Where should the utility area be located?   Preferably near the kitchen door. Here would be space for garbage and trash cans, propane gas cylinders if used, storage space for fireplace wood, and possibly even space for clothes drying, if needed.

How large an area should I plan for clothes drying?   Depends on the amount of clothes to be dried at one time. With electric driers commonly used, many homeowners only hang clothes out of doors on rare occasions. Then a portable aluminum umbrella-type drier can be set in a prepared hole in the ground, or a few lines can be run across the utility area.

How high should the screening about the utility area be?   About 6½ ft.

How about garbage cans in the utility area?   Best is the sunken metal type in the ground, with a foot pedal for lifting the lid. Trash cans or polyethylene barrels should have lids, and might be enclosed (except for the front) within a wood closet.

How can I best screen a small utility area? By planting a tight hedge of narrow evergreens; by a split sapling, woven-slat, or tightly rustic fence; or simply by a tall board fence over which interesting vines like English ivy, Dutchman's-pipe, honeysuckle, or climbing hydrangea are used. Another way is to erect a tight-fitting red-cedar sapling fence, which in itself is interesting, and on the outside train a few espaliered yews or pyracanthas.

Garden Features and Accessories

What type of bird bath is good for the small garden? Containers of concrete, clay, lead, wood, or stone are suitable, as long as they are well designed and unobtrusive. Select a design which fits your garden plan. Homemade cement-and-field-stone bird baths are not usually desirable. For a small garden a height of 2½ ft. is about right.

Are the bird baths which are set on the ground without a pedestal practical? Yes, they are very effective if well designed. Handmade ceramic or metal basins are interesting, or a hollowed stone may be used. They are usually placed in a sheltered spot surrounded by plantings to give the birds protection.

How often should you clean bird baths? As often as they look dirty or stained, which is usually 2 times a week at least in warm weather. It will help to have a special scrubbing brush for the bird bath for removing scum around the edges.

What can be used to remove algae from a bird bath? Usually water or soapy water and a scrubbing brush are all that is necessary. Borax may be added, or a bleaching disinfectant. These, however, must be well rinsed off before filling the bath with water for the birds.

I want to have an arbor. Shall I buy one or make one? First decide on why you need an arbor—for ornament, for screening, for shade? There are all sorts available, metal, white painted wood, rustic types, those made of redwood or cedar, etc. Decide what fits into your garden or patio scheme best. Consult a good picture reference book for possible designs and suggested materials. An arbor is a rather permanent garden fixture and one should be certain it fits in well with the garden scheme.

What is a pergola? A pergola is a passageway covered by an arbor which supports grape vines or large flowering vines. The structure is usually somewhat elaborate, with decorative columns and crosspieces. It is of Latin origin and is suitable to only a limited number of American gardens.

Is a pergola recommended for the small garden? The old-fashioned white painted wood pergola, used so much in gardens fifty years ago, is now out of place in most American gardens. In its place have come arbors built of thick planks and of rather heavy structure, supplying some slight shade but also support for ornamental vines to give additional shade over walks, patios, or terraces.

I want to have some statuary in my garden. Can you suggest some types? In the small garden, care must be taken not to overdo use of statuary. One well-designed piece, not too large, used as a center of interest, is sufficient. A statue is usually placed at the end of a vista or in a niche formed of evergreens. It needs a background of green plant material to fit it into the garden picture. Avoid use of pottery figures of gnomes, ducks, etc., and other novelties as being too conspicuous.

Is a bench practical in a small modern garden? Yes. One always wants to sit down in the garden when a permanent, well-placed bench is present. It can be of metal, wood, or cement or a combination of materials.

Should weather vanes be used on small properties? The use of weather vanes has been overdone in some sections. They are best used in the country, on barns, tool sheds, or other outbuildings. For a small place, get a simple style, not too large, to be used on the garage or garden house.

Do you recommend using a sundial in the garden? A sundial is very effective in the right setting as the center of interest in a rose or herb garden, or formal garden. It must, of course, be placed where the sun will hit it all day.

What is topiary work? Pruning of hedges, shrubs, or trees in specific shapes, as of animals, houses, balls, spools, figures, or geometric forms, used in formal gardens and primarily associated with medieval landscape design. Practiced today more in Europe than in America. Boxwood, yew, and privet, are employed for this purpose. Also, English ivy growing over prearranged wire frames.

Special Types of Gardens

HERB GARDENS—WHAT TO GROW

Which herbs are annuals and which perennials? I am confused over which ones to expect to come up a second year.   The annual herbs most widely used are anise, dill, summer savory, fennel, coriander, and borage. The perennial herbs include horse-radish, lemon-balm, winter savory, pot marjoram, sage, horehound, mint, tarragon, and beebalm. Parsley and caraway are, technically, biennials, but are grown as annuals. All of these grow in full sun and like a well-drained garden soil. Sow annuals as early in spring as weather permits, either in rows or broadcast.

Will you list 6 annual herbs for the kitchen garden?   Basil, borage, chervil, parsley (really biennial but treated as an annual), summer savory, and sweet marjoram.

Sweet marjoram and summer savory—two of the most popular annual herbs for culinary use.

Which 6 perennial herbs do you suggest for the kitchen herb garden?   Chives, horse-radish, mint, sage, tarragon, and thyme.

Which herbs do you suggest for a fragrant herb garden?   Bergamot, lavender, lemon-verbena, rosemary, scented geraniums, southernwood, sweet wormwood, lovage, valerian, lemon-balm, sweet Cicely, thyme, and costmary.

What herbs may be grown successfully at home, and preserved for winter use?   Try the mints (if there is a moist spot in the garden,

and care is taken to prevent the plants from overrunning their space);
also sage, thyme, parsley, caraway, dill, and anise.

What are the best combinations of herbs for tea (as a beverage)?
For flavoring tea, try mints or lemon-verbena. In combination, one
authority suggests equal parts of elder flowers and peppermint; another, peppermint and lemon-verbena. Sage and camomile, each
used alone, make tasty beverages. Never use a metal container.

I like the idea of having a few large pots of herbs set about on
our terrace. Is this practicable? Absolutely! Several herbs have interesting foliage and flowers. They withstand dry sunny situations and
their fragrance is an addition to the pleasure of terrace of patio living. (See Herbs in Pots.)

**I only have a very small garden but do want to grow a few herbs.
Where would you suggest?** A few could be grown in large clay pots
or wooden tubs on the sunny part of the terrace or patio. A small
corner of the garden (in sun) could be used to advantage, or a spot
in front of a fence, by the garage or near the kitchen door. A few
could be selected to border a walk or simply be added to the flower
or vegetable garden.

Which are the most ornamental herbs? Hyssop, thyme, lavender,
winter savory, the artemisias, borage, rue, pot-marigold, and the
sweet-scented geraniums are a few.

What are the best ones with gray foliage? Lavender, the artemisias, borage, sweet marjoram, sage, and thyme.

**In a knot garden what material do you put between the miniature
herb hedges?** Such things as marble chips, pea coal, broken clay
pots, sandstone chips, finely chipped gray gravel, and redwood bark
are a few colorful materials that make an excellent background for
the plants.

Can you clip the plants in a knot garden any time? Woody plants
such as santolina and lavender should not be clipped after mid-July,
otherwise a late clipping might force out young growth that would
not have sufficient time to mature properly before freezing weather.

What is a knot garden? A garden of low-growing plants or hedges
planted in a formal, intricate design. Common to medieval landscape
design, when colored sand was often used to form the paths or sections which outlined the beds. Now used in parks, herb gardens, and
formal gardens.

A knot garden pattern. Suggested herb plants (1) gray santolina; (2) green santolina; (3) lavender; (4) germander.

How should I start a small herb garden of a half-dozen varieties of herbs?   Plant informally in little groups, taller plants more or less in back.

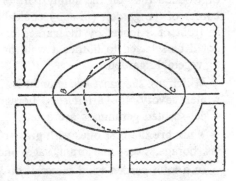

Method of laying out ellipses for a small herb garden. String is secured to stakes at B and C.

Can you give some information on herbs—some to eat and some to smell?   Good herbs for flavoring: basil (sweet) for salads, soups, and tomato sauces; chives for salads, sour cream, and pot cheese; dill for fish, shellfish, and pickles; fennel to eat like celery, or cooked; sweet marjoram, seasoning for stuffings, etc.; mints for teas and sauces; rosemary for seasoning roasts and chicken; sage for dressing; savory (summer) for flavoring vegetables, particularly string beans; thyme, seasoning for foods, salads, and sauces; tarragon, to flavor vinegar, and in chicken dishes. Herbs for scent: beebalm, lavender, lemon-verbena, mints, and scented geraniums.

Which herbs grow successfully in the house?   Basil, dittany of Crete, lemon-verbena, parsley, rosemary, sweet marjoram, tarragon, and perhaps peppermint, if the room is cool and has plenty of light.

Which herbs do you suggest for an herbaceous border? Some of them grow too tall and scraggly. Lavender, calendula, marjoram, rosemary, rue, sage, thyme, hyssop, and the gray artemisias.

Which herbs are particularly attractive to bees? Thyme, lavender, germander, beebalm, lovage, hyssop, lemon-balm, sweet Cicely, borage, and marjoram.

Can you name some herbs suitable for low hedges? Hyssop, lavender, santolina, germander, southernwood, and rue. In fairly mild climates—rosemary.

Can you suggest herbs for a usable kitchen garden for the beginner? Where can I get information as to their culture, preservation, and use? The following are particularly good for a beginner's garden: sage, tarragon, parsley, chives, shallots, basil, dill, rosemary, some of the thymes, and sweet marjoram. For further information write The Herb Society of America, 300 Massachusetts Ave., Boston, Massachusetts 02115.

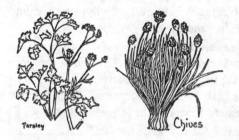

Two of the most useful culinary herbs—parsley and chives —often grown in the vegetable garden.

Which geraniums are particularly suited for planting (in summer) in an herb garden? These geraniums are botanically *Pelargonium*. The lemon-scented, peppermint-scented, apple-scented, and rose-scented are all good. (See Fragrant Gardens.)

Which herbs will tolerate part shade? Balm, bergamot, chervil, sweet fennel, tarragon, sweet-woodruff, mints, angelica, sweet Cicely, parsley, comfrey, and costmary.

Can you give me information on herbs suitable for an herb rock garden? The garden should be well drained and sunny; the soil on the lean side rather than over-rich. Almost any of the lower-growing herbs can be used, with a few taller ones for accents.

Of the varieties of herbs formerly imported, which ones can be

grown in northern and central New York? Some of them are coriander, anise, fennel, dill, cumin (*Cuminum cyminum*), and sage.

What is ironweed? Several different plants have been shown me, but I want to be sure, as I wish to use it in an old-time medical recipe. The ironweed of eastern United States is *Vernonia noveboracensis*. It usually grows in moist places, is 3 to 6 ft. high, and has open-branched cymes with many purple flowers. It has alternate linear leaves, the central vein streaked red. Blooms from August to October and is rather coarse in appearance.

I dislike the old formal design of herb gardens. Why not a simple informal border planting? Of course, this can be charming provided you study carefully the individual habits of the herbs you are going to use, and place them to look well in the final planting. Usually one should not space individual plants with large spaces in between. Plan to allow the plants to grow together. They are being grown to be clipped!

Are raised beds on the patio a good place to plant herbs? Certainly, and in this way their fragrance is more easily appreciated and they are much easier to care for and pick.

What materials should I use in making raised beds? Depends on the patio, terrace, walks, or house foundation. Use whatever goes well with what you have—brick, field stone, or concrete or raised beds of redwood or cypress. If an herb bed is to be placed along a brick walk, just a simple edging of raised bricks might prove satisfactory.

How large a space do I need for my herb garden? Actually an area only 4 ft. by 8 ft. is sufficient for all the herbs one normally needs, but one large clay pot can hold several plants—sufficient for most culinary needs.

I would like to edge a brick walk with a few herbs. Which are the best for this purpose? Basil, thyme, santolina, winter savory, and dwarf lavender. In mild climates, where it is hardy, rosemary can also be used.

Where can I obtain information on commercial herb growing? Many of the State Experiment Stations have bulletins on this subject. New York, Geneva, N.Y.; Vermont, Rutland, Vt.; Michigan, East Lansing, Mich.; Indiana, Lafayette, Ind.; Connecticut, New Haven, Conn.; Minnesota, St. Paul, Minn.; and the United States Department of Agriculture, Washington, D.C. Write to one or more of these for the latest information on the subject as well as to the Herb Society of America, Horticultural Hall, 300 Massachusetts Ave., Boston, Mass. 02115.

HERBS IN POTS

What types of containers other than clay pots might be used for herbs set out on the terrace or sun deck? Wooden tubs of various descriptions are used: an old butter tub, if you can get one, various types of redwood tubs or square containers. Plastic pots do not break and do not get disfigured outside with chemical deposits or plant growth and they stay moist longer than clay pots. Buckets: old wooden sap buckets have a special appeal.

Should I leave my potted herbs out on the terrace over winter? (New York.) No. Replant them in the open ground over winter, and possibly give them some winter protection with a good mulch.

A clay strawberry jar is an ideal container for different kinds of herb plants.

Is there any special soil treatment for the growing of herbs in containers? For drainage place a layer of cinders, gravel, or pieces of broken clay pots on the bottom. Use light, well-drained sandy soil with a little humus added. Only a very small amount of dried manure or bone meal should be added to the mixture, for these plants should not be forced into over-vigorous growth. It is not advisable to leave plants in pots or tubs over winter in the North. Rather take them out of the containers and plant in the ground over winter.

What are a few herbs for growing in pots? Lavender, dill, sage, basil, santolina, the artemisias, and fragrant-leaved geraniums. These might be clipped once or twice a season to keep them looking well.

HERB CULTURE

What general type of soil is preferred by herbs? Ordinary well-drained garden soil, lean rather than rich, and not too acid, suits the majority. Mints prefer a fairly rich, moist soil.

Do herbs thrive in sandy soils? With the possible exception of mints, which require considerable moisture, the great majority of herbs do very well in sandy soil if some humus is added and moisture is supplied in very dry weather.

I understand that most herbs need dry soil conditions. Can you suggest some for a moist, but not waterlogged, place? Angelica, bergamot, sweet Cicely, sweet flag, yellow-stripe sweet flag, lovage, mints, parsley, English pennyroyal, snakeroot, valerian (*Valeriana officinalis*), and violets.

What is the best exposure for an herb garden? A southeast exposure is ideal, but any location that gets full sunshine during the growing season will do. The soil and cultural practices, which include winter protection, are equally important.

What are the general cultural requirements for herbs? A rather poor, well-drained slightly acid or neutral soil, warmth, sunlight, and free circulation of air. Space the plants adequately, according to kind. This is a generalization; a number of herbs require distinctly different conditions.

What is the most practical arrangement of annual and perennial herbs—to interplant them, or to keep them separate? Plant the perennial kinds together and the annual kinds together. The area devoted to annuals can then readily be prepared afresh each spring and the perennial area is disturbed only every few years, when replanting becomes necessary.

Is it necessary to make more than one sowing of the various annual herbs each season? Only for quick-maturing kinds such as dill, chervil.

Is watering important in the herb garden? A few herbs (as mints) need generous supplies of moisture, but the majority develop their fragrances and flavors best when they are subjected to rather dry conditions; therefore, apply water with discrimination. Newly transplanted herbs and young plants need more attention in this respect than established plantings.

Should herbs be fertilized during the summer? The majority of true herbs require no fertilization. Feeding induces rank growth but does not favor the production of the essential oils which give to them their flavor and fragrance.

Can any non-hardy herbs be over-wintered successfully in a cold frame? Thyme, lavender, sage, and other "hardy" herbs which are often susceptible to winterkilling can be kept over winter in a cold frame. Really tender subjects, like rosemary, pineapple sage, scented geraniums, and lemon-verbena, must be kept in a temperature safely above freezing.

HARVESTING, CURING, AND STORING

Should herbs be washed before drying, and what is the appropriate time needed for this? What is a safe insecticide to use on these plants? Washing is not needed unless foliage is mud-spattered. Time needed for drying varies according to kind and environment. A rotenone or pyrethrum insecticide is recommended.

How shall I cure herbs properly so as to retain their flavor? Dry as quickly as possible in a warm, airy, well-ventilated place, *without exposure to sun.*

How does one cure herb leaves for drying? Pick them just before the plants begin to flower, any time in the day after the dew has disappeared. Tie in bundles, each of a dozen stems or so. Hang in an airy, warm, but not sunny place. When they are completely dry and crisp, strip off leaves and put in tight jars. The leaves may also be stripped fresh, right after cutting, and placed in shallow screenbottomed trays until dry.

When should herb seeds be harvested? When they have matured, and before they fall naturally from the plants.

How should herb seeds be dried? Collect the heads or seed pods and spread them in a tray made of screening, or in a thin layer on a cloth in a warm, well-ventilated room. Turn them frequently. At the end of a week or so they will be dry enough for threshing.

What is the best method of storing dried herbs? In airtight containers.

How can seeds in quantity, such as caraway, be best separated from stems and chaff? Remove as much of the stems as possible. Rub the heads or pods between the palms of the hands. If possible, do this outdoors where a breeze will help carry away the chaff. A kitchen strainer or screen is useful in the final cleaning.

What are "simples"? Herbs that possess, or are supposed to possess, medicinal virtues.

What is the "Doctrine of Signatures"? An ancient belief that plants, by the shape or form of their parts, indicated to man their medicinal uses. The spotted leaves of the lungwort showed that this plant was a cure for diseases of the lungs; the "seal" on the roots of Solomon's-seal promised the virtue of sealing or closing broken bones and wounds; and so on.

POTPOURRIS

What leaves and petals can be used for making potpourri? Any leaves or petals that have a pleasing fragrance may be used. Some of the best are rose, lavender, lemon-verbena, jasmine, marigold, stock, mignonette, heliotrope, violet, geranium, rosemary, lemon-balm, mint, southernwood, santolina, pink, wallflower, and thyme.

I want to make a potpourri of rose petals from my garden. How can I do this? Pick the rose petals (red holds its color best) when the flowers are in full bud but not completely blown. Spread them carefully on sheets of paper or strips of cheesecloth in a dry, airy room, away from the sun. Turn daily. Let them dry completely. This will take from a few days to a week. To each quart of petals add 1 oz. of orrisroot. Spices such as cloves, cinnamon, coriander, and mace may be added, if desired, ½ teaspoon of each. Keep in an airtight earthen jar.

What is "wet potpourri" and how is it made? Potpourri made by the wet method contains rose petals and the petals of any other fragrant flowers that are available. These are spread on cloths or papers to dry out partially. They are then packed in an earthenware jar with layers of table salt or coarse salt between. Add a layer of petals, then a sprinkling of salt, until the jar is filled. One oz. of orrisroot or violet powder is added, and, if desired, some cloves, allspice, and cinnamon. Put a weight on the petals and let them stand in the jar, covered, for several weeks before mixing. In addition to rose petals, lavender, lemon-verbena leaves, and geranium leaves are the most commonly used ingredients.

What is a "fixative," and for what is it used in potpourris? A fixative is used to retain the natural scent of leaves or petals and aids in preserving them. Orrisroot, violet powder, ambergris, and gum storax are common fixatives.

In making a sweet jar of flower petals, what can be used to keep the natural color of such flowers as delphinium, pansy, aconitum, and other colorful blooms? If the flowers are carefully dried, out of direct sunlight, they partially retain their color naturally. Orrisroot also seems to have a color-fixing effect.

HERB WHEELS

I would like to put plants around the spokes of an old wagon wheel that I have. How would you suggest doing this? A wagon wheel or oxcart wheel can be made the central feature of a small, formal herb garden. Select a level, sunny spot in the garden with en-riched, well-prepared soil. Place the hub down into the ground and put a few plants of each variety in between the spokes. A narrow path edged with thyme can surround the wheel. Low-growing, com-pact plants are better for a wheel-planting than tall, straggly ones.

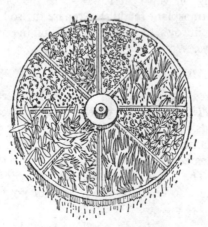

WHEEL GARDEN OF HERBS

What culinary herbs would be best in a "wheel garden"? Thyme, chives, sage, parsley, mint, lemon-balm, French tarragon, winter savory, sweet basil, sweet marjoram, chervil. Or the wheel can be planted exclusively with low-growing varieties of thyme.

Would you suggest some fragrant herbs that would look well planted in an oxcart wheel? Lemon-verbena, mint, rosemary, rose geranium, sweet Cicely, lavender, and summer savory.

SPECIFIC HERBS—ANGELICA

How do you grow angelica and what is it used for? Sow in summer as soon as seed is ripe, thin out seedlings, and transplant following spring. Soil should be moist and fairly rich. Light shade is beneficial. The seeds are slow to germinate. The plant is biennial under some conditions, so it is better to sow a few seeds each year to maintain a supply. The stems and leafstalks are used for salads and candied to decorate confections; the seeds for flavoring and for oil. The plants tend to self-sow and the resulting seedlings can be transplanted.

ANISE

Can you give some information on growing anise? It is an annual, so it must be sown each year. The seeds should be fresh because old seed will not germinate. Sow when the soil has warmed a little (about beginning of May) in rows where the plants are to stand (anise does not transplant readily). Prepare the soil deeply and make it very fine. Sow in rows 15 ins. apart and thin the plants out to 9 ins. apart in the rows. Water in very dry weather.

BALM OR LEMON-BALM

Is balm difficult to grow? Is it a useful herb? Lemon-balm (*Melisa officinalis*) is a hardy perennial of easy culture. It can be grown from seeds sown in prepared soil in July or August; the seedlings are transplanted, when large enough, to their flowering quarters. It can be propagated by division in spring. Any ordinary garden soil is satisfactory. The leaves are used for seasoning, particularly liqueurs. They are also used for salads and for potpourris.

BASIL

Can you give me information on growing basil? When should I sow the seeds? Seeds are sown outdoors after settled warm weather has arrived; or they are started indoors in April and the seedlings

Sweet Basil

transplanted outdoors later. Allow 12 ins. apart between plants. Basil yields abundantly. When cut, it repeatedly sends out new growth. Plants can be lifted in the fall and potted for winter use if desired.

BORAGE

Is borage annual or perennial? Can it be grown from seed? An annual, easily grown from seed in any good garden soil. Sow in spring when all danger of frost is past. The seedlings can be transplanted if care is exercised, but the plants are better if grown undisturbed. About 15 ins. should be allowed between plants.

CAMOMILE

Is Anthemis nobilis useful as an herb? Yes indeed, this is the old-fashioned Roman camomile, with finely cut fragrant leaves and white daisylike flowers, which have been used in making a medicinal tea. It is also used as a ground cover.

CARAWAY

How is caraway grown? From seeds sown outdoors in late May in rows 2 ft. apart. The plants are thinned to about 9 ins. apart. The first year low-growing plants are formed; the second year seeds are produced; then the plants die. Seed is most abundantly produced if the soil is not too rich. Do not water much, as this tends to keep the stems soft and causes the blossoms to fall before setting seed. Dry, sunny weather favors this crop.

CHERVIL

How is chervil grown? From seeds sown in spring where the plants are to grow. Thin plants to stand 9 ins. apart. Light shade is beneficial. Chervil is an annual. A second sowing can be made in early summer.

CHIVES

Can chives be grown from seeds or must I buy plants?   They can be grown from seeds sown outdoors early in spring (but buying a plant is easier). Thin the little plants to about ½ in. apart. They are hardy perennials, multiply rapidly, and need little attention. Divide every second year. They like a moderately moist soil.

CLARY

Is clary difficult to grow?   Clary (*Salvia sclarea*) is a biennial and dies after flowering. Sow seeds in early spring; thin to 6 ins. apart; as the plants develop, pull out every other one. Those removed can be dried. The plants bloom and set seeds the second year. A rich soil is advantageous.

CORIANDER

Is it easy to grow coriander seed?   Yes. Sow (thinly) in spring in well-drained, average soil and in sunny position. Thin to stand 9 or 10 ins. apart. Plants and fresh seeds are unpleasantly scented, but ripe seeds become very fragrant as they dry.

COSTMARY

How is costmary grown?   Propagate it from seeds or by root division. Plant in full sun or very light shade. Space plants about 3 ft. apart. Lift and replant every third year. A freely drained soil is needed. (The botanical name is *Chrysanthemum balsamita*.)

Dill

DILL

How do you grow dill?   Dill is a fast-growing annual that matures in about 70 days. Sow in early spring in well-prepared soil, in rows

2 ft. apart, where the plants are to remain. The plants grow about 3 ft. tall and make a good-sized bush. Thin out the seedlings to 3 or 4 ins. apart at first; later give a final thinning so that they stand a foot apart.

DITTANY OF CRETE

What is dittany of Crete and how is it grown in the herb garden? It is *Cimaracus dictamnus*. Increase it by seeds or cuttings. It is not hardy where winters are cold and must be wintered indoors in pots. A sandy soil, perfect drainage, and full sun are cultural desiderata.

FENNEL

Have you data on perennial fennel that grows 10 ft. tall? The common fennel (*Foeniculum vulgare*) has escaped to the wild in the South and grows 8 ft. in height. In colder climates, fennel is less tall, rarely reaching 4 ft. and usually grown as an annual.

How is Florence fennel grown? As an annual. Seeds are sown in spring where the plants are to mature. The seedlings are thinned out to 6 ins. apart. The plants mature in about 60 days.

FOXGLOVE

Is the foxglove (digitalis) a perennial? No, a biennial, although occasionally a plant will persist for 3 years. Sow seeds each June. They need a well-drained soil that is deep and fairly moist.

Can digitalis (foxglove) be grown in partial shade? Yes, if you are growing it for its decorative effect; but when raised commercially for drug purposes it must be grown in full sun, as the valuable alkaloid does not develop satisfactorily in shade-grown plants.

GARLIC

Will garlic live over winter? It is often treated as an annual since it is the young bulblets at the base of the plant that are used in cooking. If the winters are not too severe, and if winter cover is given properly, garlic can be treated as a perennial.

GINGER

Can ginger root be grown in New York State? Common ginger (*Zingiber officinale*) is a tropical plant adapted for culture only in warm climates. The wild ginger (*Asarum canadense*) is a native of our own rich woodlands. It responds to cultivation if given a rich, rather moist soil. There is also *Asarum europaeum,* a good ground cover.

HYSSOP

What are the cultural requirements of hyssop?   Give this perennial full sun or light shade, and a warm, freely drained well-limed soil. Allow about a foot between plants. Trim plants back after flowering. Easily propagated by seeds, cuttings, or root division.

LAVENDER

What is the care and use of lavender?   Grows well in any well-drained soil, not too acid, in a dry, sunny place. Protect in winter with evergreen boughs; but, even with protection, plants 3 years old or more have a way of dying back in winter. Cut dead branches back in spring after new growth near base is fairly strong. It is best propagated from cuttings of the season's growth taken in the late fall or early spring. The plants are grown for ornament and fragrance. The flowers are used in perfumes, aromatic vinegar, sachets, and are tied into bundles for use in linen closets, etc.

How can I make lavender plants bloom?   They give much more prolific bloom, with better fragrance, if grown in a light, well-drained soil high in lime content. Rich or heavy soils encourage foliage growth rather than bloom.

When should lavender flowers be harvested?   Just as soon as they are fully open.

Can lavender grow and live over winter as far north as Boston? *Lavandula officinalis* should, if given good winter protection.

Do you have to protect thyme and lavender in winter, and how? The true lavender, *Lavandula officinalis,* is hardier than others of its kind. However, it prefers a sheltered spot. Both lavender and thyme die during the winter because of excessive moisture rather than of cold. Marsh hay or evergreen boughs are good mulches. It is safer, if there is any question about the drainage, to winter both of these plants, in the North, in a cold frame.

How can I start lavender from seed?   Seeds are rather slow to germinate, and the tiny plants grow slowly. Start seeds indoors in early spring, and set out the new plants after all danger of frost is past. Do not allow them to bloom the first year. Protect through first winter by placing them in a cold frame, if possible. A well-drained soil is essential to success.

Can I propagate lavender from cuttings? Take 2-in. shoots off the main stems and branches in late fall or early spring, each with a "heel" (or portion of older wood) attached to its base. Cut the heel clean. Remove lower leaves for about 1 in. from base. Insert in well-packed sand, and keep the sand moist. Slight bottom heat will help rooting. While roots are not more than ½ in. long, put in small pots in a mixture of ½ sand, ½ soil. Keep in cool greenhouse for winter if fall-made cuttings, or in a cold frame if spring-made.

LEMON-BALM See Balm

LEMON-VERBENA

How is lemon-verbena grown? Lemon-verbena (*Aloysia triphylla*) is a tender shrub which, in cold climates, must be taken in for the winter. Cut plants back in fall; water just enough to keep them from drying out. In February bring into the light, in a cool temperature. Repot and set out again in the garden when danger of frost is past.

When should cuttings of lemon-verbena be made? In fall, when the plants are trimmed back before being brought inside; or in spring, when new growth is made. Give same treatment as advised for cuttings of lavender.

LOVAGE

Is lovage suitable for a tiny herb garden? Hardly. It is a perennial 6 or 7 ft. tall, and plants need to be spaced about a yard apart.

What soil and culture for the herb lovage that has flavor of celery? Propagate by seeds sown in early fall, or by root division in spring. Provide a rich, moist soil in full sun or light shade.

MARJORAM

Can you winter over in the house a plant of marjoram dug from the herb garden? If you refer to sweet marjoram (*Majorana hortensis*) this is the only way to keep it for another year in cold climates. It is a tender perennial, sensitive to frost. Pot the plant in September, before there is any danger of frost, and let it get accustomed to its new quarters before bringing it indoors. Cuttings can be rooted in September, keeping the young plants indoors also. It is often grown as an annual.

In what soil and situation, and how far apart, should sweet marjoram plants be set?   Give light, well-drained soil, slightly acid or neutral; full sun; space 9 or 10 ins. apart. This is a tender perennial that may be grown as an annual. Sow seed in spring. It is slow to germinate.

Is there any hardy marjoram?   Yes, what is known as wild marjoram, *Origanum vulgare,* a hardy perennial native of Europe and sometimes a weed in eastern North America. It has long been used as an essential plant in the herb garden, having aromatic leaves.

MINT

Would like a list of all mints that can be grown, and is there a sale for them and where?   The mints are very numerous. Write The Herb Society of America, 300 Massachusetts Ave., Boston, Mass. 02115 with regard to these and to their marketability.

What is the culture of peppermint? How is oil extracted from it?   Grows best in deep, rich, humusy soil which is open and well drained. The runners are planted in spring, 2 to 3 ft. apart, in shallow trenches. Keep well cultivated and free from weeds. When in full bloom the plants are cut and cured like hay. The oil is extracted by distillation with steam. For information concerning commercial cultivation ask the U. S. Department of Agriculture, Washington, D.C.

PARSLEY

Can parsley be dug in the fall and potted for winter use in the home?   Yes. No herb garden is complete without a few plants of parsley. Usually a biennial, propagated by seed best sown in early spring in a pot indoors on a warm window sill, since it is very slow in germinating.

POT-MARIGOLD

What is pot-marigold? What is it used for? Is it hard to grow?   *Calendula officinalis*—one of our most useful decorative annuals. As an herb, the flower heads were used for seasoning and coloring butter. It thrives best in cool weather. Sow outdoors in spring, or indoors in March for spring planting. Transplant 12 ins. apart. Sow again about July 1 for fall crop. The plants from this sowing will grow on into late fall and will survive light frost.

ROSEMARY

What is the best way to grow rosemary? Rosemary is a tender shrub, not hardy in the North; but it may be plunged outdoors in a sunny, sheltered spot during the summer, and carried over winter in a cool, light room. Pot in well-drained soil to which a sprinkling of lime has been added. Propagate by cuttings.

What is the best protection for rosemary in this location? (Illinois.) It is a tender shrub and must be brought in for the winter in cold climates. If there is not space for so large a plant, make a few cuttings, which will root readily in moist sand and be ready to set out in the spring.

RUE

Is rue hardy in northern gardens? Could you give its culture? Rue (*Ruta graveolens*) is hardy to Long Island, N.Y. It will not winter over outdoors in very severe climates, so it is much safer to keep it indoors during winter. It is easily grown from seeds sown early in spring in rows 18 ins. apart. Thin seedlings to 8 ins. apart, and again remove every other one. Keep the soil well cultivated. The leaves can be used whenever they are large enough. Any ordinary garden soil is satisfactory.

SAGE

Which variety of sage is used for culinary use? *Salvia officinalis*.

I have been unsuccessful in growing sage. What are its needs?
Sage enjoys best a sweet, well-drained, light sandy soil. Sow seeds in very early spring, or in August; or set out good-sized plants in early spring. Sage is not difficult. Give very little water; cultivate during the early part of the season. In spring give a light dressing of bone meal. Easily propagated by means of cuttings.

Can sage planted from seed be used and dried first year it is planted?   Yes. Don't strip the whole plant bare, however. Take only the largest leaves, or a branch here and there.

When is the best time to "pick" sage; and what is the best method of curing it?   Harvest in late summer. Cut shoots before they bloom, tie into bundles, and hang up; or strip leaves and place loosely in shallow trays in a warm, airy place, not exposed to sun.

SALAD BURNET

Is salad burnet a good herb for the herb garden?   Yes, it is easily grown and is often a weed. Usually perennial in habit, frequently found in dry, gravelly fields or pastures, it is used in salads or iced drinks. Propagated by seeds or division of the plant. Leaves have a cucumber flavor.

SAVORY

What kind of soil and culture does savory need?   There are two kinds of savory: summer savory (annual) (*Satureja hortensis*) and winter savory (perennial) (*S. montana*). Both grow best in a rather poor but well-limed soil, in an exposed sunny site. The annual kind is considered better than the perennial. The seeds are very small and are best sown indoors in pots and barely covered. Watering is done by immersing the pot in water, as the seeds wash out easily. Seedlings are set out when all danger of frost is over. Set seedlings in rows, 8 ins. between plants, 15 ins. between rows. The perennial sort can be handled in the same way.

SWEET CICELY

What are the garden requirements for growing sweet Cicely?   Sow seed in early fall, in well-drained average soil, and in light shade. When plants are mature they should stand 18 to 20 ins. apart. It is a hardy perennial and may be increased by root division.

SWEET FLAG

I want to grow sweet flag in my herb garden. Does it need full sun? Full sun is not necessary for *Acorus calamus,* but it must have moist soil. It is really a waterside plant. Propagated by division of rhizomes.

SWEET-WOODRUFF

What conditions in the garden does sweet-woodruff (Asperula odorata) need? An open, rather moist soil, where drainage is good, and shade or partial shade. A fine perennial ground-cover plant in the right location. The leaves are used to give May wine its special flavor.

TARRAGON

What soil for tarragon? Shade or sun? Almost any well-drained garden soil. Sun preferred, but will endure light shade.

Will you give me all information possible to grow tarragon? When to plant? Tarragon, a hardy perennial, needs a well-drained soil, moderately rich, with considerable lime. It does best in a lightly shaded location. This plant, since it seeds but little, is propagated by stem or root cuttings, or by division. Stem cuttings are taken any time during the summer, rooted in sand, and planted out. Root cuttings or divisions can be set out in early spring, 12 ins. apart. Do not use chemical fertilizer to force growth, as the quality of the leaves is affected by a too-rich diet.

THYME

I would like to grow thyme for seasoning. Will it stand our severe winters? (Western New York.) There are many varieties of the common thyme that may be used in the herb garden. The greatest menace to thymes during the winter is not so much cold as wetness. Wet crowns, caused by snow, will winterkill. One of the means of preventing this is to grow on rather poor soil, containing gravel or screened cinders. Do not feed in summer to force growth, and do not cut tops after September 1. A cold frame is an excellent place to keep thyme over the winter, where it will be dry. Otherwise, covering the plants with boxes to keep the snow off will help materially. Be certain their position is well drained to begin with. Seeds and plants are available from most houses listing herbs.

How can I grow common thyme? What soil? Shade? Sun? (Massachusetts.) It is best grown on a light, well-drained soil. If the soil is inclined to heaviness, work in screened cinders or gravel. Seeds can be sown in early spring outdoors, or earlier in pots indoors. Transplant seedlings 6 ins. apart. When growth is advanced, do not water much; omit fertilizer, as this tends to force soft growth that will winterkill. Do not cut foliage after September 1, as this depletes vitality. Winter protection is given by covering with light evergreen boughs, or by using brushwood with a light covering of marsh or salt hay. Lift and divide every 2 or 3 years. Grow in full sun.

Will you name several creeping thymes for planting in steps and paths? Mother-of-thyme (*Thymus serpyllum*); caraway thyme (*T. herba-barona*); woolly stem thyme (*T. lanicaulis*); common thyme (*T. vulgaris*).

WATERCRESS

How could I grow watercress for table use in my home garden that has no water? Watercress is a plant of running water, growing in the edge of clear, fresh streams. It may be grown, after a fashion, in a moist spot in the garden, and the plants will last for a time in such a location if it is shady, but they will not live through the winter unless covered with water. They become true perennials only when grown in running water. As an alternative, you can grow the garden cress, or pepper-grass, *Lepidium virginicum*. This is an annual, and furnishes salad in 3 to 4 weeks. Sow seed thickly in shallow drills 12 ins. apart. Make 2 sowings, 2 weeks apart in spring, and 2 sowings in August.

Rock Gardens

PLANNING

To build, or not to build, a rock garden is the question with us. Answerman, what counsel? Can you fit this kind of garden properly into your home landscape without the effect being unnatural? Is there a bank or slope that could be utilized in making the garden? Have you access to natural rock material that could be used? If the area is all level, is there a section where low, natural rock outcrops could be simulated? The extent of the garden will be determined by the time, labor, and money that can be spent on it. A rock garden is costly to build and time-consuming to maintain. These are the facts that need to be considered in deciding to build—or not to build.

Will I have as much color in a rock garden as in other kinds of gardens? The floral display will be concentrated between early spring and mid-June. From then on your enjoyment will come mostly from pleasing mats and mounds and spreading foliage effects; these are decidedly worth while.

How can I best fit a rock garden into my place? Use, if you have it, a somewhat steep slope, not overhung by foliage. A natural ledge of porous rock, of acceptable, weathered appearance, and provided with deep fissures, is ideal. Where such a ledge lies buried, it pays to expose and use it.

What exposure is best for a rock garden? For easy-to-grow, sun-loving plants, such as many sedums, pinks, and rock-cresses, any exposure but a north one. For gardens containing also more finicky, choicer plants, if along a building or a fence, an east exposure; otherwise, an open slope facing east or northeast As between south and north slopes, choose the latter.

Is there a rock-garden organization? Yes, the American Rock Garden Society, Secretary, 90 Pierpont Rd., Waterbury, Conn. 06705.

SOIL AND FERTILIZER

Should the rock-garden soil mixture be acid or alkaline? Some rock plants insist upon acid, some on alkaline, soil. But most will do with an approximately neutral soil; it is, therefore, best to provide this kind of mixture throughout, and then to acidify or alkalize special areas for particular plants.

Do all rock-garden plants need a specially prepared soil? No. Many robust, easy-to-grow plants, such as most sedums, pinks, and rock-cresses, will thrive in soil that would suit other garden plants. But in sharply drained places even these will be helped by an addition of some peat moss, to help retain moisture in summer.

What is a good average rock-garden mixture?   Approximately 1 part each of good garden loam, fine leafmold, peat moss, sand, and fine gravel (preferably ⅛-in. screen). The mixture should be gritty. It should let surface water penetrate promptly, but should be retentive enough to hold a reasonable supply of moisture.

What depth of prepared soil is desirable in a rock garden?   About 1 ft. For gardens made above the surrounding grade, there should be, underneath, another foot of a coarse mixture of rubble and retentive ingredients, such as peat moss, to act as a sponge.

In a rock garden is it necessary to provide the great depth of drainage that I read about in books?   For gardens laid above the grade— no. In sunken gardens or in low-lying parts, unfailing provision must be made to prevent stagnant moisture below. In our dry summer climate we must think of drainage in reverse as well—of retaining some moisture below, which later will find its way back to the surface.

I have a rock garden at the side of my house and would like to rearrange it. Can you make any suggestions concerning soil preparation and enrichment?   It should be deeply dug, and a liberal amount of peat moss added. Also incorporate cinders or coarse pebbles or rubble, leafmold, well-rotted manure or compost, and a little bone meal.

What is the best fertilizer to use for rock-garden plants, and when should I put it on?   The majority of rock-garden plants should not be heavily fed; rich feeding causes soft growth which invites disease and leaves the plants subject to winterkilling. Mix in fine bone meal or superphosphate and leafmold with the soil when preparing it, and in early spring add to established plantings a topdressing containing bone meal mixed with soil and leafmold.

CONSTRUCTION

What type of rock is best for rock gardens?   Any porous, weathered rock that will look natural in place. It is all the better if it is deep fissured. Use only one kind of rock throughout the garden.

What about tufa rock?   No rock is more acceptable to a wide diversity of plants than a soft, porous grade of tufa. But because of its glaring, bony color in sunny places it is not an attractive-looking material. In shade, and moisture, it quickly accumulates mosses and then becomes very beautiful.

Are large rocks desirable, or will small ones do as well? Construction should simulate nature. She works with massive rocks. Therefore, in gardens large or small use rocks as large as you can handle; or match smaller ones together in such manner that they will create an effect of large masses.

Can you give me a few pointers on the placing of rocks? Embed the rockwork deeply enough to create an effect of natural outcroppings. Leave no lower edges exposed to betray superficial placing. Have the several rock masses extend in parallel directions, and carry out this principle even with the lesser rocks. Match joints and stratifications carefully. Try to get the rhythm of natural ledges and outcroppings.

How shall I build a rockery in a corner of my level lawn? In the foreground of corner shrubbery create the effect of a smoothish, shelved outcropping with several broad, low shelves. Push this arrangement back far enough for the shrubs to mask the sheer drop behind.

How should I arrange a rock garden and pool in the center of a small lawn without natural elevation of rock? Create the effect of one large, flattish, or somewhat humped rock, broken, so as to provide two or more broad crevices for planting. Locate the pool, somewhat off-center, immediately against this rock effect.

What is featherock? This is a pumice rock quarried in California and only about one eighth the weight of native stone. It is often used in rock gardens or on patios, is easily cut and even hollowed out to make soil pockets for small rock plants. Some garden centers have it or can obtain it from California.

PLANTING AND CULTURE

When is the best time to plant rock gardens? If pot-grown plants are available and you can arrange to water and shade them carefully, planting may be done almost any time from spring to early autumn. Spring is a proper season everywhere. In moderately cold climates (as in lower New York State), September and October are also good months.

What rock-garden plants should one set out in early spring? Any of the sedums, pinks (dianthus), dwarf phlox, primroses, painted daisies, bellflowers, and saponarias as well as most any other rock plants.

I am planting a rock garden. What distance between the plants will be necessary? Much will depend upon the kind of plants you are using. If they are spreading kinds, such as cerastium, phlox, helianthemum, the sedums, thyme, and dianthus, set the plants about 12 ins. apart. Plants that spread more slowly, such as primula, sempervivum, saxifraga, candytuft, arenaria, aubrieta, douglasia, anemone, pulsatilla, and the dwarf achilleas, plant 6 to 8 ins. apart.

How deep should rock plants be set in the ground? Most form a spreading top that either roots as it spreads or grows directly from a central root system. The crown of the plant must not be covered. Dig a hole with a trowel; gather the loose tops in the hand; hold the plant at the side of the hole, the crown resting on the surface, the roots extending into the hole while held in position; firm the soil around the roots. When the hole is filled, the crown should be resting on the surface. A good watering will then help establish it.

The soil on the slopes in my rock garden keeps washing out, especially after planting. How can I prevent this? If a considerable stretch is exposed, set in a few good-sized rocks at irregular intervals and tilt them so that their upper surfaces slope downward into the hill. Into the surface 2 ins. incorporate screened cinders mixed with peat or leafmold. Set the plants in groups 9 to 12 ins. apart (depending on their size) and cover the spaces between the groups with peat or leafmold until the plants effect a covering.

What are the main items of upkeep in a rock garden? Weeding; thinning; repressing too-rampant growths; removal of old flower stalks; occasional division of robust plants; watering; winter covering. For the choicer, high-mountain plants, maintain a gravel mulch about their base and topdress with compost on steep slopes each spring.

When is the best time to trim and thin plants that begin to overrun a rock garden? Cut back the running kinds any time during their growing period.

Will you please discuss spring work in the rock garden? Remove winter covering when all danger of frost is over. If there is danger of cold winds and some plants have started to grow, uncover gradually. Firm back into the soil any plants that have been loosened. Replant as may be necessary. Topdress with a mixture of 3 parts good soil, 1 part old, rotted manure or compost, leafmold, or peat moss, and 1 part coarse sand, with a 6-in. potful of fine bone meal added to each wheelbarrow load. When topdressing, work this down around the crowns of the plants and over the roots of spreading kinds by hand. If a dry spell occurs in spring, give a good watering.

How should the rock garden be watered and how often? With a fine sprinkler, so as to avoid washing the soil off the roots. Frequency of watering depends upon type of soil, amount of slope, kind of plants, and whether they are established or are newly planted, amount of shade, exposure, and of course weather. If dry spells occur in spring and early autumn, watering should be done in a very thorough fashion; toward late summer, unless a very prolonged dry spell occurs, watering should be confined to such plants as primulas, globe-flowers, and other moisture-lovers. Ripening and hardening of most rock plants are necessary if they are to winter over properly.

What is the best winter cover? When applied and when removed? A single thickness of pine boughs or any narrow-leaved evergreen that will hold its leaves all winter after being cut. It is more quickly applied and removed than marsh hay. Apply after the surface has frozen solid. It is needed, not as a protection against frost, but against thawing of the soil. Remove when danger of very hard frost seems past. Just when is always something of a gamble.

Is marsh hay a good winter cover? Yes, but it is not quickly removable in the spring. Use it lightly, lest you invite mice and kindred vermin.

WHAT TO GROW

Will you please name a dozen foolproof rock-garden plants, stating flower color and season? *Alyssum* (*Aurinia*) *saxatile* 'Citrinum' (lemon-yellow; May), *Arabis albida* (double-flowered, white; April to May), *Arabis procurrens* (white, April to May), *Campanula carpatica* (blue; July), *Ceratostigma plumbaginoides* (blue; September to October), *Dianthus plumarius* (white and varicolored; June), *Phlox subulata* varieties (white, rose, dark rose, pink; May), *Sedum sieboldii* (rose; September to October), *Sedum album* (white; June), *Sedum ellacombianum* (yellow; July), *Thymus serpyllum* 'Coccineus' (deep rose; July), and *T. s.* 'Albus' (white; June to July).

Can you give a list of some of the best rock plants for spring

flowers? *Alyssum (Aurinia) saxatile, Anemone pulsatilla, Arabis albida* (double-flowered), *Aubrieta deltoides, Corydalis bulbosa, Crocus* species, *Epimedium niveum, Scilla sibirica* and *S. bifolia,* and *Tulipa kaufmanniana.*

What are the best plants for a rockery for early spring and mid-summer bloom? For early spring: *Tulipa kaufmanniana, Crocus* species, snowdrops, *Scilla sibirica,* and grape-hyacinths. Non-bulbous plants: *Arabis albida, Aubrieta deltoides,* primula, *Anemone pulsatilla, Armeria caespitosa, Alyssum (Aurinia) saxatile,* draba, epimedium, *Erysimum ruprestre,* and *Phlox subulata.* For midsummer bloom: *Dianthus plumarius, Campanula carpatica, Asarina procumbens, Bellium bellidioides, Campanula cochlearifolia, Carlina acaulis, Globularia cordifolia, Lotus corniculatus, Dianthus knappii, Linum alpinum, Linaria alpina, Nierembergia caerulea,* penstemon, *Rosa chinensis minima, Santolina viridis,* and *Ceratostigma plumbaginoides.*

Can you name 12 good perennials suitable for rock gardens, which bloom at different periods? *Phlox subulata* and varieties (April to May), *Aubrieta deltoides* (May), *Alyssum (Aurinia) saxatile* (May), *Primula polyanthus* (May), *Dianthus plumarius* (June), *Campanula carpatica* (June), *Lotus corniculatus* (July), *Veronica spicata* (June to July), *Thymus serpyllum* and its varieties (July), *Calluna vulgaris* (August to September), *Ceratostigma plumbaginoides* (September to October), *Erica* sp. and varieties, Nov. to August.

Will you list late-flowering rock plants? *Ceratostigma plumbaginoides, Allium pulchellum, A. flavum, Asarina procumbens, Calluna vulgaris* and its varieties, *Chrysogonum virginianum,* colchicums, autumn crocuses, *Saxifraga cortusaefolia,* and *Sedum sieboldii.*

What are the fastest-growing plants for a rock garden? *Cerastium tomentosum, Ajuga reptans, Thymus serpyllum* and its varieties, *Lamium maculatum, L. m. album, Phlox subulata* and its varieties, *Arabis albida,* sedums, *Saponaria ocymoides, Lotus corniculatus, Campanula carpatica,* and *Asperula odorata.*

Should I try to fill my new rock garden quickly with fast-growing plants, or do it gradually, with smaller plants? By all means the latter. Most people come to regret their first impatience, and wind up by rooting out the rampant growers, and replacing them with choicer, small plants; they are so much more delightful.

Which flowers are best to plant in a small rock garden? Such things as the drabas, *Aubrieta deltoides, Gypsophila repens, Myosotis alpestris, Nierembergia rivularis, N. caerulea, Primula vulgaris, Armeria caespitosa, Veronica prostrata, Androsace sarmentosa, A. villosa,* and *Rosa chinensis minima.* Avoid the use of coarse creeping plants; they will overrun the garden.

Can you suggest some plants for a very steep rock garden? *Thymus serpyllum* and its varieties, *Cerastium tomentosum, Sedum spurium, S. hybridum, Phlox subulata,* sempervivums, *Lotus corniculatus, Ceratostigma plumbaginoides, Asarina procumbens, Muehlenbeckia axillaris,* and *Campanula carpatica.*

Which perennial plants can I use for a very exposed location in a rock garden? *Arabis albida, Anemone pulsatilla, Phlox subulata* varieties, *Veronica prostrata, Cerastium tomentosum, Dianthus deltoides, D. plumarius, Lamium maculatum, Aquilegia canadensis, A. vulgaris, Campanula carpatica,* and *Dicentra eximia.*

Can you suggest a few small, decorative plants to fill small crevices in rocks and tiny pockets? My garden is in full sun. *Draba aizodes, Globularia repens (G. nana), Sedum dasyphyllum, Sedum acre* 'Minus', *Sedum anglicum,* and sempervivums (the tiny kinds).

Which are some good plants for shady corners in my rock garden for spring flowers? *Anemone nemorosa* (several kinds), *Brunnera macrophylla, Chrysogonum virginianum, Epimedium niveum, Iris cristata, Phlox divaricata laphamii, Phlox stolonifera, Pulmonaria saccharata,* and *Saxifraga umbrosa.*

Which perennials, not over 10 ins. in height, bloom between June 15 and September 15, and are suitable for a rock garden in shade? *Chrysogonum virginianum, Corydalis lutea, Mitchella repens, Myosotis scorpioides, Sedum ternatum, S. nevii, Allium moly, Saxifraga cortusaefolia, Arenaria montana, Gentiana asclepiadea, Cymbalaria muralis, Scilla chinensis,* and *Dicentra formosa alba.*

Which are some small summer-blooming plants for the shady rock garden? *Chrysogonum virginianum, Cotula squalida, Mitchella repens, Sedum ternatum,* and *S. nevii.*

Which are the most hardy rock-garden plants that will grow in semi-shade? *Primula polyanthus, P. veris, P. vulgaris,* epimediums, aubretias, aquilegias, *Phlox divaricata laphamii, Chrysogonum virginianum, Viola odorata, V. priceana, Vinca minor, Lysimachia num-*

mularia, Sedum ternatum, Ceratostigma plumbaginoides, Asperula odorata, trilliums, erythroniums, primroses, and dodecatheons.

Will you name rock plants that will grow and bloom in the shade of a large oak tree? *Phlox divaricata laphamii, Dicentra eximia, Chrysogonum virginianum, Asperula odorata,* erythroniums, trilliums, *Gaultheria procumbens, Mitchella repens, Vinca minor, Lysimachia nummularia,* and *Primula veris.*

Can you name several plants which will grow between rocks of a patio in very sandy soil; preferably fast growers? *Arenaria verna caespitosa, Thymus serpyllum* and its varieties, *Sedum acre, Dianthus deltoides, Muehlenbeckia axillaris, Mazus reptans,* and *Ajuga reptans.* Keep the soil reasonably moist.

Which rock plants require acid soil? Dwarf rhododendrons, azaleas, pieris, shinleaf, partridge-berry, *Cypripedium acaule,* erythroniums, galax, and shortia.

Will you name a dozen or so of the choicest and most unusual plants that I may hope to grow in my rock garden? *Androsace lanuginosa, Androsace sarmentosa, Armeria juniperifolia, Campanula cochlearifolia alba, Dianthus gratianopolitanus, D. neglectus, Saxifraga burseriana, S. irvingii,* and saxifragas.

Will all kinds of rock-garden plants grow successfully in a garden without rocks? Yes, although many of them look better against or between rocks. Many can be grown in the front of a flower garden.

ALPINES

What is the best site for alpines? A gentle slope facing northeast or northwest.

What soil is best for alpines? One that is not too rich. A neutral, porous soil, well-drained, and with grit and cinders to lighten it, will be satisfactory for most alpine plants.

Need I know a lot about alpines to have a good rock garden? No. You may use, more or less exclusively, plants from high, intermediate, or low altitudes. A good rock garden need not be filled with "highbrow" plants. It should afford a happy glimpse of nature's play with rocks and plants—be it in a mountain scree or on a roadside ledge.

Why are alpine plants so difficult to grow? Because the conditions prevailing in lowland rock gardens are so utterly different from those at or above timber line: the heavy winter pack of snow, the short summer, pure, crisp air, and chilly baths of mountain mist. One must learn gradually to devise acceptable equivalents or approximations to these conditions.

Can you name a few alpine plants not too difficult for an amateur to grow? The following high-mountain plants (not all strictly alpines) are suggested: *Armeria juniperifolia, Androsace lanuginosa, A. sarmentosa, Campanula cochlearifolia, Dianthus alpinus, Douglasia vitaliana, Gentiana acaulis,* and saxifragas.

What are the best alpine campanulas for the rock garden? *Campanula allionii, alpina, cochlearifolia, elatines, fragilis, lasiocarpa, portenschlagiana, poscharskyana, pulla, raineri,* and *tomasiniana.*

What winter care should be given alpines? Cover lightly with evergreen boughs or salt hay after the ground is frozen—usually in December.

MORAINE GARDEN

Can you explain what a moraine garden is? How is it made? A moraine is constructed for the purpose of growing certain alpine plants from high altitudes. The garden contains little or no soil, the growing medium being mostly stone chips and shale. The important factor is water. The most complete moraines have cool water circulating below the growing medium so that the roots of the plants are in a cool, moist medium much as are alpines in their native haunts. A moraine can be built in a water-tight basin 2 ft. deep and of any length and breadth. A foot-thick layer of stones is laid in the bottom. The remaining space is filled with a mixture of 5 parts crushed stone (½ in.), 1 part sand, and 1 part leafmold. Water is supplied during the growing season through a pipe at the upper end and the surplus is drawn off by one at the other end 12 ins. below the surface.

Will you give me a list of plants suitable for a moraine garden? Aethionema, androsace, *Arenaria montana, Dianthus sylvestris, Campanula speciosa, Silene acaulis,* and saxifragas. For others, consult *Rock Gardening* by H. Lincoln Foster, Houghton Mifflin Co., 1968; *All About Rock Gardens and Plants* by Walter A. Kolaga, Doubleday & Co., 1966.

PAVEMENT PLANTING

How are plants grown between the flagstones in a pavement? For the plants to succeed, the stones should be laid on sand overlying several inches of soil. Watering during hot, dry weather is very helpful.

How are plants planted between flagstones? Planting is first done as the flat stones are laid. When the spot for a plant is selected, the plant is set so that when the surface is leveled for the next flagstone, the top of the plant is resting at the correct level. The stone may have to be chipped to avoid crushing the plant.

Which plants are suitable for planting in a flagged walk? Those that will withstand much walking are: *Festuca ovina glauca, Sagina subulata,* and *Tunica saxifraga.* Others to use are *Thymus serpyllum* varieties, *Alyssum montanum, Erinus alpinus, Veronica repens,* and *Lysimachia nummularia.*

WALL GARDENS

What exposure for a wall garden? Eastern, except for shade-loving plants such as ramonda, haberlea, *Saxifraga sarmentosa,* English ivies, and certain ferns. For these a northern exposure.

What is the best type of rock for a wall garden? For an informal effect, any natural, porous rock with a good facing surface; squarish pieces, such as one might use for an ordinary dry wall, are best. A good wall garden can be made of bricks.

How does one make a wall garden? Much like a dry retaining wall, but the joints are packed with prepared soil and the stones are tilted backward to keep the soil from washing out and to direct the rain water toward the plant roots. To prevent squashing of roots, chink the horizontal joints with small pieces of stone. Place plants in position as the laying up proceeds, and firm the soil well at the back of the wall.

What special upkeep does a wall garden need? Upkeep is reduced by using suitably compact, small, rock-hugging plants. Remove all old flower stalks. Pull out weeds and excess seedlings. Prune and thin so as to maintain a balanced distribution of planting effect. On top of the wall, provide a watering trench or trough, and use it freely to prevent drying out in summer.

How are plants planted in a wall? In a wall garden, building and planting are done at the same time. If the plants are located at the joints, the soil is packed in, the plant set, a little extra soil added, and then the stones are placed. Chips placed between the stones near the plants prevent them from sinking and squeezing the plants. If planting has to be done after building, the job is more difficult. The roots must somehow be spread out in a narrow space, and the soil rammed in with a piece of stick. Don't plant fast-growing plants near slow-growing ones or the latter will be smothered.

In planting a wall, care must be taken to spot the plants with a natural-looking irregularity that avoids any studied pattern or design.

What summer upkeep is necessary for a rock wall? Keep plants well watered and weeded. Spray if necessary.

Can you tell me what spring care should be given a rockery made in an old stone wall? Trim dead pieces off plants; fill washed-out cracks with new soil. Push heaved-out plants into soil or take them out altogether and replant.

What winter cover for a wall garden? Stick a row of pine boughs into the ground thickly enough to provide shade from the brightest sun of winter. Or place a row of two-by-fours, slanting against the wall, and over them stretch a burlap cover. The pine boughs will be better looking.

Which plants are particularly suitable for use in a rock wall? All the sempervivums, *Sedum hybridum, coccineum, nevii,* and *sieboldii, Nepeta hederacea, Campanula carpatica, cochlearifolia,* and *rotundifolia, Silene caroliniana, Phlox stolonifera, Achillea ageratifolia,* and *Mazus reptans.*

Are wall gardens easy to maintain?   They are at their best in moist climates (England) where there are not long drought periods. If left unwatered in long summer droughts many of the plants will die. They require more attention than other types of gardens, especially care in watering.

BULBS FOR THE ROCK GARDEN

How should chionodoxa (glory-of-the-snow) be used in the rock garden?   Scatter the bulbs in groups of 2 dozen or more in various places among low ground covers. They may also be used effectively beneath shrubs that may form a background to the garden.

Will you give a list of crocuses suitable for the rock garden? Spring-flowering: *Crocus aureus, biflorus, chrysanthus* and its varieties, *imperati, susianus, tomasinianus.* For autumn: *cancellatus albus, longiflorus, pulchellus, speciosus* and its varieties, *zonatus.*

Can you suggest some good daffodils for the rock garden?   The best kinds are the small ones, such as *Narcissus asturiensis, cyclamineus, triandrus* (angel's tears), *concolor, bulbocodium* (hooppetticoat daffodil). The sweet jonquils and campernelles can also be used, such as *Narcissus jonquilla, j. flore-pleno,* and *odorus.*

Can you tell me kinds of tulips to plant in a rock garden and what conditions they need?   The best are the tulip species, also called "botanical" tulips. These need well-drained soil and sunshine. Plant them about 6 or 7 ins. deep. The following are among the best: *kaufmanniana, acuminata, clusiana* (lady tulip), *dasystemon, greigii, praecox, praestans, fosteriana* varieties, and *sylvestris.*

Which spring-flowering bulbs are suitable for the rock garden? Squills, glory-of-the-snow, snowdrops, spring-snowflakes, crocuses, grape-hyacinths, miniature daffodils. And also dogtooth-violets, fritillaries, calochortuses, brodiaeas, and *Iris reticulata.*

Which bulbs are suitable for a rock garden at the side and front of the house?   *Crocus* species (for fall and spring), *Galanthus nivalis* (snowdrops), *Leucojum vernum* (snowflake), *Chionodoxa luciliae* (glory-of-the-snow), muscari (grape-hyacinths), scillas (squills), narcissus species, colchicums, tulips *kaufmanniana* and its hybrids, and *dasystemon.*

When are small spring-flowering bulbs planted in the rock garden? In late August plant snowdrops, winter-aconites, autumn-flowering crocuses, and colchicums. Plant the small daffodils and crocuses in September and October.

I wish to plant a number of small bulbs in my rock garden. Should I dig up the other plants before planting the bulbs? How deep must I plant the bulbs? Unless the soil needs improving it is not necessary to remove the plants. Use a bulb trowel (a tool with a narrow concave blade), push it into the soil through the mat of plants, pull the handle toward you, and then push the bulb into the soil and smooth the plants back again. Plant these small bulbs in groups and closely together. The depth at which they are set should be, roughly, 3 times the depth of the bulb.

EVERGREENS IN A ROCK GARDEN

Which are some dwarf evergreens that can be used effectively in a rock garden? *Juniperus horizontalis* 'Wiltonii'; *Chamaecyparis obtusa* 'Nana'; *Buxus sempervirens* 'Vardar Valley'; *Chamaecyparis pisifera* 'Golden Mop'; *Calluna vulgaris* vars.; *Gaylussacia brachycera; Ilex crenata* 'Helleri'; *Pinus strobus* 'Nana'; *Tsuga canadensis* 'Cole'; *Erica* species and varieties.

Can you tell me some evergreens for a rock garden which will withstand severe winter exposure? *Arctostaphylos uva-ursi; Chamaecyparis obtusa* 'Nana'; *Taxus cuspidata* vars.; *Juniperus communis* vars.; *Juniperus horizontalis* vars.; *Chamaecyparis pisifera* 'Filifera Nana'; *Picea abies* vars.; *Picea pungens* 'Glauca Procumbens'; *Pinus sylvestris* 'Pygmaea'; *Pinus mugo; Ilex glabra* 'Compacta'.

What soil does Daphne cneorum require? This is a much-debated question! Its success seems to depend mostly upon climate. It does better in cold climates (with a winter covering) than in warmer climates. Plant in a well-drained soil to which peat moss or some form of humus has been added, away from the fiercest sun.

SHRUBS

Will you suggest some shrubs to use in a rock garden? *Rhododendron impeditum; Leucothoe fontanesiana* 'Nana'; *Berberis thunbergii* 'Crimson Pygmy'; *Calluna vulgaris* vars.; *Cotoneaster adpressa* 'Park Carpet'; *Cytisus procumbens; Euonymus fortunei* 'Gracilis'; *Ilex crenata* 'Green Cushion'; *Juniperus communis* 'Compressa';

Lavandula officinalis; Pieris japonica 'Pygmaea'; *Spiraea japonica alpina; Tsuga canadensis* 'Minima'.

Will you name a few small shrubs that look well in a small rock garden? *Spiraea decumbens, S. bullata, Cotoneaster microphylla, Berberis verruculosa, Ilex crenata* 'Helleri'. In part shade and an acid, humusy soil, *Rhododendron obtusum* and its varieties, and *R. racemosum* should be satisfactory.

Which shrubby plants would make a good background for our rock garden along the side of the garage? In east to northeast exposures: rhododendrons, azaleas, mountain-laurel, pieris, Japanese holly, and *Mahonia aquifolium.* In sunnier exposures: *Berberis koreana, Symphoricarpos chenaultii,* and perhaps an upright yew.

SPECIFIC ROCK GARDEN PLANTS

What is the proper treatment of Alyssum (Aurinia) saxatile which has grown "leggy"? It is best to raise new plants from seed. This plant does not usually last much longer than 3 years. It is inclined to rot away during winter. If it survives, wait until new shoots appear near the base of the plant, then cut the leggy, long ones away.

Does aubrieta remain in bloom for a long period? No. Its blooming season is short. However, it flowers in very early spring and is worthy of a place in the garden.

Are the plants called cinquefoils suitable for the rock garden? Can you suggest a few? Many cinquefoils (potentilla) are excellent, others are worthless weeds. *Potentilla nepalensis, tridentata,* and *verna* are worth trying. Give them full sun and well-drained, gritty soil.

How best to grow pinks in the rock garden? Dianthuses do best in a well-drained, sunny position. Do not make the soil very rich (most seem to do best in a slightly acid to near-neutral soil) and do not overwater them. They are good on gentle slopes, planted so that they can spread over the top of a rock, or in flat, well-drained pockets. Start with young, pot-grown plants if possible, and plant them out at about 9 ins. apart. Some kinds die after a time, so it is best to keep raising a few fresh plants each year.

What kinds of dianthus do you suggest for a rock garden? *Dianthus deltoides* (maiden-pink), *plumarius* (grass-pink), *gratianopolitanus* (cheddar-pink), and *neglectus* (glacier-pink).

What can I do to make Gentiana andrewsii grow? It appreciates a moist, semi-shaded situation, preferably on the edge of a pond, and a deep, humusy soil. Topdress in spring with peat moss mixed with a little dried cow manure.

Which irises are suitable for the rock garden? *Iris reticulata, gracilipes, pumila* (in many varieties), *dichotoma, cristata, cristata alba, lacustris, tectorum,* and its variety *album.*

What conditions do primulas need in the rock garden? A rich, moist soil and a shady or semi-shady situation. Some, like *Primula pulverulenta,* grow best in almost boggy conditions along the sides of streams. Practically all need plenty of moisture. If very moist conditions cannot be given, grow them in shade.

Will you suggest some primulas for the rock garden? *Primula polyantha, veris* (the cowslip), *bulleyana, denticulata, frondosa,* and *japonica.*

What care should be given leontopodium raised from seeds? The edelweiss likes a well-drained, limy soil, full sun in spring, semi-shade in summer, and light protection in winter. Either evergreen boughs or salt hay should be used, as leaves pack too hard and keep the plant waterlogged, which may result in rotting. From seed they should bloom well the second year. Carry the plants over in a cold frame, in pots, the first year.

Will you name a few penstemons that would grow in my rock garden? Are they difficult to grow? *Penstemon alpinus, heterophyllus, rupicola* and *unilateralis.* These are not difficult. They require gritty soil and do not like a position that becomes sodden in winter. They are not long-lived plants and in order to maintain them it is best to raise a few each year.

What soil is suitable for Phlox subulata? Any light, well-drained garden soil.

Where does Phlox subulata grow wild? In the eastern, western, and southern parts of the United States, on dry banks and in fields.

Do most of the western species of phlox require loose, rocky conditions in the eastern states? Yes, they seem to do better under such conditions in the East.

What are some good kinds of phlox for a rock garden? Some of the most suitable besides the various varieties of *phlox subulata* are *Phlox amoena, divaricata* (and its variety *laphamii*), *douglasii,* and *stolonifera.*

What is the best place in the rock garden for saxifragas? What kind of soil? A partially shady situation facing east or west. Soil should be gritty, open, and well-drained. Mix garden soil, leafmold, and stone chips, or screened cinders, in about equal proportion, and have a foot depth of this in which to plant. Limestone chips are also beneficial.

Which saxifragas are not too difficult to grow? *Saxifraga paniculata, apiculata, cochlearis, rosacea* (a mossy type, requiring partial shade), *hostii, macnabiana,* and *moschata.*

How many species and varieties of rock-garden sedums are there? Approximately 200. Perhaps not more than 50 distinct and useful kinds are available in nurseries.

Which are the best sedums? *Sedum album, anglicum, brevifolium, caeruleum* (annual), *dasyphyllum, ewersii, kamtschaticum, lydium, nevii, oreganum, populifolium, pilosum, rupestre, sexangulare, sieboldii, spurium ternatum, stoloniferum, hybridum,* and the self-sowing biennial *nuttallianum.*

Can I get information regarding the culture of sedums? Most are easily propagated from cuttings taken in the fall or spring. They root best in sand, either in flats or in cold frames. When well rooted, transfer them into small pots or put them directly into their permanent places in the garden. The location should ordinarily be sunny, the soil sandy and well-drained. Western-America sedums prefer a semishaded position.

Are the sunroses (Helianthemum) hardy? Do they require much care? They are not very hardy; they thrive fairly well in the vicinity of New York but farther north they are doubtful subjects. They need no more care than ordinary rock-garden plants. Give them a well-drained soil in a sunny location. Protect them in winter with salt hay or evergreen boughs, and cut them back to within a few inches of their crowns in spring, to encourage fresh growth.

Water Gardens

(See also Garden Pools)

We want a small pool for a few fish and water plants but I don't want to go to all the trouble of building one out of concrete. Can't I buy one? Yes. Various types of small pools are now available made out of Fiberglas and plastics that are extremely durable and long-lasting. Heavy-duty polyethylene film can also be easily used. Even the smallest garden can feature an aquatic display.

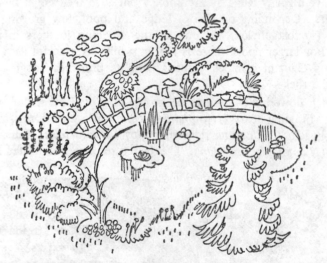

Premolded garden pools of kidney, round or rectangular shapes can be obtained from specialists. Proper plantings around their sides, especially with dwarf evergreens, makes them appear more natural.

What background materials should I use for my small informal pool? Small evergreens, yew, arborvitae, cedar, hemlock, azalea, mountain-laurel, rhododendron, leucothoe, euonymus, cotoneaster, daphne.

Can you tell me some flowering shrubs I can put around my pool? Viburnum, abelia, mock-orange, lilac, deutzia, spirea, azalea, rhododendron, mountain-laurel.

I want a formal-looking clipped hedge around the sides of my formal pool, which is at the rear of my garden. What would you suggest? Yew, hemlock, barberry, box (for sheltered positions), privet.

Can I have a successful fish pond in a plot about 9 × 15 ft.? How could anything so small be landscaped? Why not pave the area with flagstones, leaving wide cracks between stones? These could be planted with rock plants. The pool would be the central feature.

Have you any planting suggestions for rim of a pool? Astilbe, cardinal-flower, Japanese iris, loosestrife, marsh-marigold, rose-mallow, Siberian iris and *Primula japonica.*

I have a rocky ledge by my pool. What evergreen might be grown over it? Depending on size of ledge and pool, low growing bearberry (arctostaphylos), or one of the creeping junipers might be used. For larger pools, there is nothing quite as graceful as a dwarf weeping Canada hemlock planted with its branches hanging down over the rocks.

Which flowering plants can be grown in a pool other than water-lilies? Floating-heart (*Nymphoides peltatum*); true forget-me-not; water-hyacinth (*Eichornia*); water-poppy (*Hydrocleis*); water-snow-flake (*Nymphoides indicum*). The last three are not winter hardy.

A small informal pool adds interest to the garden and provides congenial conditions for moisture-loving plants.

What can be used to break the monotonous flatness of a lily pool?
Tall-growing water plants, such as American and Hindu lotus; calla; cattails (if pool is large); flowering rush; yellow and blug flags; taro; water-plantain.

With what flowers shall I border informal pool 6 × 10 ft.? *Fili-pendula vulgaris* 'Flore-pleno', *Iris ochroleuca, Trollius ledebouri, Lythrum salicaria,* hemerocallis, *Liatris pycnostachya, Myosotis scorpioides semperflorens.*

I have a hillside rock garden with an uneven 6-ft.-diameter pool. Will you give me advice as to plants for inside the pool and for outside to hold up the dirt which seems to wash away with each rain? Plant *Nymphoides peltatum* inside the pool. *Caltha palustris* (marsh-marigold) along the edge, also *Primula rosea, Trollius europaeus,* and 2 or 3 *Lobelia cardinalis* (cardinal-flower). In between plant solid with *Myosotis scorpioides,* which will hold the soil.

SPECIFIC WATER PLANTS—HINDU LOTUS

Which is the best way to keep sacred lotus (Nelumbo nucifera) through winter? If growing in a pond that is drained during the winter, cover the roots with a sufficient depth of leaves to prevent the frost penetrating to the tubers. When this plant is grown in water 2 or 3 ft. deep, usually no winter protection is necessary.

WATER-HYACINTH

How can I grow water-hyacinth? Float in 6 ins. water above a box or tub containing 6 ins. or more of soil. Keep from drifting by confining within an anchored wooden hoop. Bring plants indoors before frost.

How do you winter water-hyacinths that have been in an outside pool? Bring them indoors before the leaves are injured by cold. Float them in a container of water which has 3 or 4 ins. of soil in the bottom. Keep in a sunny window in a temperature of 55° to 60° F.

WATER-LILIES

What is proper soil for water-lilies? Heavy loam, composted for a year before use with dried cow manure in the proportion of 2 to 1. If this is out of the question, use rich soil from vegetable garden.

What shall I use to make water-lilies bloom better? Possibly your plants are starved. Divide and replant in the soil recommended above, adding a 5-in. potful of bone meal to each bushel of soil. Water-lilies need full sun all day for best results.

How large should containers be for water-lilies? Depends on the variety. Small-growing kinds can be grown in boxes 15 × 15 × 10 ins., while the tropical varieties can be grown to advantage in sizes up to 4 × 4 × 1 ft.

In a small concrete pool is it better to cover the bottom with soil or use separate boxes for water-lilies? The plants are better off if the bottom is covered with soil, but it is easier to avoid muddying the water in the pool if the soil is confined in wooden boxes or similar containers.

How deep should the water be over water-lilies? Six ins. to 3 ft. Preferably 1 ft. for tropical varieties, 1 to 2 ft. for hardy varieties, provided this is enough to prevent roots from freezing in winter.

What is the most practical way of caring for a water-lily pool in the winter? If the pool is small enough to be bridged by boards, do so and then cover with a sufficient thickness of straw or leaves to prevent the water from freezing. If the pool is drained and the water-lilies are growing in tubs, move the tubs together and cover around and over them with leaves held in place with wire netting or something similar.

Supposing the mud is not sufficiently deep to support the growth of water-lilies? Plant them in rich soil in a shallow wicker or chip basket, or fruit crate with openings sufficiently wide to allow roots to emerge, then gently slide the planted container into the pond.

How often should water-lilies be divided? Whenever the container becomes so crowded that growth is poor—usually after 3 or 4 years.

Would colored water-lilies grow where wild white ones grow in a lake with a muddy bottom? Yes.

Which water-lily can be grown in a pool fed from an underground stream? Water is cold the year round and is in dense shade. Water-lilies will not grow in such a location.

How can I plant hardy water-lilies in a natural pond? If the pond has a rich mud bottom, merely tie a heavy sod or half brick to the tuber or rhizome and drop it in the pond where water is between 1 and 3 ft. deep.

When is the best time to plant hardy water-lilies? When ice has left the pond in the spring, but they may be planted successfully up until mid-June.

Should hardy water-lilies be left outside in the pool through the winter? (New York.) Yes, if they are growing in water so deep that there is no danger of the roots freezing—18 ins. should be enough in your locality.

How early can tropical water-lilies be set out? Not until all danger of frost is past and the water has become warm—about the second week in June in the vicinity of New York.

How are tropical water-lilies planted? Pot-grown plants are commonly used. A hole is scooped in the soil of the container deep enough to receive the ball of earth about the roots, then the roots are covered with soil, taking care not to bury the crown of the plant.

Can tropical water-lilies be kept through the winter? It is difficult to carry over tropical water-lilies unless one has a sunny greenhouse. When it is possible to find small tubers around the crown of the old plant, these may be gathered in the fall, stored in sand, protected from mice, and started in an aquarium in a sunny window in April.

During the past 2 summers some sort of leafminer has eaten the leaves (making marks like Chinese ideographs) of my water-lilies. Consequently the leaves soon die. What are they and how may I get rid of them without injuring the fish in the pond? The larvae of a midge—*Chirononus modestus*. Water-lily foliage is sensitive to insecticidal sprays, so it is best, whenever possible, to use mechanical means to get rid of pests; therefore pick off infested leaves as fast as they appear, and destroy by burning, which will ultimately eliminate the miner. Or you could try one of the methyl carbamates.

We have an old pond on our place but now it is almost one solid growth of water-lilies. How can these be eradicated? By spraying the water-lily foliage with a mixture of half 2,4-D and half 2,4,5-TP in early August, applied at the rate of 1 gal. of concentrate (containing 2 lbs. of acid equivalent of 2,4-D and 2 lbs. of acid equivalent of 2,4,5-TP) in 2 gals. of water. Or sodium arsenite has proved effective as a spray—15 lbs. of sodium arsenite in 100 gals. of water.

However, check your local Pest Control Board to ascertain what the regulations are about using and spraying such chemicals.

Wildflower Gardens

WOODLAND

What is the best location for a wildflower garden? This depends on the type of flowers to be grown. Some wildflowers grow naturally in woodlands, and others in a sunny meadow. Try to make the condition in your garden most like the one which the particular plants came from.

Should a wildflower garden be attempted in an ordinary backyard garden? Certainly. An informal sort of garden can be made, using the more common types of either woodland flowers or meadow flowers.

How can a woodland wild garden be planned and arranged? A woodland garden made for wild plants should simulate natural wild conditions. There should be shade and semi-shade formed by such trees as grow in the woods. The soil for wood plants should be rich with leafmold and slightly damp. The plants are best placed in natural-looking clumps around the base of the trees. A few rocks may be used as focal points, and plants placed around them.

How does one go about starting a wildflower garden beginning with a piece of wild woodland in Vermont? It's just a small patch about ¼ acre. How do you get cardinal-flowers started to grow in such a garden? You probably have one in existence! Start by gradually replacing and replanting under and around trees, along paths, etc. You will have greatest success with the plants that grow naturally in Vermont woods. Cardinal-flower (*Lobelia cardinalis*) likes the stream sides, will grow in partial shade almost in the water, although it sometimes thrives when transplanted to garden soil with less moisture.

Will bloodroot, trillium, and columbine grow under pine trees? If not, what will grow there? The plants mentioned grow well under oak trees. They will grow under pine trees if the shade is not too great and lower branches are removed and the soil is loamy. Why not try partridge-berry for ground cover, also the club mosses? Plant Christmas fern and shield fern. Pipsissewa and shinleaf (*Pyrola elliptica*) will be dainty but difficult additions, as well as wintergreen (*Gaultheria procumbens*) and bunchberry (*Cornus canadensis*). Many worthy native plants are present and you will need a wildflower guide book to help you identify them.

What are the best methods of growing wild plants under shady conditions? Try to create the conditions in which the plants grow naturally. The amount of shade, moisture, and kind of soil are all important. If under oak trees, you may plant most of the early spring flowers, such as bloodroots, Dutchman's-breeches, partridge-berry, hepatica, bishop's cap, violets, shinleaf, wood-betony, and many ferns and club mosses, such as shield fern, polypody, Christmas fern, spleenworts. The club mosses include ground-cedar, running-pine, and staghorn. The last, however, are very difficult to transplant.

What mulching materials are suitable for woodland wild plants? Fallen leaves, leafmold, and evergreen boughs.

What soil and fertilizer should be used for wildflower planting? Generally speaking, the soil should approximate that in which the plants grow naturally. Woodland plants thrive in rich leafmold. Many prefer slightly acid soil. No artificial fertilizer should be used; well-rotted compost is next best to natural leafmold.

Should the soil around wildflowers be cultivated? The weeds should be kept out, but the soil does not need cultivating.

What plants go well with mertensia, bloodroot, and Dutchman's-breeches to fill in when their foliage dies down in late spring? Use Christmas fern or evergreen wood fern with mertensia and bloodroot; use spleenworts and grape ferns among the Dutchman's-breeches. These ferns do not have crowding habits and are almost evergreen. Their colors are good with the flowers mentioned.

Which wildflowers and trees can be established in dry, sandy, stony soil? Trees for dry, stony soil are the red-cedar (*Juniperus virginiana*), shadblow, and the locust (*Robina pseudoacacia*). Many shrubs will grow, such as bayberry, barberry, scrub oak, raspberries and blackberries, sumacs, blueberries. The blackhaw may assume the stature of a tree. Flowers include many of the flowers of the open field—daisies, asters, black-eyed Susans, pearly everlasting.

When woodland wildflowers have been transplanted from their natural habitat, should they be protected over winter? Yes, especially the first year, to prevent heaving.

Do woodland wildflowers require any special care in planting? They need the same careful planting as all flowers. Put them in well-prepared soil with enough room for the roots and do not crowd them. Tamp the soil firmly around them. Water.

My property is a gray birch grove. Which wildflowers can I plant in among the birches? Under your gray birches you can grow speedwell (*Veronica officinalis*), violets, wild strawberries, pearly everlasting, pipsissewa, shinleaf, *Phlox divaricata,* rue and wood anemones, mertensia. Ferns: Christmas fern, spleenwort, and polypody; the lycopodiums (club mosses).

Can you suggest a group of native American wildflowers for planting in a wooded lot on home grounds? *Aralia nudicaule, Aralia racemosa,* trilliums, *Dicentra eximia, Gillenia trifoliata, Shortia galacifolia, Tiarella cordifolia, Actaea alba* and *A. rubra.*

Which wildflowers will grow in a beech grove? Spring beauty (claytonia), wild columbine, harebells, hepatica, violets, mertensia, *Phlox divaricata, Trillium grandiflorum,* Jack-in-the-pulpit, red baneberry, the anemones, yellow lady's-slipper (if moist), Solomon's-seal, false Solomon's-seal, bloodroot. Ferns: Walking and the woods ferns.

Which wildflowers will grow in a woodland where there are hemlocks and oaks? A few are pink lady's-slipper, painted trillium, wood lily (*L. philadelphicum*), arbutus, bellwort, *Iris verna,* wintergreen, purple-fringed orchis, wood anemone, partridge-berry, wood aster. Shrubs: rhododendron, azalea, and mountain-laurel.

MEADOW WILDFLOWER GARDEN

Can you give me some pointers on planning and setting out a meadow wild garden? The meadow where wildflowers are to be grown should be open, sunny, and preferably fenced with either a rustic fence or rock wall. The soil for common meadow flowers should be dry, porous, and preferably a little sandy. Most meadow flowers are easily grown from seed and then transplanted. Weeds should be kept away from the plants so that they are not choked out. Room should be allowed for them to reseed themselves and form natural-looking patches.

What are the general cultural requirements for growing meadow wildflowers in the garden? The conditions should be as much like those of a meadow as possible: full sun, plenty of room for the plants, and undisturbed conditions. The soil should be porous and loamy except for moist meadow plants.

What sun-loving wildflowers are suitable for rural garden planting to give color and succession of bloom? *Phlox amoena,* April to May; *Iris cristata,* May; *Corydalis sempervirens,* May to June; *Epilobium angustifolium,* June to July; *Gillenia trifoliata,* June to August; *Campanula rotundifolia,* June to October; *Cassia marilandica,* July to August; *Asclepias tuberosa,* July to August; *Aster linariifolius,* September; *Aster ericoides,* September to October.

Which wild plants will grow well in a sunny meadow? Daisies, black-eyed Susans, the goldenrods, butterfly-weed, phlox, Joe-Pye-weed, hawkweed (devil's-paint-brush), yarrow, thistles, ironweed, lupine, pearly and sweet everlastings, American-artichoke, tansy, chicory; New England, smooth, and New York asters, trumpet creeper and bush honeysuckle, Queen Anne's lace, wild sweet pea.

BOG GARDEN

What conditions are necessary for a bog garden? Is it different from water gardening? Generally a swampy piece of ground, not under water, but where at all times there is plenty of moisture and usually too soft to walk upon. In water gardens the plants are immersed or floating. In bog gardens, the plants grow free above the soil.

What is the most practical way I can simulate bog-garden conditions in my home garden so I can grow sundews (Drosera sp.), pitcher-plant (Sarracenia purpurea), bog orchids, marsh-marigold, and other wetland plants? Pick a sunny area about 6 ft. long and 3–4 ft. wide, excavate about 2 ft. deep, and line with heavy-duty polyethylene. You can make a few perforations for drainage, but usually the plastic is severed soon enough by rodents, tree roots, and general wear and tear. Replace about a quarter of the soil, the remainder to be sphagnum peat moss. Mix the two together thoroughly, tramp solidly, and water thoroughly. Other methods for making bog gardens include the conversion of leaky fish pools by filling with soil-peat moss mixture; burying various discarded containers such as washtubs, bathtubs (and for a quite small bog garden, even a dish-pan) to their rims.

Which plants grow in wet marshland? Swamp milkweed, marsh-marigold, Joe-Pye-weed, yellow flag, blue flag, cardinal-flower, loosestrife, forget-me-not, sedges, marshmallow, water-plantain, Yellow- and White-fringed orchids, and many more.

Are tall-growing wildflowers, such as hibiscus, cardinal-flower, and lobelia, suitable for the wild garden? Yes. They are best grown in the bog garden or in a moist border.

Which wildflowers are suitable for planting near a naturalistic pool in sun and shade? *Iris pseudacorus, Iris prismatica, Aruncus sylvestris, Vernonia noveboracensis, Anemone canadensis, Asclepias incarnata, Calla palustris, Caltha palustris, Chelone glabra, Gentiana andrewsii, Hypoxis hirsuta, Lilium superbum, Parnassia glauca.*

Which wildflowers do you suggest for the edge of a slow-moving, shaded stream? Cardinal-flower, boneset, turtlehead, great lobelia, fringed and bottle gentians, forget-me-not, monkey-flower, mertensia, blue flag (iris), marsh-marigold, American globeflower. A little distance from the stream, but where they profit by some of the moisture, you can grow yellow lady's-slipper, trilliums, yellow adders-tongue, fringed polygala, Solomon's-seal, false Solomon's-seal, foamflower, Jack-in-the-pulpit, white violet, rue anemone (*Anemonella thalictroides*).

PROPAGATION OF WILDFLOWERS

Is it best to grow wildflowers from seed, or to buy the plants? Choice plants may be started from seed. Plants of most varieties may be purchased.

Which wild native plants may be started from seed and how is this done? Practically all of the field flowers, such as asters, milkweeds, goldenrods. Also columbine, pale corydalis, climbing fumitory (vine), celandine-poppy, bloodroot, early saxifrage, bishop's cap, foam-flower, and painted cup. The seeds are best started in flats in a protected cold frame. Sow in early winter or spring, using a light, sandy, leafmold or peat moss mixture.

What is a good all-around soil mixture in which to sow wildflower seeds? One half ordinary garden soil, ¼ leafmold or peat moss, and ¼ coarse sand, thoroughly mixed.

How long can wildflower seeds be kept before planting? Much depends on what kind they are. Some, such as trillium, bloodroot, and others that are produced in a more or less pulpy berry or pod, should be sown immediately before they dry at all; many other harder and thinner kinds can be kept for 5 or 6 months. A good general rule is to sow as soon as the seed is ripe, regardless of the time of the year. Germination is often erratic.

Which kinds of wildflower seeds can be sown in a cold frame late in the fall? Practically all of the perennial kinds, especially those which flower in midsummer or later.

I want to have thousands of beautiful kinds of wildflowers all over my meadow. Can't I get them by strewing handfuls of seed in all directions—a "wildflower mixture," you know, like I see advertised in the catalogues? You can try—and some success can result, depending on the quality of the seed, its freshness, soil conditions in your meadow, and the weather—but most likely, only the commonest, such as daisies and goldenrod, will catch hold and grow. Rather raise the kinds you want from seed sown in a place where they won't be overrun, and set the plants out in the meadow when they're big enough to hold their own.

What wildflowers self-sow so quickly as to become pests if planted in the garden? Goldenrod, cattails, wild carrot, jewel-weed, iron-weed, black-eyed Susan, sunflower, asters, golden ragwort, mullein, daisy, and many others.

I am not a botanist but like to identify wildflowers. Can you give me one or two references to well-illustrated books that would help me identify wildflowers from illustrations? Consult such regional wildflower guides as *A Field Guide to Wildflowers,* by Roger Tory Peterson and Margaret McKenny (Houghton Mifflin Co., 1968); *Kansas Wild Flowers,* by W. C. Stevens (University of Kansas Press, 1961).

COLLECTING WILDFLOWER PLANTS

Which wildflowers cannot be collected from the wild without breaking the conservation laws? Nearly every state has its own list of native plants under conservation, so a complete list of all protected species is impossible. Some of the more important kinds are trilliums, trailing-arbutus, mountain-laurel, all native orchids, anemone, lilies, dodecatheon, fringed gentian, cardinal-flower, birdsfoot violet, blue-bells, wild pink. However, it is only sensible conservation to collect plants from lands about to be bulldozed for highways and building.

Where can wildflowers be obtained? There are special dealers in wildflowers throughout the country who carry all types of these plants.

How do you start a wildflower preserve? Start a wildflower preserve by acquiring a spot that already has enough trees and flowers and beauty to suggest preserving. Gradually bring in groups of plants which you wish to include and see that they are planted in situations such as they seek in nature. This involves a good working knowledge of the soil and other conditions which the plants prefer and matching these conditions in the places you plant them.

May a flower preserve be joined with an arboretum? It should be a splendid addition to an arboretum.

SPECIFIC WILDFLOWERS—ANEMONES

I have tried several times to transplant rue anemone (Anemonella thalictroides) from the woods, without success. What could be wrong? They should be dug with a large ball of soil right after flowering, before the leaves die down. Take enough of the soil in which they are found to establish them in their new location. Plant in light shade. They require light, moist soil and are indifferent to acidity. The wood anemone (*A. quinquefolia*) requires moderate acidity.

What are the soil conditions required by the wood anemone (A. quinquefolia)? Moist, open woodland. Likes the borders of streams. Must have moderately acid soil. Dig with a large ball of soil just after flowering.

TRAILING-ARBUTUS

What is the botanical name for trailing-arbutus or mayflower? *Epigaea repens.*

How can I grow trailing-arbutus? Best to get pot-grown plants from a nursery, since they more easily adapt themselves to changed soil conditions. Where it grows in abundance in nature there is usually a sandy base to the soil, often ancient sandy river beds, or along the shore as on Long Island or the pine barrens of New Jersey. Soil should be light, strongly acid, and rich in organic matter, with good drainage. Plants can be propagated from cuttings in summer. Insert cuttings in a sand-peat moss mixture in a flat. Water. Cover with a flat-topped tent of polyethylene.

BLUETS

I should like to have a large patch of bluets (or quaker lady or innocence, as they are called). How can this be done? They are best in a rather moist, acid soil, in full sun. If you get them from the wild, put them in a place as much like the one they were in as possible. They should reseed themselves and form a patch.

What kinds of bluets are there besides the common quaker lady? Only one, if you are thinking of kinds that are worth planting. This one is the creeping bluet (*Houstonia serpyllifolia*), from the southern Appalachians. It is a mat-forming, rather short-lived perennial that flowers profusely for about 3 weeks in May. It will usually self-sow freely.

Dogtooth-violet (left) and bloodroot, two favorite native spring flowers.

BLOODROOT

How is bloodroot transplanted? Take care to get the whole root. Set it carefully in a well-dug soil in light shade, in early spring. Indifferent to soil acidity.

How may one germinate bloodroot seed? Collect the seed capsules just before they burst open. When seeds have ripened, they may be planted immediately in a prepared spot in the garden where they are to stay.

BUTTERFLY-WEED

Is butterfly-weed difficult to transplant from the field to the garden?   Yes, as *Asclepias tuberosa* is, as its scientific name implies, tuberous-rooted. In moving a mature specimen, a very large, thick ball of earth must be dug with it in order not to break the tubers. It can be transplanted in fall. Is one of the last things to appear above ground in spring.

Can I grow butterfly-weed from seed?   Yes. Sow in fall or spring —preferably the latter. Transplant seedlings to place where they are to grow when about 6 ins. tall, being careful not to break the very long taproots. Give full sun and well-drained soil.

CARDINAL-FLOWER (LOBELIA CARDINALIS)

Is cardinal-flower suitable for wild plantings?   Yes, if you have soil that retains some moisture. It is ideal for the edge of a stream or naturalistic pool in sun or part shade.

How can cardinal-flower be propagated?   By late-fall or early-spring sowing of fresh seed; by dividing large plants; and by pinning down a strong stalk on wet sand in August and half covering it with more sand until young plants start where the leaves join the main stem.

COLUMBINE

I have heard that wild columbine (Aquilegia canadensis) grows much taller and fuller in good garden soil than in the wild. Is this true?   Yes, but the improvement is limited to the stems and foliage; the flowers remain the same size. The result is a plant devoid of most of the grace and charm which make it so attractive in the wild. We recommend retaining its natural characteristics by giving it a rather poor, dryish soil.

What causes wild columbine to rot off at the crown when other plants flourish around it?   Columbine is used to thin, poor soil. Perhaps your soil is too moist, or the roots may be burned by too much fertilizer.

CREEPING JENNY (LYSIMACHIA NUMMULARIA)

Where can I plant creeping Jenny?   In a low, damp, pasture-like location in the sun.

DUTCHMAN'S-BREECHES

What is the botanical name for Dutchman's breeches? In what climate do they thrive? *Dicentra cucullaria.* The plant grows in thin woods and on rocky slopes, from New England south to North Carolina and west to South Dakota and Missouri. Prefers neutral soil.

FERNS

Which wild ferns can I plant in my woodland wildflower garden? Those which grow in your locality in wooded sections. Give them conditions as nearly as possible like those in which you find them. Among the best possibilities are evergreen wood fern, Christmas fern or sword fern, sensitive fern, ostrich fern, interrupted fern, royal fern. (The last three need very moist situations.)

Why can't I grow walking fern successfully in my rocky woodland? I give it just the kind of place it likes, but the leaves turn yellowish and just barely stay alive. Sounds as if the soil is acid, as is likely to be the case in a region where the rock ledges and outcrops are granite. Walking fern appears to be a lime-lover, so we suggest having your soil tested for acidity.

In what section of the United States does the climbing fern grow as native? The climbing fern, *Lygodium palmatum,* strangely enough is a native of fields in which shrubs are abundant, often in old river beds. It is found sporadically along the East Coast and abundantly in the Pine Barrens of New Jersey.

GENTIANS

Is there any way to start or plant blue gentians? Fringed gentians need a very moist situation in sun. Turn the soil, sow absolutely fresh seed on the surface in autumn, press it in, and cover with cheesecloth to prevent washing. Remove cheesecloth in spring as soon as frost is out of ground. Or, if you prefer, buy pot-grown seedlings.

Is bottle gentian a biennial? And is it hard to grow? Bottle or closed gentian (*Gentiana andrewsii*) is definitely a hardy perennial. It is easy to grow in rather heavy, dampish soil that is kept cool in summer by the shade of other plants.

HEPATICA

What sort of soil is preferred by hepaticas? Can they be placed in a wildflower garden? There are two native hepaticas: *H. acutiloba,* with pointed 3-lobed leaves, and *H. americana,* with rounded 3-lobed leaves. Common near Atlantic Seaboard. Either can be planted in the home garden in shaded locations, near rocks, if soil is suitable. A neutral soil is preferred, though the last-named is considered tolerant of slightly acid soils.

IRIS

Which wild irises can be used in the garden? *Iris cristata,* which needs a protected, moist situation and is indifferent to soil acidity; *I. verna,* wooded hills, very acid soil; *I. versicolor,* marshes, wet meadows, thickets, needs some sun; *I. prismatica,* marshes, swamps, full sun.

JACK-IN-THE-PULPIT

Can Jack-in-the-pulpits be grown in the wild garden? Yes. Give them a deeply prepared soil. If they are transplanted from the woods, take care to get all of the roots and tubers.

LYCOPODIUM (CLUB MOSS)

When is the best time to transplant such things as princess-pine? Transplant running-pine and other lycopodiums early in the spring before new growth starts. All club mosses are difficult to establish if conditions are not very close to their native habitats. May be moved any time if the place is damp enough.

MARSH-MARIGOLD

Is it difficult to transplant marsh-marigolds? No, very easy. Dig or pull the plants gently from their position in marsh or stream. Do not let roots dry out. Replant promptly in similar situation in edge of stream or naturalistic pool.

How can I propagate marsh-marigolds? The simplest way is to divide the clumps in spring, right after flowering. Merely wash the mud away from around the roots so you can see what you're doing, and separate the numerous small crowns (with their roots and leaves) with your fingers. Replant at once in bog garden or in edge of slow-moving stream or near outlet of naturalistic pool.

MERTENSIA

Is mertensia easy to grow in the garden? Yes. Though *Mertensia virginica* is found in very moist situations—chiefly along the edges of slow-moving streams—it is adaptable to partly shaded positions in the average garden.

How can I keep rabbits from eating my mertensia plants? The only way we know of is to get rid of the rabbits, by fair means or foul. Mertensia seems to be a special favorite of theirs in some localities.

ORCHIDS

How can I get wild orchids without breaking the conservation laws? Purchase them from a wildflower specialist.

How many native American cypripediums (lady's-slippers) are there? Which of these are suitable for use in the garden? There are about 10 native cypripediums, of which the following are the best for naturalistic gardening (none are suitable for gardens in the ordinary sense—they need special soil and care): *Cypripedium acaule* (pink); *C. montanum* (white); *C. calceolus pubescens* (yellow); *C. reginae*, (white and rose); *C. candidum* (white).

Can lady's-slippers be transplanted to a semi-wild garden successfully? When should transplanting be done? Yellow and pink lady's-slippers are transplanted with less risk than most other types. Best done in late summer or fall, but can be accomplished in spring if a firm root-ball is taken to prevent injury or disturbance to the roots. Be sure to include a goodly amount of the surrounding soil.

Which of our native cypripediums are perennial? How deep should roots be set? All are perennial. Roots should be set so that the growing bud, formed in fall, is just under the surface. Use rich woods soil, the surface kept from drying with a thin layer of oak leaves. Whenever you transplant these cypripediums, take as much as possible of the soil in which they have been growing.

Can you tell me what to do with a moccasin plant after it is through blooming? If by moccasin plant you mean our native pink lady's-slipper, *Cypripedium acaule*, and if it is planted in a suitable place, you need do nothing after it blooms. An oak-leaf mulch in fall is desirable.

Does showy lady's-slipper (Cypripedium reginae) require a neutral soil? (Minnesota.)   It generally is found in the wild where the soil is boggy and acid but is said to tolerate neutral soil.

Where will I find the showy orchis?   The showy orchis (*Orchis spectabilis*) and the pink lady's-slipper (*Cypripedium acaule*) inhabit rich, moist woods from Maine to Georgia, especially oak woods and hemlock groves. The showy orchis, however, is said to be tolerant of nearly neutral soil if rich enough.

Where will the purple-fringed orchis grow?   In woods, swamps, and meadows, or locations in the garden which simulate such conditions.

Where can I plant the white-fringed orchis in my wild garden?   If you have a bog garden, plant it there. Native to swamps and bogs.

Can I grow the yellow-fringed orchis in my garden?   Perhaps, if you have a strongly acid, continuously moist wild garden. It is generally not very long-lived.

PARTRIDGE-BERRY

Can partridge-berry (Mitchella repens) be grown in the wild garden?   Yes, especially if it is damp. It requires an acid, rich woods soil.

PHLOX DIVARICATA

How can I get wild blue phlox (Phlox divaricata) and what are its uses?   It can be purchased from many nurseries, especially those which deal in wild plants. Its uses are innumerable. Plant in open shade of deciduous trees. It blends well with mertensia, trilliums, and other plants of the open woodland. Self-sows. Can also be grown with tulips and candytuft in a flower garden.

PITCHER-PLANT

Can pitcher-plant (Sarracenia purpurea) be grown in the wild garden?   Yes. This is a good bog-garden subject.

SHOOTING-STAR

Is shooting-star a good wild-garden subject?   Yes. *Dodecatheon* *meadia* is a showy wildflower suitable for woodland planting in slightly acid or neutral soil.

SPRING BEAUTY (CLAYTONIA)

What are the cultural requirements of spring beauty (Claytonia)? Damp, leafmoldy soil and full shade in summer.

TRILLIUM

Which trilliums are best for the wild garden? *Trillium grandiflorum* (large-flowering white trillium); *T. nivale* (small white, earliest); *T. luteum* (yellow); *T. nervosum* (rose); *T. californicum* (sessile type in white or red).

Can trilliums be purchased? Yes, specialists in wild plants and some other nurseries list them.

How can trilliums best be propagated from seed? The best way to propagate trilliums is by division of old, large clumps. Absolutely fresh seed, sown before it has a chance to dry, may germinate the following spring, but growth is very slow and all conditions have to be just right.

VIOLETS

Are violets dug from the woods suitable for planting in the wild garden? Yes. They are easily transplanted.

What sort of conditions does birdsfoot violet need? Give a dryish, well-drained, sandy, very acid soil in full sun.

WINTERGREEN

Will you please name and describe some native wintergreens? Spotted wintergreen (*Chimaphila maculata*) with white-veined lanceolate evergreen leaves; showy white flowers, very fragrant. Pipsissewa (*Chimaphila umbellata*), rather like the above but with wedge-shaped unmarked evergreen leaves and smaller flowers, sometimes blush pink. Shinleaf (*Pyrola elliptica*), oval basal leaves, persistent but not evergreen; white flowers on 5- to 10-in. stalks, in racemes. Creeping wintergreen (*Gaultheria procumbens*), evergreen, blunt, aromatic leaves; creeping subterranean stems; blush flowers in leaf axils; edible red berries; 2 to 6 ins. tall. Flowering-wintergreen or fringed polygala (*P. paucifolia*), evergreen leaves; rose-purple,

fringed flowers, or, sometimes, white; low-growing, and spreading.
How is pipsissewa (Chimaphila umbellata) propagated? By cuttings of new growth taken the first half of July and rooted in sand and peat moss in a seed flat.

Gardens of Other Types

CHILDREN'S GARDENS

What would be a good location to give a child for a garden? A spot that has full sun all day, where the ground is in good condition and easily workable. Children are easily discouraged if their garden does not produce, so do not select any unfit "leftover" area.

Which plants would be suitable for a child to grow in his own garden? Bright, easily grown annuals, which can be raised from seed: zinnia, marigold, sweet-alyssum, and portulaca. These will give him an opportunity to learn how seeds are planted and what the plants look like as they come up. If a fence encloses his garden, morning-glories can be used to cover it.

Will you list some easy vegetables that a child might grow from seed? Carrots, beets, leaf lettuce, beans, radishes, and New Zealand spinach.

I am very much interested in planning a garden that will interest my children. Just what arrangement would you suggest? I have in mind something to go along with their own yard and playhouse. Any garden for children should be scaled down to their size. They like simple patterns and odd plants. Paths should be narrow, and all plants relatively small. Choose varieties that will stand the maximum amount of abuse. Leave plenty of play space.

GARDEN TO ATTRACT BIRDS

Which flowers attract birds? Birds (except for hummingbirds) are attracted by the seed of the plants and then only seed-eating birds. Sunflowers, *Eryngium amethystinum*, rudbeckia, coreopsis, pokeweed, lily-of-the-valley, shrub roses, partridge-berry, wild strawberry, wintergreen.

Which flowers and shrubs can I plant that are most attractive to hummingbirds? Aquilegia, delphinium, monarda, phlox, penstemon, physostegia, tritoma, flowering tobacco, flowering currant, quince.

Which vines attract birds? Vines that produce seeds or berries: bearberry, bittersweet, cranberry, dewberry, the grapes, the honeysuckles, Virginia-creeper, morning-glories.

Which evergreens attract birds? Red-cedar, fir, hemlock, the pines, yew, the junipers, arborvitae, hollies.

Which shrubs encourage birds? Most of the berried shrubs. Some are bayberry, benzoin, winterberry, blackberry, chokeberry, elderberry, hawthorn, holly, mulberry, shadbush, snowberry, the viburnums.

Which deciduous trees shall I plant to attract birds? Alders, white ash, linden, beech, the birches, hackberry, hornbeam, larch, black locust, the maples, mountain-ash, wild cherry, crab apples, oriental cherries, hawthorns.

BONSAI

What are Bonsai? These are woody trees and shrubs, painstakingly dwarfed by meticulous pruning techniques and by being grown in root-restricting pots.

Is it possible to have a garden of Bonsai? Yes. Before you enter into it wholeheartedly be certain you understand that this takes much patience and time. It should not be undertaken in areas of hot, dry summers, unless one establishes complete control of the humidity and moisture requirements of these plants.

Can Bonsai be grown and cared for in the open ground? Probably no, unless they are sunken in pots over winter. It is the restraining characteristics of the small pots that aid in causing the dwarfing. A few references on the subject of Bonsai are: *The Japanese Art of Miniature Trees and Landscapes,* by Yugi Yoshimura and Giovanna M. Halford (Charles E. Tuttle Co., 1957); *Bonsai* by Kan Yashiroda (Branford Co., 1960); *Bonsai: Special Techniques* (Brooklyn Botanic Garden Handbook, 1966).

CONTAINER GARDENING

How large should a concrete container be for a small tree? The larger the better. Small containers dry out more easily in the summer, and winter cold penetrates to the root system more quickly in the winter. Look around in your area and see what are the sizes of containers in which trees live over winter.

Is there any particular care to be given trees growing in containers on the city streets? In many northern towns such containers are taken into a cool building for the winter. Mulching the soil is helpful; watering well before the first soil freeze is almost essential.

What are some of the best plants to be grown in concrete containers along the streets of our town? In southern areas there are

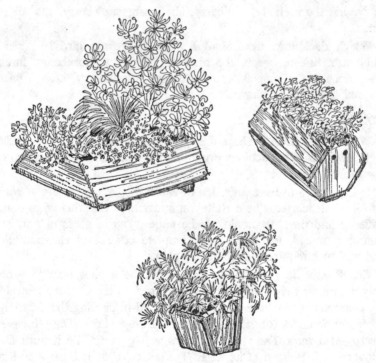

Three different shapes of wooden containers that can be constructed from redwood, drift wood or other scraps that are handy. The bottom container illustrates a shape of container suitable to fasten to a wall; the container above it (right) has holes in each end so it can hang. Screws, rather than nails, should be used to fasten the pieces of wood together.

many plants suitable for this purpose. In the North, yew, pines, andromedas, crab apples, and junipers are a few possibilities.

I have some woody shrubs and herbs in large containers on my patio. Is it safe to leave them out over winter? Probably not, unless you have no choice. Either the containers might crack from freezing soil or the plant roots might be killed by winter cold. Better take them into a cool garage or cellar for over winter, but do not let the soil dry out. If the plants must be left outside, mulch them heavily. Push the containers together so they can protect each other. Water when the soil is dry.

Our garden club wants to supply a lot of "planters" or concrete tubs for growing trees in the shopping area of the town. Is this practical? (New Hampshire.) Probably not in your area. The roots of plants do not withstand the very low temperatures the tops can withstand. The tops of American holly can withstand temperatures of 20° F. *below* zero but the roots are hardy only to 20° F. *above* zero. In a tub or planter set on the sidewalk the soil inside the tub often approximates the air temperature. If planters are used they should be removed in the fall to a barn or other building where temperatures do not go so low as outside.

In our Wisconsin town we have many small trees in tubs in the shopping area but the Park Department removes them for the winter. Is this necessary? Yes. They are taken to a cold barn or building where the tubs are not subjected to the extremely low air temperatures outside. Trees in such tubs outside over winter might easily be killed in your area.

Do trees and plants in large containers left out over winter survive? Depends on size of the container, type of plant, and the winter temperatures. Many survive if winter temperatures (of the soil in the container) do not go below 25° F. The larger the container, the better the chances for survival.

FRAGRANT GARDENS

I would like some fragrant annuals in my garden. What do you suggest? Nicotiana, nasturtium, sweet-alyssum, petunia, marigold, stock, heliotrope (tender shrub), mignonette, sweet pea.

Will you name some bulbs for a fragrant garden? *Crocus versicolor* and *C. biflorus; Scilla hispanica; Fritillaria imperialis;* hyacinths; *narcissus;* lily-of-the-valley; *Lycoris squamigera;* scented irises (rhizomes, not bulbs); *Lilium auratum, candidum, longiflorum, regale, speciosum;* tuberose.

What are some fragrant hardy flowers? *Arabis; Dianthus* species and varieties; scented bearded iris; lily-of-the-valley; *Viola odorata* and varieties; *Lavandula officinalis;* hemerocallis; buddleia; primula; clematis; sweet William; monarda; phlox; peony; roses; salvia; *Campanula lactiflora;* sweet-alyssum; wallflower.

Will you tell me which geraniums to buy for fragrance? *Pelargonium tomentosum* (mint); *P. graveolens* (rose); *P. limoneum* (lemon); *P. odoratissimum* (nutmeg).

What will give fragrance in the late garden? Chrysanthemums and sweet autumn clematis.

Which shrubs shall I plant for fragrance? *Skimmia japonica;* many viburnums; crab apples; pink and swamp azalea; *Jasminum nudiflorum* and *J. primulinum;* benzoin; magnolia; flowering almond; lilac; honeysuckle; daphne; roses; mock-orange; strawberry-shrub; English hawthorn; wisteria; witch-hazel. Tender: lemon-verbena; rosemary; heliotrope. For more information on fragrant gardens see: *The Fragrant Year,* by Helen Van Pelt Wilson and Leonie Bell (M. Barrows Co., Inc., 1967); *Gardening for Fragrance,* by Nelson Coon (Hearthside Press, Inc., 1970).

JAPANESE STONE GARDENS

The idea of having a simple garden of sand and stone sounds wonderful for the tired gardener. Could you refer me to a good book on the subject? *Japanese Stone Gardens,* by Kazuhiko Fukuda (Charles E. Tuttle Co., 1970).

ROOF GARDENS

What soil mixture should be used to fill the boxes on a roof garden? A good, friable loam is ideal. Avoid heavy clay or very sandy soil. Be sure the roof is strong enough to support the boxes.

What kind of fertilizer should I use for the plants on my roof garden? Dried manure, or a complete commercial fertilizer.

Should one use a mulch on the soil in roof-garden boxes? Yes; a mulch will help prevent sudden drying out of the soil from wind and sun on the roof. Peat moss, rotted manure, leafmold, or black polyethylene plastic film with a few holes punched in could be used.

Can one grow vegetables successfully on a roof? Yes, with full sun and good soil, quite a few can be grown. In boxes about 8 ins. deep grow lettuce, parsley, radishes, bush beans, endive, onions (from sets), New Zealand spinach, Swiss chard, and small-size tomatoes such as 'Tiny Tim'. Try stump-rooted carrots and beets. Standard tomatoes planted in deeper boxes, staked and sheltered so that they will not blow over, will thrive.

I would like to grow some herbs on my roof garden. Do you think they would be successful? Yes. Herbs are a good choice for the shallow boxes usually used on a roof. Try thyme, chives, parsley, mint, sage, and basil. (See Herbs for soil and culture.)

Will you give a list of annual flowers for growing on a roof? Marigolds, zinnias, ageratum, petunias, calendulas, sweet-alyssum, lobelia, portulaca, celosia, iberis, forget-me-nots, salvia, coreopsis, aster, scabiosa.

I am planning to make the boxes for plants on my roof garden. Can you give me some suggestions? Your boxes should be made deep enough to hold 8 to 12 ins. of soil. They can be as wide as you like. Use cypress or redwood. Provide drainage holes in the bottom of each box. The inside of the boxes can be painted with asphaltum to protect the wood, and the outside with several coats of durable outdoor paint.

I want to grow some vines on my roof. How could I effectively support them? Make an arbor over part of the roof if the winds are not too strong. This would not only be a good support for your vines, but would also supply shade and some shelter on the terrace. Otherwise, use a trellis against the side of the building, or put vine supports along the side of the building, on which to tie the vines.

I want to have a roof garden that is good-looking but will not be expensive. Will you make some suggestions? Edge the railing or wall with window boxes painted dark green or any color which fits your scheme. Grow such plants as petunia, ageratum, geranium, sweet-alyssum, marigold, and calendula. Some potted plants can be arranged about the roof. If you can get some large tubs or barrels, try a few shrubs, such as privet or forsythia, or trees, such as junipers or yews, for a background. Train vines against the wall or building. Ivy, honeysuckle, or morning-glories would do well.

What can be done on a flat roof, approximately 10 × 10 ft., on the west side of an apartment? Can soil be put on the roof to sufficient depth to raise anything successfully? Six to 8 ins. of soil will successfully grow many flowers or even a few vegetables. Check with engineer before putting this considerable weight on roof. Otherwise confine efforts to a few soil-filled boxes.

I have some large roof-garden boxes. How can I tell if the soil is sour? How can I fertilize the earth before we plant? If in doubt, have a soil test made. For most plants add ground limestone every two years. Bone meal and dried cow manure are excellent fertilizers; or use any complete commercial fertilizer. Add lime in fall or very early spring, and fertilizer at planting time.

SUNKEN GARDENS

I have a natural spot for making a sunken garden. How can I plan this? The sunken garden is viewed from above and the basic layout is very important because of this. An informal or untidy effect would spoil it. A formal garden, with a path running through the center, and a center of interest at the end, would probably work out well. If your garden is well drained, you might plan a formal rose garden; or an herb garden with thyme-planted steps and borders of fragrant plants around the four sides of the area in front of the walls. Leave the center in turf.

There is an old foundation on our property, where a house burned down. Would this make a good place for a sunken garden? Yes, it should be excellent. You may have to provide drainage, if water collects in the foundation. Build steps down into the garden of the same kind of stones as the foundation. Perennials of doubtful hardiness and shrubs, which need much protection from cold winds, can be incorporated in your planting plan.

WINDOW-BOX GARDENS

What special problems are involved in window-box gardening? First provide appropriate boxes with holes in bottom for drainage. Put in 2 or 3 ins. of cinders or broken brick, and fill with rich, porous soil. Plant with appropriate material in spring. Regular attention to watering is of prime importance. Fertilize two or three times a season.

Can you give some pointers on making window boxes? Make box to fit window space, but if the length is in excess of 3 ft. make in two sections. For good results the box should be not less than 8 ins. deep and 10 ins. wide. Use cypress or white pine at least 1 in. thick. Bore ½-in. holes, 6 ins. apart, in bottom for drainage.

What is the best soil for window boxes? One that is rich, with plenty of humus to retain moisture. Use 2 parts loam, 1 part dried manure or peat moss, with a 5-in. pot of superphosphate mixed with each bushel.

Are wooden window boxes better than those made of concrete? They are inexpensive and less weighty to handle if they have to be moved occasionally. On the other hand, they are less permanent.

Are the metal "self-watering" boxes satisfactory? Yes; but don't place too much reliance on the "self-watering" feature.

Is there any flowering plant suitable for window boxes which will last all summer and be colorful? Lantana. Get potted plants in May; usually then in flower, they will bloom until frost. They stand heat, drought, and city conditions, but are at their best when well watered and pruned occasionally to restrain lanky growth. Stand partial shade, but prefer full sun. Petunias and dwarf marigolds are also good.

Which flowers grow in window boxes? Among the most satisfactory are begonias, geraniums, fuchsias, ageratum, petunias, dwarf marigolds, torenias, pansies, sweet-alyssum, morning-glory, vinca, sedum, balsam, portulaca, lobelia.

Is there a blooming plant that will grow in window boxes under awning? (West Virginia.) None that you can be sure of. Try *Begonia semperflorens* varieties, petunias, and *Lobelia erinus* varieties.

What would you suggest for flowers (not tuberous begonias) for window boxes that are very shaded? Would like plenty of color. You will probably have difficulty with any flowering plant if the shade is heavy and continuous. Fuchsias, *Begonia semperflorens,* impatiens, torenias, and lobelias will stand as much shade as any.

What shall I plant in a window box, outdoors, on north side? (Washington.) Flowering plants: tuberous begonias, fuchsias, lobelias, torenias. Foliage plants: aucuba, boxwood, Japanese holly, dwarf yew, arborvitae, privet, English ivy, vinca, Kenilworth-ivy.

What could we plant in outdoor front-stoop window boxes which will survive New York City winter climate? Among the most satisfactory plants are small yew, arborvitae, Japanese holly, privet, and English ivy. All suffer, however, when the soil is frozen solid. Make sure soil is well soaked in fall. *Sedum acre* and *S. spectabile* will survive year in, year out.

What can be put in a window box (southern exposure) during the winter months? (Virginia.) Small evergreens, boxwood, arborvitae, junipers, spruces, with English ivy and trailing myrtle to droop over edge. This material cannot be expected to thrive permanently, however, because of poor environment.

Is it necessary to put ivy and myrtle grown in window boxes into the ground for the winter? If the soil about their roots freezes solid, they cannot take up water to replace that lost by leaves, and the plants die. Place boxes on ground, pack leaves or straw well about them, and cover with burlap or light layer of straw.

How early can pansies be planted in outdoor window boxes? (North Carolina.) Pansies are much hardier than most people realize. The established plants can be put in the outdoor window box as soon as the severe portion of winter is past. Plants grown indoors should be hardened off by gradually exposing them to cooler temperatures before setting them in the outdoor boxes. March 15, or even earlier, in your locality, might be about right.

Are hanging baskets practical? Yes, provided they are made right with plenty of moss on the outside of the soil and are never allowed to dry out.

3
Ornamental Plants and Their Culture

MOST OF our leading garden plants have their origin in wildflowers, but a few have been cultivated for so long that the original species is unknown or uncertain. They have been greatly changed by domestication, so they are quite different from the wild prototypes. Hybridizing and selection have improved the form, size, color, and garden value.

Taken as a whole, the number of different kinds and varieties of garden flowers available to the home gardener is staggering. He can easily become bewildered by the great array of different types from which to choose.

Many flower lovers prefer to specialize in one or a few groups and become experts in growing roses, irises, dahlias, chrysanthemums, or rhododendrons. There is much to recommend the practice, because the gardener comes to know his particular plants thoroughly. Those who are familiar with the interesting habits of their plants get the most fun from gardening. Most of the leading horticulturists of the country have been specialists to a certain degree, and have then in turn mastered the culture of many groups.

Plants as Garden Material

The real gardener is interested not only in the plants themselves, but also in the garden pictures he can create with them. Floriculture is a combination of both science and art. Each complements the other. To be able to grow good flowers without the skill to use them artistically in and about the home furnishes only part of the enjoyment from them that is possible. Merely using plants and flowers for decorative purposes, without understanding their culture, is an empty form of art.

Joining a garden club or special flower society is to be recommended. Such organizations are dedicated to the improvement of horticulture or to promoting the culture and development of a particular flower. Besides furnishing helpful information through their meetings and publications, they give an opportunity to become acquainted with other gardening hobbyists. The friendships and sociability encouraged by horticultural organizations are by no means a minor factor in making the world a better place in which to live.

The gardener who knows something of plant structure, plant physiology (which deals with the functions of the various plant parts), and ecology (the relation of plants to their environment) finds such knowledge helpful in dealing with problems of plant culture. Furthermore, a smattering of general botany adds greatly to the pleasures and interest which come from gardening.

Structure of the Plant. All of us know that the function of the *roots* is to anchor the plant in place and to absorb water containing dissolved nutrients from the soil. The botanists can tell us, in addition, that roots of most plants, in order to remain healthy, require air. When we know this we appreciate more the importance of cultivation which, among other things, admits the air to the soil. We can also understand why some plants fail to thrive when set in poorly drained soil from which the air is driven by waterlogging. Knowing the need of roots for air we can see the importance of adequate underdrainage for plants growing in pots and the need to avoid overwatering which drives out air from the spaces between the particles of soil.

The information that water, with its dissolved minerals, is absorbed mainly near the root tips indicates to us that fertilizers should be applied to that area where the roots are actively growing, and not in close proximity to the stem or trunk, where there are few if any actively "feeding" roots.

Plant stems, in addition to supporting the leaves and flowers, provide a connecting link which distributes water (with the dissolved nutrients absorbed by the roots and the food materials manufactured in the leaves) between the roots and other parts of the plant. The internal structure of the stem has an important part to play in some aspects of plant culture. For example, in those plants which have two or more seed leaves the stem contains a layer of actively growing cells between the bark and wood: this is the *cambium layer*. It is essential for the gardener engaged in grafting or budding to be aware of this because the cambium layer of the understock must be brought into close contact with that of scion or bud to be grafted on it; otherwise union cannot take place.

The leaves are the factories of the plant where water, containing dissolved minerals absorbed from the soil, and carbon dioxide, taken in by the leaves, are combined to form complex food substances which are then transferred by the sap to other parts of the plant where they are needed. When we realize the importance of the work carried on by the leaves we can readily understand the necessity of keeping them healthy and why we should never remove too many of them. If the work of leaves were more widely understood, there would be fewer beginners expecting a harvest of edible roots from young beets from which all the leaves have been cut for use as "greens." The function of leaves is recognized in the oft-repeated advice to leave plenty of foliage when cutting such flowers as gladioli, peonies, or tulips, and thus avoid weakening the underground parts.

The flowers produce seeds and thus provide a means of reproduction. Commonly they are "perfect": that is, the male and the female elements are contained in a single flower—as in a rose, or a sweet pea. But sometimes they are "monoecious"—that is, with stamens and pistils in separate flowers on the same plant; for example, corn, squash, and oak. In some cases the male and female flowers are "dioecious" and are produced on separate plants, as in holly and willow. While, contrary to a widespread impression, it is never necessary to have plants of both sexes growing in proximity for flowers to be produced, fruits are possible on dioecious plants only when both sexes are growing fairly close together. Also many varieties of fruits, such as apple, pear, plum, and cherry, although their flowers are "perfect," require another variety of the same kind growing near by to provide cross-pollination, because their own pollen is incapable of securing a good "set" of fruit.

Environment Is Important

Often it is helpful to the gardener to know the kind of surroundings in which the plants thrive in the wild state. The study of such environment is known as plant ecology. Some plants are found always growing in the shade; others revel in hot, dry situations. They must, in most cases, be accorded similar conditions when we grow them in our gardens. Again, some plants are more perfectly at home in heavy clay soils, while some thrive in sand. There are those which have to be grown in water, and others which languish if their feet are too wet. Some plants demand a soil with an acid reaction; some prefer a soil which is abundantly supplied with lime; and others—many of them—seem almost indifferent to the chemical reaction of the soil. It is obvious that the right kind of soil and its proper preparation are among the most important factors in plant culture.

Some knowledge of the natural environment of plants is of great help to the gardener. Plants that thrive in sheltered positions, for instance, cannot be expected to do well if fully exposed to storms and winds.

Other things also have to be considered, such as shelter and exposure to wind. Climate, of course, has a very important bearing. In some regions the extreme cold of winter prohibits us from growing some plants outdoors throughout the year, and to others the heat of summer may be inimical. Many plants are adapted to dry air; and in this group we find a large proportion which are successful as house plants. The polluted air of large cities is fatal to many plants, but there are some which can endure it; these, of course, are of special interest to those whose gardening has to be conducted in urban surroundings.

Competition for food, light, and air among themselves, and from other plants, is another environmental factor which affects growth. In order to secure room for adequate development it is necessary for us either to thin or transplant the seedlings which we raise; and it is also necessary to insure that they are not starved, smothered, or crowded by weeds.

Information bearing on these environmental factors can be obtained from observation, from books, and from the experience of friends. But sometimes if the gardener's special bent is the cultivation of rare and unusual plants, he may have to experiment for himself before he is able to discover a location and conditions in which his plants will thrive. A knowledge of the natural environment is always helpful, but there are isolated cases where plants seem to thrive better under garden conditions when their usual environment is changed. An example is our native cardinal-flower, which grows naturally in wet places, usually in shade, but which, in our garden, we find does better in the rich soil of the perennial border where it gets sun for most of the day. The wise gardener first selects plants which are adapted to the environment of his garden. If he is ambitious to grow other kinds, he must change the environment to suit them if that is possible.

Propagation of Plants

Starting new plants is an absorbing garden operation which never loses its thrill. Even an old-timer like myself, who has been an active gardener for more than forty years, can still get a kick out of watching seeds germinate (though I no longer dig them up the day after planting to see if they have started to grow!), and from inserting cuttings with the expectation of getting roots on them.

Nature increases plants by means of seeds, spores, bulbils, tubers, rhizomes, runners, offsets, suckers, and stolons. The gardener uses all these methods and in addition makes cuttings of stems, leaves,

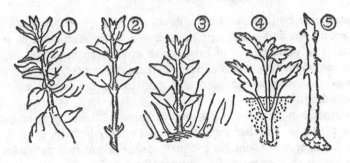

PROPAGATING PLANTS BY CUTTINGS

Many plants are readily propagated by means of cuttings —a technique which the home gardener can readily master. Most commonly used for house plants, perennials, tender annuals, and some shrubs, are softwood cuttings. In (1) above such a cutting is being made; (2) shows it trimmed, ready for (3) inserting in sand or sand and peat moss, to root. (4) Cutting properly inserted in rooting medium. (5) Hardwood cutting of rose, showing callus formed at bottom.

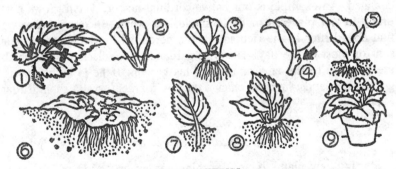

LEAF CUTTINGS

Some kinds of plants are readily propagated by leaf cuttings: (1) and (6) show begonia leaf cut across main ribs and laid flat on moist sand, with new plants starting from cuts; (2) and (3) show triangular leaf cutting of begonia; (4) and (5) leaf cutting with bud; and (7), (8), and (9) leaf cutting of African-violet, and young plant developed from it.

and roots. He also increases his plants by division, by layering, and by budding and grafting.

Several new methods, or variations of old ones, have come to the fore. Among them: the use of constant mist and plastic film, polyethylene, as aids in rooting cuttings and in general propagation. New rooting media have also come into the picture. These include: perlite, vermiculite, shredded styrofoam, and mixtures of these, often with peat moss and sphagnum moss.

The advent of fluorescent lights has made it possible for indoor gardeners to start both seeds and cuttings in the absence of natural light. This is a great advantage where window space is limited or nonexistent as well as during the winter months when light duration and intensity are usually inadequate. Many garden catalogues and stores have special units employing fluorescent tubes with a reflector.

Keeping Plants Well and Happy

The Art of Transplanting. The gardener's job is not finished when he has started or purchased his young plants. They must be properly cared for in order to get best results. The seeds can be sown where they are to mature (after proper preparation of the soil, of course); and then they have to be thinned, the soil cultivated, and weeds suppressed. Sometimes seeds are started either in pots or trays indoors or in seedbeds out of doors. Then the seedlings have to be transplanted once or oftener before the plants are installed in their permanent location. Cuttings usually are started in a propagating frame, and their subsequent treatment involves transplanting. Transplanting is usually done to temporary nursery rows, or to pots, preliminary to their final shift to the garden. In some cases, however, the rooted cuttings can be transferred directly to the garden.

Today gardeners are fortunate to find a wide selection of annual seedlings (and some biennials and perennials) sold in garden centers. These are generally in small trays containing from six to twelve plants, or in individual peat or plastic pots. The plants are usually small, but sometimes they have buds or even flowers.

Plants can easily be removed from a tray or flat by running a putty knife between the plants (through the soil and root mass) in two directions—just as you would cut a pan of fudge. Then each plant is carefully lifted and set immediately into a prepared hole in the ground. (If dry, water the growing medium before removing plants.) Plants, once they have been removed from the flat, should never be exposed to the air or sun for more than a few seconds or they will dry out and be damaged or killed. Plants grown in peat pots or Jiffy-7's should be set so that the top of the pot is *below* soil level. If left exposed, it will act as a wick and draw water from the soil. Most gardeners have found that it is a good idea to break the root-ball slightly to help roots establish quick contact with the soil into which they are being transplanted. Water transplants well to eliminate air pockets and assure intimate contact of soil and roots. If plants should exhibit excessive wilting (especially noticeable when young seedlings from indoors are planted outdoors), cover with upturned baskets or pots for a few days during the sunny hours. After that, they should be able to take the sun without wilting.

Some growers find it helpful to use a transplanting solution to lessen shock and help plants establish sooner. One such is Trans-plantone. One can also use almost any fertilizer (a quick-dissolving type such as Rapid-Gro), according to directions given for transplanting.

Transplanting is an important operation. It must be done at the right season for best results, and care must be taken to avoid undue injury to the root system. Usually trees and shrubs are transplanted when they are more or less dormant, provided the ground is unfrozen. Most of them can be moved either in spring or fall, but for best results some require spring transplanting. Frequent transplanting (every year or two), when the trees are young, produces roots that make possible transplanting, even when they are of large size, with little injury. Each transplanting inevitably shortens the wide-spreading roots, and this causes the remaining roots to branch freely. Thus the plant produces a compact mass of fibrous roots which enables it to be transplanted easily. For this reason plants obtained from a nursery (where regular transplanting is practiced) can be moved with much less loss than those which are dug from the wild.

Seedlings, and young plants in general, can be transplanted when they are actively growing because it is possible to move them with the root system almost intact. There are some exceptions among those plants which produce a deep taproot. Carrots and annual poppies, for example, cannot be transplanted with good results. Occasionally transplanting is done to promote fruitfulness, as with dwarf fruit trees, growing in rich ground, which are making excessive branch and leaf growth at the expense of flowers. The loss of roots brought about by transplanting often results in checking such vegetative growth and promoting the formation of flower buds.

Benefits of Cultivation and Mulching. Cultivation is the term applied to the loosening of the surface soil. It aids in the aeration of the soil, enables rain to penetrate more easily, and, perhaps most important, it helps keep down weeds.

Cultivation is accomplished in many ways, and a variety of tools is involved. In pots or flats a pointed stick or an old dinner fork can be used. For cultivating soil in crowded areas, there are various types of hand cultivators. In flower borders the scuffle hoe is the most useful tool, while in the vegetable garden either the scuffle hoe, draw hoe, or wheel hoe can be brought into action. In large areas, where the crops are grown in rows, power tillers or cultivators, either riding or walking, are useful.

Cultivation after rains is usually recommended to prevent the formation of a surface crust and to kill weed seedlings; but cultivation must not be done until the moisture has had a chance to penetrate and the surface is beginning to get dry. Frequent cultivation is essential to cope adequately with weeds. It is much easier to kill them while they are still in the seedling stage. Furthermore, this prevents them from stealing the food and moisture which properly belong to the cultivated crops.

A mulch is sometimes applied in order to lessen or obviate the necessity for cultivation. Paper treated to make it somewhat waterproof has in some cases been successfully used. Some plants, however, do not respond to a paper mulch and under garden conditions there are several objections to it, such as its appearance, the difficulties of anchoring it to the ground, and of working among the plants without disturbing it. Black plastic is more generally available than is paper and is very satisfactory for rows of vegetables but rather unattractive in a flower border.

Ordinarily mulches of organic materials, most of which can be incorporated with the soil at the end of the growing season to decay and form humus, are the most practical, and serve the purpose better. Mulches should be applied in a layer 2 or 3 ins. thick.

Labor Saving

The difficulty of obtaining competent help has greatly influenced modern gardening, both in garden operations and the plant materials. Even though his garden is only a small one the gardener has not been neglected by the makers of motorized equipment. In addition to power lawn mowers, either the conventional reel kinds or the rotary types with all sorts of attachments ranging from snow removal to tillers, there are many other labor-saving devices. The tedious job of trimming the whiskery grass by handshears has been eased by the electric or battery-operated trimmer.

Mulching the surface as a means of controlling weeds is another labor-saver. Among the organic materials that can be used for mulching are: buckwheat hulls, peat moss, ground corn cobs, shredded sugarcane (bagasse) sold as chicken litter, salt-meadow or marsh hay, grass clippings, sawdust, wood chips, excelsior and pulped newspaper. Most of these serve a triple purpose—that of making it easier to control weeds; conserving soil moisture by checking evaporation; and adding organic matter. Naturally there are some drawbacks to the wide use of mulches. Among them are the possibility of an increase in the slug population and the temporary depletion of available nitrogen in the soil. Fortunately these drawbacks can be counteracted by putting out slug bait containing metaldehyde or beer in saucers, and by keeping a close watch on the plants and applying quick-acting nitrogen in the form of nitrate of soda or sulfate of ammonia at the first sign of yellowing foliage.

The ready availability of bedding plants at local outlets or even by mail has eliminated the labor of sowing seeds for those who either don't have the time or don't enjoy this phase of gardening. Today one can achieve a completely planted garden (sometimes in bud or even in bloom) in a matter of hours, even in midsummer, if necessary.

There is also a trend toward making greater use of trees and shrubs for the main focal points in the garden. Once planted, most of them take care of themselves. Among the more recent introductions being used for this purpose are the 'Moraine' locust, a form of honey locust (*Gleditsia triacanthos,* var. *inermis*); a spineless variety; and a form of this, the 'Sunburst' locust, in which the new leaves are yellow.

Another new tree is a form of Schwedler maple, sold as 'Crimson King'. This, although it does not quite live up to the colored pictures in the advertisements, is an advance over the dull summer color of Schwedleri.

Watering. Plant physiologists tell us that the plant nutrients in the soil can be absorbed by the roots only when they are in solution. The necessity for abundant moisture is therefore obvious. Cultivation and mulching both have a bearing on the conservation of moisture already in the soil. In recent years the value of cultivation has been questioned by some investigators regarding the moisture-holding value of a dust mulch, but most practical gardeners still accept it.

In addition to conserving the moisture already in the soil it is sometimes necessary to *supplement* the rainfall. This is accomplished by irrigation, or by watering with the aid of a hose or watering pot. The important thing to remember about watering is that light sprinklings, which penetrate the soil only an inch or so, are not desirable, because they encourage roots to come to the surface where they are exposed to too much heat from the sun and where they may be killed by cultivation, or by drought if for any reason the daily sprinkling is neglected. When watering is done, *it should be thorough,* so that the soil is wet, if possible, to a depth of 6 to 8 ins. Do not water again until the soil begins to get dry.

The same principle should be followed when watering potted plants. Sometimes it may be desirable to let the soil become so dry that the plant is almost wilting. The soil shrinks when drying, and this opens up pore spaces, permitting the entrance of air which, as we have already seen, is a necessity for the roots of most plants.

Pruning. In a reaction against the plant butchering which went under the name of pruning many gardeners have come to look on all cutting back of plants as a practice to be avoided. Actually, however, pruning is not altogether bad. By pruning it is possible to aid the rejuvenation of sickly plants and assist in the control of insect pests and fungous diseases. Pruning can be used to correct faulty habits of growth, to promote interesting branch formations, and to bring about earlier blossoming. In certain cases it is possible to develop larger flowers on longer stems by pruning to reduce the number of flowering shoots. The complete removal of dead and dying branches is an operation that can be safely performed at any time.

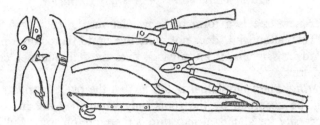

Types of pruning equipment. The pruning shears and pruning knife (left) are the most useful in the small garden.

There are several principles which are helpful to the would-be pruner:

(1) Severe pruning *when the plant is dormant* stimulates the production of strong, leafy shoots; contrariwise, pruning *when the plant is actively growing* tends to check exuberant growth and helps bring about the formation of blossom buds.

(2) Trees and shrubs which *blossom early,* in the spring, ordinarily should be pruned immediately after they flower; while those which bloom in summer or autumn, on shoots of the current season's growth, can be pruned in the spring.

(3) In general, the aim of the pruner should be to maintain the natural habit of growth of the tree or shrub. Sometimes, however, when plants of definite outline are required (as, for instance, privet hedges, or shrubs or small evergreens used as accent points in a formal garden), "shearing" or light surface pruning is practiced. This alters and controls the plant's habit of growth.

(4) Pruning, limited to *pinching out the tips* of the growing shoots, (called "pinching back") stimulates branching and develops a plant of compact habit. Chrysanthemums are commonly thus treated. The same principle is sometimes followed with woody plants, with the same purpose in view.

(5) In pruning, *no stubs should be left* which will die and decay. The cuts should be made close to the supporting branch or trunk, or just above a bud—preferably one which is pointed in the direction it is wished to have the bush or tree develop.

(6) Wounds more than an inch or so in diameter should always be painted with a protective covering to keep out moisture and spores of disease organisms.

Pruning is a complex subject full of interest and worthy of the thoughtful study of all gardeners.

Winter Protection. Gardeners everywhere commonly grow plants which are not able to survive the winter without help. In some cases this requires that the plants should be dug up and stored in a frost-free place, such as a greenhouse, cellar, or cold frame. Often sufficient protection is afforded merely by placing a mulch of insulating material on the soil over the roots. Sometimes the tops have to be covered to protect them from the effects of drying winds and winter sunshine. There are also anti-desiccants available that are sprayed on the plants one or more times through the winter to prevent excessive loss of moisture through the leaves.

Plant Supports. Some of the most useful decorative plants have twining or climbing habits. To be effectively displayed, such plants usually have to be provided with supports. These may be walls, fences, pergolas, arches, trellises, or poles stuck in the ground.

There are other plants which are not climbers but which, under garden conditions, have weak stems likely to be toppled over as a result of heavy rains or strong winds. These can be held upright by staking and tying, or by pushing twigs in between and around the clump before the plants have attained their full height.

Plant Enemies. In addition to all these operations, plants have to be protected from the various insect pests and plant diseases to which they are subject. In keeping the garden free from pests, sanitation must be practiced, plus close observation to note any departure from the normal so that remedial measures (fully discussed in Section 13) can be put into effect before much damage has been done. The wise gardener also tries to avoid growing plants known to be particularly prone to insects and diseases. Such information may have to be learned the hard way by first growing a plant and then having the fortitude to discard it if the maintenance time is beyond what one cares to provide.

—Montague Free and
Margaret C. Ohlander

Q & A *Problems of Environment*

CITY CONDITIONS

What are the best varieties of annual flowers for a small, sunny, city back-yard garden? Sweet-alyssum, China-aster, balsam, calliopsis, candytuft, celosia, cynoglossum, dianthus, impatiens, lobelia, dwarf marigold, annual phlox, portulaca, salvia, verbena, dwarf zinnia, and four-o'clock.

Which annuals would you advise for a very small half-shaded city garden? Balsam, begonia, calliopsis, campanula, celosia, cleome, impatiens, lobelia, nicotiana, petunia, torenia, vinca, viola.

Which annuals and potted plants stand shade in a city garden? Very few. Impatiens, lobelia, nicotiana, and torenia thrive in partial shade. Begonia, fuchsia, and lantana are good. Potted plants include begonia, caladium, calla, fuchsia, balsam.

How can I grow sweet peas? As a rule, they do not succeed in or around New York. Sweet peas should be planted either in late fall or *very* early spring (mid-March if possible) in full sun. They need cool weather to come to perfection. Soil is prepared 18 ins. deep, rotted or dehydrated manure or enriched compost being mixed in. Seeds are planted 2 ins. deep in a 4-in. furrow. As plants grow, trench is filled in and supports are provided for vines to climb on—twiggy branches, chicken wire, or stakes. There are also low-growing varieties that do not require support.

Which are the best varieties of perennial flowers for a small city back-yard garden? Ajuga, *Alyssum (Aurinia) saxatile, Anchusa myosotidiflora,* aquilegia, artemisia 'Silver King', astilbe, hardy aster, campanula, chrysanthemum (hardy), coreopsis, day-lily, *Dianthus barbatus,* bleedingheart (both tall and dwarf), *Eupatorium coelestinum,* gaillardia, heuchera, hosta (plantain-lily), tall bearded iris, lily-of-the-valley, mertensia, *Phlox divaricata,* platycodon, plumbago, sedum, and sempervivum in variety, tradescantia, viola.

Are there any other bulbs which furnish bloom in a city garden besides daffodils and other spring bulbs? Calla, caladium (colored leaves), tuberose for very late bloom, lilies that are listed as easy of culture and tolerant of partial shade, gladiolus for sunny, well-drained situations, and small-flowered dahlia.

How can we grow evergreen trees successfully in New York City? Select only ones that are known to be smoke- and pollution-resistant. Give them good soil, occasional fertilizer, plenty of water, and protect them from dogs. The trick is to select resistant species such as: Austrian pine, *Pinus nigra;* Japanese black pine, *P. thunbergii;* and American holly. But don't be too disappointed if they fail. None will survive in closed-in shaded places, except, possibly, Japanese yew.

Which broadleaf evergreens are suitable for a shady city garden? Andromeda, azalea, *Ilex crenata,* kalmia, leucothoe, mahonia, rhododendron, wintercreeper, abelia, pyracantha (the last two, semi-evergreen), and varieties of yew.

How shall I care for evergreens in the city? Soil should be prepared to a depth of 18 to 24 ins., incorporating peat moss and dehydrated manure. Transplant only in early fall or spring. Never allow roots to dry out, and wash foliage frequently with fine but strong spray from hose. Broadleaf evergreens require acid soil.

We don't want a paved area in our city garden, and it is too shady for a lawn. What ground covers are best? English ivy, suitable for formal as well as informal gardens; and vinca (common periwinkle) which has blue flowers in the spring. A pleasing effect is achieved with ajuga, either green or bronze-leaved, which has blue flowers in spring, good foliage all season, and is very hardy.

How can I have a good lawn in the city? Difficult unless garden gets at least 6 hours of direct sunshine. Soil should be rich and deep (at least 8 ins.) with good drainage. Prepare soil and sow a good grade of lawn seed in early September. If sod is available, it will make the quickest lawn.

What can I plant in a shady city rock garden? If you furnish proper soil, rich in leafmold, you can have an attractive planting of ferns, small-leaved ivies, and native woodland wildflowers, with small bulbs—such as chionodoxa, snowdrop, Siberian squill and crocus—for spring bloom.

Can roses be successfully grown in a city garden? Yes, providing there is abundant sunshine, deep, rich soil, and the garden is outside of congested metropolitan areas. Roses can also be grown in deep containers and planters.

What deciduous shrubs tolerate shade in a city garden? Aralia; calycanthus (sweet-shrub); deutzia; *Euonymus alatus;* rose-of-Sharon; hydrangea; kerria; privet; clethra (sweet-pepper bush); rhodotypos (jet-bead); stephanandra; viburnum in variety.

Can you recommend any distinctive shrubs for a city garden? We don't want only privet and forsythia! If your soil is good, the following will succeed: *Abelia grandiflora; Acanthopanax sieboldianus; Berberis julianae; Euonymus alatus,* brilliant red foliage in fall; *Pyracantha coccinea* (firethorn)—transplant only when young, preferably potted; stephanandra; tamarix.

Which small ornamental and flowering trees can you recommend for a city garden? *Aralia spinosa* (devils-walking-stick); flowering crab, peach, plum, Japanese cherry; flowering dogwood (only for more open situations and good, deep soil); hawthorn; honey locust; *Magnolia soulangiana* and *M. stellata;* Russian-olive; umbrella catalpa; weeping mulberry.

Would a pink hawthorn or a mountain-ash grow in a city garden? Hawthorns do very well, but mountain-ash is completely intolerant of urban conditions.

What good-sized trees stand city life? We don't want ailanthus. Catalpa, ginkgo, London plane, *Magnolia soulangiana,* Norway maple, paper mulberry, pin oak, willow oak, and willow.

We cannot build new fences for our city garden and would like vines which would cover the old ones within a year or so. What can you recommend? Fastest-growing and most tolerant perennial vines are fleece-flower (*Polygonum aubertii*); Hall's honeysuckle; kudzu vine (dies to the ground in winter but grows rapidly every summer); Virginia-creeper for shade particularly. Hyacinth bean, or morning-glories, if annuals are preferred.

Which is the fastest-growing vine to cover an old brick wall in city? Either Virginia-creeper or Boston-ivy.

It is difficult to maintain humus supply in our city garden because everything has to be carried through the house. Could I grow "green" manure? Yes. Plant winter rye seed in late September in bare places, and dig under in spring. You can also make compost from kitchen wastes in large plastic bags. (See Soils, Section 1.)

What locations and conditions in an average city house are suitable for starting seeds in flats? South or southeast window, with sunshine available for the major part of the day; fresh air without direct drafts or chilling; even temperature not exceeding 65° F. during daytime, 10° lower at night; humidity, provided by syringing, pans of water, or humidifiers; freedom from cooking or heating gas fumes. Fluorescent lights can be used when window light is insufficient.

How can we keep dogs away from plants? If the dogs belong to you, fence off a small exercise yard for them; it is an aid in training the dogs. If they do not, low wire fencing or special curved wire guards can be placed around shrubs or borders. Spraying individual plants with a solution of 40 per cent nicotine sulfate, 2 teaspoons to 1 gal. of water, is sometimes effective; as are proprietary preparations sold by garden supply dealers. Spraying must be renewed at intervals. There is also a specially treated rope that repels dogs and can be used to encircle shrubs and garden beds.

Foundation Material

What are some good, low-priced materials for foundation planting under adverse conditions? Coral-berry, five-leaved aralia, gray dogwood, jet-bead, physocarpus, privet.

Will you give suggestions as to medium-height foundation planting, without using evergreens? *Cotoneaster apiculata,* five-leaved aralia, flowering quince, Persian lilac, *Deutzia gracilis, Stephanandra incisa* 'Crispa', Mentor barberry, *Euonymus alatus* 'Compactus'.

Will you name several hardy foundation plantings which will not take up much width in the bed and will not look too dilapidated in winter? Low shrubs, in general, tend to spread horizontally. The following are narrow or compact. *Deciduous shrubs:* 'Anthony Waterer' spirea, *Berberis thunbergii* 'Erecta', dwarf privet, *Physocarpus monogynus. Evergreens:* red-cedar varieties, Chinese column juniper (both narrow, tall-growing), 'Hatfield' and 'Brown's' yews, spiny Greek juniper.

What is a good evergreen or deciduous shrub to use for foundation concealment—one that will not grow more than 2 or 3 ft. high and will not be too bushy? Most dwarf shrubs tend to be broader than tall. The following are slow-growing and can easily be kept at 3 ft. by careful pruning: *Berberis thunbergii* 'Erecta', *Picea glauca* 'Conica'; *Taxus canadensis* 'Stricta', and *Taxus media* 'Hatfieldii' (yews); *Thuja occidentalis* 'Rosenthali'.

What would be a good thing to plant between two windows to fill blank wall on south side of house in full sun? There is only 4 ft. from house to lot line and ground is sandy, from excavating cellar. Most plants die from heat. The house is Cape Cod style. *Juniperus chinensis* 'Columnaris', or *Juniperus virginiana* 'Cannaertii'. Remove the poor soil, and replace with good, light, loamy soil enriched with about ⅕ part of leafmold.

Which shrubs would be best to plant along a house that has a high foundation? These shrubs average around 4 or 5 ft. in height: coral-berry, *Cotoneaster apiculata,* fragrant sumac, mapleleaf viburnum, *Physocarpus intermedius,* hydrangea, sweet-pepper bush; Vanhoutte spirea.

What is a suitable planting on west side of house along foundation, space about 6 ft. from house to driveway? Deciduous materials: *Cotoneaster apiculata,* flowering quince, *Physocarpus monogynus,* rose-of-Sharon, rugosa rose, slender deutzia. Evergreen kinds: dwarf hemlock varieties, spiny Greek juniper, *Taxus cuspidata* 'Nana' (if kept pruned), also *Taxus media* 'Brownii', 'Hatfieldii', or 'Hicksii' (yews).

Which is best evergreen for a corner? Want a tall one that is graceful and smooth and not too spreading, for yard is small. (D.C.) Arborvitae, Chinese column juniper, red-cedar varieties.

What would be suitable foundation plantings for an old (1792) farmhouse in southern New England that is in excellent condition? Very few plants are necessary, especially if the architecture of the house is as good as it sounds. In the second place, when these houses were built, little if any foundation material was used. Sometimes a dooryard garden, enclosed by a picket fence, was planted, but usually not at the front entrance. You might consider: boxwood (Korean box is hardier than common boxwood) or Japanese holly at each side of the front door; a lilac at a corner of the house and nothing else but a low ground cover, such as vinca, in a border along the rest of the foundation. Such a simple planting would also be suitable for a modern house built along colonial lines.

What can be done with 3 ft. of space under eaves which does not get any natural moisture in summer? This space is always barren, and nothing seems to grow even though watered with the hose. Such a spot should be watered with unfailing regularity. Occasional neglect may be ruinous. Improve soil by working in leafmold or peat moss. If this is done, try *Symphoricarpos chenaultii, Berberis thunbergii* 'Erecta' (truehedge columnberry), spirea 'Anthony Waterer'. These will grow about 3 to 4 ft. high.

How can one grow shrubbery about the house that has eaves projecting 3 ft., without excessive watering? A 6-in. layer of rich compost or leafmold and peat moss at the base of roots and a generous amount of it mixed in planting soil would limit artificial watering. There are available plastic or canvas soaker hoses that can be run the length of the shrub planting and left in place all summer. To water, all one does is attach a regular hose at the end of soaker hose (or attach at faucet if possible), and allow water to run for a few hours at a time when needed.

Does close foundation planting (3 ft. away) affect walls of house in any way—possibly causing dampness on inside walls? Probably not. While the planting keeps sun and air from the walls, it also sheds rain and the roots absorb much water.

FOUNDATION MATERIAL FOR SHADE

Which plants would bloom in a location next to a garage wall where very little sun reaches the ground except in late afternoon? Bugbane, columbine, coral-bells, meadowrue, monkshood, hosta. These are all perennials. Among annuals, impatiens would be the most reliable bloomer under your conditions.

What would give me profusion of color, or at least green, on a narrow strip (about 10 ins. wide) on driveway and against the house? Strip is on the north side and therefore sunless. Ferns, goutweed (*Aegopodium podagraria* 'Variegatum'), Japanese spurge (*Pachysandra*), *Vinca minor* lily-of-the-valley, plantain-lilies, and other hosta.

What are good perennials for the shady north side of the house? It is at the front, and there is a space approximately 3 × 14 ft. between the house and the walk around the house. Astilbe in variety, balloon-flower, columbine, coral-bells, day-lily, *Eupatorium coelestinum*, plantain-lily (hosta), *Anemone japonica*.

What can I plant in shade of building under oaks, on a sandy ridge? Nothing worth trying, unless you prepare the ground thoroughly, mixing in abundant humus, leafmold, and some very old or dehydrated manure. Having prepared an acid mixture of this sort, try rhododendrons, mountain-laurel, and *Skimmia japonica*.

Can azaleas and rhododendrons be used in foundation plantings about the house? Yes, if you choose from among the small-leaved rhododendrons that remain within bounds and don't grow and spread too much. Although highly touted for the purpose, the majority of rhododendrons are not suitable for plantings near the house, as they simply grow too large. A secondary problem is that if the foundation of the house contains cement, and it usually does, rain falling against this washes a certain amount of lime into the soil in which the rhododendrons are growing, frequently causing it to become too alkaline.

Can I safely put in a foundation planting of evergreen trees where the outer branches of the street maples reach? Probably only the native yew would thrive. The Japanese yew might survive, but would not thrive. Both the shade overhead and the roots below would trouble evergreen trees.

The planting north of my house looks spindly. Which evergreens can I use to replace it? In soil well prepared with leafmold and rotted or dehydrated manure try *Taxus canadensis* and its variety 'Stricta'. In the somewhat more sunny ends, hemlock, especially its dwarf varieties, and Japanese yew. In an acid, humusy soil try *Rhododendron maximum*. At the more sunny ends: *Rhododendron carolinianum*, mountain-laurel, and *Pieris floribunda*. All of these are evergreen shrubs.

Which plants for foundation plantings are best suited for northern New England? Especially for shady north side of house? Evergreens would be best, especially the broad-leaved types, such as mountain-laurel and mountain andromeda. Because of shade only a small amount of flowers could be expected from any plants. Yews would be better.

Can you advise if there is any flowering shrub which will grow in a totally shady place in the front of the house—north side? (New York.) Few, if any, shrubs will bloom satisfactorily in complete shade. *Rhododendron maximum,* mountain-laurel, and jet-bead (*Rhodotypos scandens*) are worth trying. Among the best foliage shrubs for north exposures, totally shaded by the house (not over-hung by trees), are *Euonymus fortunei* 'Sarcoxie' and *Skimmia japonica.*

What can be planted, to grow successfully, on the north side of the house? The ground is covered with fine green moss. Prepare the ground deeply, mixing in a liberal supply of leafmold and rotted or dehydrated manure. Then you may safely try *Euonymus kiautschovicus, Symphoricarpos orbiculatus, S. albus laevigatus,* honeysuckle (*lonicera*) various kinds. If you will prepare an acid soil, such a situation may do well for rhododendrons, mountain-laurel, azalea, pieris, *Skimmia japonica.*

Which shrubbery is best for foundation planting in a very shaded spot facing west? Deciduous shrubs: *Symphoricarpos chenaultii, Rhodotypos scandens, Physocarpus monogynus, Lonicera morrowii.* Evergreen shrubs (for acid soil): *Mahonia aquifolium, Pieris floribunda, P. japonica,* mountain-laurel, and skimmia.

Which inexpensive ground and foundation plants can be used to fill in north-side foundation? Low to medium-height shrubs: *Skimmia japonica, Viburnum wrightii, Berberis triacanthophora* and *B. verruculosa, Mahonia aquifolium, Symphoricarpos orbiculatus.* Taller shrubs: *Lonicera tatarica, L. morrowii,* regel privet. Ground covers: *Pachysandra terminalis, Vinca minor.*

Which shrub can be used beside a house for sort of a hedge, to grow 5 ft. high? Not much sun hits spot, and not too good a soil. I don't want barberries. Amur river privet, five-leaved aralia, gray dogwood, Siberian pea-tree.

Ground Covers

Is it harmful for ground-ivy to grow over ground where flowers (perennials and annuals) grow? If the other plants are small, the ground-ivy (*Nepeta hederacea*) may smother them.

What ground cover flowering plants are suitable for a steep bank with northeast exposure? *Ajuga reptans,* Japanese honeysuckle, moneywort (*Lysimachia nummularia*), *Vinca minor,* English ivy.

What can I use for ground cover between sidewalk and curb, on a 2-ft. bank, 3½ ft. wide, with some shade? *Vinca minor,* 'Bowles Variety'.

We have a small, steep terrace shaded by trees. It is next to impossible to grow grass on it. Last year I planted ivy (Hedera helix 'Gracilis'), which seemed to grow only fairly well. Was our selection wise? *Hedera helix* 'Gracilis' is a well-recommended plant for dry banks and will probably do much better when it has become established. Try giving it a mulch of leafmold or well-rotted cow manure this winter.

What is the best coverage to plant where there is full sun, on a hill? Grass and weeds make it hard to cut. Honeysuckles are good, so are trailing roses. Ask your local nurseryman to supply you with suitable kinds for your region.

What is the most beautiful flowering ground cover for regal lilies in a perennial border? *Myosotis sylvatica* (forget-me-not) should please you.

Which evergreen euonymus vine would grow well as a ground cover? Purple-leaf euonymus (*E. fortunei* 'Coloratus').

What is a good ground cover to plant along house wall between two houses, space about 4 ft. wide running north and south, with steppingstone path in center? Strip gets rain but not dew. Would like something deep-rooted, short, and not viny. *Arenaria montana* (mountain sandwort), *Arenaria verna caespitosa* (moss sandwort). Both of these are very low, tufted-growing grass substitutes; they are the best plants available for planting between flagstones in a walk.

Which ground cover do you suggest to border a stream? Moneywort (*Lysimachia nummularia*) which is also known as creeping Jenny or creeping Charlie—(take your choice!), is an excellent semievergreen ground cover which might be used near the stream.

What is a good ground cover for my tulips? Pansies may be used to advantage to flower with the tulips, also forget-me-nots, especially to underplant yellow tulips. To follow these, petunias would give a good display until frost.

Will it be harmful to bulbs left in the ground if they are over-planted with annuals for summer bloom? Not if the bulbs are planted at the proper depth and the soil is enriched annually. Any kind can be used—from sweet-alyssum to zinnia—that will conform to the situation.

Is it practical to plant seeds of annuals over spring bulbs in the fall? Yes.

What is the best way to start annuals for planting in a bulb bed? Those kinds which give best results from an early start, such as ageratum, petunia, snapdragon, torenia, and verbena, can be started under glass in March and set out between the bulbs in late May. Marigold and zinnia may be transplanted at this time; or they can be sown where they are to flower, especially if a late display is most desirable. These kinds are best sown in place: sweet-alyssum, Californnia-poppy, candytuft, coreopsis, *Gilia capitata,* nigella, portu-laca, annual baby's-breath.

I have a triangular bed of tulips in the front lawn. What fairly low-growing plants can I place between the tulips after the foliage dies down? The bed is partially shaded in the morning. For color and profusion of bloom nothing will outdo petunia for the purpose, par-ticularly those of the bedding type. Other good dwarfs are ageratum, sweet-alyssum, portulaca, verbena, marigold and zinnia (in dwarf varieties).

GROUND COVERS FOR SHADE

What can I do to get grass to grow under oak trees? If trees are low-headed and dense, remove lower branches and thin top to admit more light and air. Better, perhaps, use a shade-enduring ground cover, such as ferns, pachysandra, ivy, ajuga, or gill-over-the-ground.

Grass will not grow on a terrace which is quite shady. What is the best ground cover for such a location? The terrace is about a 45° slope. Japanese pachysandra, English ivy, Hall's honeysuckle, *Ajuga reptans,* ferns, *Vinca minor, Pachistima canbyi.*

We have just planted a flowering cherry tree in our back lawn. Will you tell us what to grow around the tree? Something that blooms early spring to late fall and spreads around to cover the earth under tree. Only annuals would give you flowers from summer into au-tumn; petunias, for instance. For a permanent ground cover, try the evergreen periwinkle or Japanese spurge. The former has blue flowers in the spring; the latter no appreciable flower at all.

Which ground cover might be used under large elm trees? *Ajuga reptans,* Canada yew, English ivy, *Euonymus fortunei,* ferns, yellowroot, (*Xanthorhiza apiifolia*). Best of all, *Pachysandra terminalis,* the Japanese spurge.

What would be a good ground cover under large plantings of 3-year-old lilacs? *Veronica prostrata,* lily-of-the-valley; *Phlox divaricata,* and *P. stolonifera, Ajuga reptans.*

What will really grow under maple trees as a substitute for grass? *Pachysandra terminalis* is the court of last resort, especially under Norway maples. If this will not grow, nothing will; you might as well save time and money and stop further experimentation. Maples cast dense shade and their roots are very near the surface. Use a pebble mulch.

Is there a low-growing or creeping plant that would form a carpet for a shady pine grove in southern Vermont? The pines are young and do not shed enough needles to cover the ground. Partridgeberry; blueberries—the smooth-leaf low-bush blueberry; yellow-root (easily propagated by root division). As the pines increase in size they can be expected to kill everything beneath them.

How can I plant English ivy from cuttings for low cover under tree? Suggest rooting the cuttings first in propagating frame, then prepare soil well with leafmold, rotted or dehydrated manure. Plant rooted cuttings 6 to 8 ins. apart in early spring and keep watered until established.

Is Japanese spurge (pachysandra) better than creeping myrtle for a ground cover in the shade? Yes.

What fertilizer or special care is needed to maintain healthy pachysandra plants? Pachysandra prefers partial shade. Dig soil 8 ins. to 1 ft. and incorporate manure, compost, or leafmold before planting. If foliage of established plantation is not deep green, spread a ¼-in. layer of dehydrated manure on the surface of the soil in the fall.

Does pachysandra grow better in acid or alkaline soil? It is reasonably tolerant. If the soil is quite acid, plant pachysandra; if alkaline, use English ivy.

Sandy Soil

Which annuals grow best in very light, sandy soil? Sweet-alyssum (*Lobularia maritima*), arctotis, calendula, California-poppy, castorbean, geranium, lantana (a tender shrub treated as annual), marigold, nasturtium, petunia, *Phlox drummondii,* portulaca, *Cleome spinosa,* statice, verbena, zinnia, *Sanvitalia procumbens.*

Which hardy flowers grow best in sandy loam soil? *Penstemon barbatus,* butterfly-weed (*Asclepias tuberosa*), *Nepeta faassenii,* false-indigo, *Anthemis tinctoria, Phlox subulata, Achillea ptarmica* 'The Pearl'.

Which perennials grow best in very light, sandy soil? Achillea; *Anchusa italica; Arabis albida; Arenaria montana;* armeria in var.; *Artemisia abrotanum* (old-man); *A. stelleriana* (old-woman); *Cerastium tomentosum; Dianthus deltoides;* globe-thistle; lupine; *Nepeta faassenii;* Oriental poppy; balloon-flower; *Salvia azurea; Santolina chamaecyparissus;* sedums; yucca.

Which shrubs and trees are suitable for a sandy soil in a sunny location? With proper, ordinary care in planting and after care until established, the following commend themselves: Medium to tall shrubs—*Elaeagnus umbellatus;* hydrangea (various); hypericum; *Hippophae rhamnoides* (sea-buckthorn); *Lespedeza thunbergii;* bayberry; *Rosa rugosa; R. setigera; Robinia hispida* (rose-acacia); *Vitex agnuscastus;* tamarix. Tall-growing—Siberian pea-tree; Russian-olive; golden-rain-tree (*Koelreuteria*).

Which edging plants, preferably flowering kinds, will do well in dry, sandy soil? Several kinds of statice (armeria); *Sedum hybridum, S. ellacombianum,* and *S. spurium;* 'Silver Mound' artemisia.

Seashore

Which annuals are suitable for planting near the ocean? Sweet-alyssum (*Lobularia maritima*); California-poppy; geranium; lantana (tender shrub treated as annual); petunia; *Phlox drummondii;* portulaca; nasturtium; *Cleome spinosa;* verbena. If sufficient depth of topsoil (6 to 8 ins.) is provided, and sufficient water in dry periods, practically all annuals that grow successfully inland, provided the low-growing types are selected, if the garden is not protected from wind.

Which perennials endure salt spray and high winds? Tall-growing kinds will require staking in windy places. Among perennials able to withstand salt spray and shore conditions are Carpathian bellflower (*Campanula carpatica*); *Allium schoenoprasum;* day-lily; echinops; *Erigeron speciosus;* eryngium (sea-holly); gaillardia; bearded iris; coral-bells; perennial flax; asters; pinks; rudbeckia; sedums; *Silene maritima*; statice (armeria)—several kinds; veronica; *Yucca filamentosa,* goldenrod.

Are there any shrubs which will grow near the shore exposed to salt-laden air? Yes, but immature leaves are damaged by salt-laden fogs in spring and late spring. This applies to native shrubs also. The following are good: arrow-wood, bayberry, beach plum, chokeberry, coral-berry, groundsel-bush, highbush blueberry, inkberry (*Ilex glabra*), Japanese barberry, *Rosa rugosa* and *R. humilis,* and *R. lucida,* Russian-olive, sea-buckthorn, shadbush, sumac, winterberry, and tamarisk in several varieties.

Which trees are most suitable for seashore planting? Birch; blackjack oak (*Quercus marilandica*), but does not transplant well; Chinese elm does fairly well; hawthorn; pepperidge (*Nyssa sylvatica*), but does not transplant well; red maple; sassafras; white poplar; white willow; mulberry; shadblow; red-cedar.

Which evergreen trees resist salt air? American holly, best broadleaved evergreen; Austrian pine; Japanese black pine—best; red-cedar especially good.

Which evergreens will grow best near salt water with danger of water occasionally reaching roots? (Massachusetts.) No evergreen tree hardy in Massachusetts will *thrive* where salt water reaches the roots occasionally. Red-cedar and Japanese black pine are best bets among tall evergreens, the shore juniper (*Juniperus conferta*) among low-growing evergreens.

Will you suggest protective planting for sloping shore bank, about 18 ft., which is inclined to wash, due to wind, rain, high water?

(Chesapeake Bay area.) Toe of slope *must* first be stabilized with retaining wall of timber, boulders, or concrete. Abutting properties, if similarly subject to attack, should also receive attention. Study the vegetation of similar situations and plant that material closely on your own bank. Beach-grass, bearberry, elaeagnus, goldenrod, poverty-grass, sand blackberry, sumac, Virginia-creeper, wild grape (fox or frost grape), and wild roses are good, especially *Rosa rugosa*.

Which fertilizers are best for sandy seashore gardens? Seashore soils usually are benefited by heavy applications of humus (rotted leaves, seaweed, peat moss, grass, or other vegetation) and well-rotted barnyard manure. This is largely to improve their physical condition. Moderate applications of commercial fertilizer will help build up the nutrient content of the soil. Applications should be small but frequent.

Slopes and Banks

(*See also Ground Covers*)

I have a steep bank at the end of my lawn to the street. Can you advise the best plants to keep the soil from washing away? Cover it with plants that make a dense mat, or tangle of growth: Japanese barberry, Japanese honeysuckle (especially in shade), *Juniperus horizontalis,* matrimony-vine, *Rosa wichuraiana,* yellow-root (especially in shade). If low-growing plants are desired, Japanese spurge, or trailing myrtle.

What would you suggest to plant on a bank, across the front of our yard, about 4 ft. high off the highway and about 375 ft. long? Akebia, English ivy, Japanese honeysuckle, Japanese spurge (if shaded), memorial rose (*R. wichuraiana*), *Vinca minor,* or crown vetch.

What can I plant on a sunny south slope now covered with tufted grass? Coral-berry, five-leaved aralia, fragrant sumac, gray dogwood, jet-bead, rose-acacia, Scotch broom, crown vetch.

What can I plant on a dry, sunny slope (southern exposure, formal

surroundings) on which it is impossible to grow any grass?   Japanese barberry, box barberry, Chenault coral-berry, Tibet honeysuckle.

What can best be planted on a sandy slope that will cover well, look nice, and keep sand from blowing?   *Arenaria montana, Cerastium tomentosum, Dianthus deltoides* and *D. plumarius* (cottage pink). Mix equal parts of seed of domestic rye grass and chewings's fescue grass, and add 1 part of the seed to 10 parts of soil by bulk, and broadcast this. If your home is near the seashore, dig up roots of wild perennials, mostly weeds and grasses, that are growing above high-water mark, divide them, and plant them on your property; surround the plants with a little soil when setting them.

What are good shrubs for south slope of a gravel hill, soil loose and sandy?   Try barberry, beach plum, Scotch broom, crown vetch.

What can be used for fast coverage of a steep bank, heavy clay soil? We now have barberries, but after 2 years they are not covering very quickly, and deep gorges are being cut in the bank.   Suggest keeping barberries in but also plant clumps of Hall's honeysuckle, or bittersweet. Fill gullies with brush to catch and hold soil. Mulch slope with coarse compost or straw, to check washing.

Which flowering plants can be planted on a sandy, rocky bank?   *Phlox subulata, Gypsophila repens,* and day-lilies are suitable perennials; use a good half pailful of soil in each planting hole. Buy seed of single mixed portulaca, mix it with screened soil (1 part of seed to 10 parts of soil); broadcast the mixture.

Shade

(*See also Foundation Material in this Section and Section 2.*)

In a shaded location, which flowers will bloom in each month of the season?   The month of bloom may vary with the degree of shade and the geographical location, but one can depend upon the following plants to flower in the broader seasonal divisions of spring, summer, and fall. *Spring:* barrenwort (epimedium); bleedingheart, *Ajuga reptans, Pulmonaria saccharata,* spring bulbs (chionodoxa, muscari, scilla, etc.), *Mertensia virginica. Summer:* day-lily, foxglove, fringed bleedingheart (*Dicentra eximia*), monkshood, plantain-lily and other hosta. *Fall: Aconitum autumnale, Eupatorium coelestinum,* and *E. urticaefolium, Anemone japonica.*

Which low-growing flowering plants thrive best in shade? Epimedium in variety, *Ajuga genevensis* and *A. reptans, Dicentra eximia, Iris cristata,* lily-of-the-valley, *Pulmonaria saccharata, Lysimachia nummularia, Vinca minor,* primrose.

Which flowering plants will grow well in an area that receives only about 2 or 3 hours of strong sun daily? Iris, phlox, anemone, digitalis, coreopsis, day-lily, veronica, bleedingheart, primrose, hosta.

Due to many trees adjacent to the entire length of south side of yard, my garden stretch is damp and shady all day. What type of planting would you suggest? Arrow-wood, *Monarda didyma,* five-leaf aralia, cornelian-cherry (*Cornus mas*); mountain-laurel, plantain-lily, spice-bush (*Lindera benzoin*).

What low-growing plants can I grow to cover a small space under a cluster of oak trees? Unless utterly shaded: barrenwort (epimedium), fringed bleedingheart. If only lightly shaded: *Iris cristata* and *I. gracilipes.* Or little evergreen shrubs, in not-too-heavy shade, in acid, humus soil: *Rhododendron indicum, R. balsaminaeflorum, R. carolinianum.*

Have had no success with shade-loving plants put near trees. Have enriched the soil but trees take all moisture. Would a mulch be of use? I can use grass clippings, rotted grain straw. A garden hose is not available. If your trees are maples or elms, your problem is a difficult one. Try *Pachysandra terminalis,* Japanese spurge, planting it in the spring while the ground is moist—after first spading and raking the ground—then apply a mulch as well. This plant will often succeed where nothing else will.

Which flowers grow the best in tubs on a terrace that is shaded very heavily from a tree that is in the center? You will have to bring into bloom elsewhere, and use for temporary effects on the shaded terrace, any flowering plant that lends itself to pot culture; such as hydrangea varieties, lantana, geraniums, calla, caladiums (for colored foliage).

I have a row of Lombardy poplar trees. Can I plant flowers in front or back, or in between spaces? Yes, particularly on the sunny side: *Aquilegia canadensis, Iberis sempervirens, Digitalis purpurea,* rose 'Paul's Scarlet' climber, *Anemone japonica,* day-lilies.

What could one plant in shade of a mulberry tree? If a mere ground cover is wanted, prepare the area, working in leafmold or peat moss, compost or dehydrated manure, and plant either Japanese spurge or periwinkle; the former 6 to 9 ins. apart each way, the latter 8 to 12 ins., depending upon size of plants. If shade is not very dense, the following shrubs may, with proper preparation, be used: symphoricarpos (any), *Clethra alnifolia,* Morrow honeysuckle (about 7 ft. tall). In an acid, humus soil: *Rhododendron roseum* and *R. calendulaceum.*

Which annuals grow best in a shady location? In general annuals must have sunlight to grow satisfactorily. There are a few, however, which get along fairly well in the shade: *Begonia semperflorens,* impatiens, balsam, *Torenia fournieri,* cornflower, flowering tobacco (nicotiana), *Lobelia erinus, Vinca rosea,* monkey-flower (mimulus), nasturtium, pansy, tuberous-rooted begonias (which see).

West garden border of my house is shaded half the day; would you name 6 annuals that would bloom in it? *Begonia semperflorens, Torenia fournieri,* monkey-flower, petunia, impatiens, balsam.

Which are best annuals for partial shade and all-summer flowers? Balsam, flowering tobacco, lobelia, *Vinca rosea,* impatiens, petunia.

Will begonias grow and bloom outdoors in a spot that is shaded all day, but not densely so? And how should soil be prepared for them? They get along very well in partial shade. Soil must be moist but well drained. Work into it generous quantities of leafmold, rotted or dehydrated manure, or other humus material; also dressing of bone meal or superphosphate. (See also tuberous-rooted begonias.)

I have a semi-shady spot in my perennial border in which I have been able to grow only wild violets. Can you give me some suggestions? The ground in this spot is inclined to remain damp. Astilbe in variety, beebalm, bugbane, bugle (*Ajuga reptans*), buttercup, cardinal-flower, ferns, great blue lobelia, plantain-lily, and other forms of hosta.

Which perennials can be grown in a dry, shady place? Bugle, *Aquilegia canadensis,* moneywort, red baneberry, white snakeroot, *Aster ericoides.*

Which perennials should I plant on terraces in the shade of im-

mense forest trees high up the hill? Day-lily in variety, ferns, fox-glove, *Anemone japonica.*

What can I plant in a damp place in the shade of a neighbor's garage? Hardy primulas are good for spring, along with lily-of-the-valley. Pachysandra and English ivy are good ground covers. Foxglove, hosta, forget-me-not, ground-ivy, and periwinkle. Tuberous-rooted begonias may be planted every spring if soil is well drained.

Which shrubs will grow in a shaded place? Andromeda (*Pieris floribunda*); arrow-wood (*Viburnum dentatum*); cornelian-cherry; five-leaf aralia; jet-bead; mountain-laurel; *Rhododendron maximum;* spice-bush (*Lindera benzoin*); *Clethra alnifolia;* yellow-root (*Xanthorhiza simplicissima*); American yew.

Which shrubs can be planted near front of house shaded by tall maple trees? If the soil is full of tree roots, very few plants will get along well; try five-leaf aralia.

What kind of shrubs will grow the best along the west side of the house in almost constant shade of large oak trees? If you will prepare a deep, humusy, acid soil, this would seem fine for rhododendrons, skimmia, mahonia, azaleas, mountain-laurel, leucothoe, and pieris.

Will shrubs do well near evergreen trees? Near—yes; not *under* them, unless the evergreens are tall conifers, such as pines, with their lower branches removed.

Sun

Which shrubs will thrive along the south side of a brick house in full sun? In deeply prepared, enriched, well-drained soil, kept sufficiently moist in summer, your choice is almost unlimited. Within the limits of permissible ultimate height and width, select from catalogues any good shrubs which require no special conditions or shade. Avoid rhododendron, evergreen azalea, and, generally, evergreen shrubs.

Which shrub would suit an open, sunny, enclosed corner atop a retaining wall? Whatever you plant, prepare the soil 18 ins. deep with leafmold, old manure, and some peat moss. See that the place does not dry out in summer. Usually, for a place like this, a shrub is best which will drape its branches somewhat over the wall. You might plant any of these: *Cotoneaster racemiflora, Lespedeza thunbergii, Rosa hugonis, Spiraea arguta* or *S. thunbergii, Forsythia suspensa* varieties.

What would you suggest as a fairly low, long-blooming flower for about 2-ft. space between brick house and sidewalk on south side of house? Dwarf marigolds would be excellent. Or dwarf zinnia, or the little blue *Torenia fournieri* (wishbone-flower).

Can you suggest an edging for a 24-in.-wide border between house and driveway. South side of house. Germander, *Teucrium chamaedrys.* This may need some pruning which can be done in the spring by thrusting a spade in the soil alongside the row to check its lateral growth, using shears to trim the top growth.

Wet Ground

Are there any flowers or flowering shrubs that like wet ground throughout the year? Perennials: cardinal-flower, loosestrife (*Lythrum salicaria*), rose-mallow. Shrubs: *Viburnum dentatum, Cephalanthus occidentalis, Aronia arbutifolia,* swamp azalea (*Rhododendron viscosum*).

The boundary line of my property is quite low and wet. I have put up a 5-ft. fence. Which vines would grow in such soil (clay)? Which shrubs or hedges could I plant there as a screen? *Vines:* porcelain-vine (*Ampelopsis brevipedunculata*); Dutchman's-pipe, bittersweet, Japanese honeysuckle. *Screen: Clethra alnifolia, Viburnum cassinoides, Ilex verticillata, Lindera benzoin, Aronia arbutifolia.*

Our lot is about 1 ft. lower than the lot next door. Consequently, after a rain water stands in this spot for some time. The space is 3 × 6 ft. I would like the names of low-growing shrubs that would not interfere with the grass. The spot receives sun all day long. Do you have any other suggestion as to what to plant on the spot? *Aronia arbutifolia,* dwarf willow (*Salix purpurea* 'Gracilis'), *Ilex* *glabra,* snowberry (*Symphoricarpos*), *Itea virginica.* Pruning may be necessary to keep them low.

What shall we plant on a space which is liable to be flooded during bad storms? Rose-mallow, Japanese iris, *Lythrum salicaria.*

How should sides of a stream be treated or built up to prevent caving in? The stream, which meanders for 210 ft., is about 1 ft. deep and 18 ins. wide; it is completely dried out in the dry season. Set some large rocks in the bank, at 10 to 15 ft. apart. Plants mentioned in preceding question should hold the bank once they are established.

Which annuals grow best in wet soil in the shade? Jewel-weed and monkey-flower.

Which perennials will thrive in wet soil? Beebalm, boneset, cardinal-flower, *Iris pseudacorus,* Japanese iris, Joe-Pye-weed, *Lythrum salicaria,* marsh-marigold, rose-mallow, starwort (*Boltonia asteroides*).

What herbaceous planting is suitable for the sides of a small stream which becomes a full storm sewer after a rainfall? *Myosotis palustris semperflorens, Lysimachia nummularia, Iris pseudacorus, Lythrum salicaria.*

Which shrubs will thrive in wet soil? Buttonbush (*Cephalanthus occidentalis*), *Aronia arbutifolia* and *A. melanocarpa,* highbush blueberry, *Lindera benzoin,* Siberian dogwood, *Clethra alnifolia, Calycanthus floridus,* swamp azalea (*R. viscosa*), winterberry (*Ilex verticillata*).

Which trees will thrive in wet soil? Pin oak, red maple, swamp white oak, sycamore, sour gum (*Nyssa sylvatica*); weeping willow, *Oxydendrum arboreum, Lindera benzoin.*

What kind of trees and shrubs shall we plant around a swimming pool? *Trees:* Red maple; sour gum (*Nyssa sylvatica*); sweet-gum (*Liquidambar styraciflua*); sycamore; weeping willow. *Shrubs: Cephalanthus occidentalis, Lindera benzoin, Clethra alnifolia.* Leaves and fruits falling in the water might be objectionable, if planting is too close to pool.

Which flowering plants will grow in a boglike spot? Japanese iris, Siberian iris, astilbe, flowering rush, marsh-marigold, cardinal-flower, *Primula japonica* and *P. pulverulenta,* trollius, *Myosotis palustris,* loosestrife, Jack-in-the-pulpit, bottle gentian.

Aspects of Culture

(For soils and fertilizers in general, see also Section 1; for individual plants, see under Trees and Shrubs, Roses, Perennials, Annuals and Biennials, this section. For plant material for special decorative effects, see also Planning and Landscaping, Section 2.)

CULTIVATION

What are the reasons for cultivating the surface soil? To kill weeds and maintain a loose surface that is readily penetrated by rain. It helps also in soil aeration in those cases where a crust forms on surface.

In cultivation, should the soil be left level or mounded around plants? Generally level cultivation is best, because it exposes less surface from which soil moisture can evaporate. When it is desirable to get rid of excess soil moisture, hilling or ridging is sometimes practiced. Corn and similar crops are mounded with soil to help them stay erect; potatoes to prevent "greening" of the tubers.

How soon after a rain should one hoe the soil? When it has dried to such an extent that it no longer sticks to the hoe in sufficient amount to impede the work.

Is it desirable to cultivate the surface every week? No. Cultivate according to circumstances rather than by the calendar. Hoe after rains to prevent the formation of a crust, and to kill weeds when the surface has dried somewhat. If no more rain falls, hoe only to kill weeds.

How deep should surface soil be cultivated? This depends on character of soil, time of year, and the root formation of the plants cultivated. Sometimes it may be desirable, in some soils, to cultivate deeply—3 to 4 ins.—early in season to dry the surface. Later shallow cultivation, 1 in. deep, is preferable to avoid injury to crop roots. Modern tendency is toward shallow cultivation.

My soil forms a crust after every rain. What shall I do? Cultivate with hoe or cultivating tool to break crust; or use a mulch of organic matter. (See Mulches.) Improve soil by adding bulky organic material—strawy manure, partly decayed leaves, sedge peat, peat moss —annually until condition is cured.

Does a dust mulch really conserve soil water?   Probably not in most soils, if the soil is stirred to a depth of more than 1 or 2 ins. Moisture in the loosened soil is quickly lost by evaporation and the dust mulch is likely to absorb all the water from light showers before it has a chance to reach the soil occupied by roots.

MULCHING See also Perennials, Trees and Shrubs, etc.

What is meant by mulching?   The application of various materials —usually organic—to the soil surface to hold moisture in soil, to prevent weed growth, and, in some cases, to help keep the ground cool.

Essential small tools for the gardener—shovel, hoe, iron rake, trowel, and spading fork.

Once a mulch has been put on, is it necessary to do anything further about it?   Not much; just keep it loose. Peat moss must be watched because it is likely to pack down after a heavy rain, forming a felted surface when dry which sheds water like a roof.

Mulches are put on to conserve water in the soil. Don't they also work in the opposite direction by absorbing rain which otherwise would reach crop roots?   Yes, to some extent. Some mulch material, however—buckwheat hulls and cranberry tops, for example—allows easy penetration of water and does not absorb a great deal. Examination of soil after rain will show whether or not mulch is too thick. Peat moss is not the best mulching material because it absorbs moisture, but when mixed with leafmold, rotted manure, compost, it can be satisfactory. Peat moss's best use is in mixing into the soil.

Mulching the flower or vegetable garden, as well as around shrubs and other plantings, helps retain soil moisture and suppress weed growth.

What can I use to mulch my perennial border? I want something not unsightly. Peat moss, leafmold, buckwheat hulls, shredded sugarcane, pine needles, coconut-fiber refuse, compost.

Of what value, if any, are grass cuttings for garden beds, and how should they be used? They are of use as a water-conserving mulch, and if incorporated with the soil after they are partly decayed they add to its humus content. They should be spread in a layer of 1 to 2 ins. thick.

Is a paper mulch practicable in a small garden? Scarcely. It is objectionable on the score of appearance, and because it is difficult to anchor it. Not all plants do well under a paper mulch. In a small garden such materials as pine bark would be much better.

What are the advantages in using mulch paper in the garden? It keeps moisture in soil; it eliminates cultivation; it keeps down weeds, but is difficult to keep in place, and will tear readily.

Is polyethylene plastic film good material to use as a mulch? It can be used, but it is difficult to apply. One has to anchor it to prevent it from blowing away; and it is also essential to make provision for the ingress of water by punching holes in it. Except that it does not tear easily it has the same defects as mulching paper.

Can polyethylene be used to mulch newly planted shrubs? Yes. In this case it can be used to advantage. Cut off a square of 3 or 4 ft., slit to a little beyond the center, put it in place and anchor it by covering each corner with soil. It is desirable to punch a few holes in the plastic film so that water can get in over the entire space.

My cottage is on a salt-water beach; is it beneficial or injurious to mulch with seaweed washed up in abundance on shores? Or could the presence of salt kill plants? Seaweed makes an excellent mulch. The amount of salt present should do no damage and it is unnecessary to wash the seaweed before use.

Since peat moss is getting so high in price, would shredded sugar-cane fiber answer the purpose of peat moss for mulching, especially around acid-loving plants such as azalea and rhododendron? Yes. It works very well.

What plants would be benefited by mulching with pine needles? Pine needles are especially good for cone-bearing evergreens and acid-soil plants such as rhododendrons, but they can be used on all plants.

How about the use of well-rotted sawdust around plants, and on lawns, as a mulch? Sawdust makes a satisfactory mulch during the summer. Do not apply deeper than 1 in. unless it is mixed with sulfate of ammonia at the rate of 1 lb. to 100 sq. ft.

The busy gardener sees that rows between vegetables are mulched with straw, marsh hay, seaweed or decaying leaves.

I mulched my kitchen garden with wood chips and sawdust. The crops did not grow at all well. The foliage looked peaked and yel-

lowish. I presume this was caused by acid soil as a result of the mulch. Is there anything I can do to counteract this? It is doubtful if this condition is caused by acid soil. More likely it is due to the depletion of nitrogen by the need for nitrates of the microorganisms which bring about the breakdown of the organic matter in the mulch. Apply sulfate of ammonia—1 lb. to 100 sq. ft.; or nitrate of soda at 1½ lbs. You should test the soil and, if it shows a reaction of less than pH 5.5, pulverized limestone should be applied—the amount is contingent upon the degree of acidity plus the character of the soil (more will be needed if it is a heavy clay). Your county agricultural agent should be consulted on this matter.

I have read somewhere that when undecayed organic materials are put in or on the soil that it is necessary to add chemical fertilizer to supply food for bacteria that cause its decay. How much and what kind? Chemical fertilizer is not absolutely necessary but it is usually more convenient to obtain. Nitrogen is the element that is most likely to be lacking; this can be provided by sulfate of ammonia at 1 lb. to 100 sq. ft., or 1½ lbs. of nitrate of soda. Phosphorus can be added by superphosphate at 5 lbs. to the same area. Organic fertilizers such as poultry manure can be used at 5 lbs. to 100 sq. ft., or sheep manure at the rate of about 10 lbs. It is important to watch the behavior of the plants and if they become yellow indicating nitrogen deficiency, use quick acting nitrogen such as nitrate of soda or sulfate of ammonia, either in liquid, or dry and watered in.

WATERING

How should one water flowers? Water in at planting time if the soil is dry. When growth is active, and soil is really dry, water before the plants suffer. Mere surface sprinkling does no good. Give enough to wet the soil 6 ins. down. Cultivate the surface as soon as dry enough to work freely.

Are there any objections to spraying or watering plants in the evening? Some authorities believe that if the foliage is wet when the temperature is falling, the plants are more susceptible to attacks by disease organisms. Under outdoor conditions this is probably not important, but in greenhouse or hotbed it is wise to spray or water early in the day.

Is it harmful to water plants when sun is shining on them? Generally speaking, no. But, theoretically, it is better to water in early morning or in evening, so that water has a chance to penetrate the soil before much is lost by evaporation.

When watering newly set annuals, should water be applied to the soil, or over all by sprinkling? If water is in limited supply, leave depression around each stem and fill with water. If ample, sprinkle whole bed, making sure water penetrates several inches.

PRUNING See also under Trees, Shrubs, Evergreens, etc.

Please give us otherwise "green-fingered" amateur gardeners the real low-down on what, to me, has always been mystifying and most vexing—the art of pruning. There simply must be some fundamentals that apply. Are there not some simple rules to follow? Read the section on pruning in the introduction to this division and the answers to the pruning questions. Then, if you are still in doubt about pruning, follow the advice which Mr. Punch gave to those about to marry —"Don't."

What is the difference between shearing and pruning? Shearing is a form of pruning in which all young shoots extending beyond a definite line are cut off. Pruning proper involves cutting individual shoots or branches with a view to improving the tree or shrub.

When is the best time to trim trees? If the purpose is to check growth, it is better to prune trees when they are actively growing. Ordinarily, however, trees are pruned when they are dormant, in the fall or late winter. This stimulates strong shoot growth.

What is meant by "dormant"? Plants are said to be dormant when they are not actively growing. In deciduous trees and shrubs it is a period between leaf fall and starting into growth the following year.

Is it all right to trim trees in the winter? Yes, provided the temperature is not too low. From the standpoint of comfort for the operator and the danger of breaking surrounding branches when they are brittle from frost, it is desirable not to prune when it is very cold. However, it is preferable to wait until late winter.

How can I avoid tearing the bark on the trunk when cutting off large limbs? Make the first cut from underneath the branch, cutting upward until the saw binds. Then cut from above, which results in the removal of the branch. The stub may now be cut off with safety by sustaining it with one hand while the few last cuts with the saw are being made.

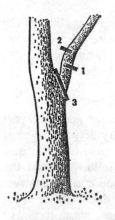

Proper way to cut off a large limb. (1) – make an "under cut" near trunk; (2) – saw off limb, leaving stub; (3) – saw off stub as close to trunk as possible.

Is there any special rule to follow when making the cuts in pruning? Yes; branches should always be cut off close to, and parallel with, the branch from which they spring. When shoots are shortened, the cut should be made just above a growth bud, pointing in the direction you wish to have the tree develop.

Should a single or double leader be developed? Generally speaking, a single leader is preferable, especially for those trees which naturally grow with a single trunk. Some trees, and all shrubs, have a diffuse habit and cannot well be restricted to a single leader.

Does pruning help make a tree bushy? Yes, if it is limited to cutting off the tips of the leading shoots. It can be done during the growing season if the tree is too vigorous.

Is it better to use hedge shears or pruning shears when trimming trees into globes, squares, etc.? If the leaves are large, as in linden, cherry-laurel, etc., it is better to use pruning shears, because the use of hedge shears results in obviously marred leaves. In the case of small-leaved trees, hedge shears can be used.

What is used to paint over wounds made in pruning? Several coatings of shellac, renewed when necessary, are excellent. Or you could use tree-wound paint, obtainable from horticultural supply houses, asphaltum paint, or white lead and linseed oil in which a little lampblack has been mixed to make it less conspicuous.

Is pruning of any help in the case of trees infested with scale insects? Yes. Branches dying as a result of attack by scale insects should be cut off. This will tend to strengthen the rest of the tree. The cut-off branches should be destroyed by burning and measures taken to kill the insects remaining.

Is pruning sometimes used as an aid in controlling plant disease? Yes; for example, canker on roses, and fire blight on trees and shrubs of the apple family. The affected limbs must be cut off well below the point of injury, and the tool used should be disinfected after every cut.

We have a young tree with the center broken off; will it grow into a tree or should we dispose of it? If there is a strong side shoot near the break, it could be trained to take the place of the broken leader. Tie a stout stake securely below the break, and let it project 2 or 3 ft. above it; then tie the side shoot to this.

How can I keep tree wounds from bleeding? Maples and birches, if pruned in spring, will bleed, but this is temporary. Another form of bleeding is caused by "slime flux," and this is often very difficult to control and may cause the bark to decay if it persists for a considerable time. Sometimes a short length of pipe is inserted to carry off the flux, or in the case of large wounds the wood is seared with a blowtorch. These practices, however, are not always effective.

What tools are necessary for pruning? For close work on trees, a narrow-bladed pruning saw is desirable. In some cases it is helpful to have one attached to a long pole to get at branches which otherwise would be difficult to reach. To cut branches ½ in. in diameter, or less, sharp pruning shears should be used, or a pruning knife. In pruning old, overgrown shrubs, long-handled "lopping" shears are useful. Small power saws, electric or gasoline, are a good investment where extensive pruning is to be done. The cut limbs can easily be cut into firewood. However, cutting large trees can be hazardous, especially if they are near buildings, so it can be more sensible to call in a tree expert.

DISBUDDING AND PINCHING

What is meant by disbudding? The removal of some flower buds while they are still small, so that those remaining will develop into flowers of larger size. Plants on which disbudding is commonly practiced include carnation, chrysanthemum, dahlia, peony, rose.

When are plants disbudded?   As soon as the buds to be removed are large enough to handle, usually about the size of a pea or bean.

How often should plants be pinched to force blooms? Should they be kept pinched as long as they bloom?   Pinching a plant delays blooming instead of forcing it, but results in a bigger, more stocky plant. Some plants, such as snapdragon, give good, bushy plants with only 1 pinching. Others, such as chrysanthemum, may be pinched 3 or 4 times until late July. A plant such as geranium, after the first pinching (soon after rooting), may be pinched just beyond each flower bud as it appears.

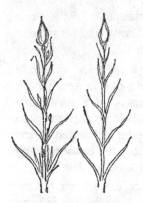

Disbudding—pinching out most of the buds in order to secure fewer but larger blooms—is often practiced with some plants, such as carnation, dahlia, chrysanthemum, and rose. Carnation at far left shows buds along stem; right shows stem after disbudding.

What plants should I pinch; and when?   These are a few examples: coleus, carnation, chrysanthemum, dahlia, fuchsia, heliotrope, iresine, salvia, and the garden geranium. One pinching, when the plants are a few inches high, may be sufficient, but in the case of coleus and chrysanthemum, pinching may be repeated more than once if extra-large plants are desired. Some woody plants are pinched back during the growing season to make them more compact.

What is meant by "terminal bud"?   The topmost bud on a shoot.

ROOT-PRUNING

What are the reasons for root-pruning?   To promote formation of fibrous roots, to induce blossoming, and to check excessive shoot and leaf growth.

How many roots should be cut off when root-pruning a tree or shrub to check growth or induce flowering? Impossible to say definitely, for each specimen is a problem in itself. Sometimes cutting the taproot is all that is necessary, and sometimes one or more horizontally spreading roots also must be cut.

What is the technique of root-pruning? If the tree or shrub is a large one, dig a trench halfway around the tree (distance from trunk depends on size of tree) and sever all thonglike roots encountered. Do the other half the following year—if necessary. Sometimes one must undermine the tree to cut the taproot.

Can I, by root-pruning ahead of time, make it possible to move some shrubs with greater safety? Yes. In the spring thrust a sharp spade into the ground to its full depth all around the shrub a few inches inside the digging circle. This will induce the formation of fibrous roots which will enable it to be easily moved the following fall or spring.

Is there any simple method of dwarfing plants? It is helpful to start off with naturally dwarf varieties. Restrict the roots by growing the plants in comparatively small containers, or by root-pruning if in the open ground. Prune the top at frequent intervals during the growing season by shortening new growth. In the case of fruit trees (which see) the use of a dwarfing understock is indicated.

SUPPORTS

What is the best method of staking perennials and annuals? The type of support varies with the subject. Those with only comparatively

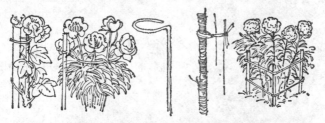

Many flowers require support, and many devices have been developed for this purpose. Detail drawing (second from right) shows proper method of securing plant stem to stake: string is first tied tight around stake; then ends are tied in a loose loop around stem.

few slender stems (delphinium, for example), should have individual slender stakes to which the stems are loosely tied. Low, bushy plants can be supported by twigs stuck in the ground around them before they have completed their growth. For others, such as peonies, wood or metal hoops, on 3 or 4 legs placed over the plants, afford the best solution.

Any pointers on staking plants?   Always maintain the natural habit of growth. Don't tie stems in a bundle and fasten to a broomstick. (See answer to preceding question.)

How can one obtain twiggy shoots for staking perennials?   Save all suitable material from shrub pruning. Keep one or more privet bushes solely for this purpose—cutting off the twigs early in the fall so that they will dry up and not grow when stuck in ground. Gray birch twigs are ideal, if available.

I want to use espaliered trees to enclose a small flower garden. How can I support them?   If in a continuous row, use galvanized wire stretched tightly on posts; or a wood fence with horizontal members. Isolated specimens are best supported on wooden trellises.

How are "espaliered" trees or shrubs supported on walls?   Sometimes by fastening directly to the wall, but this is considered undesirable where exposed to full sun in regions having hot summers. They can be fastened to wires strung on brackets 6 ins. or more from wall,

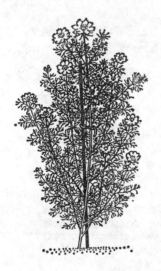

Staking an annual (cosmos). Tie is first made fast around stake and then looped loosely around stem of plant.

or on wood trellises, thus allowing circulation of air between plant and wall.

How can I attach trained shrubs directly to a wall? Use broad tape; or use cloth or leather (old gloves) cut into strips ½ in. wide, 3 to 6 ins. long, passed around branches and fastened to wall with stubby nails. Also special wall nails are obtainable from firms dealing in horticultural supplies.

I want to use vines for "accent points" in my flower garden. What is best for holding them up? Use red-cedar posts, sunk 2 to 3 ft. in the ground, or a "tepee" support.

Plant Propagation

(See also Propagation under Plant Groups.)

What are the various methods of plant propagation? Seeds, spores, bulbils, cormels, tubers, rhizomes, runners, offsets, suckers, stolons, layers, division, cuttings, grafting.

SEEDS

What are the main factors in seed germination? Quality and freshness in seed. Correct temperature, even moisture supply, and sufficient air. Some seeds must never be allowed to become really dry (usually these are stratified in a moist medium); some must be sown as soon as they are ripe; some wait a year or more before germinating; and some require an "after-ripening" period at low temperatures. However, these special treatments are necessary more often for tree and shrub seeds than for annuals, perennials, and biennials.

How can germination be hastened in hard-shell seeds? Soak in warm water overnight, or longer, to soften shell; or nick hard shell of large seeds with a sharp knife. Sometimes seeds are treated with acids, but this is not recommended for beginners.

What is meant by "stratification" of seeds? It is the term applied to the practice of storing seeds over winter, or longer, in moist material such as sand or peat moss. Seeds which lose their vitality if

RIGHT   WRONG

TRANSPLANTING SEEDLINGS

(Top left) Dig hole wide and deep enough for roots (left). (Top center) Remove only a few seedlings at a time from flat so roots don't dry out. (Top right) If soil is very dry, pour water into hole to lessen transplanting shock. (Bottom left) Use trowel to set plant in hole; water at once with transplanting solution. (Bottom center) Firm soil around plant with fingers. (Bottom right) A paper bag or other container can protect plant from wind or bright sun for a day or so.

allowed to become dry (oak, chestnut, etc.), and "2-year seeds" (hawthorn, dogwood) are commonly so treated.

Should seeds be treated with a disinfectant before planting? Yes, if trouble has been experienced in the past with seed-borne diseases.

BULBS, CORMS, AND TUBERS

What is the usual method of propagating bulbs? By digging them up when dormant and taking off small bulbs formed around the

---

STARTING SEEDS INDOORS

First moisten seed-growing medium (sphagnum moss) by adding about 1½ cups of water to about 4 cups of medium and (right) squeeze moss in bag to help it absorb water. Pour wet sphagnum moss into seed flat and (right) firm moss to make level surface for seeds.
Next open seed packet and (right) carefully sow seeds.
Cover seeds with very thin layer of moistened moss and (right) gently spray covered seeds with water.

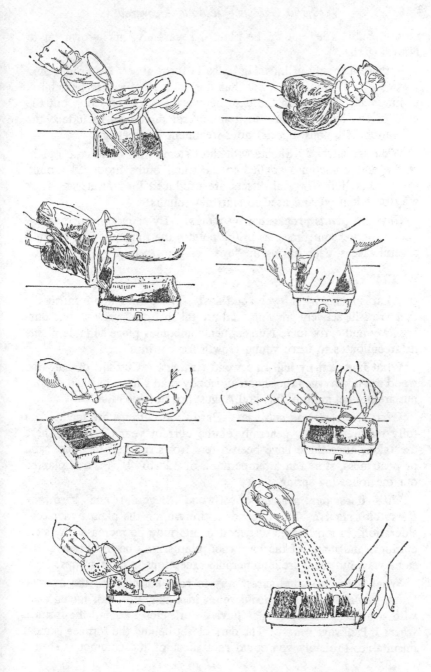

mother bulb. They should be planted separately, and grown on to flowering size.

Is there any way of inducing bulbs to form offsets for propagating purposes?   Planting shallower than normal is supposed to be helpful. Commercial growers, in the case of hyacinths, either scoop out the base of the bulb, or cut into it in several directions to induce the formation of bulbils. Special after-treatment is necessary.

What are offsets?   Shoots with short stems with a miniature plant at the end—sometimes applied to the small bulbs produced around the mother bulb. Typical offsets are produced by houseleeks. They may be taken off and used to start new plants.

How are plants propagated by tubers?   By separating or cutting, and planting. Sometimes, as in the potato, the tuber may be cut into several pieces, each having an "eye," or growth bud.

CUTTINGS

What is meant by softwood cuttings?   These are made from shoots that are still actively growing, and are taken from hardy shrubs during May and early June. Nurserymen sometimes place suitable plants in greenhouses to force young growth for cuttings.

What is meant by half-ripe wood cuttings?   Cuttings of half-ripe wood are taken when the shoots of woody plants have finished growth but are not yet mature. July and August are suitable months.

What are hardwood cuttings?   Hardwood cuttings are made from fully matured shoots, generally of the current year's growth. These are taken after there have been a few frosts, packed in moist sand or peat moss, stored in a temperature of 35° to 40° F., and planted out the following spring.

How does one propagate softwood (begonia) and hardwood (forsythia) plants?   This depends entirely upon the plant under consideration. In most cases softwood plants may be increased by stem cuttings, and many of the hardwood plants may be increased in the same way; but there are innumerable exceptions in both groups.

What is the best and surest way to root cuttings for the average home gardener? I have a cold room in cellar, no heat, facing east, with two small windows. Also have a dark closet behind the furnace where it is always warm.   The dark closet behind the furnace is most unsuitable. Probably you could root most of the commoner shrubs and house plants in the cellar room if the cuttings were placed near the window. You could also install a fluorescent light unit.

How best can one propagate plants from cuttings without greenhouse or hotbed? Many shrubs, some trees, most of the plants used for summer bedding, herbaceous perennials, many rock-garden plants, and several house plants can be propagated during the summer almost as readily in a cold frame as in a greenhouse or hotbed.

What is polyethylene? Polythene or polyethylene is the name given to a plastic film which has the properties of permitting the passage of gases and retaining water vapor.

How is polyethylene used in plant propagation? It is used in the same way as glass. Among the advantages as compared with glass are: its light weight; it usually eliminates any need for additional watering. It is also used to enclose the moist sphagnum moss when air-layering is practiced or to enclose flats of cuttings to create a moist atmosphere. The plastic is stretched over a wire frame, giving the flat the look of a flat-topped tent or miniature greenhouse.

How can I make a propagating frame? An ordinary cold frame is satisfactory; or you can use a box 10 to 12 ins. deep, covered tightly with a pane of glass. Make ½-in. drainage holes in bottom; cover with 1 in. of peat moss, and put in 4 ins. of some rooting medium (such as sand or sand and peat moss) packed down firmly. See also above for another method.

What are the essentials in using polyethylene in rooting cuttings? Thoroughly soaking the rooting medium; and completely enclosing the cuttings. When only a few cuttings are to be rooted they are put in a flower pot which is then put in a polyethylene bag and the open end is tightly closed. Or, on a slightly larger scale, a shallow wooden box (flat) can be used. In this case some kind of support is needed to keep the film from contact with the cuttings. It can be wire coat hangers. After the cuttings are inserted and have been thoroughly watered the whole is wrapped in plastic, taking care that no opening is left to permit the escape of moisture. The best way to do this is to drape the plastic over the flat and then tuck the sides and ends underneath it. The plastic can be stapled to the flat.

What is the after-treatment? The cuttings are put in a well-lighted place where they can be shaded from direct sun. In six weeks or

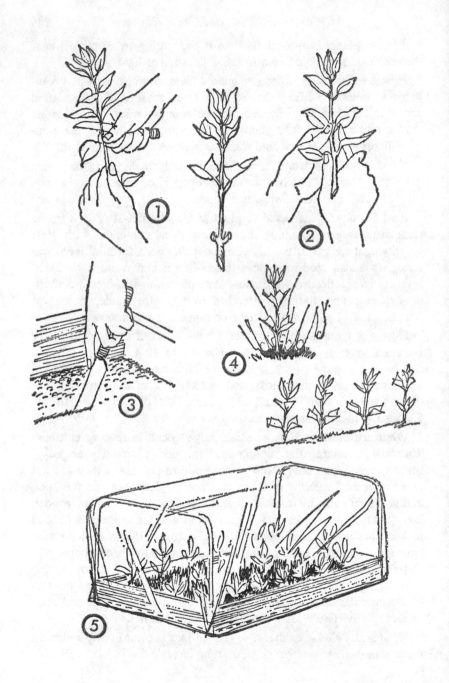

so they should be examined, and if they are rooted, gradually inure them to the outside air by loosening the cover progressively.

What is meant by the "fog box" or "constant mist" system of propagation? This is a method whereby cuttings are rooted by keeping their leaves constantly moist by subjecting them to a fine mist-like spray. Special nozzles are sold for this purpose.

I am interested in the possibilities, on a small scale, of rooting cuttings by constant mist. How does one go about it? You will need a nozzle that will deliver about 1½ gals. of water per hour, and water pressure of 30 to 50 lbs. This should be sufficient to cover an area of about one square yard. The site should be in the open in full sun; if in a windy location a windbreak may be necessary which may be of plastic fastened to a wooden frame (about 4 by 3 ft.). There must be free drainage, therefore the rooting medium should be coarse sand, and the pots or flats should be placed on a platform of galvanized hardware cloth raised an inch or two above the ground.

Is it necessary to keep the spray going all the time? No, it is not—although no great harm will accrue if it is left on night and day. It is considered desirable however to have an intermittent mist. This may be accomplished by the installation of an electronic leaf which automatically shuts off the water when it is wet and turns it on when it is dry.

What are the advantages and the drawbacks of this method of rooting cuttings by constant mist? *Pro.* It enables us to root larger cuttings than is possible by conventional means; and cuttings usually considered difficult often can be rooted with ease.

Con. On the other hand, while you may have a hundred per cent rooting, there may be great mortality when they are transplanted. The operation was successful but the patient died! Doubtless means

---

HOW TO PROPAGATE SHRUBS FROM CUTTINGS

(1 and 2) Making the cutting and trimming it, ready for planting. (3 and 4) Marking line with knife in rooting medium in flat, inserting cutting, and firming medium along row of cuttings. Water the cuttings. (5) Cuttings in flat enclosed by polyethylene. Flat must be kept out of direct sunshine. Such a propagating case rarely needs extra watering.

will be devised to overcome these defects. Many specialists now prefer the method of enclosing cuttings in plastic, as described above.

Will you please tell me something about air-layering by using plastic film? This is a method that can be used successfully outdoors on a large number of different trees and shrubs. Here is the way of it. With a sharp knife cut a slit in a stem at the point where it is desired to have roots form. (Other ways of wounding the stem are to cut a small notch in the stem or to remove a cylinder of bark, about an inch long.) The wound is wrapped with a wad of moist sphagnum moss, which is tied in place with twine, preparatory to covering it with the plastic film which should be between 2 and 4 thousandths of an inch thick.

When is the best time to make the layer? This has not yet been definitely determined. Probably early spring.

Is it a foolproof method? It is not. Care must be taken to avoid getting the medium too wet. This involves squeezing out as much of the water as possible prior to applying the moss; also in putting on the wrap it is essential to insure that no water gets in. Thus be careful to have the overlap on the under side; and see that the ties, both top and bottom, are made watertight by taping them spirally so that rain cannot seep in.

How does one know when to remove the layer? When roots are visible through the plastic. The removal of the layer is probably the most critical period. The layers, when they are rooted, should be treated for a time as though they were unrooted cuttings, by potting them, keeping them in a closed and shaded cold frame, and gradually hardening them off.

What is the best material in which to root cuttings? Sand has been most commonly used, but recently a half-and-half mixture of peat moss and sand has become popular for almost all kinds of cuttings. Sphagnum moss, vermiculite and perlite are other materials used for special purposes.

Is there any special trick in inserting cuttings? Make individual holes with a pointed stick; or make a narrow trench by drawing a blunt knife or label through the rooting medium. It is important to be sure that the bases of the cuttings touch the rooting medium and that it is well firmed about them.

Is there any reason for cutting back leaves when inserting cuttings

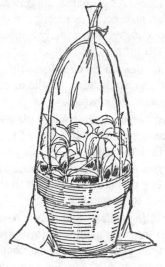

A bulb pan or a flower pot, enclosed in a polyethylene bag, makes an excellent miniature propagating case for the gardener. In it cuttings can readily be rooted.

in the rooting medium?   The reason for cutting back leaves is to prevent undue loss of moisture from the plant tissues by transpiration. Its value has been questioned by some propagators in recent years, and it is probably only necessary in the case of cuttings with very large leaves.

Why do professional growers use a powder when planting cuttings in wet sand? Is this powder a talc, or some special powder?   A root stimulant is used for the purpose of obtaining a higher percentage of rooting, to shorten the time required for the production of roots, and, in many instances, to obtain a bigger root system. Talc is sometimes the carrier with which small amounts of active chemical substances are mixed.

Which chemicals are used as stimulants for cuttings?   Many chemicals have been tried—indoleacetic acid, indolebutyric acid, naphthaleneacetic acid, etc.—and others are under trial. This is a rapidly changing field and new materials and techniques appear constantly, especially for the professional gardener and nurseryman.

Why are acids used, and what kinds, to promote good cuttings? Most cuttings root better in an acid than in a neutral or alkaline medium. Old-time propagators frequently added vinegar to water applied to cutting beds. (See answer to preceding question.)

Can anyone use root-inducing chemicals?   As prepared for general use these can be very readily applied by anyone. The most popular are in powder form. The bases of the cuttings are merely dipped into this before being inserted in the rooting medium.

How do you treat cuttings started with the aid of chemical stimulants?   The treatment of cuttings after the application of the root-inducing stimulant is the same as for untreated cuttings.

What about the use of Vitamin B₁ and hormones in rooting plants?   Vitamin B_1 is probably present in sufficient quantities in any soil reasonably well supplied with humus, so that the addition of this substance is unnecessary. If by hormones you mean the substances now on the market for facilitating the rooting of cuttings, there is little room for doubt that they are a definite aid to propagation.

What is the general treatment of cuttings after they have been placed in a propagating frame?   Keep rooting medium moist and frame closed until roots have formed, then gradually increase ventilation to harden cuttings. Frame must be in a shady location, or shaded by a double thickness of cheesecloth on sash.

How can one know when a cutting has developed roots, and is ready to be transplanted?   When it is judged that sufficient time has elapsed for roots to have developed, gently pull on one or two cuttings, and if they offer resistance it is a good indication that they have rooted. Most of the plants commonly rooted in summer produce a good root system in from 6 to 10 weeks. Many conifers, however, require as many months.

How are cuttings treated after rooting?   Those rooting early (July, August) are potted up, and the pots plunged in sand, peat moss, or ashes in a cold frame, to be planted out the following spring. Late rooters may be left in the rooting medium. Both kinds should be protected by scattering salt hay, or similar litter, among them after first severe frost.

ROOT AND LEAF CUTTINGS

When are root cuttings usually made?   Usually late in autumn for hardy plants. They should be planted ½ to 1 in. deep in sandy soil, and kept in a cool greenhouse; or the flats may be stored in a cold but frost-free place.

Does it make any difference which end of a root cutting is inserted

Rooted leaf cutting of sansevieria or snake-plant, with roots sufficiently developed for transplanting.

in soil? Yes. In order to be certain that the right end will be uppermost, it is customary to make a straight cut across the upper end of the cutting and a sloping cut at the basal end. However, with thin cuttings (such as phlox), both ends are cut straight across and the cuttings are laid flat.

How many kinds of root cuttings are usually made? When true roots, as distinguished from underground stems, are being dealt with, there is only one type of root cutting. Such cuttings are usually from 1 to 3 ins. long, depending upon their thickness.

How are cuttings of fine, stringy roots made? Cut them into lengths of an inch or a little more and lay them flat in the container in which they are to grow.

Are root cuttings more sure than stem cuttings? This depends entirely upon the plant to be propagated. The roots of all plants do not produce buds, and in these cases it is useless to attempt to reproduce them by root cuttings. In those instances where past experience has shown that a plant will produce buds on severed root pieces, this method is generally a little less trouble than stem cuttings.

What type of plant is mostly propagated by root cuttings? Many plants can be raised from root cuttings. These include apple, pear, cherry, rose, blackberry, horse-radish, phlox, trumpet creeper, daphne, locust, bouvardia, Oriental poppy, and many others. It must be understood, however, that if root cuttings are made of grafted or budded plants, it will be the understock that is propagated.

Are any indoor plants propagated by root cuttings? Not many of the more familiar house plants are propagated from root cuttings, but dracaena and bouvardia are sometimes increased in this way.

Will leaves make new plants if treated in the same way as stem cuttings? In some cases, yes. Among the plants commonly propagated in this way are African-violet, gloxinia, rex begonia, pick-a-back plant, and many succulents, such as the sedums.

Can all plants be propagated by leaf cuttings? No. Some will root —croton, for example—but never form a growth shoot. If, however, the leaf cuttings are taken with a growth bud and a sliver of the parent branch attached, they are successful in the case of most of the plants commonly increased by stem cuttings.

LAYERING

What is meant by layering? As generally understood, layering means bringing a shoot of the plant into contact with the earth with the object of having it form roots. Such shoots are slit with an upward cut, twisted, or girdled, either by having a ring of bark removed, or by encircling them with a tight wire, in order to induce the formation of roots at the injured part. This injured part must be covered with soil and kept moist.

How long before layers are ready to transplant? Many herbaceous plants will form roots in a few weeks. Shrubs layered in the spring will usually have a satisfactory root system by the end of the growing season. Some shrubs, such as rhododendrons and others that form roots slowly, require 2 years. After new roots form, the layers may be severed from the parent plant to become new plants on their own roots.

How many kinds of layering are there? Layering may be broadly divided into two classes: (a) layering in the ground, and (b) air layering. Class (a) may be divided into simple layering, serpentine layering, continuous layering, and mound layering. In all these ways it is necessary to bring the branches to ground level. Air layering (b) refers to rooting stems at points above the ground, by means of "layering pots" filled with soil; or by wrapping moist moss around the stem.

Some plants, such as the strawberry-begonia or strawberry-geranium (*Saxifraga sarmentosa*) multiply themselves by runners, which are easily rooted in pots while still attached to the parent plant.

When is layering done? Spring is the best time, as in most cases a good root system will then be developed before winter. It may be done at any time, however, but in the colder parts of the country the roots may be torn off the layers due to winter heaving if plants are layered at a later period.

New plants produced by layering. English ivy (1) rooting at each joint or leaf node. (2) "Serpentine" layering, with stem covered at intervals, to induce rooting.

What is the best kind of wood for layering? If shrubs are to be layered, stout, 1-year-old shoots are preferred, as they form a root system much more readily than older wood.

How large should the layers be? Not so large as implied by the over-optimistic advertisements of dealers! If the layer is made in the spring it should, in general, be put at the base of the shoots made the preceding year; if it is a summer job shoots of the current season are preferred.

Is there a limit to the size of branch used in layering? For practical purposes, yes. The younger they are the more readily they may be expected to root. However, layering frequently takes place when large branches, many years old, come in contact with the ground, but it may take many years before they form a root system sufficiently large to support them independently.

SUCKERS, STOLONS, AND RUNNERS

How are plants propagated by suckers?   If the plant is not grafted and is a type that produces suckers (lilac, for instance), rooted suckers can be dug up, cut back, and planted to produce new plants.

What is a stolon?   A branch which grows downward and roots at the tip, where it comes into contact with the soil. When rooted, it can be detached from the parent, dug up, and planted, to lead an independent existence. Forsythia and matrimony-vine commonly produce stolons.

How are plants propagated by runners?   Merely by digging up the runners when rooted. In special cases, to avoid root disturbance, small flower pots may be filled with earth and the developing runner fastened to the soil with a hairpin.

GRAFTING

What is meant by a "graft"?   A graft is the union of parts of 2 plants in such a manner that they will grow together to form 1 plant. It consists of 2 parts: the *understock* and the *scion*. The union of these 2, by grafting, results in a new plant having the roots of one plant and the branches, leaves, flowers, and fruit of the plant from which the scion was taken.

What is double grafting?   This refers to the practice of first grafting onto the understock a scion that will unite readily with it, and later grafting onto the first scion a second one of a kind that will unite with it but will not unite satisfactorily with the understock when grafted directly upon it.

Can any plant be grafted on any other plant?   Only those plants that are closely related can be grafted.

What is a scion?   A scion is one of the 2 parts necessary when making a graft, and consists of a short portion of stem of the plant that is to be duplicated. It usually contains 2 or more buds, and the base is cut in such manner that the cambium, a layer of actively growing tissue between bark and wood, or a part of it, will come in direct contact with the corresponding layer of the understock, which is cut to fit the scion.

What is meant by understock?   The understock is the part that constitutes the root system of a grafted or budded plant. Seedlings, or pieces of root, or rooted cuttings, are generally used as understocks. It is the part to which the scion or bud is attached that is to become the new plant.

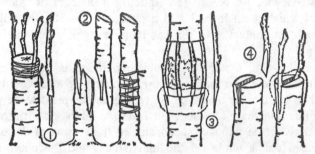

Grafting is an interesting operation which, with a little practice, any gardener can accomplish. Above are shown (1) bark grafting; (2) whip or tongue grafting; (3) bridge grafting; (4) cleft grafting. In each case the detail sketch shows how the scion (or bud wood) is cut.

When is grafting done?   Grafting is usually practiced in spring, either in the open or in greenhouses, just as the understocks are beginning to break dormancy. The understocks should be beginning growth while the scions must still be dormant. For this reason the scions are buried in the ground or kept on ice until required for grafting. Summer grafting of some ornamental trees and shrubs is also practiced.

Why are plants grafted?   To propagate horticultural varieties which do not "come true" from seed; to increase plants which are difficult to propagate by other vegetative means, such as cuttings or divisions; to modify growth of scion by use of dwarfing understocks, etc.; to hasten flowering; and to produce plants of special form as when "weeping" trees (mulberry, elm, etc.) are "worked" on a tall understock.

How are ornamental trees grafted?   In several ways, depending upon the plant being grafted. Splice, whip, veneer, and side graft are probably more commonly used than others, but saddle grafting and grafting by approach are other forms frequently employed.

What sort of roots are ornamental trees grafted on? Can any root be used? The kind of root that an ornamental tree is grafted on must be very closely related to it. Oaks cannot be grafted on elms, for example, nor beech on ash. Even in a group as large as the oaks, not all oaks can be grafted on just one kind of oak.

What is meant by budding? Budding is a form of grafting by means of which a single bud and a portion of its surrounding bark are brought in contact with the cambium layer of a suitable understock.

How is budding done? T or shield budding is the commonest form. In practice a bud and a narrow, thin strip of bark about ¾ in. in length is cut from a bud stick (a branch of the plant to be propagated). The thin sliver of wood, cut from the bud stick with the bud, may or may not be removed, according to the custom of the budder. A T-shaped cut is made on the understock, and the edges of the bark on the leg of the T lifted. The bud is then pushed down, from the top, into the cut until it is covered by the bark of the understock. It is then tied in place with raffia, soft string, a rubber strip, or a narrow strip of plastic film.

What is a bud stick? A bud stick is a shoot, usually of the current year's growth, from which buds are cut for budding.

Why is budding practiced in preference to grafting? Because only 1 bud is required to produce a new plant, consequently a given amount of scion wood will furnish more buds than scions for grafting, as each scion would require about 4 buds. In the case of stone fruits, budding insures a better union than grafting. Also, since less time is consumed in budding than in grafting, it is preferred where suitable.

When is budding done? Budding is usually a summer operation, as it can be done only when the sap is running and the bark lifts easily from the wood. June, July, and August are the usual months.

How does grafting differ from budding? The principal differences are in the time of year when each is performed, and the amount of scion or budwood required. A graft consists of an understock and a scion; i.e., a short length of shoot containing 2 or more buds. In budding, an understock is also required, but in place of a scion a single bud is inserted on the understock.

Has the plant on which the bud is placed (understock) any influence on the budded portion? Very definitely in many cases. Weak-growing garden roses are much more vigorous when budded on a suitable understock than when on their own roots. Recently dwarf apple trees have attracted much attention. Such trees are dwarf because they have been budded or grafted on understocks that cause dwarfing.

What is bark grafting? The tree is prepared as for cleft grafting (which see) but the branches are not split. Instead, a slit is made in the bark, about 1½ ins. long, from the stub down. The scions are prepared by making a sloping cut at their bases, but a shoulder is cut at the top of the slope so that the lower part of the scion, which is to be pushed under the bark, is quite thin. Several scions may be placed on one stub, depending upon its size. On large stubs the scions may be secured with brads; on smaller ones they are tied in. All must be covered with grafting wax.

What is the purpose of bridge grafting? This form of grafting is confined to the repair of tree trunks (particularly fruit trees) which have been entirely or largely girdled by rodents. Its purpose is to maintain a connection between top and roots. Unless the girdled portion is bridged in this way the tree will shortly die.

How is bridge grafting done? Trim away ragged bark. Make longitudinal slits above and below wound and loosen bark. Cut scions (from the tree being operated on) of 1-year-old wood about 3 ins. longer than the wound. Bevel each end with cuts ½ to 1 in. long; bend scion in middle; insert under slit bark; fasten with small brads. Cover points of insertion with grafting wax. Scions should be placed every 2 ins. around the trunk.

What is cleft grafting? Cleft grafting is one of the simpler forms, and involves the insertion of scions cut to a long wedge shape in a cleft of the understock. It is chiefly used in "making over" fruit trees and in grafting certain herbaceous plants.

What is the purpose of cleft grafting? The particular value of this form of grafting is in the conversion of unsuitable kinds of apples, pears, and sometimes such stone fruits as cherries and plums, to the production of fruit of better quality, or greater productiveness.

How is cleft grafting done? Cut back all branches to be grafted to leave a shapely tree; smooth over the cut faces; split each cut end with a grafting chisel. Cut scions with a wedge-shaped base about 1½ ins. long. Open cleft with end of chisel and insert scions, 2 in each cleft. See that the inner edges of bark on scions and stock are in contact. Tie in the scions on small branches; on the thicker ones this will be unnecessary. Cover scions and all parts of the cleft with grafting wax. If both scions unite, the weaker one may be cut off level with stump the following spring. At least one branch should be left to be grafted the second year, otherwise there will be an enormous growth of water sprouts.

When is cleft grafting carried out?   In spring, as soon as the buds show the first indication of swelling. The scions must be completely dormant.

What is whip grafting?   The base of the scion is cut across with a downward, long, sloping cut, about 1¼ ins. long, then an upward cut ½ in. long is made on this face, commencing about ½ in. from the lower end of the first cut. The understock is cut in a similar way. Press the tongue of the scion into the cut in the understock until the one face covers the other. Tie together with raffia or soft string, and cover the union with grafting wax; or pack in moist material and treat the same as hardwood cuttings.

What is the procedure in whip grafting if the understock is much thicker than the scion?   The first cut should be straight across. Then on one side of the understock, and near the top, cut off a strip of the same length and width as the cut face of the scion. Cut a tongue in it as previously described; tie; wax. Where scion and understock are not exactly of the same width it is most important that the inner edges of the bark of scion and understock *come in contact on one side* of the joint; otherwise they will not unite.

Cold Frames and Hotbeds

COLD FRAMES

How can I make a simple cold frame?   Use a 12-in. plank for back, a 6-in. one for front. Make ends of one 6-in. plank and half a 6-in. plank cut diagonally lengthwise (to allow for slope from back to front) cleated together. Standard sash is 6 × 3 ft., so width of frame should be 6 ft. and the length made up of units of 3 ft. plus about 1¼ in. allowance between each sash to accommodate cross ties, usually 1 in. thick. Above specifications do not allow much headroom—a height of 9 to 12 ins. front and 15 to 18 ins. in back is preferable.

What are the advantages and uses of a cold frame? Basically, it provides a protected area for sowing seeds, growing young seedlings, and rooting cuttings. In spring the additional warmth provided by the enclosed structure makes it possible to sow seeds several weeks earlier than could safely be done in the open ground. In addition, the seed bed can be protected from heavy rains which could wash out the seed. It also helps deter animals from digging in the seed bed. In winter it can be used for holding over tender perennials, rooting shrub cuttings, or giving a cold treatment to seeds or bulbs requiring such conditions.

Can I make a cold frame in December? I have a large, dry cellar where I can thaw out the soil. It is possible to construct a cold frame of wood in December, and get the soil in place ready for spring planting.

I have been informed that plants will not do so well in a cold frame constructed with concrete walls instead of wood. Is this true? No, it is not true. In fact, concrete frames can be kept more sanitary.

Since glass sash is so heavy can I use plastic or Fiberglas for the cover? Yes, both are satisfactory. However, the plastic will have a useful life of only a year or two but the cost is minimal. Although the light weight is an advantage when it comes to lifting or storing the sash, it is a disadvantage in high winds unless some means of anchoring the sash is provided.

How deep should the layer of cinders or coarse gravel be when preparing the soil in a cold frame? What should be the composition of the soil that is placed over the cinders; and how deep should it be? Cinders should be deep enough to allow for good drainage— usually 3 ins. or so. This would differ in various soils. In light, well-drained soil no gravel or cinders are used. Over this use about 6 ins. of a mixture of equal parts humus, garden soil, and sand.

How do you make a seed bed in a cold frame? If soil in frame is a sandy loam, spread a 2-in. layer of sifted leafmold and mix with the upper 6 ins. If soil is clayey, remove 6 to 8 ins. and replace with a screened mixture of sand, loam, and leafmold.

What should be added to the cold frame each year, and at which season should this addition be made?   Well-rotted manure, compost, or leafmold shortly before plants are to be set or seed sown.

How do I go about starting plants in a cold frame?   In March and April seeds of annuals and vegetables that can be transplanted may be sown, either in flats or directly in a bed of good, friable soil. Seeds of perennials can also be sown at this time. In June greenwood cuttings of some shrubs can be rooted in a few weeks if kept under rather close conditions and shaded from bright sun. In August seeds of pansy, forget-me-not, and English daisy can be sown for early-spring bloom outdoors.

What is the best way to use cold frames (of which I have quite a few) to obtain maximum year-round efficiency?   Seeds of perennials and biennials can be sown in cold frames in summer, and the seedlings transplanted and wintered over in same. A cold frame is also a convenient place in which to root greenwood cuttings of certain shrubs, inserting in sandy soil in June and July and keeping closed for a few weeks until rooted. A frame provides good conditions for seed flats of certain woody plants (as dogwood) over winter; also to winter stock plants of chrysanthemums and other perennials not reliably hardy. With the approach of spring, sow certain annual flowers and vegetables for early planting outdoors. In April and May a frame is useful to harden off greenhouse-grown plants for a short time before planting out. Any vacant space in summer could be utilized for the growing of tomatoes, melons, and cucumbers.

Is it possible to get early blooms from bulbs and other spring plants in a cold frame?   Pansies and forget-me-nots from August-sown seeds flower well in a cold frame in early spring. Good divisions of polyanthus primrose planted at the same time would also reward with nice flowers. The chaste flowers of Christmas-rose open to perfection under cold-frame protection. Potted bulbs of daffodil, tulip, scilla, and snowdrop can be plunged in the frame in October to be brought out early in the year for flowering indoors if need be, or planted directly in the frame to flower in place. Leave the sash off until freezing weather threatens, and ventilate on all warm days during winter. In very severe weather it would help to have the frames banked outside with leaves, and the sash covered with mats or similar material.

Can violets be grown in cold frames for flowering in spring? Yes. Plant strong, field-grown plants in early September. Cover with sash for a few days to help them recover, keep moist but admit some air, and shade lightly from bright sun. When established, give all light possible and plenty of air until hard freezing weather. Put mats or some other covering over the sash on very cold nights, and ventilate on every warm day in winter.

Will you tell me how to operate cold frame with plants in pots and flats? Provide a bed of sifted ashes or gravel 4 to 6 ins. deep on which to stand plants during early spring. If to be kept in frame throughout the year, pots should be buried to their rims to conserve moisture in summer and help to prevent breakage from frost in winter. (See answers to preceding questions for general management.)

Why do I have such a hard time growing plants from seeds in cold frames, even though care and thought have been used? Plants grown in frames require more careful attention than when grown in the open. Correct soil, temperature, watering, *and especially* ventilation, all are of utmost importance. Attention to these should produce satisfactory results.

What is meant by "hardening-off"? The process whereby plants are gradually inured to change in environment. For example, when moving seedlings from indoors to outdoors, they are first put in a protected frame for a few days to ease the transition to stronger light and temperature change. If one lacks a frame, the plants can be put in a somewhat protected spot for a few hours each day. If they wilt, the transition is probably being made too rapidly. When for some reason, hardening-off is not possible, it helps to spray the plants with an anti-desiccant, such as Wilt-Pruf, before setting plants outdoors.

Is it necessary to "harden off" plants before they are moved from a cold frame, greenhouse, or hotbed to open ground? Yes. A sudden change to more intense sunlight, lower humidity, and exposure to wind, is injurious to them.

I have a cold frame. When the soil freezes do I fill it in with marsh hay and close it for the winter; or do I have to give it ventilation on warm days? A light covering of salt hay put on plants when the soil freezes will give added protection. Ventilate on warm days.

If the frame is vacant, a covering of hay or leaves will keep out some frost but is hardly necessary.

How would you manage a small cold frame containing little perennial seedlings and some very choice perennial slips for rooting during winter? See that the soil is moist before hard freezing. After this, lightly cover the plants with clean litter, such as marsh hay or pine needles. Provide ventilation on warm days.

When plants are stored in a cold frame over winter, what protection should be provided? Cover with a mulch and then use a mat over the glass. Put a mulch around the outside of the frame.

Is commercial fertilizer good to put in a cold frame to give added heat? Commercial fertilizers are of no value in this respect. (See Hotbeds.)

Hotbeds

What is the difference between a hotbed and a cold frame? A cold frame has no other heat than that provided by the sun. A hotbed is heated by fermenting material, such as fresh manure, electricity, steam, or hot water.

How can I make a medium-size, manure-heated hotbed to start early tomato plants? Assuming you have the frame complete, a pit should be made 2½ ft. below ground level and the same size as the frame. Then mix 2 parts fresh stable (horse) manure with 1 part unrotted leaves. Turn 2 or 3 times at about 4-day intervals, and moisten if dry. When well heated, place mixture in the pit in 6-in. layers, each one well packed, until there is a solid 2-ft. bed, or a little more. Finish off to ground level with 4 to 6 ins. of good, fine soil in which to grow the plants.

Is it necessary to line a hotbed pit? If soil holds together, and if only a temporary hotbed is required, no. Permanent hotbed pits are usually lined with concrete or boards.

I am planning to raise flower and vegetable plants for sale to gardeners. Which is the best way of heating my beds each 6 × 17 ft.? If this is a more or less permanent proposition, the installation of electric heating cable or of electric bulbs, arranged in series, would be the best if possible. A mixture of 2 parts fresh stable manure and 1 part leaves of the previous fall would be the best fermenting material. You can, however, raise good flower and vegetable plants for home gardens in just sun-heated frames.

I expect to start a hotbed March 1. Manure is available February 15 and March 15. How can I store the February manure so I can make use of it later? The manure you gather in February can be left piled, either indoors or out, for hotbed use in March.

When is the best time to start a hotbed in northern Vermont? Late March is soon enough. Put the sash on the frames before snow-fall, so they do not have to be emptied of snow.

Does the depth of manure in a hotbed depend on climate? Yes, to some extent. Around New York City 2 ft. is the usual depth. Farther north 2 ft. 6 ins. is desirable; in the South 18 ins. or less is enough.

How much soil should be put over the manure in an outdoor hotbed? If seeds are to be sown directly in the bed, about 6 ins. of good, friable soil is sufficient. If to be sown in flats, then 1 in. or so of soil over the manure will do.

How does one know when a manure-heated hotbed is ready for sowing seeds? Stick a soil thermometer in the manure and close the frame. When the temperature *recedes* to 90° F. (it will go higher at first), it is safe to sow seeds.

Does the manure in a manure-heated hotbed have to be changed every year? Yes, it will not heat up a second time. Clear it out after the plants are removed and use it in the compost or garden.

What can be used for hotbeds in place of manure besides electricity? Under certain conditions, such as where the frames are close to a greenhouse, it is possible to heat them with steam or hot water piped from the greenhouse system. Or a pipe may be run from the house heater if the frame adjoins the house.

Is there anything besides leaves suitable to mix with manure in the making of a hotbed? If obtainable, tanbark and spent hops give good results in prolonging the period of heat in a hotbed. Chopped cornstalks can also be used.

How, or in what way, are cornstalks used for a hotbed to take

the place of manure for heating in the hotbed? Cut stalks into 1- or 2-in. lengths, wet thoroughly, pack in 2-in. layers to a total depth of 6 ins. in excess of depth when manure is used. Sprinkle each layer of 18 sq. ft. (area of standard hotbed sash) with ½ lb. cottonseed meal, ½ lb. ground limestone, and 3 oz. superphosphate. This increases heat and improves fertilizing value of cornstalks when rotted.

Can one raise hotbed plants without manure? Yes, with electric heating cable or ordinary light bulbs, arranged in series, with thermostatic control. The installation is good for some years, and the disagreeable features of the old-time hotbed procedure have been eliminated.

When and how can a hotbed be prepared to supply a small garden in town? Use special electric heating cable obtainable from a garden supply outlet. Where spring is slow in arrival, last half of March would be soon enough to start. Sun heat alone would do for an early start in the frame, as compared to outdoor sowing.

Is it necessary to ventilate hotbeds? Yes; every day except in severe weather. Tilt the sash on the side or end opposite to the direction from which the wind is blowing.

Are any special precautions necessary when watering seedlings in hotbed? Yes; because of humid air, seedlings are especially vulnerable to attack by "damping-off" fungi. Water in morning, so that leaves dry more readily. Water only when soil begins to get dry.

Do hotbeds need any special protection during cold snaps? When especially cold nights are anticipated, the sashes are covered with mats or boards as an additional protection.

How is it best to make a hotbed for seeds to be left outdoors all the year around if the seedlings should have to stay 2 or more years? In this case a cold frame will serve the purpose better than a hotbed. Depending on kinds, the seeds could be sown in the fall or spring, and the seedlings transplanted in the bed of the frame until ready to plant outside.

The Home Greenhouse

WHAT TO GROW

I am building a small greenhouse. Will you give me information on early planting of vegetables and flowers to transplant for summer production? Start about mid-February. Follow instructions given under annuals, vegetables, and propagation for details of planting. If house is to be heated, even though no higher than 45° F., chrysanthemums, azaleas, etc., and forced spring bulbs, could be used for fall and winter display.

I am building a 10 × 12 ft. home greenhouse. Can you give a few pointers as to what I can grow? Assuming the minimum temperature is 55° F., the following could be raised from seeds: begonia, calceolaria, cineraria, cyclamen, primula. Obtain plants or bulbs from dealers of the following: acacia, azalea, camellia, Easter lily, erica, gardenia, genista, gloxinia. A good book on this subject is *Gardening Under Glass,* by Jerome Eaton (Macmillan, 1972).

Which plants, besides geraniums, can be grown in a small home greenhouse maintained at 55° to 65° F., and also planted in borders during summer? Fuchsia, begonia, lantana, abutilon, acalypha, and heliotrope.

Which flowers are suitable for an amateur to grow in a small greenhouse for winter bloom? Among the easiest are calendula, stock, snapdragon, forget-me-not, daffodil, tulip, freesia, chrysanthemum, and buddleia. All of these grow in a night temperature of 45° to 50° F.

I have a glass-covered frame over the well which is outside of our home (east side); normally it is used to give light and air in basement. Will you advise which plants or vines might do well? Also what type of soil would produce best results? English ivy; chrysanthemums could be dug up and potted when budded; also such annuals as carnation, petunia, and marigold not completely flowered out could be dug from garden to finish out the season. Begonia of the bedding type (wax begonia) lifted and cut back would flower well in spring.

Bulbs: daffodil, tulip, freesia, and amaryllis should do well. For summer, coleus. A good soil mixture would be 2 parts good loam, 1 part leafmold, ½ part sand; 5-in. potful bone meal to each bushel.

Which plants, other than the little English daisy and blue forget-me-not, would be suitable to raise in a small greenhouse for small corsages? What other flowers would you suggest? Ageratum, sweet-alyssum, baby's-breath, candytuft, cornflower, lily-of-the-valley, linaria, lobelia, French marigold, annual phlox, primrose, sweetheart roses, and verbena.

Which plants will grow most successfully in my small lean-to greenhouse (southwest exposure)? (There is no heat except what comes from cellar; it is cold nights, but warm during the day.) Chrysanthemums, Jerusalem-cherry, decorative peppers, hardy bulbs, herbs.

What can I grow in a practically unheated lean-to greenhouse? Strong specimens of various early-flowering hardy perennials could be dug in fall and potted or planted to flower well in advance of their season. Hardy bulbs; St. Brigid anemone, kurume azalea, snapdragon, calendula, stock, larkspur, clarkia, nigella, *Phlox drummondii,* and chrysanthemum should all do well. Early vegetables and choice rock-garden plants could also be grown.

Am unable to heat my greenhouse. What practical use can be made of it, if any? If span-roofed and fully exposed, perhaps best to wait until March, and then sow seeds of flowers and vegetables that can be transplanted for early start outdoors. If there are benches of soil, such plants as radish, beet, lettuce, and carrot could be sown and grown inside until big enough to use. During summer, chrysanthemums could be grown to finish before winter really started. Hardy, early-flowering plants dug and planted in fall would give earlier blooms than those left outdoors.

TEMPERATURES

What temperature should be maintained in a small greenhouse? Depends on what is grown. A minimum night temperature of 50° to 55° F. will suit a large variety of plants commonly grown.

At what temperature should a small greenhouse be kept to germinate various seeds, and at same time keep seedlings at right temperature? For usual run of annuals and vegetables, night temperature of 50° to 55° F. with rise of 5° to 10° in daytime is about right. Seed pots or flats may be stood in propagating case, having slightly higher temperature until they germinate; or placed near heating pipes until seeds *start* to sprout.

Will you advise as to minimum night temperature acceptable for small greenhouse for winter growing of sweet pea, stock, snapdragon, calendula, and begonia? Fifty degrees. The sweet pea, stock, and calendula would do better at 45° F., the begonia at 55° F.

Is temperature of 65° to 70° F., maintained by hot-water heat, correct in a flower conservatory? Depends upon what is to be grown. For general-purpose house a night temperature of 50° to 55° F. (with a 5° to 10° F. rise in daytime) would be right.

We are keeping a coal furnace going in our one-wing greenhouse. How low can the temperature drop at night without harm to plants? Depends on what is being grown. Azalea, calceolaria, camellia, cineraria, cyclamen, erica, genista, hydrangea, primula, violet, and many others can endure 45° F. without injury.

I have a greenhouse built alongside of my house at the basement windows. I use it for starting vegetable and flower seeds, and heat it with warm air from the basement through the windows. What temperature should I have in it? A night temperature of at least 45° F., and better close to 55° F., would be suitable. The day temperature would vary according to sun heat, but ventilation should be increased if it rises above 65° F.

Potted plants which I place on my sunny terrace during summer have their leaves scorched when they're transferred from the greenhouse. Is there any way of overcoming this? Ventilate greenhouse as freely as possible for a week before they are moved. Keep them in a partially shaded location outdoors for a week or so before putting them on the terrace.

How does one harden off plants which have to be moved from a greenhouse into the open? By transferring them first to a cold frame, where they are gradually exposed to outdoor conditions by progressively increasing the amount of ventilation until, at the expiration of 10 days or so, the sash is entirely removed.

Is bottom heat more important than the temperature around the plants? It is under certain conditions of plant propagation, and for the growing of some plants under glass. For general culture it will not take the place of air temperature.

GENERAL CARE

What is proper soil mixture for flower seed sown in small greenhouse built off basement window? Want to avoid damping-off. One part each loam and leafmold and 2 parts sand. A formaldehyde solution (used according to directions on container) can be mixed with the soil before sowing; or pots could be prepared and drenched with boiling water a day or two previous to sowing seed, to check damping-off. Sowing seed in pure sphagnum moss generally eliminates damping-off if all equipment is sterile to begin with. One can also use one of the sterile artificial soil mixes sold for the purpose.

How is it possible to tell when soil in pots is dry? By sight, touch, and hearing. If soil looks dry, feels dry, and the pot "rings" when tapped with knuckle or stick, watering is necessary, provided the plant is in active growth.

How often should pot plants be watered? The correct answer is "when needed." The need varies with the kind of plant, its condition, and environment. When plants are in active growth, water when the soil appears to be getting dry; give enough to *wet the soil all through.*

What is the procedure in watering newly potted plants? Be sure the ball of soil is thoroughly moist at potting time. Water well immediately after potting, then wait until the soil is dry on surface. It is very easy to overwater newly potted plants. If they tend to wilt, syringing the foliage once or twice a day will be beneficial.

Is the amount of watering and damping down influenced by weather? Yes. On cloudy, moist days little is needed, especially if temperature is low. When it is sunny and dry, especially in winter when artificial heat is used, much more water must be applied to keep the air moist and plants from wilting.

Is there any way of cutting down on the need for frequently watering pot plants? Bury pots to their rims. Outdoors: in earth, ashes, sand, or peat moss. Indoors: in cinders, pebbles, peat moss, or sphagnum. If this is done, great care must be taken to avoid overwatering in damp, cloudy weather, and when plants are not actively growing.

How often should greenhouse plants be sprayed with water; and when? Tropical foliage plants can be sprayed every sunny day. This is an excellent prophylactic measure against insect pests. Generally plants in bloom should not be sprayed because of the danger of marring flowers. Spraying should be done in the morning, after plants have been watered.

How can humidity be controlled in a greenhouse? By careful attention to heating, ventilating, and wetting down of the paths and other interior surfaces, and the balancing of these factors to produce the desired result. A wet-bulb thermometer is useful to indicate the relative humidity. Special humidifiers are sold for this purpose.

Is it necessary to sprinkle frequently to keep air humid in greenhouse? Depends on what is grown. Cacti and succulents get along in dry air. Most cool-house plants—primroses, cyclamens, stocks, house plants, etc.—with moderate humidity, provided by sprinkling walks once or twice on dry, sunny days. Tropical plants from moist climates can require the sprinkling of walls, floors, and benches three or four times a day.

I have a small greenhouse heated by kerosene room heater, supplemented by thermostatically controlled electric heater. A large bucket of water is kept on top of heater to supply plenty of humidity. Temperature is kept at 55° to 60° F. Geranium growth is good, but leaves brown and fall off. Some progress in size, but in time the same thing happens. What is wrong? Probably insufficient humidity. Wet down floors once or twice a day. Install a humidifier sold for greenhouse use.

What direct effect, if any, does coal gas have on greenhouse plants? Am thinking of a small greenhouse heated by a small stove. Even minute quantities of coal gas will seriously injure or kill plants. If you have in mind placing a stove *inside* the greenhouse, drop this idea at once.

REPOTTING

When is the best time for repotting? For plants that are rapidly increasing in size, whenever the roots get crowded in the pots. For plants which have "settled down" and slowly increase in size, at the end of the resting season—usually midwinter or late winter.

When do plants need repotting? When pot is crowded with roots and available plant nutrients are exhausted. Also when, because of poor drainage, overwatering, or unsuitable soil, the roots are unhealthy.

How does one repot a plant? Prepare new pot by cleaning it and putting broken pots, small pebbles, or something similar in the bottom for drainage—from ½ in. to 2 ins., depending on size of pot, and the plant's need for quick drainage. Cover with ½ in. moss or fibrous loam. Remove plant from old pot by turning it upside down and tapping rim of pot on bench or table. Place in new pot at correct depth; fill around with new soil; tamp soil firmly with a potting stick—a small piece of lath will do. Surface soil should be a sufficient distance below rim for convenience in watering.

REPOTTING A PLANT

Removing plant from pot. Rim of pot (1) is rapped sharply on edge of bench or table to remove root-ball; (2) root-ball is loosened up to remove some of old earth; (3) crock (drainage material) and more earth removed from bottom of root-ball. Plant is now ready for repotting.

Plant is placed in larger pot, partly filled with fresh soil, and (4) more soil filled in around it. Cross section of pot (5) with crock over drainage hole. Soil is tamped in firmly (6) around old root-ball.

VENTILATION

What about ventilation in a small greenhouse? Open ventilator daily, even if it is only a mere crack, for a short time. Avoid drafts by opening on the side opposite to that from which wind is blowing. When air outside is warm and still, ventilate freely except when plants requiring high humidity are grown, when it is necessary to exercise discretion to maintain air moisture. If you must be away for most of the day or don't want to give time to ventilating, an automatic ventilating device is your answer. These are available from greenhouse suppliers.

REST

How are plants "rested"? By lowering the temperature and reducing the supply of water to their roots. Northern plants become more or less dormant in winter; some (certain bulbs) in summer, as a means of tiding themselves over during summer drought. Certain tropical plants almost completely suspend activities during the dry season.

How can I tell when my greenhouse plants need rest? By close observation, and by reading about the culture of specific plants. When a plant has grown actively for six to nine months it can indicate its need for rest by yellowing and dropping leaves; example, the poinsettia.

For how long should plants be rested? Varies with the subject; amaryllis, October to February; poinsettia, January to May; tulips, May to November. These are approximate resting periods of some commonly grown plants.

INSECTS

What are the most common insects found in the greenhouse and how are they controlled? Whiteflies, aphids, woolly aphids, mealy bugs, nematodes, red spider mites, scales, slugs, and snails. Malathion will control aphids (including woolly), whiteflies, mealy bugs, and scales. Special baits are sold for controlling slugs and snails. Some gardeners get good results with shallow saucers of beer placed at intervals on the plant bench. The slugs and snails apparently drink the beer and drown. There are materials sold for controlling nematodes, but their use is somewhat dangerous, so in small home greenhouses it's generally safer to discard any infested plant. Red spider mites can be controlled with Kelthane.

DISEASES

The leaves on some of my plants have a powdery substance on the surface. What is this and how do I get rid of it? This is powdery mildew, a fungus disease. Karathane is generally effective when sprayed according to the manufacturer's directions.

In cloudy weather the leaves of some of my plants develop a gray mold that I have been told is botrytis fungus. How can this be controlled? Use captan or any material recommended for the purpose.

SPECIFIC GREENHOUSE PLANTS

Are abutilons easy to grow in a small greenhouse? Yes. Take cuttings from outdoor plants in September, or from greenhouse plants in February. Pot in ordinary soil. Pinch tips of shoots occasionally to induce bushiness. They like sunshine and temperature about 50° F. at night. Can also be raised from seeds.

Can small plants of yellow-flowered "mimosa" (acacia) be grown in pots? Several kinds are well adapted for growing in pots in cool greenhouse (night temperature, 40° to 45° F.). Try *A. armata, A. pubescens, A. drummondii,* and *A. longifolia.*

What is the correct treatment for an acacia plant grown in a tub in a greenhouse? Cut old flowering branches back to length of 6 ins. Retub or topdress as necessary, using light, porous, peaty soil. Spray tops to encourage new growth. After danger of frost has passed place outdoors, with tub buried nearly to rim. Bring inside before freezing weather in fall. Keep cool. At all times give plenty of sun. Beware of dryness at root. Feed established plants during summer.

What is the proper way to winter an allspice tree? The allspice tree (*Pimenta officinalis*) is not suited to outdoor growing where freezing temperatures occur. If the plant is in a tub, it could be wintered in a cool greenhouse or other suitable well lighted place under cover, where the temperature range is between 40° and 50° F. Water only enough to keep the soil from getting bone dry.

How shall I plant and care for bulbs of amaryllis in greenhouse? Pot bulbs firmly in porous loam enriched with dried cow manure and superphosphate, using pots 4 ins. to 6 ins., according to size of bulbs. Leave top half of bulb out of soil. Keep nearly dry until roots form, then gradually increase water supply. Spray foliage with clear water on bright days. Temperature 60° to 65° F. at night, 70° to 75° F. by day. Give full sunlight until flowers appear, then light shade. (See also under Tender Bulbs, Section 5.)

I would like to grow anemone from seed for blooming in my

greenhouse. How is it done? Sow in April or May. Transplant individually to 2½-in. pots. Grow in summer in cool, shaded cold frame or greenhouse (pots buried to rims in sand or ashes). Repot into 4-in. pots, or plant 6 ins. apart in benches, in September. Grow in cool temperature.

Will anthurium thrive in a greenhouse where cattleya orchids grow well? Indeed they will. Both need humid atmosphere and a 60° F. temperature at night. Pot the anthuriums in a mixture of orchid peat, sphagnum, and charcoal. Keep moist at all times.

What greenhouse conditions best suit antirrhinum (snapdragons)? Night temperature 45° to 50° F.; full sunshine; free air circulation; light but rich soil; 9 ins. to 1 ft. between plants in benches; or 4-in. to 6-in. pots; judicious feeding when in vigorous growth. Avoid wetting leaves. Pinch plants in early stages to encourage branching. Propagate by seeds or cuttings.

When should snapdragon seed be sown for fall flowering? For early-spring flowering (in greenhouse)? From middle to end of May for fall. Late August or early September for spring.

I saw the interesting and beautiful flowering vine Aristolochia elegans growing at the Brooklyn Botanic Garden. I would like to grow it in my own greenhouse. Can you tell me how? It is very easy to grow. Sow seeds in light soil in spring and grow seedlings in sunny greenhouse where night temperature is 55° F. Prune plants back each spring, and topdress or repot as necessary. Unlike some aristolochia species this one is not evil-smelling.

Can you give me instructions for forcing astilbe for Easter blooming in a greenhouse? Plant strong clumps in fall in pots just large enough to hold them; plunge in cold frame; bring indoors January or later; give plenty of water and grow in light position. They need from 10 to 14 weeks, in temperature 55° to 60° F., to bring them into bloom.

What treatment should be accorded greenhouse azalea that are kept from year to year? After flowering, trim plants back lightly, repot if necessary (using an acid, peaty soil), and grow in temperature of about 60° F.; spray frequently to encourage new growth. Plunge outdoors, in sunny or partially shaded place, from June to September, then bring into cool house in light position. Never let plants suffer from lack of moisture in the soil.

I am greatly interested in the begonia and, having acquired a small lean-to greenhouse, would like to grow a collection. What temperature, etc., should I maintain? Night, 55° F., rising 5° or 10° in daytime. Shade lightly during March, April, and September; more heavily from May to August. Ventilate to keep atmosphere buoyant rather than stagnant; damp down sufficiently to keep air fairly humid. Be sure to keep house clean at all times. (See also Begonia—Section 12.)

How can I grow bouvardia? Propagate by stem or root cuttings in spring. Grow in sweet (slightly alkaline) soil that is well supplied with humus yet is porous. Give plenty of water during active growing periods. Plenty of sunlight is needed, and a greenhouse temperature of about 55° F. Keep plants pinched freely during early growth to make them bushy.

What soil does a bougainvillea (grown under glass) require? If in a pot, a rich but porous soil is needed. If planted in a ground bed, a less rich soil is preferable. Good drainage is essential, and the soil should be coarse (not sifted) and loamy.

The florists' winter-blooming buddleia—how can I grow it in the greenhouse? There are 2 types—*asiatica* (white) and *farquhari* (light pink). Root cuttings in spring; pinch out tips of young growing plants to encourage bushiness; plunge pots outdoors in summer; use good, rich soil; feed when pot-bound. Bring into greenhouse before hard freeze, and keep cool; give plenty of sun and air. Never let them suffer from dryness.

I would like to have a succession of bulbs for my greenhouse. Which bulbs shall I buy, and how plant them? Paper-white narcissus can be planted at 2-week intervals, from October 1 to January 1. Roman hyacinths, at 3-week intervals, from September to December 1. Calla-lilies are constant bloomers. Plant amaryllis in November. Lachenalia planted in September will bloom for Christmas. Try veltheimia, also. Plant tulips in November. (See also Tender Bulbs.)

Will you give instructions on raising calceolaria from seeds? Sow in shallow pans, well drained, using a prepared seed-sowing medium, or mix sand, leafmold, peat moss, and loam in equal parts, sifted through ¼-in. sieve. Firm soil, make level, sow seeds, and gently press them in with tamper. Moisten by standing pan in vessel of water for half-hour. Cover with pane of glass; shade with news-

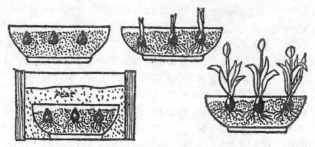

Tulips for indoor bloom: Bulbs are planted with tips level with soil surface; stored in a cold frame, pit, or cool cellar for several weeks to form roots; brought indoors to cool temperature to start top growth; and then given higher temperature and abundant water to develop their flowers.

paper. When seeds germinate, tilt glass; remove entirely after few days. Keep cool.

What conditions are needed to grow calceolarias in the greenhouse? A well-drained soil that contains a liberal amount of humus, together with some dehydrated manure and bone meal or superphosphate. Give free circulation of air; shade from strong sunshine; provide a cool, moist ash bed beneath the pots, uniform moisture, and a night temperature of 50° F.

How is it possible to force calceolarias into bloom early? By using fluorescent light to provide supplemental illumination for about 5 hours each evening from November on.

I would like to grow calendula for winter flowering in my greenhouse. Can you tell me how? Sow seed of good greenhouse strain in early August. Transplant seedlings into small pots, and later set out in benches (14 or 15 ins. apart), or pot into 5-in. pots. Use rich soil. Grow in full sun with night temperature of 45° to 50° F. Good air circulation is necessary.

Is it possible for me to grow carnations for winter bloom, along with other greenhouse plants? Yes, if the other kinds are chosen so that their needs are similar; however, carnations are usually at their best when grown in a house by themselves. They need full sunlight, free ventilation, and night temperature of 45° to 55° F. Soil must be sweet, fertile, and porous. It is usually advisable for the home gardener to buy young plants rather than attempt to propagate his own.

When should carnation cuttings be made? Late November or December or January. Select strong growths from near the base of flowering shoots and remove with a slight side twist. Insert in sand bench in greenhouse where night temperature is 50° F. Shade with cheesecloth or newspaper for a week or two.

What causes carnations to split? Splitting is caused by overfeeding, and especially by a too-high temperature, which induces rapid development. Carnations are cool-temperature plants, so growth must be gradual and the temperature at night kept evenly at about 45° to 55° F.

What are important points for a home gardener with a small greenhouse to bear in mind when growing indoor chrysanthemums in pots? Secure healthy stock. Keep plants repotted as they grow (without permitting them to become pot-bound) until they are in their flowering pots. Feed after flower buds have set. Keep greenhouse cool (night temperature of 40° to 45° F.). Full sunshine is necessary.

What kind of soil is best for growing chrysanthemums in pots? A rich mixture containing plenty of mellow, fibrous loam, rotted manure or rich compost, a good sprinkling of bone meal, or superphosphate, a generous dash of wood ashes, and sufficient sharp sand to keep the whole porous. A sandier mixture, without manure or fertilizer, is preferred for the first potting of cuttings.

Can greenhouse chrysanthemums be planted in the vegetable garden in the summer and then be dug up in fall and transplanted to soil beds in greenhouse? Yes. Plant in fertile soil. Dig up carefully before severe frost (keeping as much soil on roots as possible), replant, and then water thoroughly. Shade from bright sunshine for a few days and lightly sprinkle foliage with water to prevent wilting.

Can large chrysanthemums be grown in a greenhouse, and at what temperature? Cool (40° to 50° F.) greenhouse culture is best for large-flowered chrysanthemums. (See previous questions for culture.)

How does one propagate greenhouse chrysanthemums? After blooming, old plants are cut back close to ground and stored in a light place (just above freezing). In January or February they are placed in temperature of about 45° F., and young shoots, that soon appear, are made into cuttings when about 2 ins. long. These are inserted in sand in propagating bench.

What culture is required for cineraria?   Sow seed June to September. Transplant to flats, later to small pots. Keep repotting as plants grow, using rich, porous soil containing fair amount of humus. Grow in full sunshine during winter weather, and stand pots on cool, moist bed of pebbles. Keep moist; spray with water on sunny days. Grow cool (night temperature of 40° to 45° F.).

Do cineraria plants need much feeding?   They are heavy feeders; therefore provide rich soil, but do not use liquid fertilizers until they are well rooted in their flowering pots; then feed once or twice a week until flowers are open. Cease feeding when flowers open.

How is the fragrant, yellow-flowered cytisus handled in the greenhouse?   Its full name is *Cytisus racemosus*. After blooming, shear plants and repot, using sandy, peaty, fertile soil. Spray with clear water to encourage new growth, and grow in cool, sunny greenhouse. Plunge pots outdoors in sunny place through summer, and bring in again in fall. Night temperature of 40° to 45° F. Propagate by cuttings in spring.

Can bleedingheart (Dicentra spectabilis) be forced into bloom early in the small greenhouse?   Yes. Plant strong roots in fall or winter in pots just large enough to hold them. Bury pots to rim in cold frame; about February bring into light greenhouse (temperature of 45° to 50° F.). Keep soil moist.

What soil and culture are required for Eucharis grandiflora (Amazon- or Eucharis-lily)?   It needs tropical greenhouse conditions. Soil rich, medium, well-drained. Bulbs must be partially dried off for a month or 6 weeks twice a year, to induce blooming. Feed generously with organic fertilizer when growing.

How can I grow the tender maidenhair fern in my little greenhouse?   Adiantums are easily grown in a temperature of 60° to 65° F., if the atmosphere is kept humid. Pot in a sand-peat soil. Avoid wetting foliage, but keep soil evenly moist (except that plants can be rested by partially drying off for a couple of months in winter). Propagate by division in early spring.

Can I grow ferns in a conservatory? What is the best temperature?   Ferns do well in a conservatory. Keep the temperature above 55° F., and the house shaded in summer. Adiantum, pteris, davallia, nephrolepis (in variety) are good kinds to start with.

When should I sow forget-me-nots (myosotis) for blooming in greenhouse? Also tips on culture? Sow in May or June. Select variety recommended for greenhouse culture. Transplant seedlings 3 ins. apart in flats. Later pot, or plant in benches. Grow in cool, airy conditions. Shade from strong sunshine. Keep soil always moist.

What causes geraniums (pelargoniums) suddenly to turn yellow and then die? Gas in the air; poor drainage; overwatering; underwatering; or disease might cause this.

What is the best way to propagate geraniums that damp off or rot before rooting? Expose cuttings to sun for one day before setting in rooting medium. Water after planting, then keep on the dry side until roots are formed.

I have gerbera plants that were raised from seed in my greenhouse; the potted plants are now nearly a year old, but have never bloomed. Why? Gerberas need rich, well-drained soil. Crowns should be just above soil level. Feed with liquid fertilizer as blooming period approaches. Should be grown in cool house (night temperature of 50° F.).

Can you give me advice on how to raise and grow hydrangea for blooming in greenhouse? Propagate by cuttings from February to May. Grow in light, well-drained loam in temperature of 50° F. and full sun. Pinch once or twice before June. Keep in cold frame, water freely, and spray foliage with water during summer. From September on keep drier, and just above freezing. Start into growth in temperature of 45° F. in January or February.

How is the leopard-plant grown? The correct name is *Ligularia kaempferi.* Ordinary greenhouse culture, or conditions that suit ferns or saintpaulia (temperature around 60° F.), shade, and high humidity; but avoid wetting the leaves much.

What is Russian statice? Can I grow it in my little greenhouse? This is *Limonium suworowii.* Sow seeds in September in sandy soil. Transplant seedlings into well-drained flats, and later pot singly into 4-in. pots. Grow in full sun, in temperature of 50° to 55° F. Be careful with watering and watch out for aphids.

I have a breadfruit plant, so called. Will you tell me more about this plant, and how to care for it? Probably it is Mexican breadfruit (not related to real breadfruit) or ceriman—*Monstera deliciosa;* often sold as philodendron. Its fruits are edible. Prefers a warm, moist atmosphere, but will grow almost anywhere provided the temperature does not fall below 50° F. When planted in good soil, it is a vigorous grower, climbing high on tree trunks by means of its stem roots. It succeeds well as a pot plant.

What treatment do calanthe orchids require? Pot in spring in a mixture of fibrous loam, sand, and old cow manure, being sure drainage is perfect. Water with extreme care at first; more generously as roots take possession of soil. Shade spring and summer. Grow in warm temperature. Reduce water supply when foliage begins to die away in fall. After blooming, keep dormant pseudobulbs in warm, dry place until spring.

What kind of soil should I use for potting a cattleya orchid? Soil (in the ordinary sense) is not used for epiphytic orchids such as cattleyas. Instead they are potted in osmunda fiber (the wiry-roots of osmunda fern). With a potting stick pack the fiber firmly between and around the roots. Recently, because of the difficulty of obtaining osmunda fiber, different materials have been tried as substitutes. Among the most promising are bark fragments or wood chips; the bark of fir and birch chips have proved to be satisfactory. One advantage of using bark or chips is that they make it much easier for the beginner to pot orchids.

Would a beginner be likely to have any chance of success in raising orchids from seed? No. The raising of orchids from seed calls for specialized skill and closely controlled environment. Consult a book on orchid culture.

I have some palm tree seeds. Can you tell me how to plant these? Plant in sandy, well-drained soil in 4-in. flowerpots (in flats, if quantity is large). Space seeds about 1 in. apart, and cover about ½ in. deep. Keep moist in temperature of about 70° F.

How are pansies grown for flowering during the winter in the greenhouse? Seeds are sown in July, and resulting plants are grown in cold frame until October, when they are planted in benches, or in pans of light, fertile soil. They are grown in a light, cool greenhouse, and flowers are picked promptly to prevent seed forming.

Which primrose would you recommend for growing in a small home greenhouse (temperature of 45° to 50° F. minimum)? *Primula malacoides* (white, lavender, pink, red); *P. sinensis* (same color range); *P. kewensis* (yellow). It may be well to avoid *P. obconica* because it causes a severe dermatitis in some people.

Will you give some pointers on growing greenhouse primroses? Soil, medium loam with plenty of humus; grow in cool temperature; keep pots standing on layer of moist pebbles; shade in summer-time; keep soil moist at all times, but not waterlogged; feed dilute liquid fertilizer when final pots are filled with roots.

Can you tell me how to grow greenhouse ranunculus from seeds? Treat exactly as greenhouse anemones (which see) from seed. Both like a porous soil that is well supplied with humus.

Can I force climbing roses into bloom early in my greenhouse? Obtain strong plants in November and set in pots just big enough to contain roots easily. Use medium-heavy, fertile soil. Bury pots to rim in deep cold frame. Bring inside, in January, to temperature at first 45°, later 55° F. Spray with clear water to encourage growth. Water freely. No pruning necessary.

How should roses be pruned when they are potted, in fall, for spring forcing in the greenhouse?   Tall-growing ramblers and climbers not at all, other than removal of any dead or broken growths. Dwarf polyantha, hybrid tea, hybrid perpetual, etc.: cut back to within 9 or 10 ins. of base. Leave strong shoots longer than weak shoots.

Which classes of roses are best for blooming in tiny greenhouse during early spring?   Polyanthas and all miniature varieties would be suitable.

Would it be practical for me to grow roses for cut flowers in a very small greenhouse in which I want to grow a good many other kinds of plants?   Hardly. To grow cut-flower roses with even moderate success demands fair space and rather exacting conditions, but you could try a few plants in pots.

What makes the leaves turn yellow and fall off my miniature rose plant?   Poor drainage in the pot; not enough light; too much water; too rich a soil; too high a temperature; red spider infestation, and black-spot disease—one or more of these may be responsible.

I would like to grow salpiglossis in pots for spring blooming in the greenhouse. Is this possible?   Quite practicable. Sow seeds in sandy soil in August; transplant seedlings; and later pot them individually. Beware of burying plants too low in soil. Water with care.

Afford full sunlight and grow in temperature of 50° F. Fumigate if aphids appear.

Would it be possible to grow a bird-of-paradise flower (strelitzia) in a greenhouse built against my house? It should be. Healthy specimens need a large pot or tub, good drainage, medium-heavy soil, plenty of water, and feeding when pot-bound. They like abundant light and a night temperature of 50° to 55° F.

Can you tell me how to grow in winter the feathery stevia that is used for mixing with cut flowers? Propagate by cuttings taken from January to March. Keep plants repotted as one does chrysanthemums. Plunge pots outdoors from May to September, then bring into cool greenhouse (temperature of 45° to 50° F.). Water well at all times. Feed when pot-bound.

Are stocks good flowering plants for the home greenhouse? Yes. They can be grown either in pots or in benches. Sow seeds August to January, using rich soil. Finish in 4- to 6-in. pots. If planted in benches, set branching types 8 × 6 ins. apart; non-branching types closer. Grow in full sun and night temperature of 40° to 45° F. Avoid a highly acid soil.

Can you give instructions for growing sweet peas in a greenhouse that has scarcely any artificial heat? Sow in October in moderately fertile soil, preferably in a ground bed. Rows should be 3 ft. apart. Thin plants to 6 ins. apart. Ventilate freely, and avoid encouraging too much growth until February. Provide strings or other means of support. Feed when flower buds form. They need full sunshine. They can also be grown in 10-in. pots (though not so well), using brushwood for support.

4

Trees, Shrubs, and Vines

TREES AND SHRUBS are the backbone of any garden plan. It is they that frame the house, give it an interesting background to show it off to good advantage. They screen objectionable views and give privacy and shade where they are needed. They bring beauty and color into the garden, and if chosen carefully, they can make a beautiful setting that is of colorful interest every season of the year.

Gardeners today can obtain plants that have been introduced from all parts of the world. Nurserymen have been so busy propagating plants that there is a bewildering number available. How does one select from over 150 different crab apples, 250 different lilac varieties? Several years ago, one nurseryman offered 60 different species and varieties of mock-orange alone.

Fortunately, there are arboretums and botanical gardens about the country where one can go to see these plants, growing together and labeled. Also there are several books available in which one can find listed the better varieties—more important—why they are better. Then it is always possible to visit a nursery or garden center to see what special types of plants are offered locally. Just walking around any suburb of a large metropolitan area will provide some ideas, for in this way one can see what plants other people have bought and how they have used them in their own plantings. There is also an opportunity here to learn from others' mistakes!

With houses and gardens being considerably smaller than they were fifty years ago, there is a demand for smaller plants. Why plant an eventual 100-ft. elm if a 25-ft. crab apple will suffice? The smaller tree is attractive in all seasons, easier to care for, to spray and prune if it is necessary, and considerably cheaper to remove if that becomes a problem.

The difficult task of pruning is reduced if plants are purchased that will not grow quickly above the height wanted. The person who wants a lilac in the foundation planting, and has in mind a plant not over 5 ft. tall, covered with bloom, can easily be dismayed when that plant continually tries to grow 15–20 ft. and causes all kinds of pruning work each spring. Much better would have been to plant a 'Frosty Morn' mock-orange or an abelia, neither one of which will ever get much above 5 ft.

It pays also to learn about the susceptibility of some plants to disease and insect attacks. Why plant a European snowball, for instance, when it is known that they become covered with plant lice in the spring and need considerable spraying to keep them anywhere near good condition? The Japanese snowball would be much the better, for it is not nearly so susceptible.

Also it is advisable to pick out the trees and shrubs that you know in advance will grow under your conditions. Why fuss around with azaleas and rhododendrons if they are not hardy in your area or if you know your soil is alkaline?

When to Buy

Spring is traditionally the most popular time to buy plants, for, after a long winter indoors for gardeners over a large part of the country, the urge is to go out and see things grow. Actually, in many parts of the United States, spring *is* the best time to plant deciduous, dormant woody plants. Certainly if the plant is known to be difficult to move, it is safest to plant in the spring. Then you can purchase a plant from the nursery or garden center and plant it immediately, before it has time to dry out. If set in the ground in the early spring, the plant gets off to a good start, with a long growing season ahead to adjust to its new location.

On the other hand, if it were planted in the fall, it might have sufficient time to get its roots established, but it would have to suffer through the cold winter with trying winds and freezing and thawing soil. Many plants, especially in the colder parts of the United States, fail to survive the first winter. Early planting and a mulch aid trees and shrubs set out in the fall.

Such rugged, deciduous plants as forsythia, privet, spirea, lilac, maple, many of the oaks and crab apples can be planted in the fall in the North, as well as in the spring. It is the more difficult plants like the brooms, birches, and magnolias that might best be left for spring transplanting if there is any question about their survival in the North.

In milder parts of the South, fall planting of dormant nursery stock is just as good as spring planting. It really depends on the area, whether the fall plantings will be exposed to vicious winter winds, and whether one has taken the time to properly plant, water, and mulch the plants early in the fall.

Evergreens, both narrow-leaved and broad-leaved, are best planted in the very early fall in the North. They are always dug with a ball of soil about the roots, and planting in early September gives them time to get their roots established before the soil freezes, especially if they are mulched. The theory behind this is good to keep in mind. Evergreens always have their leaves and these give off water all the time, more on hot days than on cold days. They will lose a certain amount of water the first winter. However, if planted in the spring, their old leaves and the new growth also would lose much more—the reason why in some areas they have a difficult time staying alive, especially if their tops have not been pruned back. Even in the South, it is safer to plant evergreens in the early fall than in the spring—chiefly because they are dormant and not in active growth.

Container-grown plants are being widely offered by nurserymen and garden centers throughout the country. This innovation makes it possible to plant almost any time—in the spring, summer, or fall. It is still a good practice, though, to plant as early as possible.

There is one condition to watch for in container-grown plants. Sometimes they are grown too long in the containers, so their roots have become a solid ball. If planted out in this condition, the roots can easily strangle themselves as they grow and the plant will severely suffer. In the first place, such plants should be avoided. However, if purchased, remove the plant from its container and open up the ball of roots carefully, cutting back especially deformed roots so the ball can be placed in the planting hole in a fairly loose condition. While unnecessary fussing around with the roots of certain plants can have harmful results, some breaking up of the roots of container-bound plants has proved to be a good gardening practice.

Planting

It is at planting time that one should take the greatest care with the young tree or shrub. If the soil is poor, it should be replaced with good soil, possibly mixed with peat moss or well-rotted manure or compost. The hole itself should be ample to receive the roots, which in the case of bare-root stock, should be spread out in their normal growing condition, and not jammed into a small, tight mass.

In handling balled, as opposed to bare-root, stock, one should be very careful not to break the ball by dropping it, for then many of the young feeding roots in the ball will be broken. If it is possible to remove the burlap without breaking the ball, do so, or place the ball in the hole and then cut the strings and push the burlap down the sides of the hole, where it will eventually rot. If the plant was wrapped in polyethylene film, this must be removed.

Fill in good soil around the roots, tamping in well, and leave a small depression about the plant to catch water and prevent it from running off. Water thoroughly so the entire root area is wet; then keep it watered at regular intervals, if rains fail, to prevent the roots from drying out the first year or two. Also, it is excellent practice to mulch the newly transplanted tree or shrub, for this aids in conserving soil moisture and also keeps the weeds in check.

General Pruning

Pruning is always a dwarfing process, merely because in cutting off branches one removes so many of the food-manufacturing organs —the leaves. Therefore, if the plant is to flourish and grow as fast as possible, keep the pruning to a minimum. It is always a good idea to consider carefully why each pruning operation is to be done. There are good reasons.

In the first place one prunes at transplanting time to compensate for the number of roots that have been cut in the digging operation. It is impossible to dig all the roots, and it is unreasonable to expect a smaller proportion of roots to support the same amount of top growth with water and fertilizer. So, with deciduous bare-rooted plants, it is always safest to plan on removing at least one third of the branches at the time of transplanting. Admittedly this is hard to do, for one winds up with a much smaller plant than one has paid for! Experiments have shown that plants pruned this way at transplanting recover much faster than do unpruned plants, which sometimes die because of too much leaf area for the roots to support. (Many nurseries ship properly pruned plants.)

With evergreens and other plants that are balled-and-burlapped, the pruning need not be so severe nor is it necessary. Container-grown plants are another exception. If they have been growing in containers for some time, removal of branches is not necessary. Often, though, plants are dug and forced into containers immediately for quick sale, and so are actually merely "held" for a week or so. Such plants should also be pruned at transplanting time.

One prunes to remove dead or diseased wood, to correct bad notches on young trees, to preserve a single leader in certain trees and so prevent several leaders from taking over. Suckers are cut out at the base of some plants, such as lilacs, and certainly all suckers are cut off below the union of grafted plants.

Old shrubs can be rejuvenated, either by cutting them to the ground (in early spring), or by thinning out the older branches at the base, and then possibly reducing the height of those remaining. Such is the way to prune many lilacs, mock-oranges, spireas, and deutzias. Hedges, of course, are pruned for a purpose, and sometimes it is necessary to cut off a few limbs from a tree to give it a better shape. Girdling roots must be cut when they are noticed. When there is no good reason for pruning—don't! The plant will grow better without it.

Watering

Soils differ in the amount of water they retain, but the more humus or decaying vegetable matter in the soil the more water it will retain. Newly transplanted trees and shrubs need water to bring them through the summer droughts. It is essential that you keep track of their needs the first year or two, by checking their foliage for wilting, or by digging in the soil to see how dry it is. Trees have most of their feeding roots in the upper 18 ins. of soil, and many shrubs, such as rhododendrons, have all their feeding roots in this area. It is essential that this soil not dry out the first growing season.

Water should be applied slowly, possibly with a soil soaker, so that it sinks gradually into the soil. Applying water from the garden hose with its high pressure does little good if one hurries away to the next spot as soon as the surface soil looks "wet." If a slight depression is left around the newly transplanted shrub or tree, this helps trap the water and keeps it from running off. Checking, by digging in the soil a bit, gives an indication of how far down the water has gone. Leaving a pan out under the sprinkler gives an idea of how much water has been applied, and once you check the depth to which a certain amount of water has penetrated, it is a simple matter to repeat the timed operation the next time.

It is much better to give trees and shrubs a thorough soaking once a week during drought periods than to sprinkle them lightly each evening. Also, if it is an evergreen, don't forget to sprinkle the foliage, too, in the evening, for in this way it will take in much needed water through its leaves. Deciduous plants will benefit from having their leaves sprinkled, too. The cool of the evening is an ideal time as the plants have all night to absorb the moisture. This is also true of watering the soil.

Mulching

Mulching is provided chiefly to keep the soil from losing a lot of water by surface evaporation. It also prevents weed growth around the base of the plants. In autumn, it tends to keep the soil from freezing a little longer and thus gives the roots more time to elongate before winter arrives and the soil freezes hard. After the soil has frozen, a mulch tends to keep it frozen and prevents the disastrous "heaving" of the soil caused by freezing and thawing of late winter and early spring as temperatures moderate. Such alternate freezing and thawing causes young plants to be raised out of the soil and they can die by having their roots exposed to the elements.

In most areas of the United States, mulching has beneficial results when used on all trees and shrubs, especially newly transplanted ones. There are some, like rhododendrons, that benefit from a mulch all the time, because their feeding roots are close to the surface and they thrive in the additional moisture and cooler soil thus provided.

Many things can be used as mulching material. Peat moss, compost, ground corn cobs, ground sugarcane, leafmold, peanut shells, buckwheat hulls, ground bark, wood chips, cocoa shells, pine needles, marsh hay, seaweed, black polyethylene film, even crushed stone. Most should not be put on over 3 ins. deep. The applying of a mulch to any newly transplanted woody plant is an excellent practice, and it is a good idea to keep the mulch annually replenished for several years until the plant becomes thoroughly established.

Fertilizing

There are many kinds of fertilizers used in the feeding of trees and shrubs. Usually, it is not necessary or even advisable to fertilize a tree or shrub at transplanting time, especially if pains have been taken to provide good soil, compost, or well-rotted manure in the planting hole. It is best to let the newly transplanted tree or shrub get acclimated to its new situation for a year before it is forced into additional growth with fertilizer.

Years ago, well-rotted manure was advocated for everything. It is still an excellent source of humus and of nutritive value, but not always plentiful in all regions. As a substitute, there is the dried and granulated form readily available in bags at most garden centers. Many kinds of commercial fertilizers are available, the most common being a 5–10–5 combination. This is a general, all-purpose type.

The best time for application is in the early spring, before the plants start growing. It can be "broadcast" (by far the easier way) around the plants, or for trees growing in a lawn it might be applied by the crowbar, punch-hole method to prevent the burning of the grass, which sometimes occurs when it is broadcast over the lawn under the trees. Approximate amounts of this fertilizer might be:

deciduous trees: 2–4 lbs. per inch dia. of trunk breast high
evergreen trees: 2 lbs. per inch dia. of trunk breast high
deciduous shrubs: 3–6 lbs. per 100 sq. ft.
evergreen shrubs (exclusive of ericaceous plants): 3–6 lbs. per 100 sq. ft.

Fertilizers for ericaceous shrubs, that is, azalea, rhododendron, mountain-laurel, heath and heather and the like, are special in nature and one might refer to the section on broad-leaved evergreen shrubs for specific questions and answers dealing with this point. Several of the large fertilizer-manufacturing companies make fertilizers especially for broad-leaved evergreens and ericaceous plants, and where these are available from the nursery or garden center, they are recommended at the rates given on the bags.

The above fertilizer recommendations are based on a 5–10–5 analysis.

Actually, the amount of fertilizer applied depends on the kind and age of the plants, the type of soil, and the kind of fertilizer used. One would apply a 10–6–4 fertilizer at only one half the rate of a 5–10–5 in order to apply the same amount of nitrogen. If one were interested in obtaining more flowers on a plant that flowered poorly but grew well, one would apply a high phosphorous type fertilizer with little or no nitrogen, such as superphosphate.

When commercial fertilizers are applied, they should be watered in immediately, making certain that all the fertilizer has been washed off the foliage of any plants it has clung to.

Feeding Trees

Draw a circle on the soil under the outside limits of the branches, then another circle two thirds of the way toward the trunk. It is the area between these two circles that is to be fertilized. With a crowbar, punch 8–10-in. holes in the soil, making the holes 2 ft. apart. Divide the fertilizer (see approximate amounts of fertilizer to use above) evenly among the holes, fill in with soil, and water well. Or if you are very fussy, remove a plug of soil where each hole is to be made, punch the hole, apply the fertilizer, fill to within an inch and a half of the top with soil, then replace the plug of turf. Water in thoroughly and you probably will not notice where the holes have been punched.

It is always best, when contemplating fertilizing trees and shrubs, if you are not familiar with the process and the fertilizers, to write the State Experiment Station for their recommendations. In this way, you obtain the best information available for your area, and possibly save yourself much trouble from applying the wrong fertilizer in the wrong amount. Recommendations on the fertilizer bags or containers can also be followed.

The questions in this section have been divided into five general groups:

Deciduous Trees and Shrubs
Narrow-leaved Evergreens

Broad-leaved Evergreens
Vines
Hedges

This segregation might be kept in mind when trying to locate answers for specific problems with specific plants.

—Donald Wyman

 Deciduous Trees and Shrubs

GENERAL

What is meant by "deciduous" trees and shrubs? Those which shed their foliage in the autumn. Some, which retain their dry leaves, all or partly, through the winter, like beech and some oaks, are commonly included in "deciduous" trees.

Is it possible that a chain or a peg fastened to a tree at a certain distance from the ground will ever be further from the ground, no matter how old the tree? No, there will be no elevation of anything driven into a tree at a given point.

SOIL AND FERTILIZERS

How should I prepare the ground for planting trees and shrubs? Over a well-drained subsoil there should be, throughout the area, a foot of good topsoil. Beyond this, prepare individual planting holes for trees to a depth somewhat in excess of the depth of root-balls or root systems. Remove any excavated soil of poor quality and improve the remainder with leafmold and rotted manure or compost.

Most trees and shrubs seem to grow poorly in my soil, which is very sandy. What can I do? Select kinds especially suited for light, very sandy soil. For any others work in, around their root spread, a liberal quantity of peat moss, leafmold, compost, rotted manure, or seaweed (available from beaches if you live near the coast).

My soil, though well drained, is heavy, clayish. It bakes and cracks in summer. Will it do, generally, for trees and shrubs? You should lighten it by mixing into all planting areas, about a foot deep, a liberal quantity of fine cinders (not fine ashes) or coarse sand. At the

Trees offer more than just shade. Many show interesting bark patterns, two being the sycamore (left) and white birch (right).

same time work in some humus matter (leafmold, peat moss, rotted manure).

Few trees and shrubs succeed on my place, which adjoins a swampy tract. What can I do about this? The only cure for lack of drainage is to provide it. Either raise the level of your ground considerably, or limit your selection to those trees or shrubs which will accept the condition. Among these are aronia, swamp azalea, winterberry, buttonbush, pussy willow, tupelo, weeping willow, red maple, clethra, blueberry.

My soil is shallow, with hardpan beneath. Any special precautions when planting trees and shrubs? Before investing heavily in planting, break up the hardpan so that it will let water through. For the run of ordinary shrubs, there should be a depth of about a foot of good soil; for trees, about 2 ft. Neglect of these conditions may greatly limit your success.

What will I plant in front of an apartment house, where the soil is "sour" (of yellow clay) and the spot shady? Have tried several types of evergreens. An unpromising condition. In amply prepared pockets, try untrimmed privet, bush honeysuckle, or *Euonymus kiautschovicus*. Or, in an elaborately prepared and improved bed with acid, humusy soil, dwarf rhododendrons and mountain-laurel. If tree roots intrude, the prospects of success are poor.

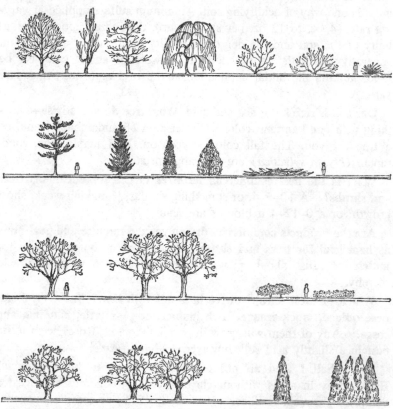

Homeowners can profit from the way landscape architects choose—and judge—trees before deciding which ones to plant. (Top row) The many forms of deciduous (leaf-losing) trees, including those of very narrow and weeping habits. (Second row from top) The shapes of conifers, of importance because these trees are evergreen all year. (Third row from top) Trees as canopies, either as single specimens or in pairs (left); and trees as walls and hedges (right). (Bottom row) The width of trees, either singly or in combination, must be considered when screening is the objective.

What do I use to make soil acid?   See Acidity in Soils, Section 1. Three to 6-in. layer of oak leafmold, rotted pine needles, or peat moss is one way of acidifying soil. Aluminum sulfate applied at varying rate (4 oz. to 12 oz. per square yard, depending upon the alkalinity of the soil and the degree of acidity required) is another, but generally less satisfactory, method. Flowers of sulfur can also be used, making the initial application at the rate of 6 oz. per square yard.

Our soil is rich but moist and acid. What tree do you advise—something with good autumn color?   Sweet-gum (liquidambar) would be a tree for you. The fall color is crimson. Red maple, sourwood, tupelo (*Nyssa sylvatica*) are also appropriate.

What is the best commercial fertilizer to use for deciduous trees and shrubs?   A 10–6–4, or something similar, if making weak, short growth; or a 0–12–4 if blooms are scant.

Are the products commercial dry pulverized manure and peat moss as beneficial for trees and shrubs as raw cow or horse manure for mulching?   Just about, provided the soil is not made too acid thereby.

Which of these shrubs thrive in a soil with lime? Barberry, Japanese quince, mock-orange, Irish juniper, crape-myrtle, nandina, and roses?   Any of them will grow in an alkaline soil. Roses seem to do best in a slightly acid soil, however.

How shall I feed an old tree which seems to be weakening? Easiest way in areas without clayey soils is to merely broadcast a complete chemical fertilizer (10–6–4, 5–10–5, or some equivalent) on the ground and wash it in thoroughly with the hose. The amount could be 2–4 lbs. of fertilizer per inch in diameter of tree trunk measured breast high, spread evenly under the branches of the tree. Another way is to dig 18-in.-deep holes with a crowbar, the holes 2 ft. apart over the same area, then divide the fertilizer equally among the holes, afterward filling them with soil. This second method does not burn the grass as much as the first. Water in thoroughly when complete. This is done in early spring or early fall.

How and when do I apply fertilizers to my shrubs?   Spring is probably the best time although October is satisfactory also. Use a commercial fertilizer (10–6–4 or 5–10–5) and merely spread it on the ground before the leaf buds open. Use the 5–10–5 at a rate of about 3–6 lbs. per 100 sq. ft., and water it in well.

TRANSPLANTING

When is the best time to transplant deciduous trees and shrubs? Either fall or spring, but the transplanting of all shrubs which are recognized as difficult to move and such trees as birch, dogwood, redbud, magnolia, yellow-wood and all tender types had best be planted in spring. Transplant before the trees or shrubs begin to leaf. In the fall, transplant as soon as most of the leaves drop.

How about evergreens? The best time for transplanting these is early in September. (See also under Evergreens, this Section.)

What is your opinion of winter planting? By this you probably mean moving in the depth of winter with a frozen ball of earth about the roots. This method is often used successfully by professional tree movers. For the average gardener, it should be avoided, except of course with very small specimens, because specialized equipment is needed to do the job successfully.

What is the advantage to be gained from a mass of fibrous roots? Ease of transplanting. Good nurserymen transplant their trees and shrubs regularly, thus inducing fibrous root growth. Or they root-prune their stock by dragging a U-shaped blade beneath the soil of the rows, thus severing wide-spreading and deep-penetrating roots. Home gardeners can root-prune trees and shrubs several months before transplanting by inserting a spade around the plant.

Can all deciduous trees be moved with bare roots? No. Experience shows that some kinds—birch, dogwood, magnolia, oak, tupelo, and all evergreens, for example—are best transplanted with a ball of earth.

How large a tree can be transplanted? It depends upon the kind of tree. Fibrous-rooted, easily transplanted kinds, with trunk up to 1 ft. in diameter if proper machinery and equipment are available, but many professional tree movers can move very large trees successfully.

I have a shade tree 10 ft. high, which was planted in the wrong place 3 years ago, that I want to transplant. How do I dig it up? Dig a trench around it 18 ins. deep. If many thick roots are encountered, keep farther away from trunk. With a digging fork carefully pick away the soil from roots, moving it into trench. Sway top back and forth to loosen remaining roots, and transplant before they dry out.

Can I dig a 6-ft. hemlock in the woods and transplant it to my garden with reasonable success?   Possibly. Dig a circle 3 ft. in diameter all around the tree with a spade in early spring. This is to cut the roots. Watch the tree during spring and summer. If it survives this treatment, then dig it carefully in early September. Keep all the roots in a tight ball and do not let this dry out. Move as quickly as possible.

When planting trees is it best to mound the soil around them, or should I leave a pocket to hold moisture to soak down to the roots? Do not mound the soil. Have it flush with the grade when planting is completed. It will then probably settle a couple of inches below grade, which is proper. A slight, saucerlike depression is advisable to facilitate watering.

Is it necessary to cut back trees and shrubs when they are transplanted? If so, how much?   Usually by about one third. If the roots are scant in relation to the top, reduce the lateral growths in the crown, leaving the leader unpruned. If the roots and tops are balanced, pruning less may be satisfactory.

Is it desirable to wrap the stems of newly planted trees with burlap? How long does one keep the wrappings on the tree?   Certain thin-barked trees like birch and yellow-wood and even beech benefit from this treatment. Leave it on for a year or two. Also, spraying the trunk with a chemical material like Wilt-Pruf gives just as good results.

Is it necessary to support the stem of a newly planted young tree? In wind-swept places, and where school children pass—yes. Before setting the tree, drive a stout stake into the center of the hole and snuggle the tree up to it. Fasten it by means of non-abrasive tape, crossed between stake and tree. Large trees are usually held firm by securing them with wires to 3 or 4 pegs driven in ground around tree several feet from it.

What should be done in the spring for fall-transplanted shade trees?   Do what necessary pruning may have been deferred in the fall planting. Check over fastenings, and prevent chafing of the bark. Replenish the mulch if necessary. Water during drought.

How can I help my newly transplanted trees (large) to form a

new and strong root system? If planted in proper soil, do not overfeed your trees, nor overwater. Keep a mulch at the base. Prevent drying out of the soil.

When transplanting trees why do suckers shoot from the ground instead of the branches? When suckers appear at the base, and no growth develops in the top, there is trouble. It is probably due to root injury and failure to prune top sufficiently at transplanting time.

Is it correct, in pruning newly fall-set shade trees of 5 to 8 ft. in height, to cut back the whip or leader one third or more as most garden books recommend? Do not cut the leader back. When necessary, reduce competing growths so as to prevent the development of future crotches.

When planting trees in the fall of the year, when is the best time to prune them? Immediately after planting.

I want to plant a double row of mixed flowering shrubs between lawn and garden, using tall and medium varieties. How far apart should they be planted in order to avoid either a sparse or a crowded appearance? As you do not give the names of the shrubs you intend to use for your border, exact directions cannot be given. As a general rule 4 to 5 ft. should be sufficient distance between plants in the front row; about 6 to 8 ft. between those in the back row.

Can most flowering shrubs and berry bushes be set out in the fall and winter, instead of waiting until spring? Shrubs (with some exceptions) and berry bushes may be safely set out in the fall; but the work should be undertaken as early as possible, while there is still sufficient warmth in the soil to develop new root growth. It is impossible to plant satisfactorily when the soil is largely composed of frozen lumps.

Could I transplant between December 15 and end of March the following: common lilac, French pussy willow, forsythia, deutzia, mock-orange, snowball, hydrangea, and bridalwreath? Do the transplanting in late March rather than in December.

Is the fall the best time of year to plant trees and shrubs in a climate as cold as that of central Vermont? No; early spring is better.

How does one go about digging up shrubs for transplanting? If they are small, thrust a spade to its full depth in a continuous circle, at a sufficient distance from center to avoid undue root injury, and pry out. Roots are likely to extend at least as far as the spread of the branches.

Is it necessary to cut back shrubs when they are transplanted? If so, how much?   Balled-and-burlapped specimens need not be pruned heavily after planting. Vigorous young shrubs of quick-growing kinds are best pruned to about half the length of main stems. Older, bare-rooted shrubs, with poorish root systems and large tops, are best pruned back to from two thirds to one half their length.

What is the reason for cutting back trees and shrubs when they are transplanted?   It reduces the plant to a size more easily supported by a disturbed root system; it reduces the area exposed to the drying effect of wind and sun, and divides the vigor of the new growth over a smaller number of growing points. (See also Pruning. Also see *Pruning Made Easy,* by Edwin F. Steffek, Henry Holt & Co., 1958.)

How low should fall-planted barberry, Vanhoutte spirea, and rose-of-Sharon be pruned?   With the barberry and spirea cut out, at about ground level, half of the strongest stems; reduce the remainder about half their length. If the rose-of-Sharon is on a single stem, it must not be cut to the ground. Cut out some of the branches at a point where they fork, and shorten the remaining ones to one fourth or one third their length.

Why do shrubs bloom well some years and others very poorly? Last spring my forsythia and flowering crab had only a few blooms. For two reasons. Some winters are cold enough to kill the flower buds of plants such as forsythia. Then too, many flowering and fruiting ornamentals, such as some crab apples, bear alternately, that is, they have profuse flowers and fruits one year and but few the next year. There is little the homeowner can do to change this sequence.

I bought some small shrubs grown in cans, but on dumping them out, I found a tight ball of roots. Should I plant anyway? Sometimes plants are grown too long in cans and when this happens the roots grow into a tight ball. Carefully open them out, unwind them, and spread them out normally in the prepared hole. If planted in a tight ball the roots might choke themselves as they enlarge and the plant would suffer seriously.

What is meant by "heeling in"?   The *temporary* planting of trees or plants, close together, in a trench or hole, with at least the roots covered, and properly watered. It serves to tide plants over an interval between their arrival and permanent planting. If so kept over winter, they should be set in a little deeper (usually at an angle of 45°) and covered, overall, with a thick layer of straw, leaves, or other mulch.

We heeled in 150 tree seedlings in November, and the weather prevented us from planting them. Will they be ruined, or can they be planted in the spring? It depends upon the kinds of trees and on the severity of the winter. It would have been much safer to have buried them, if deciduous, in a trench covered with a mulch of straw.

CARE

How can I stimulate the growth of newly planted flowering trees? If the planting hole was well prepared no special stimulant should be needed until the trees are well established. However, it is good practice to put a mulch of peat moss or black plastic on the soil over the roots in the fall.

Three years ago I started a grove of various shade trees on a plot 100 × 250 ft. There are approximately 100 trees. I am keeping the place very clean of any weeds with a small power cultivator, thereby also loosening the soil for better penetration of rain. The trees seem to do well. But am I right in keeping the plot scrupulously clean? The longer you keep the plot cultivated the more vigorously you may expect the trees to grow, but as it is an ornamental plantation and the trees are now well established and growing to your satisfaction, you can sow it down to grass. This would slow down the rate of growth a little but otherwise not be injurious.

What is the procedure to follow when watering trees and shrubs? Give thorough soaking so that soil is moist to a depth of 2 ft. If necessary, loosen topsoil with a spading fork to facilitate penetration of water. Or use a tool (obtainable from horticultural supply houses) designed to deliver water below surface by means of a hollow, pointed rod.

The grade has to be changed around my house, necessitating a "fill" averaging 2 ft. around a large oak tree. Will this harm the tree? It will probably kill it. (See following question.)

Can anything be done to help trees survive when grade over their

roots has to be raised? Build a "well" of rocks around trunk, keeping it at least a foot away. Spread a 6-in. layer of coarse gravel on soil. Lay agricultural tiles in rows, radiating from well to outer spread of roots, at end of each line, then raise the grade. The purpose of all this is to admit air to soil in which roots are growing. Unless soil is exceptionally well drained it might be wise to install drain tiles, 2 ft. below original grade, to prevent roots from suffering from too much water.

How high can the grade over roots of trees be raised safely? Depends on the kind of tree and soil in which it is growing. Six inches probably would not harm surface rooters, such as elms and maples, especially if the soil and fill is porous. Willows and ash can endure even more fill than this. The statement has been made that trees can survive a fill of 8 to 10 ft. if protected by a properly built dry well. (See above question.)

What can we do to stop a tree from "bleeding"? This depends upon the kind of tree and the cause of the bleeding. If it is merely bleeding due to pruning in spring, such trees (for example, maples and birches) should be pruned in summer. The bleeding soon stops. If it is due to "slime flux," it may be exceedingly difficult to control.

What is used to treat a decayed hole in a tree? Best thing to do is to clean out all the rotten wood, carefully, with a chisel. Then paint the cavity carefully with some good tree paint available at the garden center. These usually have some disinfectant materials in them.

Should I fill the cavity in our maple tree with cement? Usually no. This would not stop the rotting, nor would it give any strength to the tree. After cleaning it out carefully and painting (see above question) you could tack over some tin to keep out the rain and insects, then paint the tin some neutral color. In this way you could inspect the cavity every year or so, giving it another coat of paint when needed.

Will the roots of trees affect a garden? The roots of some trees are very objectionable. For instance, maples root right up to the surface of the ground, and elms are nearly as bad. Oaks and hickories are deep rooting and cause less interference with other plants. But the most serious objection to trees is to the amount of moisture they take out of the soil; and with it any soluble plant food in the vicinity.

Does smoke from a smelter damage trees and shrubs? Yes. Trees growing near a smelter may be seriously injured or killed, particularly if growing in such a position that the smoke is constantly carried to them by the prevailing wind.

Is anyone making studies of what trees and shrubs are most affected by air pollution? Yes. There is a Center for Air Environment Studies at the Pennsylvania State University, University Park, Pa. 16802. Write them for their most recent literature on the subject.

What is used to whitewash yard trees? Lime and water. But why whitewash them? Its only value is for the destruction of lichens, as its use as an insecticide is now recognized as negligible.

What is a girdling root? Sometimes one can see just at the base of the trunk of a tree, one large root crossing another. As they both enlarge, they tend to choke each other, often with serious effects to the tree. Best way to cure this situation is to cut one of the roots where the constriction occurs, thus leaving one root to enlarge normally.

How can I prevent seed formation on trees and shrubs? By cutting off the dead flowers, but of course this is only feasible on young or small plants.

PRUNING DECIDUOUS TREES AND SHRUBS

Why prune? Trees should only be pruned to remove dead branches, crossed limbs, weak crotches, to aid single-leader tree types in growing a sturdy central leader, and in some cases to "shape up" the tree. Some shrubs need pruning or thinning to keep them from becoming too dense and overgrown, and to promote flowering, as well as to cut out dead branches. Many trees and shrubs do well with no pruning.

Should all shrubs and trees be pruned? How does one know which to prune? It is not necessary to prune all of them. Some are benefited by pruning—such as most varieties of roses and certain flowering shrubs whose branches become crowded and cluttered with worn-out wood which does not bloom freely. Generally speaking, if a shrub does not give satisfaction it is worth while to try the effect of pruning. Prune, in the main, only where necessary to keep plants within their allotted space, and to keep them at the highest level of effectiveness.

Is it better to prune flowering shrubs in spring or fall? Few, if any, should be pruned in the fall in northern climates. Generally, shrubs which blossom on old wood (forsythia, for example) should be pruned in spring immediately after flowering. Those whose blossoms are produced on shoots of the current season can be pruned in the spring before growth starts.

Which shrubs should be pruned in the fall? (South Carolina.) Where severe winters are experienced it is desirable to defer pruning until the worst of the winter has passed. In your section fall pruning might be permissible for those shrubs which produce their blooms on young shoots of the current season. Examples are hybrid tea roses, peegee hydrangea, and late-blooming tamarisks.

When is the best time to prune a hedge? Hedges are best pruned when their young shoots are nearing the completion of their growth. With many hedges, one trimming at this time is sufficient; with others a second trimming can be necessary in late summer. In order to keep a fast-growing privet hedge in shipshape condition, trimming has to be done several times in a season. (See Hedges.)

What is the reason back of the recommendation to avoid, during the dormant season, the pruning of shrubs which blossom on the old wood? Because such pruning results in loss of branches which would produce flowers the following spring. Sometimes exceptional circumstances make it desirable to sacrifice flowering wood to attain a definite purpose; as, for example, when old, scraggly lilacs are cut back to rejuvenate them, reduce their height, and make a more compact bush.

Why are some shrubs pruned back every spring to mere stubs? This is done in the case of some shrubs which, though pruned back short, will flower on the new growth made after pruning. It affords a method of keeping them within limited proportions, without sacrifice of blossom. It is done with hills of snow hydrangea, vitex, abelia, spirea 'Anthony Waterer', and rose-of-Sharon.

Should you remove dead flowers from shrubs? Yes—if you want to increase the bloom of plants such as lilacs the next year. No— if you wish the plants to produce fruits, such as berrying viburnums.

Should shrubs, such as mock-orange, hills of snow hydrangea, weigela, roses, and beauty-bush, be pruned the first fall after spring planting? Shrubs usually require little if any pruning the first year after planting—certainly not in the fall. In the spring, hills of snow hydrangea and rose-of-Sharon can have the growth of the preceding year cut back two thirds.

When is the proper time for, and what is the correct method of, thinning out shrubs and bushes that have not been cared for properly for years? Should they be cut to the ground and allowed to grow up again? Indiscriminate cutting to the ground can upset the balance between root and top. Thinning out crowded branches can be done during the late fall or winter. Those shrubs which normally are pruned by shortening the shoots of the preceding year in the spring should be so treated. Any large, overgrown specimens can be cut back one third to one half, but this is done by cutting out one third to one half of the older stems at the base of the plant, possibly shortening the rest.

How many branches should be left when shrubs are espaliered against a wall? Average is about 1 ft. apart, but this is determined by the character of the shrub. Enough should be left so that the wall is well covered when the branches are clothed with leaves and shoots during the growing season.

Can narrow-leaved evergreen trees be trimmed as drastically as deciduous trees? No. One should be very careful in removing a branch, especially near the base of a tree, since new ones are seldom grown. They do not "break" as readily with new shoots. Hence, a slight pruning of the tips is about all one can do to make them thicken. This is best done in late June.

How about evergreen shrubs like yews and junipers? These are easier to prune for they usually are dense growing anyway. If needles and branchlets are below the cut, the chances are they will send out new growth.

My rhododendrons and mountain-laurel are very tall and overgrown. Can I cut them off at the base as I do privet and forsythia? Absolutely no! Pruning rhododendrons properly (unless it is just a snipping off of the young shoots) is a difficult thing to do right, partly because there are so many different kinds with varying growth habits. In order to make sure they "break," always be certain that there are some dormant leaf buds left *below* the cut. The best time for pruning broad-leaved rhododendrons is in early spring. Mountain-laurel, cut back to the ground in spring, usually produces new basal growth.

My linden tree is lopsided. Can I prune it to become a nice pyramidal tree like my neighbor's? Yes. In the early spring remove those branches or parts of them that are "out of line." Study the form of the tree carefully, taking out only such branches as make the tree appear ungainly.

WINTER PROTECTION

Are leaves good for mulching shrubs in the fall? Yes, where a mulch is desirable. Oak leaves are especially valuable around rhododendrons, and should be left in place finally to rot down.

I have read that maple leaves are not the right kind to use for a winter covering. Is this true? It all depends on what is being covered. They could be safely used as a mulch among shrubs. They are not so good as a cover for many perennials, as they tend to make a sodden mass with a smothering effect.

What is "salt" hay? It is hay from salt marshes cut and dried the same as ordinary hay. (It is often called marsh hay.) It is used for covering plants in winter as protection. It is obtained from dealers in horticultural supplies or nurserymen in your vicinity; or collect your own if you live near the coast.

Do shrubs have to be mulched for the winter with peat moss or marsh hay after their first winter? No, but it always aids root growth.

When is the proper time to remove mulching around shrubs? It is not always necessary, especially in the case of rhododendrons and related plants where a perpetual mulch is desirable.

KILLING TREE ROOTS

How can you kill tree roots growing in the sewers? Dissolve 1 lb. or more copper sulfate crystals (poisonous) in hot water and pour down a drain. If pipe is badly matted it must be cleared by plumber with Roto-Rooter machine. The copper sulfate treatment will tend to prevent the return of tree roots; but the only sure remedy is to eliminate offending trees or install root-proof pipes.

Can you tell me a sure way of killing a large buttonball tree and stopping the roots from growing without cutting the tree down? I have girdled the tree, and filled holes bored into it with copper sulfate. It should be unnecessary to do anything more to the tree; but to prevent shoots coming up from the stump, uncover the larger roots for some distance and peel the bark off them.

Is there any way to prevent elm tree feeder roots from spreading all over the lawn? I have heard that the United States Government recommends trenching the grass plot 12 × 36 ins. deep, and lining both sides and bottom of trench with tar paper. Will that work? This will work for a time. It would be better to sink a concrete trench into the ground. The deeper it is, the less the opportunity for the roots to grow underneath it and up to the surface on the other side. It may be necessary to dig down beside such a barrier every 4 or 5 years and cut all the roots growing around it.

How can I prevent roots from shrubs in a neighbor's yard from taking over in my seeding bed? They have become a very thick mat, stopping growth and preventing even the digging of dahlia tubers. Dig a trench 2 ft. deep along boundary and install a barrier below soil surface. This may be a narrow concrete wall, sheet metal, or the asphalt-impregnated roofing material which comes in rolls.

How can one combat shrub roots where shrubs and flowers are in the same bed? Chop off roots annually in the spring with a spade or a lawn edger; or install barrier as described in previous question.

What season is best for ridding property of wild cherry trees and elderberry bushes; and what is the best method? If possible, grub them out by roots with mattock; or pull up with tractor in early fall and burn when snow is on the ground. If cutting down is the only practicable method for you, do so in summer and chop off sprouts as soon as they appear. This will starve roots. There are also chemical sprays available for killing foliage as well as roots.

How can I remove a wild cherry tree and not have some shoots appear later? This tree is on a lawn. Cut down tree, grub out stump and largest roots. Any suckers that appear will be cut off when lawn is mowed. The remaining roots will soon die if no foliage is allowed to grow to nourish them.

What can I use to kill a large lilac bush; also a tree? Can be done by application of commercial weed killers to soil or foliage; but as the tops and stumps will have to be removed in any case, to avoid unsightliness, it is best to cut them down and grub out largest roots.

I cut a hickory tree down to about 20 ft. from the ground. The

tree is a foot in diameter. I would like to put a large birdhouse on the part that remains. What can I use to prevent the tree from sprouting from what remains and still have a strong pole for the birdhouse? Cut off a ring of bark at the base of the tree, or better still take all the bark off; the stump will then last longer.

What can you do when a neighbor to the south plants poplar trees and shuts off all sunlight along the entire lot line? Dig 3-ft.-deep trench along lot line, cut off all roots encountered, install barrier of asphalt roofing material, and plant shade-loving material. Cut off branches projecting over your boundary.

How best can I kill a sycamore tree which is growing so fast that it shades our perennial garden? It is about 8 or 9 years old. Is there any chemical that can be used? If so, how? The safest way to kill the tree would be by cutting off a ring of bark about 6 ins. wide all the way around the trunk. Any chemical you might use on the roots would also kill any other plants near it. Why not take it out?

What is the best method to get rid of alder and alder roots so we may greatly enlarge our vegetable garden? If there is much ground to clear, pulling them out with a tractor would be the cheapest. If there are only a few, then grub them out. Subsequent plowing would cut up the smaller roots. Also consult your county agent on the use of chemical brush killers.

How can old roots of large trees be removed from the ground when other trees are growing? If you attempt to take out the old roots there is sure to be some injury to the roots of the growing trees. The extent of the injury will depend upon how greatly the roots are intermixed. If the old roots must come out, dig them out with a grubbing ax. But it will do no harm to the growing trees if the old roots are left to decay.

Is there anything you can put on tree stumps to make them rot quicker? Drill holes in the stump with an auger, fill with saltpeter, sulfuric or nitric acid or "Ammate," then place stoppers in the hole. Use with care, as the acid will burn clothes or flesh when it comes in contact with them.

PROPAGATION

How should I store oak and maple seeds over the winter? It is better to sow as soon as ripe. This is particularly necessary with some of the white oaks. Maple and some oak seeds can be kept until spring by mixing them with sand in a box (stratification) and covering them with 6 ins. of soil outdoors.

Can trees be started from cuttings? The percentage of rooting of many kinds is so small as to make this method impractical.

What general procedure is followed in making cuttings of shrubs? Softwood cuttings are usually from 3 to 5 ins. long. Softwood cuttings must be rooted in a close, humid atmosphere such as that provided by a hotbed or polyethylene-film-covered box. Hardwood cuttings are taken in the late fall, after there have been a few frosts, stored in sand in a cool cellar (or buried in the earth) until early spring, when they are set in the open ground. (See also Mist Propagation.)

When making cuttings of shrubs and trees is the time of year, or the condition of the wood, the determining factor? Probably the condition of the wood is the more important, but as the most desirable condition occurs only at a particular time of year, there is a rather narrow range during which the best results can be obtained.

How can I propagate leucothoe? If the plant is a large clump, merely dividing the clump with a spade or even an ax in the early spring is sufficient. Cuttings can be taken, both softwood and hardwood, and rooted in a greenhouse bench with some bottom heat, or in a polyethylene-film-covered box.

Can boxwood and Japanese holly be rooted from cuttings? Easily —both by hardwood and softwood cuttings, taken either in late June (softwood) or early fall (hardwood) and placed in a sand medium in the greenhouse with some bottom heat and plenty of moisture, or in a polyethylene-film-covered box.

Generally speaking, when should I take slips from hardy shrubs? The majority root most readily during July and early August. Lilac and beauty-bush are two notable exceptions. The latter part of May, while the shoots are still growing, is the best time for lilac, and mid-June for beauty-bush.

How are slips from hardy shrubs rooted? By placing them under preserving jars, or in an electric hotbed, in a shady place. Sand, or a mixture of sand and peat moss, forms the best rooting medium. Also one can use a polyethylene-film-covered box or flat filled with sand and peat moss.

What procedure should be followed after slips taken from hardy shrubs have rooted? (Wisconsin.) They can be potted up singly, or be planted in boxes. In the northern states it is exceedingly risky to plant them in the open ground late in the fall. The pots or boxes should be stored in a cool place, such as a garage or cold cellar, where they will not be subjected to hard freezing. In the spring they should be planted in the open ground. (See also Propagation, Cuttings, this section.)

Are there any shrubs which can be increased by division? Yes. Some types of boxwood, hydrangea, rose, spirea, forsythia, kerria, etc.

I have heard about a plant propagation box covered with polyethylene film. What is it? An easy method of rooting many kinds of cuttings in the home garden is to take a greenhouse flat or wooden grocery box, fill it with a mixture of moist sand and peat moss (half and half). Make a wire support above it, 8 ins. high. Place the cuttings, moisten the rooting medium, and wrap a clear piece of polyethylene (without holes) above and below. This keeps in the moisture. It may only be necessary to moisten the mixture occasionally. Do not let it get soggy, just moist. Keep in a warm room; not too much direct sunlight. Easy to care for and if cuttings are taken at the right time it is surprising how many things will root.

Can rhododendrons and evergreen azaleas be propagated by cuttings? Yes. See under Broad-leaved Evergreens.

TREES FOR SPECIAL PURPOSES

What trees have interesting bark besides birch? Beech and yellow-wood (gray), white poplar (white), Scots pine (reddish), several species of cherries, lace-bark pine, stewartia, sycamore and cornelian-cherry (*Cornus mas*), (exfoliating), halesia and shadblow (striated).

We want some very narrow trees (not Lombardy poplar) to screen out an objectionable view at the rear of our property. Are there such? Yes. Included would be the columnar Norway maple, Temple's upright maple, the fastigiate European beech, *Liriodendron tulipifera* 'Fastigiatum', columnar English oak, red-cedar, *Juniperus chinensis* 'Mas', and arborvitae.

How can I start an arboretum? Professor Sargent, first director of the world-famous Arnold Arboretum, used to say that in order to start an arboretum one should have a thousand acres of land and a million dollars' endowment. The best advice would be to consult some recognized arboretum authority to ascertain what can best be grown in the proposed locality, how much it will cost to plant and care for it, what future purpose will be best fulfilled by the arboretum, and how this can be accomplished most economically. (See *Wyman's Gardening Encyclopedia,* by Donald Wyman, Macmillan, 1971.)

Which trees are undesirable on the home grounds because of their spreading, greedy roots? Maple, elm, and poplar.

Which food plants (shrubs or trees) can be used on a lawn of less than 1 acre, without detracting from the ornamental aspects? For beautiful blossom, any of the fruit trees. For added beauty of fruit, any of the showy-fruited apples and crab apples. If acid soil, blueberries for autumn color. For early-spring blossom and good jelly fruit, the flowering quinces. Hickories and black walnuts are very acceptable as ornamental trees.

Which tree would be a good companion for a magnolia in front of the house? If it is a star magnolia, the Arnold crab apple might do well. If it is a saucer magnolia, a fringetree could be used.

Which trees can you plant close to the house to be sure their roots will not get into the drains? The kinds will depend upon soil and the amount of space you can sacrifice for shade. Avoid the following: elms, maples, willows, and poplars.

We live in the country. Our driveway is on the north side of the house and unprotected. Driveway is east and west. On which side of the drive should trees and shrubs be planted to avoid snowdrifts? On the side away from the house, providing the winds causing those drifts come from a northerly direction.

How near the house is it safe to permit an oak or elm to grow? An elm could grow nearer than an oak (say 10 ft.), for the elm has high, wide-spreading branches and would eventually top the house. The oak, on the other hand, would have wide-spreading branches nearer the ground and might have to be twice the distance from the house so that its branches would not interfere with the building.

Will maidenhair (ginkgo), and laburnum grow in the northeast? Yes.

What tree can I get whose leaves have a silvery effect? White willow, 30 to 80 ft.; white poplar, 30 to 70 ft.; Russian-olive, 20 ft.; silver linden, 50–90 ft.

We are going to buy a few more trees with handsome foliage. We already have a hedge maple and an American beech. What else? Black oak, corktree, fernleaf beech, honey locust, especially the 'Moraine' and/or the 'Sunburst' varieties, tupelo, pin oak.

We do not like dense-leaved, heavy-looking trees, such as Norway maples. Prefer airy, delicate foliage. What do you suggest? Birch, poplar, honey locust, willow.

Are there any trees with distinctively tinted spring foliage? Not many. Here are a few: Katsura-tree (*Cercidiphyllum japonicum*); flowering cherries (*Prunus serrulata*); sourwood (*Oxydendrum arboreum*); some Japanese maple varieties; 'Crimson King' maple, purple smoketree (*Cotinus coggygria var. purpureus*).

I should like to plant a few small trees with good autumn foliage. Will you name a few? *Cornus florida*, dogwood, and its varieties; *Cercidiphyllum japonicum*, Katsura-tree; *Crataegus phaenopyrum*, Washington thorn; *Oxydendrum arboreum*, sourwood.

We would like to plant a good shade tree that would grow rapidly. Which of the following grows more rapidly: green ash, Chinese elm, silver maple, or rock maple? Chinese or Siberian elm is the fastest, with the silver maple a close second, but it is a poor ornamental, and green ash.

Can you give me some idea of a fast-growing shade tree for about a 61 × 50 ft. back yard? The Siberian elm, *Ulmus pumila*. However, it grows so fast that proper steps should be taken to prune it regularly and vigorously each year to keep it at the height you prefer.

Will you name some fast-growing trees for southern New England? Red maple, silver maple, Scots and white pines, red oak, oriental cherries, and American and green ash as well as the sycamore.

Which tree of rapid growth is best to plant for shade about a new home? Golden-rain-tree, flowering dogwood, Washington thorn, crab apple, if the house is small; red oak, sugar maple, and 'Moraine' locust.

What kind of shade tree should I plant that has a rapid growth, is well shaped, is comparatively clean during the summer, will not require spraying, and whose lower limbs, when mature, will not be less than 15 ft. from the ground? Tulip tree (*Liriodendron tulipi-*

fera) and sweet-gum (*Liquidambar styraciflua*) are favorites. Other good ones: sycamore, scarlet oak, and pin oak.

Which small ornamental flowering trees would you recommend besides fruit trees and dogwoods? Laburnum, silverbell, redbud, magnolia, golden-rain-tree, crab apple, flowering cherries, sourwood.

What is a good tree to use on a small place: one which will not have too wide root spread? Crab apple, magnolia, flowering cherry.

What type trees should be planted, on front of lot, for decorative purposes, where large trees are not desired because of their effect on the lawn? Are dogwoods, flowering cherries, etc., suitable? Dogwoods and crab apples are both superior to flowering cherries for this purpose.

What kinds of trees can be planted in a pasture used by hogs (that they will not root out or eat)? Hawthorn.

Can you name a few small trees with decorative fruit? *Cornus florida* (dogwood); *Crataegus phaenopyrum* (Washington thorn); and *C. mollis* (downy hawthorn); *Sorbus aucuparia* (European mountain-ash); siebold viburnum (Viburnum sieboldii).

Which trees provide food for birds? Cherries, mulberry, mountain-ash, hawthorn, small-fruited flowering crab apple, flowering dogwood, hollies, fringetree, tree viburnums.

Which are the best deciduous trees for specimen lawn planting? Flowering cherry, weeping willow, Norway maple, dogwood, beech, and 'Moraine' locust. Among the fruits, apple is best, although crab apple is more often used.

Will you name some lawn trees good for the windy southern New England coast? Red maple, red oak, poplar (especially white poplar and quaking aspen), sassafras, white willow, sour gum.

Can you suggest a shade tree nice for a back yard? Canoe birch; yellow-wood, red oak.

What are the best deciduous trees to plant for shade on landscaped grounds? Maple, apple, red oak, birch, buttonball, lindens are good.

How does one identify the sex in shade trees? The only certain way is to study the flower, when open. Those with flowers having both stamens and pistils are bisexual. Most trees, especially fruits, are of this type. Then there are trees like the hollies, ginkgo, willows, and mulberries which have only pistillate or fruiting flowers on one tree—these are the female or fruit-bearing trees. Staminate (male) flowers are produced on a separate tree. These latter are the male or non-fruiting trees.

Specific Trees

AILANTHUS

Of what special value is the ailanthus tree?   It is useful in city back yards, where it grows rapidly and endures almost any soil conditions, smoke, and dust.

Why do some ailanthus trees give off a disagreeable odor when in flower?   These are the male, or staminate, trees. The female, or pistillate, plants are inoffensive.

What is the ultimate height of the tree-of-heaven (ailanthus)? Sixty feet.

BIRCH

What is the difference between the paper birch and the gray birch? Paper birch bark peels off in shreds; gray birch does not. Paper birch has horizontal black marks on its bark; gray birch has triangular black patches. Gray birch has softer wood, subject to fungous disease, and is comparatively short-lived (20 to 30 years), while paper birch survives more than twice that long.

Which species of birch has white bark and several stems that come from the ground?   Gray birch (*Betula populifolia*).

I bought some white birch trees and when they came the bark was gray instead of white. Did they send the wrong trees?   Probably not. When very young the bark is gray; turns white later.

Would a weeping birch make a good tree to plant in front of a house?   No. This is a variety of the European birch, all of which are susceptible to the pernicious bronze birch borer. The best birch is the canoe or paper birch, native all over New England, and a splendid ornamental, very resistant to the bronze birch borer.

Are birch and sycamore trees suitable for shade on a small property? Birch trees would be better because they are considerably smaller. The sycamore takes a great deal of room.

At what time of the year should weeping white birch trees be planted? (Missouri.) In the spring is best. In the case of large specimens, balled, burlapped, and platformed, autumn or winter should be safe in your climate.

When is proper time for transplanting birches? (New York.) In the spring, before growth starts. In the milder parts of the state, balled-and-burlapped trees may be moved in the fall.

Is it practical to plant white birch in this locality (25 miles east of Pittsburgh, Pennsylvania)? Please give directions for type of soil, and any special care necessary to keep it healthy. Yes, it can be planted. All it needs is a good, well-drained soil, preferably on the sandy side. Susceptible to serious infestations of leafminers which can be kept in check by a systemic insecticide.

Last spring we planted a 14-ft. paper birch tree (it was balled in burlap). It did not fully leaf out and was attacked by aphids for which we sprayed. The tree did not seem to do well. Is there anything we can do for it this spring to make it healthier? Birch trees do not transplant too readily, but if yours was properly balled it should survive. Try placing a mulch of old or dried manure, leaf-mold or compost over the surface of the soil occupied by the roots. Put this on in May, after the soil has had time to absorb some warmth. Do not let the soil become too dry.

What is the life span of birch trees? Can they be planted near fruit trees? Yes, the birch tree—especially the paper or canoe birch (*Betula papyrifera*)—will live to be 50 to 75 years old or more. These trees do not send up suckers, nor do they harm fruit trees in any way.

Vandals have removed a cylinder of bark 6 or 8 ins. wide from my canoe birch. Will it harm the tree? Yes, if the inner bark has been removed. The leaves may start into growth because the sap passes up through the wood to the branches, but the roots will ultimately die of starvation because the food which nourishes them passes downward through the bark. If the injury is discovered early enough, it can sometimes be repaired by bridge grafting—which see.

If a young white birch tree is pruned, do the branches need to be treated where pruned? It is unnecessary to paint wounds when they are less than ½ to 1 in. in diameter. Large wounds should be covered with tree paint or something similar to keep out moisture and spores of disease organisms.

Can white birch be raised from cuttings?   It is next to impossible to root white birch from cuttings.

BLACK TUPELO   See Sour gum.

BUCKEYE   See Horse-chestnut.

BUTTONBALL   See Sycamore.

CATALPA

What is the origin of the so-called umbrella tree?   This is a dwarf form of catalpa (*C. bignonioides* 'Nana'), usually grafted or budded, at a height of 6 ft. or so, on straight, single-stemmed plants of *Catalpa bignonioides*.

I have 2 catalpa trees; bark is becoming loose and the part of one top looks rather dead. Can I save these trees?   Your description suggests root trouble, possibly due to poor drainage; or frost injury. Cut out all dead branches, and note whether the wood below the loose bark is also dead, for if it is you may have difficulty saving the trees. If the grade has been changed, this may have produced conditions unfavorable to the trees.

How do you prune an umbrella (catalpa) tree?   It is the practice to cut it back annually if a formal effect is desired. Prune in spring just before growth starts. It may, however, be left unpruned; then the head will present a more natural appearance and increase considerably in size over pruned specimens.

Should all the branches of the so-called umbrella tree be cut away in the fall?   It is the usual practice to cut them in the fall, but this leaves an ugly stubby knob. If pruning has to be done, delay it until just before growth starts in the spring. (See preceding question.)

Is there any special way of trimming a catalpa tree if it has branched out too close to the ground? Mine is about 2 ft. from ground and the leaves are so heavy they smother the grass underneath.   The lower branches may be cut off to raise the head of the tree. It should be done gradually, taking not more than 1 or 2 in any one year.

CHINESE ELM

How far apart and how close to the house should Chinese elms be planted? How close to septic tank and drainage bed? Keep them some 25 ft. away from drains. If you have in mind a row of them, plant no closer than 25 ft. apart, and at least 20 ft. from the house. A single tree might be set closer to the house if for some reason that should seem desirable.

What is wrong when a Chinese elm does not thrive? It is impossible to give a definite answer without more information. The soil may be at fault, but more probably you have not had it long enough for it to become established. Or it may have the Dutch elm disease.

When and how should I prune a Chinese elm, now about 10 ft. high, and very bushy, with lowest branch about 3 ft. from ground? Growing V-shape on top. If a high-headed tree is required, prune by removing 1 or 2 of the lowermost branches every year. This can be done in early spring before growth starts. It might be desirable to eliminate the "V," because of the danger of splitting, by removing the weaker of the 2 branches forming it.

How should I trim Chinese elm trees for effective shade? Cutting back the tips of the main shoots will stimulate branching and thus make the head more compact to provide denser shade.

Will you give suggestions for pruning (not trimming) Chinese elms to globe shape and square shape? When trees are trimmed to formal shape by shearing them, usually no further pruning is necessary.

I planted 2 Chinese elms which have grown along entirely different lines. One grew very rapidly, with spreading, upright branches and sparse foliage. The other grew slower, with dense foliage, and has a tendency to droop, very similar to a weeping maple. Since I prefer the second, could you tell me whether there are 2 varieties, and the name of the second? There are many variations in the Chinese (also called Siberian) elms, unnamed as yet. Ask some nurseryman to propagate the one you like from cuttings.

CORKTREE (PHELLODENDRON)

What does a Chinese corktree (Phellodendron amurense) look like? It is a round-headed, wide-spreading tree. The leaves are compound, with 7 to 13 leaflets, aromatic and handsome.

ELM

Should I plant an elm? Many have been lost in our town from the Dutch elm disease. Unfortunately it is better not to plant elms now. There are many other trees making good substitutes. (See below.)

What is the best time to plant American elms? Either in early spring or in autumn, after the leaves drop.

At what season should elm trees be trimmed? During the growing season, if it is desired to check growth. Otherwise pruning can be done in the fall or late winter.

Our elm was killed by the Dutch elm disease. Should I plant another? No. Select a good substitute like sugar maple, Katsura-tree, yellow-wood, beech, 'Moraine' locust, sweet-gum, oak, linden, or zelkova 'Village Green'.

EUONYMUS

Can you tell me why euonymus does not have berries in the fall? It has white blossoms in the spring, and was supposed to have berries in the fall. Euonymus species frequently perform in this fashion. They are probably alternate-bearing, like fruit trees. It may also have been that weather conditions were such that when the pollen was ripe it was not distributed properly by wind or insects. Fertilize with a complete fertilizer containing ample amounts of available phosphorus and potash. This could be done in the very early spring.

GINKGO

For what special uses is the ginkgo suitable? The ginkgo, or maidenhair, is quick growing and useful as a city tree. It is picturesque and erratic in its habit of growth and is remarkably insect and disease resistant. Autumn color is clear yellow.

Will you tell me something of the history of the ginkgo tree? How long has it been grown in this country? The ginkgo, since ancient times, has grown about temples in China. It is sole survivor of a large group of plants with a long geological ancestry, perhaps unchanged for a million years. Is probably more ancient than any other tree except the dawn-redwood, *Metasequoia glyptostroboides*. Introduced in this country in the early nineteenth century.

When and how shall I transplant two 5-ft. ginkgo trees, standing 4 ins. apart, with roots intertwined? In the spring, before growth starts. Try to untangle the roots carefully without breaking them. If you can do no better, save the roots of one intact and cut those of the other if necessary. Set as deeply as they stood. Water them well. Mulch the base, and prevent soil drying.

GOLDEN-CHAIN See Laburnum.

HONEY LOCUST

Is the honey locust good for the small place? I have recently seen one without thorns. The thornless honey locust (*Gleditsia triacanthos* 'Inermis') is a very desirable, lacy-leaved tree. It can, however, grow too tall for a small property. It is more slender than the common honey locust, which is undesirable under certain conditions because of the vicious thorns on trunk and branches and its habit of suckering freely.

HORNBEAM

What is the difference between the American and the European hornbeam? The native tree reaches a height of about 30 ft. while the European one grows to 50 ft. and is more vigorous when young. The European is more treelike; the American tree is hardier in the North.

HORSE-CHESTNUT (BUCKEYE)

What is the difference (if any) between horse-chestnut and a buckeye? Generally speaking, the horse-chestnut has five to seven leaflets in a cluster, while the buckeye has only five. Also the horse-chestnut attains greater height, and the fruits, flowers, and leaves are larger. We commonly think of *Aesculus hippocastanum* as "the" horse-chestnut. This is a native of Europe. The members of the *Aesculus* genus native in America we commonly consider buckeyes.

Is the horse-chestnut a good lawn tree? It is not considered so any more for it is rather untidy. There are many better lawn trees available, such as lindens, oaks, crab apples, mountain-ash, and beeches.

How long will it take for a 35-ft. horse-chestnut tree to re-establish after transplanting? It is about 10 ins. in diameter at base. If successfully moved into a suitably moist, well-drained soil, it will probably take two years for the tree to resume approximately normal growth.

JAPANESE PAGODA TREE   See Sophora.

LARCH

We have a tree which looks like a pyramidal evergreen but loses its foliage in winter. What is it?   A larch; probably the European larch (*Larix decidua*).

Is the larch a desirable lawn tree?   Yes. The European larch is best for lawns, while the American larch (commonly known as tamarack and hackmatack) is best in low, moist places.

Would a larch tree make a good growth in rather heavy clay soil? (Ohio.)   Yes, it might grow well in a heavy clay soil, but it prefers a cool, rather moist atmosphere such as that of the lower mountainous regions of the northern and northeastern United States.

How and when should a larch be transplanted? (New Jersey.) In fall or spring, with a ball of earth.

LINDEN

Are lindens good lawn trees?   Yes, indeed, and one, the littleleaf European linden (*Tilia cordata*), is excellent for urban street tree planting. The dense pyramidal habit and fragrant flowers in early July are outstanding. Other specimen trees would be the pendant silver linden (*T. petiolaris*) and the silver linden (*T. tomentosa.*)

LIQUIDAMBAR (SWEET-GUM)

In the late fall I purchased from an Ohio nursery a sweet-gum or liquidambar tree 10 ft. high. It was then covered with bright red leaves—beautiful fall coloring. Here it has not shown any fall coloring, only a drab yellow; why? (Pennsylvania.)   It should have a western exposure and plenty of available nitrogen to make vigorous growth. Often it takes several years after transplanting to really "reach its stride." Soil conditions often affect coloring.

MAPLE

I would like to have a maple tree but haven't much room. What shall I select?   The Amur maple is comparatively small, its leaves are handsome, turning a brilliant scarlet in the fall, but it casts a rather heavy shade.

What kind of hard maple has reddish or purplish leaves all summer? The Schwedler maple has a reddish tinge to the foliage throughout the season. 'Crimson King' is an improvement on Schwedler, with red leaves throughout the summer.

What kind of maple is Acer negundo? Commonly called boxelder or ash-leaved maple; this is a large, rapid-growing tree which withstands cold, dryness, and strong winds, but has very weak wood and splits easily. Best used only in dry areas where other maples will not grow.

Will you please tell me the common names of the following maples: Acer circinatum, A. macrophyllum, A. floridanum, and A. grandidentatum? 1. Vine maple; 2. bigleaf maple; 3. Florida maple; 4. bigtooth maple.

In what kind of soil and location do hard maples thrive? In any not utterly sandy soil of fair quality; not too acid and well drained.

I have a maple tree facing northwest, which gets a lot of wind. The branches are very short and high up. Can you advise how to get a fuller and shadier tree? It is probable that on the windy side the branches will always be shortest, as it is so exposed. You might try feeding it with a good tree food, or mulching the ground under the branches with dried manure or compost.

What is best time to transplant maple trees about 12 to 15 ft. high? In the spring, before growth has started; or in the autumn, after leaves have dropped.

My maple grows very thick and casts too dense a shade. How can I overcome this? Thin out superfluous branches during the summer months. Do this in such a way that the tree has a pleasing branch pattern. In some instances you may find it necessary to cut branches up to 10 ft. long. Always make the cuts close to the parent branch.

How can the top 6 ins. of soil be kept clear of roots of a 30-year-old hard maple? This is a surface-rooting tree, and there is no means of preventing the roots coming to the surface without injuring the tree in the attempt.

How hardy is Japanese red maple? What sub-zero temperatures

can it endure? Probably cannot live through consistently sub-zero winters.

What location and what kind of soil should the Japanese maple (the cut-leaved variety) have? A well-drained, open situation and a light loam of fair quality, but not necessarily rich. Mulch the soil around newly planted trees.

Would you recommend covering with burlap my Japanese red maple tree? (New York.) If you do not mind the appearance, this is a good idea. Japanese maples are subject to winter injury. They may stand uninjured for a number of years, and then some abnormal winter condition will cause one side of the tree to die.

My Japanese maple has unsightly, withered leaf edges. I am told that the soil isn't right. Is that so? Condition is probably caused by sunscorch during the period of soft spring growth, at which time the leaves are extremely sensitive. All you can do is provide some slight protection from the brightest sun in the spring.

How can one root cuttings of Japanese maple? Take cuttings in June and place them in a shaded cold frame or polyethylene-covered box. Unless you have had some experience with the propagation of plants you may not be very successful. Usually propagated by grafting or seeds.

What is the Norway maple like? A large, massive, quick-growing tree with big, dark-green foliage. It creates a shade so dense, and its roots are so greedy, that practically nothing can be made to grow under it.

When is the best time to cut large lower limbs on Norway maples? Should cuts be painted? If so, with what? As soon as the leaves have fallen; or in summer. When the wound has dried, paint with shellac, tree-wound paint, or white lead and linseed oil.

Why does a red maple tree turn green in the summer? This is quite normal.

When is the proper time of year to prune an ornamental red maple tree? In the spring. If it is a matter of promoting bushiness and checking growth, shoots can be shortened during the growing season.

I have a silver maple tree on which the leaves dry up before fall. One other silver maple tree on the same place is all green. What can

be the reason? Probably a difference in soil or moisture conditions. However, it can be due to a leaf blight.

I should like to transplant some soft maples. How much should they be pruned? It would depend upon the relative proportions of roots and tops. If roots are scant and coarse, reduce the length of side branches by as much as one half, leaving the leader intact.

What causes the bark on a large soft maple tree to split and hang in tatters? Apparently the tree is otherwise healthy. It is natural for the bark on old soft maples to peel off; this need cause no alarm, provided the bark immediately below that which is peeling is in good condition.

When and how does one plant and care for sugar maple trees? Where can they be bought? Sugar maples can be purchased (by that name) from many nurseries. Plant in the spring, before growth has started; or in autumn after the leaves have dropped. They require no special care or coddling and will thrive in any well-drained soil of fair quality.

MOUNTAIN-ASH

What can be done to make mountain-ash produce more berries? Does it need a special soil? Mountain-ash or rowan-tree (*Sorbus aucuparia*) will grow well in any reasonably good garden soil. However, if your trees have reached the age where they can be expected to fruit heavily, and fail to do so, they can be in need of fertilizer.

Would the mountain-ash be hardy here where dogwood trees are not? (Northern Maine.) Yes.

How close to house can I plant a mountain-ash tree? I want its shade to fall on our terrace. As close as is consistent with comfort and convenience. As close, if you wish, as 5 or 10 ft. It would develop more perfectly if set at least 15 ft. away.

Is a mountain-ash 6 ft. high easily transplanted in the fall? (New Jersey.) In New Jersey—yes.

I have a 3-year-old mountain-ash. Would moving harm the tree; and could you advise as to the best time? Move it in the spring. Dig the entire root system. Have the hole large enough to accommodate it in a natural position. Water well, and place a mulch about the base.

Why doesn't my mountain-ash, age 5 years, bloom? If your tree is healthy, it should bloom within the next year or two. When the growth is very vigorous, blooming is sometimes delayed; but it is too early to worry about that on a 5-year-old tree.

What treatment will encourage bloom on young mountain-ash trees? As they get older they should flower more freely, but there is no treatment that will insure equally free flowering every year. Whatever the age of the tree, in some years it will flower more profusely than in others. Make sure the supplies of phosphates and potash in the soil are adequate.

Why does my mountain-ash have a tree full of blossoms but only about 10 clusters of red berries in the fall? The tree is 6 years old. Weather conditions at flowering time may have been too cold or too wet, so that only partial pollination took place.

My mountain-ash is weak. Bloomed with heavy crop of seeds, then became thin. When may I prune? Some branches are weak and broken. It is in an open northeast location. The production of a heavy crop of seeds is a severe drain upon the resources of a tree and may account for the appearance of thinness. Feed it at least after every heavy fruiting. Cut out the broken branches immediately. Any other pruning should be done in spring before growth starts. Have you looked for borers in the trunk? (See Section 13.)

I planted a small mountain-ash tree this summer. The branches are long and growing more perpendicular than I like. Would pruning help? If so, when should it be done? Shorten the young shoots about one half in late winter. During the growing season, if any shoots show excessive vigor, pinch out their tips.

I know that the berries of mountain-ash are bright orange, but what are the blooms like? Broad clusters of small creamy-white flowers in May.

OAK

Which are the fastest-growing oaks? Red oak and pin oak.

How can I identify the different oaks? Black (*Quercus velutina*), bark very dark brown; inner bark orange; leaves to 10 ins. long, 7 to 9 ins. broad, toothed lobes, shining dark green above. White (*Q. alba*), very light bark; leaves to 9 ins. long; 5 to 9 rounded lobes. Red (*Q. rubra*), leaves to 9 ins. long; 7 to 11 pointed lobes, indented halfway to middle; pale beneath. Scarlet (*Q. coccinea*), leaves to 6 ins. long; 7 to 9 very deep, pointed lobes; bright green. Pin (*Q. palustris*), pyramidal form; lower branches drooping; leaves to 5 ins. long; 5 to 7 oblong, pointed lobes; bright green.

When is the best time to transplant oak trees?   In the spring, before growth starts.

Why must a pin oak be transplanted in the spring only?   Practice indicates that bare-rooted pin oaks are better planted in the spring only. Balled, burlapped, and platformed trees are often moved successfully in the fall.

When and how should a small oak, grown from seed, be transplanted?   In the spring, before growth commences. Dig out the whole root system. Have the hole wide enough to accommodate it; water the soil thoroughly; place a mulch at the base and see that the roots do not lack moisture at any time.

In transplanting red oak trees is it wise to cut the tap root? When transplanting oak trees not previously transplanted, it is inevitable. Young trees can survive it, but old trees will resent it and are, therefore, poor planting risks.

How should I feed a pin oak?   See under Soils and Fertilizers, this Section.

What does my soil need to make white oak leaves turn red in the fall instead of just drying up? Also, my pin oak leaves turned brown with very little of the normal red.   White oak leaves seldom turn red —usually purplish—in the fall. Pin oak leaves should turn a brilliant red some seasons when climatic conditions are just right. If your tree has a full western exposure, has plenty of nitrogenous fertilizer, and the weather is just right, it should turn the desired red. But the reasons vary considerably from year to year, some years resulting in "good" color and other years being decidedly "poor."

PEPPERIDGE   See Sour gum.

PLANE   See Sycamore.

POPLAR

During heavy, wet, unseasonable snow, when leaves were on trees, several bolleana poplars with trunks over 4 ins. in diameter broke off and had to be trimmed 'way down. What trimming shall I do on upright branches from low side branches? Paint wounds; leave up-right branches to develop.

What time of year should Lombardy poplars be topped? Ordinarily Lombardy poplars are not planted in situations where it is necessary to cut off their tops. If it has to be done, they can be cut back at any time without injury. Cutting back during the growing season checks growth; during the dormant season it promotes strong, leafy shoots.

How can I choose new leaders for some Lombardy poplars which lost their tops due to a severe wind and rain storm? Select the strongest shoot near to the top and center of the tree to make a new leader. Cut off the splintered stub just above the shoot. Make a slanting cut which will shed rain, and paint the wound.

SASSAFRAS

Is it easy to transplant sassafras trees from the wild? No, it is very difficult. This interesting tree, with large, various-shaped leaves which turn brilliant yellow, rose, and scarlet, is not easily transplanted. Choose trees not more than 6–8 ft. high—the smaller the better.

My yard has numerous sassafras trees growing. Do they have any ill effect on the soil? No. They are desirable trees, especially when they reach maturity. Picturesque in winter because of their gnarled branches; very wind resistant.

SOPHORA (JAPANESE PAGODA TREE)

What is the Japanese pagoda tree like? What is its scientific name? *Sophora japonica* is called Japanese pagoda tree or Chinese scholar tree. It has a rounded top with leafage which suggests the locust and casts a light shade. In summer it has small, yellowish-white, pealike flowers in large panicles. Hardy as far north as Massachusetts. Though it can attain a height of 60 ft., it remains small for many years.

SOUR GUM (NYSSA SYLVATICA)

I am told that a sour gum (also known as black gum, black tupelo, and pepperidge) would be appropriate for a place with poor drainage. What is this tree like? In silhouette when young a little like pin oak. Slow-growing, moisture-loving, attaining a great height; very hardy; distinguished tree; noted for scarlet and crimson foliage in autumn; difficult to transplant. The foliage is a dark glossy green.

SWEET-GUM   See Liquidambar.

SYCAMORE (PLANE, BUTTONBALL)

Sycamore, plane tree, or buttonball tree—which is the correct name?   All three common names are used for sycamore.

What is the best plane tree for city streets?   London plane (*Platanus acerifolia*).

What is the difference in appearance between the bark of the American plane and that of the London plane?   When the bark is shed the trunk of the American is white; the London plane is yellowish.

What is the rate of growth of a plane tree?   When young, averages about 2 or 3 ft. of growth in height each good growing season.

Does London plane prefer spring or fall planting? What are best soil conditions?   Plant in early spring or in the fall. It will grow well in any good soil.

Does the plane tree shed its bark untidily?   Yes; but the white or yellowish inner bark thus disclosed is definitely decorative.

Can a sycamore root about 3 ins. in diameter growing out of slope be removed without harming tree?   If the tree is well provided with roots on the side away from the slope, cutting off the root should not hurt the tree. As soon as the cut surface is dry, paint it with a good tree paint.

When is the best time to cut large lower limbs on sycamore?   This can be done in late winter or early spring before growth begins. It is not advisable to cut off more than 1 or 2 limbs at one time because of the danger of promoting excessive sappy growth.

TULIP TREE (LIRIODENDRON TULIPIFERA)

Which tree is it that grows tall and stately and has cream, green, and orange tulip-shaped flowers in June? In autumn the coloring is yellow.   Tulip tree (*Liriodendron tulipifera*). It does not flower, however, until it has attained good size—probably 10 years or more after planting.

Is it possible to grow tulip trees in northern New York State?
Near Rochester and Buffalo—yes. In the upper Adirondacks—no.

How shall I prune a tulip tree that was transplanted this spring, having three or four new shoots at the base? The original tree died. Before growth starts in the spring remove all shoots but the strongest. Avoid leaving any stubs which might decay.

TUPELO, BLACK   See Sour gum.

WILLOW

What is a good willow (not weeping)?   White willow (*Salix alba*).

When is the best time to move a willow tree?   In the spring, before growth starts.

Can a 4-year-old weeping willow be moved from one side of lawn to the other side without injuring the roots?   It can be moved safely, but not without cutting some of the roots. This will not be serious. Willows move easily in moist soils.

How far should a weeping willow tree be planted from a sewer? Are their roots a particular menace to sewer pipes?   At least 25 ft. or 30 ft. away. Their roots are very likely to be troublesome.

Will the roots of willow trees damage concrete pits, septic tanks, or drilled wells? I am anxious to plant a pair near these things and have been told that the roots damage underground constructions. The roots of willows will enter the tiniest crevices where they may obtain moisture, and unless all joints are screw joints or are filled with lead you may have considerable trouble in a few years.

Is a weeping willow tree self-pruning? I notice all the small limbs have dropped off; or is this caused by a disease?   Many willows shed some of their twigs annually by the development of what the botanist calls "abscission layers." Probably this is what your tree has been doing. Not a disease, but it certainly is not a neat habit.

Decorative Flowering Trees

CHERRY

Are there flowering cherry trees whose leaves unfold brown and then turn green? Yes. Among these are Sargent cherry with single pink blossoms, and Kwanzan cherry with double pink ones.

Which flowering cherry trees have white and pale pink flowers? Try 2 beauties, 'Naden' with semi-double fragrant blossoms in pink and white, and 'Shirotae' with double white flowers.

I once saw a cherry tree blooming in autumn. What was it? It must have been autumn cherry (*Prunus subhirtella* 'Autumnalis'), pink, which blooms in spring and again sparingly in the fall.

What is the best way to propagate Nanking cherry (*Prunus tomentosa)*? Either from seeds, which should be stored cool, 40° to 50° F., in moist sand over winter; or from cuttings taken in July and placed under a bell jar or in a polyethylene-enclosed flat; or in a cold frame kept closed until roots are formed.

Is there a narrow or columnar Japanese cherry? Yes, a beauty named 'Amanogawa', with semi-double pink flowers 1¾ ins. in diameter.

CRAB, FLOWERING

I have a sunny space alongside my house about 10 ft. wide. Will you recommend a flowering tree that will not spread too much and will not grow over 20 ft. tall? Any one of 20 different kinds of crab apples, especially 'Dorothea' crab apple.

Would you advise spring planting of flowering crab? Yes.

What is the best way to move flowering crab apple trees 3 ins. in diameter, about 8 ft. high? Balled, burlapped, and platformed— preferably in the spring; but safe enough in the autumn, after the leaves have dropped.

Can you recommend a few decorative crab apple trees? Arnold crab (*Malus arnoldiana*) with single pink and white blossoms; carmine crab (*M. atrosanguinea*), blossoms deep pink and red fruits; 'Dorothea' with double pink blossoms, 2 ins. in diameter, and yellow fruits; and the cherry crab (*M. robusta*) with white flowers and red and yellow fruits. There are nearly 100 others being offered by American nurserymen.

Is the Bechtel crab apple still a popular ornamental? No. Although it has double pink flowers, the fruits are only green and not ornamental. There are many much better Oriental crab apples with both good flowers and ornamental fruits.

Do crab apples make the same type of growth as apples? In some cases, but most make a much finer texture, are dense and rounded in habit, and can be grown with branches touching the ground on all sides. 'Van Eseltine' is narrow and upright in habit, the tea crab is vase-shaped, 'Red Jade' has pendulous branches.

I live in Wisconsin. Are crab apples hardy here? Yes, they can be grown wherever there are apple trees.

What care does the dolgo crab tree need in winter? No more care is needed than would be given an apple tree. A mulch of rotted manure or compost spread around in the fall would be helpful.

Is there any way of preventing a flowering crab apple from increasing in size too rapidly, without loss of the flower display? Yes. Shorten young shoots each season, about ½ when they are ⅔ grown.

DOGWOODS

Does the flowering dogwood tree come in any color except white? Yes, there are pink or rose forms.

What is the Japanese flowering dogwood like? Similar to our native flowering dogwood, but the flowers (bracts) are pointed instead of blunt. The Japanese species (*Cornus kousa*) blooms a few weeks later. The berries grow together in a head and appear to resemble large raspberries.

Should soil for dogwood be acid or alkaline? It grows well in both, if not extreme. Slightly acid preferred.

What is the best fertilizer for dogwoods? How applied and when? Flowering dogwood (*Cornus florida*) is usually planted in spring. In such cases mix a 10–6–4 with a good compost at the rate of 4-in.

potful to a wheelbarrow of soil, and use this to fill about the ball of soil. Thereafter, if necessary, fall applications of 10–6–4. A 4-in. tree (diameter of trunk) will need 10 lbs. applied over the area covered by spread of branches and a little beyond.

I have been told that white flowering dogwood (Cornus florida) would not bloom if planted in an unprotected place, but only if in a wooded place. Is this true? (Michigan.) This may be true in the colder parts of Michigan, where the wooded areas give it winter protection and prevent its buds from winterkilling from too severe cold. Farther south the dogwood will do well either in the open or in wooded areas.

When is the best time to move dogwood from the woods to a garden? In the spring only—before growth starts.

Should the pink dogwoods be planted at a different time from the white kind? (Kentucky.) Both white and pink dogwoods can be planted at the same time. Transplant with a ball of earth—not bare root, unless plants are very young.

Are dogwood trees, 3 to 4 ft., hardy in northern New York? In Rochester and Buffalo—yes; but in the Adirondacks these trees are frequently subjected to such low temperatures that winterkilling results.

How soon after transplanting wild dogwood do they bloom? From 1 to 5 years, depending on the size and age of the plant and the growing conditions.

What would cause a white dogwood to show only 2 bracts to a flower, every flower, every season? Winter injury—the outside bracts being killed or stunted by severe weather. Also there may be individuals in which this is characteristic. Such specimens should be replaced with normal plants.

What makes all the buds fall from my white dogwood in the spring? They set perfectly in the fall, but just drop off. They are frequently killed by severe winters. This is especially true in central to northern New England.

Can dogwood be grown in this section? Our soil is alkaline. My tree had about 6 leaves on all summer. (Utah.) Give it the best garden soil you have available. Mix acid leafmold with it. The chances are the summers are too hot and the winters too cold for flowering dogwood (*Cornus florida*) to amount to very much in many sections of Utah.

I have a white dogwood tree 5 or 6 years old. Appears to be very healthy, but does not blossom. What should be done? Merely have patience; and try working superphosphate into the soil about the roots.

My pink dogwood has faded to a dirty white. Is there anything I can fertilize with and bring back to original lovely pink? Possibly a heavy application of a nitrogenous fertilizer would help. It might be that the pink-flowering part has died and you now have the white-flowering understock left in its place, since pink dogwoods are usually grafted plants. If this is the case, and the understock only remains, it will never have pink flowers.

What is the treatment to insure blooming of red dogwood? Every well-established flowering dogwood should bloom if the soil is normal. If it does not, a 3-ft. ditch 18 ins. deep could be dug around the tree several feet from the base. Superphosphate should be mixed with the soil as it is returned to the ditch. This treatment frequently results in aiding the flowering of dogwoods, and of wisterias.

A transplanted twin (2-stemmed) wild dogwood bloomed for the first time this year. When is the proper time to cut the shoot or twin which does not bloom? Any time, preferably just after flowering. However, both branches will bloom eventually.

When is the best time to prune and transplant a dogwood tree? Ours has small flowers, and is getting too large. The branches have fallen over the ground and rooted themselves. Can I use these in any way? Dogwoods are best pruned in the spring after flowering, and are most easily moved in early spring. The branches that have rooted can be cut off and transplanted, and in this way might make separate plants.

What winter protection should be provided for very young dogwood trees? Mulching the roots with peat moss, rotted manure, or compost would help the first year or two.

Is it true that there are 2 kinds of dogwood trees—male and female? No; dogwood flowers are "perfect," having both stamens and pistil in the same flower. They are borne in clusters and form the center of what commonly is considered the dogwood "flower." The large "petals" are really bracts or modified leaves surrounding the clusters of the tiny *true* flowers.

Is it difficult to grow dogwoods from seed? (North Carolina.) No. Sow 1 in. deep in late fall; protect carefully from mice; and leave outdoors all winter to freeze. Germination will begin in spring, and may continue for a year. Transplant when 4 ins. high.

Will pink dogwood tree seedlings bloom true? Probably not. They should be propagated either by grafts or budding to insure the young plants having the identical characteristics of the parents. These are termed asexual methods of propagation. Propagation by seed is the sexual method.

Can I propagate pink or red flowering dogwood from seeds? The seedlings are not likely to be red-flowered. The usual method is to graft scions of a colored form on seedling understocks of the common flowering dogwood. Layering is practicable if it is possible to bend the branches down to earth to root them. (See Propagation.)

RUSSIAN-OLIVE (ELAEAGNUS) See Shrubs.

FRINGETREE (CHIONANTHUS)

Is the fringetree native? What is it like? Yes. This tree or large shrub bears loose, shredlike tassels of fragrant green-white flowers, in May or June, and has glossy tapering leaves. Male plant has larger flower trusses, but female has plumlike fruits in September.

GOLDEN-RAIN-TREE (KOELREUTERIA)

Is there any tree I can get that has yellow flowers? Golden-rain-tree and laburnum, which see.

I want to try an uncommon flowering tree. What do you advise? Please describe same. The golden-rain-tree (*Koelreuteria paniculata*) is a small, decorative tree with rounded top. Large panicles of small yellow flowers bloom in July or August. In September it has papery pods, and the foliage turns bright yellow.

Would a golden-rain-tree be appropriate on a small informal place? We like yellow blossoms. (Mid-New England.) Excellent, if given a sheltered location; otherwise branches can be killed back during severe winters. It likes full sun.

GORDONIA (FRANKLINIA)

What is Franklinia alatamaha (also known as Gordonia alatamaha)? A beautiful shrub or small tree originally from Georgia. Introduced to cultivation in 1790 by John Bartram, who discovered it on one of his plant-collecting trips to the South; it has since never been found in the wild. It has handsome, glossy, bright green leaves about 5 ins. long. In autumn its foliage turns orange-red and it bears cup-shaped, fragrant white flowers to 3 ins. across, with handsome golden anthers. A large specimen in Bartram's Garden near Philadelphia was long supposed to be the only living specimen. All other specimens in cultivation are believed to have been propagated from the Bartram tree, which is now dead. Its common names include Franklin-tree and gordonia, the last probably because it has been shunted back and forth between two genera, *Franklinia* and *Gordonia*.

Does the "lost tree" (Franklinia) have any special requirements? Mine does not grow well. It prefers a moist but well-drained soil. Not reliably hardy inland far north of New York City.

Does the Franklin-tree require an acid or alkaline soil? There is a conflict of opinion on this point. Usually it is considered that an acid soil is preferred, but some have found that it responds to an application of lime.

Is loblolly bay (Gordonia lasianthus) hardy in Pennsylvania? Probably not. Native from Virginia to Florida. *Franklinia alatamaha* (see previous questions), if sheltered, can be hardy to Massachusetts.

HAWTHORN

What color are the flowers and berries of the hawthorns? To choose a few popular kinds—Washington thorn and cockspur thorn have white flowers; English hawthorn has several varieties, single and double, varying in color from white to scarlet. These all have red berries, the Washington thorn bearing the most decorative ones.

What is a "May Day tree"? Perhaps you mean the May-tree of England, also called English hawthorn, which is a hawthorn, *Crataegus oxyacantha*.

Do you need two trees to make hawthorns bloom? No.

I transplanted a hawthorn tree in November. Is it natural that the leaves should die in a few days? I cut back all the tips of the branches at the time of transplanting. If planted with bare roots (which would be hardly advisable), then any leaves left on the tree would promptly wither. But this would not be harmful so late in the season.

What is the reason why a very flourishing pink hawthorn tree starts

to shed its leaves in early August and has new leaves and even blossoms in September? Can this condition be corrected? The fact that the hawthorn sheds its leaves in August suggests that the tree has been attacked by spider mites, or by a leaf blight. For the spider mites use diluted miscible oil as a dormant spray; for the blight, use Bordeaux mixture. See also Section 13.

When should red hawthorn trained on a wall be pruned? It should be pruned, after flowering, by shortening new shoots as they are produced during the summer. The following spring, before growth begins, thin out some of the weakest shoots if they appear to be crowded.

How shall I prune my Paul's double-scarlet hawthorn? If it is growing vigorously, and you wish to keep it within bounds, shorten the leading shoots in July. If growth is weak, cut out branches in late winter, having in mind the desirability of maintaining its interesting branch pattern.

LABURNUM

I saw in June a small tree that had flowers like wisteria, only yellow in color. What was it? Golden-chain laburnum (*L. anagyroides*).

How hardy is the Laburnum watereri? This is probably the hardiest of the laburnums. However, it is not reliably hardy much farther than 50 miles north of New York City.

Will you describe necessary soil, exposure, and give any other suggestions for culture of "golden tree," which I understand is a variety of laburnum? (Massachusetts.) These trees prefer a sandy soil, not too acid, which must be well drained. Protection from cold winds is also necessary.

Will you give some advice on the culture of Laburnum watereri? I have had difficulty growing this tree. This should not present any difficulties provided it is growing in a well-drained position. (See previous question.) Do aphids attack it? If so, spray with malathion or nicotine whenever they are present; otherwise they can completely ruin the new growth.

MAGNOLIA

Are Magnolia fraseri, macrophylla, kobus, and soulangiana 'Lennei' hardy in Pennsylvania? Yes. All these should be hardy in Pennsylvania except in the very coldest areas.

Are the following varieties of magnolias good for southern New York: M. virginiana (sweet bay), M. acuminata (cucumber tree), and M. obovata (whiteleaf Japanese magnolia)? Yes.

Would any magnolia trees be hardy north of New York City? Would their leaves be evergreen? Leaves would not be evergreen. The cucumber tree, the saucer magnolia, the star magnolia, and the sweet bay (or swamp magnolia) are hardy in Boston.

Will a magnolia tree grow around Woodridge, New York? Certainly. The star magnolia, the cucumber tree (*Magnolia acuminata*), or any one of several varieties of the beautiful saucer magnolia should all do well.

Sweet or acid soil for magnolias? Slightly acid, pH 6.5.

When is the best time to transplant magnolias? In the spring, even during, or immediately after, the flowering period. Move with as good a ball of fibrous roots as it is possible to obtain.

Should a small potted magnolia tree be kept growing in the house in sunny window for the winter, to be planted outdoors in the spring? Do not attempt to keep the magnolia growing through the winter, as it requires a rest at that time. Keep it in a cool cellar or garage, but do not allow the soil to become entirely dry. It should be planted in the garden in the spring.

When can I move magnolia trees from woods to garden, and what treatment should be given? In the spring. The cucumber tree (*Magnolia acuminata*) is not easily transplanted from the wild. Get as many of the fibrous root ends as possible. Have the hole wide enough to accommodate them. Mulch the soil over the roots. Wrap the trunk with burlap, and spray tops with Wilt-Pruf *before digging*.

What are the "rules" for growing magnolias? Magnolias require rich soil, therefore the addition of rotted cow manure or compost is advisable. While they require a moist soil for best results, it is equally important that it be well drained. For most, a position with full exposure to the sun is desirable.

Will you give the year-around treatment which would be best for the growth of Magnolia soulangiana in my locality? Particularly the establishment of young trees. (Pennsylvania.) Once the plants begin to grow satisfactorily after they are planted in the garden, they require little in the way of extra attention. A mulch over the roots, particularly a mulch of rotted cow manure or compost will feed them and keep the roots cool in summer.

How can I get results with a magnolia in this district? (Pennsylvania.) The star magnolia is the easiest to grow and is also the hardiest. If it is given a good soil it should do well. The many varieties of the saucer magnolia (*Magnolia soulangiana*) can also be grown with no particular attention other than the supplying of good soil.

Our Magnolia soulangiana, planted in October, had scant bloom and very few leaves the following spring and summer. Will it survive? We mulched with cow manure in fall. What else can be done? Magnolias frequently make very little growth during the year after they are transplanted. Mulching is beneficial. For the first winter at least, protect from sun and wind with a screen of burlap, evergreen branches, or boards. It should make good growth after the first year.

What can I do to make a magnolia bloom? I have had the tree for 5 years and it is 7 ft. high, grows well, but has never bloomed. It is possible that you have a seedling of one of the tree magnolias, in which case it might be several years more before the tree blooms. As the growth is satisfactory, do not worry. Some tree types take nearly 20 years to bear their first flowers. However, 'Merrill', a recent hybrid with large, double white flowers, will bloom only 3–4 years after it is grafted. Star and the saucer magnolias usually bloom a year or so after transplanting.

I have a Magnolia soulangiana which was in bloom when I bought it from the nursery; it bloomed the next season but hasn't bloomed for two seasons. What should be done? Magnolias resent moving and sometimes take a few years to become established after transplanting. If it is planted in good soil in a well-drained position it will soon resume its flowering. If you have any doubt about the quality of the soil, topdress it with cow manure.

How do you cut back a Magnolia virginiana (6 to 7 ft. tall) when transplanting? Reduce the main stems to about ⅔. If it appears to be making good growth, do not cut it.

My young magnolia produced many sucker shoots this summer. Should they be cut or left on? If the shoots originate from below the ground line, they probably come from the understock on which the magnolia is grafted, and should be cut off. If, however, they come from *above* the ground line, they may be left, provided they are not too crowded and do not spoil the looks of the tree.

How should I protect magnolias, planted in spring, during the first winter? (Michigan.) Sometimes it is advisable to wrap the trunks in burlap, especially for the first winter. If the plants are small, you might build a burlap screen about them for the winter and even partly fill it with leaves, which would aid in protecting the roots from too-severe winter cold.

Do young magnolia plants (4 to 5 years) need winter protection? The magnolias commonly grown should not need protection at that age unless your garden is so situated as to be exposed to northwest winds. If that is the case, erect a screen on that side of the plants.

Can you start a new magnolia from cuttings from an old tree? If so, how can it be done? Some of the magnolias may be rooted, but they are very difficult. Sideshoots, about 5 ins. long, are generally the most successful. Cut very close to the branch, so that a little of the old wood is taken also. They must be kept in close, humid conditions until rooted. A cold frame or polyethylene-covered box in a place out of the sun would be required. *Magnolia stellata* (and possibly others) can be easily rooted by the "mist" method.

A branch was broken from my young magnolia bush. It has one bud on it. I placed it in a bottle of water and it started blooming. How can I grow roots on it? You can't! (See answer to preceding question.)

Where and how should magnolia seeds be planted? Soak in water until fleshy covering can be removed. Plant seeds at once, before they dry out, ½ in. deep in soil of cold frame, or in cool place over winter. They will germinate the following spring.

PEACH, FLOWERING

When is the best time to transplant a flowering peach? (New Jersey.) In early fall or in spring.

PEAR

What is the 'Bradford' pear? It is a hybrid, a fast-growing seedling of *Pyrus calleryana,* selected by the U. S. Department of Agriculture, that is proving a good street and garden tree in the vicinity of Washington, D.C., although perfectly hardy north to Boston. A standard tree, 5 ft. tall, with white flowers and brilliant scarlet autumn foliage. The small fruits, only ½ in. long, have no economic value.

PLUM

How and when shall I prune purpleleaf plum (Prunus cerasifera 'Atropurpurea')? Severe pruning of trees related to plums and the stone fruits generally is to be avoided. Unless there is some urgent reason to the contrary, pruning of the Pissard plum should be restricted to shortening "wild" (too energetic) shoots during the growing season.

REDBUD (CERCIS)

Which other native tree would make a good companion to the white-flowered dogwood? The redbud; it flowers simultaneously and likes a similar environment.

What does redbud look like? In open places it has wide crown and grows 15 or more ft. high. In shaded and crowded quarters it will grow taller and slimmer. It has deep pink, pea-shaped flowers which grow in clusters along the stems. The leaves which follow are large and roundish, turning bright yellow in the fall.

Can redbud be successfully moved in fall? Redbud is not one of the easiest shrubs to move, and spring is much safer than fall for the operation. Move it with a ball of earth, held by burlap, attached to the roots and, unless the ball is very firm, do not attempt to remove the burlap when the plant is in its new position.

This is the second year for a redbud tree. Will it bloom this spring if I move it quite early? Do not expect redbuds to flower much the first spring after transplanting. Do not transplant them unless necessary. They are not very good-natured about being moved.

Why does my redbud tree not bloom freely? Has grown nicely, but has very few blossoms. Redbuds, dogwoods, and some other flowering trees often fail to produce flowers during periods of vigorous growth. Do not feed your tree with nitrogenous fertilizers.

SHADBLOW (AMELANCHIER)

What is a good small flowering tree for light woodland? Serviceberry (*Amelanchier canadensis*); also called shadblow or shadbush. It has delicate white flowers in spring.

Does the serviceberry grow well near the salt water's edge?   Yes.
Thicket serviceberry, *Amelanchier oblongifolia,* endures salt-laden
winds.

SILVERBELL (HALESIA)

Is the silverbell a desirable small tree?   Yes. Its main attraction
is in spring, when the dainty white flowers are produced, but its
striated bark can be of interest in all seasons.

Where would the silverbell be attractive?   On the edge of woodland in company with a ground cover of Virginia bluebells, violets,
and other woodland flowers.

SMOKETREE (COTINUS)

What gives the smoketree its name?   When the seed pods form
in June they produce whorls of gray-lavender hairs. As they become
full blown the bush seems enveloped in a whorl of smoke.

What would be the reason for my young smoketree not growing
taller? I have had it 6 years and it is only the same height as when
I bought it.   Either it is being recurrently killed by cold winters,
or the soil is not to its liking. Would suggest fertilizing with well-
rotted manure or rich compost in the fall, *after* digging it up and
examining the roots and transplanting it to some new situation which
you know has fertile soil.

Why does my smoketree blossom but not set any seeds? The blossom stems wither and drop off. It is more than 20 years old.   The
sexes are sometimes on separate individuals and this particular plant
is probably the male or staminate type which never bears fruits.

I have a smoketree 6 years old and more than 10 ft. high. Why
doesn't it bloom? It gets leaves, but no flower buds.   You may have
the native smoketree (*Cotinus obovatus*), which blooms sparingly.
The European (*Cotinus coggygria*) is more floriferous.

How should a smoketree be trimmed to tree form, instead of a
bush?   No attempt should be made to change common smoketree
(*Cotinus coggygria*) to tree form—it naturally forms a bush. American smoketree is occasionally seen as a tree. This form can be encouraged by the gradual removal of the lower branches, starting when
the tree is young.

YELLOW-WOOD (CLADRASTIS)

What tree is it that has white flowers resembling wisteria? It has a sweet perfume. I saw it at night and it was beautiful. It was probably yellow-wood, *Cladrastis lutea.*

Will yellow-wood resist high winds? No. The wood is inclined to be brittle.

Deciduous Shrubs

WHAT TO GROW

Can you give me a list of uncommon, but worth-while, hardy shrubs? *Berberis mentorensis; Buddleia alternifolia; Corylopsis glabrescens; Cotoneaster divaricata; Euonymus alatus* and *E. europaeus; Kerria japonica* 'Variegata'; *Rubus deliciosus* (thimbleberry); *Shepherdia argentea* (buffaloberry); *Symphoricarpus orbiculatus* (coral-berry); *Viburnum burkwoodii; V. carlcephalum.*

Could you suggest good shrubs with interesting winter habit? Flowers not essential. Regel privet, five-leaf aralia, shrub dogwoods with colored branches, cork bark or winged euonymus, and several varieties of Japanese barberry.

We have a step bank between the house and sidewalk, filled with boulders. It is impossible to grow grass between them and keep it looking neat. What do you suggest? Best shrubs would include the Arnold dwarf forsythia and *Stephanandra incisa* 'Crispa'. Both are deciduous, about 3 ft. tall, and root wherever their branches touch moist soil. *Juniperus horizontalis* varieties (evergreen) would also be good. The memorial rose (*Rosa wichuraiana*) has long been used for this purpose and it is semi-evergreen.

Will you name a few pretty shrubs, besides lilacs and forsythia, that grow rather heavy and would make a "wall" for an out-of-door room? Beauty-bush (*Kolkwitzia amabilis*); gray dogwood (*Cornus racemosa*); honeysuckle; *Viburnum dilatatum.*

Which shrubs will give us bloom in the garden from spring to fall? We have a narrow strip on one side of our house. March—February daphne (*D. mezereum*); April—*Corylopsis spicata*, forsythia, *Abeliophyllum distichum;* May—*Spiraea prunifolia, S.* x *arguta*, Vanhoutte spirea, *Viburnum carlcephalum*, lilacs; June—mock-orange, beautybush, various shrub roses; July—snowhill hydrangea, clethra, vitex; August—peegee hydrangea, rose-of-Sharon, buddleia; September—firethorn (orange berries). You didn't say how wide your "narrow strip" is. Consult a book like *Shrubs and Vines for American Gardens*, by Donald Wyman (Macmillan, 1969) for detailed information on these and other shrubs.

Will you list some dwarf shrubs? *Deutzia gracilis; Juniperus procumbens* 'Nana'; *Pinus mugo* (selected very dwarf forms); *Tsuga canadensis* 'Cole'; *Ilex crenata* 'Helleri'; dwarf boxwood; *Spiraea bumalda; Spiraea japonica alpina;* Rhododendron 'Veesprite'; several dwarf yews; heaths and heathers; *Daphne cneorum;* 'Gumpo' azaleas; *Leiophyllum buxifolium* (sand-myrtle).

Can you name some shrubs which can be trained against a wall in espalier fashion? *Abeliophyllum distichum; Kerria japonica;* firethorn (*Pyracantha coccinea*); *Forsythia suspensa;* yew; *Cotoneaster horizontalis* and others; flowering almond; *Jasminum nudiflorum;* privet; peach; golden-chain (*Laburnum anagyroides*).

Which shrub can be planted near a window as a screen and stand trimming? If by trimming you mean close shearing, privet will take it. As an irregular bush that will tolerate removal of some growths and still flower, try forsythia; but prune out old growths right after blooming.

BERRIES

In order to have a continuous succession of colorful berries along a long drive, which shrubs should be planted? The drive has very little sun in summer. To provide fruits throughout late summer and winter, use the following: barberries; cornelian-cherry (*Cornus mas*); red-stemmed dogwood; gray-stemmed dogwood; many viburnums including *Viburnum wrightii, V. dilatatum, V. sieboldii, V. acerifolium, V. trilobum.*

Can you name a few shrubs with outstandingly bright fruit? *Aronia arbutifolia; Berberis thunbergii, B. koreana;* callicarpa; *Cotoneaster dielsiana, C. franchetii; Euonymus europaeus; Ilex ver-*

ticillata; Lonicera tatarica; Rosa rugosa, R. eglanteria; Symplocos paniculata; and nandina.

Are there any shrubs with decorative fruit colors other than the usual bright reds? Asiatic sweetleaf (*Symplocos paniculata*), turquoise; yellowberry flowering dogwood; gray dogwood, white berries on red stalks; privet, black; Chenault coral-berry (*Symphoricarpos chenaultii*), pink; beautyberry (*Callicarpa japonica*), metallic purple; *Viburnum cassinoides,* berries first white, then pink, finally black.

What are some of the best of berried shrubs? Aronia, mahonia, barberry, viburnum, shrubby dogwood, cotoneaster, Asiatic sweetleaf, pyracantha, holly, and privet.

BIRDS

Which shrubs, easily grown in part shade, will attract birds? Buckthorn (*Rhamnus cathartica*); fragrant thimbleberry (*Rubus odoratus*) red (*R. strigosus*) and blackcap (*R. orientalis*) raspberries; red-berried elder (*Sambucus pubens*); viburnum species; shadblow (*Amelanchier canadensis*); chokeberry (*Aronia arbutifolia*); *Cornus alba, C. mas,* and *C. racemosa; Ilex glabra; Lonicera morrowii.*

What shrubs should I plant to attract birds to my garden? (Vermont.) Bush honeysuckle, chokeberry, cotoneaster, honeysuckle, shadbush, spice-bush, wild roses, and most other berry-bearing shrubs.

BLOOM IN ABUNDANCE

We would like succession of bloom in our shrub border. Our place is informal and we like native plants. Can you help us? February and March—vernal witch-hazel; April—spice-bush, cornelian-cherry, shadblow, redbud; May—pinkshell azalea, dogwood, rose-acacia, red chokeberry, rhododendron, viburnum—various; June—silky dogwood and gray dogwood, mountain-laurel, snow azalea, rhododendron, prairie rose, flowering raspberry; July—Jersey-tea (*Ceanothus americanus*), showy cinquefoil, summersweet (*Clethra alnifolia*); August, September, and October—colored foliage and pods and berries; witch-hazel (*Hamamelis virginiana*).

What shrubs can be planted to bloom from early spring until late fall? To obtain a succession of bloom, one must plant several plants which bloom in sequence. *Hamamelis mollis* (earliest); *Abelia grandiflora,* 12 to 15 weeks; *Potentilla fruticosa,* 10 to 12 weeks; *Spiraea* *bumalda* 'Anthony Waterer', 8 to 10 weeks; forsythia in variety, 3 to 4 weeks; vitex, 8 to 10 weeks; *Hibiscus syriacus,* 8 to 10 weeks; azaleas; lilacs; rhododendrons; roses; hydrangeas; rose-of-Sharon; common witch-hazel (latest). (See preceding question.)

Can you name some shrubs with fragrant flowers? Honeysuckle (*Lonicera fragrantissima*); mock-orange (*Philadelphus coronarius* and *P. virginalis*); *Viburnum carlesii;* clethra; common lilac; *Daphne cneorum;* strawberry-bush (*Calycanthus floridus*).

We are planting a little old-fashioned summer cottage with old-time shrubs. Can you remind us of a few blooming from June to September? June—rose-acacia, mock-orange, sweet azalea, shrub roses, *Spiraea bumalda,* lilacs, hydrangea; July—strawberry-bush, smokebush, hydrangea; August—summersweet, rose-of-Sharon.

Will you name 5 deciduous shrubs desirable for flowers, berries, and foliage color? *Aronia arbutifolia, Berberis koreana, Viburnum prunifolium, Vaccinium corymbosum, Cornus alba* 'Gouchaultii'.

FOLIAGE

Which shrubs have distinctive autumn color, other than the brilliant reds and orange shades? Here are a few: *Abelia grandiflora* (reddish-bronze); *Cotoneaster divaricata* (purplish); *Mahonia aquifolium* (chestnut and bronze tints); *Viburnum carlesii* (purplish-red); *V. tomentosum* (purplish).

Can you name some shrubs with outstandingly bright autumn foliage? *Berberis koreana, B. vernae, B. thunbergii; Cotoneaster adpressa; Euonymus alatus* and *E. alatus* 'Compactus'; fothergilla; *Franklinia alatamaha; Itea virginica; Rhododendron arborescens, R. schlippenbachii,* and *R. obtusum kaempferi; Rhus aromatica; Stephanandra incisa; Vaccinium corymbosum; Xanthorhiza simplicissima.*

I am partial to shrubs with foliage of a fine, lacy quality. Can you mention a few? *Acer palmatum dissectum* varieties; *Abelia grandiflora; Cotoneaster dielsiana; Neillia sinensis; Rosa hugonis* and *R. eglanteria; Spiraea arguta, S. thunbergii; Symphoricarpos chenaultii;* tamarisk; *Stephanandra incisa* 'Crispa'.

Will you name a few shrubs with aromatic foliage? *Calycanthus floridus, Comptonia asplenifolia, Cotinus* species, *Elsholtzia stauntonii, Lindera aestivale, Rhus aromatica, Rosa eglanteria,* bayberry, lavender.

Specific Shrubs

ABELIA

How would abelias harmonize with broad-leaved evergreens?
Very well; they like peaty soil as the evergreens do, but not too much
shade.

**Are Abelia grandiflora and the crape-myrtle hardy in the Pittsburgh,
Pennsylvania, area?** *Abelia grandiflora* is hardy in Pittsburgh, but
the crape-myrtle may not prove completely hardy. Certainly it should
be tried only in the most protected areas.

How long is the blooming season of Abelia grandiflora? From
June or July to late October, or even November.

ABELIOPHYLLUM

Is there such a plant as "white-forsythia"? *Abeliophyllum
distichum* is often called that although it is not a true forsythia. It is
a shrub from Korea, growing 5 ft. tall with dense clusters of white
flowers, especially conspicuous because they are borne in early spring
before the leaves appear, just before forsythia blooms. The flower
buds are not reliably hardy north of southern Connecticut.

ARALIA, FIVE-LEAF (ACANTHOPANAX)

**A nurseryman recommends acanthopanax for planting in shade.
Is it any good?** Yes! Flowers and fruits negligible; beautiful
5-parted, lacy leaves; fast-growing, well shaped; will grow under trees
or in any shaded place, or in full sun; drought resistant. Height about
5 ft.

ALMOND (PRUNUS TRILOBA)

How do you prune a flowering almond (Prunus triloba)? The
flowers are produced on the shoots made the preceding year, therefore, as soon as the flowers fade, cut back flowering shoots to within
2 ins. of the point of origin.

Can I root cuttings of an almond?   Yes. The cuttings must be taken in July and placed in a cold frame, or glass-covered box, in order to have the requisite moist, humid conditions to induce rooting.

AMORPHA

What is the indigobush? Is it hardy in northern Ohio?   Indigobush (*Amorpha fruticosa*) is somewhat weedy, with purplish flowers, in spikes, during June and July. Will grow in poor soil, and should be hardy in northern Ohio.

AZALEA, DECIDUOUS

Why do I have trouble growing azaleas dug from the woods when those purchased from the nurserymen do very well indeed?   Most plants growing in the woods have considerably longer but fewer roots than if they were grown in the nursery, where they are periodically root-pruned. In digging azaleas in the woods, usually much of the root system is cut off.

I have two plants of pinxterbloom and two of rose azalea. They have been in the ground for 3 years and both of the former have bloomed each year, but the latter never have. Why? What degree of temperature is the minimum under which the pinxterbloom will bloom?   Both these azalea species need acid soil, and if grown in identical conditions the one should bloom if the other does. Pinxterbloom will bloom even though temperatures fall considerably below zero.

I have a wild azalea. How can it be made to bloom?   If collected in Massachusetts this is probably pinxterbloom (*Rhododendron nudiflorum*). If given acid soil, plenty of water, and a mulch of pine needles, oak leaves, or peat moss and compost, it will undoubtedly bloom well in two years' time.

What can you combine with azaleas for summer and fall bloom? Soil is part clay. Have put oak-leaf mulch around azaleas, but nothing else seems to thrive.   For a midsummer shrub, try *Clethra alnifolia*. For autumn flower, the low, matting, blue-flowered ceratostigma. For both of these the clay soil should be lightened with compost and peat moss.

(For questions on soil and care of azaleas, see Broad-leaved Evergreens.)

What conditions are necessary for the growth of Ghent azaleas?
These deciduous hybrid azaleas need a fairly open situation and deep-drained acid soil. At least one third of it should be humus-forming oak leafmold or peat moss.

Where and in what soil should I plant pinkshell azalea (Rhododendron roseum)? Light shade, such as that given by thin woodland. Deep, moist soil with plenty of humus.

When is the best time to set out azaleas? (Georgia.) In your region, late summer and fall planting only are preferable. Most varieties of azaleas, however, can be transplanted in full bloom, if they are carefully dug and immediately replanted.

At what season of the year should a wild azalea be transplanted?
It can be transplanted either in the fall after its leaves have dropped or in the early spring, before new growth starts. Spring is the preferred season. It should be carefully dug to preserve all roots, with soil adhering to them. The roots should not be allowed to dry out while plant is being moved.

What types of azaleas would be hardy for this section of the country? The temperature often goes to 20° F. below, but not for any great length of time. (New York.) Many azaleas can be grown in northern New York and New England and in fact grow in the woods as natives. Some are flame, torch, pinxterbloom, roseshell, pinkshell, royal, sweet, and swamp. Many of the Exbury, Knaphill, and Ghent hybrids are also worth a trial, and will grow and bloom even when temperatures drop as low as 20° F. below zero.

What are the best varieties of azaleas to plant in southern New York State? Practically any of the azaleas except the evergreen Kurume and the Indian varieties. Many of the colorful Exbury and Knaphill hybrids are hardy even as far north as central Maine.

How can I lengthen the period of bloom in azaleas? By selecting types which bloom successively. The following species should insure two months of continuous flowers from early July to late August: Korean, pinkshell, pinxterbloom, flame, sweet, swamp.

Are there any azaleas which will grow in swampy places? Swamp azalea grows naturally in swampy ground. Pinkshell is also satisfactory.

Are the Exbury and Knaphill azaleas superior to our native azaleas,

such as the flame azalea (R. calendulaceum) and pinxterbloom (R. nudiflorum)? No easy answer is possible—perhaps it's all a matter of personal taste! The clarity of colors and their range and the size of each floret are spectacular in the Exbury, Knaphill, and other deciduous hybrid azaleas. Yet the natives, several of which have been used in the breeding which has achieved the hybrids, have undeniable beauty and grace, especially when grown informally in an open woodland.

BARBERRY

What is Korean barberry? A very decorative shrub growing 6 to 7 ft. high, erect when young and then spreading and arching. Thick, broad, wedge-shaped leaves turning orange-red in autumn. Small, but showy yellow flowers in spring, followed by scarlet berries in fall.

Is there a barberry suitable for a very low hedge? Yes. Box barberry (*Berberis thunbergii* 'Minor'), very like a miniature of the well-known Japanese barberry. There is also a variety called truehedge columnberry. It grows narrower and more erect. Good for its fine autumn color. Best is the dwarf red-leaved variety 'Crimson Pygmy', not over 2 ft. high.

When shall I transplant a barberry bush 3 years old? How far apart? When to prune? Barberry bushes of the kinds that lose their leaves every fall can be transplanted in spring or fall, while they are leafless. Evergreen kinds are better transplanted in spring. If they are to be planted in a shrub border where every plant is to be allowed enough room for normal development, the smaller kinds can be allowed 4 to 5 ft. and the taller ones 6 to 7 ft. at least. Pruning should be done immediately after transplanting.

When shall I prune barberry? Barberry ordinarily requires little if any pruning, except in those cases when a special shape is desired, as in hedges, or in a formal graden. Then the practice is to shear it when the new shoots have almost completed their growth in late spring.

I want to drastically prune my barberry. Should it be done in spring or fall? If it has to be cut back, do it in the spring. It may suffer from winter injury if done in the fall.

If Japanese barberry is trimmed to the ground in December, is it possible to transplant same in the spring to another spot in garden?

If any small part of the stems were left above ground, you may safely move it in the spring. If cut clear to the ground, then wait until new growth starts.

How can the truehedge columnberry barberry be raised from seed? This plant is a "cultivar." It will not reproduce itself from seed.

How can I best propagate Japanese barberry? The simplest method is from seeds, which should be stored in a cool place in moist sand over winter, and sown very early in spring. Or they may be rooted from cuttings taken in July and kept in a closed hotbed or polyethylene-covered box (See Propagation) until rooted.

BAYBERRY (MYRICA)

When is proper time to transplant bayberry bushes? (New Jersey.) Spring; or, in New Jersey, early autumn.

Wild bayberries were planted on the north side of house. Will these grow? Not a good situation. They prefer open situations, and will take only very light, partial shade.

What is proper cultivation of bayberry? Where may it be obtained? It is by nature a shrub of open, sunny, sandy coastal tracts. Therefore, in cultivation, it should be kept out of shade. It is a poor-soil shrub. Plant it, balled-and-burlapped, in the spring, in non-alkaline soil. Few nurseries grow it. One may have to obtain it from dealers in native plants.

BEARBERRY (ARCTOSTAPHYLOS)

Is bearberry (Arctostaphylos uva-ursi) a good ground cover to plant just back of a dry retaining wall? Yes, one of the best if there's plenty of sun and the soil is well drained and sandy. Be sure to get only pot-grown plants from a reliable nursery; wild plants are *very* difficult to transplant.

What conditions are necessary for growth of bearberry? Full sun or light shade, well drained and aerated, very sandy soil, and acid.

BEAUTY-BUSH (KOLKWITZIA)

I've heard about kolkwitzia. What is it like? Beauty-bush is top ranking. It suggests weigela, but is finer by far. Flowers are smaller, more abundant, and a pale pink with yellow throat, in early June.

Slow-growing. Ultimate height to 9 ft. and nearly as broad, making it ultimately a very large shrub.

Last year I planted a beauty-bush. It has not bloomed and has thrown out only one new shoot. It gets morning sun and careful attention. Should it not have flowered? Next spring prune back the one shoot. It will probably branch out and begin to form a solid shrub. It might flower the following spring. The beauty-bush often doesn't flower at an early age.

What kind of fertilizer should be used on a beauty-bush to get it to bloom? No need for special fertilizer. This shrub often does not flower at an early age. Wait. It is worth waiting for.

Should a beauty-bush (Kolkwitzia amabilis) be pruned? If so, when? If the bush is crowded, cut away the oldest flowering branches to the ground immediately after the flowers have faded. Otherwise, little or no pruning required.

How can I start new plants from my beauty-bush? Either from seeds, which take several years to reach flowering stage; or from cuttings. Cuttings must be of soft wood, i.e., taken from the tips of the shoots while they are still growing actively. If taken at a later stage, they will form a large callus but generally fail to form roots. Softwood cuttings can only be rooted in a shaded cold frame or polyethylene-enclosed box.

BENZOIN

At approximately what age does Lindera benzoin (spice-bush) flower? Does it make a good screening shrub? How far apart should it be planted for that effect? Is it thoroughly winter hardy in Connecticut? It begins to flower when 5 to 8 years old. In New England it grows to about 8 to 10 ft. tall. Makes a fair screen, with plants set 5 to 6 ft. apart. It is relatively pest free and requires no special attention, and should be thoroughly hardy in Connecticut, where it is native.

BLUEBERRY

I want to grow blueberries for their ornamental foliage. Any special soil requirements? Make soil acid by mixing with it rotted oak leaves (which see), rotted pine needles, or peat moss. Maintaining a

3-in. layer of oak leaves or peat moss on soil over roots is a good plan to help keep soil moist.

BROOM (CYTISUS)

What is the scientific name of the shrub called "Scotch broom"? It has yellow flowers similar to sweet peas, with the seed borne in a pod like peas. Has it commercial possibilities? *Cytisus scoparius.* Probably no commercial possibilities except as an ornamental. Is used in a limited way for making brooms, in basketry, for thatching, etc., especially in Europe.

What soil is best for Scotch broom? It succeeds well in many places in poor, almost barren sand dunes, roadsides, and embankments. It prefers a light, sandy soil, non-alkaline. The admixture of a little peat moss will be helpful. Plant in well-drained, open places. Start with small plants—pot-grown, if you can get them.

BUTTERFLY-BUSH (BUDDLEIA)

Which kinds of buddleia bloom in late summer? There are several, but the varieties of *Buddleia davidii,* with flowers ranging from mauve to deep purple, are the best.

Which buddleia is the most reliably hardy? *Buddleia alternifolia,* which has short, dense clusters of fragrant blue flowers in May.

Where would be the best place to plant buddleia? In a sunny place or shady place? Makes its best growth in full sun.

How should buddleias be planted? Buddleia, dug from a nursery, should be planted in spring. Probably the roots will have been roughly pruned when the plant is received, but before planting they should have any ragged ends cut clean. Plant an inch or two deeper than previously, and pack the soil carefully between the roots. Cut the stems back to 2 ins. from the point where growth started the previous spring. Give full sun.

Is it too late to prune branches of buddleia in April? I understand they should be cut late in November. Spring is the correct time to prune buddleias. They should not be cut back in the fall because of the danger that a severe winter will injure them and necessitate still more pruning in the spring.

Is it advisable to debud the first spikes of buddleias? No particular advantage to be gained from this practice.

Should butterfly-bush be cut down every year in Pennsylvania? In your section the effects of winter are almost certain to make pruning necessary. Wait until the buds begin to grow in the spring, then cut the top down to vigorous shoots.

Is Buddleia alternifolia pruned in the same way as the butterfly-bush buddleias? No. Its flowers are produced on old wood; therefore pruning should be done immediately *after* flowering, merely thinning out crowded shoots and shaping up bush.

What care should be given buddleia (butterfly-bush or summer-lilac) for winter protection? A mulch of littery material around the base is all that may be needed. It is advisable not to cut the tops back until spring.

Can butterfly-bushes be grown from slips? If so, how is it done? When are cuttings made? Yes. The cuttings, 4 to 5 ins. long, are made in July or August, from side shoots. Cut off the bottom pair of leaves, and make a clean cut through the stem, just below the joint from which the leaves were cut. Insert one third of their length in sand, in a propagating case.

CARYOPTERIS

What is caryopteris like? The one commonly grown (*Caryopteris incana*) is a shrub bearing bluish flowers. It is not fully hardy in the North, where it is treated as a perennial herb.

How should one prune caryopteris, and when? Wait until the buds swell in spring and then cut back each branch to a strong-growing bud. If winterkilled to ground, remove dead stalks in early spring.

CHASTE-TREE (VITEX)

Is chaste-tree really a tree? Mine is more like a shrub. It may develop into a small tree in a favorable climate. In the North its young branches often are killed by low temperatures, which make it assume a shrubby habit.

Does chaste-tree (Vitex agnus-castus) require acid soil? It appears to reach its best development in a sandy peat. This would indicate a preference for a non-alkaline but not highly acid soil. It grows readily enough in average, light garden soils.

How and when is proper time to prune chaste-tree (Vitex agnus-

castus)? This blossoms on shoots of the current season and should be cut back in spring. Wait until growth begins (it is a late starter) and cut back the branches to strong-growing buds.

COTONEASTER

What are some of the best cotoneasters for border planting? *C. hupehensis,* 6 ft. high; *C. salicifolia floccosa,* 10 ft.; *C. zabelii miniata,* 6 to 8 ft.

We are looking for a cotoneaster which is lower growing than C. horizontalis. What do you suggest? *C. adpressa* grows only 9 to 12 ins. high; has glossy berries in fall like *C. horizontalis,* but it is hardier. Also *C. microphylla thymifolia,* 1–2 ft.; *C. dammeri,* 1 ft.; and *C. congesta,* 3 ft.

How can I grow the cotoneasters successfully? Give them a sunny position, in well-drained soil. *Protect young plants from rabbits* in rural districts.

CRAPE-MYRTLE (LAGERSTROEMIA)

What kind of soil does crape-myrtle need? It has no special requirements, and will thrive in any ordinary garden soil.

What is the proper care of crape-myrtle as to fertilizer, trimming, watering, and winter protection, if needed? (Maryland.) Fertilize by mulching with compost or rotted manure in the fall, which will also help protect the roots against winter injury. If in an exposed location, cover the top with evergreen branches. Shorten shoots of the preceding year ½ to ⅔ in the spring. Cut back flowering shoots when the blossoms have faded. Water only during droughty periods.

Why did my 8-year-old crape-myrtle fail to bloom the past summer? Two of them have always bloomed beautifully until last season. (Kentucky.) The chances are that they were injured by the very severe winter.

Can you advise why my crape-myrtle shrubs do not bloom? (Brooklyn, New York.) I have had these shrubs for 4 years and protect them each winter. They bloomed only the first year after planting. Winter injury and not enough heat during the growing season. They bloom freely about once in 10 years as far north as this. Grow in the warmest, sunniest situation; cut back in the spring to strong-growing shoots.

The crape-myrtle, an old bush, very tall and about 10 ft. from an oak, is thrifty as to foliage but no blooms. We have a stratum of clay soil but have put in many tons of topsoil and plenty of fertilizer. What is wrong? The proximity of the oak may be a factor in the failure of the crape-myrtle to bloom. Omit nitrogenous fertilizers and try the effect of an application of superphosphate to the soil over the roots, at the rate of 6 oz. per square yard. Maybe the soil is too acid and would be helped by an application of ground limestone.

Can a crape-myrtle be protected sufficiently to winter safely out of doors in a climate where the temperature falls to 10° to 15° F. below zero? No.

How shall I care for crape-myrtle, and do the plants need pruning? (California.) Not satisfactory in southern California. Pruning consists of cutting back the shoots, immediately after flowering, to encourage new growth and further flowering.

CYDONIA (CHAENOMELES SPECIOSA) See Quince, Flowering.

DAPHNE

What is the name of the daphne which blooms very early? February daphne (*D. mezereum*). It is valued for its early blooming, and lilac-purple fragrant flowers. Height may reach 3 ft.; stiff, erect; deciduous.

Why do the leaves of a Daphne mezereum turn yellow and drop off during the months of August and September? It is characteristic of this species to shed its leaves during drought in late summer.

DEUTZIA

Are there any low-growing deutzias? If so, when do they bloom? *Deutzia gracilis,* with white flowers in May; *Deutzia rosea* has pinkish flowers, otherwise resembles the preceding.

What are the advantages of the tall deutzias? Are they interesting in winter? Their flowers are showy; otherwise their foliage and their branch pattern are uninteresting.

When should I transplant deutzias? In spring or early fall.

When is the proper time to trim deutzias? They should be pruned by cutting out worn-out and crowded flowering shoots immediately after the blossoms have faded.

DOGWOOD (CORNUS) (See also under Decorative Flowering Trees.)

Which dogwood shrubs have colored twigs in winter? *Cornus alba* (Tartarian d.), bright red twigs; *Cornus sericea* (red Osier d.), deep red; *Cornus* 'Flaviramea' (golden-twig d.), yellow; *Cornus racemosa* (gray d.), gray; *Cornus sanguinea* (blood-twig d.), dark blood-red; *Cornus sanguinea* 'Viridissima' (green-twig d.), green.

What color are the berries of the dogwood shrubs? Tartarian dogwood, whitish; silky dogwood, pale blue; blood-twig dogwood, black; pagoda dogwood, dark blue; red Osier dogwood, white or bluish; gray dogwood, white.

How are the shrubby dogwoods used to best advantage? In masses as open woodland border, or as an informal hedgerow planting of mixed shrubs.

I have had a Cornus mas (cornelian-cherry) for 3 years, but it has not grown. Can you prescribe? Takes a few years to become established. If you have given it good soil, fertilized it occasionally with well-rotted manure, compost, or a complete commercial fertilizer, and given it plenty of water, you have done the best you can for it.

ENKIANTHUS

What is Enkianthus campanulatus like? A graceful, upright shrub with an ultimate height of 12 to 15 ft., but slow-growing. In May and June it bears drooping clusters of yellowish bell-shaped flowers, similar to blueberry flowers. Its chief value is in its foliage, turning brilliant orange and scarlet in the fall.

What deciduous shrub with good autumn color can we put in among the evergreens at the east and west side of our house? *Enkianthus perulatus,* growing to 6 ft., would be a good choice because, like the broad-leaved evergreens, it prefers acid soil. Use *E. campanulatus* if a taller shrub is required.

EUONYMUS

I have seen a shrub which has curious corky flanged bark on its branches. Its leaves turn deep rose in the autumn. What is it? Winged euonymus (*E. alatus*).

FORSYTHIA

What different kinds of forsythia are there? About 5 species; several varieties. Among the best are, urnlike in form *F. intermedia* 'Spectabilis'; and fountainlike (or drooping), *F. suspensa,* and the heavily flowered variety 'Karl Sax'.

There is such a difference in the number of flowers on forsythias that I wonder if it is due to soil or location; or if there is more than one kind of plant. (Arkansas.) There are several kinds of forsythia. *Forsythia intermedia* 'Spectabilis' is a very showy one.

What is the hardiest forsythia? A species called *F. ovata,* earliest to bloom; flowers, however, are less effective and more amber in color.

When is the best time to transplant forsythia? Does it require cultivation? This shrub may be safely transplanted in spring or fall, any time that it is leafless. Cultivation to remove weeds around newly transplanted shrubs for a period of 1 or 2 years is decidedly beneficial.

Our forsythia had a late fall bloom this year. Will that impair the spring bloom? Yes, for the flower buds are formed in the summer, and if some open then the bloom the following spring will be just so much reduced.

Why do forsythias bloom around the bottom of bushes only? Because in cold areas the flower buds—present all winter long—are killed by low temperatures except where they are protected by a blanket of snow or fallen leaves or mulch.

I have forsythia on southwest corner of our house, about 6 years old; used to bloom in spring; now blooms in October and November. Why? The chances are the autumns have been unusually mild in this particular location.

Why doesn't my forsythia bloom? The buds seem to dry up. They have been killed by winter cold. Try *Forsythia ovata.* This is the most hardy of all the forsythias.

How and when should forsythia be pruned? Cut out some of the oldest branches annually, making the cut not far from the base of the bush. This can be done in February, and the cut branches brought indoors and placed in water to force them into bloom; or wait until the bush has flowered, and prune it immediately after the flowers have faded.

How do you prune forsythia when it has grown too high? Thin out some of the older stems a few inches above the ground level. Sometimes by removing a major number of the taller older stems, those left will be much lower. If not, reduce those that remain to the desired height but never cut them off in a horizontal line, for this disfigures the bush.

How can I keep forsythia bushes from getting so awfully straggling? Make them more compact by pinching out the tips of strong-growing shoots during late spring and early summer. Comparatively compact varieties, such as *F. viridissima* and *F. ovata,* are preferable if there is an objection to a straggling habit.

Can forsythia or goldenbells be pruned in fall as well as in spring? Usually the shrub gets very awkward after spring pruning. Forsythia produces its flowers on preceding year's growth, and any cutting back during the time it is dormant results in a diminution of the floral display in the spring. Try pinching out the tips of strong-growing shoots during the growing season.

When is proper time to trim weeping forsythia? The beauty of this variety is in its long, trailing growth. It should not be trimmed in the usual sense of cutting back the tips. Thinning out crowded branches is permissible in the spring immediately after the flowers have faded.

HAZELNUT

Are there any garden forms of the European hazelnut that are grown for their beauty rather than the production of nuts? There are two outstanding ones. One is a variety of the filbert (*Corylus maxima* 'Purpurea'). The other is the European hazel (*Corylus avellana* var. 'Contorta'), which is interesting rather than beautiful. The leaves of 'Purpurea' are dark purple, especially in early spring; and in 'Contorta' the stems are twisted and curled in a way that makes it an excellent example of living sculpture.

HONEYSUCKLE (LONICERA)

Are the fruits of the honeysuckle ornamental? Yes, they are small round berries, blue, red, or yellow. It is the red and yellow ones on such plants as the Amur, Tatarian, and fragrant honeysuckles that make a display and are most attractive to the birds. There are some yellow fruited varieties also.

Can you mention a few desirable honeysuckle shrubs? Fragrant honeysuckle—April, white; Morrow honeysuckle—May, cream-yellow; blueleaf honeysuckle—May, pink; Amur honeysuckle—May, white; and Tatarian honeysuckle—May, rose and white.

How can I best propagate honeysuckle? In order to have plants of uniform kind, it is best to root the plants from cuttings. Many of them root quite readily from hardwood cuttings, and this is the simplest way. Or they can be raised from cuttings taken in July and kept in a closed polyethylene-covered flat, until rooted.

HYDRANGEA

Will you tell me what is the real name of the hydrangea with pink or blue flowers? Bigleaf hydrangea (*Hydrangea macrophylla*). There are many varieties of this species, both with blue flowers and with pink flowers. 'Rosea' is a popular variety with pink flowers.

What are some hydrangeas other than the usual peegee and snow hill? Try panicle hydrangea, the parent of peegee, with flowers more opened out, not so "top-heavy"; climbing hydrangea (*H. anomala petiolaris*), as vine or shrub; oakleaf hydrangea, with interesting foliage.

What exposure to sun should hydrangeas have? The common species do best in full sun, although they will stand slight shade.

Do oakleaf hydrangeas need a shady or sunny location? Partial shade.

What plant foods do hydrangeas need and when? They require no special fertilizer treatment. The use of well-rotted manure or compost or a mixed commercial fertilizer in the spring is satisfactory.

Can a hydrangea be transplanted in my state in the month of October or November? (New York.) Yes.

Would transplanting a large hydrangea into another section of the garden cause injury to the plant? No, not permanently, if properly done. Transplant in early spring.

When is the best time to move hydrangeas? Either fall or early spring for very hardy types; spring in the case of "French" hydrangeas.

Should a potted hydrangea with a large beautiful blue flower which came from a greenhouse be transplanted to the outdoors? (Kansas.) It probably would not live over winter.

My mother gave us a 4-year-old hydrangea to plant in our garden. Could you tell me what to do to make it bloom next year? Protect canes from winter injury by covering them in the fall with a bushel basket or leaves held in place by chicken wire or something similar. Do not cut back the canes in the spring any more than is necessary to remove injured tips.

Does peegee hydrangea require any special care? I don't seem to be able to grow them. One of easiest shrubs to grow. Needs no special care.

Why do the leaves on my pink hydrangeas appear yellow and mottled? The soil is too sweet or alkaline. Have it tested and add aluminum sulfate to reduce the pH value to 6.8 or lower.

What would cause a hydrangea to stop flowering after having bloomed beautifully for 3 seasons? Too much shade, poor soil, over-fertilization, improper pruning, and winter injury are some of the more important factors that affect the flowering of hydrangeas.

Why do my French hydrangeas bloom some years and not others? (New York.) Cold injury to the flower buds is the most common reason for failure to flower. The flower buds are formed in the fall, and if the winter is severe they may be killed even though the plant is not seriously injured.

Why has my hydrangea plant (French type) not bloomed for 15 years, even though it grows well and is kept pruned? (Massachusetts.) Undoubtedly the flower buds which form in the fall are killed during the winter. Give more winter protection by covering with leaves, held in place by chicken wire, etc. Pruning at the wrong time of year (each spring or fall) will prevent flowering by removing the flower buds. Prune immediately *after* blooming (late July).

After blooming should the old flowers be cut from hydrangeas? Not necessarily, unless they are unsightly.

Do hydrangeas bloom on old or new wood? Some common species, such as *Hydrangea paniculata* 'Grandiflora' and the hills of snow type, bloom on new wood, and can be pruned in the early spring. On a few other types, particularly the common greenhouse or French (*Hydrangea macrophylla*) varieties, the buds originate near the tips of the canes formed the preceding year, and should be pruned *after* flowering, or not at all.

How near to the ground do you prune hydrangeas? This depends on the species. *Hydrangea arborescens* can be cut off at the ground each year. (See preceding answer.)

When is the proper time to cut back a blue hydrangea? This species (often called French hydrangea) should be pruned immediately after flowering. Pruning in the fall or in the early spring will reduce the number of flowers or prevent flowering.

What is the best way to prune a standard hydrangea? Since round, uniform tops are desired, all branches should be cut back so that only 2 or 3 buds are left at the base of each old stem. Pruning should be done on this type (*Hydrangea paniculata* 'Grandiflora') in the early spring.

How should peegee hydrangeas be pruned? This is the strong-growing shrubby type which sometimes almost attains the dimensions of a small tree. It blossoms on shoots of the current season, and if large heads of bloom are desired, the shoots of the preceding year should be cut back to one bud in the spring.

When should the oakleaf hydrangea be pruned? Immediately after flowering. This is another species, like the French type, in which the flower buds form in the fall. Since the buds are likely to be injured during severe winters, the plants should be protected by mulching.

Why do my hydrangeas have so many leaves and so few flowers? Too much nitrogenous fertilizer and improper pruning can encourage the growth of foliage instead of flowers. In warm climates the common French hydrangeas may not set flower buds in the fall because of high temperatures.

What care should be given blue hydrangeas in an eastern exposure for the winter? Wrap in burlap or straw, and mulch soil heavily with leaves.

Can blue hydrangeas be propagated? Yes, by cuttings. However, the flowers may appear as pink when grown under different soil conditions.

What causes pink hydrangeas to turn blue? Experiments have conclusively demonstrated that the presence of aluminum in the tissue of hydrangea flowers causes the blue coloration.

Can all kinds of hydrangeas be made to produce blue flowers? No. Only the pink varieties of the common greenhouse or French hydrangea (*Hydrangea macrophylla*) will turn blue.

Will my hydrangeas be blue if I plant them in an acid soil? Pink varieties of the common greenhouse or French hydrangea produce blue flowers when grown in acid soil (pH 5.5 or below). Soil acidity is an indirect factor in the production of blue flowers because of its relationship to the solubility of aluminum in the soil. The aluminum is soluble and can be absorbed by the plants when the soil is acid (pH 5.5 or below). In neutral or slightly alkaline soil the aluminum is insoluble.

What chemical will change the color of hydrangea flowers to blue? Aluminum sulfate is the most effective chemical, but common alum (potassium alum) will also bring about the blue color.

Can dry aluminum sulfate be mixed with the soil to produce blue flowers? Dry aluminum sulfate can be used in the spring at the rate of 1 lb. for each square yard of ground area. It may be necessary to repeat the treatment for several years. Aluminum sulfate can also be mixed with the soil when it is prepared. The soil should be tested to determine its reaction (pH). If the soil is neutral, mix in thoroughly ½ lb. for each bushel.

How does one make hydrangeas growing in pots have blue flowers? Water 5 to 8 times, at weekly intervals, with a 2½ per cent solution of aluminum sulfate (1 lb. to 5 gals. water). Use 1 gal. to each plant.

If rusty nails are put in the soil will a hydrangea produce blue flowers? Rusty nails or any other form of metallic iron has no effect upon flower color. Potassium alum (common alum), however, will induce blue coloration.

How can I make a blue-flowering hydrangea produce pink flowers? The soil should be made neutral or very slightly alkaline (pH 6.7 to 7.2) by the addition of lime. Too much lime will cause mottling of the leaves, as the result of a lack of iron. The required amount of lime should be deeply and thoroughly mixed with the soil. It is best to lift the plants in the fall, shake off as much soil as possible, and replant them in the specially prepared lime soil.

How can one prevent discoloring of hydrangea flowers? Flowers of intermediate hues between pink and blue are produced when the soil reaction is between pH 6 and 6.5. If pure blue flowers are desired, add aluminum sulfate to make the soil more acid (pH 5.5). For pink flowers, add lime to bring the soil reaction to pH 6.8 to 7.0.

KERRIA

What is Kerria japonica? This shrub grows 4 to 8 ft. high and produces bright yellow flowers. Variety 'Pleniflora' is double and more vigorous. Both have green stems. It is a shrub of easy culture, and does well in part shade. There are also varieties with variegated foliage.

I have an old kerria shrub, but only 1 or 2 branches bloom. How can I treat or prune it? Winter injury or crowded branches can be responsible for its failure to bloom. Cut out weak shoots in spring and remove flowering branches as soon as the flowers have faded.

How can I best propagate Kerria japonica 'Pleniflora'? Either by means of cuttings in July, which must be kept in close, humid, shady conditions until rooted; or by hardwood cuttings, taken in late fall, buried in the soil over winter, and set in the garden in early spring.

LILAC (SYRINGA)

What are the best lilacs (French hybrids) in each color? White —'Marie Legnay', 'Mme. Lemoine'; violet—'De Miribel'; blue— 'Bleautre', 'Firmament'; pink—'Alice Eastwood', 'Lucie Baltet'; purple—'Sunset', 'Ludwig Spaeth'; two-tone—'Sensation'.

Are there ever-blooming lilac bushes? No.

What are so-called "own-root" lilacs? Those lilacs so propagated that the roots and tops are from one continuous piece of plant, i.e., not grafted with two pieces grown together as one. Hence, they are not susceptible to the serious graft-blight disease. "Own-root" lilacs are the best kind to buy.

Would you consider a Syringa amurensis japonica (Japanese tree lilac) a good lawn specimen tree? How tall does it grow? Yes. It may grow 40 ft. high and more but usually is under 20 ft. and is comparatively slow-growing.

What is the difference between lilac species and the other, or common, lilacs? Lilac species are the wild lilacs of the world found growing in uninhabited places. The "common lilacs" are usually considered either natural hybrids, which have appeared in gardens, or (more frequently) as the direct result of hybridizing efforts, mostly of *Syringa vulgaris.*

Why are French hybrid lilacs so called? Because hybridizers in France have had much to do with their production.

What kind of soil and nourishment are best for lilacs? Any fair, not too heavy, well-drained, alkaline or slightly acid garden soil. If needed, every other year apply a 3-in. mulch of rotted cow manure or compost alternated with a dose of limestone. Do not feed them unless the need is indicated, lest they grow too tall and must be cut back.

Please advise when to plant a lilac bush; spring or fall? Either. Lilacs are among the easiest of plants to transplant and will grow under almost any conditions.

I planted a lilac the last of November. Was it too late? Probably; but if ground didn't freeze until late December this date for planting should have been satisfactory.

Can a large lilac bush be moved and continue blooming—that is, without waiting several more years? Yes, if moved with a large ball of soil about the roots, and if the branches are pruned back ⅓ in the operation.

How long do lilacs have to be planted before blooming? This depends on many things, such as soil, skill of transplanting in the soil, etc. Some plants, grown properly, will bloom profusely when only 4 ft. tall. Others may take years before they will start to bloom.

I transplanted a lilac bush. Should the leaves be stripped at the bottom in the spring or left alone? Always prune off some of the branches when transplanting; approximately ⅓ of the total branches is a good average. Stripping off the leaves is not a good practice in this case.

What is the ultimate height of the French lilacs? Depends on the variety; 10 to 25 ft.

Which lilacs, if any, will thrive with only forenoon sunshine?
All lilacs need sunshine. The less sunshine they have the fewer the flowers.

Will you give me information pertaining to the culture, pruning, and general care of own-root, French hybrid lilacs, for specimen bloom? I have a collection of young plants comprising 12 varieties.
The general care of these lilacs is no different from that of any others. For specimen blooms, cutting out a few of the weakest flowering shoots in winter is helpful. Read other questions and answers.

Why do the leaves on new lilac bushes turn brown? Transplanting injury, lack of sufficient water, too much fertilizer, or air pollution.

We have lilacs of different species, some more than 10 years old. The foliage always looks clean, but the plants never have any buds or flowers. Neighbors have flowers on their lilacs. Why not ours?
When lilacs fail to bloom, 4 things can be tried, since every lilac should bloom if grown properly: 1. Thin out some of the branches at the base of the plant. 2. Root-prune by digging a 2-ft. ditch around the plants. 3. When the soil is removed from the ditch mix with it a generous amount of superphosphate (about 8 oz. to every 3 ft. of ditch) and return the soil to the ditch. 4. Apply limestone if soil is acid. One of these methods, or a combination of all, should force the plant to bloom. Some lilacs, like many other plants, are alternate-blooming, flowering profusely one year and sparsely or not at all the next. This, unfortunately, is to be expected.

Why do lilacs fail to bloom even though flower buds are formed?
This may be due to severe drought in the late summer after the buds have been formed.

We have old-fashioned lilacs, large clumps 8 or 10 years old, that have only 5 or 6 blossoms each year. Can you suggest what is cause for not blooming freely? Probably too many young suckers at the base. Cut out most of these and you probably will be repaid with good blooms.

I have some Persian lilacs, also French lilacs, none of which seem to do well. What kind of soil and conditions do they require? They need a good alkaline soil with sufficient moisture throughout the summer. Try applying limestone in spring and a 3-in. mulch of manure or compost in fall to see if they help.

How does one prune lilacs to keep them a decent height and still have blooms? Do not give all the pruning in one year, but over a period of several years. Do not allow them to become too dense, for this forces them to grow high. Allow each branch room to grow. Thin out older branches by cutting them off at the base of the plant. Remove all but a few suckers.

Should lilacs be pruned? Yes, prune out most of the young suckers and all of the dead or diseased wood. Some of the older branches could be cut out also, to allow more light to reach the branches in the center of the plant. Prune just *after* blooming.

My lilacs are 10 ft. tall. How can I bring them down to eye-level height? In 2 ways: 1. Cut them down to within a foot of the ground and so start entirely new plants. 2. If this is too drastic, do the same thing, but over a period of 3 years, hence thinning out only ⅓ of the branches each year and allowing for continuous bloom.

Will severe pruning force old-fashioned lilacs to give more bloom? Yes, it may; but do not expect flowers for a year or two.

What is the best way to cut back very old, tall, uncared-for lilac bushes? Cut them down nearly to the ground.

What is the best way to start growth again on lilac bushes—all the growth seems to be at the top, leaving the lower part very unsightly. Can it be done? Yes; cut back to within a foot of the ground, and start all over again.

What can be done, if anything, to prevent lilacs from suckering? There is no preventive measure, but once started this suckering habit should be stopped immediately merely by cutting out a majority of the young suckers.

Should any suckers be allowed on French hybrid lilacs? Yes, if they have been propagated on their own roots. However, if they have been grafted, the suckers from the understock may prove to be either California privet or some very different lilac. Therefore *all* should be cut out of grafted plants.

My French hybrid lilacs were propagated by cuttings and are growing on their "own roots." Can I allow suckers to grow? Yes—to some extent. A few of these can be allowed to grow to replace the older branches which are cut out or to allow the bush to increase in size. Do not allow all to grow, however, as the bush will become too dense, and flower formation will be decreased.

Is it necessary, or better, for the bushes, to cut off dead flowers from lilacs before they bloom again? Yes. Cut them off as soon as they are finished blooming. This prevents seed formation and allows more nourishment to go to the flower buds for the next year.

What is the proper time and method of root-pruning lilacs to bring them into bloom? Dig a 2-ft. trench in spring slightly within the outside limit of the branches, in this way cutting all roots encountered.

How can you stop lilacs from spreading into your neighbor's yard? Sink a concrete barrier down in the soil, or continually dig and cut roots on that side of the plant.

How do you start new bushes from an old lilac bush? The best method is to raise a new stock from cuttings; or, if it is not a grafted plant, rooted suckers may be dug up, tops cut back ½, and planted.

I have a lilac bush 'President Grevy'; one branch has flowers of a different color, pale pink with a yellow center. How can I propagate this sport? It is not from the rootstock, as it appears on a bush 10 ft. high. Either by cuttings, or by grafting or budding it on California privet. This privet is not recommended as an understock, but in order to work up a stock of the "sport" that has occurred on your lilac, you would be justified in using it until you could obtain enough plants on their own roots.

When should lilac cuttings be made? While the shoots are still growing, usually about the middle of May. Make cuttings 5 to 6 ins. long; remove bottom leaves; make a clean cut through stem ¼ in. below place where leaves were attached. However, lilacs are sometimes raised from hardwood cuttings (taken in early winter) which are planted in boxes of sand and kept in cool but frostproof sheds until spring, when rooting takes place.

How is lilac best rooted from cuttings? Outdoors, cold frame, or greenhouse? Either in propagating cases in a greenhouse, or in a shaded hotbed. The cuttings are placed in sand and kept in a close, humid atmosphere until rooted. (See preceding question.)

How is Persian lilac propagated? Either from seeds sown in spring, or from cuttings in May. Also from suckers.

The leaves of my lilacs are a gray-green instead of true shade.

What is the remedy? The chances are they have mildew. This happens especially in the late summer or during a moist season. It is not serious and can be ignored. Dusting with powdered sulfur as soon as mildew appears is the remedy.

What is lilac "graft blight"? This is a disease occurring on plants which have been grafted on California privet understock. A plant which has this disease will look sickly, have yellowish leaves, and may die even in good growing weather. The only remedy is to dig up and destroy such a plant.

How can one eliminate chlorosis in lilacs? This is not well understood. Chlorosis occurs even on healthy plants growing in normal soil during dry seasons. During the following year the same chlorotic plants may appear healthy. About all one can do is to see that they have some fertilizer and lime, and water thoroughly during dry spells.

MIMOSA (ALBIZZIA JULIBRISSIN)

Will a mimosa tree survive a Michigan winter? The hardiest mimosa—*Albizzia julibrissin rosea*—might be tried in southern Michigan. This proves fairly hardy in Boston, Massachusetts. The mimosa of the South will not be hardy.

Are you supposed to prune mimosa (Albizzia) trees? Yes, when they require it to make them shapely. Where they grow rapidly, they incline to be too flexible and "weak-backed" unless pruned.

MOCK-ORANGE (PHILADELPHUS)

Which are some of the best mock-oranges? The old-fashioned sweet mock-orange (*Philadelphus coronarius*); 'Avalanche' with single very fragrant flowers and gracefully arching branches; 'Conquête', 'Mont Blanc' with single flowers 1¼ ins. in diameter; double-flowered varieties like 'Albâtre', 'Argentine', 'Bannière', 'Girandole', 'Minnesota Snowflake' with 2-in. flowers and able to withstand temperatures to −30° F., and the ever-popular 'Virginal', all of which are fragrant.

Will you give me information on the comparative merits (ease of growth, hardiness, floriferousness, fragrance, shape, and height) of the following hybrid mock-oranges: 'Bannière', nivalis, 'Norma', 'Pavillon Blanc', 'Pyramidale', and 'Voie Lactée'? These are all of approximately equal hardiness—not reliably hardy north of Philadelphia—but they are being grown as far north as Boston. They are all about 5 to 7 ft. tall; equally easy to grow; but vary in beauty and amount of flowers and fragrance. Using another hybrid, 'Avalanche', as a basis for good flower and the old-fashioned fragrant *P. coronarius* as best for fragrance, and rating these both at 10 points, the varieties could be rated as follows: 'Bannière'—flower, 5; fragrance, 4; *nivalis*—flower, 3; fragrance, 6; 'Norma'—flower, 6; fragrance, 4; 'Pavillon Blanc'—flower, 2; fragrance, 0; 'Pyramidale'—flower, 3; fragrance, 0; 'Voie Lactée'—flower, 2; fragrance, 2.

I once saw some mock-oranges with large double flowers. What might they have been?   'Virginal', or perhaps 'Argentine'; beautiful with flowers 2 ins. across. There are several others of equal size also available.

Why don't my mock-oranges, planted last spring, bloom? They have so much brush in them.   They need a year or two in order to recuperate from the shock of transplanting. Thin out a few of the branches if they are too crowded.

Although pruned, why does mock-orange 'Virginal' not bush out, but grow only lanky shoots at the top?   This variety is naturally gawky. It can be made a little more compact by pinching out the tips of lanky shoots when they are actively growing.

How should I trim an overgrown mock-orange bush?   Thin it out during winter by cutting the oldest branches as near the ground line as possible. Shorten those remaining about ⅓, if it seems necessary. This drastic treatment will result in few, if any, flowers the following spring.

When and how is the best way to prune a mock-orange shrub?   Immediately after flowering by cutting out the oldest and weakest shoots, making the cuts as near the ground line as possible.

PRIVET (See also Hedges, this section.)

If a privet is not pruned, what kind of flowers does it have? And berries?   Cream-white flowers in small panicles somewhat like lilacs, but with a sweet (but to some distressing) odor in midsummer. Berries are black.

What is the name of a privet which forms a broad bush?   Regel privet—*Ligustrum obtusifolium regelianum.*

What is the best time to prune Amur River privet? When grown as a bush, needs no pruning. As a hedge it should be sheared when the new growth is 6 to 8 ins. long. Repeat shearing in August.

QUINCE, FLOWERING (CHAENOMELES SPECIOSA)

What colors are to be had in flowering quinces? When do they bloom? Today many nurserymen offer their own varieties, often grown from seed. They are hybrids or varieties of the species *Chaenomeles speciosa* and range in color of flower from pure white, through pink to deep red. Single- and double-flowered varieties are available. They bloom in early May. Flowering quince has been variously known as *Cydonia japonica, Chaenomeles japonica,* but the current classification is as *Chaenomeles speciosa.* The designation *Chaenomeles japonica* is reserved for the Japanese quince, a low-growing species which flowers in spring before the leaves develop. (See following question and answer.)

What kinds of flowering quince bushes are there? Are some varieties taller than others? The tall shrub *Chaenomeles speciosa* grows to about 6 ft. high. The dwarf species (*C. japonica*) is a broad, low shrub, growing to 3 ft. high. A still lower variety (*C. j. alpina*) spreads into a low patch seldom over 1½ ft. high.

I have a flowering quince (red) that does not bloom, although the plant is 6 years old. The sprout was taken from a beautiful bush which blooms each year. This plant has never bloomed and it's planted beside 2 other quinces that bloom each year. Why? It may well be that the original plant was a grafted plant and the understock was the common quince, which blooms only after reaching some size. Would suggest that you check the two in foliage. If they differ, discard yours. If they do not differ, check them again when the parent is in flower next spring.

The blossoms of my flowering quince are produced toward the center of the bush and are not well displayed. Can this be avoided? Yes. Prune the bush by shortening the new shoots as they are produced throughout the summer. This will cause the formation of flower spurs near the tips of the branches.

I have a shrub in my garden that I have been told is a variety of flowering quince. It has never bloomed and I was wondering what could be done to force it to bloom. Would pruning help? Summer pruning will help, as described in the preceding answer. The incorporation of superphosphate in the soil over the roots, at the rate of 6 oz. per square yard, may be helpful. Root-pruning (which see) should be resorted to if these measures fail.

How can I propagate my flowering quince? The flowering quince can be treated in the same manner as flowering almond (which see).

Is the fruit of the so-called "burning bush," or Chaenomeles speciosa, edible? It is very sour, but can be used in making jellies. Incidentally "burning bush" is a misnomer as an English name for this shrub. It is more correctly applied to the wahoo, or strawberry-bush, *Euonymus americanus* or to *E. alatus,* which see.

ROSE-ACACIA (ROBINIA)

What is a rose-acacia? A hardy shrub (*Robinia hispida*) native to the Allegheny Mountains. Grows to 3 ft. with dark, rich green foliage and racemes of rose-colored, pealike blossoms in late spring.

Where shall I plant a rose-acacia shrub? In a spot protected from heavy winds, in light soil. Good for dry banks and as a screen. It suckers freely and, if neglected, forms a dense thicket.

Do rose-acacia shrubs have to be grafted stock to bloom, or can they be taken from old plants? No. If the old plants spread from year to year by suckers then it is a simple matter to dig up and replant some of the suckers, and so form new plants. However, rose-acacia is sometimes grafted high to form "standards," in which case any growth taken from the base would merely increase the understock, probably black locust (*Robinia pseudoacacia*).

ROSE-OF-SHARON (HIBISCUS SYRIACUS)

What colors does the rose-of-Sharon come in? White, pink, purple, red, and blue, both single- and double-flowered varieties.

The most beautiful rose-of-Sharon I have seen has single lavender-blue flowers with carmine eye. What is its name? 'Coelestis', an old favorite. A newer blue-flowered variety is 'Blue Bird'.

What is shrub-althea? Same as rose-of-Sharon, *Hibiscus syriacus*.

What kind of soil does rose-of-Sharon thrive in? Mine was doing poorly. I put lime around it and it died. It needs a deep soil which has plenty of water—even a tendency to be very moist occasionally.

A complete fertilizer and *water* would possibly have saved your plant.

Can rose-of-Sharon shrubs or trees be transplanted in the fall? Can be safely transplanted in fall except in places subjected to high, cold winds during the winter.

What is the correct care of rose-of-Sharon? (Maine.) There are many places in Maine where the rose-of-Sharon simply will not grow because of winter cold. Where it will survive, cut back the last year's shoots to about 4 buds early in the spring. This heavy pruning usually results in heavy flower production—providing, of course, it has good soil.

What is the cause of my rose-of-Sharon buds falling off before they open? Partly a varietal characteristic. Other factors might be insufficient phosphorus or potash in the soil; too little soil moisture; or attack by aphids.

When and how should rose-of-Sharon (Hibiscus syriacus) be pruned? Blossoms are produced on shoots of the current season, so the shoots of the preceding year can be cut back to within 3–4 buds of their point of origin in spring, with no loss of blooms. However, this heavy pruning makes an ungainly bush, and many good gardeners prefer to prune them lightly or let them go unpruned.

What are the best conditions for rose-of-Sharon? Can it be budded or grafted? Rose-of-Sharon (*Hibiscus syriacus*) will grow quite well in any reasonably good garden soil. It may be budded or grafted, but this trouble hardly seems justified, as most of the varieties root very readily from cuttings taken in the summer.

RUSSIAN-OLIVE (ELAEAGNUS)

What shrub would give a distinct silvery effect? Russian-olive (*Elaeagnus angustifolius*), with narrow leaves, silvery on reverse side, a shrub to 20 ft. high; silverberry (*E. commutatus*)—bushy, to 12 ft., leaves silver on both sides, fast-growing; cherry elaeagnus (*E. multiflorus*), leaves silvery beneath, grows 4 to 9 ft.

Does elaeagnus have flowers or fruits? Flowers inconspicuous but strongly fragrant in *E. angustifolus,* silverberry, and *E. umbellatus.* Small, yellow-silvery berries on silverberry; brown-red berries on *E. umbellatus.*

In what manner and how severely should Russian-olive (Elaeagnus angustifolius) be pruned if 3 years old and about 15 ft. high? Usually needs no pruning when growing in poor, dry soil and a sunny location to which it is adapted. Yours evidently is in rich ground and should be pruned by shortening lanky growths about midsummer.

SNOWBERRY (SYMPHORICARPOS)

How and when should the snowberry bush (Symphoricarpos albus) be trimmed? If it is behaving itself by producing plenty of fruits on a shapely bush, leave it alone. If not, cut it down to the ground in late winter.

SPIREA (SPIRAEA)

I would like to know if I should snip the tips of bridalwreaths? If so, when? Do not snip off the tips, as this spoils the grace of the bush. Instead, cut out some of the old shoots at the base as soon as the blossoms have faded.

Is it possible to trim and drastically reduce bridalwreath (Spiraea prunifolia) in size? Yes; cut back all flowering shoots immediately after the flowers have faded. Shorten those remaining, if necessary, to reduce to the height required.

How should spirea 'Anthony Waterer' be pruned? This is a late bloomer, producing its flowers on shoots of the current season; therefore, it may be cut back about ½ in the spring, just as growth begins.

We have a number of spirea plants on an old lot which are much too large and tall for our present building lot. How drastically can these shrubs be pruned? Spireas in general can withstand severe pruning. It may be done in late winter, but this results (in the case of early-blooming varieties) in no blooms the following season. They can be cut to within a few inches of the ground.

STEPHANANDRA

What is stephanandra? The cutleaf stephanandra has finely cut leaves and terminal spikes of small, greenish-white flowers 2 ins. long in June. It is from Japan. It grows about 7 ft. tall in a graceful arching manner.

Is stephanandra a good ornamental shrub for my garden? (Connecticut.) Probably only mediocre, but its recent variety 'Crispa' has become extremely popular, especially for planting on banks or in rocky areas. Only about 3 ft. tall, it roots vigorously wherever its branches touch the soil. Easily propagated by merely digging up the rooted branches, preferably in the spring. Don't plant in the rock garden as it quickly outgrows its space and can become a pest.

SUMAC

Can fragrant sumac be closely trimmed, down to say 4 ins.? When? Yes; in the spring before growth starts. But better leave it a little longer than 4 ins.

SWEET-SHRUB (CALYCANTHUS)

What color are the flowers of sweet-shrub (Calycanthus)? When does it bloom? Reddish or purplish brown. Blooms in June and July.

Is calycanthus a difficult shrub? We planted one, pruned it, and gave it plenty of water, but it slowly died after having come out in full leaf. Calycanthus should not present any great difficulty, though it is sometimes slow to start into vigorous growth after moving. The treatment you gave your plant appears to be correct. If you make another attempt, cut out at least half of the older stems at ground level, and reduce the remainder about half their length. Be careful not to give too much water.

A sweet-shrub bush which formerly produced very fragrant flowers now continues to have lovely blooms which, however, have no scent. Is there anything that can be done? No, unless you wish to try fertilizing it heavily with well-rotted manure or some complete commercial fertilizer. Sometimes increased vigor produced in this manner will make the flowers more fragrant. It is a good idea to "smell" the flowers of this shrub before purchase, as apparently some scentless forms have been propagated.

TAMARISK

What does a tamarisk (Tamarix) look like? Handsome, picturesque shrub with a plumy effect. Leaves resemble heather. Flowers pink to white. Some of the hardiest (to southern New England) are *T. parviflora, T. pentandra,* and *T. odessana.*

I have been told that the tamarisks can stand ocean spray and wind. Is that true? (Massachusetts.) Yes. It is one of the finest of all shrubs for shore planting, and thrives in sandy soil.

When and how is a tamarisk pruned? We have one which has six or seven long branches which begin at the ground level and sprawl. Pruning depends on the group to which it belongs. Some bloom early on old wood, while others flower on wood of the current season. The first type should be cut back severely after flowering; the latter in the spring. In both cases the (approximately) 1-year-old shoots should be cut back ½ to ⅔.

VIBURNUM

Which viburnums do you recommend for autumn coloring and fruiting? Linden viburnum (*V. dilatatum*); witherod (*V. cassinoides*); Wright or Oriental (*V. wrightii*); mapleleaf (*V. acerifolium*); blackhaw (*V. prunifolium*).

Which viburnums have the most effective flowers? Double-file viburnum (*V. plicatum tomentosum*); Japanese snowball (*V. plicatum*). The former has flat flower heads which lie along the top of the horizontal branches.

Which viburnum would lend itself best to foundation planting? None, except possibly *Viburnum plicatum* 'Mariesii' because of its horizontal branching, good flowers and fruits, and then the house must be a large one. About the only location for it would be at a corner. The low-growing *V. opulus* 'Nanum' could be used as a hedge under a bay or picture window.

Which viburnum will stand the most shade for woodland planting? Mapleleaf viburnum, also called dockmackie (*V. acerifolium*).

Is there a low, compact viburnum? Yes; dwarf cranberry-bush (*V. opulus* 'Nanum'), to 2½ ft. high, and *V. opulus* 'Globosum', about 5 ft. high.

Does Viburnum carlesii prefer a neutral soil? It will grow well enough in any approximately neutral garden soil of good quality, not likely to become parched.

Why is Viburnum carlesii so difficult to grow on its own roots, and Viburnum burkwoodii so easy when the plants are practically identical? This is one of nature's many as-yet-unanswered questions. In fact, *V. carlesii* is one of the parents of *V. burkwoodii*—which only makes the answer more difficult.

Why did my Viburnum dilatatum fail to produce berries? It may have been that a cool rainy spell predominated just when the pollen was ripe. This would have prevented insect activity and wind from disseminating the pollen at the proper time. Also with this species, it is essential to plant two to three plants—all grown from seeds (not grown from cuttings of the same plant) to insure fruiting.

Can you suggest reasons why three Japanese snowballs (Viburnum plicatum tomentosum) I planted died? The European snowball (V. opulus 'Roseum') and American cranberry-bush (V. trilobum) lived. Possibly killed by winter. The Japanese snowball is not so hardy as the European.

When and how can I prune my snowball bush (viburnum) which has grown too high and too shaggy? You might take a chance on cutting it back immediately after flowering; or in early spring if you are prepared to sacrifice the season's crop of bloom; but often snowball bushes do not respond well to severe pruning.

I have a snowball bush 5 or 6 years old that has never bloomed. What is wrong with it? The flower buds have probably been killed by winter cold or lack of nutrients in soil.

WEIGELA

Is there a weigela with very showy blooms? Yes, variety 'Bristol Ruby', with red blossoms; or 'Eva Rathke' or 'Vanicek', both of which have a tendency to recurrent bloom from June to August.

What is the best way to treat a weigela bush that is very old and produces very few flowers? Thin out the bush by removing some of the oldest branches during the winter. Cut them as near as possible to the ground line. Annual pruning should consist of the removal of worn-out flowering branches as soon as the blossoms have faded.

WILLOW, PUSSY

Will a pussy willow do well in dry soil? Pussy willow (*Salix discolor*) adapts itself to a dry soil but prefers a moist. In dry soil it may become quite susceptible to diseases, and it will grow more slowly and remain smaller.

Why does my pussy willow burst forth in December and not in spring? (Massachusetts.) Mild winter days frequently force pussy willows into premature growth, especially if the tree is growing in a protected spot.

When is best time to prune pussy willows? If it is desired to have the "pussies" develop on long, wandlike shoots, the tree should be pruned severely before growth starts by cutting back all of the shoots made the preceding year to 1 or 2 buds. Otherwise no pruning is necessary.

Is it best to let a pussy willow grow in a bush or tree form? How tall should it grow? It is best to keep it in bush form by pruning out any central leader that may appear. The height depends upon conditions, varying from 10 to 20 ft.

The florist sells long branches of pussy willows with much larger "pussies" than I can grow. What are these? These are the so-called French pussy willows (*Salix caprea*) with larger flowers than our native *S. discolor*. Long shoots are grown by heavily fertilizing the plants and cutting the branches back severely each spring, thus forcing vigorous growth.

How can I start pussy willows in the ground? What time of year? As soon as the frost is out of the ground in spring, make cuttings 8 to 10 ins. long. Place ¾ of the cutting in the ground. Or root shoots indoors in water, then plant them.

WINTERBERRY (ILEX VERTICILLATA)

I have seen a shrub in the wild which in fall has shining scarlet berries close to the stem after the leaves are gone. What is it? Probably winterberry (*Ilex verticillata*), a deciduous holly.

How can winterberry or black-alder be used? In a shrub border, preferably in moist soil. It grows somewhat lank, so plant it in back

Two good plants for autumn and winter color—American holly and its relative, the native winterberry. The latter is much hardier, but is not evergreen.

of lower shrubs as, for instance, inkberry (*Ilex glabra*), an evergreen relative.

Does winterberry require "wet feet" or does it grow in spite of the water? Winterberry is a shrub often found in the wild state in swampy ground. However, it grows quite successfully in any good garden soil, provided it is not too dry.

Will you tell me the best way to move, transplant, and grow the winterberry holly? Dig it carefully in the very early spring, with or without a ball of earth about the roots. Place in a good garden loam, slightly on the moist side if possible. Prune back one third. Water well.

WITCH-HAZEL (HAMAMELIS)

Where would you plant a witch-hazel? In the woodland, or in the rear of a shrub border, or near a window of the house so the blossoms may be enjoyed from indoors at close range. They are not showy, but valued for their late winter or late fall bloom.

What is the ultimate height of the witch-hazel? The tallest witch-hazel your answer man has seen was an old specimen of the native *H. virginiana,* some 40 ft. high. That is exceptional. Another native species, *H. vernalis,* usually remains less than 8 ft. high.

When do the witch-hazels bloom? October or November—native witch-hazel; February or March—Japanese, Chinese, and vernal.

Will witch-hazel grow in half shade? Is it worth growing? Witch-hazels are eminently suited for planting as undershrubs in wooded places. Their unseasonal flowers are more interesting than spectacular. Showiest in flower is the Chinese (*H. mollis*). Where open woodland situations are to be planted, the witch-hazels are well worth while.

Narrow-Leaved Evergreens

WHAT TO GROW

What does coniferous mean? It means cone-bearing. Among the cone-bearing trees are fir, spruce, pine, Douglas-fir, and hemlock.

I have recently bought a new property of several acres and believe there will be space for me to plant many coniferous evergreens—both

among the dwarf and standard kinds. Can you recommend any books on this subject? *Manual of Cultivated Conifers,* by Marinus Nyhoff (The Hague, The Netherlands, 1965); *Dwarf Conifers, A Complete Guide,* by H. J. Welch (Charles T. Branford Co., Newton, Mass., 1966); *Handbook on Conifers* (Brooklyn Botanic Garden, Brooklyn, N.Y., 1969); *Conifers for Your Garden,* by Adrian Bloom (Floraprint Ltd., Nottingham, England).

What are retinosporas?   This is a term applied to juvenile or immature forms of false-cypress (*Chamaecyparis*) and arborvitae (*Thuja*).

What are the best evergreen trees for specimen lawn planting? (Northern New England.)   Douglas-fir, white fir, hemlock, white and red pine; arborvitae, yew, and Hinoki false-cypress if small trees are preferred.

I want to put some evergreens back of my white birch trees. What would harmonize?   Hemlock or red pine.

Would like a few dignified evergreen trees. What do you suggest that would in time become very large?   Hemlock, white pine, red pine, firs, and most spruces where climates are not too hot.

Will you recommend some medium-size, erect-growing evergreen trees?   Arborvitae (*Thuja occidentalis*); red-cedar (*Juniperus virginiana*); Chinese juniper (*J. chinensis*); upright yew (*Taxus cuspidata* and *T. media* varieties).

Can you suggest some drooping evergreen trees to plant beside our garden pool?   Weeping hemlock, weeping Norway spruce, weeping Douglas-fir.

We are planting a wildflower sanctuary in our woodland. Which evergreens would be the best to introduce there?   Hemlock, rhododendrons, Canada yew, white pine (if not too shady).

What is the fastest-growing evergreen?   In the northern United States this is probably the hemlock, although the white pine might run first when grown in good soil.

Are there any evergreen trees with berries?   Red-cedars and other junipers have blue-gray berries, and the yews sometimes have red berries, but they usually drop quickly.

What are some evergreens that can be grown for Christmas decorations?   Hollies, all kinds, both deciduous and evergreen; pine, spruce, fir, hemlock, arborvitae, juniper, yew, mountain andromeda, Japanese andromeda, mountain-laurel. Spruce and hemlock quickly drop their needles when cut unless stood in water.

I wish to set out 50 or 75 evergreens for use later as cut Christmas trees. What kind of trees would you recommend for western Pennsylvania? Douglas-fir (*Pseudotsuga menziesii*) and Scots pine. Balsam fir is best if it will grow in your section.

LOW-GROWING EVERGREENS

What evergreens, 4 to 6 ft. high, are spreading in habit? Common and Pfitzer juniper, Japanese yew, Sargent weeping hemlock.

Two shapes found among junipers; the prostrate or spreading varieties are desirable for banks or as ground covers.

Which low evergreens could be used to edge our terrace in a sunny, dry location? *Juniperus conferta, J. communis* varieties, *J. horizontalis* varieties, and *Ruscus aculeatus*.

Which formal evergreen would be suitable for each side of our sunny front door? *Picea glauca* 'Conica', the dwarf Alberta spruce.

Is there a dwarf evergreen with red berries in winter? Yes, dwarf forms of Japanese yew.

Are there any evergreens that will remain low—not more than 2 ft.? *Buxus microphylla* 'Compacta'; *Buxus* 'Curly Locks'; *Chamaecyparis obtusa* 'Nana' and var. 'Pygmaea'; *Gaylussacia brachycera;* several varieties of *Ilex crenata; Juniperus procumbens* 'Nana'; the dwarf leucothoe and 'Cole' dwarf hemlock. All will remain under 2 ft. tall.

Are there low-growing conifers suitable for a rock garden? Spreading English yew, dwarf Japanese yew, dwarf Hinoki falsecypress, 'Andorra' juniper, 'Bar Harbor' juniper; dwarf forms of Japanese holly and Norway spruce.

For picturesque effects in the rock garden, or in more or less formal plantings, such evergreens as mugho pine and the Oriental or Chinese arborvitae are selected.

Which evergreens would make suitable foundation planting for the four sides of a large farmhouse? Are fruit-bearing bushes practical for such use? Evergreens would be selected from the rhododendrons (for shady areas), yews, arborvitaes, and junipers. Yes, fruit-bearing shrubs, such as the blueberry, viburnum, and cotoneaster, would be assets in such a planting.

For foundation plantings choose low-growing evergreens that stay low (such as Pfitzer juniper). Dwarf Alberta spruce (right) is a very slow-growing conifer especially desirable as an accent in the rock garden or among other dwarf evergreens.

CULTURE

What kind of soil is best for evergreens? A soil suitable for most kinds is a good loam, well drained, but somewhat retentive of moisture. On such a soil, additional nourishment can be supplied for yews, which like a rather rich diet. Junipers, pines, and Douglas-fir should not require it. Most broad-leaved evergreens need an acid soil.

Can good results be expected from evergreen trees planted on land stripped of its topsoil? Such land is not suited for the intensive cultivation of evergreen trees, but pockets can be prepared for occasional trees. In a clayish subsoil, prepare these pockets by mixing in cinders and peat moss; in sandy soil, work in plenty of peat moss.

Our soil is dry. Would pines and junipers be advisable? Yes, most pines and junipers tolerate dry soil.

What is the best fertilizer for dwarf evergreens? Some, including dwarf junipers and pines, will require none, unless the soil is very poor. Arborvitae, yews, and chamaecyparis like some fertilizer. The best way to apply nourishment to established plants is by applying a topdressing of leafmold or peat moss mixed with old manure or dried manure before snow falls.

Do evergreens need a leaf-and-manure fertilizer? In planting— depending upon the quality of the soil—mix more or less leafmold and old manure or compost with the planting soil. For established evergreens in good soil, nothing more than a topdressing of the same. Yews like a topdressing of dried manure or compost.

Can evergreens be fed in winter? A rich mulch of compost or a mixture of dried manure and peat moss, applied in the fall, is satisfactory. It is unwise to spread commercial fertilizers on the ground in the winter, as melting snows or rain will take it away without its penetrating the soil. Best time is October or very early spring.

How often should bone meal be placed around evergreens? Do not use bone meal. Use, rather, somewhat acid artificial fertilizers; or, still better, topdressings of leafmold or compost or old manure. (See previous question.)

TRANSPLANTING

How are evergreens transplanted? Very small specimens are moved with a ball of earth, held in place by burlap, attached to their roots. Large specimens should be moved with a platform beneath them, installed by someone with experience.

When is it best to transplant small evergreens and how? Either early September or early spring. Dig a hole twice as wide and twice as deep as the root system of the plant; have plenty of good soil available; be certain there is drainage at the bottom of the hole. Set in plant carefully—no deeper in soil than it formerly grew—untie burlap and remove it (if possible without the root-ball collapsing, otherwise tuck it in between the side of the hole and the root-ball), fill in soil, make firm, and water thoroughly. Leave a slight depression in soil about plant so that it will receive plenty of water until it becomes well established.

I would like to change several little evergreens to another location. When and how do I go about it? If plants are small, dig them in the spring with the best possible root-ball. Plant in a friable soil mixed with leafmold, compost, or dried manure. Water thoroughly; mulch the base to prevent drying out. If larger trees, transplant either in spring or early autumn.

When is the best time of the year to plant little evergreens (seedlings)? In the spring, when the ground has dried and warmed so that it is friable; and before the evergreens have started growth.

When is the best time to transplant evergreens? For well-grown nursery grades, spring, before growth has started; or early autumn, from August 1 on. For plants that have not been transplanted recently, spring is best. Large trees, properly balled and platformed, can be moved in the spring, or as late into the autumn as the ground can be dug.

Evergreens planted with the burlap on do not grow for me, although I have raised beautiful evergreens. Should I remove burlap instead of slitting it? Unless it might break a weak root-ball, remove the burlap; at least open the knots, spread it out in the bottom of the hole, or cut it off close to the base of the ball.

How early in the spring can evergreens be transplanted? Wait till all frost is out of the ground and the soil has dried off and warmed up, so that it is thoroughly workable. Transplant evergreens before they have started into growth.

When does the fall planting season for evergreens begin? Generally, as soon as the early summer growth has become hardened. In the case of pines, spruces, and firs, this means as soon as the annual growth has been completed and has hardened and the terminal buds firmly "set." In dry seasons, one usually waits for a favorable moist spell of weather.

In New York, what are the best months for planting evergreens? And what months in spring and fall are the deadlines for planting? Plant preferably in early September (first choice); or March to April (second choice).

Which evergreens could be planted in December? In lower New York State, large specimens of the hardy kinds, if properly balled and platformed and moved by professionals. December is late for smaller evergreens, and one might best wait until early spring.

Is it O.K. to move evergreens in midwinter, so long as the ground is not frozen, but may freeze up any time after the planting? Safe enough for large trees, dug with solid fibrous root-balls, carefully planted, well watered, mulched, and moved by professionals. Not advisable for small evergreens; unsafe for trees that have not been previously transplanted.

Why do I lose so many evergreens, purchased with solid-looking balls and tightly burlapped? Possibly because these good-looking trees had been dug and kept out of the ground for some time prior to your purchase. Freshly dug trees, promptly planted, stand a far better chance of succeeding than "pre-dug" stock.

I often find roots of dead evergreens packed hard in a dry ball, despite repeated soakings. How come? Root-balls dug in clayish soil, or puddled in clay, when planted in a lighter soil may easily become caked hard, so that water cannot penetrate them. Loosen the surface of hard-looking balls before planting.

Why do so many evergreen trees die after transplanting? There are many possible causes. Trees may not have had fibrous root systems; they may have been dug with inadequate root-balls, or planted at the wrong season; they may have perished from drought; or they may have been tender kinds.

Will oak sawdust, if it is put in the ground while transplanting evergreens, help them or do harm? On a soil deficient in humus, rotted (not fresh) hardwood sawdust may be helpful. Or use leafmold, peat moss, or old manure.

Our water supply comes from a deep well and is quite hard. We have planted many seedling evergreens. Will it be harmful to use well water on them; and will it injure the foliage should any get on it? Alkaline water is definitely harmful to all broad-leaved evergreens, and might injure some narrow-leaved ones, such as pines, hemlocks, spruce, fir, false-cypress. Foliage will be injured through damage done to the whole plant by introducing alkali into soil, not by contact of water with leaves.

Should one cultivate around evergreens? Cultivation at the base of established evergreens can disturb surface roots and do more harm than good. Keep the soil from caking, rather, by means of a mulch of leafmold or compost, with perhaps a little old or dried manure.

Should one at all times keep a mulch about the base of evergreen trees? Mulch all newly planted evergreens. While a mulch will be helpful to many established evergreens, not all kinds require it if planted in a suitable soil.

What is the reason that evergreens, such as pyramidal arborvitae or Scots pines, turn a rusty brown and lose their needles? This may represent only a normal shedding of old foliage. Drought and soil exhaustion may cause premature shedding. Vigorous growth and proper sanitation tend to reduce it.

My arborvitae has a lot of brown leaves. I have dusted it with sulfur. Can you give any advice? Prevent caking of the soil, and see that the roots do not lack water. Just before ground freezes, give a very thorough soaking. Keep a mulch of leafmold or compost about base.

I have poor luck with mugo pine and Koster blue spruce. I lost two mugos, and the spruce doesn't look well. What is wrong? Both kinds, unless transplanted frequently in the nursery, make coarse roots, which mean great risk in transplanting. Most losses are due to this. Secure transplanted, fibrous-rooted plants. These will usually grow right along in any fair soil, if planted where they get sun.

Would the exhaust from autos, blowing into the evergreens, cause their death? Repeated and protracted exposure to these gases can cause the death of evergreens, especially hot exhaust gas on a cold winter day.

Should healthy evergreen trees turn yellowish? Color is not a natural condition. No. A yellowish discoloring may indicate any of several causes of trouble: poor drainage, overwatering, or a poor quality of soil.

In the planting about our house one corner plant died 6 months after planting. A reset did the same. The soil was examined, and

no lime pocket was found, nor sign of insect trouble. All other plants
are doing well. What may have been the trouble? Corner plants
often suffer from a strong draft of air. This can be fatal to newly
planted trees. A windscreen might prevent the trouble.

I have red-cedars and Pfitzer junipers, planted 2 years ago. They
are not growing and look dry, although I have tried to treat them
right. I hoe around them and water thoroughly. They are on west
side of terrace (not very close to terrace) and pretty far apart. What
do they need? Examine them for spider mites. If these are found,
spray promptly and repeatedly with malathion. The ground may be
hard and poor. Cultivate and apply a mulch.

Do evergreen trees need shade or sun? Nearly all prefer an open
situation. The native yew prefers shade. Balsam fir and hemlock prefer
a situation open overhead, but some partial protection from the
brightest winter sun.

When is the best time to apply a dormant oil spray to evergreens
(in central Pennsylvania)? What should the temperature be? Early
spring; but this kind of spray should always be used on evergreens
most carefully, for if too strong, it will quickly burn the foliage and
possibly kill the plant. It will remove "bloom" from types such as
blue spruce. Temperature should be under 65° F.

How can I straighten spruce and other evergreens bent from snow-
storms? Pull them back into position. Light trees may be held in
place by stakes; larger ones by guy wires or ropes fastened to pegs
in the ground, or to overhead points. After a snowstorm, go over
your evergreens and brush off snow with a broom or the back of
a rake.

PRUNING

When and how should an evergreen be trimmed to make it bushy
instead of a tall tree? Different kinds can be trimmed at different
times, but the season which will suit all is in late June or July period
of soft spring growth. In upright growing kinds, trim both top and
side branches so as to avoid a chopped-off effect.

What can one do to train evergreens to be bushy instead of tall
and straggly? Trim them annually, from the start. And see that those
which like a rich soil, such as yews and chamaecyparis, are kept supplied with a nourishing topdressing. Don't grow them in shade.

Can evergreen trees, which have been allowed to grow too tall near the house, be trimmed back? It can be done with the kinds which will "break" readily from the old wood; but not with pines, firs, spruce, hemlock, or Douglas-fir. Trimming back, however, can leave large evergreens in an unsightly condition.

Can evergreen trees be kept low by cutting the tops? Yes; but a radical "topping" will spoil the appearance and natural beauty of most—especially pines, spruces, and firs, which will not "break" from the old wood, and will remain stunted. An exception is when evergreens are used as a hedge.

Is it advisable to heavily prune small evergreens to control shape? With the exception of erect-growing pines, spruces, firs, and Douglas-fir (which are best left with a minimum of pruning), most young evergreens will be benefited by pruning uneven shoots that they will eventually make more solid and compact plants.

Does it harm a spruce or pine to cut branches from it for indoor purposes? It may not threaten the life of a large tree, but can spoil its appearance if overdone.

Can evergreens be trimmed in winter? Never prune them during freezing weather. Do not trim in winter any of those evergreens which make one annual shoot terminated by a prominent bud or "candle," like pine, spruce, fir, and Douglas-fir. These should be trimmed in early summer. Young "candles" of pine may be shortened before the needles develop.

WINTER PROTECTION

Will you outline winter care of untransplanted seedling evergreens, and of once- or twice-transplanted ones? For the seedlings and once-transplanted, a covering with dry leaves in late autumn; for the twice-transplanted, a mulch over the ground and light branches (not necessarily evergreen) laid over the rows or beds. Water the plants thoroughly just before winter hard freezing and previous to applying mulch.

How should pines and junipers be cared for during the winter? If well established, no special winter protection is needed. In the case of newly set plants a mulch of leaves or other littery material, applied as the ground is about to freeze, might be helpful and would certainly do no harm.

How should I care for Douglas-fir, Serbian spruce, Austrian pine, and mugo pine in the winter? (New York.) The evergreens mentioned are quite hardy in New York and need no special winter protection.

Is it true that I shouldn't mulch with oak leaves around my small firs? There is nothing harmful to firs in oak leaves; but in a planting near the house, for instance, the leaves may be too loose to be the best mulching material.

What is proper procedure for protecting low evergreen shrubs and trees in the winter (located at the seashore with only the house to protect them)? If the soil is dry, give a good watering before the ground freezes, then put on a mulch of leaves or litter several inches deep. Protection from wind is probably important, and this may be afforded by sticking evergreen boughs in the ground around them. In some cases it may be advisable to erect a temporary windbreak made of boards or burlap.

Will it be worth while to cover bases of evergreens with partly decayed leaves now (January) after the ground has been covered with snow for some time? The trees were planted in October. If the snow is likely to remain all winter, there is no need for a mulch at this time; but if a midwinter thaw occurs, then it would be advisable to spread leaves to curtail bad effect of alternate freezing and thawing.

Is there any way to prevent windburn on evergreen trees? The injury referred to is probably the scorched appearance of foliage sometimes noted in the spring, especially on firs. This is caused by the sun in winter and can be prevented largely by placing trees so that they will have some slight protection from the brightest sun in winter.

How shall I take care of evergreens in winter, when they cannot be watered? There is not much to be done in this case. In some cases, such as small specimens in a foundation planting, or in a very exposed position, evergreen boughs could be stuck in the ground around them to give some protection from winter sun and wind.

PROPAGATION: SEED AND CUTTINGS

Is it possible for an amateur to raise evergreens from seeds? Yes, providing one has reasonable patience and is prepared to give careful attention to the seeds and seedlings. (See following questions.)

How can I grow evergreens from seed? Sow fall-collected seed in spring in shallow boxes filled with light, well-drained soil. Cover, to about diameter of seed, with sifted soil. Place flats in cool, shaded cold frame and keep evenly moist. When watering, avoid disturbing surface soil. Transplant when large enough to handle.

How do you keep seeds of evergreens until planting time? Store in tins, jars, or tight paper bags that are nearly airtight, in a cool, dry place.

When should evergreen tree seed be planted; and how old should the seed be? Seed collected in fall should be sown in spring. Older seed, kept under proper conditions, will germinate, but viability becomes progressively less with each passing year.

Can evergreens be propagated by using the clippings for cuttings? (Wisconsin.) Most of the yews, junipers, False-cypresses (chamaecyparis), arborvitaes, and some of the spruces can be propagated by means of clippings. These can be taken in late August, but as a rule many of them do not form roots before winter, therefore a greenhouse is desirable, particularly in your climate. If you have a greenhouse (night temperature 50° to 55° F.) you could also take cuttings in November and December.

What is best temperature to root pines and spruces from slips in hothouse beds? The percentage of pine cuttings that can be rooted is so small as to make this method almost valueless. A very few of the spruces can be rooted, and for these a greenhouse with a night temperature of 50° to 55° F. is required.

Will you describe the simplest way to start cuttings of arborvitaes and junipers? Take the cuttings in the latter part of August, and set them out, about 1½ ins. apart, in boxes of sand. The boxes should not be more than 4 ins. deep, but any convenient size; the sand must be made firm before the cuttings are put in. Then cover the box and cuttings with polyethylene film after watering thoroughly. Keep them in a hotbed until there is the possibility of the sand freezing, then place them in a cool, frostproof storage for the winter. If covered tightly with polyethylene film, they may need water only once a week, or even less often.

Should boxes filled with sharp sand and leafmold, containing cuttings of yew and boxwood, be placed in deep shade, or in semishade, for best results? The important thing is that the cuttings must not be directly exposed to the sun, except possibly very early in the morning or late in the evening.

Specific Evergreens

ARBORVITAE   (See also Hedges.)

Which arborvitae would be best in our northern climate, to serve as a boundary-line screen?   Pyramidal arborvitae, *Thuja occidentalis* 'Fastigiata'.

Would an arborvitae stand city conditions?   Not very well but it will grow in the city if conditions are not too severe. Needs good moist soil and sunshine for at least half of the day.

Will golden arborvitae do as well in shade as in sun?   No. All "colored" evergreens require full sun to bring out their peculiar coloring.

When is the best time to plant arborvitae? What soil?   Plant in early fall, up to October 1; small plants a foot or so tall only in the spring. Dig them with solid root-ball. Set as deeply as they formerly stood. Fill around the ball with friable soil enriched with compost or peat moss, and water this down well. When settled, add more soil, leaving a slight depression around the plant to catch rain water. Mulch the base, and in dry weather administer occasional soakings.

Why are arborvitaes so hard to grow?   They are by nature lovers of open situations and moist soils. Their use in foundation plantings, which is rarely suitable, therefore, is highly artificial and unnatural. (See previous questions.)

Can an arborvitae be pruned if the tree becomes too tall and thin? When is the proper pruning time?   This can be done effectively in the case of quite young plants. Pruning and topping will do little good to old plants. Pruning should be done during the period of soft spring growth. To improve the denseness of old plants, apply a nutritious topdressing of leafmold and rotted manure or compost.

When and how is the best time to trim arborvitae?   During the period of soft spring growth, shear the outer surface slightly, trimming the extremities of the soft growths. Close shearing results in a dense, formal appearance; light shearing in a less formal appearance.

CEDAR

Could I grow a cedar-of-Lebanon here? What is its botanical name? (Southern Pennsylvania.) *Cedrus libani* would probably grow for you, but it is not hardy much farther north, though a hardy strain of the cedar-of-Lebanon has been introduced by the Arnold Arboretum near Boston and has been growing there since 1903.

CRYPTOMERIA

What is the cryptomeria like? The Japanese temple-cedar or cryptomeria is a rapid-growing evergreen tree with tufted branches. It attains 125 ft. in Japan. It is not hardy much above Zone VI. In this country it is handsome when young, but soon becomes scrawny.

FALSE-CYPRESS

I have a tiny dwarf tree which has frondlike foliage and seems very tolerant and hardy, and looks very well in the rock garden. What is it? It is probably dwarf Hinoki-cypress (*Chamaecyparis obtusa* 'Nana').

FIR

What does the Nikko fir (Abies homolepis) look like? Large, broadly pyramidal evergreen tree with spreading upturned branches, and glossy dark-green leaves. Needles spread upward forming a V over the twig. Identify it by its grooved branchlets.

What is a good fir as a specimen tree? (New Hampshire.) White fir (*Abies concolor*).

Which of the evergreens is very dark in color, of pyramidal form, tall, and with pendulous branches? This is probably the Douglas-fir (*Pseudotsuga menziesii*), one of the best.

Will you suggest some good fir trees? Douglas-fir, white fir, Nikko fir, Nordmann fir, Veitch fir, Fraser fir.

Can we grow fir trees in a dry, rather hot part of the East? Probably not; they require a cool, somewhat humid climate; but if you must try one, the white fir would probably do best.

Can one grow a balsam fir in New Jersey? Probably not. It does best north of Connecticut; or in mountains south of Virginia.

Do fir trees grow well in a fairly sandy soil? How early in spring can they be planted? Yes, in a somewhat sandy soil, enriched with leafmold or other humus matter. Best time to plant them is the early fall.

How can I grow Christmas trees in Massachusetts? In New England the "Christmas tree" is usually the balsam fir (*Abies balsamea*), which requires the cool, moist climate of the mountains. It has a difficult time in the warmer areas about Boston, and on Cape Cod. If the climate is right, young trees 6 to 18 ins. high can be set out in any field and be expected to begin to yield suitable Christmas trees in from 7 to 10 years. However, because of the time element involved, only marginal land should be used for this purpose. Write your local State Experiment Station for the most recent bulletin on the subject.

Is it wise to buy a tubbed fir Christmas tree and then, on a mild day, after the holidays, plant it outdoors (the hole having been previously dug and filled with leaves)? From a viewpoint of gardening economy better buy proper kinds and grades of trees for ornamental use, in the proper seasons, and buy your Christmas trees cheaply, without balls. However, many living Christmas trees are successfully set out after the holidays, following the method you mention.

How does one plant trees used indoors as Christmas trees? Prepare the planting hole in advance. Fill and heap it over with leaves. Have planting soil ready indoors. Keep the tree moist; remove it promptly, after use, to a cool place. Plant on a frost-free day, and water thoroughly. Apply a thick mulch, and place a burlap screen around it.

How can I prune a fir tree which is growing too tall and narrow? Does it need fertilizing? The soil is very poor. Many fir trees grow naturally tall and narrow. It is not practicable to prune back a fir tree after it has reached any great size. In poor soil, apply a nutritious mulch of leafmold and compost at the base.

HEATHS AND HEATHERS

I want to plant a little "sheet" of heath. What kind of soil? Choose a well-drained, sunny situation. Prepare a cushion, fully a foot deep, made up of about half garden loam, and half peat moss. (If your soil is heavy clay, add sand and more peat moss.)

Can heather (Calluna vulgaris) be satisfactorily grown out of doors in the vicinity of New York? Scotch heather grows quite well in acid soils, along the eastern seacoast. The plants often kill back during very cold and windy winters so should be mulched with evergreen boughs or marsh hay.

Should Scotch heather be pruned? Early-blooming varieties should be cut back to the *base* of the flowering shoots as soon as the blossoms have faded. In sections where heather suffers from winter injury, pruning should be done in early spring just as growth is beginning. Such yearly pruning (technically, "shearing") keeps the plants shapely and floriferous.

Which is more hardy—the heaths (Erica) or the heathers (Calluna vulgaris)? Which would be more likely to survive in Ithaca, N.Y.? Generally, there are more winter-hardy forms of *Erica carnea,* such as the well-known 'Springwood Pink', than there are among the many varieties of *Calluna vulgaris.* (However, there are other species of *Erica,* such as *E. hyemalis,* which are not hardy in northern regions and can only be grown as pot plants there.) In Ithaca, most of the varieties of *E. carnea* should be winter-hardy, especially with a good snow cover for protection.

Does Scotch heather bloom in winter? No. Heather (*Calluna vulgaris* and its varieties) blooms in the summer. You are thinking of heath, probably varieties of *Erica carnea,* which often start flowering around Thanksgiving and Christmas. However, their major flower display is usually in early spring.

Can I divide heaths and heathers? Not too well, although sometimes the plants form layers, which when removed, make new plants fairly quickly—depending on the variety.

I would like to make a small heath and heather garden, but the only sunny area I have directly adjoins our terrace. Would the plants look all right there? Yes, it sounds like an excellent location and, as you relax on the terrace, you will be able to look down on the intricate patterns of the plants. Try to keep your access areas to the terrace obvious enough so guests and family members won't trample the plants.

Are heaths and heathers hard to grow? No, if consideration is given to soil, mulching, and pruning, as mentioned in the first three questions at the beginning of this section.

I am planning a heath and heather garden. What other plants can I use with them? Many dwarf conifers, such as *Juniperus communis* 'Compressa'; dwarf small-leaved rhododendrons, such as *Rhododendron impeditum* and *R. intricatum;* and the evergreen azaleas such as the 'Gumpo' varieties. Larger-leaved and taller-growing rhododendrons and azaleas can be introduced as background plantings to your garden.

HEMLOCK

We have an extremely shady garden. Would any evergreens do well for us? Hemlocks and yew only.

Which evergreen trees obtained in ordinary woods would be best to put around a home? I wish to stunt their growth. How is this done? Hemlocks would be best of all, for they can be kept at any height merely by trimming or clipping their new growth, once or twice a year, in the early summer and late summer or early fall.

What type of soil is best for young hemlocks? Do they require much water? A light loam, rich in humus. In an ordinary garden soil, up to 25 per cent of leafmold or other humus can be worked in; in a light, sandy soil twice this amount. Hemlocks should not be permitted to suffer for lack of water; but do not keep the soil drenched.

When is the best time to transplant hemlocks? (New York.) In early autumn, during favorable, moist weather, up to about October 15.

What conditions and methods are advocated for most successful transplanting of hemlocks from woods in same locality? The safest method is to root-prune the tree a year in advance of moving. When actually transplanting, the roots should all be carefully dug in a tight ball of earth and *not allowed to dry out* while the plant is being moved from one place to the other.

Can a 25-ft. hemlock, once transplanted, regain new needles on branches now bare, due to moving of tree to different spot in garden? If the bare branches do not develop new leaves during the spring following transplanting, they never will. In that case, remove the dead branches.

What is the proper care of hemlock trees? They prefer a situation sheltered from strong winds and a soil very rich in humus. They revel in leafmold. Use lots of it when planting, and apply a leaf mulch about the base. Do not let them get dry, and, in dry autumns, soak the soil thoroughly just before winter. If set in a sun-scorched place, partial shade will be helpful in establishing seedling trees.

Why do hemlocks die back soon after planting? They should not. The trouble can be due to one or more of several causes: lack of a good, solid, fibrous root-ball when transplanted; improper planting; lack of humus in the soil; lack of water; or windy exposure.

How would you propagate hemlock from cuttings? Do they need heat? Propagating by cuttings is difficult but it can be done with a very small percentage of rooting. Take softwood cuttings in early July, place in mixture of sand and peat moss in a greenhouse bench with bottom heat, or under constant mist, which see.

JUNIPER

Which juniper would grow tall, compact, and narrow? Canaert red-cedar. Or one of the Chinese junipers, such as *J. chinensis* 'Columnaris', would be good.

Are Irish junipers of same family as red-cedar trees? Can they be safely planted near apple trees? Yes, they both belong to the genus *Juniperus*. They serve as alternate hosts for the cedar-apple rust, and should not be grown within several hundred yards of apple trees.

Will Irish juniper do well in an east foundation planting? Mine don't look very good. Red spider might be the trouble, as they were not sprayed this year. A northeast exposure would be better. This juniper is subject to winter burn on the sunny side. Spider mites are often injurious; but the effect would spread over the entire tree, not merely on the sunny side.

How can I keep my Irish juniper from turning brown each spring? Keep the brightest sun in winter from the foliage, either by locating the junipers in a northeast exposure, or by means of a burlap screen or other protection.

Are cedar and red-cedar the same thing? No. The word "cedar," when correctly used, applies to the genus *Cedrus*—a group of trees native in North Africa, and southwest Asia. These are quite different from our native "red-cedar" (*Juniperus virginiana*) of the eastern United States.

What is the best time of year to transplant red-cedar from a field? Cedars over 7 ft. high should be root-pruned in September and moved a year later. This will insure a fibrous root system, so necessary to successful transplanting.

What can be done to improve the appearance of red-cedar trees planted in front of a house? Examine them for the presence of spider mites. If these are present, spray promptly and repeatedly. Cultivate the surface lightly, without disturbing roots. Mulch with leafmold or rich compost. See that there is no lack of moisture. Red-cedars should not be used in a foundation planting.

What time of year should I plant a spreading juniper? Spring, after the ground has become thoroughly workable, before growth has started; or early autumn. In lower New York State, up to about November 1. In dry autumns, take advantage of such wet spells as may come along.

What fertilizer do spreading junipers need? Established, thriving plants, in soil of fair quality, need none. In poor soil, apply a top-dressing of leafmold or peat moss mixed with compost. Avoid alkaline fertilizers.

What winter and summer care does an erect juniper, 2 to 3 ft. high, require? Is it possible to prevent dead branches at the base? Is this due to dogs? Examine branches for spider mites. If found, spray promptly. See that the soil does not cake. Apply a mulch. Dogs can well be responsible for injury to lower branches.

When are junipers pruned; and how? The principal annual pruning is done during the period of soft spring growth. If a formal appearance is desired, a second, lighter pruning can be given, about September 1, to upright-growing kinds like the red-cedar.

Can I cut about 27 ins. off the top of a Meyer juniper without damaging the tree for summer growth? Our tree is too tall. Yes, you can reduce the height by cutting back. It will produce new growth below the cut, which will eventually cover the stubbed effect.

Please tell me the right way to trim Savin junipers. Can the long branches be trimmed back? For proper development, Savin junipers should be pruned rather heavily in their young stages. This will make them bushy. When old branches are pruned back, they can be slow in producing new growth and the effect can be unsightly.

After the top is broken off a silver juniper, Juniperus virginiana glauca, will it ever be a nicely shaped tree? It will readily develop a new leader of acceptable appearance within 2 or 3 years. The process may be helped by staking up the new leader and pruning back competing growths.

How long does it take for juniper berries to ripen; and when is the time to pick them? Some junipers will never have berries. Only the female (pistillate-flowering) trees bear fruit. The Rocky Mountain juniper (*Juniperus scopulorum*) and several other junipers take 2 years to mature their fruits. These could be picked in the late summer or early fall of the second year. The female trees of *J. virginiana* should bear fruit every year if weather conditions are just right.

How do nurserymen increase junipers? I have done it by slicing a branch and burying it until it roots, but there must be a quicker way. Either by cuttings or grafting. Cuttings are placed in the greenhouse in summer or early winter. Cuttings of some junipers will remain alive and in good condition for more than 2 years without rooting. Grafting is done early in the year.

Can I start Pfitzer's juniper from cuttings? It is possible but this juniper does not root too readily. Make cuttings, about 5 ins. long, in latter half of August and place in greenhouse bench with bottom heat. (See Propagation, this section.)

PINE

Which is the more satisfactory, red pine or Austrian pine? They are similar, but the former is less susceptible to insect pests than the latter in some areas.

We like pine trees, but our soil is moist. Would any of them do well? White pine (*Pinus strobus*) and pitch pine (*P. rigida*) are occasionally found growing wild in swamps in New Jersey. In the South, longleaf pine (*P. palustris*) could be planted.

We were advised to buy pine trees for our garden near the windy

seashore. Is Scots pine a good choice?   Yes. Japanese black pine is most resistant to wind and salt spray, however.

I would like to plant a pine tree which is not coarse in texture. What do you suggest?   Use either white pine or Japanese red pine.

How can I tell the principal pine trees apart?   Many of them by the length of their "needles," and the number of each cluster (fascicle). White pine—5 in a cluster, 5 ins. long (soft bluish); Austrian pine—2 in a cluster, 6½ ins. long (stiff); Scots pine—2 in a cluster, 3 ins. long (twisted); red pine—2 in a cluster, 6 ins. long (glossy); Japanese black pine—2 in a cluster, 4½ ins. long (sharp-pointed).

What is the best fertilizer to keep a pine tree healthy and growing? Is bone meal O.K.?   Bone meal (superphosphate is better) when transplanting, but it is not a complete fertilizer, which can be applied later on. However, if the soil is of good quality and the tree healthy, no feeding will be required. At the slightest sign of soil exhaustion, apply a topdressing of leafmold or peat moss mixed with rotted manure or compost.

Can pine trees be planted all year round?   No. Not during the period of soft growth, from May to August.

I have some fine 4-year-old white pine and Norway pine. When is the best time to transplant them, and should they be in full sun or partial shade? (Wisconsin.)   Transplant in early spring, before growth starts. Mulch the surface. An open situation is best, but some temporary shading would be desirable.

When is the best time to transplant pine trees? (New York.)   In the latitude of New York City, fibrous-rooted trees can be transplanted either in the spring, or in the autumn, between August 1 and November 1. Pines not previously transplanted had better be planted in the spring only, with as good a root-ball as possible.

How should pine trees be transplanted?   Untransplanted trees over 6 ft. high should be root-pruned (which see) in September and moved a year later. Transplanted trees with fibrous root systems can be dug with a ball of roots, burlapped, in the spring or in early autumn. Water down the filling soil. Fill the hole flush with the grade. Mulch soil over roots.

Is it too late to transplant pine trees that were set out as seedlings, and are now about 10 ft. tall?   No. Root-prune (which see) them in September; move them a year later, or in the spring of the second year. They should then have developed sufficient fibrous roots to facilitate successful transplanting.

How old can pine trees be transplanted safely?   There's no age limit. The only limits are those set by available machinery for moving, and by obstructions in the path of travel.

Should grass be kept away from the ground around young pines? Yes.

When and how does one prune mugo pines?   When the candle-like spring growths have about reached their full length, but before the leaves have spread out, cut these "candles" back partly. When they are reduced to ¼ or ⅓ their length each year, a mugo pine will form a dense, cushionlike plant.

I have a matched pair of mugo pines. One is getting larger than the other. Is it possible to trim them back?   Yes. In the annual pruning of the candlelike spring growths, cut those on the larger plant a little farther back than those on the smaller plant. This ought, in a year or two, tend to even the two plants up. Do not prune into the old wood.

What can be done to save young pine trees badly browned by the heat from burning brush?   If the scorched branches produce new leaves in the spring following injury, no harm will have been done. If not, nothing can restore the damage; cut off the burned parts.

Will you please tell me what makes our pines so thin looking, and with brown edges?   Probably unsuitable environment, such as inadequate underdrainage, or too much shade.

Are new pine trees started by seeds or cuttings?   Pine trees are started from seeds sown in spring. Some varieties are grafted. Most species and varieties are exceedingly difficult to raise from cuttings.

Can pine trees be grown from seed?   Yes. Seed ripens September to November, the cones that produce the seed being 2 or 3 years old. Collect cones before seed has shed and place in shallow boxes in warm, dry place. (See answers to other inquiries.)

Is there any disease that pine trees catch from fruit trees?   No, but the white-pine blister rust lives for part of its life on gooseberry and currant bushes. This is a very serious disease.

RED-CEDAR   (See Juniper).

SPRUCE

Which are some of the outstanding spruce trees?   Oriental spruce (*Picea orientalis*); Serbian spruce (*P. omorika*); Colorado spruce (*P. pungens*)—some varieties of this are bluish in tone.

What is the best fertilizer for blue spruce?   An occasional top-dressing of leafmold or peat moss with compost mixed into it. When planting, mix leafmold and some rotted manure or compost with the planting soil.

I have planted spruce trees in oyster shell. I was advised to use sulfate of ammonia and pine needles to make the soil acid. Was it wrong?   Oyster shell is not suitable for evergreens. Add a large quantity of acid humus material, such as peat moss, hemlock or pine-needle leafmold.

What type of soil is suitable for spruce trees?   A good loam, enriched with humus. Untransplanted trees over 6 ft. high should be root-pruned in September and moved a year later. Trees previously transplanted should be dug with a good ball, either in spring or in early autumn. Water the soil after planting. Fill flush with the grade. Mulch.

Should ground be frozen to remove spruce and pine from woods to lawns?   Not necessarily. The main thing is to secure an adequate, solid ball of fibrous roots and earth. Large trees are sometimes most conveniently moved with frozen balls.

How much space should be available in front of a house to plant a blue spruce?   It should have an area 20 ft. or more in diameter in which to grow.

In a blue spruce, successfully transplanted last year, the old foliage has lost its bright color. Will it return?   This happens often when in transplanting or transit a blue spruce is tied in tightly or crowded. The blue, waxy coat of the foliage rubs off and does not renew itself. Subsequent new growth will eventually cover the dull inner foliage. The color rubs off most readily on the soft new growth.

I have had little success with blue spruces. Will you give information on their culture?   Be sure to procure transplanted, fibrous-rooted plants. Plant in a well-drained, sunny place in any fair, loamy soil. Plant in the spring before growth starts, or shortly after August 1, during suitable damp weather. Water plentifully; mulch the base. Keep the roots moist, but not too wet, and in dry autumns soak thoroughly just before winter.

What is the proper care for Norway spruce and blue spruce seedlings, now 1½ ins. high?   Assuming that they were planted in well-prepared planting beds, merely keep under lath shades, and maintain soil moisture with a light, fine surface mulch.

Can you prune and shape a blue spruce? If so, when is the proper time?   Yes. Prune only during the period of soft spring growth. The shaping process can sometimes be aided by tying in misdirected branches and staking a crooked leader.

How shall I trim sides of Colorado blue spruce too wide for parking space?   If this involves cutting into old wood, it will not be found practicable. Better move the whole tree back from the drive, if possible.

I have a blue spruce which is growing lopsided. How shall I trim it?   If the leader is crooked, stake it. If any branches can be tied into place, do this before you use the pruning shears. If it is a matter of one or more protruding branches in an otherwise well-balanced plant, then reduce these branches as necessary.

How does one prune blue spruces to prevent them from growing too large?   They are by nature tall-growing trees. They can be kept down artificially by means of annual prunings or shearings during the period of soft growth in spring. This involves the snipping off of the extremities of the shoots.

In two spruce trees that serve as windbreaks the lower branches are dying. How can I improve their appearance and discourage any great increase in height?   Once the lower branches have died, nothing will bring them back to life, and no new growth will replace them. To prevent further loss of lower branches, remove all crowding nearby growths which shut out light. Keep a mulch about the base; eventually cut off top shoots if necessary.

Can I get information about propagating blue spruce? Can they be increased by cuttings?   They can be rooted from cuttings, but not very readily. Use shoots of one year's growth with a very small "heel" of old wood, inserted in January in a propagating case in a warm greenhouse. Usually they are grafted by nurserymen. For detailed information consult *Plant Propagation,* by John Mahlstede and Ernest S. Haber (John Wiley and Sons, 1957).

How can Moerheim blue spruce be propagated?   Usually propagated by grafting.

How, when, and where should one plant seeds of Norway spruce and Colorado blue spruce?   Sow ¼ in. deep in a bed of fine soil, shaded by lath screens, until seeds have germinated; or in flats in cold frame in spring.

Will handling spruce and red-cedar Christmas trees, after they have been in the house, cause a bad case of poison on the hands and face?   Such a difficulty is not common. Some individuals might be allergic to the resins in these trees, but cases of poisoning are rare. Sometimes handling needle-leaved evergreens causes a temporary irritation to the skin on hands, but it soon disappears. Could you have had a potted plant of *Primula obconica* in the house at the same time? This primrose causes a severe skin poisoning, similar to that of poison-ivy, on those who are allergic to it.

YEW

Which yews grow in tree form?   English yew and the single-stem Japanese yew; but they rarely attain great height in this country except in the Pacific Northwest.

Which yews make narrow upright growth?   Hatfield, Hicks, and Irish yew (where winters are not severe); also Japanese upright yew, and the variety 'Stovehenii'.

Hemlock will not survive here but we have had best success with Japanese yew. What else shall we plant?   There are several varieties of yew, available from nurserymen, which differ in shape and height. These could be used.

Do dwarf yews prefer an acid soil?   No, they will grow well in either acid or alkaline soils.

When is the best time to move yews?   Either in spring, before growth starts, or in early September.

Should dwarf Japanese yew be fed? If so, what and when?   Not necessarily. If their color is good, leave them alone. Dwarf Japanese yews always grow slowly. Well-rotted manure makes a good fertilizer, when needed, or even commercial fertilizers when used according to directions.

I have two Japanese yews. One has retained its dark green, but the other has a slight yellow cast. Why? Frequently Japanese yews are grown from seed. Then there are wide differences in the resulting plants. Height, shape, and color of foliage are all variables in such instances.

My Japanese yew is dying. I have given it plenty of water and fertilizer, sprayed the foliage, all to no avail. What is the trouble with it; and how can I correct it? The roots of this plant are probably being attacked by the grubs of the strawberry root weevil. Chlordane is the usual remedy for this pest. Consult your county agent for local recommendations and timing.

I planted two yews four years ago. One seems to be dying. It has been this way for two seasons. Foliage is green but very thin. There are no grubs around roots. This is a condition frequently related with finding aphis on the roots. If this is not the case, the explanation could be in some peculiar soil condition. Would suggest digging the plant, removing the soil about the roots, and transplanting in some other situation.

When is the best time to trim Japanese yew? Just after growth has been completed, in late June or early July.

Should yew trees be trimmed in August, or are they prettier left untrimmed? Usually they are prettier untrimmed when grown as specimens, but some years a small amount of trimming (which really can be done any time) is necessary to keep certain branches from growing too much out of proportion to the rest of the plant.

Should low-spreading yews, in foundation plantings, be pruned? Not if they stay low and do not grow out of proportion to the other plants.

Should the branches of Taxus cuspidata be tied for winter protection or supported in some way? The branches break easily. This might be done if they are growing in situations where snow and ice will accumulate on them, as under the eaves of the house.

How can I best propagate Japanese yew for a hedge? Take cuttings 6–7 ins. long at the end of June, place them in sand in an electric hotbed (temperature about 75° F.), keep watered and shaded, and they should be rooted by fall. Pot them and keep in a cool place (not freezing) over winter, then plant out after all danger of frost is over.

Can I propagate yew from seed? Yes. Collect seed in fall, clean off the fleshy part, stratify seed in peat moss or sand at room temperature for five months, then three months in the refrigerator at 40° F., then sow.

Can you advise how to grow Japanese yew from seeds? Clean the fleshy pulp from the seed; stratify by placing alternate layers of moist peat moss and seeds in a box; keep at a temperature of 30° to 40° F., possibly in refrigerator, and sow in the early spring. Some seeds may not germinate for a full year, so don't be discouraged if they all do not come up the first year.

How can I raise seedlings from berries on a Hicks yew? This can be done (see preceding question), but Hicks yew is a hybrid and seedlings of it will not all have the characteristic upright shape of the Hicks yew. A better method would be to propagate by cuttings taken in early summer.

Broad-Leaved Evergreens

CULTURE

What fertilizer ingredients, in what formula, would you suggest for feeding ericaceous plants, and at the same time maintain acidity in the soil? Tankage or cottonseed meal applied at the rate of 5 lbs. per 100 sq. ft. is satisfactory for small plants. For large plants use 6–10–6 fertilizer in which cottonseed or soybean meal is used to supply one fourth to one half of the nitrogen. Apply at the rate of 2 to 3 lbs. per 100 sq. ft. of bed area. If the soil is sufficiently acid, 7½ lbs. nitrate of soda, 10 lbs. superphosphate, 2½ lbs. sulfate of potash could be used to approximate the above formula. (See also Azalea and Rhododendron.)

What does "ericaceous" mean? This term is applied to the plant family Ericaceae, consisting mainly of shrubs, very small plants, and small trees which require a sandy, peaty acid soil. Among the

Ericaceae are the following: andromeda, arbutus, heath, heather, enkianthus, wintergreen, blueberry, mountain-laurel, sand-myrtle, leucothoe, pieris, rhododendron (including azalea). Some are evergreen, others, deciduous.

What kinds of native shrubs, besides azaleas, need acid soil? Rhododendrons and all other broad-leaved evergreens; blueberries, huckleberries, and bayberries. As a general rule, provide acid soil conditions for all kinds that grow naturally in oak or evergreen woods.

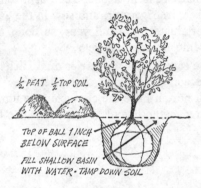

½ PEAT ½ TOP SOIL

TOP OF BALL 1 INCH
BELOW SURFACE

FILL SHALLOW BASIN
WITH WATER - TAMP DOWN SOIL

PLANTING A BROAD-LEAVED EVERGREEN

Which broad-leaved evergreens will grow best in New York City? Japanese holly (*Ilex crenata*); inkberry (*Ilex glabra*); drooping leucothoe (*Leucothoe fontanesiana*); Oregon holly-grape (*Mahonia aquifolium*); *Pieris floribunda* and *japonica,* and *Rhododendron obtusum* 'Amoenum'.

What soil is best for mountain-laurel? Moist, acid, bountifully supplied with humus. Grows well in rhododendron soils.

Do rhododendrons, mountain-laurel, etc. require special soil? Yes. A well-drained subsoil beneath, 12 to 18 ins. of topsoil containing up to 50 per cent acid humus matter. A totally uncongenial soil should be removed bodily, and replaced with a suitable compost. For acid humus, use pine, spruce, hemlock, or oak leafmold; or peat moss. Peat moss, mixed with well-rotted manure or compost, and added to soil makes a good medium for plants of this type. Soil acidity should be 4.5–6.5 pH.

Can I condition my alkaline soil for rhododendrons? Yes. Sulfur is the safest way. See Introduction to Soils, Part 1, for directions.

My soil is very acid, but rhododendrons do not grow well; why? The soil may be too acid, and poorly drained. Bring it up to pH 5.5 by adding pulverized dolomitic limestone (a soil test will indicate how much lime you need). Dig out bed to a depth of 18 ins., put in 6 ins. cinders, and return soil mixed with limestone and peat moss.

How can I be certain a soil is acid? Send samples to your county agricultural agent or to State Agricultural Experiment Station for testing; or buy one of several soil-testing kits available for just this purpose. (See Acidity in Section 1.)

Our soil is definitely alkaline, but I want to grow azaleas and rhododendrons. What should I do? The best way is to excavate the soil in the area for planting to an approximate depth of 2½ ft. Place in the excavation only acid soil rich in humus. Sphagnum peat moss is an acceptable source of humus.

With a soil only slightly alkaline, how does one make it acid with a minimum amount of trouble? The second best way of acquiring an acid soil is to apply aluminum sulfate to the soil in question, at rates depending on the alkalinity, or pH. Following figures indicate reaction of soil at start, and amount of aluminum sulfate per square yard: pH 5.5 to 6.0, ¼ lb.; pH 6.5 to 7.0, ½ lb.; pH 7.0 to 8.0, ¾ lb. This should be well watered in, and the soil again tested at the end of 2 weeks. If the soil has not reached the desired acidity, to a depth of 6 to 12 ins., apply sulfur at one sixth of the rate given above.

How acid should soil be for azaleas and rhododendrons? For most of them, pH 5 to 6.

Should a soil in which azaleas and rhododendrons are growing be tested more than once a year? Only if the plants fail to grow well.

Will coffee and tea grounds sprinkled around azaleas help to acidify the soil? Would this practice be harmful? No, it would not acidify soil to any marked degree.

What is the best time of year to feed azaleas? They can be fed either in early spring or fall.

We use cottonseed meal for fertilizer a great deal down here. Can

this be used on azaleas? (South Carolina.)   Yes. A mixture of 2 lbs. of cottonseed meal and 1 lb. of ammonium sulfate, used at the rate of 1 to 2 lbs. per 100 sq. ft., makes a very good acid fertilizer. (See also under Rhododendron.)

What type of soil does wild azalea (or pinxterbloom) require? A normally moist, acid soil.

I would like to grow rhododendrons here. How can I make soil acid? (Illinois.)   See under Azaleas for method of making soil acid. In Illinois, especially the northwestern part, the summers are very hot and dry and the winters very cold, which is extremely hard on rhododendrons. Precautions should be taken to give foliage and roots plenty of moisture in the summer; also to give winter protection, especially in exposed situations.

My soil is very dry, and some of my rhododendrons have died. What should I do?   Mix decomposed vegetable matter (rotted manure, rotted oak leaves or pine needles, compost, and peat moss) with the soil. Then apply a mulch of rotting oak leaves, pine needles, or peat moss mixed with compost about the base of the plants. All these help to conserve moisture.

What fertilizer should one give rhododendrons growing in a poor, sandy soil?   Add decaying vegetable material, such as rotted manure, decaying oak leaves, pine needles, and peat moss. Chemical fertilizers alone added to a poor, sandy soil would not be sufficient.

Is flowers of sulfur a desirable fertilizer for azaleas and rhododendrons?   It acts as a fertilizer, for in making the soil more acid it releases certain materials which were not formerly available to the plant.

What summer and winter care do azaleas need?   Water thoroughly during drought in summer. Mulch with oak leaves, pine needles, or peat moss to maintain acidity and to protect roots in winter. Tender varieties should have evergreen boughs or burlap screens placed about them.

Is it possible to grow rhododendron and azalea successfully in Ohio? What are the soil requirements?   Yes. Evergreen azaleas are easier to grow than the evergreen rhododendrons, but both can be grown from Maine to Florida, and west to the Mississippi River, providing they have acid soil, plenty of moisture, and not too severe winter temperatures.

What is the proper treatment for azaleas the year round? Our bushes are not blooming. (Minnesota.) Many azaleas, especially in the colder parts of the United States, have their flower buds killed by very low temperatures. Plant only the hardiest kinds in cold areas, such as the pinkshell azalea, pinxterbloom, and some of the Ghent hybrids.

How can I grow azaleas (which come from West Virginia) between lakes Ontario and Seneca, in soil that is not naturally acid? First make the soil acid. Practically anything which is hardy in the mountains of West Virginia will prove hardy in central New York.

How do you pinch back evergreen azaleas? Merely pinch off end of growing twigs. This will force several side buds to grow, and will result in a bushier shrub.

How should azaleas be pruned? Cut out diseased or dying branches from the base of the plant. Often it is advisable to cut off a few twigs here and there to force thick growth. Otherwise they need little pruning.

Should seed pods be pruned from azaleas? Cut off dead flowers before seed pods form, then more strength will go into flower-bud formation for the next year.

What should azaleas be sprayed for? Lacebug and red spider are the most serious pests of azaleas.

Will rhododendrons grow in full sun? Yes, if you mean the small-leaved kinds, but partial shade is best for the large-leaved types.

Are there any particular requirements, as to sun or shade, for rhododendrons? Rhododendrons bloom most profusely in the full sun; but if grown in partial shade they will bloom sufficiently well to be attractive. In deep shade most varieties bloom very little.

Do rhododendrons and azaleas need the same growing conditions? Yes, except that large-leaved rhododendrons will grow better in shaded situations protected from wind.

When should rhododendrons be planted? Preferably in spring, then in late summer.

Where should rhododendrons be planted? Where they get some shade and some filtered sunlight. Also, they should be protected from high winter winds. Their roots should not be allowed to dry out at any time.

My place is exposed to wind from the ocean. Will rhododendrons thrive?   No. In any case they need shelter from strong wind—especially in winter.

How old must rhododendrons be to bloom? Mine are five years old, growing well in prepared acid soil and partial shade, but do not bloom.   Many rhododendrons bloom when they are about five years old. This particular plant may be growing too fast vegetatively. Root-pruning might be practiced by pushing a spade into the soil around the base of the plant, not too near the stem. Or you might try superphosphate (15 to 20 per cent), applied beneath the mulch, at the rate of 4 oz. per square yard. Some varieties and species bloom at earlier ages than others.

Can you tell me why my rhododendron did not bloom although it has healthy foliage and growing conditions (acid) are favorable?   Is it receiving too much shade? Or it may have been that the flower buds were killed by an unusually cold winter. Also, rhododendrons are like many other ornamentals in that they bloom profusely one year and very little the next. There is little that the amateur can do about this "alternate-bearing" habit of some kinds.

How is Rhododendron maximum made to bloom better?   This species does best only in the shade. Ornamentally it is not so good as the earlier-flowering hybrids, because the flowers appear after the new growth has started, and this frequently hides the flowers. Plenty of moisture, acid soil, and an acid mulch are helpful aids.

Are all broad-leaved evergreens transplanted with a ball of soil about their roots?   Absolutely, yes! This applies specifically to boxwood, daphne, holly, inkberry, and all azaleas and rhododendrons. The idea is to dig as many of the fibrous feeding roots as possible, enclosed in a tight burlapped ball of soil so the ball does not break up. If this happens, many fibrous roots are broken and the plant can fail to survive. Handle the ball as carefully as possible and do not let it dry out!

Do I take the wrapping material off the ball at transplanting time?   Yes, if you can do it without breaking the ball. If you can't, set the ball in the prepared hole, cut all tied strings and ropes, carefully roll back the wrapping material and push to the bottom of the hole, without breaking the ball.

WINTER PROTECTION

Do azaleas and rhododendrons need winter protection in the vicinity of New York? How is this best provided? Only the more tender evergreen sorts need the kind of protection provided by a burlap screen or pine boughs, so placed about the plant as to protect it from high winds and sun. All azaleas will do better if provided with a mulch of some acid material (oak leaves, pine needles, or compost) about their roots in winter.

Should broad-leaved evergreens be covered completely for the winter? If by this is meant the complete covering of the leaves, the answer is: No! But if a mere shading of the plant is meant, this proves helpful when tender varieties are being grown.

Should young azaleas be protected for the winter if they are not sheltered by shrubs? The evergreen varieties might well be mulched since these are the least hardy. Mulching material should be light, allowing air circulation. Use evergreen boughs, marsh hay, or oak leaves.

How can potted azaleas purchased at the florist and full of buds and flowers be taken care of so as to bloom again? Most of the florists' potted azaleas are Kurume azaleas, and are not hardy north of Philadelphia, Pennsylvania. They will grow out of doors the first summer but will be killed by winter cold in most northern regions. In the South, such plants can be planted out of doors in acid soil, protected the first winter, and usually come through in fine shape. In the North, such potted plants can be summered outdoors by plunging the pot to its rim in soil. Bring indoors before winter.

Should azaleas and rhododendrons have a mulch about their roots? Why? Yes. Because their roots are shallow and grow best when the soil is cool and moist. In the winter a mulch protects the roots against extremely low temperatures.

Is it good to mulch azaleas and rhododendrons with manure? Not if it is fresh. Well-rotted manure can be used without injury to the plants.

When should a mulch be applied to azaleas and rhododendrons? It is well to put a mulch over the roots just before winter weather sets in. This, if not more than a few inches deep, can be left on until time to place new mulching material for the next winter.

What makes a good mulching material for azaleas and rhododendrons and other broad-leaved evergreens?   Oak leaves, pine needles, and acid peat moss mixed with compost. Upon decomposition all these are beneficial to the growth of this type of plant.

I have no oak leaves but plenty of maple leaves. Could I use these as a mulch?   It would be better to use peat moss mixed with compost instead. Maple leaves tend to pack closely when wet, thus keeping air from the plant roots. When very tightly packed, they frequently "cake" and have been known to kill azaleas for this reason. Also, maple leaves are alkaline when decomposed.

Would it be helpful or harmful to tie burlap sacks around the branches of my camellia and to cover the buds, in winter?   It would be harmful. Air must circulate about these plants in the winter, and wrapping stems and branches would not permit this. It is far better to build a screen of burlap about them, open at the top to permit free air circulation at all times, but also giving a screening and shading protection.

What is the best protection for rhododendrons exposed to strong winds?   Burlap screens, or screens of evergreen boughs, so designed and placed as to give protection from winds, and some shade during winter months—especially February and March. Snow fencing can also be used.

When should leafmold mulch be applied to rhododendrons? Any time, especially after planting. Renew as necessary.

PROPAGATION

Are azaleas, rhododendrons, and other ericaceous plants propagated by seed?   Yes, depending upon the kind and the purpose for which they are needed. Any of the wild forms, native or exotic, can be raised from seeds, as the seedlings will reproduce the characters of the parent. Hybrid forms and "sports" should not be reproduced from seeds, but by cuttings.

How can I start ericaceous plants from seed?   Collect seed pods in late fall when they are ready to open. Keep dry, and in late fall shake seeds out on milled or ground sphagnum moss 1 in. deep on top of acid soil well firmed in pots. Keep moss moist, preferably by

using a fine mist spray from time to time or enclose pots in polyethylene. In several months seedlings should be of right size to transplant into flats or small pots. They develop well under fluorescent
lights.

Can azaleas be propagated by cuttings?   It is exceedingly difficult
to root cuttings of deciduous azaleas, but the evergreen varieties can
be rooted with great success in July. The cuttings should be about
3 ins. long, taken (just after new growth is completed) from the tips
of the shoots and placed in a rooting mixture of sand and peat moss
in a flat tightly enclosed by polyethylene after being thoroughly watered. Keep the flat out of direct sun.

What is the type of graft used on rhododendron?   The veneer
graft is most commonly used. The understock is not cut back at the
time of grafting. A downward, slanting cut is made on the stem of
the understock, about 1½ ins. long and about one third of the way
through the stem. A second cut into the stem (at the base of the
first) removes the piece of bark and attached wood. The base of the
scion is cut to correspond to the cuts on the understock. Few rhododendrons are grafted today.

How should rhododendrons be separated?   Rhododendrons as a
rule should not be "separated" in the same sense that one thinks of
separating perennials. They grow as individual plants, often in
clumps. Any attempt to divide these clumps would probably prove
disastrous.

Specific Broad-Leaved Evergreens

AZALEAS, EVERGREEN

How can I grow the evergreen azaleas?   They need much the
same conditions as rhododendron. See questions and answers on
Culture above.

**A group of Hinodegiri azaleas have become too large. Can they
be clipped rather severely, after next bloom, without injury or serious
loss of future bloom?**   Yes, they withstand heavy pruning.

Will you discuss winter protection for azaleas in this region? Mine fail to blossom in the spring; most of the leaves are brown and new growth is slow to start. During the summer they grow well. (Northern New York.)   The evergreen types are not hardy in northern New York. If you build a screen of burlap or pine boughs, this might help to bring them through in better condition; but if the flower buds are killed, even with this protection, then the thing to do is to plant a hardier variety. *Rhododendron calendulaceum, R. nudiflorum,* and *R. viscosum* are among the hardiest of the deciduous azaleas.

What are the Glenn Dale hybrid azaleas? Would they be hardy in Connecticut near the coast?   The Glenn Dale hybrids are the breeding results of B. Y. Morrison, formerly head of the Division of Plant Exploration and Introduction of the U.S.D.A. at Glenn Dale, Maryland. The breeding aim was to obtain evergreen azaleas hardy in the Middle Atlantic states that would bloom from April to June. Of the 400 or so named varieties introduced in 1940 and for several years thereafter, many are probably not available from commercial nurserymen. Most of the Glenn Dales would be hardy in your region. A few of the more outstanding of these hybrids that should be available include: 'Copperman', late, orange-red; 'Mary Margaret', late, orange-red; 'Martha Hitchcock', late, white with magenta margins; 'Gaity', late, red; 'Fashion', midseason, hose-in-hose orange-red; 'Pixie', early, white striped with red; 'Aphrodite', midseason, dusty pink; 'Geisha', early, white striped red.

BOXWOOD

I have heard about Korean box; what is it like?   It does not grow more than 3 ft. high, resembles dwarf box, and is the hardiest of all the boxwoods, but the foliage often turns brownish.

In making an English box garden in a space 50 × 75 ft., what should spacing be?   This depends on the height at which the box bushes will be kept. If a height of 3 to 4 ft. is desired, then plants could be spaced 18 ins. apart for a hedge. Single specimens, if allowed to grow unclipped should be allowed a space at least 5 ft. in diameter.

What fertilizer should I use on boxwood?   Well-rotted manure or rich compost is best. Commercially prepared chemical fertilizers should be used with discretion, for fear of burning the foliage.

What is the best time of year to move large boxwoods? Commercial tree movers transplant them at any time of year. The home gardener might best do it in early spring, or very early fall.

Would small boxwood plants, of which we have a number to be transplanted, do well along a cemented parkway about the building? How far apart should these be planted? When? These would grow satisfactorily if given good soil and sufficient room. They should be set 10 ins. apart if this is the dwarf variety, *Buxus sempervirens* 'Suffruticosa'. Transplant in early spring.

Should boxwood be covered for a time after transplanting? If the weather is very hot, shading with a burlap screen will help cut down the water loss. Also syringing the foliage during the evenings of hot days will aid young boxwoods in pulling through. Covering such young plants the first winter is a good practice.

What winter and summer care do boxwoods require? A thick mulch of leaves or straw on soil for the winter; plenty of water during hot, dry summer weather.

Many of the leaves of my boxwood drop off in midsummer, and the plants become unsightly. What causes this? Probably the boxwood leafminer, the most serious of boxwood pests. The tiny maggots tunnel within the leaves, causing irregular swellings or blisters in the leaf. Spray with methoxychlor, diazinon, or malathion in early spring.

What material should I use to spray my boxwoods for boxwood leafminer? Timing is most important. Keep a close watch on the under sides of the leaves during late April and early May and when the pupae are beginning to get active it is necessary to spray right away with malathion. A better way to determine the timing is to open some of the blisters and if the pupae have black heads it is time to spray. When the infestation is heavy one spraying is not sufficient; so, spray with malathion early in summer. Follow directions on the containers and observe all precautions.

When is the best time to trim boxwood? Late June.

Can boxwood be trimmed close to the ground in order to thicken the growth at the base of the plant, where many of the limbs are

very lanky? In the case of old plants with very thick trunks and branches it is practically impossible to coax new growth from the base. In young plants, this may be feasible, but cutting heavy branches back severely should be avoided.

How shall I protect old, very large, and dense boxwood during winter? Prune out any dead or diseased branches. Thoroughly water, if ground is dry. This is frequently necessary, for winter injury may result if they enter winter with dry roots. Cover with burlap supported on wood frames if injured by winter in previous years.

What makes some box turn reddish brown in winter? Is there any remedy? Either too-low temperatures, or too much bright, warm sun while the ground is still frozen. The remedy is to protect the boxwood with a screen of wood, burlap, or pine boughs.

What makes boxwood winterkill? Many complex physiological factors. The chief cause for winterkilling is bright, warm sunshine in early spring, while the ground remains frozen. Another cause is low temperature.

Is the true dwarf box hardy in Boston? It will survive with protection, but is not reliably hardy there.

How can I root cuttings of boxwood? Put them in polyethylene-enclosed boxes of sharp sand or a mixture of sand and peat moss in July or August. Remove to a frost-proof building during the winter months.

CAMELLIA   See also Regional Section and Specific Tender Shrubs, this section.

In a southern garden I saw an evergreen shrub that I became very much interested in. The owner called it Camellia japonica. It had a double flower like a rose and as large. Please tell me where I can buy this shrub? (Pennsylvania.) Camellias in many beautiful forms and colors can be obtained from southern nurseries. *C. sasanqua* and possibly *C. japonica* will be hardy with you in Pennsylvania if you live in the moderate areas. They probably would not survive in the western part of the state and certainly not in the mountains. Pick as protected a location as you have with some shade in winter and summer. Some camellias are being successfully grown in New Jersey, on Long Island, and on Cape Cod, but they are mainly shrubs for mild climates.

DAPHNE

I have tried Daphne cneorum many times and had no luck. I tried full sun; half shade; shade in sandy soil enriched with fertilizer; wet soil; dry soil; and also clay soil. Can you advise? As a matter of fact, it grows in *both* acid and alkaline types of soil. What is more important is that the soil should be a sandy loam and well-drained. Shade has little to do with it. Such successive failures as indicated above would point to the possibility that the acidity or alkalinity of the soil might be at fault, and the soil should be made nearer the neutral point.

Is it possible to transplant a daphne which has been in one place for 5 years? (Michigan.) If the daphne is growing satisfactorily in its present position, it would be better not to attempt to move it. If it must be moved, transplant in spring, with a ball of earth attached to the roots.

What is the proper method of pruning Daphne cneorum? My plants sprawl all over the place. It is the nature of this species to be wide-spreading. Pinching out the tips of the growing shoots will help keep it more compact.

Can Daphne odora be pruned? Daphnes are inclined to resent severe pruning. You can keep them compact by pinching out the tips of the growing shoots.

Should a daphne plant receive special protection during the winter? Generally it seems desirable to protect *Daphne cneorum* from winter sun and wind, though some plants come through perfectly without, even when exposed to morning sun. A loosely arranged overcoat of pine branches is sufficient.

How can an amateur best propagate the dwarf daphne? The rose daphne can be rooted from cuttings, but with difficulty, by usual means. Under constant mist 100 per cent rooting can be expected. Shoots can be layered in the usual way. Another method (mound layering) is to place sandy soil in among the shoots in the form of a mound, leaving only a few inches of the ends of the shoots protruding. At the end of the season the earth is drawn away and the rooted shoots are potted singly. The great objection to the latter method is that the resulting plants are rather spindly.

EUONYMUS

Which evergreen euonymus does not climb but remains a shrub?
E. japonicus, not reliably hardy north of Washington, D.C., and varieties of *E. fortunei.* One is the variety *carrierei.* Another is *E. fortunei* 'Vegetus', but this will climb if near a wall.

HOLLY (ILEX)

What is the difference between Osmanthus aquifolium and holly?
Osmanthus is often mistaken for holly because of the similarity of the foliage, but they are easily distinguished by the opposite leaves of osmanthus and the alternate leaves of holly. There is no close botanical relationship between the two.

What is the hardiest kind of holly? We have a "Christmas garden" and would like to add this to it. (Massachusetts.)   The American holly (*Ilex opaca*) might grow near the coast, or if protected; English holly probably would not. *Ilex pedunculosa* and the native inkberry, *I. glabra,* are the hardiest, but they do not look like the Christmas holly. Also the deciduous winterberry (*Ilex verticillata*) is very hardy, and has beautiful Christmas-red berries.

Does the American holly grow low or high?   Both the American and English hollies are trees, growing eventually to 50 ft. or more in height.

What kind of soil does the American holly prefer?   A light, sandy soil, containing some decaying leafmold. Heavy clay soils should be avoided in planting hollies.

What fertilizer shall I use for American holly?   If it is growing well, do not apply any fertilizer. Well-rotted leafmold, worked well into the soil, is about the best material which can be applied. Rotted manure or compost can be applied in the late fall as a mulch. Hollies prefer a light, sandy soil.

When is the best time to plant a holly tree?   In early September; or early April, just as the new leaf buds begin to open.

When and how is it best to transplant holly, especially in a hedge?
In areas where the climate is moist, either spring or very early fall. In the eastern United States very early spring is usually best. The plants should be dug carefully with a ball of earth about the roots. If planted as a hedge, space 2 ft. apart.

How can I most successfully transplant hollies? The safest way is to move them with a ball of earth about the roots. If they are to be dug up in the woods, sizable trees should be root-pruned (which see) a year in advance of transplanting.

Is it possible to raise holly that is used for Christmas decorations in Maine, or is that too far north? Maine is too far north. The northernmost limit for American holly is Cape Cod. English holly can be grown very little in the northeast except on Cape Cod and Long Island and farther south near the coast.

Can I get holly to grow in my garden? (Michigan.) It is doubtful if either the American or the English holly will grow in Michigan except in extremely well-protected situations.

Is it true that in Ohio holly should be planted where the winter sun will not hit it? It is not the winter sun so much as the high, dry winds of late winter which injure holly trees. If these are prevalent, it will pay to protect the holly trees from such winds.

Where is the beautiful English holly grown commercially? In the moist regions of Oregon and Washington.

Have set out native American hollies, using leafmold and soil from the woods as a fill around the roots. How should I fertilize and care for them from now on? You have done the best possible. Keep the soil moist, sprinkle the tops in the evening of hot days throughout the first summer. If you have good soil, do not fertilize until one year after transplanting.

How shall I care for small holly trees? Water well, especially through the first summer after transplanting. Apply a mulch of well-rotted leafmold in the fall, and place a protective screening of burlap or pine boughs about them the first few winters.

Why do some English holly trees have no berries? The male or pollen-bearing trees never have berries. Only the trees with the female or pistillate flowers will fruit.

I have a thriving grafted English holly which sets a good berry crop each year. When the berries are half formed, they all drop. Have tried less water, more water, and fertilizer—with no results. Why? This sounds very much as if the female flowers had not been properly fertilized with pollen. A male tree should be near by to make certain pollination occurs.

We have a female English holly which flowers, but no berries set. Tried grafting male cuttings, but none took. Would you suggest trying budding instead? If so, what type of bud and when and where on the limbs should I do the budding?   English hollies can easily be budded. Use the shield bud, commonly used in propagating peaches. Insert buds in August or very early September. Be certain that only the pointed leaf buds found on the more vigorous shoots are used. Insert buds only on the current year's growth. (See Propagation.)

What is the matter with a holly tree that has stopped producing berries, even though male trees are present?   Such incidents are difficult to explain. Some trees are alternate in their bearing habit, having a large crop of fruits one year and very few fruits the next. Sometimes a cold, rainy season, just when the pollen is ripe, prevents its distribution by wind and insects.

A holly tree purchased three years ago, which then had berries, has failed to produce them since. The pH of the soil is 5.4, and there is a male tree within 70 ft. Why does it fail to bear?   It may be recuperating from the shock of transplanting. Fertilize and water well. Berries will soon be formed if the near-by tree really is a male.

When and to what extent should holly trees be pruned?   Pruning, especially of fruiting plants, might be done just before Christmas, by cutting short branches for decoration. Other pruning should be limited to taking out dead or diseased wood and crossed branches. Slight trimming, to make the tree dense and compact in habit, can be done during early spring, before growth starts.

How can one tell sex of a lone holly plant? I want to buy more but don't know sex needed.   Observe the flowers, which are very small and inconspicuous, and appear in late spring. The pistillate or fruiting flowers have a well-developed pistil in the center, and undeveloped stamens. In the male flowers the pistil is small and undeveloped, and the stamens bear pollen.

Should you plant more than one Burford holly for it to bear berries?   No, the Chinese holly (*Ilex cornuta*) (of which the Burford holly is a variety) is unique among the hollies in this respect. The fruiting plants will bear fruits even though their flowers do not receive pollen from male plants.

How is English or American holly propagated from cuttings?   In a greenhouse, either in sand or a mixture of sand and peat. Use cuttings 4 to 5 ins. long taken in August or September. Shade with cheesecloth.

Does inkberry (Ilex glabra) have attractive fruits? If not, why is it popular? While the inconspicuous flowers are small, it has attractive black berries and glossy leaves, somewhat like box. It is hardy and shade enduring and able to withstand city growing conditions.

Recently I admired an evergreen hedge which the owner said was a holly. It had rather small, glistening leaves without the "points" on holly foliage. Could this have been a holly? Yes, probably a form of Japanese holly (*Ilex crenata*), and possibly the form known as 'Convexa', which has foliage resembling boxwood. The Japanese holly is a superior evergreen shrub, quite hardy, and with many named forms. (Not all hollies have prickly foliage, nor are they all evergreens.)

MAGNOLIA See also Flowering Trees.

Is Magnolia grandiflora hardy in the North? There is a large specimen growing in a sheltered spot in Brooklyn, New York, but it is not usually hardy north of Washington, D.C.

MAHONIA

Is Oregon holly-grape the low-growing shrub with leaflets something like holly? This is *Mahonia aquifolium* (Oregon holly-grape). The leaves vary in color from deep green to rich purple-red. If its environment is suitable and not too exposed, it has yellow flowers followed by little grapelike bunches of bluish-black berries. It prefers half shade.

Which is the hardiest kind of mahonia for use as a ground cover? *M. repens.*

What exposure suits the mahonia? A northeast exposure, where it gets enough winter sun to bring out the bronzy colors in the foliage, but not enough sun and wind to scorch the leaves.

Is mahonia (Oregon holly-grape) hardy at sub-zero temperature? Yes, it will withstand temperatures of 5° to 10° F. below zero. Persistent temperatures any lower than this will probably cause injury.

How and when shall I trim mahonia, planted on north side of the house? Some of it grows upright, but part lies almost on ground. I

thought there was only one kind of mahonia, but I seem to have two different kinds. There are several kinds, two of which are commonly grown in the East, one upright and shrubby—*Mahonia aquifolium,* and another which is really a ground cover—*Mahonia repens.* They can best be pruned in spring. *M. bealei* is dubiously hardy in most northern areas but is excellent in the southern states.

MOUNTAIN-LAUREL (KALMIA LATIFOLIA)

When does mountain-laurel bloom, and what color are the blossoms? Will it stand shade? Deep pink buds and pink-white flower clusters, in early June. Sun or shade.

What are some uses for mountain-laurel? Mass plantings in woodland or as occasional accents among azalea, rhododendron, leucothoe, ferns, hemlock.

When is the proper time to transplant the wild mountain-laurel? In the early spring, before the buds have started growth.

Is mountain-laurel hardy in Cleveland, Ohio, without any protective covering? Yes; but be certain the soil in which it is planted is acid.

In transplanting mountain-laurel from woods have been generally unsuccessful, even with utmost care exercised on basis of rules governing growth of this plant. Any specific reasons? Sounds like soil trouble. Perhaps by bringing in considerable leafmold and soil from woods you could succeed in growing it. Add peat moss to your soil also.

Will you give proper culture for Kalmia latifolia? Mine is seven or eight years old and has never bloomed, though it seems to be healthy. If the plant is healthy, this shows it to be growing in good soil. You might try the effect of superphosphate (15 to 20 per cent) applied beneath the mulch, at the rate of 4 oz. per square yard. Perhaps the shade is too dense.

LEUCOTHOE

What is Leucothoe fontanesiana? How is it used? An evergreen with arching stems clothed with handsome long racemes of fragrant white flowers and long, oval leathery leaves. Acid soil and partial shade. Good for woodland plantings, with rhododendron, mountain-laurel, and hemlock.

PIERIS

When do the "andromedas" bloom? What are the blossoms like?
Mountain andromeda (*Pieris floribunda*) has erect panicles of small
cream-colored waxy bells in May. Japanese andromeda (*Pieris japonica*), drooping panicles slightly longer than on the mountain andromeda, in April to May. The flowers appear in spring.

Would Japanese andromeda be hardy in northern New England?
No; but our native mountain andromeda probably would be.

**What is the difference between our native mountain andromeda
and the Japanese species?** The native (*Pieris floribunda*), though
hardier, is not so easily content nor is it as handsome of leaf and
flower as *P. japonica*. The latter is better suited to formal plantings
and the former to woodlands.

**Which andromeda has leaves that turn reddish bronze in winter
and new spring leaves with a rose-colored cast?** Japanese andromeda.

What soil is required by the andromedas? Moist, peaty or sandy
soil. Part shade desirable.

**Would Pieris japonica stand through the winter on Long Island,
if planted on a north or west exposure, with a leafmold mulch?** Yes,
there should be no problem if the winter winds are not too high.

Is there any insect that attacks the leaves of pieris? The lacebug
is the most serious pest of pieris foliage. This is a small insect with
lacelike wings appearing on the under surface of the leaves. It appears
in May and June, to be followed by a second infestation later in
the summer.

**When should pieris be sprayed to control the lacebug? What mate-
rial should be used?** Spray as soon as the insects appear, usually
in June. Several materials are available for control. Use diazinon,
Cygon, or malathion according to directions. Spray forcibly on the
under surfaces of the foliage, on a cloudy day when the temperature
does not exceed 80° F. Spraying in full, hot sunshine will burn the
foliage. Lacebug infestations disappear when pieris plants are moved
into a more shady location.

PYRACANTHA

Are any of the pyracanthas hardy? Yes. *P. coccinea,* or firethorn, is hardy in the middle states. Sometimes winterkills in the vicinity of New York City. The varieties 'Lalandei' and 'Kasan' are hardiest.

Would like to plant two pyracanthas, one either side of large living-room window, to grow against house. However, there are three small oak trees, about 9 to 12 ft. distant, on front lawn. Would their shade cause the pyracantha not to fruit? Planting where you suggest would not be advisable. For an abundance of berries full light is needed. Though the oaks may not be very big at present, it is probable that in a few years they would cast a shade too dense for the pyracanthas to fruit satisfactorily.

When is the best time to transplant Pyracantha coccinea 'Lalandei'? A difficult plant to move successfully, particularly if it has attained any size. Spring is the most suitable season, and it must be moved with a ball of earth. Do not attempt to remove the burlap when re-planting.

What can one do to make pyracantha bushes have more berries? Keep in good health and growing vigorously. They frequently bear good crops only in alternate years. A fertilizer rich in superphosphate, combined with root-pruning if bush is growing vigorously, might aid in increasing fruit production. Full sunshine, or at least uninterrupted light, is a requisite.

Firethorn—one of the most color-ful of berried shrubs for winter.

How should pyracanthas be treated when dead branches appear? Pyracanthas are susceptible to fire blight, a serious disease of apples and pears, their close relatives. When this appears, cut out the branches immediately and burn them. The cut should be made considerably below the injured part.

Last year my pyracantha was full of berries. This year it had none, Why? How can I keep it from growing so tall? Most berried shrubs are alternate in their bearing, producing heavy crops one year and light crops the next. Pyracantha can be restrained at any height by pruning—preferably in summer.

How are pyracantha cuttings rooted? Take the cuttings in July and place them in 3 to 4 ins. of sand in a fairly deep box. Enclose the box with polyethylene, and keep it in a position out of the sun but with good light; or root them in a cold frame.

RHODODENDRON

Which types of rhododendron are the hardiest and the most satisfactory for growth in northern New England as mass planting, not as specimen plants? The giant rosebay (*Rhododendron maximum*) is the hardiest of all the rhododendrons. It is not so colorful as some of the hybrids, but it can be used for massing.

What color are the flowers of different native rhododendrons? Carolina rhododendron, pink; Catawba rhododendron, rosy-purple; rosebay (*R. maximum*), pale pink.

How tall does the Carolina rhododendron grow? Six to 8 ft. maximum height; usually less under cultivation.

What are some of the hardiest rhododendron species for the Boston area? *Rhododendron catawbiense; R. carolinianum; R. maximum; R. mucronulatum; R. smirnowii; R. racemosum; R. laetevirens;* and, in most areas, *R. yakusimanum.*

The foliage of many of my rhododendron plants folds tightly in the winter. Will this do harm? On the contrary, this is a natural phenomenon which occurs with many rhododendrons when the weather is cold (below freezing) and dry. The curling or folding reduces the exposed leaf surfaces and conserves moisture.

What are some of the hardiest rhododendron hybrids? 'Boule de Neige', white; 'Nova Zembla', red; 'County of York', white; 'Caroline', fragrant, mauve; 'Vernus', early, pink; 'Ramapo', violet; 'Windbeam', pink; 'Wyanokie', white; 'Scintillation', pink; 'Catawbiense Album', white; 'Ignatius Sargent', red.

I have recently become interested in rhododendrons. Where can I find detailed information on these plants? In *Rhododendrons of the World*, by David Leach (Charles Scribner's Sons, New York,

1961); *Rhododendrons and Their Relatives, a Handbook* (Brooklyn Botanic Garden, Brooklyn, N.Y., 1971); *Rhododendrons in America,* by Ted Van Veen (Sweeney, Krist & Dimm, Inc., Portland, Oregon, 1969). Also join the American Rhododendron Society (see Sources for Further Information, Plant Societies).

Is there a rhododendron with fragrant flowers? Yes. There are several species with fragrant flowers and many hybrids of these species have inherited this desirable characteristic. Some are hardy only in the benign climates of the Pacific Northwest, but one very hardy hybrid, suitable for colder climates, is 'Caroline'. Its pale mauve flowers have a delicious perfume. There are others.

Can I successfully propagate rhododendrons from cuttings? Once considered nearly impossible for the home gardener, but with the advent of polyethylene and root-inducing hormone powders, such propagation is possible for the amateur. Take the cuttings from new growth in late summer, remove all but three or four leaves, and after dipping the end of the stem in the rooting powder (available from garden centers and seed houses), insert the cutting in a half-and-half mixture of sand and peat moss in a flat or pot. Water thoroughly. Then enclose the flat or pot in a tent of polyethylene, stretching it over a flat-topped wire frame. The polyethylene should be stapled or fastened securely so a humid atmosphere exists within the flat. Keep the flat out of direct sunshine but where it receives light. For faster rooting and growth, the flat can be kept in a frost-free room over winter with the temperature of the sand-peat moss mixture at about 70° F. Rhododendrons and evergreen azaleas respond well to fluorescent lights. Slower but eventual rooting can result if the flat remains in a protected site outdoors all winter.

SKIMMIA

Would you recommend growing Skimmia japonica as far north as Long Island, N.Y.? Yes. This evergreen appears to be more hardy than once believed, but it should be in the shade and protected from strong winds.

I have had a skimmia for two years and while it always flowers, it never bears berries. What is wrong? You must be growing the male plant. As with some hollies, both a female and male plant are necessary for fruiting of *Skimmia japonica*. (See next question.)

I have heard that there is a skimmia species in which both female and male flowers and berries are borne on the same plant. What is it? This is true. The plant is *Skimmia reevesiana,* and it is similar to *S. japonica* but seldom reaches over 1½ ft. in height.

VIBURNUM, EVERGREEN

Is there a good evergreen viburnum? Yes, the leatherleaf viburnum (*V. rhytidophyllum*), with long, oval, leathery wrinkled leaves. Protect from too much winter sun. Not reliably hardy north of New York.

Specific Tender Shrubs

ACACIA

Can we grow the yellow-blossomed acacia trees one sees in California? (Connecticut.) No, they will not endure temperatures much below 20° F.

Where can I get plants of the acacia with small yellow blossoms? Can it be grown in the garden? (Missouri.) Many California nurseries can supply acacias. They are either trees or shrubs. They are not hardy where winter temperatures drop below 20° F. above zero.

BAY TREE (LAURUS)

How hardy is bay tree or sweet bay and when is the best time to trim to formal shape? It is not really hardy north of Philadelphia, Pennsylvania. Trim when the new shoots have almost completed their growth. A second trimming may be necessary if the first stimulates the production of new shoots.

CAMELLIA

At what pH do camellias grow best? Will they do better at 5.7 to 6.2 or from 6 to 7? Camellias are less particular in this regard than gardenias and some other plants. They should thrive in either of the soils mentioned, providing it is physically in good condition and is fertile.

What soil preparation is necessary for camellias? (California.) Make the soil rich and friable to a depth of at least a foot, or, better still, 2 ft. Mix with it very generous amounts of leafmold or peat moss and very old rotted manure. Good compost can also be used.

What is the best fertilizer for camellias? When should it be applied? Old cow manure (or dehydrated manure or cottonseed meal, plus compost) applied as a mulch at the beginning of the growing season, followed, a few weeks later, by a light dressing of any complete fertilizer.

What is the best way to start and grow camellias? For outdoor culture, prepare ground so that it is rich and well drained but retentive of moisture. Select a lightly shaded position. Obtain good plants. If possible, visit gardens and nurseries where camellias are grown and familiarize yourself with their needs.

When is best time to move Camellia japonica? During the dormant season, in winter or in early spring.

Can camellias be forced to bloom earlier? If so, how? They can be encouraged to bloom early by planting them in sheltered locations; a more certain method is to grow them in pots, tubs, or planted out in ground beds in a cool, airy greenhouse.

What causes few blossoms rather than many on a well-fertilized camellia bush? Possibly the plant is in too dense shade. Some protection from strong sunlight is helpful, but lack of sufficient light is harmful. Also overfertilization may result in too vigorous growth at expense of flower production.

What is it that eats holes in camellia leaves? Have never found anything on them, and no spray that I have used seems to do any good. Probably the Asiatic beetle or the black vine weevil. Before specific advice can be given, a surer diagnosis is desirable. Send specimens to your State Agricultural Experiment Station.

What causes my camellia leaves to fall off? Damage to roots due to careless transplanting; waterlogged soil; lack of sufficient water, particularly during growing season; or spray damage.

What causes the leaves of an apparently healthy camellia plant to turn brown just before coming into blossom? This can be due to very cold weather, disease, or extreme drought. Spray injury could also be responsible.

My camellia has rusty coat on buds, and they do not open in the spring. What should I do? (Texas.) You seemingly have a variety unsuited to outdoor conditions. There are some kinds that are satisfactory in greenhouses, but not outdoors. Replace plant with variety recommended by local nurseryman.

Will frequent sprinkling of camellias while in bud cause the buds to rot and drop off? I understand they should be sprinkled during hot weather. Spraying of the foliage during hot weather is beneficial. Make sure, however, that the ground also is kept moist to a good depth. Do not be deceived by merely wetting the surface.

Why do many full buds fall off my red camellias late in the season? They are planted on the east side of the house, with just the morning sun. Should they be moved? The commonest reason for bud-dropping is lack of sufficient moisture at the roots of the plant. This is particularly true of secondary buds that develop if a late frost has killed early growth. Certain diseases also cause bud-dropping.

Can I increase my favorite camellia by layering? Yes. In June or July, nick a low branch with a knife, bend to the ground, hollow out a little trench, and lay the branch in this. Cover with sandy soil and use a brick or other heavy object to prevent motion. Be sure that the layer is kept constantly moist.

How and when can we start camellias from cuttings? July. Select firm, young growths, 3 or 4 ins. long; cut away lower leaves and cut stem horizontally below joint with sharp knife. Plant firmly in sand or sand and peat moss. Keep lightly shaded, moist, and in humid atmosphere. Slight bottom heat helps rooting.

What makes the buds on my 'Soeur Therese' camellia turn brown on edges of petals? This can be due to flower-blight disease. Send specimens to your Agricultural Experiment Station for examination.

What is the scurfy white substance on the under side of my camellia leaves? This is tea scale, and must be controlled by carefully spraying with a white-oil emulsion or Cygon after flowering.

The leaves on one of my camellias have large, dark spots, and drop off the tree. What causes this? Possibly the black mold disease, which is often associated with another infection called spot disease. Grow your plants under pines or in light shade.

GARDENIA   See also House Plants, Section 12.

I know cape-jasmine (gardenia) requires acid soil. I have fed copperas and aluminum sulfate, but still the leaves are yellow and smutty-looking, and no blooms. Can anything be done?   Use more natural methods of acidifying the soil. Mix oak leafmold, rotted pine needles, or granulated peat moss with the soil, 1 to 3. The smutty appearance is indicative of the presence of scale insects. Spray with malathion to get rid of them.

When is the best time to transplant a gardenia, crowded in its present location?   At the very beginning of the growing season, when new shoots and leaves are observed to be starting.

Can gardenia plants remain outside in garden all year 'round? (New York.)   Even with protection gardenias are not hardy in New York. Southeastern Virginia is about as far north as *Gardenia jasminoides* can be successfully grown outdoors.

How can I make gardenias bloom in my yard?   The Cape-jasmine or *Gardenia jasminoides* needs a sheltered, sunny position, a moist (not waterlogged) acid soil, and protection from frost.

Is it necessary to protect small gardenia plants by building a frame around them, and wrapping with sacks?   They need protection of this kind if there is danger that they will encounter frost.

JASMINE

Which jasmines are hardy in the North?   None reliably hardy though *Jasminum nudiflorum* (a good wall shrub), blooming very early before leaves appear, can be grown in the vicinity of New York City if given a southern exposure with the protection of a sheltering wall. *J. humile,* an erect evergreen to 20 ft. with yellow flowers, and *J. officinale,* climbing, with white flowers, are grown near the seaboard in the Middle Atlantic states.

Can jasmine (the flowers of which are used for tea) be grown as far north as Cleveland, Ohio?   Not very well. In a protected spot it might live through the winter; normally one would expect it not to be hardy.

OLEANDER

How can I succeed with oleanders in my garden? (California.)   They are easily grown out of doors in the South. Watch for scale.

Will you tell me how to start slips of oleanders? Cuttings taken in July and August root readily in sand if kept in close, humid surroundings such as a hotbed or polyethylene-covered box. Or shoots may be kept in water until rooted, and then potted in soil.

POMEGRANATE

What soil is best for pomegranate? A heavy, deep loam. Suited only to tropical and subtropical climates, or for the greenhouse.

When should a pomegranate (flowering) be pruned? Shorten strong-growing shoots about one third when they have almost attained their full length.

Hedges and Windbreaks

WHAT TO GROW

What would be the best kind of hedge to set out on the north side of a lot? This depends on the height. For under 6 ft. a yew hedge would be good, but expensive. For over 6 ft. a hemlock or white pine hedge. These are evergreens and so would give protection 365 days a year. Evergreen hedges cost more, but they are worth it for their winter protection.

Which flowering hedge would look well around a vegetable garden? It should be low so that it will not shade the vegetables. Spirea 'Anthony Waterer', with its flat-topped, deep rose-red flowers would give color to the area. Prune back after it has bloomed and more blossoms should follow. Also *Berberis thunbergii* 'Minor' would be good. Why don't you select something attractive but more practical? For example, a blueberry or raspberry hedge—kept pruned to about 4–5 ft.

Which flowering shrubs would make good hedge plants, even if unpruned? Barberry, especially upright-growing types; *Abelia grandiflora;* Siberian pea tree (*Caragana*); Japanese quince, especially the variety 'Spitfire'; deutzia; hydrangea, bush honeysuckle, spirea, common lilac, many of the viburnums. Unpruned privet makes a good tall hedge or screen.

What are the beautiful hedges made of that one sees in England? Can they be grown here? (Maryland.) Many different species are used. Perhaps you have reference to the English hawthorn and English holly combination. This could be done here by substituting American holly for the less-hardy English species where the latter is not hardy.

What would be a good low deciduous hedge, not above 2 ft. high, to put around a sunken garden? One of the dwarf barberries (*Berberis thunbergii* 'Minor'); slender deutzia; the dwarf cranberry-bush viburnum (*Viburnum opulus* 'Nanum').

What would be good as a fairly high deciduous hedge for screening? Acanthopanax, corkbark or winged euonymus, rose-of-Sharon, privet, buckthorn, Vanhoutte's spirea, various lilacs.

Could you suggest some good deciduous trees which would screen our garage driveway from our terrace—something natural-looking for an informal place where there is plenty of room? (Massachusetts.) Tallhedge (*Rhamnus frangula* 'Columnaris') is vigorous, tall, and narrow, grows 12 ft. tall, and needs no clipping.

What is the name of a hedge plant that would grow at least 6 ft. tall? I do not want privet or barberry. The one I have in mind has dark berries on it. The American cranberry-bush with red berries (*Viburnum trilobum*); or the glossy buckthorn with red and black berries (*Rhamnus frangula*).

What is the difference between buckthorn (Rhamnus cathartica) and alder buckthorn (R. frangula)? Which is better for a hedge? (Maine.) The former (for Maine), because it is hardier than alder buckthorn. The latter, however, has pointed glossy leaves, while the former has dull rounded ones.

What is the best fast-growing hedge for screening (not privet)? (North Carolina.) Myrtle (*Myrtus communis*); cherry-laurel (*Prunus laurocerasus*); Portuguese cherry-laurel (*Prunus lusitanica*).

Is a flower border or a shrub border better to screen a vegetable garden from view? Either kind of border would be proper; shrubs would be the more permanent. Why not plant a yew hedge, which would not take up more than 2½ to 3 ft. of width; or a single, informal row of *Spiraea Vanhouttei;* or bush fruits, such as blueberries or gooseberries?

What hedges are recommended for the lazy gardener who prefers not to have the work of clipping every week? Truehedge column-berry; the upright privet; true dwarf box, dwarf winged euonymus, the dwarf hedge yew, and other similar plants are ideal for the lazy man's hedge. They need practically no clipping. At most this need be done but once every other year.

What hedge would be best for city property—one that would need least attention? One of the best would be the five-leaved aralia (*Acanthopanax sieboldianus*). Japanese barberry hedges are also good under adverse conditions; and privet, of course—but this needs attention.

Can you suggest a neat, small, broad-leaved evergreen shrub to use at the edge of a terrace? (We want to have the plants untrimmed, but not more than a few feet high.) English ivy trained on a frame; boxleaf holly (*Ilex crenata* 'Convexa'); dwarf box; *Euonymus fortunei vegetus*. Warty barberry (*Berberis verruculosa*).

What is the rate of growth of a Canadian hemlock hedge? Which low shrubs would go well in front of it? A well-established young hemlock hedge in good soil will average at least 18 ins. a year. Such a hedge in itself is very beautiful, but if shrubs have to be placed in front of it, some low-growing types—coral-berry (*Symphoricarpos*), slender deutzia, roses, Oriental quinces, and the like—might be used.

What kind of evergreen can I grow for a hedge, not more than 6 ft. high, that will keep a neat shape without shearing? Hicks yew will do this, although it will take quite a few years for it to grow 6 ft. high if small plants are purchased. Farther south the Irish yew would be ideal.

What could be used for a low evergreen hedge (not box) for between vegetable garden and lawn? A yew called *Taxus canadensis* 'Stricta', or *Ilex crenata* 'Convexa' (commonly called the convex-leaved Japanese holly) would answer.

Would spruce trees make good hedges? (New Hampshire.) Yes. Norway spruce (*Picea abies*) either trimmed or untrimmed; also various forms of white spruce (*P. glauca*). Why not a hemlock hedge, which would be better.

Are there any evergreen barberries for hedge purposes? Yes; Juliana barberry, with black berries, grows to about 5 ft. *Berberis ver-*

ruculosa, with tiny holly-like leaves, growing about half as tall, is also suitable.

What hedge material would give a soft, blue-gray tone? Moss retinospora (*Chamaecyparis pisifera* 'Squarrosa').

Can you give us advice on which evergreens to grow across the front of our place to form a hedge that people can neither see over nor through? Either *Ilex crenata,* red-cedar, American arborvitae, or hemlock (all are evergreen).

Could we have an evergreen hedge, unclipped, which would have berries? Yes, firethorn (pyracantha) or *Taxus cuspidata* 'Nana'.

Which evergreen would make a handsome hedge that, without trimming, need never exceed 6 ft.—preferably less? Dwarf Hinoki-cypress (*Chamaecyparis obtusa* 'Compacta'). Also, other dwarf forms of this evergreen.

Which trees, other than native hemlock, make a good hedge? Northern exposure, semi-clay soil. The hedge is wanted for beauty as well as to serve as a windbreak. White pine, red pine, red-cedar, Serbian spruce.

Which tall evergreen—not too expensive—would you suggest for use as a fence along boundary line? Hemlock or white pine.

FERTILIZERS AND PLANTING

What is a good fertilizer for hedges? Any complete commercial fertilizer. For instance, 5–10–5 might be applied at the rate of 5 to 10 lbs. per 100 ft. of hedge, depending on the size of the plants.

How shall I plan a hedge? Decide whether you want it low or high, thorny or flowering, evergreen or deciduous. Just why you want it. Then select the best plant material to fit the need.

How does one plant a hedge? Dig a trench 2 ft. wide, 1 to 2 ft. deep, close to property lines, but at a safe distance away from sidewalk or street, so hedge will have plenty of space to expand up to the size at which it is to be permanently maintained. Put well-rotted manure or compost on bottom of trench, then some good soil, and tramp firm. Space plants 1 to 3 ft. apart (depending on size), filling in soil about their roots. Make firm, and water well. Cut back severely if a deciduous shrub is being used.

How far apart (approximately) should 6- to 8-ft. shrubs be planted

for screening purposes? It depends upon the kinds used and on how quickly you want a solid screen. For instance, rose-of-Sharon might be set 6 to 7 ft. apart and the Morrow honeysuckle 8 to 10 ft. while the tallhedge (*Rhamnus frangula* 'Columnaris') need be only 4 ft.

When is the best time to move a hedge of flowering shrubs? Should they be cut back? We want to keep them as large as possible for a screen. They can be moved after leaves have fallen in the autumn; or in the early spring. In transplanting, their tops should be cut back about one third for best results.

TRIMMING AND TRAINING

What is the best way to prune hedges? Different sorts of plants used as hedges demand different treatments. Large plants like white pine and spruce should be allowed to retain approximately their outline. Hemlock hedges should always be much wider at the bottom than at the top. Large privet hedges should also be somewhat wider at the bottom, although smaller ones can be trimmed with the sides vertical. Regel privet and other shrubs of that sort should be allowed to grow as naturally as possible. Hedges of dwarf yew should be broader than they are high. Dwarf boxwood and other edging plants can be trimmed to a rectangular shape.

How should one prune a deciduous hedge the first year? Cut back to within 6 to 12 ins. of the ground at planting time. Lightly shear whenever new shoots reach a height of 10 to 12 ins. if a close, compact hedge is needed.

Should hedges be trimmed to any special shape? Wider at bottom, preferably with a rounded top.

Do all hedge plants have to be trimmed several times in the season? No. Most evergreens can be kept tidy with one shearing. The same is true of such deciduous shrubs as barberry, buckthorn, rose-of-Sharon, and spirea.

Should hedges be trimmed during the winter? This can be done with no injury to deciduous hedges, if hardy. It is best to let it go until spring, however.

How shall I cut a hedge to make it grow? Cutting or pruning never makes a hedge "grow." It is good soil, fertilizer, and plenty of water offered the roots which really make the hedge grow.

I have heard that constant trimming devitalizes a hedge. Is this true? Yes, to some extent. Privet, for example, sheared every 3 weeks is more likely to succumb to the effect of a severe winter than one sheared only 2 or 3 times during the growing season.

Are electric hedge shears satisfactory? Yes; a good type will do the work in about one fourth the time required with hand shears.

Is it necessary to cultivate the soil along a hedge? Yes. Primarily to keep out weeds, which might grow and choke lower branches of hedge, especially when it is small. Or apply a mulch to suppress the weeds.

Specific Hedge Plants

ARBORVITAE

How shall I plant an arborvitae hedge? (Topsoil is rather poor and only 9 ins. deep.) Dig a trench 2 ft. wide and 1½ ft. deep. Put topsoil on one side. Either remove 9 ins. of subsoil and replace with good soil; or take out 3 ins. and fork in 4 to 5 ins. of rotted manure, compost, or peat moss and make firm by tramping. Return topsoil, and proceed with planting. The young trees should be set from 18 ins. to 3 ft. apart, according to their size.

When and how should an arborvitae hedge, about 18 ins. high, be trimmed? Top it evenly, during the period of spring growth, to about 1 ft. high. Thereafter, if you want a solid hedge, permit it to gain each year not more than 6 ins., until the desired height has been reached. From then on keep it closely sheared.

BARBERRY

What is the best treatment to produce a thriving barberry hedge? Give it good soil to grow in from the start. Fertilize with rotted manure or commercial fertilizers once a year if needed. Keep watered during very dry spells. In trimming, keep the hedge slightly wider at the base than at the top.

When, and in what manner, should barberry and privet hedges be trimmed? Always trim hedges so that they are wider at the base than the top, thus giving the lower branches plenty of exposure. Trimming might best be done when the young shoots are half grown, or nearly full grown, in late spring. However, trimming can be done without injury at practically any time.

BOXWOOD

What time of year is best for planting a boxwood hedge? Either early spring or early fall.

CHINESE ELM

To make Chinese elms form a thick hedge, what procedure should be followed? Cut them back hard. Any plants up to 3 ins. in diameter at the base (and possibly larger) could be cut back to within 6 ins. of the ground. Then a trimming before active growth has stopped, and another a month later, will aid in forcing bushy growth.

TRUEHEDGE COLUMNBERRY

I planted a hedge of truehedge columnberry, 18 to 24 ins. tall, last spring, cutting back half the growth, and trimming the new growth occasionally throughout the summer. Although no plants were lost they did not bush out enough from the base. What procedure shall I follow? How far should they be cut back next spring? These plants never will bush out at the base, for this is a columnar or upright-growing variety. If the shoots at the base have their ends pinched off occasionally, this may help somewhat. It is only necessary to trim the tops once a year. If the plants are still too far apart to make a hedge, move them closer together.

MONTEREY CYPRESS

What is the cause of scant foliage on lower part of a Monterey cypress hedge? (California.) Not sufficient room at the base. Hedges should be *wider* at the base than the top; this gives the lower branches plenty of sunlight and exposure. When hedges are clipped perpendicularly, or narrower at the base than at the top, the lower branches can be expected to become sickly and die.

HEMLOCK

What is the best way to grow a thick hemlock hedge and yet not stop its upward growth too much? Allow it to elongate upward a full year untrimmed, then merely trim off the terminal buds of the branches several times during the next season. If it thickens up well in that year, allow it to grow with little trimming the next, and so on. This would be true of most evergreen hedges.

Will a hemlock hedge thrive in a northwestern exposure without protection from sweeping winds?   Depends on the area. If in the middle states, or in the South, yes. If in the extreme northern parts of Minnesota, Illinois, Wisconsin, where winds are high and extremely cold, some "burning" might result in winter. If in Midwest, where winds are very hot and very dry in summer, the answer is, No!

In planting 18-in. hemlock bushes for a hedge, should spacing be 2 ft. or less?   Best spacing would be 18 ins. apart.

When do you shear a hemlock hedge?   Shorten new growth about the end of June.

CHERRY-LAUREL

When is best time to prune a cherry-laurel hedge?   This can be pruned any time; the best time (i.e., when one trimming would do the most good) is when the new shoots have nearly completed their growth for the current year. To avoid cutting leaves, use pruning shears rather than hedge shears.

LILAC

How about purple lilac for a hedge?   It makes a splendid tall hedge, but you must remember that the more it is clipped the more flower buds are removed. Also, in many places it must be sprayed annually for bad infestations of lilac scale.

CARAGANA

At what season should a caragana hedge be trimmed for the first time?   At the time it is planted; not again until the very early spring of the next year.

WHITE PINE

How does one trim white pine into a compact hedge, solid from the ground up?   Trim during the period of soft growth, reducing the new, candlelike growth, but not pruning into old wood. Permit only a slight annual gain in height. Shape the hedge so that it tapers up from a wide base to a narrower, rounded top. Keep the base free from weeds.

PRIVET

I want to plant a waxleaf privet hedge. Please tell me how tall this privet grows? How far apart to set plants? And if they need lime. (New Jersey.)   This privet, untrimmed, can grow to 30 ft. in height. For a hedge, space 18 to 36 ins. apart, and keep trimmed to height desired. Privets grow well in either acid or alkaline soil, but this species would be hardy only from southern New Jersey southward.

In the first warm spell can I broadcast bone meal around my California privet hedge so that it can get a quick start in spring? I planted the hedge last May.   You can, but the "early start" would be doubtful for bone meal is very slow in taking effect. You might better use a commercial fertilizer, such as 5–10–5.

How low should a privet hedge be cut when planted?   Shorten all branches at least two thirds.

What is the procedure in trimming a newly planted privet hedge to make it bushy?   Shear it whenever the new shoots attain a length of about 1 ft., cutting them back one half.

What is the best thing to do with an old overgrown privet hedge?   Cut it off 6 ins. above the ground in the early spring, and in this way force it to start anew.

How often is it necessary to shear a privet hedge?   About three times during the growing season, giving the last clipping early in September. It is better to shear every few weeks if a very trim hedge is required.

I was unable to trim and shape privet hedge last fall. Now it is unsightly. When is the earliest time to trim?   A privet hedge can be trimmed any time of year except late summer, when a trimming might force new growth which would not mature by winter.

What makes privet hedge die from the roots?   The common privet (*Ligustrum vulgare*) is subject to a serious blight which kills the plants and for which there is no known cure. Better use some other kind; they all do well in normal soils.

When is the time to make cuttings of privet hedges? How do you go about doing it?   Late spring or early summer is best. Take 6-in.

cuttings of the new wood, and place them in sand in a hotbed, with some bottom heat if possible. Keep moist but not wet, shade, and they should be rooted in four weeks or less.

SPIREA

At what time of the year should a spirea hedge be trimmed? Just after it has flowered, then one gets the full benefit of the flowers.

How can you get a hedge of spirea in which the plants were set 2½ ft. apart to grow together at the bottom? Best plan would be to cut it down to the ground and thus force it to make bushy new growth. If it doesn't grow together then, reset the plants 18 ins. apart—as they should have been set in the first place.

SPRUCE

I planted a hedge of 6- to 8-ft. Norway spruces 3 ft. apart. How should I trim them so that they will stay thick and rich at their base? Top in the spring to 5½ or 6 ft. Thereafter, in the annual shearing, allow only little gain in height. Trim sides no more than necessary for an even appearance. Shape the hedge so that it tapers from a wide base to a narrow, rounded top.

TAMARISK

Can tamarisk be used for a hedge? It makes an excellent informal hedge. If late-blooming species, cut back in spring. If a May- or June-flowering species, cut back when flowers have faded.

WILLOW

Can you tell me whether a golden willow hedge would be suitable for a boundary around a farm building? (Iowa.) If a tall, quick-growing hedge is required, and there is plenty of room, the willow would be quite suitable.

YEW

What distance apart should Japanese yew (2 to 3 ft.) be planted for a straight border-line hedge? Eighteen inches is best, but if this costs too much, 24 to 30 ins. would do. It would take the hedge a longer time to grow together in the second instance.

When is the best time to trim a yew hedge? It can be trimmed almost any time. Trim "wild" shoots in spring; give main shearing at end of June.

ROSA MULTIFLORA

Do you approve the use of Rosa multiflora as a hedge plant? It grows much too large for use on small properties but is satisfactory for a country property or estate. A 3-year-old hedge can be 8 ft. high and 12 ft. across.

Windbreaks

For how great a distance does a windbreak exert its influence? About twenty times its height.

Which trees are suitable for use as windbreaks? If soil is sandy, red pine and Scots pine. For sandy loam, white pine, Douglas-fir, spruce. For heavy soil, arborvitae, balsam fir, white spruce.

We need a windbreak on the west line of our property. The spot is quite shaded. Would Scots or Jack pine thrive there? No, not in shade. Use hemlock if height is needed; or Japanese yew, upright form.

Which evergreens are best to use for windbreak? We get heavy windstorms from the southwest, and the garden is on a hill sloping to the south. Red pine.

What can I plant for a hedge and windbreak—something that will grow fast? There is a strong north wind all summer; space is ample. The Siberian elm is one of the fastest-growing trees we have. Plant it thickly, about 5 ft. apart, if the hedge is to be over 20 ft. high; about 3 ft. apart if hedge is to be nearer 10 ft. high. It is one of our best trees for dry climatic conditions.

I haven't much room on my property but would like a windbreak on the north and west sides. Any suggestions? Plant arborvitae; red-cedar; upright form of Japanese yew; or white pine. Keep in bounds by annual pruning.

What would make a good windbreak for a garden that is exposed on all sides? Closely set evergreens, such as red-cedar, hemlock, or arborvitae, are good. A 6-ft. paling fence or a storm fence might also help.

Vines and Their Culture

How do different vines climb? By clinging rootlets, such as English ivy, trumpet creeper, euonymus; by adhesive disks, such as Boston-ivy; by coiling tendrils, as balloon-vine, *Cobaea scandens,* sweet pea; by stems which twine, such as wisteria, bittersweet.

Is any special preparation needed before planting vines to grow on a house? Make sure there is sufficient depth (1½ ft.), and width (2 ft.) of good soil. All too often the planting area next to a foundation is filled with builder's rubbish.

WHAT TO GROW See also Landscaping.

I have a partially shaded back yard in the city. Which flowering vines could be grown on the fence? Cinnamon-vine (*Dioscorea batatas*); silver fleece-vine (*Polygonum aubertii*); wisteria. The last will bloom only if it can climb to where there is sun. All these vines need a trellis, or to be supported in some way.

Which flowering vines would look well growing over a stone wall? We would like to enjoy seeing the flowers from our porch, 100 ft. away. Perennial pea, wisteria, clematis, hyacinth-bean, trumpet vine, rambler roses.

Which flowering vines will cling, without support, to the wall of our garage? Trumpet creeper; climbing hydrangea; Boston-ivy.

Which vines shall I grow on our clapboard house, which will need painting occasionally? Do *not* use clinging vines, such as the ivies, climbing hydrangea, or trumpet creeper; nor wisteria, which will thrust strong stems between the clapboards, sometimes destroying them. Honeysuckle, silver fleece-vine, clematis, akebia, should do well. A trellis hinged at bottom will be advisable so you can lay it (with the vine) down at painting time.

Which hardy flowering vines will stand the winter in southwest

corner of Massachusetts? **Elevation 1,800 ft.** Bittersweet, trumpet creeper, sweet-autumn clematis.

Which vines would you suggest for growing on stone walls, chimneys, and house walls? *Euonymus fortunei;* ivy (*Hedera*), small-leaved varieties; Boston-ivy.

Which vines will grow and climb in oak shade? Virginia-creeper, wild grape, bittersweet.

Which are the best climbing vines for this area (S. E. New York)? Clematis, bittersweet, Hall's honeysuckle, silver fleece-vine, and wisteria.

Which vines will thrive in water? None, in the northern United States.

What kind of a flowering vine or climber will grow every year to a height of 15 or 20 ft. on the north side of a house, where it would get the early morning and late-afternoon sun? Sweet-autumn clematis, silver fleece-vine. Also *Cobaea scandens,* an annual.

Which vine can be planted on top of a ledge where soil is very shallow and dry in ordinary years? Foliage is desired to keep dust from house. Very few vines would do well under such circumstances, but bittersweet and sweet-autumn clematis might be tried. Virginia-creeper is another possibility.

Which flowering vines are satisfactory for use on the north side of a house, in shade during most of the day? It is improbable that any flowering vine will thrive very well, but you might try trumpet honeysuckle, climbing hydrangea, or silver fleece-vine. *Cobaea scandens,* annual, and mountain fringe (adlumia), a biennial, might do well.

What are some of the easiest-grown and most beautiful flowering perennial vines? Wisteria, honeysuckles, trumpet creeper, silver fleece-vine, sweet-autumn clematis.

I have a terrace 13 × 14 ft.; sunny most of the day. I want to "grow a roof." What would you suggest? Something that will grow fast and give protection in summer, and at the same time something that will be decorative and useful as a more permanent screen. How about a grape vine? How long would it take to provide a screen, and how many should I plant? The soil is sandy. Grape vines would serve well. Plant 4 on each of two opposite sides. It will take at least 3 to 4 years to cover this area. The kudzu-vine might cover the areas in a shorter time—but it has no grapes!

Which woody vines are good for screening purposes? Kudzu-vine is probably the best, for it is the fastest-growing. Dutchman's-pipe makes a very dense screen with its large rounded leaves. The bower actinidia, Virginia-creeper, and grapes are also possibilities, although the last ones have rather coarse foliage. None are evergreen.

Which vine gives quickest growth for trellis at window for shade? Kudzu-vine grows the fastest (and the most!) of any of our "perennial" vines. Where it is not hardy, bittersweet, the five-leaf akebia, or the bower actinidia, might be used. All these are rapid-growing vines and have smaller and more interesting leaves than the large, coarse-leaved *Vitis coignetiae,* which is about the fastest-growing of the grapes.

Which flowering vine would be pretty to cover top of cave, the end and sides of which will be planted as a rock garden? Sweet-autumn clematis, or rambler roses.

Is there an evergreen vine which will cling to a wall in shade? English ivy (*Hedera helix*); wintercreeper (*Euonymus fortunei radicans*).

Which evergreen vine do you recommend to hang down from the top of a driveway wall? Wintercreeper, or English ivy, where hardy.

What is the best creeping vine for walls of stucco? *Euonymus fortunei* or one of its varieties is very good. Boston-ivy usually adheres well also.

Which ivy can I plant by the doorway that will hang down from the top in a place that is shaded most of the time? Either Boston-ivy or English ivy; the last being evergreen. Give both good soil in which to grow; keep moist during dry weather.

Is there some small-leaved vine which will cling to rocks? I would like something besides ivy and euonymus. (Delaware.) Creeping fig (*Ficus pumila*). Its small leaves lie flat. Not reliably hardy north of Baltimore, though it has been known to survive 80 miles north of New York City.

Annual Vines

We have rented a summer cottage and would like to grow some annual vines to cover lattice. What would be appropriate, easy to grow, and have attractive flowers? Morning-glory, moonflower, scarlet runner bean, hyacinth-bean (*Dolichos*), cup-and-saucer vine (*Cobaea scandens*).

Which vine can be grown over a poultry fence to provide shade, and for concealment? Have tried 'Heavenly Blue' morning-glory, but chickens eat it. Is there any annual vine distasteful to poultry? Try climbing nasturtiums, hyacinth-bean, wild cucumber, Japanese hop (humulus), scarlet runner bean, and cardinal-climber. Mix seeds together, sow quite thickly along the bottom of your fence, on outside. Chickens may take some and leave enough of others to give you a show. If necessary, thin to stand about 1 ft. apart.

Can you suggest vines—annuals—which will grow in a place which has shade ¾ of the day? Try cup-and-saucer vine (*Cobaea scandens*), hyacinth-bean, morning-glory, and cardinal-climber.

Will you give the correct information of how to grow Adlumia fungosa or mountain fringe from seed? I have not been at all successful. Reproduce the conditions natural to this native plant of the northeast United States. Give it a cool, damp situation, as it would be in woodland, protected from sun and wind, with shrubs to climb on. It is a biennial, sometimes grown as an annual.

What does the scarlet runner bean look like? It resembles in leaf and habit the pole beans we grow in our vegetable gardens, but the blossoms are larger and scarlet in color. The pods and green beans are edible.

I saw a beautiful vine twining on strings to cover a cellar window wall. It had purple sweet-pea-like flowers in late summer, and then broad, flat, red-purple beans. What was it? Hyacinth-bean (*Dolichos*) of easy culture.

Is the cup-and-saucer vine (Cobaea scandens) a satisfactory annual? Yes, if started indoors 6 weeks before ground warms up.

Plant individual seeds in peat pots or Jiffy-7 peat pots so the roots won't be disturbed at planting time. Set out at tomato-planting time. Grows to the top of a 3-story house in one season. Lovely foliage, tendrils; showy buds, flowers, and seed pods late summer and autumn. Foliage colors red-purple in light frosts. Grows on until hard freeze.

Is moonflower a good annual vine? Yes. Large leaves, beautiful, fragrant, night-blooming flowers in late summer and autumn. Give it something to climb high on. Start indoors. (See cup-and-saucer vine.)

What is the proper procedure in propagating moonflowers? Sow seeds. Proceed as suggested for morning-glories below or start seeds in individual peat pots indoors in early April.

Is there a variety of moonflower which climbs and has colored flowers? Moonflower is a twining night-bloomer with white flowers. There are also pink varieties. Twining day-bloomers are morning-glories.

Which large-flowered morning-glories are best? 'Heavenly Blue', 'Scarlett O'Hara'—crimson; 'Pearly Gates'—a white sport of 'Heavenly Blue'. Start indoors in peat pots for early bloom in the North.

I would like some morning-glories for a window box; not the large-flowered varieties. You want the Japanese type (*Ipomoea nil*), which are to be had in white, crimson, purple, blue, and other colors. They grow 2 to 8 ft. high, while 'Heavenly Blue' grows 10 to 20 ft. The dwarf morning-glories grow only about a foot high.

Should I plant morning-glories in the same place a second time? Theoretically it is wrong; but practically there is little objection. Dig the soil deeply, and work in decayed manure or compost; if, after a few seasons, morning-glories seem to be doing less well, sow instead hyacinth-bean, *Cobaea scandens,* or tall nasturtiums.

Will you tell me how to make 'Heavenly Blue' morning-glories grow? Dig soil 1 ft. deep, mixing superphosphate with it, ¼ lb. per square yard. Sow seeds about ½ in. deep and 2 ins. apart, after soaking in water overnight. Thin out to 6 ins. from plant to plant. Make your sowings at the base of a fence, trellis, or some similar support.

Do morning-glories require a rich soil? Soil of average quality is good enough. If it is too high in nitrogen, you may have large plants with small flowers; if you work in a balanced fertilizer, however, they should have large flowers and remain in bloom for a longer period each day.

Had some 'Heavenly Blue' morning-glories and watched for seed, with no success. Shouldn't they have formed seeds?   They grow readily from seeds which you purchase. It is possible that fertile seeds cannot be collected in your part of the country. Seeds are produced in large quantities for the trade in southern California.

Is there any known way to keep morning-glories open longer in the morning?   No.

When picking morning-glories, how do you keep them open in the house in a container?   Cut buds at sunset, selecting those ready to open. Keep in water up to their necks in a cool cellar overnight. Clip stems and place in position in morning. Moonflowers cut in late afternoon will open in containers indoors.

How tall will climbing nasturtiums grow? How do they cling?   To 6 ft. They climb by means of coiling leaf stalks.

SWEET PEA   See Annual Flowers, Section 8.

Woody Vines

AKEBIA

What do you recommend to mask an ugly leader pipe near our front entrance?   *Akebia quinata* deserves such a place where one views it closely. It has dainty oval leaves, five to a group, and a decorative manner of growth. It will festoon itself around any upright support. At intervals along a leader pipe the vine will have to be tied up. Sun or shade suits akebia.

Is there any vine, except English ivy, that remains green during the winter, and that is suitable for covering the side of a frame building? The five-leaf akebia (*Akebia quinata*) is worthy of a trial. It climbs by twining and would have to be supplied with wire for support. It is not completely evergreen, but leaves remain on the vine long into the winter. Another evergreen vine, *Euonymus fortunei radicans,* would satisfy these requirements but it is susceptible to serious infestations of scale.

Does akebia have flowers? Small rose-purple waxy flowers neither conspicuous nor numerous, but very interesting at close range and fragrant.

AMPELOPSIS AND PARTHENOCISSUS

I have cement blocks about 4 ft. high on the 3 sides of my porch and would like to know what will grow up and cling to these blocks so they will not be conspicuous. It is on the north side, therefore there is not much sun. Wintercreeper or St. Paul Virginia-creeper (*Parthenocissus quinquefolia saint-paulii*).

What plant will cover a stone wall where the location is hot, dry southern exposure? The ordinary ivy which flourishes on the north wall does not thrive here. Boston-ivy or St. Paul Virginia-creeper.

Which deciduous ivy is the best to cover a stone wall? What kind of soil? Should it be covered by a mulch for the winter? The Boston-ivy, St. Paul Virginia-creeper, or even the Virginia-creeper could be used to cover a stone wall. These do not need any special soil, simply a good garden loam. No winter mulch is required.

How shall I order an "ivy" which has deeply cut leaves and berries which turn lilac to bright blue? This is porcelain ampelopsis (*Ampelopsis brevipedunculata*).

Which deciduous "ivy" has the best autumn coloring? Virginia-creeper (not a true ivy) has the most brilliant crimson foliage in autumn, together with the Boston-ivy (*Parthenocissus tricuspidata*).

Where would Virginia-creeper grow? In the woods, on the ground, up a tree, in the sun or shade, along a wall, on the sand dunes. Very hardy and very adaptable.

What kinds of deciduous clinging vines are there? Among them are Virginia-creeper and its several smaller-leaved varieties. Then there is Boston-ivy and its small-leaved varieties, trumpet creeper and climbing hydrangea.

BITTERSWEET

I have heard that the Oriental species of bittersweet is better than our native kind. Is that so? It is more vigorous and has better foliage, but the fruits are about the same.

How would bittersweet look growing on a trellis by the front door?
As it is rather rampant, we doubt if you would like it there. Its chief
charm is in its dark bare stems with their clinging berries in fall and
winter. A clematis would be better.

**If bittersweet seeds are planted, how long will it take before the
vine produces berries? Does bittersweet prefer acid soil?** About 3
years. They grow well in either acid or alkaline soil.

At what time of year can bittersweet be planted? Spring or fall.

Will bittersweet climb on a stone chimney? No. It is a *twining*
vine not a *clinging* one.

How can I make my small patch of bittersweet larger? Allow
some of the shoots to touch the ground, cover portions of them with
soil, and they will soon take root, especially if you cut part way
through the vine on the under side of the portion to be covered with
soil.

**What causes blossoms to fall from stems at base of a bittersweet
vine?** Probably the male flower blossoms, which never have any
fruits and fall off the plant after the pollen has been dispersed.

**I have several bittersweet vines on trellises. The clusters which I
gather in fall are usually small and imperfect. Is there anything I can
do so that these vines will produce clusters such as I see in the florist
shops in the fall?** Be certain that 1 or 2 strong male or pollen-
bearing plants are close by, preferably growing in with the fruiting
vines. Another method is to note when they bloom in June, obtain
cut branches of male flowers from some distant plant, put in bottle
of water, and tie up in your fruiting vine. Leave there for 2 weeks and
the pollen distributed by insects and winds will fertilize the pistillate
or fruit-bearing flowers, insuring a good crop of fruits.

**Should bittersweet be pruned while growing? Mine grows 4 or 5
ft. high and then starts long runners 7 or 8 ft. long and of course
there is no trellis for them.** Yes, it can be pruned while growing.

**I have a bittersweet vine. When should the berries be picked for
winter bouquets?** Any time after heavy frosts.

**I have read that only the female plants of bittersweet have berries.
How can you sort the seedlings to discard male plants?** They can't
be sorted as seedlings. It is necessary to wait until they are old
enough to bloom.

CLEMATIS

I am interested in clematis. Which species or variety is best in bloom, and easy to care for?   *Clematis paniculata,* the sweet-autumn clematis, is one of the easiest of all to grow. The Jackman clematis can be grown fairly easily if the soil is alkaline.

Which clematis is it that one sees in our woodland?   Rock clematis, *Clematis verticillaris,* blooming in May or June; or virgin's-bower, *C. virginiana,* with white flowers in August to September. Must climb into sunlight to bloom well.

Could you tell us the name of a clematis with rosy-pink flowers about 2 ins. across? There are 4 petals and yellow stamens. Bloom in May.   Pink anemone clematis (*C. montana rubens*).

Is there any clematis with red flowers that is easier to grow than the big-flowered hybrids?   Scarlet clematis (*C. texensis*) is a native of Texas. Grows to about 6 ft., with flowers about 1 in. long; blooms July to September.

Can you tell me of a yellow clematis that would grow in Maine? I saw a beautiful small variety (on the ground) in Canada but could not find its name.   *Clematis tangutica,* the golden clematis, is certainly worthy of a trial. It is the best of the yellow-flowered species, a native of China. Will need winter protection.

What is the best exposure for Jackman clematis? (Illinois.)   In Illinois as protected a situation as possible, but not complete shade. All clematis bloom better where the vines reach full sun, but they like shade at their bases.

What fertilizer does clematis need? Should one cultivate around it, or are the roots near the surface of the ground?   Most clematis varieties require lime and a cool, moist soil, best supplied by a mulch of leafmold. Roots are very near the surface.

Is it always necessary to shade the roots and lower stem portions of clematis?   This is necessary on most of the many large-flowered hybrids, but it is not necessary on our native clematis types nor on the sweet-autumn clematis.

What type of trellis is best for clematis?   Chicken-wire netting supported in rigidly upright position on a light frame.

Will different varieties of clematis, planted very close, "cross,"

thus spoiling the species? No, this will not change the plants or flowers a particle. Seeds from the flowers might yield seedlings of mixed parentage.

How can I grow large-flowered clematis? They do well for 6 months or a year, and then die. Unfortunately many large-flowered clematis are susceptible to a rather serious disease which kills them during the summer months. No manure should be applied, nor should water be allowed to stand at the base of the plants. If the disease occurs, spray with wettable sulfur at once, and again in a week or ten days.

How and when should one prune clematis? Those which bloom on old wood (such as *C. florida, montana,* and *patens*) need little or no pruning beyond the removal of dead or diseased wood. The *lanuginosa, jackmanii,* and *viticella* types bloom on wood of the current season, and may be cut back in spring before growth begins.

A white clematis, planted in the fall, grew about 10 or 12 ft. the following summer, but did not flower. Should I have pinched it back after it was 3 or 4 ft. high? No. Let it grow and gain nourishment; it will bloom the second or third year.

When and how should Clematis paniculata be pruned? In many places in New England this clematis will be killed to the ground by winter cold. In such places it should be pruned back, in early spring, to just above where the buds break. In situations where it does not kill to the ground, merely cutting out some of the older wood is all that is necessary.

Should clematis be pruned in fall or summer? I notice some cut them down to ground, but I have never cut mine and have lovely vines. What is the best preventive for aphis? If you have lovely vines, continue the same treatment. Cutting them down does not help. (See preceding questions.) Aphis can be controlled by spraying with malathion or diazinon.

Should a Clematis jackmanii be trimmed or pruned in springtime? Yes; but only if the vine is cluttered up with a mass of unproductive or dead shoots.

Can you start clematis from cuttings? Clematis are rather difficult to propagate. This can be done either by cuttings or seeds. For the amateur, sowing the seed in the fall is the easier method. Many of our large-flowered hybrids must be propagated by cuttings, or by grafting.

DUTCHMAN'S-PIPE

Which vine would make a good solid screen to hide the compost pile? Please describe Dutchman's-pipe. Dutchman's-pipe would be fine if grown on a series of vertical cords or slats. The big roundish leaves, 10 ins. in diameter, overlap each other. Flowers, nondescript in color, resemble a Dutchman's-pipe.

EUONYMUS FORTUNEI (WINTERCREEPER, EVERGREEN-BITTERSWEET)

Which one of the wintercreeper vines has berries like bittersweet? The best of the berried varieties is the bigleaf wintercreeper (*E. fortunei vegetus*).

Our wintercreeper is especially noticed because of its leaves, which are variegated, sometimes with white or pinkish tones. What variety could it be? Silver-edge wintercreeper (*E. fortunei* 'Gracilis').

Which euonymus vine has very tiny leaves? Baby wintercreeper (*Euonymus fortunei* 'Minimus').

Which is the hardiest of all evergreen vines that will cling to a stone wall? Wintercreeper (*Euonymus fortunei*) and its varieties.

Is Euonymus fortunei the new name for what we used to call Euonymus radicans? Yes. It is now *Euonymus fortunei radicans*. (Until the botanists decide to change it again!)

I have a euonymus which I thought would climb on a wall, but it remains a bush. What is the trouble? It must be the variety called glossy wintercreeper (*E. fortunei carrierei*) which is shrubby, non-climbing. There is another shrubby variety which remains so unless planted near a wall (*E. fortunei vegetus*), the bigleaf wintercreeper.

GRAPE   See Fruits—Section 11.

HONEYSUCKLE

Which honeysuckle has flowers that are yellowish on the inside and rose-purple outside? Everblooming honeysuckle (*Lonicera heckrottii*).

Please describe the scarlet trumpet honeysuckle (Lonicera sem-

pervirens). **I believe it used to grow in gardens long ago.** Yes, it is long in cultivation. Orange-scarlet flowers with long tubes, yellow inside, produced from May to August.

What low-growing variety of honeysuckle would you recommend for a northern exposure, with semi-shade? Hall's honeysuckle—but watch out; it is a pernicious weed if it gets out of bounds.

What low vine may one plant under the shade of a large maple tree, but unprotected from the wind; one which will grow with myrtle, where grass will not? You might try Hall's honeysuckle, but it is very difficult to coax anything to grow under most maples.

Our honeysuckle vine (2 years old this past spring) had only one spray of bloom. Why? The foliage is beautiful and healthy-looking. It needs time to become well established before it will bloom properly.

My honeysuckle lost all leaves in midsummer, then bore leaves and blooms and seeds at one time. What should be done this year? Give it more water. This was probably due to unusually dry weather.

Does Japanese honeysuckle eventually work its way into water drains? Should it be planted near them? Like the roots of most plants it probably will, but usually the roots won't do much damage in this respect.

How does one trim out honeysuckle which is very thick, and about 12 ft. high? If there is too much wood, it may be necessary to cut it off at the base and start all over again.

Will you tell me whether honeysuckle vine can be pruned, and at what time of the year? Prune it in the early spring when the buds are breaking. Unless the vine is to be restrained within a limited area, it is necessary to prune out only dead or diseased wood.

What is the proper way to prune a honeysuckle for profuse blooming? Mine is a cutting about 3 years old, with very few flowers. Is a trellis necessary? Don't prune; allow it to grow profusely on some support, and if good soil, plenty of water, and sunshine are available, it will soon bloom well.

HYDRANGEA

How tall does the climbing hydrangea grow? How does it climb? *Hydrangea anomala petiolaris* can grow 50 ft. or more in time, but it is slow. It clings to a wall without support, sends out branches at right angles to the wall, and blooms in June.

What kind of flowers does the climbing hydrangea have? Flowers are white, in round, flat, open clusters, resembling some of the viburnum flowers; small fertile flowers in the center, large sterile flowers on the perimeter of the cluster.

IVY

How can one tell whether an ivy is a variety that will be hardy if placed outdoors? We want to plant some on a new cottage chimney. Try several. The hardiest evergreen variety is the Baltic ivy (*Hedera helix* 'Baltica'). If this winterkills, no English ivy will grow there. You might also try the varieties 'Bulgaria' and '238th Street'.

What does Baltic ivy look like? Its leaves are slightly smaller than those of the typical English ivy, and the white veins are often more prominent.

Which evergreen vine can I plant on north side of brick house? English ivy, if a tall-growing kind is required; otherwise, use winter-creeper, which is hardier.

Which vine is suitable for planting on a west slope, to cover up ground and stay green all the year round—one that won't spread too much? Baltic ivy.

WISTERIA

I have had a wisteria for several years that has not flowered. What can I do? The time-honored recommendation is to root-prune around the plant (use a sharp spade, inserting it deeply in a circle around the stem, as though you were going to transplant); then make a shallow trench into which superphosphate (use several pounds for each inch in trunk diameter) is poured and then mixed in the soil, after which the trench is filled with soil; and finally, prune back vigorous vegetative shoot growth. The pruning can be done in summer and perhaps again in fall or winter.

How do I prune a wisteria? The objective in pruning a wisteria is to keep the growth restricted to force spurlike shoots which produce flowers. In summer cut back the shoots at about the seventh leaf; in winter the shoots are further shortened—to within 1–3 ins. of their base. At this time, the future flowers will be readily apparent in the bud stage.

I have grown several wisteria plants from seed, but they have not flowered. It's better to buy grafted or cutting-grown wisteria vines from a specialist. Some species are slow to come into flower and seed-grown plants are known to be even slower. However, you might try root-pruning, drastic top-pruning, and adding superphosphate, as recommended above.

I would like to grow a wisteria plant up an oak tree. Will the vine hurt the tree? Yes. Wisteria is a twining vine and eventually its heavy trunk can strangle the tree.

Should wisterias be grown in rich or lean soil? Probably a soil on the lean side is to be preferred, as too rich a soil can stimulate vegetative growth at the expense of flower production. However, if the space in which the wisteria grows is at all restricted, such as might be the case near a house, yearly fertilizer applications in spring might be necessary, especially if the vine is flowering abundantly.

Can I grow a wisteria in a large tub on my terrace? Yes. Start with a fairly rich soil mixture (see above question). A wisteria trained in tree formation would also be satisfactory.

5

Bulbs, Tubers, and Corms

NO FLOWERS are more rewarding for the time and room required for their culture than the various bulbs and other bulb-like plants—those which form tubers and corms instead of true bulbs. A considerable number produce flowers very early in spring when our spirits—and our gardens—need their gaiety. Others add brilliant color to the garden scene all summer. A few extend the bulb-flowering season well into the fall.

There are still many gardens, however, where one looks in vain for any sight of bulbs other than a few daffodils, perhaps a planting of that ubiquitous tulip, 'Red Emperor', and a dahlia or two. The owners of such gardens are overlooking a wide range of easily grown plants which could provide them with beautiful and interesting flowers, very literally, from one end of the year to the other, for there are a number of bulbs and corms that may readily be flowered indoors too. The most easily obtained and grown of these are commented on in the following pages. You can add to your store of garden pleasures by becoming acquainted with them.

National organizations made up of specialists and devoted amateur growers have developed for some of the very popular types of bulbs. Many of these publish bulletins, have annual conventions, and sponsor seasonal shows. Many also have regional and local affiliates. Dues are usually nominal. A local garden club or agricultural and horticultural schools and societies will be able to provide current addresses. If you are enthusiastic about a particular genus, you'll find kindred company in the following: American Begonia Society, American Daffodil Society, American Dahlia Society, North American

Gladiolus Council, American Gloxinia and Gesneriad Society, or North American Lily Society.

—*Bebe Miles*

 The Hardy Kinds

WHAT TO GROW

Which hardy bulbs may be used in permanent plantings?   Among the most satisfactory are daffodil, hyacinth, grape-hyacinth, squill, chionodoxa, snowdrop, crocus, the hybrid lilies, allium, colchicum, and camassia. Tulips may give several years' bloom without being taken up, especially if planted deep (to 10 ins.).

Which bulbs can be left in the ground the year round?   Allium, brodiea, calochortus, camassia, chionodoxa, colchicum, crocus, erythronium, fritillaria, grape-hyacinth, hyacinth, tulip, daffodil, iris, leucojum, lily, puschkinia, scilla, shooting-star, snowdrop, snowflake, sternbergia, and anemone.

We have spring-flowering bulbs. Which hardy bulbs shall I plant for summer bloom?   Hardy kinds: summer-hyacinth, hardy begonia (*B. evansiana*), lycoris, hybrid lilies, sternbergia, colchicum, fall-flowering crocus, and some of the flowering onions (allium).

CULTURE

What kind of soil should I use for spring-flowering bulbs?   A rather light, but fertile and well-drained, slightly acid soil is best. Avoid the use of fresh manure. Very old manure and superphosphate are good fertilizers.

Bulbs do not multiply readily in the soil in my garden. Tulips do not last over 3 years. What element in the soil is lacking?   Possibly your soil is not suitable, but this is not unusual for tulips. Heavy, clayey soils are not conducive to increase. Most bulbs prefer a loose, fertile soil that has been well worked to a depth of 10 or 12 ins.

Does well-rotted manure above, but not touching, the bulbs rot them?   No. But it is much better to spade the manure under before planting, so that it is well below the bulbs, but not in direct contact with them.

How deep should bulbs be planted? No general rule can be applied to all bulbs. Some lilies should be planted 8 or 9 ins. deep, others 2 ins. deep; so the depth varies. If possible, obtain specific information for each kind before planting. If this is not available, a rough rule that can be followed in the case of the hardy spring-flowering bulbs is to cover them with soil equal in depth to 2 or 3 times the diameter of the bulb.

How late in the fall can bulbs be planted? Bulbs planted in December will grow and thrive, and instances are known of January-planted bulbs succeeding. But much earlier planting is recommended.

Early-flowering bulbs arrived after sub-zero weather and snow. How can I take care of them over winter and when can I plant them? They are winter-aconites, scillas, tulips, etc. Keep in cool, dry place and plant any time when ground thaws, up to January. After that plant bulbs in pots or flats of soil and cover with 6-in. layer of sand or cinders outdoors. They cannot be kept over winter out of the soil.

How can I tell which end goes up when planting a bulb? Generally there will be vestiges of roots at the bottom of the bulb. The top is usually more tapered, and a shoot or eye may be visible as a clue. Tubers often show "eyes" on the top.

Can you plant bulbs in spring that call for planting in fall? Certain hardy, summer-flowering bulbs can be held in cold storage and planted in spring as, for instance, lilies; but fall planting is better. Spring-flowering bulbs must be planted in fall.

Can a person plant bulbs of all kinds in spring? Only summer- and fall-blooming kinds can be planted at that time.

When do I order and plant autumn-flowering bulbs such as fall crocus, sternbergia, and colchicum? Order as early in summer as possible and plant immediately on arrival.

Can you take up crocus and daffodil bulbs, separate, and replant them as soon as the leaves die down? Or must you wait until fall? It is always best to transplant narcissi before mid-July.

Should bulbs be watered after planting? This is usually not necessary. Very little moisture is needed for their early root growth, but in case of a long, dry spell with no rain within a month after planting, a thorough watering is beneficial.

What is the best way to handle the small bulbs one finds growing on older bulbs?   Plant them separately in specially prepared nursery beds where the soil is loose and fertile. Grow them in these beds until they reach blooming size.

What can be done with spring-blooming bulbs which come through the ground in winter, due to a warm spell?   If planted very shallowly, cover with a layer of soil or whatever plant litter is available. However, some bulbs make early foliage naturally.

If true bulbs have their flower bud within them, do they need full sunshine in order to bloom?   Yes, they need sunshine and moisture to bring the blooms to maturity.

Does it inhibit next year's bloom to pick flowers of bulbous plants? No; not if most of the foliage is left. This is needed to manufacture food that feeds the bulb and produces the next year's bloom. Removal of flower heads before they set seed aids the bulb.

What can I do with the unsightly foliage of my spring-flowering bulbs after bloom is over?   Removal of foliage before it has matured (turned yellow and wilted) is sure to prevent normal bloom the following year, as the maturing foliage provides nutrients for the flowers to come. Water in dry spells to keep foliage growing as long as possible. Place later-flowering plants in front of and around bulbs to detract from the maturing foliage. An example would be Christmas ferns among naturalized daffodils.

Do spring-flowering bulbs need fertilizer after planting?   An application of a complete plant food should be applied and gently raked into the surface each spring. In light, sandy soil a second application in late spring after bloom is over is also advisable.

Do you advise the use of a summer mulch on bulb beds?   Yes, by all means. A mulch of shredded bark, pine needles, buckwheat hulls, shredded sugarcane or other similar material may be applied early in spring after weeding and fertilizing. If bed is later overplanted with annuals, the mulch remaining on the bed will help to control weeds and retain moisture through the summer heat.

What causes bulbs to disappear in the soil? Such hardy bulbs as daffodils, tulips, lilies, and iris are examples.   Unsuitable soil or poor drainage; cutting the flowers without leaving sufficient foliage to make food to fatten up the bulbs; cutting of leaves before they wither naturally; and disease or the depredations of rodents.

How short a rest period should bulbs have after being taken up from the soil? This varies with the kind of bulb. Colchicums and lilies, for example, should be replanted with least possible delay, as also should daffodils. Tulips can be stored out of ground for 3 months or more without harm.

Should tulips, daffodils, and hyacinths have mulch (leaves) over them in fall? When should they be uncovered? Not necessary except in extremely cold sections unless you are in an area subject to frequent alternate freezing and thawing. Damage is then from "heaving" of roots and bulbs from soil. Under these conditions cover *after* the ground has frozen hard, with leaves, compost, marsh hay. This keeps ground uniformly cool and prevents damage to roots by heaving. Uncover gradually when growth appears.

RODENTS

Have had much trouble losing lily and tulip bulbs in winter. Some rodent makes burrows 3 ins. below surface of ground. Have used wire baskets in planting, but to no avail. Also poison and traps. What can I do? You may have to encircle the whole bed with fine mesh wire netting, 12 ins. wide, buried vertically, and extending 2 to 3 ins. above ground surface. Do not *mulch* bed until ground is well frozen. Liberal addition of pebbles or stone chips to the soil when planting a bulb bed discourages mice.

Do moles eat bulbs? No, moles are carniverous, but mice use mole runs and destroy many bulbs. Consult your county agent for regional suggestions to combat rodents. If it is any consolation to you, there are "on" and "off" years for these pests!

We have heavy populations of both field and pine mice. Are there any spring bulbs they will not destroy? All rodents love tulips and crocus but will not touch any of the many kinds of narcissus bulbs.

Rabbits eat my tulip buds and devour crocus plants, flowers and all. What can I do? Dried blood sprinkled heavily around the plants can give temporary protection. Try covering your plantings loosely with boughs cut from your Christmas tree. Leave them on tulips until stems are a foot tall. Don't remove from crocus until clover is in leaf. A cat or dog can help, too!

What can I do about deer eating tulips and lilies? Ordinarily deer will not touch narcissus, so use these for open areas and keep tulips, crocus, and lilies closer to house. Double the number of susceptible bulbs you plant—some for you and some for the "critters"!

Specific Hardy Bulbs

ALLIUM

Do flowering alliums possess that unpleasant onion odor? No— unless the stems or leaves are crushed or bruised. In fact, flowers of many alliums are decidedly pleasant to smell.

What are the best flowering onions for outdoor gardens? Many species of allium are excellent for planting in borders. Among the best are *neapolitanum* (white); *azureum* (blue); *flavum* (yellow); *aflatunense* and *rosenbachianum* (purple lilac); and *albopilosum* (violet). Shorter kinds ideal for rock gardens and foreground planting are *karataviense* (silvery lilac); *moly* (yellow); *roseum grandiflorum* (rose); *stellatum* (pink); and *schoenoprasum* (rosy purple). *A. giganteum* bears large violet flower heads as high as 5 ft. in early summer.

What soil and treatment do summer-flowering onions require? A rather light, well-drained loam is best, although they will thrive in most soils, providing drainage is good. *A. moly* flourishes in partial shade, but full sunshine is preferred by most species. Divide and transplant whenever crowded: either fall or early spring. Most are very easy to grow.

ANEMONE

Will anemone tubers survive winter in New York (Long Island) if planted in fall? Will they bloom if planted in spring? If so, when should they be planted in the vicinity of New York? Rock-garden tuberous-rooted kinds (such as *apennina, blanda, ranunculoides, quinquefolia,* and *nemorosa*), are hardy and should be planted in fall. The florists' tuberous-rooted kinds are not hardy. You might try storing them in a cool place (40° F.) over winter, and planting them in the spring, or order from a spring catalogue and plant on arrival.

How should one plant tuberous anemones, such as nemorosa, blanda, etc.? Plant in early fall in porous soil containing generous proportion of humus. Set tubers 2 or 3 ins. apart, and cover about 2 ins. deep. Light woodland shade is needed.

ARUM

I have a lilylike plant which produces a flower, dark purplish in color, almost black, on a stem 8 ins. tall, with leaves 5 × 3 ins. It seems to be hardy as it survives our occasional frosts. It becomes dormant in summer. Could you please identify? Probably black-calla (*Arum palaestinum*). It needs a winter mulch in the North.

BELAMCANDA

Can you tell me something about a plant called blackberry-lily? *Belamcanda chinensis,* a hardy iris relative from the Orient, is now naturalized in many parts of this country. Easily grown in sun or light shade and propagated by seeds or division. Orange summer flowers, spotted with purple-brown, are followed by blackberry-like fruits much prized for dried arrangements.

BRODIAEA

What treatment do brodiaeas, such as grandiflora, capitata, and ixioides, need in the garden? Plant in fall in gritty soil in full sun. Set bulbs about 2 ins. apart and cover 3 or 4 ins. deep. Protect with light winter covering of marsh hay or similar material.

Can you tell me the name of the floral firecracker plant? *Brodiaea coccinea,* one of the many fine species of this genus native to western America. The flowers bear a close resemblance to a gaily-colored bunch of firecrackers.

CALOCHORTUS

Can calochortus (or mariposa-tulip) be successfully grown in the Middle Atlantic states? Yes, but they are not very easy to keep from year to year. Plant at twice their own depth, late in fall, in specially prepared, very gritty soil. Mulch well to prevent heaving.

Water freely when growing, but keep bed as dry as possible in late summer and fall. They need sunshine, demand perfect drainage.

CAMASSIA

Will you tell me something of camassias and their care? They thrive in any good garden soil that is not too dry; prefer full sun or light shade; bloom in May (flowers blue or white), then die down. Plant in early fall, so that bulbs are 4 ins. below surface and 7 or 8 ins. apart. Do not transplant as long as they bloom well.

Are camassias good garden flowers? Very good indeed, and worthy of being more widely planted. Most of them are native Americans and are of easy culture. Apart from their garden value, their spires of starry flowers are excellent for cutting purposes.

CHIONODOXA

Does the bulb glory-of-the-snow (chionodoxa) need any special care? One of the easiest and loveliest of hardy spring-flowering bulbs. Plant in fall in any fairly good soil, 3 ins. deep, 2 or 3 ins. apart. Do not disturb for many years. Topdress every 2 or 3 years with fertilized soil. They increase and improve with passing of years. Excellent for planting in low-growing ground covers such as vinca or bearberry. Good pink and white forms exist as well as many blues.

COLCHICUM

How deep should colchicum be planted; and how often divided? Cover the tops of the bulbs with not more than 3 ins. of soil. Divide every third or fourth year.

What soil and situation are best for colchicums and when should they be planted? Soil should be rich and reasonably moist (but not wet). Light shade. Plant in early August. They often self-sow.

Why did my colchicum have no leaves with the flowers? This is normal. Colchicum foliage is produced in spring. A low ground cover such as vinca or thyme sets off the early fall flowers admirably. American colonists called them "naked ladies"!

CONVALLARIA (LILY-OF-THE-VALLEY)

Can lilies-of-the-valley be grown in an absolutely shady place?

Yes. They will grow in dense shade if the soil is fairly good, but will probably not bloom so freely as when in partial shade.

How can I grow lily-of-the-valley? What kind of soil? I have no success. A moist, but not wet, soil that contains generous amounts of humus. Improve soil by spading in rotted manure, leafmold, peat moss, before planting. Lily-of-the-valley prefers light shade. Plant in spring. Each year in early spring the bed may be topdressed with leafmold, compost, or rotted manure. Do not allow the plants to become overcrowded.

The garden in which I have very fine clumps of giant lilies-of-the-valley has been okayed as to soil, sunshine, and shade; they have splendid foliage. Why is it they do not multiply, and produce only a few stems of bloom? The soil is basically clay, though it has been enriched. If the soil is very rich, the foliage will be good, but flowers scarce. Let the plants become firmly established, then they will flower when the excess nutrients are used up.

Is there any difference in size of lilies-of-the-valley, or can you make them grow to be a good size? How? The largest-flowered variety is named *fortunei*. Old, worn-out plantings usually produce few small flowers. Lift, separate, and replant in newly fertilized soil every 3 or 4 years. Make sure shade is not too dense.

How do you grow clumps of lily-of-the-valley for forcing for cut blossoms? Plant clumps in very rich, sandy loam. When pips are ¼ to ⅜ in. thick and ⅞ to 1 in. long, cut away from clumps with as much root as possible. Wrap in bundles and place in cold storage, 28° to 32° F., for at least 3 months. Best results however are obtained from specially prepared pips.

Are the roots of the lily-of-the-valley poisonous? Yes. The druggists' convallaria, which is used as a heart tonic, is made from lily-of-the-valley roots. Red fall berries are toxic too.

CROCUS

When shall I plant crocus and how? Spring-flowering kinds in September and October. Plant in light, fertile soil, in sunny place. If among grass, only where grass can remain uncut until leaves have died away in late spring. Plant 2 or 3 ins. apart and about 3 ins. deep. Fall-blooming kinds should be planted in July or August; or transplanted in June or early July after foliage dies down.

Should crocus be planted in beds, or with grass, to look natural? They appear best when planted among some low ground cover, such as creeping thyme, creeping phlox, or vinca. Without the competition of grass roots, crocus thrive and multiply, so in a few years a planting will make a bright splash in the foreground of a garden even without an underplanting. Fall types, however, look much better with a ground cover; clove pinks are ideal. Other garden situations for crocus groupings include within or near stone steps or walls, in soil spaces between steppingstones on terraces, and under shrubs and small trees such as forsythia, cornelian-cherry, and birch.

DAFFODILS (NARCISSUS)

Many of the early spring-blooming plants would not be worth a second glance if it were not for the fact that they are harbingers of spring. Daffodils, on the other hand, would be important even if they bloomed in June or August.

The daffodils belong to the genus *Narcissus,* and the two names are used interchangeably. One species (*N. jonquilla*) and its hybrids are often called jonquils, but they are still daffodils. Over 10,000 varieties have been introduced. The color range of the group is largely yellow, orange, and white, but hybridizing has produced good varieties with apricot and pink tones as well as some with green markings.

Daffodils have much to recommend them. While a given species

While daffodils are not shade lovers, they do well along woodland paths and in drifts within the woodland if they receive sun in the spring.

or variety may not succeed in all parts of the country, there are types that do well in warm climates, and others that thrive where winters are severe. They are highly prized in rock gardens, borders and in small intimate gardens, and they may be naturalized in woodlands and meadows. They are also fine as cut flowers. Many are very fragrant.

What type of soil is needed to grow daffodils? Any garden soil is suitable, providing it is deep, well drained, and reasonably fertile. Avoid planting in hot, barren soils or where the soil remains wet for long periods. They will not survive in wet soils.

What is correct preparation of soil for planting daffodils? Elaborate preparation is unnecessary, although some specialists might go to the trouble of spading the soil 12 ins. deep and placing rich compost or rotted manure in the bottom of the trench or area. The homeowner can either spade the area to be planted and incorporate about 3–5 lbs. of a complete fertilizer such as 5–10–5 to 100 sq. ft. in the soil; or place the bulbs where he wishes them to grow and dig individual holes for each bulb. Mixing about the same amount of superphosphate in the soil before planting is also recommended, especially in sandy soils. A quick way to prepare the soil for daffodils, especially in large plantings and naturalized groupings, is to rototill the soil to a depth of 8 or 10 ins.

Can you tell me how to prepare a bed in which to grow daffodils for exhibition? The classic recommendation is to excavate a trench 18 ins. deep, dig into the bottom a 6-in. layer of well-rotted manure or rich compost and on this spread a generous sprinkling of bone meal or superphosphate. Cover with 6 ins. of good topsoil (without manure), set bulbs on this, and cover with any fairly good soil.

How should one fertilize daffodils that do not need lifting and replanting? Topdress in early fall with superphosphate and in early spring with a complete fertilizer and compost or old, well-rotted manure.

Is superphosphate a safe fertilizer to use on daffodil beds? Yes. It may be forked in at planting time.

With what can I feed my daffodils to increase size of blooms for exhibition? Dilute liquid cow manure applied at intervals in spring, from the time flower scapes appear, helps immensely. Keep beds well watered. If reduction in size and quantity of bloom is caused by overcrowding of bulbs, fertilizer does not help. When foliage becomes crowded and bloom falls off (4 to 6 years after planting), dig after foliage matures, separate bulbs and replant.

What type of situation is best adapted for daffodils?   A slight slope, sheltered from drying winds, with deep and well-drained soil.

Can daffodils be naturalized among trees?   Light deciduous woodland affords an ideal location for daffodils which, under such conditions, thrive and increase abundantly. Plant them on the fringes of the tree branches but never to the north of a tree and never under evergreens in deep shade.

A good way to use daffodils is in informal or naturalized plantings under a tree.

When is the best time to plant daffodils?   August, September, or October, with preference for the earlier dates. If bulbs do not arrive until November—then plant them then.

Daffodil bulbs ordered from seedsman usually do not arrive until fall, yet I am told to transplant those that are in my garden in July. Why?   Bulbs in storage remain dormant for some considerable time after those in the garden have developed new roots. Bulbs are harmed by moving after root growth is far advanced. Early planting is always advisable.

Can daffodil bulbs be planted as late as December?   Yes; dormant bulbs can be planted any time before the ground freezes solid. Well-stored bulbs have been planted with success as late as February. Earlier planting, however, is much to be preferred.

Is it true that if you transplant daffodils in spring, they will not bloom? If so, why? It is scarcely possible for them to bloom satisfactorily if removed from the soil during peak growth. By spring the bulbs have a fully developed root system and the disturbance of transplanting causes a serious setback. If taken up in clumps of soil, with roots intact, they probably will bloom fairly well.

About what distance should be left between full-sized daffodil bulbs when planting? It depends upon the effect desired, and also upon the variety, because bulb sizes vary considerably. A minimum distance of from 3 to 6 ins. should be allowed. For colonizing, the bulbs should be set in a pleasingly informal pattern rather than evenly spaced.

How deep are daffodils planted? In light soils large bulbs are set with their bases 6 to 8 ins. deep; in heavier soils, 5 to 7 ins. deep. Small bulbs should be planted shallower than those of larger size.

Does deep planting encourage daffodils to multiply? No. On the contrary, it checks rapid division. Shallow planting induces rapid multiplication. Deep planting tends to build up strong-flowering bulbs and lengthens the years between transplantings.

Can daffodils be interplanted with tulips to produce early flowers and thus extend the blooming season of the planting? Yes. This is an entirely satisfactory combination—especially in small gardens.

How are daffodils cared for? Plant in good deep soil. Water during dry weather, especially after flowering, to keep foliage green as long as possible. Remove faded flowers. Fertilize yearly. Give sun at least half the day.

What are the moisture requirements of daffodils grown outdoors? They need ample supplies during the growing season, particularly in spring, when the flower scapes and foliage are developing.

When should daffodils be lifted for storage through the summer? Or is it better to leave them in the ground all year? Summer storage is not recommended for daffodils. If they must be dug, July is the best time. Store in dry place, as cool as possible down to 50° F.

What time of the year should daffodils be separated? June or July is the best time; wait until the foliage has fully matured, so the bulbs are quite dormant. If you dig when the leaves are just browning, you can trace the bulbs best and avoid slicing into any with the fork. After separation, replant at once. However, bulbs can be transplanted earlier—even in bloom, if they are replanted at once and watered.

Do daffodil bulbs naturalized among trees have to be dug and re-planted at intervals?   Yes, whenever they become so crowded the quantity and quality of the blooms have deteriorated. This may be as often as every third year, or as infrequently as every 5 or 10 years. Remember growing trees cast increasing shade each year, so conditions gradually change. Move bulbs out to periphery of branches.

Daffodils left in one place too long (right) produce excessive foliage and few flowers. Dividing old clumps and re-planting will result in blooms like those at left.

Will daffodils bloom the spring after they have been divided and reset?   Yes, if of blooming size: 1½ to 2 ins. diameter for trumpet varieties, 1 to 1½ ins. for smaller varieties; and ⅝ to 1 in. for the *triandrus, cyclamineus,* and *jonquilla* types.

What should be done with clumps of daffodils that won't bloom? After the foliage has died down, dig them up, separate the bulbs, fertilize the soil, and replant.

How can I get miniature daffodils to bloom every spring?   Plant in a sheltered place in moist, but not waterlogged, soil. Water freely during dry periods whenever foliage is present. Dig up, separate, and replant every 3 years. Miniature hybrids are easier than true species.

Can daffodil bulbs which have bloomed indoors in pots be stored after blooming, to be used next year?   Not for forcing again. If kept well-watered until ground is in satisfactory condition, they may be planted outdoors and will bloom in future years.

I have heard that it is harmful to cut the foliage off daffodils when they have finished blooming. Is this so?   Yes; the leaves are needed to produce food to plump up the bulbs in readiness for next season's flowering. Never remove foliage until it has died down, or at least turned yellow. Encourage it to grow as long as possible by watering during dry spells.

Is it harmful to "braid" daffodil foliage after flowering? Generally yes. The leaves can be bruised, and fewer surfaces will be available to catch sunlight and manufacture food. Next year's flowers depend absolutely on this year's foliage.

Daffodils planted the end of September are now (late October) through the ground. Will they survive? Probably. Throw an additional 2 ins. of soil over them. They were planted too shallowly.

Can you tell me why double daffodils do not mature their blooms? Hundreds of stems come up with empty cases at the tops. They are overcrowded and are robbing each other of nutrients and moisture. Dig up the bulbs, separate them, enrich the bed, and replant. Water thoroughly during dry weather in the spring.

What is the simplest way for a home gardener to increase a limited stock of a choice daffodil? Plant bulbs shallowly (about 4 ins. deep) in a well-prepared bed—preferably in a cold frame. Give good cultural care and lift, divide, and replant every second year.

Is there any rapid method of vegetatively propagating daffodils? In summer large bulbs can be sliced vertically into many sections (each containing a small portion of the basal plate). The sections are then planted in peat moss and sand. Mild bottom heat stimulates production of new bulblets.

How are daffodils raised from seeds? Sow in late August in rows 6 ins. apart in a well-prepared seed bed in a cold frame. Cover seeds ¾ in. deep. Shade the bed, keep uniformly moist, weeded, and covered with marsh hay or other protection during winter. Allow seedlings two summers' growth, then lift and replant with wider spacing. Expect at least 7 years before blooming.

Why can't I get daffodil seeds to come up? It is possible that the seeds are not fertile, or perhaps your cultural care is incorrect. Hand pollination of the flowers should result in fertile seed. Some hybrids are sterile, however. See previous question.

Are daffodils subject to pests and diseases? Several diseases and some insect pests may be troublesome, but these usually do not appear in garden plantings. If trouble is suspected, remove affected bulbs and send samples to your State Agricultural Experiment Station for diagnosis and advice.

Is the hot-water treatment of daffodil bulbs effective?   Yes, as a control for eelworms, bulb flies, and mites. The treatment consists of soaking for 4 hours in water maintained at 110° to 111.5° F. One pint of formalin to each 25 gals. of water is added if basal rot is present. Bulbs must not be treated too early or too late in the season. There are now many new chemical miticides on the market.

What is the difference between a daffodil and a narcissus?   These names are interchangeable, although "daffodil" is applied particularly, but not exclusively, to those kinds which have large, well-developed trumpets. *Narcissus* is the botanical name for the entire group.

What is a jonquil? A jonquil hybrid?   The true jonquil is *Narcissus jonquilla,* a species that has slender, rushlike foliage and sweet-scented flowers in clusters. Jonquil hybrids are horticultural developments of this species, usually with larger flowers.

How do I decide what daffodils to choose from catalogue listings?   The various species are usually italicized as: *N. cyclamineus.* Most varieties in the trade are hybrids and labeled: *N.* 'February Gold'. These are usually showier and easier to grow than true species. Large bulb firms group their offerings according to divisions developed by the American Daffodil Society. These classifications indicate the bloodlines of a daffodil hybrid. More importantly, they make it easier to select your daffodils. By planting clumps from different classes, you will obtain a longer season of bloom and a wider color range, and enjoy flowers of quite varied form and size.

Can you recommend some good daffodils in each of the various classes?   Fashions change among daffodils, too. Reasonably priced varieties in the current catalogue of a reputable dealer are the best guides for all but the specialist. Local chapters of the American Daffodil Society have up-to-date advice on good varieties for specific areas, and they often sponsor spring shows where you can see for yourself.

What determines the division or class of a daffodil?   It can be its parentage. Thus *cyclamineus, triandrus, jonquilla, tazetta,* and *poeticus* daffodil hybrids all exhibit clearly the distinguishing characteristics of their particular parent.

Doesn't size have anything to do with classification? Yes, and so does form. Any double flower belongs in the double division. The size of its cup or trumpet in relation to the length of its outer petal segments (perianth) determines whether a daffodil is listed as a trumpet, a large-cup, or a small-cup.

I want something other than yellow daffodils. What do I choose? Most of the daffodils with bright-colored cups are either large-cups (Div. II) or small-cups (Div. III). Colors of cups range from red-orange to apricot and pink. Outer petals of these are generally yellow or white. There are pure whites in almost every class from big trumpets to dainty *triandrus* hybrids.

Are cluster-flowered (tazetta) daffodils less hardy? They do not do well in the most northern states, but they are perfectly hardy in the mid-Atlantic region, for example.

What is a split daffodil? Through irradiation and selective breeding a race of daffodils has been developed which does not have a center cup. Instead the trumpet has been "split" into petal segments which lie more or less flat against the outer perianth.

What daffodils are outstandingly fragrant? Choose hybrids which are listed as *jonquilla, tazetta* (cluster-flowered), or *poeticus* types. One cut specimen of the easy species *N. jonquilla simplex* perfumes a whole room.

What are some early-flowering daffodils? Hybrids in the *cyclamineus* division such as 'Peeping Tom' are your best bet for first blooms. Give them a warm spot facing south for extra earliness.

Please name some late-blooming daffodils. Choose hybrids from catalogue descriptions of the following types: *triandrus, jonquilla, poeticus, tazetta,* and white small-cups. A touch of afternoon shade prolongs their flowering.

What is the double white narcissus that looks like a gardenia, smells sweet but does not bloom very freely? *N. alba plena odorata* is a notoriously shy bloomer. It prefers a moist situation. Try instead 'Cheerfulness', 'White Lion', or 'White Marvel', all white doubles.

ERANTHIS (WINTER-ACONITE)

I have not had success with winter-aconites, although I planted them in a favorable situation early in October. Can you suggest cause

of failure? Too late planting. They should have been planted as soon as available. They quickly deteriorate when kept out of ground.

What conditions do winter-aconites (eranthis) need? A woodsy, non-acid soil in light shade. They often do well on gentle slopes, and once planted should be left undisturbed. Set tubers 3 ins. deep and about same distance apart. Water well once immediately after planting.

EREMURUS

Are Foxtail-lilies hardy? These stately (5- to 12-ft.) members of the lily family produce from star-shaped, fibrous rootstocks, rosettes of narrow leaves which send up blooming stalks bearing heavy racemes of bell-shaped white, pink, yellow or orange flowers in late spring. They are hardy to Zone 4 if heavily mulched after ground freezes hard. Do not remove mulch until late spring frosts are past as early spring growth may be frost-nipped. For this reason a northern exposure is desirable. Handle brittle tubers carefully.

ERYTHRONIUM

What are the habits and culture of dogtooth-violets? Erythroniums are woodland plants which like humusy soil and partial shade. Many prefer a moist situation. European varieties are usually offered by color. Native American species vary greatly and are offered by specialists in wildflowers.

What is the proper depth for planting dogtooth-violet bulbs, and how late can they be planted for spring blooming? Plant with top of bulb 3 ins. below surface. September is latest month for planting. They quickly deteriorate if kept out of soil long.

Are the trout-lilies or dogtooth-violets easily grown in gardens? They are among the loveliest of plants for lightly shaded places where soil is deep and humusy and possibly moist. Unfortunately many of them gradually deteriorate when planted in eastern gardens, but they are well worth replanting from time to time.

FRITILLARIA

What is the guinea hen flower? *Fritillaria meleagris.* The speckled, pendant blooms are more curious than beautiful. A good rock garden subject. Western sources offer several good native species.

What is the culture for crown imperial? *Fritillaria imperialis,* like many others of its genus, is capricious, sometimes doing well, and then again, for no apparent reason, failing to thrive. Plant in early fall in deep rich soil, in light shade. Leave undisturbed as long as it continues to thrive. Too warm a situation may encourage premature spring growth.

GALANTHUS (SNOWDROP)

I am very fond of snowdrops. Where and how shall I plant them? Plant in early fall, setting bulbs 3 to 4 ins. deep and about 3 ins. apart. If possible, choose a porous soil that contains fair amount of humus, and a lightly shaded position. They multiply fairly rapidly if congenially located. Try the giant *Galanthus elwesii* for earliest flowers.

How often should snowdrops (Galanthus nivalais) be lifted and transplanted? Do not disturb unless absolutely necessary; they do best left alone. If transplanting is imperative, do it after foliage dies down. Do not keep bulbs out of ground longer than necessary.

HYACINTH

Can hyacinth bulbs be planted outside in November for spring flowers? Yes, but a month earlier is preferable.

Can I plant hyacinth bulbs in the spring? If so, will they bloom the first summer? Only the so-called summer-hyacinth (*Galtonia candicans*) can be planted at this time. It blooms the first summer. The spring-flowering Dutch hyacinths are planted in fall and bloom in spring.

Will hyacinths be injured if moved after the leaves show? Yes, they will suffer somewhat. If absolutely necessary take care to keep a large ball of soil intact about the roots.

Will Hyacinthus amethystinus grow in light shade? When does it bloom? Yes. It blooms end of May and early June in vicinity of New York. A fine species for the home garden. The very early *H. azureum* is a tiny gem. Plant bulbs of both in fall, 3 to 4 ins. deep.

HYPOXIS HIRSUTA

What is the little lily-like yellow flower with grass-like foliage that blooms so long? A native American, *Hypoxis hirsuta* is often called gold star-grass. It blooms from May to November at Philadelphia. Order from wildflower specialists. Plant in humusy soil and half shade. It is in the amaryllis family.

LEUCOCRINUM

Are star-lilies annuals or perennials? I have had them in the house summer and winter so far, but they increase so fast, I won't have room for them all another winter. Will they stand the winter in the flower bed? Star-lilies or sand-lilies (leucocrinum) are hardy perennials. They are native from Nebraska to the Pacific coast.

LEUCOJUM

A friend gave me a clump of leucojum which I greatly admired in her garden 2 years ago. They have never bloomed in mine. Why? This plant dislikes root disturbance and the transplanting may have caused it to skip blooming for a couple of years. Leucojums enjoy a soil rich in leafmold and a sunny or very lightly shaded position.

I bought bulbs of Leucojum vernum, which books say grows 6 ins. tall. Mine grew 2½ ft. Was the soil too rich? The plant often sold as *Leucojum vernum* (spring snowflake) is the later-blooming and much taller *L. aestivum* (summer snowflake). The former has but 2 flowers on each stem; the latter usually 4 to 6.

LILIES

Today's gardener is luckier than his forebears, for he has at his command new races of lilies for which growth success is almost guaranteed. Lilies have been called both the most fascinating and the most exasperating of all garden flowers: fascinating because of their beauty of form and coloring; exasperating because of frequent failures and disappointments. Now with the new hybrids available everywhere no one need temporize about planting lilies. Few ornamental bulbs have as great decorative value or are better adapted to modern gardens. Because they are closely linked with art and religion, they are interesting for aesthetic reasons, too.

In nature different species are found under the most diverse conditions: some grow at high altitudes, others at low; some inhabit the desert, while others are found in damp meadows. They come from both dry and humid climates, and from cold and warm regions. Is it any wonder that as a group they used to appear capricious when included in a garden planting?

While lilies have been cultivated in gardens for a long time, it is only in this century that they have really been domesticated. Previous efforts to hybridize the wild species had proved almost futile. Once a few hybrids were obtained, however, these intercrossed readily. The result has been new races or groups of man-made lilies which are infinitely easier to grow in gardens than were their progenitors. Today lilies have become flowers for every garden. They are invaluable for cutting as well as for the landscape effects. Flower forms and colors are unbelievably diverse, and bloom is spread from June to September. Most of the first hybrids were quite tall, but lower-growing selections are now on the market, too.

How should soil be treated before planting lilies? Well-drained garden soil that is in good condition requires no special treatment. Spade it well, allow it to settle, and plant the bulbs. It is desirable to mix some peat moss or other humus into most soils before planting.

Do lilies require "sweet" or acid soil? Most hybrid lilies prefer soil slightly on the acid side, but the madonna lily (*L. candidum*) needs some limestone. The foliage of a few kinds becomes chlorotic or yellowish in alkaline soil. *Lilium hansonii, speciosum, canadense,* and *superbum* are some of these; add generous amounts of peat moss when planting them. *L. philadelphicum* demands highly acid soil.

What kind of fertilizer is best for lilies? A good garden fertilizer, or almost any complete fertilizer that is relatively high in potash. One good formula is 5–10–10. Manure should not be used, as it may encourage losses from basal rot.

Can bone meal and cottonseed meal be used in ground where lily bulbs are to be planted? Yes, they are satisfactory but superphosphate would be more efficient than bone meal.

When is the best time to fertilize lilies? Early spring.

How should hardy lily bulbs be planted? The ground should be deeply dug and compost or peat moss added. Small bulbs should go 3 to 4 ins. deep; 5 to 6 ins. is about right for large bulbs. Madonna and chalcedonicum lilies and their hybrids should be covered 1 to 2 ins. Shallower figure is for heavy soils; deeper for light sandy types.

When is the best time to plant most lilies? As early in fall as you can obtain the bulbs. If necessary, mulch the spot well with thick newspapers and leaves to prevent freezing until the bulbs arrive. Then plant them immediately. Bulb suppliers have improved storage techniques, so it is now possible to get some good American bulbs in spring as well; but the selection is not nearly as complete as in fall.

When is the best time to divide and transplant various kinds of lilies? When the tops begin to die. Somewhat earlier or somewhat later lifting will not materially affect the performance of the plants the following year. Lilies are never completely dormant; don't leave bulbs out of the ground even overnight.

How often should lilies be divided and reset? Only when the number of stems indicates that the plants are becoming crowded. Lilies often resent moving. Plant far enough apart so they can remain undisturbed for some years. Never set closer than 6 ins.; a foot is better for vigorous hybrids.

Can you tell me how to take up lilies? The leaves often stay green until cold weather. Also, how about the roots? I was always afraid to cut off roots, so I just took the plants up and set them in a new place, although I wanted to ship them. If necessary to replant, do so in fall about a month before ground freezes hard. Ship with roots intact.

Should lilies be moved in spring? How deep should they be planted? They may be moved if taken up early with considerable soil about their roots. Plant at the same depth in the new site as they were before being moved. Fall, however, is much wiser.

Why are the new American hybrid lilies so much better than the old species for gardens? Many are grown from seed and are thus disease-free; extreme care is exercised to keep propagating areas clean by the American growers. These lilies also have built-in hybrid vigor and resistance to disease. Many of the old bulb species came from foreign sources, which meant long shipping delays as well.

What should a beginner look for when purchasing lily bulbs? Buy reasonably priced hybrids from American-grown sources. These are lilies which have proved themselves.

Just what is a "stem-rooting" lily? Many garden lilies are stem-rooting; that is, they produce most of their roots from the stem that grows upward from the bulb.

Why do lilies become spindly after a season or two? Some lilies fail to bloom because they become crowded; others because of disease or frost injury to the growing point. Trees or shrubbery may provide too much competition for sunshine or soil moisture. Most lilies need sun on the leaves most of the day but shade to keep their roots cool; use mulch or a ground cover.

Examples of modern lilies: Aurelian Hybrids

Does Lilium speciosum rubrum bloom in August; and can it be planted in spring? It blooms in late August or September. It may be planted in spring. Try the hybrid speciosums such as Jamboree Strain or Imperial Crimson Strain.

I cannot grow auratum lilies. What do they need? They usually fail because they become infected with mosaic disease. Try again with mosaic-free bulbs, planted away from other lilies, in ground that has not grown lilies recently. A surer bet is one of the new hybrid auratums such as Imperial Gold.

If different kinds of lily bulbs are planted in the same bed, will the different species "mix"? They will not "mix" if by "mixing" is meant that the pollen of one kind will influence adjoining plants so

New hybrid speciosum lilies, the Imperial Crimson strain.

that their flowers change. However, any seed that formed would be a mixture of all the different kinds.

Should Easter lily bulbs be taken up and dried before replanting? No. If it is necessary to move them, take them up late in the season and replant promptly.

I planted lilies 4 years ago. Should I have taken them out since and transplanted them? Lilies that are doing well need not be transplanted until they become crowded, which condition will be manifested by their numerous short, weak stems.

Why do lilies "run out" in this section? (Pennsylvania.) Because of their susceptibility to obscure virus diseases, certain lilies, such as *L. auratum,* are not long-lived in many sections. Others, such as the tiger lily, thrive despite the diseases. Try some of the new hybrids in a fresh spot.

How shall I plant and care for lilies of various kinds? Plant madonna lilies in late August or September; all others when bulbs are received. Madonna lilies are covered 1 to 2 ins. deep to top of bulb; most others 3 to 6 ins., depending on size of bulb and kind of soil (see under Planting). In cold sections mulch for winter with straw or marsh hay or leaves weighed down with branches after ground freezes. During the growing season mulch with shredded pine bark or other porous material, especially in warmer areas. Remove weeds, fertilize with a complete fertilizer, and water if season is dry.

Will you give me some information about growing madonna lilies? Mine have always failed. Deep planting is a common cause of failure. The top of the bulb should not be more than 2 ins. from surface of the ground. Any good garden soil, well drained, and a sunny site are suitable. Use organic fertilizer and a sprinkle of lime, but no manure or peat moss near the bulbs. Spray, if necessary, against botrytis blight, which see. Unfortunately many stocks of madonna lilies are badly infected with disease. Buy only American-grown bulbs from a reputable dealer. Unhappily, too, the madonna has proved more difficult to hybridize even for such a miracle worker as Jan de Graaff, the father of many of the modern hybrids.

What are the cultural requirements of most lilies? What ground cover shall I use over them? Any good, well-drained garden soil in full sun or light afternoon shade. Low-growing, shallow-rooted plants such as pansies, violas, Scotch pinks, arabis, and low-growing ferns are the best ground covers for lilies.

Can the ground where lilies are growing be hoed? Yes, but with extreme care. Many lilies appear late in spring and careless hoeing may result in chopping the shoots off below ground. Lily roots are near the surface and are damaged by deep hoeing. A summer mulch of leafmold, lawn mowings, shredded bark or bagasse will eliminate the necessity for much cultivation.

What sort of mulch should be used around madonna lilies? Marble chips, shredded bark, buckwheat hulls. They do not want anything highly acid.

Does it harm lily bulbs to cut the flowers? Unfortunately, yes. One can scarcely avoid removing a considerable proportion of the foliage together with the blooms, and these leaves are needed to manufacture food to build up the bulbs for the next season's growth. Some kinds can be cut every second year without serious damage.

How do you get long stems on lilies? Long stems are produced on well-grown plants that are free from disease. Cultural requirements are a fertile soil well supplied with organic matter, mulching to conserve moisture, and the annual application of a complete commercial fertilizer. Old plants with numerous stems should be divided, and the bulbs replaced in enriched soil.

Should lily blooms be left on plants, or should they be picked off before seeding? Remove flowers as they fade. This favors the development of larger plants the following year.

Should lily stems, after they have dried up and died, be left, or should they be cut off or pulled off? They should be removed lest they harbor disease. They can be pulled up gently if it is desired to save the bulblets which are found at the bases of the stems of certain species; otherwise they should be cut off.

At what time of year should lily bulbs be dug? Do not dig unless it is necessary to move them to another location or divide them. Take them up when the tops begin to die.

Do we cover lilies because they are not quite hardy, or to prevent freezing and thawing? Lilies are mulched to prevent damage to the bulbs from low temperatures and to prevent injury to the roots from alternate freezing and thawing.

At what temperature should lily bulbs be kept during winter? They are hardy and should be left in the ground over winter. In cold regions protect with a 6- or 8-in. straw mulch. (See next question.)

My lily bulbs arrived too late to plant outside. I have buried them in sand in a cold fruit cellar. Will they be all right? Yes, if temperature is kept just above freezing. It would have been better, however, to have potted them before storing in the cellar. Knock gently from pots and plant outside in spring at proper depth.

Can lily species be grown from seed? Seeds of such lilies as *Lilium regale, tenuifolium, amabile, concolor, formosanum, henryi,* and *willmottiae* germinate promptly. Plant in early spring in flats of good soil, and leave in a cold frame, under lath shades, for 2 seasons. Water and weed regularly, and mulch or cover the flats with boards during winter. At the end of the second summer plant the seedlings out in nursery beds for another year or two, mulching the beds for winter. Plant seeds of *L. auratum, speciosum, martagon,* and native American lilies in spring. They will not send up leaves until the following spring. If the flats are stacked during the first summer no weeding, and only occasional watering, will be necessary. At end of the third season the plants should be large enough for the nursery bed. Hybrid lilies will not ordinarily breed true from seed, but you may get some interesting variations.

What is the most successful way to propagate regal lilies, and how long before blossoms may be expected from seed? By seed. The larger seedlings should bloom during their third season.

Our madonna lily set seed after it bloomed. Could I plant the seed this winter in a box in the house? Madonna lily seeds can be started in flats in the house any time during the winter.

When and how should lily bulblets be planted? Remove bulblets borne at bases of the stems when stems are cut down in fall. Plant them in a nursery row for a year or two until they are large enough to transplant to the border. Bulbils borne in the axils of leaves of some varieties may be planted about 1 in. deep as soon as they begin to drop from the plants.

How can I propagate the gold-banded lily (Lilium auratum)? Remove the bulblets from the bases of the stems in the fall and plant them out in a nursery for a year or two until they are large enough for the border. This is often a difficult lily.

I have three madonna lily bulbs grown from scales I took from large bulbs last August. What should I do with them until next August? I have them potted in the house now. Keep them growing in the pots until next August, when they may be planted in the garden.

Can small bulbs of lilies that appear almost on top of the ground be separated from the main plant and be planted deeper to increase the stock? Yes. To prevent crowding, bulblets which form near the surface of the ground on the bases of the stems, should be removed every year or two, and planted elsewhere.

How do you separate lily bulbs when you wish to start new plants? Dig, and break up the clumps in late fall. The small bulbs on the bases of the stems may also be saved. Lilies which do not increase by bulb division nor by stem bulblets may be propagated by removing a few of the scales from the bulbs as soon as the flowers fade and planting these an inch deep in a light soil. These vegetative ways of propagating work for both hybrid and species lilies.

What is the best way to avoid mosaic disease in lilies? Plant only bulbs known, or guaranteed, to be free from mosaic. Your best bet is American-grown hybrids. Or grow the bulbs from seed away from all lilies and other bulbous plants. When you see any sign of disease, dig up the plant and burn it at once.

What is the treatment for basal rot in madonna lilies? It is caused by a fungus. If detected before the bulbs have rotted much, remove decayed tissue, dip bulb for 20 mins. in 1 part formaldehyde to 50 parts water, and replant in a new location.

What is the recommended treatment for botrytis blight of lilies? Spray at weekly intervals with Bordeaux mixture. This disease is most serious in wet seasons.

How can I prevent field mice from destroying lily bulbs? Plant the bulbs in cages of wire netting of a large enough mesh to let the stems grow through. Or mix generous quantities of pebbles or gravel in the soil atop the bulbs.

Is it true that L. philippinense and tiger lilies are disease carriers and should be removed from the garden? They may or may not have mosaic disease. Foreign stock, often vegetatively produced, is more likely to carry disease than seed-grown American bulbs. Our lily growers also use new acreage, less likely to harbor disease microorganisms.

How can I decide which of the hundreds of new hybrids to buy? Preferences for color, height, and blooming season should be your guides while studying catalogues. Attend one of the shows sponsored by the North American Lily Society or its local affiliates and see some of them for yourself.

Please tell me what new hybrid lilies to choose for my garden. June: Mid-Century Hybrids, Martagon Hybrids, Del Norte Hybrids; July: Harlequin Hybrids, Fiesta Hybrids, Bellingham Hybrids, Aurelian Hybrids; August: Potomac Hybrids, Jamboree Hybrids, Imperial Hybrids.

What lilies are long-lived? Healthy bulbs give long life. Buy only American-grown bulbs from a reliable dealer.

What is the difference between a strain of lilies and a named hybrid clone? Hybrid strains are developed by crossing two different lilies. Often grown directly from seed, a general strain will show some color variation, but selected strains will be generally of the same hue. For example, Pink Perfection Strain, Golden Splendor Strain, and Green Magic Strain are all selections of Aurelian Hybrids. A clone is a named variety selected for outstanding characteristics. It is vegetatively produced and all bulbs sold under the name give identical flowers. Examples are 'Enchantment', 'Shuksan', 'American Eagle'.

What is the botanical name of the commonly used Easter lily? *Lilium longiflorum.* Several improved varieties of this lily have shorter, stocky stems for pot growing. Not reliably hardy outside in the North, however.

Can lilies be forced to bloom indoors? In addition to the well-known Easter lily, several hybrids are excellent for forcing during the winter. Try any of the Mid-Century Hybrids such as 'Enchantment', 'Cinnebar', 'Harmony', and 'Joan Evans'. The pink and ivory 'Corsage' is reported excellent, too.

LYCORIS SQUAMIGERA (RESURRECTION-LILY)

Which lily is it that shows its leaves in the spring, then dies, and in August sends up stalks which have a pink-lavender bloom? *Lycoris squamigera,* sometimes sold as *Amaryllis hallii.* It is not a lily and is a member of the amaryllis family.

How shall I care for Lycoris squamigera? Plant in September in light, loose soil, either in full sun or light woodland shade. Set bulbs so tops are 5 ins. deep and spaced 5 or 6 ins. apart. Leave undisturbed for many years. Ferns make a good companion planting.

Why has Lycoris squamigera failed to bloom since transplanting two years ago? It is in a sunny, well-drained location. Bulbs multiplied, but sent up no flower stems. It often happens that transplanted bulbs of this species refuse to bloom for 2 or 3 years after transplanting.

I have 2 lycoris bulbs now 4 years old. They came up in the spring, and the leaves are healthy and long; they die down in July but never bloom. Can you help me? Maybe you planted small bulbs. If in a suitable soil (deep, light, well drained) and location (full sun or light shade) they should grow and eventually flower.

When do you dig Lycoris squamigera? Some say after the foliage dies and before they bloom; others, after they bloom. Best time for transplanting is immediately after foliage dies.

MUSCARI (GRAPE-HYACINTH)

How late can grape-hyacinth (muscari) bulbs be planted? They can be planted any time before the ground freezes hard; but it is better to plant them in early fall.

Do grape-hyacinths multiply? If so, when can one transplant them? Yes; they multiply freely. Self-sown seedlings come up in great numbers. Lift bulbs as soon as foliage has died down and transplant immediately; or store in cool, dry place until fall.

Can I keep grape-hyacinth bulbs, without planting, till next spring? No. If you cannot plant them in open ground, plant them closely together in shallow boxes of soil. Stand outdoors and cover with leaves or hay during winter.

When should grape-hyacinths, which have been undisturbed for years, be reset? To what depth? They can be lifted and replanted when the foliage has died and become completely brown. Plant 2 ins. apart, and cover tops of bulbs with 3 ins. of soil.

I have 2 varieties of muscari; one sends up top growth in fall. Which variety is it? How do I care for them over winter? The nomenclature of the species and varieties of muscari is very confused. Several of them produce foliage in the fall. They are quite hardy and require no special winter attention.

ORNITHOGALUM

Can you give me some information about ornithogalums? (Texas.) More than 100 kinds exist. They are natives of Europe, Asia, and particularly Africa, belonging to the lily family. Many kinds should be hardy in Texas. They need a fertile, sandy soil. The article in Bailey's *Standard Cyclopedia of Horticulture,* available in most libraries, although written many years ago, would be of interest and help to you.

Is the very fragrant Ornithogalum arabicum hardy in the vicinity of New York City? Not generally so, although it will winter and bloom if given a very sheltered position, porous soil, and winter protection. *O. nutans* is hardier, and *O. umbellatum* (star-of-Bethlehem) has become a weed in parts of the East.

PUSCHKINIA

Will you give me directions for growing a scilla-like bulbous plant called puschkinia? Plant in early fall about 3 ins. deep and same distance apart, in light, well-drained, fertile soil, either in full sun or very light shade. A fine, hardy early-blooming bulb which increases well into colonies if left undisturbed. It has attractive light blue flowers which appear about the time forsythia blooms.

SCILLA

What is the best way to plant and care for the blue scilla? Plant *S. sibirica* in fall in deep, loose soil that is fairly fertile. It thrives for years without disturbance. Do not remove foliage until it has completely died down. The scillas, with large, potatolike bulbs (*S. hispanica* and *S. nonscripta*), are set 5 ins. deep. Other kinds about 3 ins. deep. *S. bifolia* is one of the earliest spring bulbs.

Which scillas are best adapted for planting in a shaded situation, in soil containing lots of leafmold? The Spanish bluebell (*Scilla hispanica*) and the English bluebell (*Scilla nonscripta*). Both may be had in blue-, pink-, and white-flowered forms. Most catalogues list these as *S. campanulata,* although their genus is now *Endymion* officially.

STERNBERGIA

What is the name of the rich golden-yellow flower that looks like a crocus (but more substantial) and blooms in September? *Sternbergia lutea*. Plant bulbs 4 or 5 ins. deep in August, in quite porous soil and sheltered situation where snow seldom lies long. Mulch with shredded pine bark. Sternbergia must have winter sun on its foliage and resents root disturbance. Overplant with annual sweet-alyssum since it flowers before the leaves develop much. They die down naturally every June.

TULIPS

The spring garden would indeed be dull without tulips. They are one of the "musts" of the mixed flower garden because they are un-surpassed in their wide array of harmonious colors and stately forms. The range of hues covers the entire spectrum and all its tints and shades except pure blue. What artist would not revel in tubes of tulip colors as a medium for painting garden pictures?

For generations tulips grew in the fields and gardens near Con-stantinople before they found their way to Holland in 1571. Few plants have been molded to such an extent into the economic and social life of a nation. Even though grown in all the temperate re-gions, they are still thought of as Dutch.

In the course of history tulips have had their ups and downs. Soon after their introduction into Holland they reached a peak of popu-larity never before or since achieved by any plant. Men speculated and gambled with them as is done today in cotton, corn, and oil. The prices of new varieties soared to staggering heights. A single bulb of the variety Semper Augustus once sold for 13,000 florins, the equiva-lent of $6,500. Then came the crash; and the economic and financial structure of the entire nation was threatened. The popularity of tulips vanished, and for years they were hidden in the small home gardens of the poorer people of Holland, only to rise again and become a leading industry.

Tulips are valuable in many kinds of garden planting. Their best use is in the border, where they combine beautifully with other spring-flowering plants. Do not line them up in rows like soldiers. In small groups of a single kind they offer friendliness and charm whether you plant early dwarfs in a warm niche or dramatic Darwins as a focal point.

They are also useful for formal beds where they take on an appropriate quality of stiffness and constraint. In swaths of a single color they will lead the eye however the designer fancies. Early-flowering types are the easiest to force for winter decoration inside. Finally, for flower arrangements their form is distinctive and their coloring delightful.

Hybridization in the last few decades has produced new groups of tulips ideal for home gardeners. The Fosteriana 'Red Emperor' was perhaps the most famous of these man-made wonders, but it has been joined by a wide range of others. Earliest are the Kaufmanniana hybrids. They are followed by the Fosteriana hybrids, the Greigi hybrids, and the Darwin hybrids. The season ends with the traditional tall Darwins. By planting groups of the various kinds of hybrids plus some of the true species, which are charmers, too, it is possible to have almost three months of tulip bloom.

What kind of soil suits tulips best?   A fertile, well-drained, light loam, at least 12 ins. deep. They will grow satisfactorily, however, in a wide variety of soils.

Will tulips grow well in a position that is located in a wet spot in my garden?   No. Good subsurface drainage is of the utmost importance in growing tulips. The bulbs will quickly rot in waterlogged soil.

Is it necessary to change the soil yearly in beds where tulips are planted?   It is easier for most home gardeners to change the location in the garden than to move all that soil. In fact, tulips can be planted in the same ground for many years before diseases become a problem.

What can I add to my garden soil to make my tulip bulbs grow larger?   Superphosphate and commercial fertilizer, mixed with the soil at planting time, and rich compost or well-rotted manure, set 2 ins. under the bulb with a soil separation layer between the bases of the bulbs and the manure, will aid.

What common fertilizers are good for tulips?   Superphosphate, dried and shredded cattle manure, sheep manure, and commercial fertilizers, such as a 4–8–4 or 5–10–5.

Is it worth while to put commercial fertilizer on a tulip planting in

late fall? Yes, but better in spring. Apply and water it in immediately.

What is the best fertilizer for tulips? Complete commercial fertilizers, of low-nitrogen content, and superphosphate are satisfactory. Avoid all fresh manures. Liquid manures should be used only in weak dilutions.

Is it well to put manure on my tulip bed? Manure is practically wasted when put on the surface. It should be used only in the bottom of the bed. Best winter covers for tulip beds are marsh hay, clean straw, pine bark, and rough compost.

When is the best time to plant tulips? October 15 to November 1, except where a short growing season makes earlier planting necessary.

How late can one plant tulips and still hope for fair results? (Ohio.) December 15 in your section. Their stems will be shorter, and their blooms not so large as those of earlier-planted bulbs.

How can I save tulip bulbs which are not in the ground at the time of the first hard freeze? Build a fire over the frozen ground and thaw it out, or else chop through the crust and plant. Tulips cannot be held a full year out of the ground.

Could tulip bulbs be planted in January or February if the weather permits? Yes, if sound and well preserved. By February the flower buds contained in the bulbs are usually dead. However, this procedure may result in saving the bulbs so that they will flower the following year.

How does one obtain even results from tulip plantings? Flowers all the same height, and all of one kind blooming together with flowers of the same size? By planting good-quality, even-sized bulbs of one variety at the correct season and setting them all at the same depth. Professional gardeners accomplish this by removing soil from the bed, placing the bulbs, and then refilling with soil. For the very best results new bulbs of the same variety or the same type should be planted each fall.

Is it true that tulip bulbs do better when planted 10 or 12 ins. deep as stated by some bulb growers? Deep planting prevents tulips splitting up and saves the task of digging and separating them every 2 to 3 years. Large bulbs may do well planted with their bases at this depth but shallower planting is usually more advisable if bulbs are small. Deep planting retards breaking up of each bulb into several smaller ones and therefore makes it possible to leave the planting undisturbed for several years. Perfect drainage is a must for deep planting, however. A high water table in a wet year will wreak havoc.

Do you agree that if tulips are planted 9 ins. deep they'll never have to be moved? No; but they will need replanting less frequently than shallowly planted bulbs.

What happens if you plant tulip bulbs too deeply or too shallowly? If planted too deeply, small bulbs will waste their strength pushing through to the ground level. If too shallowly, they may heave out of the ground, or freeze completely.

What do you think of treating tulips as annuals, that is, plant new bulbs every fall, enjoy the flowers in the spring, and then pull the plants and discard? My Yankee soul is appalled at such waste! Healthy tulips planted fairly deep in well-drained loam often increase to delightful clumps before having eventually to be separated because of crowding.

In planting 1,000 tulips in beds 36 ins. wide should I remove the soil to a depth of 6 or 8 ins. and replace after setting the bulbs? I want to plant annuals without lifting tulips. Your method is quite satisfactory, but it is quicker to prepare the bed and then plunge the bulbs into the ground, using a long-shanked trowel. Annuals can be planted over bulbs planted 6 ins. deep or deeper.

How can I get larger tulip blooms? I plant only top-size bulbs obtained from a reputable dealer. Fertilize each September with 5 lbs. of a 4–8–4 fertilizer to each 100 sq. ft. of bed. Water freely during dry periods in spring. Do not remove leaves when cutting flowers. Remove faded flower heads to prevent seed production. Never remove leaves or dig bulbs until tops have dried completely. However, you always have the largest tulip flowers the first spring after planting. Thereafter the flowers tend to get smaller as the bulbs split. One solution is to treat the bulbs as "annuals." Discard after blooming; plant new top-size bulbs in the fall.

Will tulips bloom as well the second year after planting as they do the first? Generally, no. However, if the soil is well prepared, moisture is provided during the growing season, and the flowers are removed immediately after blooming (but the foliage left intact), there often is little difference between the quality of the first and second year's blooms. Some varieties deteriorate quickly, though, after one year.

Could tulips be satisfactorily grown in a porch box 5 ft. long, 15 ins. wide, and a foot deep; northwest exposure? Possibly—for one spring's bloom. Drainage must be adequate and boxes shouldn't freeze solid. Pack and mulch with straw or marsh hay.

Can tulip bulbs which have been forced be made to produce flowers outside? If so, how? They can be planted outside if the soil is well fertilized, but the number of flowers as well as their size may be disappointingly small for several years. If you intend to try this, be sure to keep the forced plants watered and growing so that they retain their foliage as long as possible. It's really not worth the trouble.

Can tulips be left in year after year? I have some that have been in for some years and they look very good. As long as the bulbs continue producing satisfactory blooms, keep them in the ground. Cut flowers off as soon as they fade. Keep watering the bed in dry weather until the foliage has completely died down. Fertilize in spring.

Will tulip bulbs bloom again if flowers are cut? They should bloom the following year providing most of the foliage is left to die down naturally.

If all that comes up from a tulip bulb is one large leaf and no bloom stalk, will that bulb, or the increase from it, ever bloom? This indicates either need for digging and separation or immaturity. First-year bulblets produce only one big leaf. Both the bulb and its increase can eventually bloom if planted in enriched soil. This "growing on," however, may prove tiresome, and for practical purposes it is often better to discard such weakened bulbs and start afresh with new stock.

Last year I lost about 1,000 tulips. Do they run out? One bed was replanted after bulbs were lifted and separated, but many died. Would lack of snow affect them thus? (Minnesota.) No. Losses may be caused by disease, rodents, or high watertable. In your section shallowly planted bulbs need the protection of a winter mulch.

What is the best method of producing tulips from bulbs which have bloomed 2 years and now show nothing but leaves? Dig the bulbs in July or early August. Replant only those having a diameter of 1 in. or more in fresh soil. Set small bulbs in rows, in vegetable garden or elsewhere, to grow on or discard entirely.

Is it advisable to prevent small tulip bulbs from blooming the first year, thus to obtain larger bulbs for the next year? Yes; but do not remove buds until they show color.

There are many ways to use tulips in the garden. They are stately enough to be planted in rows along walks.

Can tulips be lifted and packed in soil until the tops are dry so as to save the bulbs; or should they be planted deeper so I can plant "glads" above them? Tulips can be lifted, carefully "heeled in" in a shallow trench, and watered frequently until their tops are fully dried. They may then be separated and stored and be replanted in the fall. It would be easier to discard them and start with fresh bulbs in the fall.

Should tulip bulbs be taken up each year and separated? Should they be covered with leaves in the fall? No. Dig them and separate them only when bloom falls off unless the ground is wanted for other purposes. (See answer above.) A winter mulch is desirable where temperatures go much below zero. Bulbs planted deeply or in heavy soil require separation less frequently than those in light soils or that are shallowly planted.

Is it all right to dig tulips in the fall for transplanting? Tulips can be dug and transplanted as late as October 1. An earlier date is better, however, as vigorous new root growth begins in October and continues until hard freeze.

Can tulips be moved in spring before blooming? No, it is impractical and will prevent the bulbs from blooming. It is also dangerous to the future welfare of the bulbs.

Do tulips need to be cured in the sun after digging? They should not be exposed to the sun, even a 30-minute exposure to full sunshine may crack the coats on the bulbs. Cure them by storing in a cool, dry place protected from sunlight.

What is the best way to store tulip bulbs through summer? Dry them thoroughly, dust well with sulfur, and hang them in ventilated bags from the rafters of a cool, dry cellar, shed, or garage.

How can I keep tulips over winter, to plant in spring? This is not a good practice. If it must be done, store at 34° to 40° F. Tulips cannot be kept over safely for periods longer than 6 to 8 months.

When do you reset tulip bulbs that have been lifted and stored through the summer? No sooner than September 15. October 15 is better, if the bulbs are storing well.

What should be done with small tulip bulbs taken up in spring but not planted the following fall? They are hardly worth bothering with. Small bulbs will have wasted most of their substance by being stored so long.

Is it important to cover the ground after planting tulip bulbs when the weather is freezing? In very cold sections it is wise to cover tulip plantings with marsh hay or a similar protection. Apply this after the ground is frozen. Do *not* use manure for mulching tulips as it sometimes harbors botrytis blight.

How is the breeding of tulips accomplished by the home gardener? By the same methods used for most other flowers. Ripe pollen is transferred, with a camel's-hair brush, from the stamens of the male parent to the receptive stigma of the seed-bearing parent. All stamens are removed from the female parent before they ripen and shed pollen, and the flower is covered with a paper or plastic bag, to prevent accidental pollination.

Is it true that it takes 7 years to grow tulips from seeds? During this time is there any top growth? No. Tulips often produce blooms in 3 years from seed. Top growth appears on the young seedlings.

Could you give detailed directions for growing tulips from seeds? Seeds should be planted in light, well-drained soil in a cold frame in summer. Dig the bulblets the following year when the foliage has died down, and plant them 3 or 4 ins. deep in nursery beds in fall. The soil should be enriched for the young bulbs. It is a tedious process that appeals only to the most interested amateurs and to breeders of new varieties.

How do tulip bulbs multiply? By offsets (young bulbs), which grow from the base of the mother bulb. These are separated and are grown on to flowering size in specially prepared nursery beds.

How can the little tulip bulbs be taken care of so that they can produce full-size bulbs that will flower? When tulip bulbs are dug up, there are so many little ones. Immediately replant the small bulbs 3 to 4 ins. deep in good soil, or they may be stored in a cool place in a mixture of *slightly* moist peat moss and sand to be replanted in fall. Small bulbs are often immature when dug. They have high water content and little stored food. Loss of water causes withering, so do not store dry. Allow flower buds (if any) to develop the next spring until they show color, then nip them off. Encourage foliage to grow as long as possible. Have soil well-enriched at all times.

Are tulips subject to disease? Tulip diseases include fire blight, gray bulb rot, shanking, root rot, and mosaic. For all of the above, destruction of infected stock and a change of soil or sterilization of the infected soil are the only effective remedies.

Last year some of my tulips had small greenish spots on the leaves; the spots grew larger and many of the leaves turned yellow. Some buds failed to open. What was the trouble; and what can I do? Botrytis or "fire" blight. Remove and burn infected leaves; dig bulbs each year, and burn all showing infection. Replant in a new location, where no tulips have been grown for several years.

What causes new colors and varieties to appear in tulip beds after a few years? Do the bulbils or offshoots produce other varieties? Are the new forms seedlings? Change of color is usually due to disease mosaic. Infected plants should be removed or the virus will spread through the entire planting. It is unlikely there would be any self-sown seedlings.

Do moles eat tulip bulbs during winter or early spring? Moles are carniverous and therefore do not eat bulbs, but mice and other pests can follow the mole runs and destroy the bulbs. However, mice exist without the help of moles and are very destructive among tulip plantings. Some years they are worse than other years. Their prevalence in a region can be another reason for treating tulips as annuals.

What can I do to keep pocket gophers from eating tulip bulbs? (Idaho.) Use commercial rodent repellents, poisons, or cyanogas in the form of dust forced through a special air pump made for the purpose. Plant the bulbs nearer your house.

How do you prevent mice and squirrels from eating tulip bulbs? There is no easy way. You can try planting the bulbs in wire-mesh baskets, experiment with rodent repellents, keep cats—and plant so many tulips that some will be overlooked by the pests.

What tulip types are generally available? What are their characteristics? *Species or "botanical" tulips and their hybrids:* Many of them low-growing and very early; a few like the Fosterianas ('Red Emperor' was the first), very large. Hybrids of species like the Kaufmanniana, Fosteriana, and Greigii are among the most spectacular for early color. Darwin hybrids contain some of the largest tulips known and bloom later than the Fosteriana hybrids but earlier than the regular Darwins. *Single Early Tulips:* Bloom just after early species. There are many fine yellow and orange varieties in this group and many are fragrant. They are 10 to 16 ins. in height. *Double Early Tulips:* Double form of Single Early class; long-lasting, especially when cut. Good for massing. *Late Doubles:* Often called peony-flowered and are also long-lasting but taller. *Cottage:* Tulips with tall, flexible stems, yellows and oranges but no purples, lavenders, or bronzes. *Darwin:* The largest group with big, globular flowers on very tall stems; colors range from white, yellow, and orange through pinks, salmons, and reds to lavenders and deep purples. *Breeder:* Bloom after Darwin tulips and produce large, stiff-stemmed, cup-shaped flowers in golds, bronzes, browns, purples. *Parrot:* Late-flowering with laciniated and twisted petals, excellent for arrangements. *Fringed or Crystal Tulips:* Finely cut petal edges but no twisting. *Lily-flowering:* Bloom late with graceful, goblet-shaped blooms with pointed, recurved petals.

What types of tulips give the earliest bloom? Two fine species (*T. pulchella violacea* and *T. turkestanica*) usually bloom in March at Philadelphia. The many water-lily tulip hybrids (Kaufmanniana) are also very early.

What tulips are best for midseason bloom? Select your favorite colors from among those listed as Cottage, Darwin hybrids, and Greigii hybrids.

What are bouquet tulips?   Also known as branching or multi-flowered tulips, they produce from 3 to 11 flowers on one main stem from one bulb. In a small garden, a few bulbs will make a good splash of color.

What tulips are good for flower arrangements?   All tulips are excellent in bouquets. For unusual effects raise some from the following classes: fringed, viridiflora, broken, and parrot.

How shall I select late-flowering varieties of tulips?   From the catalogue of a reputable dealer, select kinds which appeal and which are within your price limit (the highest-priced varieties are usually the newest). Make your selection from the Darwin, cottage, and lily sections. If possible, visit tulip plantings in May and make your selections then.

Are the early-single, and early-double types of tulips satisfactory for spring bedding?   Yes. They are lower-growing and earlier-flowering than the Darwins and cottage tulips. Try also Kaufmanniana and Greigii hybrids in groups of a single variety for mass effects.

Which of the "botanical" tulips are most satisfactory for the average garden?   *Tulipa kaufmanniana* (the water-lily tulip); *clusiana* (the lady tulip); *sylvestris* (the Florentine tulip); *praestans,* red; *tarda* (*dasystemon*), yellow; *pulchella,* purply red; *turkestanica,* cream; *persica,* yellow and bronze.

Tender Bulbs, Corms, Tubers

(*See also House Plants*)

GENERAL

How often should bulbs be watered when being forced in a dark, cool room?   Until growth starts, just enough to keep soil moist. All forced bulbs, while in active growth, require constant supplies of moisture, and should never be allowed to dry out.

Do the following need to be placed in dark to form roots: freesias, St. Brigid anemone, ranunculus?   Freesias, no. Anemone and ranunculus preferably, but not necessarily. All should be started in cool temperatures.

How long a rest period must bulbs that have been forced in pots have before being replanted?   Hardy bulbs, such as narcissus, tulips, hyacinths, etc., should be discarded or planted out of doors after forcing. Tender subjects, such as hippeastrum, haemanthus, oxalis, lachenalia, etc., should be rested from the time the leaves have died away naturally and completely, until they show evidence of starting into growth again.

Can I store bulbs in an old-fashioned cellar which is damp?   If too damp, many bulbs will rot. Suggest you make provision for better ventilation, which should result in drier conditions.

ACHIMENES

How are achimenes grown?   Pot rhizomes about 1 in. apart and ½ in. deep in pans of sandy, humusy soil early in spring. Water sparingly at first, more freely as growth develops. Temperature 60° to 65° F.; atmosphere moist. Keep air dry and cooler when flowers appear; shade from strong sun; feed when actively growing. Gradually dry off at end of growing season and store when dormant. Achimenes increase prodigiously each season.

Achimenes died after blooming. How long do bulbs remain dormant, and where shall I keep them during this period?   From late summer until March or April plants remain dormant. Keep rhizomes mixed with dry sand, stored in temperature of 45° to 50° F. during this period.

ACIDANTHERA

Can acidanthera be grown outdoors, like gladiolus?   Yes, except in far northern states where it is better to start early by planting several bulbs together in good soil in large pots or tubs indoors; grow outside during summer and bring into cool situation indoors before frost; after blooming, dry off and rest. In other sections plant outdoors in sunny garden bed rich in humus after all danger of frost is past and treat as for gladiolus.

AGAPANTHUS

Is the blue African-lily hardy, or must it be protected (in New

Jersey)?   Agapanthus is not hardy where more than very light frosts are experienced. In New Jersey and similar climates it should be wintered in a light, cool, frostproof cellar or some similar situation.

ALSTROEMERIA

Is alstroemeria hardy in New York? How is it grown?   *A. aurantiaca* survives on Long Island when established; however, most kinds need protection of a cold frame, or may be grown by planting out in spring and lifting and storing in cool cellar through winter. They need an abundance of moisture (without stagnation) during growing season.

AMARYLLIS

What is an amaryllis?   *Amaryllis belladonna* of South Africa is the only plant to which the name amaryllis truly belongs. It is tender north of Washington, D.C. Requires deep planting and full sun. The name is commonly applied to hippeastrums, which hail from South America, as well as to sprekelia (Mexico), lycoris (Asia), sometimes to vallota (South Africa), and occasionally to crinum and other genera.

Will red and white amaryllis (hippeastrum) bulbs bloom in a summer garden?   The florists' amaryllis, or, as it is more correctly named, hippeastrum, cannot be successfully grown as a garden plant except in warm regions, such as Florida and California.

Is there a way to have amaryllis (hippeastrum) bloom at a more desirable time?   They are typically winter and spring bloomers. The exact time of flowering can be controlled to some extent by varying the temperature in which they are grown, by the methods employed to ripen them off in the fall, and by delaying their restarting.

Do amaryllis (hippeastrum) bulbs absolutely need to rest?   Yes. However, some individual bulbs exhibit much less of a tendency to go completely dormant, and lose all of their foliage during the rest period, than others. Withholding water in late summer is a good way to force dormancy.

During the past summer my older amaryllis (hippeastrum) bulbs have grown some new bulbs. I will soon have to rest the large bulbs. How can I save the small ones? Would it be safe to separate them?   Rest young bulbs with mother bulb, and separate at potting time.

Plant young bulbs individually in small pots of sandy soil, and give same treatment as older specimen. These bulbs prefer to be pot-bound.

BABIANA

I have a bulb called babiana. Will you please tell me how to care for it? Exactly same treatment as freesia, which see.

BEGONIA (TUBEROUS-ROOTED)

Are tuberous-rooted begonias annuals? They are tender perennials. They bloom the first season if seed is sown very early indoors.

Do tuberous-rooted begonias need any special attention except shade? The stems on mine seemed so brittle, the flowers fell off almost before they were open, and the tubers diminished considerably in size. They need a loose, woodsy soil containing plenty of humus, even moisture, good drainage, and shelter from strong winds and hard rain. They like well-rotted cow manure. They need light—not total—shade to flower properly.

Where can I plant, and how can I start and care for, tuberous-rooted begonias? Purchase tubers in early spring. Plant in pots of light soil indoors for 6 or 8 weeks before plants are to be set outside. Set plants in open ground when all danger of cold weather has passed. Sheltered, shaded position necessary and soil enriched liberally with humus. Keep moist throughout summer.

What is proper soil mixture for tuberous begonias to grow in planters placed on ground outside? One part good garden soil, one part coarse sand or vermiculite, one and one half parts flaky leaf-mold or peat moss. Add superphosphate, 1 pint to a bushel of compost. You may vary this mixture somewhat, but result should be a rich, but porous, humusy soil. Well-rotted manure or rich compost can also be added.

Will growing plants of tuberous-rooted begonias, set out in May or June, do as well as the tubers? Well-established plants set out from pots after the weather has become warm and settled should do as well as, and will produce earlier flowers than, tubers set in the open ground.

Should tuberous begonias be lifted before or after first hard frost?

Before the first killing frost. A light frost that just touches the foliage will not harm them.

What should be done to tuberous begonias in the fall? (Outdoor grown.) Lift them before severe frost, and spread out in flats (leaving soil adhering to roots). Put in sunny, airy place, and allow to ripen. When stems and leaves have died, clean and store the tubers in dry sand, soil, or peat moss, in a temperature of 40° to 50° F.

My tuberous-rooted begonias "run out." Is there a way to grow them so they will bloom year after year? Too heavy a soil, strong competition from the roots of other plants, lack of fertility, or any other factor that discourages growth may account for this. If grown under favorable conditions, they will last for many years.

How can I grow tuberous-rooted begonias indoors? Start tubers in flats of leafmold or peat moss in temperature of 60° to 70° F. When growth is 2 or 3 ins. high, pot into 4-in. pots, using loose, rich soil. Later pot into larger pots as needed, but *avoid overpotting*. Keep moist at all times; feed established plants; shade from bright sunshine; keep atmosphere moist; they do well under lights.

Can tuberous begonias be used in house when taken from garden? No, at least not the same year. After a season's growth in the garden they need a winter's rest. They may be started into growth again the following spring.

Do tuberous begonias grown as house plants need a rest period? Yes indeed. They must be dried off and completely rested during the winter. At end of summer, plants begin dying back naturally.

How can one propagate tuberous begonias? From seed. By rooting cuttings made from the young growths or by carefully cutting the tuber into pieces. This last operation is done in spring just after growth has started. Be sure that each piece of tuber retains a growing sprout. Dust cut surfaces with fine sulfur before potting up.

Will a cutting from a tuberous-rooted begonia grow a bulb or tuberous root, and will it bloom? Cuttings taken in early spring (they are made from the very young shoots) and inserted in a moist, warm sand propagating bed will bloom well the first season. They will form tubers that may be stored in the usual way through the winter.

CALADIUM

I bought a beautiful potted plant of fancy-leaved caladium, but it

began to die in fall. What did I do wrong? It is natural for this plant to lose its foliage in fall, remain dormant through the winter, then start into growth again in spring.

Would it be practicable to plant the beautiful colored-leaved caladiums out of doors in summer, dig them in fall, and store them in cellar through winter? This is just what you are supposed to do! Select a partially shaded location. Prepare soil well and incorporate humus with it. Plant tubers after ground has warmed up. Water freely in dry weather.

How can I care for tubers of colored-leaved caladiums that have been dormant through winter in pots of soil in which they grew last season? To start into new growth, remove tubers from old soil and place in shallow boxes of leafmold or peat moss, just covering tubers. Keep moist and in temperature of 70° to 80° F. When growth has started, pot up again, using a light, rich, humusy soil.

CANNA

Will you please let me know how to cut cannas to plant in spring? Use a sharp knife and cut so that each division consists of one good eye on a substantial piece of rootstock. Allow to dry overnight before planting.

How early should cannas be started? They can be started indoors as early as February 1, and then potted into 4-in. pots. For roots that are to be planted outdoors without potting, start 4 to 6 weeks before planting (after danger of frost).

What is the proper method of starting cannas in the house? Water sparingly until growth has started, then heavily. Use bottom heat to start.

What is the best soil for cannas, and how deep should they be planted? Any ordinary soil. Plant so that the "eye" is less than 2 ins. below the surface.

How shall I care for canna roots during winter? Dry thoroughly after digging. Dust lightly with sulfur and cover with clean sand or peat moss kept slightly moist. Store in cool, dark place and inspect often to see if drying occurs. If too dry, sprinkle sand or soil with water occasionally.

Are there any cannas suitable for a small garden? There are "dwarf" cannas in several colors which seldom grow over 30 ins.

How should canna roots be divided before storing for the winter?
Do not divide in fall. Store whole, and cut in spring.

Cannas planted last year grew large and healthy, but very few de-veloped flowers; they were small and poor. Why? Poor, runout planting stock is most likely responsible. Too much nitrogen could also be the cause. Cannas need fertilizer containing high phosphoric content. Lack of sunshine may also be responsible.

Is it a good plan to dig cannas and store the roots over the winter? (Georgia.) No. In the lower South it is a good practice to allow cannas to grow without moving until the clumps become very matted. Every 3 or 4 years dig the clumps, sometime during the winter, sepa-rate the roots, and set the divisions in new beds of well-enriched soil.

CLIVIA

Will you please tell how to grow clivias in pots? Pot in rich, well-drained soil. Do not repot oftener than absolutely necessary. Water to keep soil always moist; shade from sun; feed when growing ac-tively. Give winter temperature of 50° to 60° F. In summer keep outdoors in shade.

COLOCASIA (ELEPHANT'S-EAR)

Is the elephant's-ear a kind of caladium? How do you grow it? Often sold as *Caladium esculentum,* but correct name is colocasia. Plant tubers in pots indoors in spring. After all danger of frost has passed, set outdoors in moist, rich soil. After first frost, lift, dry off, and store in a cellar or similar place.

DAHLIAS

Few flowers have attained such wide popularity as the dahlia. Yielding readily to the handiwork of plant breeders, it has produced innumerable forms and colors. In the early days the breeding work was aimed at increasing the size of bloom. When flowers were ob-tained as large as dinner plates, the gardening public began to feel they were coarse and too big to be artistic. The hybridizers were not disheartened, but proceeded to develop miniature types. Today the size of different varieties varies from ½ to 15 ins. in diameter, and the plants are from 18 ins. to 7 ft. in height!

The colors, clear and rich, include all the hues except clear blue.

The petals have a crystalline texture which gives a luminous or translucent quality to the color. In addition to the pure spectrum hues, they embrace the rich, warm tones of the sunrise and the soft, full tints of the sunset. There are flower forms to suit any fancy. Some varieties are dense, full, and formal; others are loose, shaggy, and carefree. There are ball-shaped types, singles, and some even mimic the forms of other flowers, such as the peony, orchid, and anemone.

The dahlia hails from Mexico, where it may be found growing at altitudes from 4,000 to 8,000 ft., among the broken rocks of lava beds and where the temperature is moderate and rains are frequent. As with other plants, its native habitat provides an indication of its cultural needs: good drainage, plenty of moisture, cool temperatures.

In garden plantings the lower-growing dahlias are not combined with other plants to the extent they might well be. Many gardeners feel that they are difficult to use except by themselves in mass plantings. Yet when placed in the perennial border or in front of shrub plantings, they give a magnificent effect. Dahlias should be more generously used in the flower gardens of America to give added color in the late summer and fall.

Even gardeners who do not want the chores of storing tubers over the winter can enjoy dahlias quite inexpensively. Fine varieties, both single and double, are available through seed. Started early in the house, the seedlings develop quickly into bushy plants in the garden. Needing no staking, these lower-growing types are perfect for bedding and yield cut flowers until frost. The tubers they form, of course, can be gathered in the fall by the provident gardener, or they can be discarded.

What type of soil do dahlias need? They will grow in a wide variety. Important points are porosity and free drainage, reasonable humus content, and sufficient retentiveness, so that the plants do not suffer from lack of moisture. Any good vegetable garden soil is satisfactory.

What is the best way to prepare soil for dahlias? Spade and then broadcast to every 100 sq. ft., or to every 10 dahlia hills, 5 lbs. bone meal or superphosphate mixed with 1 lb. of muriate or sulfate of potash. Leave until day of planting, then thoroughly rake in the fertilizer, breaking all lumps and making the ground smooth. In sandy soil, add peat moss. Dahlias in any kind of soil respond to soil enriched with compost or well-rotted manure.

Can dahlias be planted in the same place every year? What is best to plant to enrich the soil? (Pennsylvania.) Yes. After roots are dug, spade and plant winter rye. If your soil is acid, broadcast ground limestone. Cow manure spread over the winter rye and turned under just before it goes into stalk (usually in Pennsylvania about the first week in May) would be beneficial.

Will you suggest a fertilizing program for dahlias? At planting time broadcast 5 lbs. bone meal mixed with 1 lb. muriate of potash to each 100 sq. ft. of ground, or to each 10 hills. About July 10 give each plant a handful of a complete fertilizer (5–10–10 or 5–10–5). Finally, about August 25, when buds appear, mix 3 lbs. superphosphate, 4 lbs. dried manure, and ½ lb. muriate of potash together and rake this amount into every 10 hills. Do not apply closer than 6 ins., nor more than 18 ins. away from stems.

Have saved wood ashes from my fireplace. Should I use them on my dahlia bed? Yes indeed; they are a valuable source of potash. Be sure to store in a dry place, then either dig the ashes into the ground at planting time, using up to 10 to 15 lbs. per 100 sq. ft., or apply them as a topdressing in early September.

Is liquid manure good for dahlias? Excellent. A diluted solution, made from either cow manure or chicken manure and applied at weekly intervals while the flower buds are developing, increases both size and quality.

What is best location for dahlias? They need free circulation of air, direct sunlight for at least 6 to 7 hours each day, freedom from competition with roots of large trees or dense shrubbery, and a fertile, well-drained soil.

Do dahlias thrive best in full sun or part shade? Full sun.

In planting dahlias, should they be kept a certain distance from other flowers? Not more than is necessary to permit both the dahlias and the other flowers to grow and develop satisfactorily. Dahlias should not be crowded. Set the taller kinds from 3 to 4 ft. apart; somewhat less for the miniatures and pompons.

How soon can dahlias be planted in pots indoors before they are

transplanted outdoors? For May planting outdoors, pot during April.

What is the proper planting time for dahlias? After all danger of frost has passed, usually about May 15 in the vicinity of New York City.

Can the tubers formed by the dahlia that one buys in pots and sets out in late spring be held over and used the following year? Yes. They are entirely satisfactory.

Which is better, to leave dahlias in bunches or to plant the tubers separately? I have mine put away in bunches for the winter. Leave in bunches to store, but always divide the clumps before planting.

If the necks of dahlia tubers are injured, will the plants bloom? No. Dahlia tubers with broken necks will not grow.

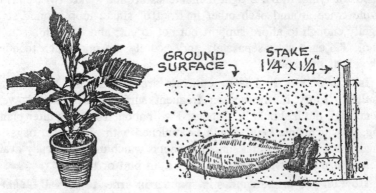

Left—pot-grown dahlia plant. Right—correct method of planting: one root, with strong eye, cut from clump.

Can dwarf or "bedding" dahlias be started in 3- or 4-in. pots and be planted out after tulips are dug? Start seed, sowing in flats or bulb pans, indoors in March. Grow on, transplanting into pots of suitable size, and set out in open garden beds when all danger of frost is over and ground has warmed up.

Dahlia catalogues list plants as well as roots of certain varieties. I would like to try plants next season. How do you handle them? When received, remove from carton but leave in pots. Soak in shallow water to freshen. Set out in late afternoon or on a cloudy day.

Dig holes 6 ins. deep; remove plants from pots; set so root-balls are just covered with soil, and leave finished surface around plants 3 ins. below grade. If following day is sunny, shade. Plants will take hold in a few days. Gradually fill holes with soil as plants grow.

How are dahlia tubers planted after clumps have been divided? First set stout stakes in place; at base of each stake, dig a wide hole 6 ins. deep; loosen up bottom. Lay tuber horizontally, with neck near stake and with eye pointing upward. Cover with soil so that tuber is just hidden. As eye grows, keep filling in soil so that it is kept just covered until surface grade is reached. Small types need no staking.

I am afraid my method of tying up dahlias is not very successful. They are always damaged in storms. What do you suggest? Plant in a position not too exposed to wind. Sisal binder twine is good for tying. Make 2 tight half hitches around stake; twist ends of twine twice around each other in front of stake; loop around stem tightly enough to afford support but not to cut; and tie with a square knot. Tie each stem separately and securely; do not bunch together like sheaf of wheat.

Is it necessary to hoe or cultivate around dahlias? What about mulch? Early in the season frequent surface cultivation is very beneficial, but it should be dispensed with about 10 weeks after planting, at which time beds should be mulched with pine bark, bagasse, buckwheat hulls, or other similar products which may be locally available. Do not cultivate when plants are in bud or bloom.

How do you prune dahlias in summer in order to get fall blooms? Allow only one main stalk to grow. When plants reach about 10 ins. in height, pinch out their centers just above the second pair of leaves. Side branches which develop should be pinched also. Remove any flower buds that appear before August 1.

How much water do dahlias require? Unless weather is very dry, they need none until they commence to bloom. Then water thoroughly, soaking the ground every week or 10 days whenever rainfall is insufficient.

How are dahlias disbudded so that they have large blooms? When the buds appear (usually in clusters of three), pinch out all except the central one of each group. New lateral shoots will appear. All of these below the remaining bud, except the 2 nearest to the main stalk, should be pinched out. This will not only produce large blooms, but will keep plants low and bushy and will encourage the development of long stems.

What is the proper method to produce strong-stemmed dahlias that will support large blooms when cut? Remove all but 1 stalk from each plant. After 3 sets of leaves develop on this, pinch out its tip. Laterals will soon grow and eventually become main branches. All laterals and sublaterals other than the 4 main branches should be pinched out, except for the 2 sublaterals that develop near the base of each flowering stem.

How are exhibition dahlias grown? By planting healthy stock of suitable varieties, and by intelligent attention to cultivation, watering, spraying, disbranching, disbudding, and fertilization.

How many days should one allow from planting time for blooms of giant dahlias to develop for show? From 80 to 120 days, depending on the variety. A hot, dry season may cause blooms to mature from 10 to 15 days later than normal.

When and how do you cut dahlia flowers for exhibition? After sunset on the evening before the show. Cut with long stems, trim off any leaves not needed, and immediately stand the stems in water. Carry indoors and then trim the base of each stem by cutting it slantwise under water. Keep in a cool, dark place until they are packed for transportation.

How do I dig and divide dahlia tubers? After the first frost, dig up clumps carefully with a fork. Turn upside down and allow them to dry in the sun for 4 to 5 hours. Let some soil cling to the clumps to guard necks from breaking and prevent excessive drying during storage. Do not divide until some months later (March or April).

What care do you suggest if part of the dahlia bulb is injured in lifting? Remove injured tubers with a sharp knife or pruning shears. Sprinkle the cut surface with sulfur.

How shall I store dahlia tubers? In a cool (45° to 55° F.) cellar, or in barrels or boxes lined with newspaper and placed where the temperature is not more than 55° nor less than 40°. Examine periodically to see that they are not becoming mildewed nor drying up.

Should dahlia roots be wrapped in paper or packed in earth for winter storage? Either. Allow soil to cling to clumps to prevent excessive drying. Peat moss makes a good material in which to store them.

What is your opinion of the practice of washing dahlia tubers as opposed to leaving on soil? Either may be satisfactory. If soil is left, it tends to prevent excessive drying and reduces danger of necks of roots being broken. If tubers are washed, make sure that they are well dried before storing. Pack in peat moss.

Can dahlias be stored out of doors if buried below the frost line? Yes, if well below the frost line. They will not survive if the tubers are frozen.

What makes dahlia roots rot after they are dug? We put ours in the garage, and in about 3 weeks they had all rotted. Probably the temperature went down below freezing. There are also several rot organisms which affect stored dahlia roots.

A short time after digging my dahlias, the roots shriveled and became soft. What was the reason? They were dug after the first frost. You probably kept them in a warm place and thus dried them out too fast.

Why do my dahlia tubers sprout after storing? They were put away in peat moss in the cellar. Storage place is too warm. Take care they are not near a heater. Temperature during storage should not be above 55° F.

My dahlia bulbs in storage are beginning to sprout. I have them packed in sand. Will this harm them? Not if it happens in spring when planting time is approaching. Sprouting in winter weakens roots and should be prevented by storage at 40° to 55° F.

What causes large dahlias to wilt as soon as cut? Large-flowered dahlias always wilt if cut during the day. Cut in late evening, well after the sun is down, or *very* early in the morning. Dipping ends of the stems in boiling water for 1 or 2 minutes has a tendency to keep the flowers fresh.

We have dahlias which never bloom. Does their age have anything to do with it? Not if they are healthy. Dahlia "stunt," a virus disease, and tarnished plant bug often prevent flowering.

Why do dahlias with large flowers have very thin stems? The excess buds were pinched out. Some varieties naturally have weak stems. Excess nitrogen and too little potash also cause this condition.

My dahlia garden is between two buildings. I get very good plants, but the frost kills the buds before they bloom. Is there any way to speed the blooming of dahlias? Your plants may not receive sufficient sun. Plants in shade tend to become soft and to bloom late. Possibly you have late-flowering varieties. These should be planted early.

Why do my dahlias have so many leaves and so few flowers? Probably because of too much shade or too much fertilizer. Attention to pruning and disbudding may help.

Can Coltness Gem dahlias be carried over from year to year by storing the tubers? I want particular colors; otherwise the ease with which they are propagated from seeds would make winter storage foolish. Yes, treat the roots exactly as you do other dahlias; label by color.

Why do some dahlias, of varieties supposed to be tall, stay low? Very possibly because they are infected with mosaic disease or "stunt." Check with a skilled grower or with your State Agricultural Experiment Station. Destroy diseased plants.

My dahlias make good growth and lots of flowers but never form tubers. What can I do to encourage the plants to grow large, plump bulbs that will keep over winter? Probably you use an unbalanced fertilizer. Excess nitrogen will cause the condition you describe. Try more potash and phosphate. There are some dahlias, particularly choice varieties, that are very poor root producers. If the plant was grown from a cutting made *between* the joints, it would bloom, but would not form tubers.

I planted dahlias, took great pains with them, and although they were very thrifty they did not flower. They bloomed last year. What is the cause? Lack of blooms may be caused by not enough sunshine, surface cultivation continued late in the season, too much nitrogenous fertilizer, insects or disease.

Some years my dahlias bloom; other years they don't. What is wrong? Weather conditions have some effect on the blooming of dahlias. If water is not supplied artificially, a dry season may cause poor blooming. See other questions.

How can I stop my dahlias from growing 9 ft. tall, with very little bloom? Probably too much shade, or fertilizer containing too much nitrogen. Allow only one main stalk to grow from each plant, disbranch, and disbud as described in other answers.

Why do my dahlias refuse to bloom? They have plenty of water and fertilizer and are planted in good garden soil. They have southern exposure. The plants grow strongly but have few, poor blooms. Is the air circulation good? Dahlias should not be planted along the side of a house or close to a hedge. They may be infected with insects such as thrips, leafhoppers, borers, or tarnished plant bug; or with mosaic or "stunt." Try a change of stock. Dahlias planted in same soil year after year sometimes deteriorate.

I have a dahlia that grows about 8 ft. tall and has lots of buds, but they never open up. Why? It grows lots of nice tubers. These symptoms are suggestive of tarnished plant bug injury.

What causes imperfect dahlia blooms? Diseases, as stunt; pests, as leafhoppers, tarnished plant bug, and thrips; unfavorable weather conditions.

Has anyone discovered the cause of the variation in color in some bicolored dahlias? The exact cause is not definitely known. Bicolored varieties seem to be particularly unstable and tend to run back to solid colors.

For what particular purposes are dwarf dahlias suited? For decorative garden beds or borders, for providing cut flowers, and for exhibiting at flower shows. They need no staking.

I have heard that dahlia bulbs were used as a food. Is there any reason why they should not be so used; are they habit-forming or harmful in any way? According to the authoritative Sturtevant's *Notes on Edible Plants,* "it was first cultivated for its tubers, but these were found to be uneatable." Ancient Mexicans are said to have used them for food, however.

How are dahlias propagated? By division of the clumps of roots; by cuttings; by seeds; and, much more rarely, by grafting.

How are dahlias increased by cuttings? Undivided clumps are planted in a cool greenhouse in January or February. Cuttings, each with sliver of tuber attached at the base, are prepared when shoots are 3 ins. or so long, and are inserted in a propagating bench (bottom heat 65° F.; atmosphere, 5° lower), or in a flat. Shade and a "close" atmosphere are supplied. When roots are an inch long, cuttings are potted up individually. Ordinary stem cuttings may also be used, but the basal cut should be made just below a node. It is scarcely practical to use this method unless a greenhouse is available.

What types of dahlias bloom the first year from seed? All types. The Coltness and Unwin hybrids and others that are grown chiefly for mass-color effects in the garden, rather than for perfection of their individual blooms, are the kinds most commonly raised from seeds.

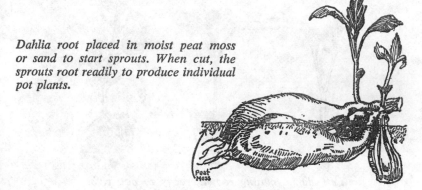

Dahlia root placed in moist peat moss or sand to start sprouts. When cut, the sprouts root readily to produce individual pot plants.

How can I save seeds from my dahlias? After petals have fallen, allow the flower head to dry on the plant (wax paper or plastic is sometimes wrapped around heads so that they dry quicker). Gather heads before killing frost and place them in a dry cellar until they have fully dried out. As a rule seeds saved from dahlias grown in the vicinity of New York are not fertile. The best seeds are produced in California, where the growing season is much longer.

How should dahlia seeds be started? Sow in pots or flats of light, sandy soil, February to March, in temperature of 60° F. Transplant seedlings (when second pairs of leaves have developed) individually into small pots. Grow on in a sunny location, with temperature of 55°. When roots crowd small pots, replant into 4-in. pots or into open ground if already warm enough.

Is it necessary to remove the tubers from seedling dahlias, and when? No; the small tubers are left on and set out with the seedling plants.

How can I hybridize dahlias? Some large dahlia growers maintain beehives in their gardens, and the bees carry the pollen from plant to plant. Others employ hand pollination, which involves using a camel's-hair brush to transfer the pollen of one variety to the pistil of another.

How are new varieties of dahlias developed? They are selected from seedlings. Some responsible dahlia growers make a specialty of raising and selling dahlia seed saved from the leading exhibition varieties.

Left—dahlia cutting rooted, ready to pot; right—dahlia seedling, ready for transplanting. (Note small tuber already beginning to form.)

How were the giant dahlias developed from smaller ones? By systematic breeding, based on hand cross-pollination, and by carefully selecting the most promising seedlings. This work has been going on a long time. The Aztecs were doing it in Mexico when the Europeans arrived.

Can dahlias be divided immediately after they are dug in fall, or must they wait until spring when they are sprouted? Is any special instrument used for this purpose? It is better to wait until spring, when eyes are visible. Use any good, sharp knife with a stout, fairly long blade.

How should dahlia clumps be divided? By using a sharp knife and pruning shears. Each division of a clump should include a portion of the old stem attached to the neck of a tuber; on each should be a visible eye capable of developing into a sprout. After dividing, let tubers air dry overnight before planting.

Is there any danger of dividing dahlias too much? Yes; unless you are experienced there is a danger of cutting into undeveloped eyes.

How can I divide dahlia bulbs when absolutely no eyes are visible? *Do not* divide until eyes appear. If clumps are slow in "eying up," put them in a flat with damp peat moss and place in a warmer, well-ventilated spot. This will cause eyes to develop in a few days. If eyes fail to appear, the stock is "blind" and will not produce plants.

Should each clump of dahlia roots be separated so as to plant only 1 root in a place? Yes. Be sure each division has an eye (bud) from which a shoot will develop.

Are dahlia bulbs which shrivel up after division any good? They will probably produce weak plants. After dahlia roots are divided, they should be kept in slightly damp peat moss until planting time.

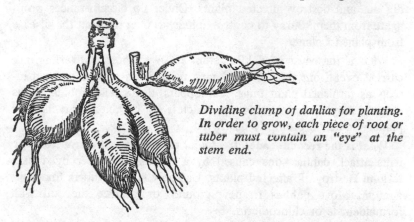

Dividing clump of dahlias for planting. In order to grow, each piece of root or tuber must contain an "eye" at the stem end.

How can I know a live dahlia tuber from one that will not grow, when dividing for spring planting? Roots that will grow possess eyes (buds) which usually appear on part of the stalk or old stem of the clump. Many clumps produce "blind" roots. These should not be planted.

Do mice eat dahlia tubers? Yes. They can be very troublesome. Wire mesh baskets as recommended for tulips around the tubers can help (leave room at top for sprout to come through). Keep weeds down; mice do not like to cross open areas. They can also get into stored tubers; inspect frequently and set traps if necessary.

Do rabbits eat dahlias?   They can level a bed of new shoots but seldom bother established plants. If rabbits are a problem in your area, at planting time protect each tuber site with a circle of chicken wire which can be removed later. Or cut the bottoms off cardboard milk containers and push these into the soil a few inches when shoots appear; the container also acts as a wind screen to protect tender new shoots until they harden off. Dried blood applied around the shoots is often an effective deterrent against rabbits.

My dahlias are not growing well. I suspect mosaic disease. What are the symptoms?   The plants are usually dwarfed; the leaves are smaller than normal and show a yellowish mosaic, or spotting. Pale-green bands are often developed along the midribs and larger secondary veins.

Is there any cure for mosaic disease of dahlias?   No. Ruthlessly dig out and destroy affected plants. Under no circumstances propagate from them. Spray to control aphids, as they transmit the disease from plant to plant.

What is the cause of dahlia "stunt"?   A temporary dwarfing, not carried over from year to year, may result from attacks of such insects as tarnished plant bugs, leafhoppers, thrips, and aphids. Virus diseases may cause real stunting, which is not curable. Virus-infected plants should be promptly destroyed.

What is the recommended treatment for dahlia wilt disease?   Two wilts attack dahlias—one caused by a fungus, the other by a bacterium. Destroy all affected plants. Use only healthy tubers for propagation. Move dahlias to new ground, or sterilize the soil with formaldehyde or chloropicrin.

How can I recognize and control red spider mite on dahlias?   It is commonest in hot, dry weather. The leaves become yellowish or pale brown. With a hand lens the insects, usually covered with a fine web, can be seen crawling on the under sides of the leaves. Forcible spraying with clear water to wash them off is helpful.

My dahlias are attacked by small bugs that jump off the leaves when disturbed. The leaves are turning yellow and becoming brittle. No holes appear in the leaves. What is insect, and what remedy do you suggest?   This is leafhopper. Spray at weekly intervals with a pyrethrum or all-purpose spray. Destroy all weeds in vicinity.

I have had a lot of trouble with corn borers in dahlias. How can I check their ravages? Spray or dust twice a week with rotenone from August to October inclusive. Pick off infested blooms. Burn old stalks at end of season.

Does more than one kind of borer attack dahlias? Yes. The common stalk borer hatches out in May, eats a hole in the stem, and usually remains until August. Watch for holes in stems and probe with fine wire to kill borers. Destroy all coarse weeds in the vicinity.

I have found large shell-less snails eating dahlia flowers. Can I do anything other than hand-pick? Clean up all rubbish and debris. Slugs hide under stones, bricks, boards, etc., during the day. Spread metaldehyde around according to directions or use alcohol or beer poured in a flat container the slugs can climb onto.

How can I learn more about dahlia growing and exhibiting? Join one of the numerous local societies devoted to dahlias; there are also several regional groups and the parent American Dahlia Society. Or watch in your local paper for notices in the fall of dahlia shows.

How important are the classifications of dahlias made by the A.D.S.? These divisions are used in all shows sponsored by the A.D.S. For the casual gardener these groupings offer quick ways to pick varieties by size, flower form, and color from the catalogues. Very extensive collections will have a key as an aid.

What is the meaning of initials like FD, SC, etc. after named dahlias in catalogues? These identify flower forms. FD means formal decorative, SC=semi-cactus, M=miniature, BA=large ball-shaped, POM=small ball-shaped, etc. Look for a key in the catalogue or consult A.D.S. lists for complete descriptions.

What is the difference between cactus and decorative dahlias? Cactus types have more or less tubular petals, while petals of decorative types are more flat than tubular.

What are the round ball-like dahlias called in catalogues? These may be listed as ball or pompon, depending on their size.

What are some good dahlias for cutting? Those classed as pompons and miniatures are particularly good for bouquets.

Is there a definite trend toward small-flowering varieties of dahlias? Yes; largely because they require less space and less attention in regard to disbranching, disbudding, and staking. In many ways they are more useful than the large-flowering types both in the garden and as cut flowers. They are usually listed in catalogues as miniature or dwarf bedding dahlias. Pompons are excellent, too.

EUCHARIS (AMAZON-LILY)

Will you give me the recommended method of growing the Amazon-lily? *Eucharis grandiflora* bulbs should be planted, several together, in large pots containing rich, well-drained, fibrous soil. Avoid repotting unless necessary. Give temperature of 65° to 75° F., plenty of moisture when growing, and shade from bright sun. Foliage is evergreen, so plants should never be dried off completely. Eucharis sometimes blooms twice a year, outside in summer and inside in late winter. A month after any flowering, begin to withhold water until foliage almost wilts. Continue this regime for 4 to 6 weeks, then resume regular watering and fertilizing.

FREESIA

What conditions are necessary for growing freesias successfully? Well-drained but fertile soil; strict care in matter of watering; cool (45° to 55° F.), airy growing conditions; and fullest possible exposure to sunshine. Sound, healthy corms of fair size are a prerequisite.

What is the secret of watering freesias? When first potted, give thorough soaking; place in cool situation; and cover with several inches of leafmold or coarse compost. When growth starts, remove mulch, and water to keep soil only just moist. Freesias abhor too much water during their early stages of growth. Gradually increase supply of water as leaves develop, and water generously when well rooted and in full growth. After blooming, water freely until foliage begins to fade, then gradually reduce, and finally withhold water entirely.

Do freesias need a high temperature? Quite the contrary. They thrive best where the night temperature does not exceed 45° or 50° F., with a daytime rise of 5° to 10° permitted.

How shall I fertilize freesias grown in pots in winter? Mix superphosphate with potting soil. When flower buds begin to show, feed at weekly intervals with dilute liquid fertilizer.

Is it possible to grow freesias outdoors? Specially prepared bulbs are now available through spring bulb catalogues.

GLADIOLUS

The gladiolus species, from which the modern garden varieties have been developed, grow wild along the shores of the Mediterranean Sea and in South Africa. The true species are of little significance as garden plants, although a few are offered for fall planting. In areas where winters are not too severe they bloom in May and June. While the flowers are small and the colors limited, they do add an interesting note to the late spring garden.

It is a far cry from any of the wildlings to the glorious flowers we know today as gladiolus. They are available in heights from a few feet to giants taller than the average person although such giants should be considered novelties rather than legitimate garden subjects. Every color of the rainbow is represented, even green. The individual florets of modern varieties are set closely together along the spike with most having flaring open petals. An increasing number are frilled or ruffled. Many have contrasting color in the throats.

All-America Gladiolus Selections sponsored by the North American Gladiolus Council are announced every year. These winners have been tested in gardens around the country and represent outstanding new varieties.

Mirroring today's smaller homes and gardens, many of the newer gladiolus are smaller in stature than the huge florist's spikes once so popular. These miniatures average about 30 ins. in height, seldom need staking, and should increase the gladiolus' popularity with modern gardeners. Of late many All-America winners are in this class, and flower arrangers are delighted with their daintier spikes.

The ease with which gladiolus can be grown anywhere in the United States undoubtedly contributes to their popularity. They are not particular in their soil requirements. They do well in warm exposures. While they tolerate neglect better than many other plants, they also respond to good treatment. Of upright growth, they require little room, so that large quantities of flowers can be produced in a limited area. They are therefore ideal for small gardens.

Usually they are grown in beds or in rows in the cutting garden. However, if combined with other plants in the mixed border they will add much color interest and a good vertical line. Gladiolus, however, are more important as cut flowers than as decorative garden plants.

They keep exceptionally well, and the form of the spike is especially well adapted for use in various types of arrangements.

Do gladiolus take the strength out of the soil? I have 20 acres on which gladiolus have been planted for the last 2 years, but the soil has been fertilized each time they were planted. Gladiolus do not exhaust the soil, particularly if fertilizer is used, but repeated growing in the same soil can result in an increase in disease, and this may make bulbs unsalable.

I am interested in raising gladiolus bulbs. Does the soil have to be very fertile for best results? Fertile, but not excessively rich.

What is your suggestion for the best fertilizer to be used for gladiolus? A 5–10–10 mixture. Avoid animal manures, as they are apt to cause disease in the corms.

Which fertilizer shall I use when I plant gladiolus in my flower border? Providing the soil is in good condition, almost any complete fertilizer will be satisfactory. Bone meal, superphosphate, and unleached wood ashes are excellent. Avoid fresh manure; leafmold or peat moss and, of course, commercial fertilizers are satisfactory.

What type soil should gladiolus have to be most successful? A well-drained, sandy loam in which gladiolus have not been grown for the past 3 years.

Will gladiolus grow in sandy soil? Fine specimens can be grown in sandy soil if enough moisture is supplied. Better mix peat moss in the soil before planting, though.

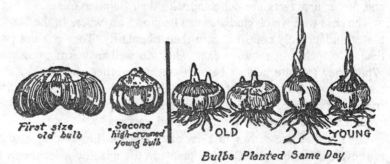

Gladiolus corms: Small, "high-crowned" young corms are preferable to larger-sized, old flat ones.

How am I to pick out the right kind of gladiolus corms to plant?
Best for planting are clean No. 1 corms 1½ ins. or more in diameter,
with small scars, which proves they were grown from small corms.
Very large, flat corms are less desirable than moderate-sized ones
with greater depth.

Do gladiolus prefer sun all day, or partial shade? Full sun, although they can be grown in partial shade.

How early can gladiolus be set out? As soon as frost is out of the
ground. Little is gained by extra-early planting, and sometimes later
plantings bloom first. Many catalogues list early, midseason, and late
varieties to help stretch the flowering period. If you have a favorite,
successional plantings will allow you to have it in bloom over a long
period of time.

When is best time to plant gladiolus; and how deep? Make first
planting about May 1, and follow with successional plantings up to
early July. Set corms 4 to 6 ins. deep. In warmer climates, planting
times are earlier, of course.

**When should I plant gladiolus to bloom in September and mid-
October?** Between June 15 and July 1.

**Will the flowers of late gladiolus be as large as if the bulbs were
planted early?** Late flowers should be larger than early ones of the
same variety, because cool nights produce larger flowers and better
color in gladiolus.

**How deep do you advise planting gladiolus; and how far apart in
rows?** Four ins. deep in heavy soil and 5 to 6 ins. in light, sandy
soil. Three ins. apart is close enough in the rows for good spikes.
Space rows 18 to 30 ins. apart.

What is the best method for planting gladiolus? In rows, like
vegetables, for cutting. They can then be given better care and will
produce better spikes. In the garden use clumps of a single variety
for focal points.

Can gladiolus bulbs be planted too closely to each other? The
old rule is to plant the diameter of the corms apart, but small sizes,
at least, should be given more room.

How deep should the cormels be planted? About 2 ins. deep.

**The gladiolus bulbs which I planted along the borders of my shrub-
bery failed to grow well. What is wrong?** Gladiolus are not able to

compete successfully with the roots of strong-growing trees and shrubs. Try planting in well-prepared soil away from the influence of roots.

Can gladiolus corms be used after not having been planted one year? Gladiolus corms are of little use the second year; but bulblets are still good the second year, and those of hard-to-sprout varieties grow better then. Soak them in tepid water for 2 or 3 days first.

What is the best way of supporting gladiolus so they do not fall over? Tie to individual slender stakes, or place stakes at intervals along both sides of the rows and stretch strings from stake to stake.

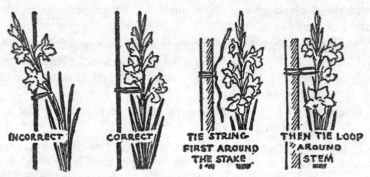

INCORRECT   CORRECT   TIE STRING FIRST AROUND THE STAKE   THEN TIE LOOP AROUND STEM

Method of staking gladiolus spike to prevent injury by wind.

Do gladiolus need much watering? The soil must be well drained, but they need an abundance of moisture, and if the season is at all dry they should be watered liberally, particularly after the sixth or seventh leaf begins to develop.

How are gladiolus corms grown to such mammoth sizes as 4 to 5 ins. in diameter? Some varieties under good conditions make 4- and 5-in. corms, but a good, thick 1½-in. corm is more satisfactory.

Do gladiolus corms need to be taken up every year? They are killed by freezing, and so should be dug and stored in a cool, dry cellar over winter.

How can I keep my late gladiolus from sprouting? To keep your corms from sprouting store them in a cool, dry, dark place, in slatted or screen-bottom trays. The temperature should be evenly maintained, at as near 40° F. as possible.

Taking up gladiolus for winter storage. Plants are loosened in the soil, pulled up gently to save the cormels, and placed in flats to dry before cleaning. Tops can be cut off just above corms to save space.

What can I do with gladiolus that I failed to take up last fall? Are they ruined? (Kentucky.) Gladiolus are only half-hardy and ordinarily will freeze and rot if left in the ground over winter, unless they are in a well-drained soil and are covered with a heavy layer of protective mulch.

When should gladiolus corms be taken up in fall? When the leaves start to turn brown. A good new corm is formed 6 weeks after blooming.

Should gladiolus corms be trimmed close before storing? The tops should be cut off close to the corm at digging time. The husk should never be removed while in storage, as it helps the corm to retain its moisture.

How can I store gladiolus corms to keep them from shrinking and drying out in winter? If stored in a cool cellar, they will not shrink or dry out. The ideal temperature is 40° F. Never allow them to freeze. Try hanging them in bags made from the legs of old nylon stockings.

Will a light frost on gladiolus corms ruin them; and how can I tell if they are still all right? A light frost will not harm the corms. If they are badly frosted, they will dry out and become very light in weight.

Why do gladiolus corms produce large blooms one year and none or very poor ones the next? Possibly your bulbs were dug too soon after blooming, or perhaps you cut the stems too low when picking flowers. Corm diseases or thrips may be factors; or poor growing conditions.

Why do my gladiolus bulbs exhaust themselves within 2 or 3 years and produce inferior blooms?   Varieties vary greatly in this respect; some will produce good spikes for a number of years, others for only a single season. Gladiolus scab is often responsible.

What makes my gladiolus flower stems develop crooked necks? Not all varieties of gladiolus "crook," but those which do should be planted so that they bloom in the cool weather of fall.

Will small gladiolus corms, such as No. 6 size, bloom the first season if planted early enough?   No. 6 size corms of most varieties will bloom, although the spikes will be short and the flowers few.

I have 200 gladiolus seeds planted and they have grown 8 ins. tall and have fallen over. They look healthy. Will they be all right? Gladiolus, the first year from seed, look like grass. They should form small, mature corms in about 12 weeks.

Why don't gladiolus bloom all at one time?   Blooming time varies according to the size of the corms and the variety. Larger corms bloom soonest. Catalogues of gladiolus specialists often list number of growing days necessary before planting. It may vary from 60 to 150 days.

Are gladiolus true to color?   They normally come true to color, although color sports often appear among the smoky shades.

What makes gladiolus of different colors gradually change to one color after a few years?   Many people think that gladiolus change color. What actually happens is that the more robust-growing varieties in a mixture outlive and out-multiply the weaker-growing ones.

My gladiolus bulbs end up with a growth on the bottom. Is this natural, or is it a disease? If so, what is the treatment?   Gladiolus in growing form new corms on the tops of the old ones; the old corms remain attached to the bases of the new ones; they are easily removed 3 or 4 weeks after digging. Often a cluster of tiny cormels grow from the base of the new corm, and are a means of propagation.

What is the best way to increase gladiolus?   By saving and planting the small bulblets that form around the large corms.

How are gladiolus corms raised from the many small corms that develop on each large one?   The small corms are stored through the

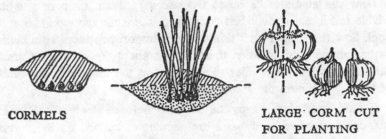

CORMELS   LARGE CORM CUT
FOR PLANTING

*The cormels, planted early in spring, like peas,
produce by autumn small corms, some of which
usually flower the following year. Right—large old
corms, with more than one sprout, can be cut before planting, to increase stock of a favorite variety.*

winter, and are planted in rows in well-prepared soil much as are
larger corms (except that they are not set so deeply). They are then
grown on to flowering size.

**What is the best way to get gladiolus bulblets to sprout quickly
and evenly?** Soak them in tepid water for 2 or 3 days, before planting. Also plant them as closely together as 20 to the foot as they
seem to like company.

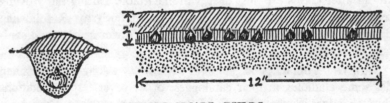

FROM SMALL BULBS

*Small gladiolus corms are planted out in nursery
rows to grow on into flowering-sized bulbs for
another year.*

**In the propagation of gladiolus, what is the procedure of handling
the bulblets or cormlets gathered from old bulbs, until the next planting season?** Dust with malathion, and store in a cool, dry place in
an open crate.

How are new varieties of gladiolus developed? They are raised
from seeds. Most improvements are obtained from seeds collected
from hand-pollinated flowers.

How can gladiolus be raised from seeds? Plant them in a light, friable soil in an outdoor bed early in spring, while the ground is still cool. Sow the seeds rather thinly in shallow drills, spaced so a cultivator can be used between them. Cover about ¼ in. deep. Corms the size of a pea or smaller should develop the first year, and most of these will bloom the second year.

Should gladiolus corms be treated before planting? Certain fungous and bacterial diseases are sometimes carried on the corms as are thrips. If these are suspected, disinfect by soaking for 20 minutes, just before planting, in a solution of 1 part mercuric chloride in 1,000 parts of water, by weight. Rinse thoroughly in clear water immediately before planting.

What should be done to stop wireworms from damaging gladiolus bulbs? Wireworms are usually bad only in newly made gardens, or where trash is allowed to accumulate.

How can I check the ravages of cutworms among my gladiolus? Clean the ground of all weeds and other unwanted growth in fall. Use a poison bait.

What is the most satisfactory method of combating gladiolus thrips? In fall after corms are dug, dust with malathion. During the growing season if thrips or aphis appear, spray with Meta-Systox-R, following directions on label carefully. Keep weeds cut down nearby as a sanitary measure.

How can I obtain good gladiolus varieties? Almost all seedsmen list some gladiolus in their catalogues; order several spring editions through advertisements in any of the garden magazines. Corms are often available locally through garden centers in spring. Choose colors to harmonize with your indoors since gladiolus make wonderful cut flowers. Plant at least 10 of a kind so you'll have enough for bouquets.

What are the uses of miniature gladiolus? Please name a few varieties. Miniatures are generally useful in mixed border plantings and especially as cut flowers. They are more informal than the standard varieties and the spikes are more graceful for use in arrangements. Also they seldom need staking. All-America miniatures are excellent choices. Catalogues also list such smaller-sized varieties as 'Butterfly', 'Primulinus', 'Nanus', or Baby hybrids.

GLORIOSA (GLORIOSA-LILY)

Can gloriosa be grown out of doors in summer? Yes. Plant strong tubers in pots of light, humusy soil in March or April and grow as container plants outside after the weather warms up. Or start plants in the sunny border after all danger of frost has passed. Lift tubers before frost and store in dry sand or peat moss through winter in temperatures between 50° and 60° F. Container plants may be rested dry in the same pot, but replace soil every year before beginning growth cycle. This is one of the rare vining tubers. The plants climb by means of barbed tendrils at the ends of the leaves, so place a cord trellis or brushwood for support.

HAEMANTHUS

Are haemanthus adapted for growing indoors? They are both interesting and beautiful as house plants or greenhouse plants. Some of the best are *katharinae, coccineus, multiflorus,* and *albiflos.*

How should I care for blood-lilies (haemanthus)? Water freely when leaves are in evidence; keep dry at other times. Give full sunshine, well-drained soil, and repot every 3 or 4 years at beginning of growing season. Feed when in active leaf growth. Temperature 50° to 60° F.

HEDYCHIUM (GINGER-LILY)

Is the ginger-lily (hedychium) adaptable for growing outdoors in the North? Only in sheltered, warm situations, and then the roots must be lifted in fall and stored in sand in a frostproof cellar over winter. Plant outdoors after all danger of frost has passed, and give abundance of water when growing.

HYDROSME (SNAKE-PALM)

Can snake-palm—the one that has a flower like a big purplish calla-lily, and a huge, finely cut umbrella leaf—be grown outdoors in summer? Yes, and its foliage is both distinctive and decorative. Plant in good soil in sun or light shade and it will quickly grow. Its name is *Hydrosme rivieri.* The huge flower is evil-smelling, but this is not too critical when the plants are grown outdoors.

HYMENOCALLIS (PERUVIAN-DAFFODIL)

How can I raise Hymenocallis calathina? Plant out after ground is warm, weather is settled, and absolutely all danger of frost has passed, in sunny, well-drained border in fertile soil. Cover to depth about 3 times the diameter of the bulb. Dig before first frost; do not remove foliage but allow to dry on the bulb and store *with fleshy basal roots intact* at a temperature of about 60° F. Leave some soil on roots for the winter; wash this off with hose before replanting.

I planted Peruvian-daffodils—bulbs as large as those of amaryllis. On taking up this November, the bulbs were very much smaller. Why was this? Unsatisfactory cultural conditions. Soil perhaps too heavy, or not fertile, or not enough sun. They probably will not bloom so well next year.

Should Hymenocallis (formerly Ismene) calathina (Peruvian-daffodil) be stored in dry sand over winter, or left spread out? Either way is satisfactory. It should be kept in temperature of at least 50° F. Leave roots on.

IXIA

Will you give me cultural directions for ixia and sparaxis? Read answers under Freesia. Ixia and sparaxis need exactly the same treatment.

LACHENALIA (CAPE-COWSLIP)

Will you give me the detailed cultural needs of lachenalia (cape-cowslips)? Plant bulbs close together in early fall, in pots or hanging baskets containing light soil. Treat same as freesias.

Which varieties of lachenalia would you recommend to a beginner? *Pendula* (red and yellow) and *aurea* (golden yellow) are the easiest to find.

LEUCOCORYNE (GLORY-OF-THE-SUN)

What is glory-of-the-sun, and how is it grown? A tender, bulbous plant from the uplands of Chile named *Leucocoryne ixioides*. It is handled indoors like freesias. Avoid high temperatures and grow in sunny, airy situation. Blooms late winter and spring.

LYCORIS RADIATA

I have 3 bulbs of Lycoris radiata in a pot in the house. They have been potted since September. Why haven't they bloomed? Is there anything I can do to encourage bloom? *Lycoris radiata* often passes its bloom season. July and August are best months to plant these. Work a tablespoonful of superphosphate for each bulb into the surface soil.

MONTBRETIA

Will you describe culture of montbretia? It needs essentially the same care as gladiolus. The corms are, however, rather hardier, and in favored places may be left in ground over winter if given a very heavy mulch.

OXALIS

How should one grow the tender kinds of oxalis bulbs? Pot during August in light, fertile soil. Space bulbs 2 or 3 ins. apart just below surface. Water carefully at first; freely when growth has developed. Give plenty of sunshine; temperature of 50° to 60° F. Feed when pots are filled with roots. After flowering, gradually reduce water, and finally dry completely and rest.

POLIANTHES (TUBEROSE)

Will you give me some information on tuberoses? (Washington, D.C.) Purchase good bulbs of tuberose (*Polianthes tuberosa*), plant outdoors in full sun and light, fertile soil after ground has warmed up. Lift in fall and store dry in temperature of 60° F.

RANUNCULUS

Ranunculus bulbs sent from California arrived after ground was frozen. Can I successfully plant them in spring? How should I treat them during winter? Store in dry sand or peat moss in cool but frostproof cellar or shed. Plant 2 ins. deep, 6 ins. apart, as soon as ground can be worked in spring. Make soil friable with plenty of leafmold and sand. Position should be moist and lightly shaded. Tuberous-rooted varieties are dug and stored through winter.

SCHIZOSTYLIS (KAFIR-LILY)

Will you give me instructions for growing the Kafir-lily (schizostylis) in New Jersey?   Plant in spring in well-prepared, light, fertile soil in a deep cold frame. Keep sash off in summer, but protect in fall and winter. Water freely during growing season.

SPREKELIA (JACOBEAN-LILY)

In California I saw a lily called Jacobean-lily that looked like a curious crimson orchid. What is it? How can one grow it?   *Sprekelia formosissima* (sometimes sold as *Amaryllis formosissima*). Plant bulbs 6 ins. deep in light, fertile loam, in a sunny position after all danger of frost is over. Water freely when foliage is above ground and fertilize while in active growth with any complete fertilizer. In cold climates lift after first frost and store bulbs above freezing through winter; remove tops but *leave roots on.* Sprekelia also makes an interesting pot plant for indoors and is usually offered for such use in fall catalogues.

TIGRIDIA

What soil and situation do tigerflowers (tigridias) prefer?   A warm, well-drained soil and a sunny situation. Plant same time as gladiolus. Take up and store in same way.

TUBEROSE   See Polianthes

OTHER BULBS

I understand there are a number of South African bulbs that need very much the same treatment as freesias. Will you please list some of these?   Ixia, sparaxis, babiana, antholyza, tritonia, crocosmia, lapeirousia, ornithogalum, and lachenalia.

What is the best way of propagating ixia, sparaxis, tritonia, and similar South African or "cape" bulbs?   They all multiply quickly by offsets. These can be removed and planted in bulb pans, about an inch apart, at potting time. They are also very readily raised from seed.

6
Roses

ROSES ARE so closely associated with the painting, literature, music, and even the politics of the world that they have for many centuries been an integral part of our culture. The rose is the very symbol of beauty and loveliness. Since the dawn of history it has been admired, appreciated, and linked with all kinds of human activities. It would be difficult to find an individual who could not recognize a rose—the best known and most loved of all our cultivated plants, and truly the "queen of flowers." Its majestic form, gorgeous colorings, and delightful perfume are unsurpassed. Even the thorns command respect. It is the standard of perfection by which all other flowers are judged.

Contrary to widely held opinions, roses are not difficult to grow. Their presence around long-deserted houses is evidence of their tenacity.

Many new homeowners harbor the mistaken idea that roses are specialists' plants, and that the beginning gardener, with very limited space at his disposal, would do well not to attempt growing them—except of course, for the ubiquitous climber or two at the front door or along a fence.

It is quite true that such roses are better than none at all, but no true flower lover will—or should—be content until he has in his garden at least a half dozen or so of the modern bush roses to provide flowers for enjoyment both in the garden and as cut flower decoration indoors.

The often-heard argument that roses "require so much care" scarcely seems to hold when one considers that the modern garden varieties give flowers almost continuously from late May into October or November, while most other hardy flowers are in bloom for little more than two or three weeks. And many of the splendid new varieties developed during the last decade or two, especially in Floribunda and the new Grandiflora groups, have remarkable vigor and hardiness. The development of improved "all-purpose" controls for insect pests and diseases has greatly simplified rose culture for the amateur and gone far to assure success even to the least experienced beginner, so we have really reached the day when there should be roses in *every* garden.

Roses give more in proportion to time spent than any other flower. They respond to every bit of attention but they do survive some neglect, given a good start in life. Roses provide about seven months of bloom in the Middle Atlantic states and even more in warmer climates. They are versatile enough for many landscape purposes, as they vary from tall shrubs suitable for accent or background planting to dwarf polyanthas for edging and tiny miniatures for pots. They can be used as boundary hedges or to line a driveway or walk. They climb over fences and walls and sprawl as ground covers. They can be planted in small groups through the perennial border as well as grown by themselves in formal beds. More and more roses are now being grown in tubs on patios or penthouse terraces and the many Mini-Rose Shows in February and March attest to the popularity of miniature roses grown indoors under lights.

More than 10,000 worldwide rose cultivars (varieties) are registered with the International Registration Authority, and the *Handbook for Selecting Roses,* published by the American Rose Society, lists about 1,000 varieties as presumably currently available in this country. Unfortunately, as fine new roses flood the market, many old favorites disappear. Except for firms that specialize in old roses, individual nurseries seldom offer more than 100 to 200 varieties in a year. To find the rose you want, you may have to hunt through catalogues of nurseries in several different states. Remember that it does not matter where your rose is grown—California, Georgia, Ohio, Oregon, Pennsylvania, New York, or Texas—so long as it is a variety hardy in your climate. Naturally a tender tea from the South may not live in New York, but a hybrid tea from that area will do very well, if it can be procured for your best planting time.

—*Cynthia Westcott*

SELECTING PLANTS

What are the main types or classes of roses?

HYBRID PERPETUAL, abbreviated as HP. Vigorous, hardy roses, mostly June-blooming, but some varieties repeat during the summer and autumn.

HYBRID TEA, HT, or IIIA in numerical classification. Derived from crossing the more tender tea roses with hybrid perpetuals. Flowers usually produced singly and intermittently through the season. Bushes in this popular class are usually planted in separate beds.

GRANDIFLORA, Gr, IIIB. Flowers with form of hybrid teas, borne singly or in clusters.

FLORIBUNDA, F., IIIC. A hybrid between polyantha and the tea rose, hardy, with larger flowers than the polyantha and produced abundantly all season.

POLYANTHA, Pol., IIID. Usually small plant bearing large clusters of small flowers, hardy, recurrent.

MINIATURE, Min., IIIE. Fairy roses, flowers less than 1 in. across, single or in clusters; plants seldom more than 12 ins. high.

LARGE-FLOWERED CLIMBER. Large flowers and mostly recurrent bloom, produced on old wood.

RAMBLER, R. Usually one annual bloom of small flowers in large clusters on new wood.

TEA, T. Fragrant roses, blooming profusely in the South, a few varieties surviving in the North.

SHRUB, S. This is a catchall class, including many rose species and their hybrids.

There are also climbing forms of hybrid teas, grandifloras, floribundas, and polyanthas. In rose shows these are classed as hybrid teas, etc., and not as climbers.

Tree or standard roses are manufactured by budding a hybrid tea or other type at the top of a straight trunk.

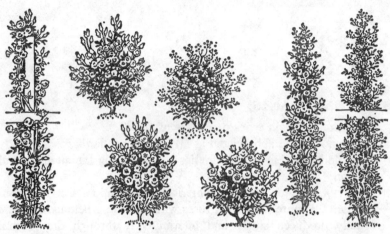

Types of roses: left, Climbing Hybrid Tea; center top, Hybrid Perpetual and Polyantha; center bottom, Hybrid Tea and Floribunda; right, Large-flowered Climber and Rambler.

What about rose colors? Roses are color-classified into the following groups: ab, apricot blend; dr, dark red; dy, deep yellow; lp, light pink; dp, deep pink; m, mauve; mp, medium pink; my, medium yellow; ob, orange and orange blend; or, orange red; pb, pink blend; r, russet; rb, red blend; w, white or near white; yb, yellow blend.

What are the standard rose grades? No. 1, three or more strong canes; No. 1½, two or more strong canes; No. 2, two or more canes; No. 3, one cane. The best grades will have longer canes but these are usually cut back before they are mailed from the nursery.

What age plants should be purchased? Two-year-old field-grown plants, with the No. 1 grade, usually give the best results.

Is it advantageous to buy climbing roses that are 5 or 6 years old?

No, the younger, 2-year plant becomes established sooner and is more successful.

Are cheap roses offered by nurseries a good investment? No, you get what you pay for. The original cost of a good rose is small compared to later care. Cheap roses may be poor grade or outworn bench roses from a greenhouse.

Should one buy budded or own-root stock? Almost all roses sold by nurseries are budded stock. Sometimes hedge roses are on their own roots.

General Culture

LOCATION

Can you grow roses in semi-shade? Roses need at least 6 hours of full sunlight each day to grow well, but some manage to bloom with a little less. Morning sun is preferable; light shade in the afternoon is an advantage in hot weather.

Do roses require a special type of soil? Almost any garden soil can be amended to grow roses. The ideal type is a well-aerated, slightly acid, medium-heavy loam containing an abundance of organic matter. Sandy soils and clay soils can both be improved by plenty of organic matter—peat moss, leafmold, well-rotted manure, compost.

Do roses like wet or dry feet? Roses require good drainage. Dig a hole 18 ins. deep, fill it with water. If this does not soak away in a few hours choose another location or have tile drains installed.

SOIL PREPARATION

How deep should the soil be prepared for a rose bed? The old rule was 2 to 3 ft.; now we find 18 ins. is sufficient, even though the roots may go much deeper.

How do you prepare a new rose bed? The standard method has been as follows: Remove the soil to a depth of approximatcly 18 ins., keeping the topsoil and subsoil separate. Next put back a 6-in. layer of the topsoil in the bottom of the bed. Add 3 ins. of compost, peat moss, or other type of organic matter; fork it in thoroughly. Shovel in another 6-in. layer, and work in more organic matter; last, fill the bed with the subsoil mixed with more organic matter.

Is there a short cut?   Yes, you can take out the first spade depth and then improve the second 9 ins. of soil in place. Fork it thoroughly, incorporating plenty of peat moss, some dehydrated manure or rotted manure, and superphosphate, about 3 lbs. per 100 sq. ft. Work in more of the same as you replace the topsoil.

Should you use lime as you prepare the bed?   Only if a soil test shows a pH value of 5 or lower. Use ground limestone or common agricultural lime (not hydrated lime) at the rate of 3 to 6 lbs. per 100 sq. ft. of ground area, depending on the degree of acidity.

Why will roses not do well in a sweet or alkaline soil?   The iron in an alkaline soil is insoluble, and thus unavailable to plants. All garden plants require iron to form chlorophyll (the green coloring matter in the leaves); absorption of iron is interfered with in a lightly alkaline soil.

What is the appearance of rose plants when the soil is too alkaline? The veins of the leaves become dark green and the area between mottled with yellow. In severe cases, the leaves may become almost pure white.

How do you acidify soil for roses?   Soil may be made slightly acid by mixing in finely powdered sulfur, 1 to 3 lbs. per 100 sq. ft.

Can aluminum sulfate be used to acidify soil for roses?   Aluminum sulfate is less desirable than powdered sulfur. It is more expensive, less easy to obtain, and more has to be used. In large quantities, it may be harmful, but it is quick-acting.

Will peat moss, used in preparing the bed, acidify the soil?   Peat moss, if used in large enough quantities, will temporarily increase soil acidity. Its effect is not permanent and the peat moss-soil mixture gradually returns to nearly the pH value of the original soil. It is, of course, highly important as a source of humus and in improving the mechanical condition of the soil.

What special treatments do roses growing in a sandy soil require? Working into the soil an abundance of organic material; watering during dry periods; and 2 or 3 applications of a mixed commercial fertilizer during the growing season.

Is it necessary to have a clay soil for success with roses? Not at all. Some of the best rose gardens are found in regions where the soil is light and sandy. Almost any type of soil can be improved for roses by proper treatment.

How much peat moss should be used? On very heavy clay soils as much as 50 per cent by volume may be incorporated. Ordinarily 25 per cent by volume is satisfactory. This means 1 bu. of peat to each 3 bu. of soil.

How should peat moss be used in preparing the soil for roses? It is best to mix it thoroughly with the soil if a new bed is being prepared. Where individual plants are set in to replace those that have died, mix the peat moss with the soil that is used to fill in around the plant.

Should the peat moss be moistened before it is mixed with the soil? It is not necessary, but a thorough soaking of the soil and added ingredients is necessary after planting.

What kind of peat moss is best? Any of the commonly available brands of peat moss (sphagnum moss peat) are satisfactory. It should be fibrous and thoroughly granulated. The more thoroughly decomposed sedge and muck peats are less beneficial.

Can both peat moss and manure be used? Yes, they make an excellent combination. A mixture of 1 bu. of manure, 2 bu. of peat moss, and 10 bu. of soil is ideal.

What kinds of organic material can be used in preparing rose soil, other than peat moss and manure? Leafmold is satisfactory and can be used at the rate of 1 bu. to 5 bu. of soil. Compost, muck, seaweed, and various commercial organic materials can be used.

I have access to chicken manure. Can it be used on roses? If so, when? It is a satisfactory fertilizer if it has been allowed to rot somewhat before using. It is advisable to put it on in the late fall or very early spring; or mix with soil at planting time.

How much chicken manure can be used on roses? One bu. for each 100 sq. ft. can be used with safety.

PLANTING

What is the best time to plant roses? It depends on where you live. Spring planting is safest in Minnesota and winter planting, mid-December to mid-February, is best in California and much of the South. November planting is sometimes recommended for winter blooms in Florida. For the temperate states, November planting allows first choice of varieties from the nursery and the bushes are out of the ground a very short time, but in many nurseries the roses are not hardened off enough to ship in the fall before your ground becomes frozen. Spring planting is therefore somewhat safer.

How can roses be kept if they arrive before planting time? Nurserymen try to ship plants for arrival at your correct planting time; set them out immediately if you can. If you must wait a few days, keep the unopened package in a cool place.

Should rose plants be heeled in if planting is too long delayed? Yes. Dig a trench about 12 ins. deep; pack the plants closely in the trench, at an angle, and cover roots and part of the canes with soil. Plant within 3 weeks.

What do I do when ready to plant? Unpack the box in the shade and away from wind; trim off broken roots or canes, then put in a pail of water. You can plant immediately or let soak for a few hours, but not longer than overnight.

How may one prepare the soil for individual plants set in to fill out a bed? Dig a hole large enough to accommodate the plant. Mix the required amount of peat moss with the soil that was removed, and use the mixture to fill in around the plant.

How deep should roses be planted? In most areas the bud union (a "bump" at top of roots) should be at ground level. If this "bump" is exposed to the sun there will be more basal breaks. In very cold climates the bush is set an inch or two deeper and in the South the bud union is placed an inch or two above ground level.

How far apart should roses be planted? In favorable climates where they make vigorous growth, they should be farther apart than in cold areas. An average would be 2 ft. apart for most hybrid tea and floribunda varieties, 3 ft. for hybrid perpetuals, 6 to 8 ft. for climbers, but about 1 ft. for miniatures.

How large a hole should be dug for a rose plant? It depends on the size of the root system but if the roots are too long, they should be cut off and not coiled around in the hole. You may need a hole about 18 ins. across and 12 ins. or more deep.

Should the roots be placed straight downward or spread out horizontally? Usually you make a soil mound in the hole and spread the roots out and down over this.

Is it necessary to firm the soil when planting rosebushes? Yes, as you add the soil, firm it in with your fingers and then, when the hole is ⅔ full, step around the bush, so that no air space is left. Then fill the hole with water and let it soak away before you add the rest of the soil, which is left loose. After that, mound soil around the canes to about 8 ins.

In planting roses, the soil should be thoroughly firmed about the roots.

Why do you mound the soil around newly planted bushes in spring? To keep the canes from drying out while the root system becomes established. This is very important in giving the rose a good start in life. Remove this extra soil in a couple of weeks in spring; leave it on all winter after fall planting.

Are potted roses satisfactory and how late in the season can they be planted? Rose plants grown in large tar-paper pots are available from many rose growers and at local garden centers. If you cannot plant dormant, bare-root roses early in the season it is wise to buy potted roses. There is a better selection in May and June, but they can be planted as long as they are available.

How should potted roses be planted? Dig a large hole, cut off the bottom of the pot, and set in the hole. Slit the tar paper down the side and carefully remove it without breaking the root-ball. Fill in around the ball with earth mixed with peat moss. The bud union should be at ground level as with other roses, but you do not mound after planting a potted rose—which is usually in full growth and even in flower.

TRANSPLANTING

Should rosebushes be moved periodically? No. Once a rose is established, it is best not to move it.

Can old rosebushes be transplanted? Transplanting old bushes (10 to 15 years) is advisable only on a limited scale. Old plants do not send out new roots readily and it can take them several years to become re-established. Transplant in the fall and take as much soil as possible with the roots.

How can I move a large climbing rose without danger of losing it? Do not try to move the plant without drastic pruning. Cut out all but 4 or 5 young, vigorous canes. Lift the plant carefully with a ball of soil.

Is it better to move an old rosebush than to buy a new one? Not unless it is an old favorite no longer available.

Can roses be transplanted after the ground begins to freeze or should they be stored over winter in the basement in case it is necessary to move them? Move to the new location even if the ground is somewhat frozen. If you know they must be moved, mulch the new location with straw or leaves to keep it from freezing. After transplanting, mound soil as high as possible around the canes.

PRUNING

Do you prune new bushes when planting? They are usually pruned sufficiently in the nursery. Wait until they start to grow and then some limited pruning may be required. If so, cut back to the new shoots.

Is it better to prune in the fall or in spring? Always in spring. In autumn you may cut back extra tall canes that might whip in the wind, but leave the rest to spring—unless you are an exhibitor cutting back to fit under rose cones for winter.

Does severe pruning result in more vigorous plants? Not usually. Exhibitors may prune and feed rather heavily but for long-lived, vigorous bushes you need plenty of foliage to manufacture food. Moderate pruning allows more flowers that are still of excellent size.

How far back do you cut hybrid tea roses in the spring? That depends on the amount of winter injury. Cut back to sound wood,

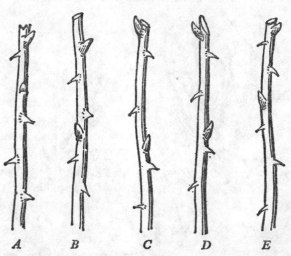

*How to prune a rose. A – ragged cut, won't heal. B – cut too far above
bud. C – cut too close to bud. D – cut too slanting, comes below bud.
E – Right! Slight slant about ¼ inch above bud.*

preferably the size of a lead pencil, remove diseased or weak growth,
branches that cross each other in the center of the bush, and any
candelabra-type of growth.

How far above a bud should a cut be made?   Make a slanting cut
in the direction of the bud and as close to it as is safe—leaving not
more than a ¼-in. stub.

Is it always necessary to make the cut where a bud points outward?
Not always, but it helps to keep the interior of the bush open. It is
more important to cut above a sound bud that is starting to grow.
With a sprawling variety like 'Crimson Glory', cutting to some inside
buds keeps the bush more upright.

Should roses be pruned with a knife or pruning shears?   Use
pruning shears rather than a knife. A good pair of sharp, pruning,
curved-edge shears are fine and less apt to injure canes than the
straight-cut type of pruning shears. For old heavy canes you may
need lopping shears.

Do you prune grandifloras the same way as hybrid teas?   Essentially. Some, like 'Queen Elizabeth', are rather tall and might be
pruned somewhat higher.

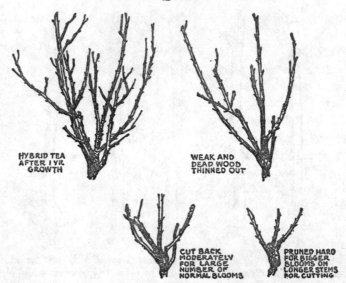

Pruning garden or bush roses of the hybrid-tea type.

What about polyanthas and floribundas? Remove all the dead and injured wood, but for masses of color display, cut back less than hybrid teas.

Are the large-flowered climbers pruned any differently from the ramblers? Yes. Old-fashioned ramblers, such as 'Dorothy Perkins', usually bloom on canes produced the previous summer. Hence, after June bloom, some of the old canes are removed at ground level and the new ones tied to supports.

The large-flowered climbers bloom on older wood. Clean out dead wood, etc. in spring and prune as necessary for the space. Some varieties, such as 'Mrs. Arthur Curtiss James' and 'Dr. J. H. Nicolas', do best if the main canes are trained horizontally and the lateral growth cut back to a foot or so from the cane.

How should shrub roses be pruned? A few of the older canes should be cut back to the ground each spring to encourage the growth of basal shoots. This helps rejuvenate the plants. If growth becomes thick, remove some of the upper branches.

How are tree roses pruned? Remove all weak or dead wood from the top and cut back the main canes to about 6 to 8 ins. from the crown. Take off all suckers that start to develop on the trunk, or from the base.

What is the best way to cut off fading flowers? Removal of dead blooms is another pruning operation. On newly planted or low-growing bushes make the cut above the first 5-leaflet leaf and close to it. If flowers are wanted for the house, canes on established bushes can be cut lower, but never below the last two leaves on a cane.

How do you summer-prune large-flowered climbers? If the variety repeats bloom through the summer, cut off the fading flowers, as for hybrid teas, and shorten the lateral canes as necessary to prevent too vigorous growth. If the climber is a once-bloomer, leave the dead flowers to produce attractive hips (seeds) in the fall.

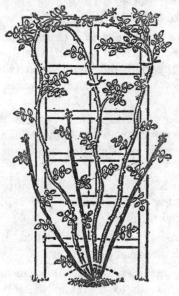

Climbing roses of the rambler type, which flower on new wood of the current season's growth, are pruned, just after flowering, by cutting old canes back to the ground (as indicated by dotted lines in sketch), thus leaving room for the husky new canes.

FERTILIZING

When is the best time to fertilize roses? Feed established roses soon after pruning but wait several months before feeding newly planted bushes—except for any fertilizer mixed in the planting hole.

Are commercial fertilizers good for roses? A mixed commercial fertilizer, 5–10–5 or comparable grade, is satisfactory. Apply one to two trowelfuls per bush, lightly worked into the soil but not touching the canes. Mixing this with dehydrated cow manure is helpful, or you may prefer a special rose food with an organic base.

How often do roses need fertilizer?   One rule has been a ground feeding in early spring, another about the time of heavy June bloom, and a third in early August. Some rosarians make lighter feedings more often, and exhibitors may feed quite heavily before a rose show.

Can you feed through the foliage?   Yes. Foliar feeding makes a very good supplement. Make one good ground feeding after pruning and then add a foliar food (Rapid-Gro or Miracle-Gro) to the pesticide spray every week or two during the summer. In this case, omit the later ground feedings. In most areas, do not feed after mid-August, allowing the bush to harden its growth for winter.

How can one tell when roses need fertilizer?   The leaves are a light yellowish-green, plants fail to make lush, vigorous growth.

How do roses look when they are overfertilized?   Usually the growth is stunted, stems short, flowers small. New shoots fail to develop promptly after the first blooming period; midsummer and fall bloom is reduced. The tips of the feeding roots, normally white, appear brown.

What can be done if roses have been overfertilized?   Very heavy watering on several days in succession will leach out some of the excess nutrients. Working in peat moss or shredded sugarcane (bagasse) may help.

Can manure be used as a fertilizer?   Manure is an excellent source of organic matter in the soil and a rather weak fertilizer. Use it in conjunction with a complete commercial fertilizer.

Is horse manure satisfactory for roses?   Yes. If well-rotted, it can be applied as a mulch or mixed with the soil at planting time.

Is there any danger in using bone meal on roses?   Bone meal contains a large portion of lime, which tends to "sweeten" the soil. If the soil is already neutral or alkaline bone meal might make the pH too high for best growth. However, bone meal is usually applied to supply phosphorus, and for this purpose, it is too slow-acting. Superphosphate is better.

Is there anything better than bone meal as a fertilizer for roses? Superphosphate is quicker-acting and more effective as a source of phosphorus. It can be used at the rate of 3 lbs. per 100 sq. ft. It is best used in the initial preparation of a bed; thereafter the "complete" commercial fertilizer should supply sufficient phosphorus.

Are wood ashes good for roses?   Yes, if the soil is acid; they contain potash and lime. Use at rate of 4–5 oz. per square yard. If the soil is neutral, the ashes might make it too alkaline.

Are there any roses that should not be fertilized?   Yes, the shrub rose *Rosa hugonis* does best in poor soil; it can die if fed.

Can cottonseed meal be used as a rose fertilizer without making the soil too acid?   Yes, unless the soil already has a low pH. It is often used as a base in special rose foods.

MULCHING

Is it better to cultivate or to mulch rose beds?   Mulching is preferable because it reduces the amount of labor, helps to retain soil moisture, keeps the soil cool, and does not disturb the roots. If there is no mulch, there should be *very shallow* cultivation every week or so.

What materials are best for mulching?   Whatever is readily available in your area: buckwheat hulls, cocoa shells, bagasse (sugarcane refuse), ground corn cobs, wood chips, pine needles, or sometimes partially decayed leaves.

Is peat moss a good mulch?   Peat moss is far better incorporated into the soil and not used on top. As a mulch, it cakes readily so that water flows off the bed rather than down into it.

When do you apply the mulch?   In spring, after pruning and fertilizing. Cultivate the soil first, to remove all weeds. If no winter protection is required, the mulch may be left in place all year, adding a little more as it decomposes.

Can mulches be worked into the soil to increase the organic content?   Some can, but buckwheat hulls can be slightly injurious to plant growth in the soil. They are best left on top and not used too deep; about an inch of mulch is sufficient.

WATERING

Is it a good plan to water roses in dry weather?   Roses like plenty of water. They will make more growth and produce more flowers if *thoroughly* watered about once a week, unless there is sufficient rainfall.

What is the best way to water roses?   To be most effective the soil should be soaked to a depth of at least 5 or 6 ins. A light sprinkling on top does more harm than good. It is best not to wet the foliage because this spreads the black-spot disease, but if you must use an overhead sprinkler, water in the morning so the foliage can dry off before evening.

How can roses be watered without wetting the foliage?   Use a soil-soaker hose (a hose perforated with holes) or a Waterwand; or let a gentle stream of water from the hose flow over a board into the bed. Some ardent rosarians install subirrigation systems.

What happens in a prolonged drought when water is restricted? The roses will survive but go into semi-dormancy, producing few new flowers. Never fertilize unless you can also water. Mulching helps conserve soil moisture.

PEST CONTROL For more detailed information see Section 13, Plant Troubles and Their Control.

What are the most common and harmful rose pests?   The more common insects include aphids, leafhoppers, roseslugs, rose chafers, Japanese beetles, and thrips; sometimes borers, rose scale, rose midge, rose curculio, budworms, and leaf tiers. Red spiders (mites, not true insects) are almost always present. Black spot is the most devastating rose disease, causing defoliation and occasionally death if uncontrolled. Powdery mildew, more common in late summer, is conspicuous with its powdery white coating over the foliage and may deform buds and flowers but it is not lethal. Rust and cankers are occasional problems.

Some common diseases of roses.

What is the best way to keep roses healthy? Start at time of spring pruning by cutting below the work of pith borers and removing cankered canes. Then, beginning when the leaves are fully out, spray weekly with an all-purpose mixture. This should include one or two insecticides, usually malathion and carbaryl (Sevin), sometimes methoxychlor or Meta-Systox-R or dimethoate; a miticide, Kelthane, Tedion, or chlorobenzilate; and a fungicide, folpet (Phaltan), maneb, or Benlate. The latter is best for powdery mildew but no better than folpet for black spot. Maneb has been used more in the South for black spot and zineb on the West Coast for rust. Satisfactory combinations of these materials are available under many trade names. The chemical ingredients of a spray mixture are always listed on the container.

Does spraying give better control of rose pests than dusting? It is somewhat more effective but either will do if the pesticide is applied often enough and the under sides of the foliage are protected.

I read an article on roses which said that they should be sprayed with 4–4–50 Bordeaux mixture. Should I? No, this remedy is outmoded. The copper in it is too strong for roses and can cause defoliation nearly as bad as black spot. The newer fungicides are much safer.

Are there any roses that don't require spraying? Yes, there are some that survive for years without spraying—despite visitations by an occasional pest. Try 'The Fairy', a shrub polyantha, or 'Vanguard', a hybrid rugosa, or the climber 'New Dawn', or 'Betty Prior', a floribunda. Most hybrid teas are so susceptible to black spot that they do need some treatment.

How can mice be controlled in the rose garden? Poisoned grain should be placed under the mulch, at frequent intervals in small open containers that will protect it from becoming wet. A jelly tumbler laid on its side and covered with a piece of board serves the purpose. However, mice populations fluctuate from year to year. Some years they do very little damage. A cat or two is a help and less tedious than preparing the poison grain.

SUMMER CARE AND PROBLEMS

Should roses be disbudded? Yes, if cut roses are desired for the home or exhibition. For garden display, there can be partial disbudding of hybrid teas and hybrid perpetuals, but not of polyanthas and floribundas, buds of which are left to produce an abundance of flowers.

How does one disbud roses?   Just as soon as the secondary buds become visible, pinch them out, leaving the largest or top one to flower.

How do I recognize a sucker?   A sucker is a rose shoot arising from the rootstock of a budded or grafted plant. It will come from below the bud union and the foliage will differ from that of the good rose. Multiflora understock has dull, light-green foliage and, if allowed to bloom, small white flowers. 'Dr. Huey' understock has reddish foliage and red flowers.

How do I get rid of suckers?   Cut them out just as soon as noticed but be sure you don't confuse them with basal breaks of the budded rose.

Do all suckers have 7 leaflets to a leaf?   Not all; some understocks have 5 leaflets and some hybrid teas and climbers can produce leaves with seven leaflets. You must note the type of foliage rather than the number of leaflets to be sure that a new shoot is understock rather than a good basal break.

Can roses revert to a wild form?   No. If you see flowers of a different type and color from the variety purchased it means that the growth from the understock has overpowered and killed the budded rose. Discard and order another plant.

Should I keep tree roses on which the top has died but which are sending up new shoots from the base?   No, these are understock and the plant is worthless.

What causes roses to be lighter-colored at some seasons than at others?   The more foliage on the plant the brighter and more intense the coloring. Cool weather increases the color because less of the food from which the pigment is manufactured is used up in respiration. Rose blooms are always paler and smaller in summer heat and sun.

Will iron or rusty cans have any effect in changing the color or shading of a rose?   No.

Why are my 'Talisman' roses pale yellow instead of their real

color? Perhaps the plant was incorrectly labeled, perhaps too-bright sun.

Some of the shoots on my new hybrid tea did not develop into flower buds. Why? No one knows for sure the reason for these blind shoots. It happens more frequently on new bushes and some varieties are more apt to have blind shoots than others. Usually, if you cut the shoot back a few inches it will later produce a flower.

WINTER PROTECTION

Is winter protection necessary? Definitely *yes* in Minnesota, Maine, and other cold states, definitely *not* in the South and California, and probably not in many other areas. After growing roses for 50 years in New York and New Jersey, I now believe that the necessity for winter protection in this region is a myth. I mounded roses as recommended for the first half of this period but no rose has been hilled in the past 25 years. I have lost a few bushes to crowding, too much shade, too deep planting, crown gall, and chipmunks but never, to my knowledge, to lack of winter protection.

Summer treatment is the key to winter safety. A rose without plenty of food reserve in its canes, depleted by repeated defoliation from black spot, may die no matter how well protected for winter.

If protection is necessary, what is the best method? Mounding (hilling) has been the standard method. Hoeing up soil from between plants can disturb or expose roots; bring it in from the vegetable garden or the annual garden or compost pile. Pour about a pail into the center of each bush, making a natural hill, about 8 ins. high. In temperate climates, do not add straw or salt hay; this encourages field or pine mice and is too difficult to remove in spring.

When should the soil be mounded? After frost but before the ground freezes hard—November in southern New York.

Can leaves be used for winter protection? In regions where there is alternate freezing and thawing, leaves keep the canes too wet and encourage canker fungi. In Vermont, where things stay frozen, I have seen roses that wintered well, covered with 3 ft. of leaves, held in place with a chicken wire fence, and no soil mounds.

Is manure satisfactory for mounding around roses? Not for mounding. It should never touch the canes, but rotted manure can be applied to the valleys between soil mounds after the ground freezes.

Is it all right to use peat moss around roses for winter protection? Peat moss retains too much moisture and increases canker diseases. It is much better put into the soil when the bed is prepared.

Should tar-paper collars be placed around rose plants to hold the soil high around the stems? No. Unless they are covered on top they will let in too much rain and keep the canes wet.

Is it all right to cut hybrid teas to about 8 ins. from the ground before protecting for winter? No. Prune as little as possible in autumn. If you are using rose cones (see next question) instead of mounding, you may have to cut back to 12 to 18 ins., depending on height of cone.

What are rose cones? Lightweight cone-shaped covers made of plastic or styrofoam, with a lid on top that can be opened for air when it is too warm. The cone is used in place of a soil mound but the cone has to be held in place with earth or stones. Cones are mostly used by ardent rose exhibitors.

Is it all right to cover rosebushes with peach baskets during the winter? If the temperature goes very low, mound up with soil before putting on the basket.

How do I winter roses in Minnesota? Some rosarians in your state have adopted what they call the Minnesota tip method. They dig trenches between the rows of roses, loosen the roots on one side of a bush, tip it into the trench, and cover with more soil.

How should climbing roses be protected? When the temperature does not drop below 0° F., no protection is needed for the hardy varieties. Where temperatures between 0° and 10° below can be expected, mound soil over the base of plants. In more severe climates remove the canes from their support and pin close to the ground, then cover with soil.

How can tree roses be protected in cold climates? Remove the stake, loosen one side of the earth ball, lay the rose down on the ground, or into a trench, and cover top, trunk, and exposed roots with soil.

Is wrapping with burlap sufficient protection for tree roses in New York State? Not unless the winter is very mild and the plants are in a sheltered situation. Sometimes hybrid perpetual trees winter without much protection.

Do miniature roses require special protection? Miniatures are very hardy. If floribundas winter without protection in your area, so will miniatures. I never cover them near New York City. Miniatures can, however, be brought into the house in January (after some freezing weather), pruned a little, and forced on the window sill or under lights. Return them to the garden in May.

How shall I treat a rosebush that has been growing on the patio all summer in a tub? Move it into an unheated garage. If the tub is very large, so that the roots cannot freeze, it might be left outside in a sheltered location. A gardener who grows floribundas and climbers on a New York City terrace reports that they winter there safely without protection. But the minimum size of container is 14 ins. in all dimensions and preferably larger.

DISPLAYING ROSES

What time of day should roses be cut, either for the house or for exhibition? Late afternoon is best, with early morning next choice.

How long a stem should be taken? Only as long as actually needed, with a little leeway for later trimming. The less foliage removed from the plant, the better. Be sure to leave at least two leaves above where the stem joins the main cane. And cut just above a leaf, without leaving any stub.

CUT POINTED BUDS WHEN FAIRLY TIGHT   GLOBULAR VARIETIES WHEN PARTLY OPEN   2 LEAVES AND EYES LEFT ON STEM   TO DEVELOP NEW BUDS

How to cut a rose.

Do you plunge cut rose stems into cold water? Contrary to former advice, it is best to place cut stems into warm water immediately; it rises faster in the stem. If water is not available as the roses are cut and they start to wilt, they can be revived. Bring a shallow pan of water to boiling, turn off the heat, and insert the lower inch of stem while you count to 10.

What further conditioning is done? Keep containers in a cool, dark place away from drafts. If they must be held for exhibition more than overnight, keep in a refrigerator at about 35° F.

Are the flower preservatives satisfactory for keeping roses? Yes, they do prolong the life of cut roses. Sugar may be just as effective.

Can you time rose blooming for a show by pruning? Hard pruning in spring means bloom about a week later than moderate pruning. For a fall show, roses are pruned back a little about 40 to 55 days before the show, the number of days depending on the variety.

How are roses judged? Points are given for form, color, substance, stem and foliage, balance and proportion, and size, with emphasis on form.

What is meant by form? When judged, the rose should be at perfection of its possible beauty. For heavy-petaled hybrid teas, this means ⅔ to ¾ open with petals unfurling in a circular pattern around a well-defined center. Roses with fewer petals are at their best when ½ to ⅔ open.

Is disbudding obligatory? Single-flowered hybrid teas should be grown naturally, but all other hybrid teas and all hybrid perpetuals must be disbudded. Grandifloras can be exhibited in a show disbudded as a single stem or as an inflorescence. Floribundas and polyanthas are not disbudded. Old garden roses (types in existence before 1867) are shown as they grow naturally, although unwanted side growth can be discreetly removed.

How do you select the right color class in a show? You must know the name of the variety and then look up the color class in the *Handbook for Selecting Roses,* published annually by the American Rose Society. There are 16 authorized color classes but not all are used in every show schedule.

Propagation

GENERAL

What different methods can be used to propagate roses? Rose varieties can be propagated by budding, grafting, cuttings, and layering.

Are own-root rose plants propagated at home as satisfactory as budded stock? They are much slower in getting started, but will usually develop into equally good plants. Some gardeners consider them longer-lived and more productive.

What is the "union" of a rose plant? The place where the bud of the desired variety was inserted on the understock in the propagation of the plant. It can usually be seen as a jointlike swollen area 2 or 3 ins. above the roots. It is just below the region from which all main branches of the plant arise.

BUDDING

Are roses propagated by budding or grafting? Most outdoor roses are budded.

What is meant by budding? Budding is a method of vegetative propagation. It means to graft by inserting a bud of one variety into the bark of another.

Why are outdoor roses budded instead of grafted? It is the simpler method for large-scale production and requires less greenhouse space and equipment.

What is the best time to bud roses? Usually in July and early August, but it can be done at any time when the bark slips readily.

How do you bud roses? Grow or procure an understock of *Rosa multiflora* or some similar species. Make a T-shaped slit in the bark just at the ground level. From the stem of the desired variety cut out a well-developed bud with the petiole of the leaf attached. Pick out the wood attached to the bark. Open the slit on the understock and insert the bud so that the bark fits close to the wood of the understock.

Wrap firmly with raffia or soft twine, but be careful not to injure the shoot bud. After 3 or 4 weeks remove the binding.

Should a home gardener try to bud roses? Yes. It is fun to do. Do not be discouraged if unsuccessful at the first attempt. Some enjoy it as a hobby and some use it to get roses no longer available commercially. But it is an infringement of the Federal Plant Patent Act to reproduce patented roses while the patent is in force.

CUTTINGS

Can roses be grown from cuttings or "slips"? Yes.

When is the best time to root rose cuttings? Rose stems will root best about the time the petals fall.

Where can one find the best cuttings on a rosebush? The flower stems make the best cuttings.

How long should a rose cutting be? Four to 5 ins. is the right length. It should contain 3 nodes.

Will a slip from a grafted plant be like the variety or the understock? It will be the same as the variety.

Will all varieties of roses root readily? The hybrid teas, polyanthas, floribundas, and most of the climbers will root easily. Hybrid perpetuals and many of the shrub and species roses do not root so well.

Should the leaves be removed from rose cuttings? Leaves that will be below the surface of the rooting medium (usually sand) in which the cuttings are placed should be removed; others should be left on.

Should the blossom be left on a rose cutting? Never. The middle and lower part of the stem make better cuttings.

What is the best material for rooting rose cuttings? Clean, sharp, medium coarse sand or a mixture of sand and peat moss.

What conditions are necessary for rooting rose cuttings? Keep the rooting medium moist. Shade during first few days with newspaper or cheesecloth. Take out any cuttings that appear to be rotting, and any leaves that fall off.

Are root-growth substances helpful in rooting roses? Yes. They usually cause cuttings to root more quickly and to produce a better root system.

Can rose cuttings be rooted in soil under a glass jar? Yes, if only a few plants are needed.

What special precautions need to be taken in rooting cuttings under a fruit jar? Select a place where the jar is shaded during the hot part of the day. Keep soil moist at all times. Do not put more than 3 cuttings under a single jar.

How long before cuttings rooted under a jar can be moved? If the cuttings are taken early in the summer, they are usually large enough to move by fall. They will need to be protected by mounding soil over them.

How does one go about removing the glass jar? Don't let too much growth develop before removing it. Select a cloudy day. Remove the jar. If the sun comes out, shade the cuttings with newspaper for a few days.

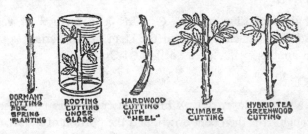

DORMANT CUTTING FOR SPRING PLANTING · ROOTING CUTTING UNDER GLASS · HARDWOOD CUTTING WITH "HEEL" · CLIMBER CUTTING · HYBRID TEA GREENWOOD CUTTING

New rose plants from cuttings.

Can cuttings be rooted in a cold frame? Yes. The soil should be removed and clean, sharp, medium coarse sand put in to a depth of 4 ins. or so. It may be necessary to keep the cuttings shaded with cheesecloth.

Can seed flats filled with sand be used for rooting rose cuttings? Yes, but they must be watched very carefully to make sure the sand doesn't dry out. Enclosing the flat in polyethylene should help.

Will spring rose cuttings withstand the winter if left in the garden? Yes, if completely covered with soil and if they are in a place where the drainage is good.

How should rose cuttings rooted during the winter be cared for? Plant out of doors in the early spring in good soil. Keep them well watered.

Where should one transplant rose "slips" (cuttings) after they are rooted? They can be planted in their permanent location, or in a nursery bed or cold frame.

How long before a cutting from a climbing rose will bloom? Ordinarily some flowers can be expected the second year after the cutting was rooted.

Can a new shoot which has come up about a foot from the original plant of variety 'Blaze' be moved? If possible, this shoot should be allowed to bloom before it is transplanted to make certain it is the same variety and not a sucker from the understock. Cut the root connection between it and the main plant the spring before it is moved. It will then develop a good root system of its own and will transplant easily.

GRAFTING

What does grafting mean? Grafting is a method of vegetative propagation by which a piece of the stem of the variety is made to grow on another plant. (See Section 3—Grafting.)

LAYERING

How are roses layered? A branch is cut a little more than halfway through. It is then bent down, and the portion of the stem where the cut was made is buried in the soil. When the branch appears to be rooted, it is severed from the plant. After a year it can be moved where desired.

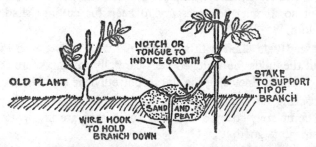

Propagating a rose by layering. New plants of many climbers can readily be obtained by this method.

SEEDS

Do roses come true from seed? Only wild species. Named varieties are hybrid plants, and every seedling will be different.

How can roses be made to set seeds? Some varieties are comparatively sterile and will set little or no seed. Try putting pollen from other varieties on the stigmas.

How does one germinate rose seed? Place the seed in small, unstoppered bottles in moist peat moss and store in a refrigerator for 3 months at 41° F. Plant seeds in soil containing ⅓ peat moss, ⅓ sand, and ⅓ soil. Keep moist and at a temperature of about 68° F. Sometimes seed planted in a protected cold frame in the fall will germinate the following spring and summer.

HYBRIDIZING

How do you "cross" roses? While the flower is still in the bud stage carefully remove all stamens before the pollen is shed. Cover emasculated flower with a cellophane or paper bag. When stigmas have developed, place some pollen of the plant selected for the male parent on them. It is desirable to repeat the pollination on several successive days. Remove the paper bag when the seed pod starts to develop.

UNDERSTOCKS

What is meant by a rose understock? Garden roses are not grown on their own roots but are budded on the stem of a wild rose grown for the purpose. The stem, upon which the rose is budded or grafted, is called the understock. (See Budding and Grafting above.)

How can one propagate his own understocks? Make hardwood cuttings 6 to 8 ins. long of smooth 1-year-old shoots of *Rosa multiflora* or other species. Remove the 2 lower eyes to prevent suckering. Callus in moist peat moss or sand at 45° F. Plant out of doors in the early spring, or root inside and plant out later. Bud during July or early August.

Where may understocks be obtained? Few rose growers offer them except in large quantities. Try rose-growing concerns.

What understocks are used for tree roses? *Rosa rugosa, Rosa* *canina,* and occasionally *Rosa multiflora.* Sometimes 'Dr. Huey' with 'De la Grifferaie' for stem portion.

Roses for Every Purpose

AUSTRIAN BRIAR

Are Austrian briars old-fashioned roses? Yes, they are hardy, bright-colored, once-blooming shrubs, derived from the species *Rosa foetida.* 'Austrian Copper' is brilliant orange-scarlet, with yellow on the reverse petals, single. 'Persian Yellow' and Harison's Yellow have small, semi-double yellow flowers.

BLACK ROSE

Is the so-called "black rose" really black? There is no truly black rose. Dark maroon 'Nigrette', 'Matador', and 'Zulu Queen' have been called black.

BLUE ROSE

Is a blue rose possible? The nearest hybridizers have come to it are mauve roses, the first of which was 'Sterling Silver'. Some red roses turn bluish as they age and there have been fraudulent claims for the violet 'Veilchenblau' as a blue rose.

BORDERS

Which rose is best to border a walk? Almost any floribunda would do and you can select from tall growers, like 'Betty Prior', medium-height 'Spartan' or 'Fashion'. Repeat-blooming hybrid rugosas would be good, such as 'Frau Dagmar Hartopp' with single pink flowers or the shrub 'Gartendirektor Otto Linne', with clusters of deep pink flowers continuously produced.

What is available for low borders? The pygmy floribundas seem to have disappeared from the market, but there are still some low polyanthas. Orange 'Margo Koster' is ideal. 'Salmon Cameo' and pink 'Cecile Brunner', 'Pinkie', or 'China Doll' are other possibilities.

What, besides miniature roses, can be used to border rose beds?
Ageratum, lobelia, sweet-alyssum, or dwarf marigolds. Don't use
primroses; they increase the red-spider problem.

CABBAGE

**Can you give me any information about the cabbage rose? Is it
suitable for the garden?** The cabbage rose (*Rosa centifolia*) is one
of the oldest roses to be cultivated. It is an excellent garden plant,
being fragrant, hardy, and producing quantities of bloom during June.

CLIMBERS

**Can I have climbers that bloom every month like hybrid teas?
(Northern New York.)** There are many large-flowered climbers that
are hardy and repeat during the summer. White: 'White Dawn',
'Pax' (a semi-climbing hybrid musk); yellow: 'Golden Showers';
pink: 'Blossomtime', 'Clair Matin', 'Dr. J. H. Nicolas', 'Inspiration',
'New Dawn', 'Rhonda'; red: 'Blaze', 'Don Juan'. Climbing hybrid teas
might not be hardy in your area but climbing 'Crimson Glory' winters
well in New Jersey.

What climbing roses are recommended for northern Vermont?
Any of the above should do if properly protected by removing the
canes from their support and pinning them close to the ground for
winter. 'Mary Wallace', a lovely pink June bloomer, seems very hardy
in Maine.

**What is the red climbing rose, somewhat like 'Paul's Scarlet'
climber, that blooms in the fall?** 'Blaze', the improved form, blooms
profusely in June and repeats all season if old flowers are promptly
cut off.

Are the climbing forms of 'World's Fair', 'Pinocchio', and 'Summer Snow' really everblooming? None of the climbing sports of
bush varieties seem to bloom as freely as the originals. These 3, however, produce flowers more or less continually through the summer,
although never in the quantity they do in June. 'Summer Snow' may
be the only one now available as a climber.

**What is the difference between a rambler and a large-flowered
climber?** Any tall-growing roses that require the support of an arbor, trellis, or similar structure, or can be trained to one, can be
classed as climbing roses. A rambler is one type of climber and is

distinguished by its long, slender canes, produced the previous season, and dense clusters of small flowers. The varieties 'Dorothy Perkins' and 'Crimson Rambler' are typical but they tend to mildew very badly. 'Chevy Chase' is a much improved 'Crimson Rambler' that seldom mildews, but it is now hard to find. 'Tausendschön' is a rose-pink rambler available from nurseries specializing in old roses. Ramblers bloom only once; they do not repeat. Most large-flowered climbers repeat during the season and they bloom on old wood.

DAMASK

Can you give me some information on the damask rose? The damask rose (*Rosa damascena*) was introduced to Europe from Asia Minor in the sixteenth century. It is one of the oldest roses in cultivation and is second only to the cabbage rose in the intensity of its perfume. It makes a good garden shrub that is hardy. *Rosa damascena* 'Trigintipetala' is used in southeastern Europe for making the celebrated attar of roses. This form is red and is also known as 'Kazanlik'. 'Marie Louise' is a deep pink damask.

How tall do damask roses grow and are they hardy? They are very hardy and grow to about 5 ft.

Is York and Lancaster a damask rose? Yes, it is white, striped with pink.

Is there a white damask? 'Mme. Hardy' has large, very full, very fragrant white flowers, occasionally tinged flesh-pink, in clusters.

EARLY BLOOMERS

What are the earliest roses to bloom? The single yellow *Rosa hugonis,* often called Father Hugo rose, blooms in early May near New York City. Yellow-white *Rosa primula* may be even earlier but is hard to obtain. By mid-May some of the Kordes roses, like 'Frühlingsmorgen', may start, along with the pink hybrid rugosa 'Frau Dagmar Hartopp', while fragrant double-yellow 'Agnes' and salmon-pink 'Vanguard' follow a bit later.

FLORIBUNDA

What are floribunda roses? Technically, they are hybrid or large-flowered polyanthas. They originated through hybridizing polyanthas with hybrid teas. The flowers are larger than those of the polyantha group but in growth and flowering habit are much like them. Because of the cluster form and repeat habit, they are very colorful all season.

What are some good floribunda roses?   White: 'Ivory Fashion', 'Iceberg', 'Saratoga'; yellow: 'Spanish Sun', 'Yellow Cushion'; yellow blend: 'Golden Slippers', 'Redgold'; pink: 'Betty Prior', 'Bon Bon', 'Gene Boerner', 'Gruss an Aachen'; pink blend: 'Fabergé', 'Fashion', 'Vogue'; orange blend: 'Orangeade', 'Woburn Abbey'; orange red: 'Fire King', 'Ginger', 'Sarabande', 'Spartan'; red: 'Europeana', 'Frensham', 'Red Pinocchio'; mauve: 'Angel Face', 'Lilac Charm', 'Lilac Dawn'.

Do floribundas have a longer blooming period than hybrid teas? Not by the calendar. Hybrid teas usually come into bloom a week or more ahead of floribundas, but the latter produce more flowers during the summer.

Are there floribundas especially good for corsages?   Yes. White 'Corsage' is fine for small flowers, 'Cupid's Charm', a pink blend of hybrid-tea quality, is excellent for this purpose, along with yellow blend 'Little Darling'.

Can floribundas be used with other flowers?   Some gardeners use them for accents in the flower border, choosing those of medium height and grouping two or three together.

FRAGRANCE

Is it true that modern roses have lost their fragrance?   This is a base canard. A few popular modern roses, like 'Peace', have little or no fragrance, but there are many with some fragrance and an increasing number that are outstandingly fragrant. The American Rose Foundation has awarded the Gamble Fragrance Medal to the hybridizers of 'Crimson Glory', 'Chrysler Imperial', 'Sutter's Gold', 'Tiffany', 'Granada', and 'Fragrant Cloud'.

Please name some fragrant roses.   In addition to those noted above, 'Candy Stripe', 'Christian Dior', 'Electron', 'Lemon Spice', 'Mr. Lincoln', 'Oklahoma', 'Pink Peace', 'Sweet Afton', and 'Tropicana' among hybrid teas have delightful scent. Grandiflora 'Apricot Nectar' is very fragrant and so are climbers 'Don Juan' and 'Clair Matin'. 'City of York', a once-blooming climber, is so fragrant it scents an entire yard, but it is now rather hard to find in nurseries.

FRENCH ROSES

Will you please name some old-fashioned French roses? 'Cardinal de Richelieu', dark purplish-red; 'Duc de Valny', large, double red to rose pink; *Rosa gallica* 'Officinalis' (the apothecary rose), semi-double, rose-red, very fragrant; Rosa mundi (*R. gallica* 'Versicolor'), white to pale pink, striped red (also incorrectly called York and Lancaster).

GRANDIFLORAS

What are grandiflora roses? A relatively new class of roses with the free-flowering habit of the floribundas and the perfection of flower form and size of hybrid teas. Some are taller than hybrid teas, with more vigor; the flowers are borne singly as well as in sprays. Pink 'Queen Elizabeth' was the first rose to be named in this class, in 1954, and it remains one of the best.

What are some outstanding grandifloras? Quite a number, including 'Apricot Nectar'; 'Camelot', 'Lucky Lady', and 'Pink Parfait', pink; 'Carrousel', 'John S. Armstrong', and 'Scarlet Knight', red; 'Olé' and 'Montezuma', orange-red; 'Granada', red blend; 'Mt. Shasta', white.

GREEN ROSE

I have been told that there is a rose called the "green rose." What is it like? The green rose (*Rosa chinensis viridiflora*) originated about 1855 and is still available as a novelty, but is certainly not a beauty. The petals are just narrow green leaves so that the flower is very disappointing. It is sometimes used in flower arrangements before the buds open, as the foliage has a tint of bronze.

Is the green rose a climber? No. It belongs to the group of China roses (see above). Aside from its interest as a curiosity, it is of no garden value.

GREENHOUSE ROSES

How do you grow roses in a small greenhouse? Plant in bench in good soil. Keep moist, but not soaked. Keep the temperature as near 60° F. at night and 68° F. during the day as possible. Use plants propagated for greenhouse culture rather than those for out-of-doors, because the former are budded on *Rosa manetti* understock and are better adapted for growing in a greenhouse. Potted miniature roses, on their own roots, should do very well in a greenhouse.

GROUND COVERS

What rose is satisfactory for planting as a ground cover? *Rosa wichuraiana,* the memorial rose, has creeping branches with half-evergreen foliage and fragrant white flowers. 'Max Graf', a hybrid rugosa, has a trailing habit and single, bright pink flowers and attractive foliage. 'Mermaid', with yellow flowers, can cover anything —banks or fences—in warm climates, but it usually winterkills near New York. The white polyantha 'Sea Foam', with shiny dark foliage, is more of a shrub but it is recommended for covering banks.

HEDGES

What is the rose often advertised as a living fence? This is *Rosa multiflora,* which has small, blackberry-like flowers. It is a prolific grower and does make an impenetrable hedge but it is suited to the farm and large properties rather than suburban lots. It may grow 10 ft. wide and keeping it trimmed is a thorny, impossible task.

What other roses can be planted as a hedge? 'Betty Prior' or many other floribundas, some of the lower-growing hybrid rugosas, or the everblooming shrubs 'Belinda' or 'Gartendirektor Otto Linne'. The shrub polyantha 'The Fairy' or 'Sea Foam' will make, in 2 or 3 years, an impenetrable hedge about 3 ft. high. This will keep out dogs, but some yearly cleaning out is a rather scratchy job. A new race of "vase" roses will be good for hedges.

HYBRID PERPETUALS

How do hybrid perpetuals differ from hybrid teas? The hybrid perpetuals were the progenitors of the hybrid teas and in their heyday ranked first in popularity. They have a decided Victorian quality in the largeness, fullness, and boldness of their blooms, but lack the refinement in form of hybrid teas. The colors include purest white, deepest crimson, and the innumerable hues linking these two extremes. The plants are vigorous, rather coarse, and quite hardy. There is profuse June bloom and some varieties have recurrent bloom.

What are a few of the best hybrid perpetuals? 'Frau Karl Druschki' is tops. It has large flowers of hybrid tea form, pure white, produced repeatedly. 'Henry Nevard' has very large, fragrant, crimson-scarlet blooms and also repeats. 'General Jacqueminot' has recurrent, very fragrant clear red flowers. 'Mrs. John Laing' and 'Baronness Rothschild' have huge, clear pink flowers.

Can hybrid perpetuals be planted in a bed with hybrid teas? It is better to keep them separated. They take more room and those that do not repeat rather spoil a rose bed in summer. Use them as shrubs. However, if space is a problem, there is no reason why the two kinds can't be combined in one large bed or border.

HYBRID TEAS

What are hybrid tea roses? As a class they are moderately vigorous and hardy, requiring some protection in colder states. Their chief merit is their frequency of bloom, a characteristic that gives them the common term "monthly roses." In variety, richness, and delicacy of their coloring, and their perfection of form and pleasing fragrance, they are not equaled by any other type.

What is the difference between a hybrid tea and a monthly rose? They are the same thing.

What are some of the best hybrid teas? The following are highly rated hybrid teas, presently available, grouped according to color class.

White or near white—'Blanche Mallerin', 'Garden Party', 'John F. Kennedy', 'Matterhorn', 'Pascali', 'White Masterpiece'.

Yellow or yellow blend—'Eclipse', 'Golden Gate', 'Irish Gold', 'King's Ransom', 'Peace'.

Pink—'Charlotte Armstrong', 'Electron', 'Miss All-American Beauty', 'Pink Favorite', 'Royal Highness', 'South Seas', 'Swarthmore'.

Pink blend—'Chicago Peace', 'Confidence', 'First Prize', 'Helen Traubel', 'Portrait', 'Tiffany'.

Apricot blend—'Medallion'.

Orange-red—'Fragrant Cloud', 'Tropicana', 'Simon Bolivar'.

Red—'Crimson Glory', 'Big Ben', 'Chrysler Imperial', 'Gypsy', 'Mr. Lincoln', 'Oklahoma', 'Proud Land'.

Mauve—'Blue Moon', 'Lady X'. 'Sterling Silver' has beautiful flowers but the plant does better in the greenhouse.

What varieties of single hybrid teas are worth while? 'Dainty Bess', with 5 pink petals and maroon stamens, is most desirable and still offered by many nurseries. White 'Innocence', yellow 'Cecil' and 'Irish Fireflame', orange, veined-crimson, are sometimes available. 'Oriental Charm' is a red semi-double (9 to 12 petals) that is taking prizes in rose shows.

Are the new varieties of hybrid teas as hardy and strong as the older ones? Yes, many of them may be somewhat more hardy.

Where does one purchase older varieties? One or two nurseries specialize in older roses. 'La France', the first hybrid tea, introduced in 1867, is still offered, along with white 'Kaiserin Auguste Viktoria', pink 'Mme. Caroline Testout' and 'Edith Nellie Perkins', yellow 'Duchess of Wellington'.

I know nothing about hybrid tea roses, but wish to have a rose garden. What are the best varieties to purchase as a beginner? (Nebraska). Any of the modern hybrid teas mentioned here should survive with enough winter protection. You may need up to 12 ins. of soil with some covering on top. Iowa State University is now breeding roses that are hardy without such protection and that will bloom like hybrid teas. These are being made available to nurserymen and should do well in Nebraska. 'Prairie Princess' is on the market, also 'Country Dancer', 'Music Maker', and others.

I have only a few hours a week to spend in my garden, but I want some roses. Can I grow hybrid teas? Why not? Start with a few and then add more as you see how little time they take. Spraying up to 300 roses takes only about an hour a week and cutting off dead blooms takes only a few minutes as you stroll around enjoying the roses. Plan a little time in spring to plant, prune, feed, and mulch and you will not have to do too much later.

MINIATURE ROSES

What are "fairy roses"? Another name for the miniature roses that are forms of *Rosa chinensis minima*.

What are miniature roses? They are naturally dwarf, growing from 5 to 15 ins. tall, with flowers an inch or less across. They are like tiny hybrid teas, with plant, foliage, buds, and flowers in perfect scale, but the pleasure they give is immeasurable. There are many gardeners growing these miniature roses indoors under fluorescent lights, but the plants are hardy outdoors, wintering better than do hybrid teas in very cold climates.

Are there many varieties of miniature roses?   Yes, a great many, with more introduced each year. Several nurseries devote themselves exclusively to production and sale of miniatures.

Please name some of the best.   'Baby Darling', 'Beauty Secret', 'Cinderella', 'Dian', 'Janna', 'Judy Fischer', 'Pixie Rose', 'Red Imp', 'Starina', 'Sweet Fairy' (fragrant), 'Simplex' (white single), 'Toy Clown' are a few, but there are many others. 'Baby Masquerade' always attracts attention with its changing red, orange, and yellow colors, but it grows considerably taller than most miniatures.

I have heard about a miniature moss rose; is there such a thing? 'Tiny Kara' has its buds heavily covered with soft moss; 'Fairy Moss' is another variety with mossy buds.

How do you grow miniatures indoors?   Keep pots on damp pebbles in a cool, sunny window or 3 to 6 ins. below fluorescent lights. Plant out in the garden in spring, pot up in the fall, let go dormant for 6 to 8 weeks, then bring indoors, pruning as necessary.

MOSS

What are moss roses?   A type of the cabbage rose, *Rosa centifolia*. The bud of the flower is enclosed in a mossy envelope. Much of the great fragrance comes from the mossy glands. Moss roses are very old, having been in cultivation for centuries, and a number are still available from nurseries specializing in old roses. Among the best are 'Crested Moss' (found on a convent wall in Switzerland in 1827), 'Communis' ('Old Pink Moss'), 'Comtesse de Murinais', 'Deuil de Paul Fontaine', 'Mme. Louis Leveque', 'Salet', 'Striped Moss'. Most moss roses have one annual flowering in June, fairly lengthy, but 'Salet' may repeat through the season.

POLYANTHA ROSES

What are polyantha roses?   The term "polyantha" (meaning many flowers) well describes the class. The plants are usually dwarf and give a continuous profusion of small flowers in large clusters. They are especially hardy, but less adapted for cutting than other types. For garden display they are unequaled. They were formerly called "baby ramblers" because the flower clusters were similar to those produced on older varieties of ramblers.

What varieties of polyanthas are worth while?   'Cameo', 'Cecile

Brunner', 'China Doll', and 'Pinkie', all pink; 'Margo Koster', orange to salmon; 'Mother's Day', a red sport of 'Margo'; 'White Koster', pure white. Taller than these are 'Mrs. R. M. Finch', light pink; 'Orange Triumph', an orange-red; and 'The Fairy', but the latter is best classed as a small shrub.

ROSE RATINGS

The pictures in the catalogues are all enticing. How can you tell if a variety is really good? Two excellent ways. The American Rose Society rates rose varieties, from reports sent in by amateur rosarians all over the country. The results are published each year in the *Handbook for Selecting Roses,* and anyone can procure a copy by sending 10 cents to the society.

All-America Rose Selections, Inc., rates roses by sending professionals to judge roses for 2 years as they are grown in 22 test gardens across the country. Each year the coveted AARS award is given to a very few varieties, seldom more than 2 or 3, and roses thus designated are sold with an AARS tag. The AARS roses for 1973 were 'Electron', 'Gypsy', and 'Medallion'. Those for 1974 are 'Perfume Delight', a bright pink, fragrant hybrid tea, and two floribundas, pink-orange 'Bahia' and 'Bon Bon', a pink and white bicolor.

If you buy AARS roses or those with an American Rose Society rating of 7.5 or above you should have success if you do your part in giving the rose a good start.

RUGOSA ROSES

Will you tell me something about rugosa roses? This hardy species and its many fine hybrids are among the toughest and most long-lived of all roses. They are suitable for planting at the seashore, where they make themselves thoroughly at home in sandy soil. They grow in the very cold sections of the West where few roses can survive and they can be used as large shrubs or hedges wherever there is room for them. The species (*Rosa rugosa*) has deep rose or white flowers. Rugosa foliage is shining dark green and rugose (wrinkled). For some of the best hybrids, see under Shrubs.

SCOTCH

What are Scotch roses? A strain of old-fashioned roses with fine foliage and spiny growth. Hardy, disease-resistant, they can be planted with shrubs or as specimens. Harison's Yellow, 6 to 8 ft., is semi-double; 'Stanwell Perpetual', double, pink, constant bloomer; 'Frühlingsgold', single, yellow, very fragrant; 'Frühlingsmorgen', pink and yellow with maroon stamens and huge red hips. Scotch roses are varieties or hybrids of *Rosa spinosissima.*

SHRUBS

What are shrub roses? Many of the more vigorous, hardy roses can be used in the garden in the same fashion as any flowering shrub. Some are officially classed as shrubs and some are listed as species or in the rugosa or other groups. 'Golden Wings', with very large, sulfur-yellow single flowers, was introduced as a hybrid tea, but when it proved to be exceptionally vigorous, too tall and broad ever to be planted with hybrid teas, it was reclassified as a shrub. 'The Fairy', with continuous clusters of small pink flowers, is still classed as a polyantha, but it is really a shrub, spreading to 4 to 5 ft. and 3 to 4 ft. high. 'Sea Foam' has the same habit and the same type of flowers, but white, and is officially a shrub. 'Sparrieshoop', with light pink, fragrant flowers, sometimes repeating, is halfway between a shrub and a climber and so is 'Pax', which repeats its creamy white, almost single, blooms on willowy canes all summer.

Please list some good rugosa shrubs. 'Therese Bugnet', hardy in Alaska, has fragrant pink flowers. Other good rugosas include 'Agnes', yellow; 'Conrad F. Meyer', pink; 'Frau Dagmar Hartopp', pink, and a relatively low bush; 'Grootendorst Supreme', red; 'Pink Grootendorst', clear pink, fringed petals; *R. rugosa alba,* white; 'Sarah Van Fleet', pink; 'Vanguard', large, double, salmon-pink, very fragrant flowers, not recurrent.

SPECIES

What are species roses? Please name some. The species are the wild roses from which cultivated roses have been bred. Some of those most suitable for the garden are *Rosa hugonis* (Father Hugo rose), yellow, early, 6 to 8 ft.; *Rosa rugosa,* red or white single; *Rosa setigera* (prairie rose), large, single, pink, 6 to 8 ft. *Rosa multiflora* has small white flowers in large trusses and is chiefly desirable for red hips which attract birds. Other species are *R. centifolia, R. chinensis, R. eglanteria* (the sweetbriar rose which has ripe-pineapple-scented foliage), *R. foetida, R. spinosissima, R. damascena.*

SUPPORTS

How can I support my climbing roses?   On a split-rail fence; over a trellis bought or made for the purpose; over an arch; or on cedar posts with crossbars added for extra support (the latter method is especially suited to pillar-type roses).

What is a pillar rose?   The term "pillar" refers more to a method of support than to an actual type of rose. Roses adapted to a post or pillar include some climbing varieties that do not have excessively long canes and some of the tall-growing hybrid perpetual varieties.

How can an overgrown rambler be attached to the side of a house? The plant should be properly pruned, by cutting off, at the ground level, all but the new basal shoots. These can be trained as desired by tying them with soft twine to nails driven into the side of the house. However, the house wall is not an ideal form of support. The roses will interfere with painting and other aspects of maintenance. It is better to use some form of latticework, which should be held out from the wall itself at least 6 ins. or, preferably, a foot.

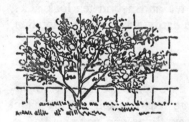

Trellis support for climbing and semi-climbing (pillar) roses.

If it is a large-flowered climber rather than a rambler, do you still cut out everything but new basal shoots?   Keep some of the older canes but prune the laterals (side growth) back to within a foot of the cane.

SWEETBRIAR HYBRIDS

What are hybrid sweetbriars?   They are hybrids of *Rosa eglanteria,* having scented foliage, single or semi-double flowers on arching canes, and strong growth. The species, with small, pink single flowers, has been known since 1551 and is commonly found in pastures. The hybrid 'Lady Penzance' has single pink flowers with yellow centers.

'Lord Penzance' is fawn-colored with fragrant flowers as well as foliage.

TEA ROSES

Why are varieties of roses called "tea roses"?   Because the scent of the flowers resembles fresh green tea leaves (not the beverage). Pink and yellow forms of *Rosa odorata* were brought to England from China in 1824 and thence to the United States. They are mostly grown in the South and on the Pacific coast, although a few may survive elsewhere. In mild, moist climates they are very recurrent and grow without much care, being tolerant of black spot and intolerant of pruning. The fragrant flowers are of medium size without bold colors and are well-formed.

What varieties of tea roses are available?   'Catherine Mermet', flesh-pink; 'Duchess de Brabant', rosy pink; 'Maman Cochet', cream to pink; 'Safrano', yellow; 'William R. Smith', pink blend; and a few others.

What is the difference between the tea rose and a hybrid tea?   The hybrid tea rose is descended from the tea, which is one of the parents of the hybrid tea. In appearance the tea and hybrid tea look alike, but the hybrid tea is more vigorous and hardy, has a wider adaptation, and has bolder colors.

TERRACES AND PATIOS

My property is limited and I don't have space for a real rose garden. Could I grow a few roses in large redwood tubs on my patio, which received enough sun to keep geraniums and petunias flowering abundantly?   Yes, select floribunda and grandiflora varieties, as they are more floriferous than hybrid teas. You can also grow miniature roses in planters or in clay pots sunk in window boxes filled with peat moss (do not overwater!).

Why did the roses on my terrace, which did well during the summer, die over winter, when rosebushes set in the open ground near the terrace wintered well?   The roots of container-grown plants are much more subject to winter damage from low temperatures than are the roots of plants in the ground. Most plants grown in containers need special care to survive the winter. One suggestion is to group containers together in areas protected from winter sunshine and wind and then pack their sides and tops with marsh hay, straw, leaves, ever-green boughs, or whatever is at hand. It would be simpler to move containers to a garage or other enclosure for the winter, and if heavy tubs are on casters this might be possible. Of course, city gardeners don't have garage space and will have to take their chances with the winter elements. And the few roses grown in containers can always be replaced in the spring—when necessary.

Do roses grown in pots need any special care? They require the same attention as roses growing in gardens, plus the added care needed by a plant restricted to a pot. Each tub or container should have holes to drain off excess water, and watering the soil thoroughly, before it becomes bone-dry, is most important. A regular fertilizing schedule is essential, since the roots of container-grown plants cannot forage for nutrients as can roots in a garden.

I need two tall accents in tubs on each side of steps leading down from my terrace. Would tree roses be satisfactory? What would I do with them over winter? Tubbed tree roses should make rather formal, yet most attractive, accents. In cold climates, about the only way to carry the bushes safely through the winter would be to remove them carefully from the tubs in late fall and bury them horizontally in a trench covered with soil. After the ground freezes they should be covered with evergreen boughs or rough compost. In spring, re-plant the bushes in tubs or open ground.

TREE ROSES

What is a tree (standard) rose? Instead of the bud being inserted close to the ground (as is done in propagating other types), tree roses are budded near the top of a tall understock cane. The plant that develops from the bud is therefore on a trunk or standard. The trunk, usually of *Rosa rugosa* stock, is itself often on a different root-stalk, so 3 roses are involved in creating a tree rose.

Can tree roses be grown in cold climates? They are difficult to grow in cold climates because they are hard to winter. In regions where the temperature does not drop below 10° F. they are usually satisfactory. A hybrid perpetual, such as 'Frau Karl Druschki', used as a tree rose, may suffer less winter injury.

WALLS

I have a low rock retaining wall in front of my house that is 175 ft. long. Should roses be planted on the inside, which is on a level with the yard, or on the outside, so they would have the wall for support? Plant on the inside so the rose stems can overhang the wall.

What rose varieties would you suggest for a low rock retaining wall? (Kansas.)   *Rosa wichuraiana* or 'Max Graf'.

The American Rose Center

What is the American Rose Center?   A dream come true, it is the home of the American Rose Society and a mecca for all gardeners. Administered by the tax-exempt American Rose Foundation, the Center is located in Shreveport, Louisiana, on a 118-acre tract donated to the Foundation. There are 3 connected buildings: administrative-editorial; laboratories-offices; and auditorium-showroom. In addition to a display garden of 30,000 roses, there will be gardens for testing cultivars, for experiment and research, for old roses, for international collections, for tree roses. There will be memorial gardens and landscape demonstration plots. Besides roses, many flowering shrubs and trees—azaleas, camellias, crape-myrtles, dogwoods, etc.—are being planted through the natural wooded areas. To learn all about roses, visit the American Rose Center in Shreveport.

7
Perennials

FEW GARDENERS today have the space or will to make the 100-ft. long, 8–10-ft.-wide borders that are still seen in England. But perennials can assume an important role in even the smallest garden, whether they be used as a few plants for accent or by the dozens. Besides near permanence, they offer a certain decorative quality that's hard to achieve with annuals, shrubs, or bulbs.

The perennial gardens of today and tomorrow will be much simplified so care will be minimal, their impact on the landscape maximal. For example, a classic combination of three favorites—peonies, bearded iris, and day-lilies—can border a driveway and provide color from spring until fall if the varieties have been carefully selected to spread the bloom sequence. The peonies and iris will flower first, then day-lilies will flower over most of the summer, according to variety. The area itself need be no more than 4 ft. wide and 25 ft. long and the gardener has only to master the simple needs of three rugged perennials that grow well under similar conditions. Such a narrow border eases maintenance considerably since all plants can be reached without actually stepping into the garden.

Another popular approach to a perennial garden is the irregularly shaped island garden, perhaps with a few large boulders or a small tree placed strategically for accent. Again, this garden is easy to work in, and different effects can be had from the various sides. In such a garden it's possible to accommodate both sun- and shade-lovers as well as rock garden plants. Or annuals and perennials can be mixed. If only a few plants are desired, an attractive mulch or perennial ground cover can be used to fill the remaining spaces.

The single accent perennial is very effective, but it must be chosen with great care as it has to be decorative in bloom as well as out of bloom. Dramatic accents that come to mind are a clump of peonies or day-lilies by a garden gate, a grouping of Japanese iris by a small pool, or an ornamental grass by a garden seat.

Not to be overlooked is the use of perennials as ground covers to replace high-maintenance lawn areas. Such perennials as ajuga, lily-of-the-valley, sweet-woodruff, and sedum offer a great deal more eye appeal than grass or gravel under certain circumstances.

For the advanced gardener who enjoys combining colors and textures to weave living tapestry, there is no better group of plants to work with than perennials. The challenge is there and the possibilities are limitless. The cost is reasonable, the results fairly soon achieved. The scene can be changed frequently—not so easily done with more permanent shrub plantings.

—*Margaret C. Ohlander*

WHAT TO GROW

What is a hardy herbaceous perennial?   A plant which lives for a few or several years, whose tops die in winter, but are renewed, from the same roots, each spring.

What is the average age of perennial plants sold by leading nurseries?   About 1 to 2 years old.

Can you suggest a selection of 24 perennials of easy culture, for succession of bloom?   Spring: lily-of-the-valley, forget-me-not, coral-bells, violet, bleedingheart (tall and dwarf), dwarf iris, mertensia, *Phlox divaricata,* ajuga. Summer: *Campanula carpatica, C. carpatica alba, C. lactiflora,* and *C. persicifolia;* astilbe, coreopsis, eupatorium, gaillardia, day-lily, bearded iris (tall), rose-mallow, hosta, platycodon, hollyhock. Late summer and fall: plumbago, rudbeckia, chrysanthemum, hardy aster, helenium.

What bright-colored perennials can I use on the north side of my red brick house to make an attractive rear terrace?   Aquilegia hybrids, *Brunnera macrophylla, Monarda fistulosa, Anemone hupe-hensis* and *A. magellanica, Dianthus deltoides* and *D. arenarius, Phlox subulata* varieties, *Ceratostigma plumbaginoides, Veronica incana.*

Can you list a few perennials that will bloom well with little or no care, and that will not look unkempt before and after blooming? Any variety of hosta (funkia), any of the numerous day-lilies, pe-onies, phlox, *Eupatorium rugosum, Aster novae-angliae,* ajuga, ar-temisia, baptisia, thermopsis, coreopsis, echinops, *Iris sibirica, Rudbeckia speciosa, Sedum spectabile,* achillea, *Dicentra eximia.*

What would be an interesting layout for a perennial bed that is backed with shrubbery? First set out groups of delphiniums—3 or 4 to a group—spaced at irregular intervals over the bed 8 to 12 ft. apart, depending upon size of bed. Then set out hollyhocks in same manner—2 to 3 plants in each group. Intersperse in the same way varieties of summer phlox, then various hardy asters. This will give distribution of bloom. If spaces are left, fill in with Oriental poppy, achillea, aconitum, *Anemone japonica, Campanula persicifolia,* cush-ion chrysanthemums, dianthus species and varieties, gaillardia, gypso-phila 'Bristol Fairy', helenium, heliopsis. These will lend support to the 4 main kinds at different parts of the season. The principle is to weave the pattern back and forth across the border.

What are good combinations of ordinary perennials in border? The over-all border plan should be based upon the distribution of bloom over the planting and over the season. Color combinations, although effective at the moment, leave gaps in the planting unless planned to be followed up with other plants. Some good color com-binations are lupines, anthemis 'Moonlight' and *Oenothera missouri-ensis;* poppy 'Helen Elizabeth', Shasta daisy, and *Linum perenne;* purple iris and *Aquilegia chrysantha;* delphinium hybrids, *Thermopsis caroliniana* and pyrethrum. These are but a few of the countless com-binations possible. Be sure that all flowers selected for a combination bloom at the same time, as usually their season is short.

I have a collection of 24 varieties of day-lilies for continuous bloom during the season. They are all in shades of cream and yellow. Which hardy perennials do you suggest for harmonizing bloom from early spring to fall in a border? Siberian iris, bearded iris, astilbe, cimicifuga, delphinium, *Salvia azurea,* regal lily, veronica 'Blue

Champion', goatsbeard, (*Aruncus sylvester*), *Platycodon grandiflorum*, liatris.

FOR SPECIAL PURPOSES

Which perennials can be planted around Oriental poppies to cover their unsightly fading foliage? *Anemone japonica, Gypsophila paniculata* 'Bristol Fairy', *Thalictrum aquilegifolium*, hardy chrysanthemums, *Eupatorium coelestinum*. This latter perennial starts very late in spring and fills out by midsummer.

My yard is made up of rock and ashes. Which perennials will grow well here? Everything seems to burn up from heat of sun. *Euphorbia myrsinites, Tunica saxifraga, Sedum acre, Silene maritima, Saponaria ocymoides, Nepeta* x *faassenii, Lathyrus latifolius, Echinops ritro*.

What makes the best plant or flower (perennial) for cemeteries? For shade: *Ajuga reptans, Dicentra eximia*, vinca 'Bowles Variety'. For sun: *Dianthus plumarius, Sedum spectabile, Sedum acre, Aegopodium podograria*.

Which perennial can I grow in a small bed bordering my terrace? The terrace faces north, and I want something at least 1 ft. high. *Dicentra eximia, Phlox divaricata laphamii, Nepeta* x *faassenii*.

Which are the best perennials to grow in a border along an active red-cedar hedge? If there is at least a half day of sun: hardy asters; *Eupatorium coelestinum*, helenium, *Heliopsis scabra, Nepeta* x *faassenii, Oenothera youngii, Phlox arendsii* hybrids, and summer phlox are some of the most satisfactory.

Which perennial flowers can be satisfactorily grown in a city backyard garden where there is practically no sunlight? *Ajuga reptans* and *A. genevensis, Dicentra eximia, Mertensia virginica*, day-lily, *Pulmonaria saccharata*, and *P. angustifolia azurea, Phlox arendsii* and *Phlox divaricata*.

Can you suggest perennials for small plot of ground facing the east? House is the background. Violets and lily-of-the-valley not successful. Aquilegia, anemone, *Phlox arendsii* and *P. divaricata*, anchusa, epimedium, monarda, *Hosta* (*Funkia*) *sieboldii* and *H. coerulea*.

What are some easily grown blue-flowered perennials? Veronica 'Crater Lake Blue', *Veronica longifolia subsessilis*, delphinium 'Belladonna', tradescantia 'J. C. Weyland', *Platycodon grandiflorum, Campanula persicifolia grandiflora, Ceratostigma plumbaginoides.*

What should one plant on north, east, and south fences to act as a screen, and also as a background for perennial borders? *Clematis montana rubens, Lathyrus latifolius, Polygonum aubertii,* bignonia 'Mme. Galen'.

Will you name some very hardy perennials? Achillea, ajuga, aquilegia, artemisia, astilbe, coreopsis, dicentra (bleedingheart), eupatorium, day-lily, lythrum, mertensia, *Nepeta* x *faassenii,* peony, platycodon.

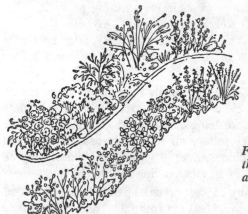

Facing flower gardens follow the lines of a gracefully meandering path.

I am interested in perennial flowers that require little work, after once being started, and are also good for cutting. Will you name a few? Astilbe, bearded iris, hardy chrysanthemum, *Helenium autumnale, Coreopsis grandiflora,* peonies, hardy asters, *Gypsophila paniculata* 'Bristol Fairy', lily-of-the-valley, *Platycodon grandiflorum,* gaillardia, nepeta, day-lily.

Am interested in a small flower garden, including some for cutting. Which flowers would you recommend as of easy culture, and hardy? Any good varieties of bearded iris, any good varieties of hardy phlox, *Heliopsis scabra* 'Incomparabilis', *Gypsophila paniculata, Helenium autumnale,* delphinium 'Belladonna' and delphinium hybrids, *Dianthus plumarius, Dicentra eximia* and *D. spectabilis.*

Are there any shade-tolerant perennials?   Aconite, ajuga, anemone, aquilegia, astilbe, bleedingheart, bugbane, Carpathian bluebell, day-lily, doronicum, epimedium, ferns, eupatorium, lily-of-the-valley, *Lobelia cardinalis* and *L. siphilitica,* mertensia, *Monarda didyma, Phlox divaricata,* hosta, plumbago, primula, thalictrum, vinca, and viola.

What are the best types of hardy flowers for a sunny, dry place? *Alyssum (Aurinia) saxatile, Veronica incana, Cerastium tomentosum, Aethionema grandiflorum, Arenaria montana, Arabis albida (alpina),* *Linum perenne,* dictamnus, heliopsis, iris (bearded), day-lily, *Oenothera fruticosa* (sundrops).

Can you give me the names of some low-growing perennials that can be used for a border? *Iberis sempervirens, Alyssum (Aurinia) saxatile* 'Compacta', *Ceratostigma plumbaginoides, Aster novi-belgi* dwarf varieties, polyanthus primrose, *Sedum hybridum* and *S. sieboldii, Veronica incana.*

What low-growing, neat, easy perennials with good foliage can be used for edging?   Ajuga, either with deep green foliage, or variety 'Bronze Beauty', with bronze leaves, is a good choice; it has blue flowers in the spring, husky foliage all season, spreads rapidly, and stands shade and city conditions. Several varieties of sedum may be used for edging, if controlled from spreading too much.

Will you name some bushy edging perennial plants for along walks? *Epimedium alpinum rubrum,* best in partial shade; *Campanula carpatica, Lamium maculatum, Iberis sempervirens, Aegopodium podagraria variegatum,* hosta (various kinds), *Lirope muscari* and its striped variety, *variegata; Sedum hybridum, S. spurium* and *S. sieboldi.*

Can you give a list of low perennials to be grown in beds along a flagstone-walk? *Achillea tomentosa, Ajuga genevensis, Alyssum (Aurinia) saxatile* 'Citrina', *Anemone japonica,* aster (cushion type), *Campanula carpatica,* cushion chrysanthemums, dianthus, various species and varieties, *Nepeta* x *faassenii, Phlox subulata* varieties, pyrethrum varieties, *Veronica incana.*

Will you name some perennials for planting along the front of the border? *Alyssum (Aurinia) saxatile* 'Compacta', *Dianthus plumarius, Statice longifolia, Ceratostigma plumbaginoides,* dwarf asters,

Veronica spicata nana, Arabis alpina, Silene maritima, Tunica saxi-fraga, Veronica incana, Nepeta x *faassenii.*

What are some medium-height perennials for the center of the border? Astilbe, *Campanula persicifolia* varieties, Artemisia 'Silver King', *Achillea ptarmica, Aquilegia coerulea, Paradisea liliastrum, Dicentra eximia, Eupatorium coelestinum, Veronica longifolia subses-silis, Gypsophila paniculata.*

Which are the best tall-growing perennials for a border? *Bocconia cordata, Thalictrum glaucum* and *aquilegifolium, Phlox paniculata* hybrids, *Helenium autumnale, Rudbeckia purpurea,* delphinium hybrids, asters (tall named varieties), *Cimicifuga racemosa, Campanula pyramidalis, Echinops ritro.*

Will you give list of plants for a small perennial border with succession of bloom as long as possible and no plants which are difficult to obtain? *Arabis albida fl. pl., Phlox subulata,* bearded iris, astilbe, veronica 'Blue Champion', day-lily, heuchera, dianthus, phlox 'Miss Lingard', Shasta daisy, hardy asters, coreopsis, gaillardia, *Heliopsis scabra,* helenium varieties, cushion chrysanthemums, nepeta.

Can you give me a list of perennials to use in a border 2 to 3 ft. wide and 50 ft. long, that would keep it looking well all season? *Brunnera macrophylla, Dicentra eximia,* delphinium 'Belladonna', *Dianthus caesius,* gaillardia, geum, *Gypsophila repens* 'Bodger', nepeta, pyrethrum, summer phlox, *Heliopsis scabra, Eupatorium coelestinum,* hardy asters, cushion chrysanthemums. Constant color can be secured only by introducing annuals for later summer bloom.

Will you suggest varieties for a perennial bed 30 × 10 ft., so as to have continuous bloom from early spring to late fall? Make a selection from the following: *March:* crocus, snowdrop, squill, winter-aconite (all bulbs and tubers). *April:* rock-cress, goldentuft, hepatica, moss phlox. *May:* perennial candytuft, columbine, globe-flower, iris, Virginia cowslip, bleedingheart, polyanthus primrose, astilbe. *June:* Japanese iris, early phlox, Shasta daisy, painted daisy, pinks, coral-bells, Oriental poppy, hybrid columbines, lemon-lily, delphinium, hollyhock. *July:* baby's-breath, false dragonhead, butterfly-weed, loosestrife, Carpathian bluebell, perennial sunflower, balloonflower. *August:* plantain-lily, rose-mallow, sneezeweed, cone-flower, cardinal-flower, hardy asters, sea-lavender. *September:* Japanese anemone, hardy asters, perennial sunflowers, goldenrod, showy stonecrop, hardy chrysanthemums. *October:* monkshood, hardy asters, leadwort (ceratostigma), hardy chrysanthemums, helianthus, *Salvia pitcheri.*

Is there a perennial that blooms nearly all summer? No—despite claims in catalogues! *Heliopsis scabra, Gaillardia aristata, Nepeta* x *faassenii,* and *Dicentra eximia* all come very near it.

Which dwarf border plants bloom over the longest period of time? *Silene maritima, Dianthus deltoides,* viola 'Jersey Gem', *Tunica saxifraga flore-pleno, Nepeta* x *faassenii.*

SOIL PREPARATION

How deep should soil be prepared for new border? For best results, the soil should be dug and prepared not less than 18 ins., and preferably 24 ins., deep.

How shall I prepare new ground for perennials? Dig the ground to a depth of at least 18 ins., mixing in well-rotted or dehydrated cow manure, leafmold, peat moss, or compost, with superphosphate, 10 lbs. to 100 sq. ft.

In preparing a border, should all stones be removed? Should soil be screened? For perennials, annuals, and shrubs, stones the size of a lemon or smaller may be left in the soil. Do not screen the soil.

Is sand or clay better subsoil for perennial border? If sand is too loose and porous, drainage will be excessive; if clay is hard packed, drainage will be stopped. Generally speaking, a sandy subsoil is preferable. Hard clay should be broken up and lightened with peat moss, cinders, gravel, or sand.

What element is lacking in the soil when perennials have good color and flower well but lack sufficient strength to stand upright and spread all over the beds? Possibly insufficient phosphorus and potash; but crowded planting, too much watering, and overfeeding with nitrogenous manures will cause weak stems. However, many perennials need support by staking.

For 20 years we have had a perennial border. The last 5 years it has deteriorated; replacements, fertilizer, etc., have not solved the problem. Maple and elm trees grow near; sunshine is one hour a day. Can any soil be improved to overcome lack of sunshine? Nothing can be done to improve the soil so that it will overcome the lack of sunshine and greedy tree roots.

Why don't my plants near red-cedar trees thrive? Are there any perennials that will grow fairly well in the shade of trees? The soil may be "poisoned" by accumulation of years of dead red-cedar foliage. Try removing this periodically. Give the surface a light application of ground limestone and a generous supply of rotted manure, compost, peat moss, or leafmold. Work till the ground is in good "tilth." Most shade plants, especially the "woodsy" ones, will grow well if soil is friable and not super-acid. Some are ferns, dicentra, *Mahonia repens, Vinca minor,* hepatica, *Pachysandra terminalis,* primula, *Ceratostigma plumbaginoides, Phlox divaricata, P. carolina* and *P. ovata,* aquilegia.

FERTILIZERS

Which is the better time to put fertilizer on perennials—spring or fall? Chemical fertilizer is best put on when plants are actively growing. Superphosphate and animal manures can be worked into soil when planting.

Will fresh sheep manure hurt perennials? No; providing it is not put on too heavily, and is not allowed to come in contact with the roots. Use 1 lb. to 10 sq. ft. and cultivate into surface soil.

What is a good fertilizer for asters, larkspur, peonies, and delphiniums? Well-rotted or dehydrated barnyard manure, supplemented during the growing season by a balanced commercial fertilizer. A little lime may be needed if the soil is acid.

Is there anything to be gained by fertilizing perennials during the growing season? In some cases, yes. Many kinds—phlox, delphinium, chrysanthemums, etc.—are helped by supplementary feedings of liquid manure or quick-acting commercial fertilizer, applied when flowers are about to be formed. Whether or not this is necessary depends on character of soil, the initial preparation of the border, and annual routine practices to maintain its fertility.

How do you prepare and fertilize perennial beds in the spring so as not to disturb the plants? By forking in the manure, compost, or fertilizer lightly.

Do all perennials need lime? My soil is cleared-off pine woodland. Most garden flowers need a soil near the neutral point or slightly acid. Your county agricultural agent probably would be glad to advise you on how much lime to apply to your soil after you have it tested.

PLANTING AND TRANSPLANTING

What is the method of planting perennials? Make a hole of sufficient size, with spade or trowel (depending on the size of the root system), to accommodate the roots without crowding. Put plant in hole no deeper than it grew in nursery. Work soil between and over the roots, and pack *firmly*. Soak with water.

Is it all right to plant perennials when soil is sopping wet? No. Soil structure can be harmed as a result. Wait until soil is crumbly but still moist.

When is the best time to remake a perennial border? September and early October. Early spring is also good, but early-blooming plants should be replanted in the fall, except for those on the border line of hardiness in the region. However, a certain amount of rearranging is possible throughout the growing season.

Is August a good month to revamp borders? Definitely not. It is the hottest and driest month as a rule, and newly transplanted stock (with the exceptions noted below) is likely to suffer.

Which perennials should be moved in midsummer or early fall? Bearded iris can be moved in July and August; bleedingheart, Christmas-rose, peonies in late August and September; Oriental poppies in August; madonna lilies as soon as tops wither.

Should all perennials be cut back either after replanting or transplanting in fall? Tall perennials are better if cut back before being moved. Whatever foliage remains down near the soil matters little in the fall.

What is the time for dividing and transplanting perennials in northern Maine: fall, or spring? Fall, if it can be done at least 4 weeks before heavy freezing. It can be done in spring, too; but as early as possible.

In making over perennial borders, which plants should not be disturbed in the fall? What can I do about them? None of the late-blooming ones, such as chrysanthemums, hardy asters. Replant all early and midsummer bloomers, except those likely to suffer winter injury. Dig around others without disturbing them; transplant in the spring.

Should flowers be planted in straight rows or staggered? The effect is better in a staggered planting. When they are grown for cut flowers only, it is more convenient to have them in rows.

When is the correct time to plant perennials in the spring? Will they bloom the same year? Plant as early as the soil can be worked. Plants, if large enough, will flower the same season.

My nurseryman sells perennials in pots and other containers from spring to fall. He says they can be planted any time during the growing season. Is this true? Yes. More and more plants, including trees, shrubs, and roses, are being handled in this way. Obviously the rules about spring and fall planting only don't apply because pot-grown plants suffer no disturbance in transplanting.

CULTURE

What constitutes good year-round care of a perennial border? In spring (when frost has left the ground) remove winter mulch. If rotted manure or partly rotted leaves were used, leave finer portions and lightly fork into soil, along with topdressing of complete fertilizer. Reset any plants heaved out of ground by frost. More mulch can be applied to suppress weeds and prevent formation of surface crust. Support those plants which need it. Water thoroughly when necessary. Put on more mulch after first severe frost.

What is the best way to keep down weeds in a border of perennials? Use a narrow scuffle hoe frequently to chop off weeds before they attain much size. Run the hoe through the soil about an inch below the surface. Weeds among the flowers must be pulled out by hand. Certain mulching materials also help to keep down weeds.

How close and how deep shall I keep soil worked around different plants? Depth depends on the type of plants; shallow-rooted plants need shallow cultivation; deep-rooted plants will take deeper cultivation. All can be worked close, but with care not to cut stems.

Will straw mulch help in weed control and hold moisture? If not, what will help besides pulling and hoeing? A straw mulch or any like material helps in summer to keep down weeds and hold moisture.

Which flowers should be pinched back to become bushy? Can poppies or lilies be so treated? Chrysanthemums, hardy asters, helenium, some tall-growing veronicas and penstemons. Most plants that tend to send shoots from the axils of the leaves can be pinched. Poppies and lilies should not be pinched.

When is best time to cut back perennials; and how far? This can be done in the late autumn, when the herbaceous stems have died down. Cut down to within an inch of the soil for most plants. Some plants have a clump or rosette of green leaves which should not be cut off; just cut the old flower stems. Some gardeners prefer to wait until spring before cutting off the tops of the perennials. Their argument is that it helps to prevent winter injury because snow and tree leaves are held by the stems.

Why do some hardy perennials die off after 1 or 2 luxuriant seasons? Most perennials need dividing and transplanting after 2 or 3 years. Many are short-lived. Some do not overwinter very well; still others succumb to diseases or insects.

How often should perennials be watered? No definite time can be set; the kind of soil, the needs of the various plants, as well as other factors, have an influence. See that at all times during the growing season the soil is kept moist. This is the safest rule in mixed plantings.

Can plants be watered too much to bloom? I have some shade from maple trees and my soil gets hard if I don't water often. I have very little bloom on my perennials and roses. Iris do quite well. Shade, rather than too much water, is responsible for lack of bloom. Use shade-tolerant plants. Improve soil by adding humus-forming materials.

Is it true that water should not touch leaves of perennials? There is scant danger from water on the leaves doing any harm.

Do you have to water perennial flowers in the winter, or do you just cover them? No watering is then needed, there being no activity. Merely cover them after the ground is frozen.

WINTER PROTECTION

What is the theory back of covering plants for the winter? The theory varies with the kind of plant. Plants that are not hardy are covered *before* hard freezing to protect them from low temperatures which would destroy the cells and thus kill the plant. Truly hardy plants are covered *after* the ground freezes; not to protect them from cold, but to keep them cold. The theory here is to prevent fluctuation of ground temperature, resulting in alternate freezing and thawing, which cause the injury. A mild spell in late winter, followed by a sudden hard freeze, is dangerous. In some cases merely shading plants from the winter sun is sufficient. Most winterkilling occurs in late winter or early spring.

Shall or shall we not let mother nature blanket our border garden with maple and locust leaves and if so, when shall we remove the leaves? This is not the best way of protecting most garden perennials. Maple leaves tend to make a sodden mass and smother to death any but the more robust plants. Light, litterlike material, such as marsh hay, through which air can circulate, is best. Covering should be removed gradually when signs of pushing growth are observed underneath. Take off the final covering on a dull day.

Is it necessary to protect newly planted perennials for the winter? What is best method? It is advisable, in colder regions, to protect plants for the first winter. Marsh hay, peat moss, evergreen branches, or cornstalks can be used. Lay loosely, so as not to smother plants; do not put on until after first hard freeze.

I planted perennial seeds in my cold frame in July. They have made good growth. Can I leave them in the frame until the spring? Should I put a mulch in the frame after December? A mulch will help. You may want to cover them earlier than December, depending on when you get heavy freezing. Seedlings from seed sown in July ought to make strong plants by late fall, particularly if planted out in a bed. If they are hardy perennials and are well grown, they do not need cold-frame protection.

How much winter coverage is needed on established perennial beds of iris, phlox, tulips, and various small plants? How early should this be put on? What is best type? (New York.) A covering of about 3 ins. is sufficient for the average planting of perennials. Wait until the ground has frozen before putting it on. Use some litterlike material that will not pack down, such as marsh hay, pine needles, or evergreen branches.

Is peat moss a good winter covering for my garden of peonies, iris, hollyhocks, delphiniums, nicotiana, dicentra? Peonies and bearded iris should not be covered in winter. This favors rot. Delphiniums are better if covered with several inches of coarse ashes. Nicotiana is not hardy in the North. Hollyhocks and dicentra are the only ones that might benefit from the peat moss. Peat moss is not a good mulch; it is better used as a soil conditioner at planting time.

In mulching plants, do you wait till the ground is frozen? As a rule it is best to wait until the ground has frozen before putting on a protective mulch. Delay up to this point helps to harden the plants somewhat and also encourages rodents to find winter quarters elsewhere.

Should perennials be carefully covered in very changeable climates in the fall? It seems that we always cover or uncover at wrong times, and plants are more tender. It is really the changeable conditions in winter that make covering advisable. The covering is not to keep out cold but to protect against bad effect of alternate spells of freezing and thawing. Delay it as long as possible in the fall; at least until the ground freezes. With the approach of spring, partially remove the covering; watch the plants and the weather; complete it on a dull day if possible.

Which perennials need a winter mulch, and which prefer none? And what kind of mulch? Most perennials—except those with heavy green tops like tritoma—are the better for a winter mulch, particularly in regions of alternate freezing and thawing. Leafmold, marsh hay, and evergreen boughs are some of the better materials. Light covering is to be strictly observed.

Propagation of Perennials

SEED

When is the best time to sow perennials in a greenhouse? In late February or early March, in a greenhouse of moderate temperature. With most kinds, seedlings will soon be large enough to be transplanted into flats, from which they can be set outside in a nursery bed in May. In this way only the usual summer cultivation is required and strong plants will be available for fall planting in the border if need be.

Can perennials be raised successfully from fall-sown seed? Where winter is severe and a cold frame is available, seeds of perennials can be sown in fall, so as to remain dormant for an earlier start in spring than would be obtained from spring sowing under similar conditions. Losses would be great in trying to carry small seedlings over winter.

Can you provide specific list of best planting dates for popular perennials from seed? If greenhouse space is available, in March; if only a cold frame, in April; if no glass protection, outdoors in May. Some growers prefer to sow in August, thus securing the advantage of fresh seed of the current season; but sowing in the first half of the year insures huskier young plants, better able to face their first winter.

What is the latest date for planting perennial seeds for bloom in following spring? Possibly in early August; but May sowing is better.

If you have no sunny window available, can you start perennial seedlings indoors? Yes. Under fluorescent lights.

Is it advisable to sow seeds of perennials in the open ground? Yes. Make a special seed bed by mixing in fine leafmold or peat moss and sand in the top 3 or 4 ins. of soil. Sow as early in May as possible and keep the soil moist. A good method would be to sow in seed pans or flats, bury these to the rims in sand or coal ashes, and cover with polyethylene until germination.

Can any perennials be grown from seed by simply scattering the seeds where they are to bloom? There is no doubt it could be done with certain kinds; but it is not the best, nor, in the long run, the easiest method.

Should perennial seedlings be transplanted? If the seeds were sown during the summer, transplant when they have developed their first true leaves. Water immediately, and if possible provide light shade for a few days. Cultivate and water when necessary to promote growth.

Why do seeds I save come up so well, while seeds I buy, especially perennial, do so poorly? Because, being home-grown, they are fresh;

and they may be sown soon after ripening if need be. Buy only from a reliable dealer.

Which perennials grow from seed easiest? Aquilegia hybrids, *Campanula persicifolia* in variety, delphinium hybrids, *Coreopsis grandiflora*, erigeron, *Gaillardia grandiflora*, heliopsis, *Heuchera sanguinea*, *Lilium regale*, *Lupinus polyphyllus* hybrids, primroses.

Can Thalictrum dipterocarpum seeds be planted in late fall or early winter? Will they bloom the following season? Yes, under glass; but they probably would not be strong enough to flower the following season.

What is the best method of raising thermopsis from seed? Sow the seed when ripe in a flat of sandy soil, and keep it in a cold frame over winter. If seed is at hand in March, sow then and grow under fluorescent lights, first placing it in hot water to soak overnight.

How can I raise trollius from seed? Sow the seed when ripe in a flat of rather porous soil. Keep it in a shaded cold frame, and as far as can be possible maintain cool, moist conditions. It will probably not germinate until the second year.

CUTTINGS

How are perennials propagated by cuttings? Cut off young shoots in spring when they are about 3 ins. long, making the cut below ground if possible. Insert in sand in hotbed, or in propagating case in cool greenhouse. Also, by non-flowering shoots in summer.

Will you tell me how to start slips in sand—such as chrysanthemum and carnation? Use a box about 10 ins. deep; make drainage holes in the bottom; put in 1-in. layer of coarse cinders or perlite, and cover this with peat moss; add 3 ins. sand, tamped firm. Cover the box with polyethylene, and keep it where there is good light but out of sun. Chrysanthemum cuttings are taken from the base of old plants in spring; carnations can be rooted in August.

DIVISION

What is the best way to divide most perennials? Dig up the plants and pry the rootstock apart into pieces of suitable size with the help of *two* spading forks; or hand forks if the plant is small.

When should perennials be divided? Early bloomers in early fall, late bloomers in spring. Bearded irises and Oriental poppies in summer.

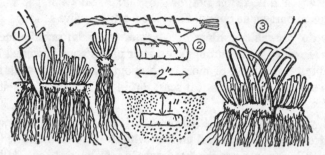

PROPAGATING HARDY PERENNIALS

Clumps or crowns can be cut apart with knife or spade (1); or torn apart with two digging forks (3). Root cuttings (2) of some subjects (Oriental poppy, phlox, platycodon), buried about an inch deep, quickly form new plants.

HYBRIDIZING

How are flowers crossed by hand so that they produce seed? Remove anthers from the flowers you want for the seed bearer before the pollen is ripe. Cover flower with transparent bag. When stigma is ripe (or sticky), put on the ripe pollen from the male parent, return the bag, and tie securely.

How does one go about producing a new color in a perennial? By taking the pollen from the flower of one species or variety and placing it upon the stigma of another. Both should belong to the same genus.

Specific Perennial Plants

ALYSSUM (AURINIA)

What soil is needed to raise Alyssum (Aurinia) saxatile? It grows best in a light, porous soil with good drainage and sun.

Alyssum lives but one year for me. Why is this? It needs a well-drained soil and full sun in order to live from year to year. Remove flower heads before they set seed.

Does alyssum need full sun for growing? It does best in full sun; will grow in part shade but not flower so freely, nor live so long.

How do you make cuttings of Alyssum (Aurinia) saxatile that will root and grow? Take cuttings soon after plants have flowered. Make them about 3 ins. long, or more, with about 1 in. of bare stem below the leaves; cut just below a leaf scar. Put in sand; water; keep shaded for a few days.

Will you explain how Alyssum (Aurinia) saxatile 'Compacta' is raised from seed? I have had no luck with it. It may be raised from seed sown in summer and wintered over in a frame or bed and planted out in spring; also, sow in spring and plant out early in fall.

ANCHUSA

Will you please give cultural care of anchusa 'Dropmore'? Good garden loam, with fair moisture and full sun. Divide roots every 3 years.

Is Anchusa azurea 'Dropmore' a true perennial, or should it be treated as an annual? Is it hardy in Massachusetts? It is a perennial and should be hardy in Massachusetts. However, it is not a long-lived perennial, and often dies in cold winters.

ASTERS

When should hardy aster seeds be planted? Can be sown in a greenhouse in March; cold frame in April; or outdoors in May.

When is best time to put out hardy asters? In spring before they have more than an inch or two of growth.

How can I keep aster (Michaelmas daisies) from growing too high? Pinching them back in early summer should help them stay bushy.

Which is a strong-growing hardy aster—preferably blue? 'Violetta' grows to 3 ft. or more, with lavender-blue flowers. Also 'Blue Radiance' and 'Eventide' are good strong blue varieties.

ASTILBE

Are the garden forms of astilbe that flower in late spring related to the shrub spirea? No, but can't blame you for wondering, as many nurserymen and catalogues persist in labeling these herbaceous perennials—which are decidedly non-woody—as "spirea." The flowers are fluffy, like some of those of spirea.

I would like to grow astilbe plants in my flower garden but have been told I can't as they require constantly wet soil. My garden's soil is average, but phlox and day-lilies thrive in it. I always water the garden during drought. You should be able to grow astilbe under the conditions you describe. While the plants of astilbe revel in moist, rich soil, they also adapt to more average conditions. When planting, add rich compost, leafmold, or peat moss to the planting holes so soil moisture will be retained.

BABY'S-BREATH (GYPSOPHILA)

What kind of soil for growing perennial baby's-breath? It will grow in any reasonably good soil; it does not have to be rich, but should be well drained and deep, and not more than slightly acid.

Can perennial gypsophila be successfully transplanted? Yes, if care is taken not to break the fleshy roots. It is best done in the spring.

What's wrong when gypsophila petals are so small you can barely see them? Probably you have a poor seedling or another plant, *Galium aristatum,* which is sometimes sold as baby's-breath which it resembles.

I have a 'Bristol Fairy' baby's-breath that grows beautifully but never blooms. Can anything be done to make it bloom? Some do not bloom when planted in too rich a soil. Try transplanting it (being careful not to break the long roots), and lime the soil.

How is gypsophila 'Bristol Fairy' propagated? Propagation is done by division, by cuttings, or by grafting on pieces of roots.

Does gypsophila 'Bristol Fairy' come true from seed? No.

BLEEDINGHEART (DICENTRA)

I had a large bleedingheart die last winter; was this because I covered it with leaves? Probably you used too many leaves and smothered the plant; or perhaps you covered it too early. Wait until the soil is frozen, then cover lightly. Remove gradually in spring. Mice will eat the roots.

My bleedingheart plants grew to large, healthy bushes but would not bloom. Why?　Probably planted in too dense shade.

When is the best time to move bleedinghearts?　In early autumn, or very early spring.

When is the correct time to divide bleedingheart?　September.

CACTI

What are the hardiest kinds of cacti?　*Opuntia compressa* (*vulgaris*), *O. fragilis, Echinocereus viridiflorus,* and *Pediocactus simpsonii.*

Are there any varieties of cactus, other than opuntia, that can be left outside all winter in south Jersey?　You might try *Echinocereus viridiflorus* and *Pediocactus simpsonii.*

Will cactus from the Arizona desert thrive in Oklahoma?　Those native from north of Phoenix will possibly grow if given a thoroughly well-drained and sheltered position.

Can spineless cacti be grown in a climate which is hot and dry in the summer and cold and wet in the winter?　No. The spineless opuntias do not thrive where wet winters are experienced.

What are names of some cacti that will live out of doors in south-central North Carolina?　*Opuntia compressa* (*vulgaris*), *O. fragilis, O. rhodantha,* (*O. xanthostemma*), *O. polyacantha, O. imbricata, O. basilaris, O. ursina, Echinocereus viridiflorus, E. reichenbachii, E. baileyi,* and *Pediocactus simpsonii.*

CANDYTUFT

How can I propagate Iberis sempervirens (evergreen candytuft)?　By seeds sown in spring; by dividing the old plants in autumn or spring; or by cuttings made in summer of the young growth inserted in a cold frame.

What is the best way to get a quantity of evergreen iberis, for edging, from seed?　Sow in an outdoor bed in May or June. Transplant seedlings to nursery beds, allowing 6 to 8 ins. between plants. Set in flowering quarters in fall, or following spring.

Will you give me proper culture for iberis? Mine is all dying.　Iberis usually grows satisfactorily in any well-drained garden soil not too acid, and needs no special care. There are perennial and annual iberis. The perennial kind sometimes does better when plants are cut back to within a couple of inches of the crown after they have flowered.

CARNATIONS (DIANTHUS)

Is it possible to grow the English border carnation in the East? The heat of summers is not favorable to their culture, nor are they winter hardy in this region. Some success can be attained by sowing seeds in a greenhouse in February, potting the seedlings, and planting out in May in as cool a spot as possible; a little shade in July and August will help. Pinch them several times to make them branch; give some support to keep the plants from sprawling. Keep nearly all the buds removed until late summer, and let them flower in fall. Summer flowers are inferior.

What kind of fertilizer is best for carnations? The basic need is for some kind of humus; rotted or dehydrated manure is the best. Peat moss, compost, or leafmold can be substituted, but to these lime and fertilizer must be added. To a bushel of any of the above, add ½ lb. of pulverized limestone and 1 lb. of complete fertilizer. Mix thoroughly and spread this 3 ins. deep and mix with the soil. When plants begin to bloom, feed with pulverized sheep manure, dried blood, or tankage, dehydrated manure, ½ lb. per square yard.

The soil here is sandy. Water supply very limited. Will carnations get along on natural rainfall? It will not be possible to get the best returns under these conditions. Set the plants out as early as possible, while the weather is cool. In July put on old leaves, grass clippings, or weeds as a mulch, and maintain it. This will assist in keeping the roots cool. Don't let the plants exhaust themselves by overflowering. Remove most of the buds until cool weather sets in.

Will you give the culture of hardy carnations? Sow seeds indoors in March in a soil mixture containing equal parts of loam, sand and leafmold. Transplant the seedlings into flats 2 ins. apart or into peat pots. Plant outside in May, about 12 ins. apart. Prepare the bed by forking in leafmold or peat; add 10 lbs. dried cow or sheep manure to 100 sq. ft. Water after planting; pinch out the tips to induce branching. Keep the soil stirred until the end of June, then mulch with old leaves or compost. Keep the plants watered; disbud for larger blooms.

What is the follow-up care of carnation seedlings; also winter care as far north as Pennsylvania? After hardening off the seedlings in a cold frame, set them out in the open in May in a well-prepared bed. (See previous questions.)

How can I grow pinks and carnations in upright clumps instead of spreading all over the ground?   Pinks and carnations have a tendency to spread, although some of the improved Marguerite strain are less inclined than others. Insert small pieces of twiggy brush among the plants while they are still small. This will tend to hold them upright. A little tying here and there will keep them tidy.

I am able to raise most kinds of flowers except hardy carnations. Just what do they need to do well?   They need a well-drained soil. The plants should be set out early to become well developed before hot weather. Give them plenty of moisture during hot weather. Some believe in keeping the buds removed until late summer because they flower best in cool weather.

Why do my carnations have thin stems? The flowers are large, but the stems are so small they will not stand up.   Try applying superphosphate to the soil, 4 oz. per square yard. Look to the variety; this sometimes is a vital fault that no amount of care will eliminate.

I have 2 choice carnation plants now 2 years old. One is full of buds and blooms, the other has not even a bud. Why?   The fault in the non-blooming plant is in the way it was propagated—hard growth from non-blooming stock. Discard it, and propagate from the plant that blooms.

I read in a magazine that if you take cuttings from perennial pinks in October they would grow indoors. Did this, but they are not thriving. Why?   What the article probably meant was to take the cuttings in October and winter the young plants over in the house and plant out in spring. They are not house plants. They need full sun, and bloom only in summer. In any case, cuttings are better if taken in August.

Our pinks formed large plants their second year but did not blossom. In the same soil sweet Williams did very well. What do you suggest?   The soil may be a little too rich or too wet, or lacking in lime. A well-drained soil, full sun, and the chance to ripen off in fall are necessary. Do not feed or water after August.

Which dianthus species are dependably hardy?   *Dianthus arenar-*

ius, arvernensis, plumarius (cottage pink), *deltoides* (maiden pink), *petraeus, gratianopolitanus* (cheddar pink), *pavonius.*

Which kind of pinks are perennial? Is it better to sow new seed every spring? The most important perennial pink in the garden is *Dianthus plumarius,* of which several varieties, both single and double, are grown. *D. alpinus, D. gratianopolitanus, D. deltoides, D. knappii,* and *D. pavonius* can be grown in rock gardens. It should not be necessary to sow seed every spring. Named varieties of *D. plumarius* are propagated from cuttings or divisions.

The Scotch or dwarf pink in its usual form is too straggly. Can you name a dwarf compact variety that is better in this respect? *Dianthus deltoides* 'Brilliant', *D. arvernensis, D. subacaulis, D. gratianopolitanus.*

CHRISTMAS-ROSE (HELLEBORE)

What is the botanical name of the Christmas-rose? *Helleborus niger.*

How should I start a bed of Christmas-roses? Select a position in partial shade where the soil is rich and moist; add well-rotted manure, compost, or leafmold. Obtain young plants from dealers and set out in early spring.

I have a Christmas-rose that I have had for 3 or 4 years, and last February was the first time it bloomed. Now I would like to move it. Will that set it back again for 3 or 4 years? The Christmas-rose does not like to be disturbed, and if you move it again it will in all probability set it back for a few years. Moving carefully with a very large soil-ball would help, but it would be best to leave it where it is.

What location should I transplant my Christmas-rose to? It doesn't do anything on the south side of the house. The southerly aspect is too warm. Put in a cooler spot, and let it get established. Never allow it to become dry. See preceding answer.

Do Christmas-roses need much sun? Christmas-roses do best in partial shade, where they are not subject to being dried out in summer.

What makes my Christmas-rose die down, then get new leaves, but no bloom? Has not bloomed this year. The plant failed to set flower buds due to some factor like drying out in summer, or poor soil. It may have been disturbed during cultural operations.

Will you tell me how to divide a Christmas-rose? Mine is doing wonderfully well, but I would like to give some away. Best divided in late summer or autumn by taking a spading fork and lifting the side shoots without disturbing the main plant. It resents any disturbance, and when well established should be left alone.

I planted a Christmas-rose in spring a year ago. It seems to be showing no signs of buds; in fact, no new shoots have come up this fall. It is in a well-drained spot, partially shaded, and covered with a box, one side of which is glass. What is the proper care? How early shall I cover it? What kind of fertilizer? Put fertilizer on in spring. Do not cover the plant at all. A few leaves drifting in among the stems is enough covering. Let the plant become well established, and avoid all disturbance. (See answers to preceding questions.)

How can I start Christmas-roses from seed? Sow, as soon as ripe, in a mixture of soil, leafmold, and sand in cold frame, and keep moist. They are slow to germinate, and will probably take from 3 to 5 years to reach flowering size.

CHRYSANTHEMUM

The garden chrysanthemum, originally an oriental plant, has been so changed through centuries of cultivation that it scarcely resembles the species from which it was derived. In the year 1750 it was introduced into English gardens but at that time created very little interest. About a century later it was brought to America, and for years was grown only as a greenhouse plant. Within the last half century it has become a prominent garden flower—a result of the successful development of hardier and earlier-flowering types and varieties.

Chrysanthemums in the garden give a profusion of bloom in bright autumn colors as a grand finale to the gardening season. Light frosts do little damage to either the flowers or the foliage. If planted in protected spots, they will often remain attractive until mid-November in the latitude of New York State. Farther south, and in other milder climates, they are even better adapted, and a much larger selection of varieties can be used.

While hardy chrysanthemums are comparatively easy to grow, they will not stand neglect. They need to be divided and reset every second or third year, and kept well fertilized and free of disease and insect pests. Considerable care should be given to the selection of varieties for outdoor planting. There are many kinds in the trade, but only relatively few of these bloom early enough in the fall, or are sufficiently hardy where winters are severe, to be dependable garden plants.

What type of soil is best for hardy chrysanthemums? Any friable, free-working soil is satisfactory. It should be well drained yet reasonably retentive of moisture and of goodly depth.

How should a bed for chrysanthemums be prepared and fertilized? Spade it deeply (without bringing up large quantities of unkind subsoil), incorporate a 3- or 4-in. layer of rotted manure or compost and a dressing of superphosphate. If manure is not available, substitute compost and commercial fertilizer. Lime, if necessary, to keep soil approximately neutral.

How shall I prepare a bed for chrysanthemums? My ground is quite low and has a heavy clay subsoil. Spade or plow in fall, adding manure, compost, leafmold, or peat moss. In early spring apply a dressing of lime, and a week or so before plants are set out, fork in a light application of complete fertilizer. Chrysanthemums will not succeed in waterlogged soil.

Do hardy chrysanthemums like lime or limestone in the soil? They prefer pH 6 to 7. They have much the same requirements in this respect as the general run of garden vegetables.

What should chrysanthemums, carried over in a cold frame for winter, be fed? And when? Do not feed while in cold frame. Add rotted manure and superphosphate, or complete fertilizer, to outdoor beds prior to planting; possibly a light side dressing of complete fertilizer when half grown. Liquid fertilizer applied in late summer and early fall works wonders.

How can manure be used on cushion chrysanthemums? How freely? Around second-year plants work a 2-in. covering well into the soil together with some superphosphate and a dusting of wood ashes. Prepare soil for new plantings as for other hardy chrysanthemums.

Do cushion chrysanthemums need summer feeding? No. Not if soil is fairly good.

When should one plant chrysanthemums? In the spring.

Where should chrysanthemums be planted? Any location that receives sunshine at least ⅔ of the day, providing soil and air circulation are good. Avoid overhanging eaves, walls, and stuffy corners. Don't crowd them among other plants.

What is the best way to plant hardy chrysanthemums? In well-prepared soil make a hole with a trowel or spade, of ample size to accommodate roots. Set plant in position; spread out roots; work soil in among them and press soil firm with fingers. Do not plant when soil is wet and sticky. Water after planting.

How often should chrysanthemums be replanted? Strong-growing kinds should be divided every year; moderate-growing, every second year.

Would it be advisable to divide and reset chrysanthemums in fall after they have finished blooming? No. It is safer to do this in spring. (See following questions.)

When is best time to divide hardy chrysanthemums? How? In spring, as soon as shoots are 3 to 4 ins. high. Dig up clump; discard old center portion; separate young offshoots; plant as single divisions, 10 or 12 ins. apart, in carefully prepared soil.

Is spring or fall the best time to transplant chrysanthemums that are in a too-shady place? Spring is best, but if necessary they can be moved any time during the growing season if thoroughly watered first and carefully lifted with a good ball of soil.

Can hardy chrysanthemums be moved when in bloom? Yes. Be sure soil is moist; take up clump with a good root-ball; replant immediately. Firm soil around roots; shade for 2 or 3 days; and *don't neglect watering.*

What is the best way to store early chrysanthemums during winter in Washington? Lift plants and place in cold frame. If left in garden, cover lightly with evergreen branches, leaves, or similar protection.

What is the best way to care for chrysanthemums after they stop blooming in fall? Cut stems back close to ground. If brown foliage appeared during summer, burn stems and all dropped leaves—they harbor insects. Cover lightly with evergreen branches and dry leaves.

What is winter care for chrysanthemums, without a cold frame, in southern Vermont? A blanket of evergreen branches intermingled with leaves would make best covering. Apply when soil is slightly frozen. Good soil drainage is an important factor.

Can well-rotted manure be placed on top of chrysanthemums as a winter mulch? Yes, but not close to the crowns. Pack dry leaves immediately around the plants themselves.

When should chrysanthemums be covered, before or after frost? After the first killing frost and when the soil is slightly frozen.

How can I keep a cushion chrysanthemum over winter? (Minnesota.) Cushion chrysanthemums should winter over in Minnesota with a light blanket of evergreen branches and dry leaves applied when ground is lightly frozen.

How may I protect large-flowering chrysanthemum blooms in the outdoor garden? A double-thick cheesecloth covering stretched over a framework affords considerable protection. Avoid growing varieties that are late in flowering.

Can you take a non-hardy chrysanthemum, cut it off a few inches from the ground, keep it inside until spring, and then set it out? Yes, if you pot the roots and carry the plant over in a cool, well-lighted cellar or room. Soil must be kept slightly moist. There are, of course, many reliable hardy chrysanthemums that do not require this attention.

Is December 1 too late to put a chrysanthemum plant outdoors that has been in bloom in the house for about 4 weeks? Too late for sure results in most northern areas. If planted in a sheltered corner and covered lightly, it has a fifty-fifty chance.

Would semi-hardy chrysanthemums winter in soil in a barn cellar? Should the cellar be dark or light? A well-lighted barn cellar that is cool should do. Be careful that soil does not dry out.

Just how do you care for cushion chrysanthemums? I know they are heavy feeders and I care for them very well, but why do they bloom one year and not the next? Divide every second year. Water copiously, but only when needed during dry periods. Reasonable feeding should be sufficient. Tarnished plant bug and other insect injury can prevent flowering.

How should chrysanthemums (cushion type) be cared for to bloom freely so they look like pictures in the catalogues? Choose sunny location. Don't crowd together or among other plants. Add a complete general purpose garden fertilizer plus compost or other form of humus to the soil under your plants. Cultivate frequently but lightly and water copiously when needed. Divide plants every other year.

Will you give me information on how to grow large chrysanthemums out of doors?   Grow 1 to 2 stems only to each plant; remove all side buds. Shading with black sateen cloth to hasten blooming, or special protection, may be necessary.

Have read that covering chrysanthemums with black cloth for a certain time during the day brings them into bloom earlier. Will you give me detailed instructions for its use?   There is a special black sateen cloth made for this purpose. Starting in mid-July, completely darken the plants from 5 P.M. until 7 A.M. Discontinue when the buds show color.

Can the blooms of large, exhibition chrysanthemums grown outside in the garden be hastened by enclosing them in darkened frames? If so, when should these frames be applied? I am an amateur but sell quite a few flowers to florists.   Yes. Build framework of wood and cover with black cloth so as to be as nearly light-proof as possible. (See reply to previous question.)

What care should be given exhibition chrysanthemums?   They require careful attention to all details of cultivation, such as propagating, soil preparation, watering, staking, disbudding, etc. When buds appear, apply liquid fertilizer every week or 10 days until the flowers begin to open.

Will you please give culture on pompon chrysanthemums?   Pompons are easily grown in the garden. Good rich soil, thorough watering when needed, and frequent cultivation are the essentials. Only tallest varieties require pinching.

How should I care for chrysanthemums in the spring?   Divide and replant if they have been growing 2 years in same place; if possible give them a different location. Otherwise fork some manure, compost, or fertilizer into surface soil.

My chrysanthemums have been in 3 years and are large clumps. Should they be thinned out? Into what size clumps?   Strong-growing chrysanthemums should be divided every year; moderate-growing kinds every 2 years. Do this in spring, leaving each division with 1 or 2 shoots.

How do florists manage to keep the foliage on chrysanthemums

green down to the ground? By starting with young plants, taking care that they are never allowed to dry out, but are not overwatered. Most florists spray the plants every 10 days so that insects cannot get a start.

How can I grow many-branched chrysanthemums? Keep plants young by frequent division and pinch them back 2 or 3 times during growing season. Keep staked; and watered during dry periods.

What is the correct way to disbud chrysanthemums? Many plants produce larger flowers if just 1 (the terminal) bud remains on each branch. Remove unwanted buds by rubbing them out with thumb and finger when they are ⅛ in. or so in diameter.

When should chrysanthemums be pinched back? Tall-growing types, at intervals during spring and early summer. Give first pinch when 9 to 12 ins. high, second when about 15 ins. high, and possibly a third in late July. Cushion-type varieties require no pinching.

Should I pinch every shoot on a chrysanthemum, or just the center one? All strong shoots are cut back early in season to cause low, bushy growth.

Should cushion and pompon chrysanthemums be pinched back in spring? All cushions and many pompons branch naturally and do not require pinching. A few of the taller pompon varieties should be pinched.

What is the best method of pruning and disbudding hardy chrysanthemums? "Pruning" consists of pinching out the tips of the shoots when plants are 9 ins. high, and the tips of all subsequent side

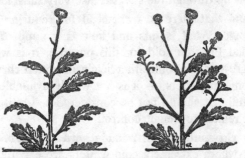

Disbudding a chrysanthemum. In order to secure a flower of large size, the top terminal bud (of the several which form) only is left.

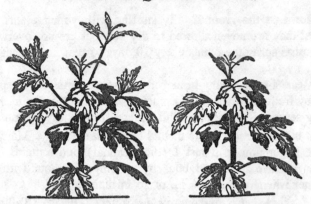

Pruning or "pinching" a chrysanthemum. In order to throw the plant's strength to the terminal bud, or a crown bud, side shoots or laterals are removed.

branches when they are 6 ins. long. This practice is discontinued in late July. Disbudding consists of removing many of the young flower buds so that the one or more allowed to remain on each stem will develop into especially fine blooms.

What is the proper way to stake chrysanthemums? Each year the weight of mine bends over the stems. Wooden or bamboo stakes can be pushed into the ground near the plants and the stems neatly tied to these. Place supports *before they begin to flower,* and try to preserve the natural habit of plant. Avoid tying so that plant is bunched together like a shock of corn. Brushwood staking inserted so shoots grow up through the sticks is also very satisfactory.

I understand that there is a chemical for reducing the height of chrysanthemums. What is this and how is it applied? There is a chemical called Phosfon sold for this purpose. It is widely used by commercial growers for controlling height of potted chrysanthemums, less so by home gardeners, as it is not widely available and must be applied carefully. It should not be considered a substitute for proper culture, as it relates to height control.

Are hardy chrysanthemums reliably hardy throughout the United States? Not where extremely cold winters are experienced.

Is there anything one can do to make chrysanthemums bloom earlier in the fall? I had several new varieties this year and they

budded so late that they didn't bloom at all. When selecting new varieties, choose early-flowering kinds.

Why didn't my chrysanthemums bloom this fall? They are the old-fashioned type and are planted on the south side of my house. Was it because they need dividing and transplanting, or because of an early freeze? Old-fashioned chrysanthemums naturally bloom late and are sometimes caught by an early freeze. Why not try some of the many good kinds that flower in September and October?

My chrysanthemums grow very tall but have weak stems and few blooms. What shall I do? Divide them in the spring; pinch back (nip out tips of growing shoots with thumbnail), starting when plants are about 6 ins. tall and continuing every 2 weeks until mid-July. This will make plants bushy and more floriferous. Grow in full sunlight.

If seedling chrysanthemums bloom in October the first year and in August the second year (in the same place and about same conditions), what is likely to be their regular season of blooming? From mid-September on if your plants are divided and reset every second year, as they should be.

Two chrysanthemums, full of buds that seemed ready to burst several weeks prior to freezing weather, did not bloom. Can their blooming season be hastened in any way? Your varieties are too late for your particular locality. Try earlier kinds. The *buds* of some varieties are not frost hardy, even though the flowers may be.

How can I keep chrysanthemums from growing out of bounds? Both hardy and exhibition types are 5 to 6 ft. tall. Use phosphates rather than nitrates for fertilizing. Grow in full sun and do not crowd. Pinch back vigorous shoots during May, June, and July.

Our cushion chrysanthemums have very few blossoms. This is their second year. What is wrong? They should be at their best in their second year. Don't crowd. Prepare soil deeply and water copiously whenever needed during summer. They do best in full sun. Tarnished plant bug may prevent flowering.

I had a fine collection of chrysanthemums, but each blooming season I find that I have more bronze colors and less yellows, reds. Do they revert? Chrysanthemums do sometimes exhibit the phenomenon known as mutation; but more probably self-sown seeds have germinated and reverted to other colors. The bronze varieties are especially vigorous, and would take the lead.

Do different chrysanthemums mix and change color if planted closely together? (Louisiana.)   No. But seedlings which differ in color can spring up among the parent plants. This would be very likely in your climate.

How can I best increase choice chrysanthemums?   If hotbed or greenhouse facilities are available, take cuttings (in February or March) from stock plants kept over winter in a cold frame. Root in sand, transplant to pots or flats of soil, and set outdoors in April. Plants wintered outdoors can be taken up and divided in early spring.

What is the method of splitting or dividing a cushion chrysanthemum plant?   Same as any hardy chrysanthemum. (See previous and following replies.)

Will you please tell me how to divide or thin chrysanthemum plants?   Lift just as new growth appears in spring. With hands, knife, or a small hand fork pry off from outsides of old clumps small divisions, each consisting of 2 or 3 shoots, with roots attached. Plant divisions 1½ to 2 ft. apart in well-prepared soil.

Is it better to start new chrysanthemums from slips, or to divide old plants?   Cuttings or small healthy divisions give equally good results. The former are better, however, if stock plants are infested with nematodes.

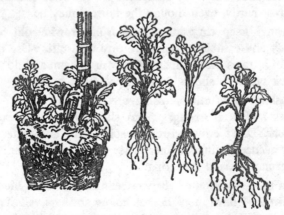

Old chrysanthemum plant, and young growths with roots removed to provide new plants.

Will chrysanthemums grow from cuttings made from tips of shoots that are removed when plants are pinched back? Yes.

When is the proper time to start to root chrysanthemum cuttings for best results? For large plants, cuttings should be started indoors in late February and the cuttings taken in March. Cuttings taken in April and May are quite satisfactory, but plants are smaller.

How can I graft several colors on a single chrysanthemum plant? Grow a strong, early-started, young plant to a single stem. At the desired height, say 2½ ft., pinch the tip out to promote side branches. On these insert the grafts. A humid atmosphere should be maintained after grafting and the grafts should be kept sealed with polyethylene until they have formed a good union.

Can one buy seeds of the large-flowering-type chrysanthemums? They are listed by a few large seed houses. More readily available from seed are low-growing, small-flowered varieties, both single and double. This is an inexpensive way to acquire chrysanthemums. Seed germinates readily if sown early outdoors in a cold frame. Plants should flower by fall. In cold climates select the earliest flowering Korean chrysanthemums.

How can I grow chrysanthemums from seeds to get blooms first year? Start seeds indoors during March. Transplant once to flats or a cold frame before planting in outdoor garden.

What insects and diseases commonly attack hardy chrysanthemums? See Chrysanthemums—Section 13.

Why didn't my hardy chrysanthemums bloom this year? The leaves turned like dusty-miller leaves. Evidently the plants were badly mildewed. Do not plant too closely together or in shade.

What spray do you recommend for black aphids on outdoor chrysanthemums? Spray with malathion or diazinon.

How can I control chrysanthemum leafspot disease? First be sure you have this disease. The effects of leaf nematodes are often mistaken for it. Leafspot produces in the diseased areas masses of white spores which are easily seen with a hand lens. To control, pick off and burn infected leaves; spray with zineb, ferbam, or Dithane M-45; avoid wetting leaves when watering.

What is care of fall-blooming chrysanthemums? Mine die down every fall, lose their leaves (which turn black or brown), and flower

very late. They are probably infested with leaf nematodes (eelworms). After blooming, cut back close to ground. Remove and burn all stems and leaves, which harbor this pest over winter. In spring propagate from tip cuttings and set plants in new location in good soil, or in soil disinfected with formaldehyde or chloropicrin.

My chrysanthemum blooms turn brown before fully opening. Why? Foliage is in good condition. Send a few affected leaves to your State Agricultural Experiment Station to be checked for leaf nematodes. (See previous reply.)

In cold climates, how can one be assured of buying plants that will bloom before killing frost? Buy from a specialist and be guided by the blooming dates given for each variety. If your area is different from where the catalogue comes from, dates can vary a week or two since the dates are usually based on blooming time in the nurseries' growing fields.

I have always admired the big chrysanthemums worn as corsages. Can these be grown in the garden and what should I ask for? These are known as "football" chrysanthemums. They can be grown, but need a little more attention to disbudding and staking than regular varieties. In cold climates they need protection from frost as they are rather late to bloom.

Is there a difference in hardiness of chrysanthemum varieties? Apparently there is. If you live in very cold regions try to buy those developed in northerly regions. The University of Minnesota and the University of Nebraska have introduced quite a few varieties.

What is a cascade chrysanthemum? These are plants grown so that they cascade down over a pot on a special frame. Sometimes they are trained up a frame. Special varieties are used for this purpose so it's best to consult the catalogue of a chrysanthemum specialist.

What are spider chrysanthemums? These have long narrow petals, curled at the tip. They are very exotic-looking and because the flowers are somewhat delicate, they are generally grown in a greenhouse or with some form of protection against the elements.

COLUMBINE (AQUILEGIA)

My columbines never grow into healthy plants, as I have seen others do. They have full sun, and the other plants around the columbines grow very well. Why? They need a well-drained sandy loam, neutral or slightly acid. Prepare ground at least a foot deep; incorporate a 2-in. layer of rotted manure or rich compost; space plants at least 9 ins. apart.

What is the best location for columbines? What fertilizer? Most any location except a hot, dry, windy one; light shade, too, is beneficial. Topdressing of leafmold, with well-rotted manure or compost, in early spring, is good.

What is the proper way to plant columbines? I planted them in rich woods soil in a spot that got sun in the morning, shade later in the day, fairly well drained. They never came up. The soil and position should be all right. You probably planted them too deeply, and the crowns rotted. They are subject to a soft rot.

From a planting of 15 columbines only 2 bloomed. Could you supply any information as to their culture? See preceding answers. When established, the others probably will bloom.

Can columbine seedlings, coming from seed planted in August, be transplanted next spring? Yes.

Is it possible to transplant old columbine plants? When? Yes. Best done in early spring. Water until established. Don't plant too deeply.

How shall I divide columbines? Lift the clumps, shake off the soil, and gently pull the plant apart, taking care not to break the roots.

DAY-LILY (HEMEROCALLIS)

When is best time to plant day-lilies? How? Spring or summer planting is all right. They can even be lifted in full bloom if a good clump of soil is taken and care is used not to damage the roots. Plants must be watered deeply and kept well-watered for a week or two. Dig soil deeply, adding well-rotted cow manure, leafmold, peat moss, or compost; dig holes deep enough when planting so that roots are not crowded, and set plants with crown just level with soil.

Do day-lilies have to be planted in the shade? No. Day-lilies will grow in full sun if the soil is rich and moist, but otherwise do better in light or partial shade.

Can day-lilies be successfully grown planted among other perennials in a border? Yes, providing you give them space enough to grow—at least 3 ft.

What is the cause of day-lilies failing to blossom? Failure to bloom is most commonly due to too-dense shade, or plants being overcrowded and the soil exhausted.

How can I get lemon-lilies (Hemerocallis flava) to bloom? Divide and replant in full sun in soil that has been dug deeply (18 ins.) and enriched with a 3-in. layer of rotted manure, leafmold, peat moss, or compost, plus bone meal or superphosphate at the rate of 6 oz. per square yard.

How shall I divide day-lilies? These are sometimes hard to divide, especially old clumps. The best method is to first dig up clumps, then push two spading forks through the clump, back to back, and pry the clump apart.

Can you give me the name of an exquisite, dainty, lemon-yellow day-lily, which blooms profusely in early spring? Foliage same as dark day-lily, only light and much daintier. In all probability the lemon-lily, *Hemerocallis flava*. This species is fragrant.

What is the main blooming season for day-lilies? This is July and August. However, some bloom in June and others in September and October.

What is the orange day-lily that I see growing wild by the wayside? This is *Hemerocallis fulva*. It's a fairly rampant grower and is best used where it can multiply. There are better orange hybrids for garden use.

Are there any miniature day-lilies? Yes, they are becoming increasingly popular and a few more new varieties are listed each year. In general the flowers are smaller than for the taller varieties but they are showy nonetheless.

Will you name some good varieties of day-lilies that will give a succession of bloom, from the earliest to the latest? Check a catalogue of a day-lily specialist and choose a good assortment from each group—early, early-midseason, midseason, midseason-late, and late. Here are a few suggestions. *Early:* 'Channel Islands', creamy yellow; 'Chartreuse Queen', chartreuse; 'Jake Russell', gold. *Early-midseason:* 'Annie Welch', soft pink; 'Bold Ruler', deep rose; 'Buried Treasure', light yellow; 'Carey Queen', red; 'Cashmere', creamy yellow brushed with rose on petal tips; 'Chipper Cherry', cherry red. *Midseason:* 'Glowing Lights', apricot pink; 'June Prom', pale orange; 'Lexington', yellow. *Midseason-late:* 'Fairy Delight', pink; 'Hall of Fame', pink; 'Party Partner', pale apricot. *Late:* 'Claudia Ann', dusty rose; 'Diamond Deb', peach; 'Holiday Harvest', yellow; 'Luminaire', copper.

Is there such a thing as a double day-lily? I have one and thought maybe it was a freak. Yes. There are quite a few. Two doubles are 'Kwanso' and 'Double Gold'.

Can you tell me how to hybridize day-lilies? The flowers which are to be used as the seed bearer should be emasculated (remove anthers) and enclosed in a waxed or cellophane bag; when the stigma becomes sticky, the ripe pollen from another variety is transferred to it.

What is the best time of day to hybridize the day-lily? From about 12 noon until 2 P.M., as the pollen will be driest at that time.

DELPHINIUM

The modern delphinium is one of the most spectacular of our garden flowers. Most common garden hybrids are tall-growing, and are best used toward the back of a mixed border where they create strong vertical lines and accent points. However, a new dwarfer strain is being developed by the famous English seedhouse of Blackmore & Langdon, so look for these in your catalogue. While the clear blue colors are most highly prized, sparkling whites, rich violets, and soft, pleasing mauves are available. Some have yellow or red flowers, but

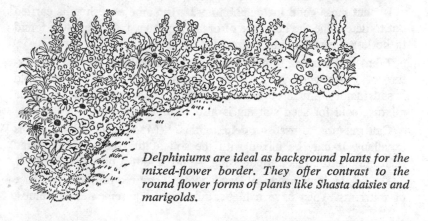

Delphiniums are ideal as background plants for the mixed-flower border. They offer contrast to the round flower forms of plants like Shasta daisies and marigolds.

they are not so easy to grow in the average garden; nor are the flower spikes as showy as those of the more common types.

The geographic distribution of delphinium species is more or less limited to the Northern Hemisphere, but they are used in gardens on every continent. While their culture varies in different regions, they are grown successfully throughout the United States and Canada.

There are 4 main types of delphiniums. The erect and tall-growing elatum or garden hybrids bear single or double flowers in dense spikes. The 'Belladonna' and 'Bellamosum' types are dwarfer, with more finely cut foliage and looser spikes. The two are essentially much alike in habit of growth, but the 'Belladonna' has light-blue or white flowers, while in the 'Bellamosum' type the flowers are dark blue. The Chinese delphinium is comparatively dwarf, seldom attaining a height of more than 3 ft. The foliage is finely cut and the clear blue or white flowers are borne in a loose, informal arrangement. They are the easiest to grow, and especially valuable for cutting to be used with other flowers in mixed bouquets or arrangements. The delphinium annual is the larkspur.

What kind of soil is desirable for delphiniums? A rich, friable loam containing a high percentage of organic matter.

How can one increase the amount of organic matter in the soil for delphiniums? Experiments have shown that thoroughly decomposed leafmold is the best organic matter to use. Oak leafmold is less desirable than other types. Mix the leafmold with soil at the rate of 8 to 10 bu. per 100 sq. ft.; or 1 bu. of leafmold to 8 bu. of soil. Rich compost should also be satisfactory.

Is peat moss good for delphiniums? In some experiments carried out to determine the best type of organic matter, peat moss was found to be less desirable than leafmold.

What soil mixture is best for starting delphinium seeds? A mixture of 1 part good garden loam, 1 part sand, and 1 part leafmold is satisfactory. Sift through a sieve having ¼-in. mesh. A commercial mixture sold for seed starting is also suitable.

Can manure be used on delphiniums? Manure, if well rotted, is excellent. It may be mixed with the soil at the time it is prepared or it may be used as a topdressing. Apply about 5 bu. per 100 sq. ft.

Do delphiniums need fertilizer? Yes. They require an abundance of nutrients. They have a higher nitrogen requirement than almost any other garden flower. Unless the soil is already very rich they should be fertilized at least twice a year with a complete commercial fertilizer.

When should delphiniums be fertilized? Make the first application in spring when the new shoots are about 4 ins. tall. A second application can be made about 5 weeks later.

Do delphiniums require lime? They do best in a slightly acid soil (pH 6.8). If the organic matter content is very high, they will do well over a much wider range of pH values (pH 5.5 to 7.2). Lime is required only when a pH test shows that the reaction is pH 6.5 or below.

What type of lime should be used for delphiniums; and how should it be applied? Ground limestone is best. Where soil is very acid or very heavy, hydrated lime or wood ashes can be used. Spread it evenly over soil surface and work it into the top 3 or 4 ins.

Should lime be applied to delphiniums every year? No, only when a soil test indicates it is necessary.

How can one tell by observing the plants when the soil is too "sweet" for delphiniums? The leaves appear mottled with yellow or, in severe cases, with white. The veins usually retain their dark-green color. A pH test of the soil will confirm the plant symptoms.

In what situation should delphiniums be planted? In full sun or very light shade and, if possible, with some protection from strong winds.

How far apart should delphiniums be planted? In perennial borders, 2 to 3 ft. each way. In cut-flower garden, 3 to 4 ft. between rows and 2 ft. between plants in rows.

When should delphiniums be transplanted? Very early spring is best; but they can be transplanted with success in fall, or immediately after their first period of bloom.

When should full-grown delphiniums be moved? In very early spring, if possible before growth starts. Move with a large ball of soil.

How can I keep my delphiniums healthy? Give them a rich, well-drained soil. Fertilize twice a year. Spray with a miticide.

How can delphiniums be made to bloom in the fall as well as during their regular season? By cutting the flowering stems off as soon as possible after they have finished blooming. New shoots will then come up and flower in the early fall.

How can delphiniums be staked?   Begin when the plant is about 3 ft. high, and place three 6-ft. stakes in the form of a triangle around it. Tie a band of raffia or soft twine around the stakes about 1 ft. above the ground. As the plant grows, tie additional bands around the stakes. If desired, individual stakes can be used for large-flowering spikes. This latter method is to be preferred in decorative plantings.

Should delphiniums be watered?   Delphiniums require large quantities of water, especially during, and just prior to, the flowering period. They will be improved by thorough watering when the weather is dry.

What winter care should be given delphinium seedlings started in a cold frame in August?   Cover with about 2 ins. of medium-coarse clean sand. Later mulch with straw or salt hay. Put sash on the frame to keep out snow and rain.

Should young delphinium plants, set out in the fall, be mulched? It is always well to protect seedlings transplanted in the fall from heaving. Covering the plants with about 2 ins. of sand, and later mulching lightly with marsh hay or straw, will give the necessary protection.

Should established delphiniums be covered over winter?   In all but the coldest climates this is unnecessary. Delphiniums are more likely to be killed by poor drainage, smothering, or diseases than by low temperatures.

Should a beginner buy delphinium plants or start them from seeds? Either is satisfactory, but most delphinium growers prefer to start their own plants. Purchase only the best plants or seeds. Inferior strains are unsatisfactory.

Do seeds from hybrid delphiniums produce desirable plants?   If seeds are saved from superior plants they will probably be satisfactory but they are seldom as good as the plants that seeds were collected from. It is usually best to buy seeds from reliable growers who have taken special pains in producing them. Try to buy fresh seed.

Why have my delphiniums failed since I moved them and replanted them 1 ft. from a hedge where they get south sun?   Probably the moving is responsible. They may do better when they become re-established. However, you have set them too near the hedge. They should be at least 2 or 3 ft. away and kept well fertilized and watered.

How can I prevent my delphiniums from growing tall and having brittle stems even though I withhold nitrogen? Vigorous delphiniums are likely to be brittle and to break off during wind- and rainstorms. Withholding nitrogen will not make the stems less brittle; in fact, it may make them more so. Nothing can be done except to stake the plants adequately.

Can delphiniums have their tops pinched out, like zinnias, to make them branch? No, the shoots that arise from the bases of the plants terminate in flower spikes. When the growing point is removed, the lateral buds do not develop as they do with zinnias.

How can I keep delphiniums alive during the hot summer months? They can be grown in light shade or cloth houses. In the open keep them well watered but don't let the soil remain soggy.

Why do delphiniums freeze in winter? Delphiniums are really very hardy plants. It is seldom that they are killed by low temperatures. They are more likely to be smothered by snow, ice, or poor drainage. Diseases, especially crown-rot, can develop during the fall, winter, or early spring, and kill the plants. Heaving is another hazard. Some leading growers consider the English strains hardier than the American strains developed on the Pacific coast.

How long will delphiniums live? Where the crown-rot diseases are not serious, they live indefinitely. However, since these organisms are widespread over much of the United States, from 3 to 5 years is the expected life of the ordinary plant.

How can Delphinium cardinale be wintered in cold climates? It can't. This species is tender and will not stand freezing. It can be carried over winter only in a greenhouse, and even then it is not very successful.

How can delphiniums be grown in a warm climate, such as Florida? Grow them as annuals by sowing seeds early each spring. The plants are not usually successfully carried over a second year.

Is there a truly perennial delphinium? In their native habitats many species persist for years, but under garden conditions they are more subject to diseases and are less long-lived.

Why do some delphiniums live longer than others? Natural variation in vigor, disease resistance, etc., account for the difference in longevity.

What is the best temperature for germinating delphinium seeds? The optimum is 55° F.

What is the best way to raise delphiniums from seed? Many different methods are successful; it is difficult to state which is best. Where many plants are needed, sow in well-prepared soil in a cold frame in August. Leave the seedlings in the frame over winter and transplant to the garden in spring.

Does it speed germination to refrigerate seeds? If seed is fresh (recently harvested) it does not need refrigeration before sowing. When not fresh (as in spring), refrigeration in an airtight container in the refrigerator for several weeks will help. If seed is to be stored over winter, keep it in the refrigerator in an airtight jar.

What conditions are necessary for growing delphinium seedlings? Good light, plenty of moisture (but the soil must not be kept soaked), and a temperature of 55° to 60° F.

Can delphinium seeds be sown in the open ground? Yes. If you do so, prepare a bed with special care where the tiny seedlings can be protected. It is really better, however, to sow in a cold frame or in seed flats.

When should delphiniums be started indoors? Seeds can be sown any time between February 1 and May 1. If started early, many of the plants will bloom the first year.

How thick should delphinium seeds be sown and how deep should they be covered? Sow in rows spaced about 2 ins. apart. The seeds in the rows should be about ¼ in. apart. Cover so that seeds are barely out of sight.

Should delphinium seeds be disinfected? And how? Disinfecting is desirable, especially where the soil is not sterilized. The use of a disinfectant, sold for the purpose, is satisfactory. Merely place a pinch of the powder in the seed package and shake until seeds are evenly covered.

Is it necessary to sterilize soil in which delphinium seeds are sown? Not necessary, but it is good insurance. Measure out 2½ tablespoonfuls of formaldehyde (40 per cent strength) for each bushel of prepared soil; dilute with 4 or 5 times its volume of water; add to soil, and mix very thoroughly. Place soil in seed boxes, saving a little for covering the seed; stack the boxes one above the other to confine the fumes for a day or two, then uncover them. When the odor is no longer perceptible it is safe to sow the seeds.

Will delphinium seeds sown indoors in spring produce flowers in summer? If sown indoors before April 1 most of the plants will bloom in late August or early September.

Should delphinium seedlings grown indoors be transplanted, or may one wait until they can be planted outdoors? Transplant to flats as soon as big enough to handle conveniently. Use a soil mixture of 1 part leafmold, 2 parts garden loam, and ½ part sand. Good drainage must be provided so that soil never remains soggy. Seedlings can be put in individual peat pots.

Is it wise to divide delphiniums that have grown to a large size; and how often should this be done? Ordinarily it is better to start new plants from seeds, but old clumps can be divided if they have become too large; this will usually not be until they are at least 3 years old.

How are delphiniums divided; and how large should the divisions be? Lift the plants, shake off the soil, and cut the clumps apart with a strong knife. Replant immediately in well-prepared soil. Each division should contain 3 to 5 shoots.

My delphiniums suffer from "blacks"; they are deformed and stunted and marked with black streaks and blotches. What is wrong? This "disease" is not a disease at all but is caused by an infestation of an exceedingly minute pest—the cyclamen mite. Cut off and burn badly infested shoots. Spray from early spring to flowering time with Kelthane or Thiodane about once a week. Avoid planting delphiniums near strawberries, which are also host to this mite.

What is a cure for crown-rot of delphiniums? Crown-rot is really a name for a group of diseases. All are very difficult to control. Sterilize the soil with Terrachlor and destroy infected plants. When possible, plant delphiniums on ground where the plants have not been previously grown.

I planted some delphiniums but several were eaten off by slugs. How can I prevent a recurrence? Use Metaldehyde, according to directions.

Is mildew on delphiniums caused by the soil?   No. Mildew is a fungous disease that infects the leaves. It is controlled by spraying the plants with Benlate or Karathane. Avoid setting plants too closely together.

How many colors of delphiniums are there?   If all the species are considered, they cover an unusually wide range. The garden hybrids contain white and tones of blue, violet, and mauve. *Delphinium nudicaule* is orange and red; *D. cardinale* is clear red; *D. sulphureum* and *D. zalil* are yellow.

Is there a true pink perennial delphinium?   The variety 'Pink Sensation' comes nearest to this description.

How can I get the colors I want by growing my own delphiniums from seed?   The Pacific Giant Hybrids exist in blue and light blue, violet and dark blue, white, and in pastel and mixed shades.

I have heard of a delphinium called 'Connecticut Yankee'. I believe it was developed by a famous photographer. What is this?   This strain was developed by the well-known photographer Edward Steichen. The bush-type plants are about 30 ins. tall, which makes them excellent subjects for the average garden. The color range includes shades of blue and purple. Flowers are large and single. Foliage resembles that of delphinium species more than the regular hybrids. If seed is sown outdoors in early spring, plants will usually bloom by August.

EREMURUS

When is the best time to plant eremurus (foxtail-lily), spring or fall? Will 2- or 3-year-old plants bloom the first season after planting, or must they be older? (Wyoming.)   Plant in fall, since top growth begins early in spring. Usually plants younger than 4 years bloom little, if at all. For first season results, 4-year-old plants are set out. They will require a winter mulch (10 or 12 ins. of coal ashes) to protect the roots from too-severe freezing in Wyoming.

Does eremurus (foxtail-lily) require a special kind of culture?   It is best to give it a deep, well-prepared soil but see that it is well drained. Work in some superphosphate each fall.

How do you plant foxtail-lily (eremurus)? Do you spread the roots out or do you plant with the roots down, like Oriental poppy?   They should be planted with the roots spread out flat. The roots will snap off if bent when planting.

How deep should 4-year-old eremurus roots be planted? Plant so that the crown is about 2 ins. below the soil surface. Too-deep planting is apt to cause the crown to rot, especially in a heavy soil.

I have some 3-year-old eremurus in a lining-out bed. What care do they require; and do they prefer light or heavy soil? Plant in sheltered position in rich, well-drained soil, in full sun, with the fleshy roots spread out and the bud 2 ins. under the soil. Plant in late September, and cover before winter with a loose mulch.

Can eremurus be divided, and when? They can be divided only with difficulty, unless they make offsets freely. Early fall is the best time. Each division must have a bud, or eye.

Can eremurus be raised from seed? When and how long until bloom? Can be raised from seed sown in flats or pots in late autumn or spring. Will bloom from seed in about 4 to 6 years.

EUPATORIUM (HARDY-AGERATUM)

How deep should the hardy-ageratum be planted? It is shallow rooting; plant about 2 ins. deep. The roots are stringy; merely spread them out and cover. This species is not related to the familiar ageratum grown as an annual, but is a relative of Joe-Pye-weed, a popular native plant.

When should hardy-ageratum be moved? It is best done in spring before growth starts.

How often do you have to move hardy-ageratum? Probably best lifted and transplanted every year or two, as it grows into quite a mat which usually dies out in the center.

HARDY FUCHSIA

Is hardy fuchsia (Fuchsia magellanica) a shrub, or can it be included among herbaceous perennials? It is really a low-growing shrub, but in northern climates it is often killed down to ground by the winter, making it in effect an herbaceous perennial.

In what kind of soil should a hardy fuchsia be planted? I had no luck with mine. A light, well-drained garden loam with some leafmold added. It is often planted in rock gardens. Keep it out of exposed situations, and try a light winter cover.

GERBERA

What care does gerbera require—including cultivation, pests, and diseases? (New York.) This South African perennial is not hardy, although it can be grown outside in sheltered situations if given winter protection, or lifted in fall and wintered over in a cold frame. More commonly grown as greenhouse plant. Grow in well-drained, fairly rich soil; keep crowns just above soil level. Fertilize in spring with liquid fertilizer. Propagate from seeds (slow to germinate) or, better, by cuttings of side shoots. Spray for leaf roller and green fly, two of its worst enemies.

What garden soil, exposure, moisture, food, for gerbera? (They are hardy here.) (Delaware.) Best in well-drained soil in full sun. Water only in dry weather. Apply weak liquid fertilizer in spring and early summer.

I have some gerbera roots. I have them in a box 18 ins. underground covered with leaves and soil. Will they smother, or will I have to install an air vent pipe? The covering is too deep. Tender plants cannot be wintered over by burying them. Without a cold frame or like protection it is difficult to over-winter gerberas. An air vent would be of little help. Plant them next to a building; erect a wooden frame around them. Cover with hay and give air in mild weather.

How can I grow gerbera outside? Should be grown in full sun in well-drained soil. Plant only in spring and give cold frame protection for the winter. They are not hardy in northern gardens.

Do gerbera roots need dividing; and when? They do not require dividing very often; but when the clumps get large and begin to fail, divide in spring.

HELIOPSIS

Where should heliopsis be planted? In what type of soil? Plant in full sun, in any garden soil. Will probably flower better in a fairly dry situation.

Is there a double-flowered heliopsis? Yes, the variety 'Golden Plume' is a fine golden yellow double that blooms from July to October.

Does heliopsis require frequent division? The plants are very vigorous so they tend to become crowded after about 3 years. At that time it is advisable to divide them in early spring.

HOLLYHOCKS

Do hollyhocks take an excessive amount of moisture away from surrounding plants? Not enough to harm near-by plants. The ground around hollyhocks usually looks dry because their large leaves shed a lot of rain.

IRISES

Irises have always been favorites among garden flowers because of their sparkling hues and exquisite forms. The many species are distributed throughout the Temperate Zone and are therefore adapted to culture in most of the civilized world. Like roses, irises have been a part of our historical and legendary heritage. They were named in honor of the goddess of the rainbow, the messenger of Zeus and Hera. In medieval times the fleur-de-lis became the emblem of France and its abstract form has been widely used as a motif in many forms of art.

While some iris species have not responded to the efforts of plant breeders as readily as many other kinds of plants, considerable development has taken place, particularly in the tall-bearded iris group. Much of this work can be attributed to amateur gardeners. Size, substance, coloring, and garden value have been greatly improved. Many of the species used in American gardens need no improvement to make them worth-while garden subjects.

Irises are adaptable to many diverse uses in the landscape. They are often used as one of the important features in a mixed perennial border, but they are just as stunning when used as single accents by a wall or rock outcropping, for example. With today's emphasis on minimum maintenance, the border limited to three perennials—peonies, bearded irises, and day-lilies—has gained deserved popularity for the extensive period (early summer to late summer) of bloom provided and—because all these plants grow under similar conditions —easy care.

Do irises grow better in low, moist ground, or in dry soil? In sun or shade? Bearded irises require sharp drainage. Beardless kinds (such as Japanese varieties) need plenty of moisture but not waterlogged soil. The yellow flag of Europe and our native *Iris versicolor* succeed even in swamp conditions. Most do best in full sun.

What is the correct soil for bearded irises? Any good garden soil. Add bone meal or superphosphate and gypsum when remaking the beds. If heavy, lighten with sand or ashes. They require good drainage.

Do Japanese irises require acid soil? Yes, or at least a soil that is not alkaline. Never apply lime, bone meal, or wood ashes.

For Japanese and Siberian irises, what soil preparation is required? Spade deeply; incorporate plenty of humus—old rotted manure, leafmold, peat moss, or compost. Also, if the soil is somewhat poor, add a dressing of cottonseed meal, pulverized sheep manure, or general fertilizer. Never apply lime, bone meal, or wood ashes to Japanese iris. Siberian iris are tolerant of alkaline soil, but prefer one that is somewhat acid.

What kind of soil is good for Dutch irises? Any fertile, well-drained garden soil other than heavy clay. This is true for all bulbous irises.

Is manure good for irises? Animal manure should not be used on bearded irises, but the beardless species (including the Japanese and Siberian irises) appreciate well-rotted manure.

What is the best time of year to feed ordinary bearded irises; and how? Fertilizer, usually a 5–10–10, is best applied during periods of active growth. For bearded iris this is in early spring and about a month after blooming. A large clump of iris can use a handful (about ½ cup) in spring, about half of that for the second application. Apply fertilizer around the rhizomes, but not directly on them. Follow the fertilizing with a good soaking with a repeat soaking again in a day or two.

Should beds of bearded irises be fertilized each spring? Not if ground was well prepared and fertilized at planting time.

What fertilizer do you recommend for ordinary bearded irises? Superphosphate and unleached wood ashes together with a commercial fertilizer low in nitrogen. Mix with soil when beds are made.

Do bearded irises require lime? Only if the soil is decidedly acid.

Are wood ashes good fertilizer for iris? When should they be applied? Yes. They are generally best applied in spring. If they are saved from a stove or fireplace, store dry until time of application since their value is quickly lost in the rain. They supply from 5 to 25 per cent of potash as well as 30 to 35 per cent of lime. Water in after applying at rate of 4–5 oz. per square yard.

What is the best fertilizer to use on Japanese irises? Rotted cow manure (or if this is not available leafmold or peat moss fortified with a light dressing of complete fertilizer). A fertilizer formulated for rhododendrons and azaleas (acid-loving plants) is good. Apply as a mulch in May or early June. In fall, mulch with manure, leaves, or peat moss.

Are irises more attractive planted together or scattered in clumps throughout the garden? By themselves they are not attractive over the greater part of the year. Clumps of one variety in front of evergreens are very effective. Many people interplant irises with day-lilies.

When, where, and how do you plant bearded irises? Main planting time is in June or July after flowering, in good garden soil. However, they can also be planted in spring and fall. June planting allows maximum time for recuperation before blooming the next year. Plant rhizomes level with surface in well-drained, sunny beds. In light, sandy soil the rhizomes can be covered an inch or so; but in heavy soils they should be left with the tops exposed. Buy your stock from a reliable dealer so you will receive good, healthy rhizomes.

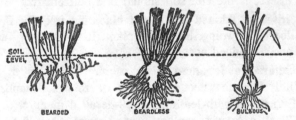

Planting depth for bearded, beardless, and bulbous irises.

What distances should be allowed between irises when planting? Tall-bearded, 9 to 18 ins.; dwarf-bearded, 6 to 9 ins.; Japanese and Siberian, 18 to 24 ins.; bulbous, 4 to 5 ins. with 12 ins. between rows.

At what distance apart should purchased divisions of tall-bearded irises be set? For a substantial effect the first year after planting,

8 or 9 ins. A better spacing is 16 or 18 ins., but this takes 2 years to produce a good display.

Should iris rhizomes be dried out before replanting? Not unless the rhizomes are rotted from disease, because if the feeding roots are dried no new growth results until new ones develop. Irises can be divided and transplanted without much setback, providing their roots are kept out of the sun and they are replanted immediately.

Will irises bloom if they are moved early in spring? The Japanese and Siberians usually do; the tall-bearded sometimes (but with short bloom stalks). If possible, avoid moving bearded irises until after the blooming season.

When and how deep should Japanese irises be planted? Early spring, before growth starts, or late August. Crowns should be set 2 ins. below the surface.

Can we grow irises successfully? We have a lot of shade. Ordinary garden irises will not thrive in shade. Certain wild species, such as *Iris cristata, gracilipes, verna,* and *foetidissima,* are satisfactory in partial shade. Bearded iris will produce a few flowers in light shade.

How often should I transplant irises? Whenever they become so crowded that the rhizomes are growing over one another. This will usually mean about every 3 years.

Can irises be replanted in the same bed? Yes, if redug and fertilized. If disease is present, soil should first be sterilized.

Should irises be thinned out if not blooming freely? If lack of bloom is due to crowding, lift and replant. If some other cause, get diagnosis and be guided accordingly.

What culture do Japanese irises require? Bed must be well drained (it is fatal to select a location where water stands during winter). Enrich soil with leafmold, well-decayed manure, or garden compost. Plant in August; replant every 3 years. They like plenty of water before and during blooming season. Never plant in alkaline soil or where lime has been used.

Can you suggest a helpful book on iris? I am interested in making them my hobby. One comprehensive book is *The Iris Book,* by Molly Price (D. Van Nostrand Company, Inc., New York, N.Y., 1966).

What are the conditions favorable to the growth of Siberian irises?

Plenty of sunshine, well-drained, rich, slightly acid soil. They like plenty of rotted manure or rich compost, also plenty of moisture from spring until blooming is over.

Do the Dutch, English, and Spanish irises all get same culture? In general, yes. Plant bulbs 4 to 5 ins. deep, October to November, in sunny location and in good, well-drained loam. Let remain for 2 years, then lift and replant in a new location. They are gross feeders and deplete the soil very quickly. In severe climates a winter mulch is beneficial.

How are bulbous irises handled in the South? Dutch, English, and Spanish irises are dug after blooming and are stored in a cool shed until late fall, when they are replanted. This is because they make fall growth, and if left in ground the flower stalks are usually killed by a freeze in late winter. When lifted and replanted in late fall, stalks do not develop until spring.

Do Dutch irises have to be dug up each year? Not unless they have suffered winter losses. In that case try planting as late in autumn as weather permits. The following year dig the bulbs when the foliage dies down, and store in a cool location until autumn. In extreme climates a winter mulch is beneficial.

When is the best time to move Dutch irises? As soon as the foliage has died down. In the South many people lift them at this time and store in airy containers in a cool shed until late fall.

What is correct culture of oncocyclus irises? These natives of the Near and Middle East require a dormant season, without moisture. Grow them in pots or cold frames so they are kept dry from mid-June to mid-December.

What culture do spuria iris require? These are best planted in early fall. They can take a year or more to bloom after moving. Grow in sun or partial shade, in neutral to slightly acid soil. This iris is a heavy feeder, so fertilize each spring with a complete fertilizer (5–10–10) or use rotted or dehydrated manure.

When do you divide and replant Siberian irises? Late August or September.

I have a large garden of Japanese irises that were planted 4 years ago. When should I divide and reset? They seem to be getting

crowded. Immediately after blooming season, in September, or just before growth starts in spring.

How much watering and cultivating do irises need?   Bearded irises ordinarily need no watering. Japanese and other beardless types need plenty of moisture until flowering is through. Cultivate shallowly and sufficiently often to keep surface loose and free of weeds.

What care should be given iris rhizomes after the blooming season? If overcrowded, divide them. Remove flower stalks immediately after flowering, and be on the alert for signs of borers or rots. Keep all dead foliage cleaned off.

Does it injure iris plants to take green foliage off in the late fall? Leaves turning brown should always be removed promptly. Green foliage should not be removed nor cut back in late fall because this may adversely affect next year's bloom.

When leaves are forbidden as winter protection for bearded irises, what can be used?   No protection is necessary unless rhizomes have been planted in late fall. Evergreen boughs then make the best protection. Marsh hay or excelsior can also be used.

Would you cover iris roots? I have over 400 different kinds and it would be quite a task to cover them all.   No. They only need protection if planted in late fall, and then only because their root growth will not be sufficient to keep them from heaving. A few irises of Californian origin need to be planted in sheltered spots.

How can I transport irises to shows?   Obtain large florists' boxes. String tape across them in several places so that stalks can be suspended without blooms touching bottoms or sides. Keep boxes level; or if this is impossible, then tie each stalk to the tapes.

How should I prepare irises for exhibition at my local garden-club shows?   Bloom stalks should have at least 2 open flowers. Three would be better. These should be the first blooms. After cutting, stand in water for 30 minutes or longer. Foliage should be displayed with flower stalks. Dead or torn blooms count heavily against you. Varieties should be correctly labeled.

Is there any special organization of iris growers?   Yes. The American Iris Society. Each member receives the society's well-illustrated bulletins. The address of the Secretary of the Society is 2315 Tower Grove Ave., St. Louis, Mo. 63110.

I have tried for many years to raise red and pink irises, but can't make them live over winter. What is the reason?   Try planting earlier in summer, so that plants become established before winter. You might also look for varieties developed by northern hybridizers.

Why won't Japanese irises bloom for me?   Too much shade? Alkaline soil? Dry soil? Water settling around crowns in winter? Any of the above may be responsible.

My bearded irises grow and look well, but bloom rarely. What is the reason? They have been established more than 2 years. They get full sun at least half a day.   Most likely they are overcrowded and need dividing. Some varieties of tall-bearded irises require dividing every year for good bloom.

Are all bearded irises robust growers?   No. Certain varieties, especially dark-colored ones, are less vigorous than others. Some that have originated in southern California are tender, and do not do well in cold parts of the country.

Do irises change colors from year to year?   No. But in different gardens the same iris can vary somewhat in color intensity, due to cultural and environmental conditions. Slight variations can occur in different locations in the same garden.

After a few years does a mixed planting of irises gradually lose color and turn white?   No. What sometimes happens is that the faster and more vigorous growers crowd out slower-growing varieties.

Why do irises stop blooming after being separated, even though carefully taken apart at right season? They are free of pests and were planted at right depth.   Perhaps soil is deficient or exhausted. Try remaking beds and adding superphosphate and perhaps lime. Sunshine is important.

I planted irises two years ago, half of them grew to enormous size and bloomed, but the others remained small and spindly. How can I make these perk up and bloom?   Robust varieties produce a representative bloom stalk the first year after planting, others take 2 years to become established. Furthermore, varieties vary in height; it may be that you have some of the intermediate varieties growing together with tall-bearded sorts.

My irises (early dwarfs and Siberians) bloomed the first year but not the following 2 years. What is wrong?   Perhaps they do not get enough sunshine, or they may be too crowded, and in need of dividing. Siberians are gross feeders; they require plenty of fertilizer.

My irises do not do well; they have decreased in size and stopped blooming. The soil is stiff clay. What would you advise? Perhaps your soil is so heavy that just enough feeding roots develop to keep your plants alive, but not enough to build strong plants. Lift, divide, and replant in well-drained beds improved by addition of coal cinders or sand, superphosphate, and a dressing of agricultural lime if soil test shows need of it. Incorporate organic matter.

What is the difference between the Dykes Medal and Dykes Memorial Medal? No difference. The complete name is the Dykes Memorial Medal, but it is generally spoken of as the Dykes Medal. Most catalogues of iris generally indicate winners of this medal.

How should I divide tall-bearded irises? After flowering cut the leaves back halfway, lift the clumps, then with a sharp knife cut the rhizomes into pieces so that each has one (or, if preferred, 2 or 3) strong fan of leaves attached. Be sure divisions are disease-free before replanting. Divide every 3 or 4 years.

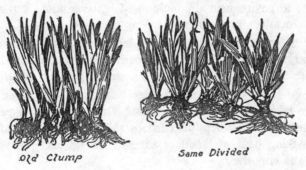

Old Clump   *Same Divided*

A clump of bearded iris, divided for replanting.

How are Japanese irises divided? When? It is quite a job if the clumps are large. A heavy-bladed knife or billhook is the best tool. Cut the leaves halfway back and then chop the rootstock into pieces each having 3 or 4 growths. Discard old, lifeless material. Save only young, vigorous portions. Do this work in September, in shade, and keep the roots from drying out.

Should iris seeds picked in fall be planted fall or spring? In fall;

if planted in spring they will not germinate until following year. Plant in open ground or in a cold frame—the latter preferred. In a cold frame they start coming up in late February, and should be transplanted in late June to nursery beds.

Typical divisions of tall-bearded, dwarf-bearded, and beardless irises.

How do you grow irises from seed? After seed is harvested plant immediately in a cold frame, or save until late fall and plant in open ground. If sown earlier outdoors, young seedlings come up and are heaved out during winter. Be sure soil is well prepared and on light side. Transplant the seedlings, in late June, to a nursery bed, spacing at least a foot apart each way. Nearly all should bloom the following year.

My iris leaves are spotted. What shall I do? This is leafspot disease. Cut back diseased foliage and burn it. If this is not done, it will spread disease through garden. Be sure and keep all dead leaves picked off, and in 2 years you will have eliminated the disease. Leaves may also be dusted or sprayed with zineb. Avoid splashing water on leaves as this spreads the disease.

Are irises subject to virus disease? Iris mosaic disease attacks both bearded and bulbous kinds, causing mottling or yellow striping of leaves, and lack of vigor. Destroy all infected plants.

My iris roots have rotted, and watery streaks appear on the leaves. What is the cause? Bacterial soft rot. It often gains entrance through wounds made by the iris borer. Dig and destroy rotted plants; sterilize soil by soaking with ½ cup Clorox in ½ cup water. Also pour on rhizomes and leave them exposed to the air until healing takes place. Avoid planting diseased rhizomes. Sterilize knives and tools with the solution, as disease is spread by these. Clean off and burn dead leaves and rubbish in fall.

How can I control thrips on Japanese irises?   By spraying or dusting with diazinon or Sevin.

Grayish plant lice have attacked my iris roots underground. What control measures shall I take?   Root aphids are destroyed by soaking the soil with nicotine sulfate, 2 teaspoonfuls to 1 gal. water; or by the use of malathion (follow directions on the package).

What controls are recommended for iris borers?   Clean up and burn all old leaves and debris in fall, and if winter covering has been used burn this in early spring. In severe infestations spray with Thiodane, Sevin, malathion, or Cygon in spring.

How are irises classified?   Broadly classified into bulbous and rhizomatous. In the bulbous group are included Dutch, Spanish, English, Reticulata, and Juno. In the rhizomatous are found the bearded (Euopogon, Aril, Oncocyclus, Regelia, and Pseudoregelia), and beardless iris (including Siberian, spuria, Louisiana, and crested).

Which group of irises is most useful in the home garden?   Undoubtedly the tall-bearded (often miscalled German irises). The Japanese and Siberian groups are also very useful.

In reading about the flowers of bearded iris, I often come across these terms which I don't fully understand—amoena, plicata, variegata, blend, bicolor, bitone, and self. Can you tell me what they mean?   *Amoena:* tinted white standards and colored falls; *plicata:* stitched or stippled margin color on a white background; *variegata:* yellow or near yellow standards with deeper falls which may be either veined or solid tones of brown or purple; *blend:* combination of two or more colors (one always being yellow); *bicolor:* light or medium standards in one color and deeper contrasting falls in another color; *bitone:* two tones of the same color; *self:* uniform color.

Do all bearded iris bloom at the same time?   No, there is considerable variation. The catalogues of iris specialists are very helpful on this point. For each variety they indicate the relative blooming period as VE (very early), E (early), EM (early-midseason), M (midseason), ML (midseason-late), L (late), VL (very late).

What is meant by dwarf, lilliput, and intermediate when referring to bearded iris?   Miniature dwarf iris are under 10 ins. tall; lilliput or standard dwarf-bearded, 10 to 15 ins. tall; and intermediate 15 to 28 ins. tall. Most tall-bearded iris are about 36 ins., but a few can reach 40 ins.

Can you tell me the relative bloom times of the various irises?
This varies in different localities. However, in the New York City
area it starts usually in March or April with *Iris reticulata* and is soon
followed by the miniature dwarf-bearded (April–May); then the
dwarf-bearded, aril, and intermediate bearded (May); then tall-
bearded and Siberian (May–June); followed by Dutch, Louisiana,
spuria, and Japanese (June–July). Last to bloom are the reblooming
bearded (late July, August, September).

**Which is better, cheap collections with many irises or a few good
new varieties?** Not always are high-priced varieties better than
older, inexpensive kinds. Unless immediate effect is imperative, there
is no doubt that a few good irises are to be preferred to a lot of poor
ones. They soon multiply.

**Is the bulbous iris Juno known by any other name? Can I obtain
hybrids in the Juno group?** No. It and other species of the Juno
group are rare in American gardens. Only a few hybrids exist. They
are only suited for skilled growers and comparatively mild climates.

LUPINE

What can I use to build up soil for lupines? They need a well-
drained medium soil. Use sand, leafmold, and well-rotted manure.
Lime should not be used on lupines, as they require an acid soil.

**One authority says acid soil, another a lime soil for perennial
lupines. What is your opinion?** Most lupines seem to do better in
an acid soil.

What should I use to fertilize lupines? Well-rotted compost, cow
manure, or any general garden fertilizer.

Will you give soil and cultural directions for Russell lupines? Russell lupines thrive in any good garden soil in full sun. Seed should be
planted in August, about ½ in. deep, and soon after it has ripened.
The spikes do not grow so large here as in England. It is, however,
one of our finest perennials. Lupines are short-lived and may not
persist after the first year. The soil must be well drained.

**What is the best way of raising the improved types of perennial
lupine from seed indoors? I have had poor germination.** Sow individual seeds in small pots of sandy soil, first nicking the hard seed
coat with the point of a knife. Sown in March and started in a green-

house the seedlings will show in a week and be ready to plant outdoors, without the roots being disturbed, in May. Or nick the seed or
place in hot water for an overnight soak, and sow thinly outdoors in
April if the soil is in friable condition.

Will lupine seeds "stratified" come up following year?   They
should. If kept over winter in a seed container germination is aided by
making a nick in seed coat with a sharp knife.

Can lupines be transplanted? Do they last many years?   Old plants
do not like to be disturbed and are very hard to transplant. Young
plants can be transplanted in very early spring if care is used to protect
the roots. Lupines are short-lived. For a constant supply sow seed
each year.

Is there a dwarf form of lupine?   There are several fine dwarf
forms that grow only 18 ins. tall. Check seed catalogues.

**I was told that lupine seed should be treated with an inoculant
(Legume-Aid) the same as for pea seed. Is this true?**   Since lupines
are legumes, it generally improves the germination to treat the seed.
However, it's not absolutely necessary.

MONKSHOOD (ACONITUM)

How often should aconitum be divided?   These plants flower very
freely when they are in established clumps, and can be left undisturbed for years.

How deep shall I plant aconitum, and in what kind of soil?   They
are best planted with the crown about 1 in. down, in rich, moist soil,
neutral or slightly acid.

Do aconitums need winter protection?   They are hardy but should
be protected for the first and second winter after planting.

When should I sow seed of monkshood?   In late autumn, using
fresh seed.

Will monkshood grow in shade?   They do best in partial shade.

**Will you name several kinds of monkshood that would be suc-
cessful?**   *Aconitum fischeri, A. napellus* 'Sparks Variety', *A. henryi*,
and *A. anthora*.

Is it advisable to plant monkshood? I have heard it is poisonous.
Monkshood does contain poison. It is said to have been mistaken for

horse-radish on occasions and eaten with fatal results. But it is widely grown in gardens, as are many other poisonous plants.

PENSTEMONS

I have several penstemon plants which stayed green long after frost. Is it a hardy variety? You may have plants of the bedding penstemon, which is not hardy but which stay green until late. The other kinds are hardy, and, with the exception of the alpine sorts, are treated like ordinary perennials. Many of them remain green until long after frost.

How do you trim and care for large penstemons? They need no trimming. The wiry stems of the tall kinds need support, best supplied by using twiggy brush inserted among the plants when they are about a foot tall. Growing up through this, with loose stems tied up and the tops of the brush cut away when flower buds form, they will be held neatly and securely. Cut the stems after flowering, and top-dress with bone meal.

How is it best to divide penstemon plants? Lift the plants in early spring, pull them gently apart, and replant.

PEONIES

The modern peony is the achievement of years of steadfast devotion and effort on the part of plant breeders. For more than 2,000 years the peony has been cultivated in China, not alone for its highly prized flowers, but for its roots, which in early times were used for food and medicinal purposes. It was named in honor of Paeon, the physician of the gods, who—according to mythology—received the first peony on Mt. Olympus from the hands of Leto.

Present-day gardeners are inclined to take the peony for granted because it has become so common. The very fact that it is common only serves to emphasize its many worth-while qualities. Hardiness, permanence, ease of culture, and freedom from pests are but a few of its merits. Diversity in flower form, attractive colors, clean habit of growth, and deep-green foliage combine to produce a plant of exceptional value for mass plantings or for the mixed border. Peonies rank high as cut flowers because of their extraordinary keeping qualities. They are primarily plants for the North, for they require the low temperatures of winter to break the dormancy of the buds before spring growth will take place.

There are two main classes of peonies—herbaceous and tree. The herbaceous peonies die back to the ground each year while the tree peonies merely drop their leaves, and the somewhat woody stems persist year after year. Tree peonies are generally taller than the herbaceous, the flowers are somewhat larger, and in general they bloom a week or two earlier. Both are valuable garden subjects and although herbaceous peonies outsell tree peonies, the latter are fast gaining popularity as good varieties become more readily available.

Some horticulturists consider that the interest in peonies is on the wane; that their potentiality for further improvement is exhausted. This does not seem to be the case, however, for within the last few years several new varieties have been introduced that eclipse all previous originations in perfection of form and color. They have always been garden favorites and will continue to be so.

What type of soil is best for peonies?   They grow well in a wide range of soil types. Any rich, friable garden soil is satisfactory.

Is a very heavy soil satisfactory for peonies?   Yes, providing it is well-drained. Some form of organic material, such as well-rotted manure, peat moss, or leafmold, should be added to make it more friable.

Will peonies thrive in a sandy soil?   Sandy soil is well suited to peony growing if its fertility is maintained. Well-rotted manure or rich compost and commercial fertilizer should be used.

What is the proper method of preparing the soil for peonies?   Spade it to a depth of 12 to 18 ins. Thoroughly work in some well-rotted manure or other form of organic material at the rate of 4 bu. per 100 sq. ft. Incorporate 3 lbs. of superphosphate to each 100 sq. ft. If the soil is acid apply lime (5 lbs. per 100 sq. ft.) several weeks before planting.

Do peonies need lime?   Peonies grow best in a slightly acid soil (pH 5.5 to 6.5). If the soil is very acid (below pH 5), the addition of ground limestone is beneficial.

What kind and how much fertilizer should I use for peonies?   A mixed commercial fertilizer of 4–12–4 or 5–10–5 analysis is satisfactory. Use 4 lbs. for each 100 sq. ft. Well-rotted manure is also satisfactory. Avoid the use of fresh manure.

When peonies are planted in the fall should they be fertilized then, or the following spring?   Work fertilizer thoroughly into the soil before planting. No additional fertilizer will be needed the spring following; but each succeeding spring use a mixed commercial fertilizer.

Do peonies need fertilizer; and when should it be applied? Yes. Apply commercial fertilizer in spring. When growth is about 4 ins. high work it into the soil around the plants. Rotted manure makes a good fertilizer to put on in the fall.

Should peonies be planted in full sun? The best results are obtained when the plants are exposed to full sunlight. They should be protected from strong winds.

Can peonies be grown in partial shade? While they do best in full sun, they will grow satisfactorily in light shade. They require at least 6 hours a day of direct sunlight for good results.

Does the peony plant need to be kept away from other flowers in the beds? Providing they are properly spaced and cultural conditions are right, other plants exert no influence whatever on the blooming of peonies. They are often used in mixed perennial borders, and are excellent for the purpose.

When should peonies be planted? In the fall or early spring.

How deep do herbaceous peonies need to be planted? The crown, from which the buds arise, should be only 1 to 2 ins. below the soil level.

Does it matter whether the eye of a herbaceous peony is 1 in. or 2 ins. below the surface? No. It is important, however, not to exceed 2 ins. If planted too shallowly, there is danger of the roots being heaved out during winter.

I planted peonies the last of November; was it too late? Planting can be done any time until the ground freezes, but the ideal months are September and October. This gives them an opportunity to become partially established before winter.

I planted peonies in a temporary location in late November. When and how should I transplant them to their permanent place? It would be desirable to leave them where they are until October, when moving would be much easier. However, you can move them in spring as soon as the ground has thawed, and replant immediately.

If I move peony plants in spring will they bloom the same year? Yes, if moved *very* early, before growth starts. The soil must be kept moist at all times.

Will peony roots, which have been kept in the cellar all winter, grow satisfactorily? It is never advisable to treat them in this manner. However, if they have not dried out, and appear to be in good condition, they will survive. It may take 3 or 4 years before they regain their full vigor.

Will peonies bloom the first summer after transplanting? Usually; if the plants are vigorous and were not divided into small pieces; and if the transplanting was done at the right time. The blooms may not be so large and perfect as those produced in succeeding years.

Why does it take peonies so long to bloom after dividing? Dividing the clumps is a severe operation; it results in the loss of roots in which food is stored. Dividing at an improper time causes recovery to be especially slow. If the divisions are very small, it may take 2 to 3 years before the plants are sufficiently vigorous to bloom.

How do you recognize healthy peony roots suitable for planting? They should be approximately 1 in. in diameter, smooth, free from bruises, and each containing at least 1 plump bud and several smaller ones. No decay should be evident near the cut surface.

How can you bring an old peony border back into bloom? If the plants are very old, it is advisable to divide the clumps and replant them in well-prepared soil. Keeping the bed free of weeds by shallow cultivation, and applying fertilizer in the spring, will increase the quality and quantity of the flowers.

Is it necessary to dig up peony roots every year and break them up to obtain more blossoms? No. It is best not to divide and transplant peonies any oftener than is necessary to maintain vigorous growth. Ordinarily every 5 to 8 years is often enough. Better-quality blooms can be had by fertilizing and making certain that the plants do not lack moisture at the time they come into flower.

Should peonies be disbudded? Size and quality of flowers are improved by disbudding. The practice is advisable if blooms are to be used for cut flowers, or for exhibition purposes. In the garden, where mass color effects are desirable, it is not important.

When should peonies be disbudded? The earlier the better. Ordinarily it can be done when the plants are about 18 ins. tall. Just as soon as the secondary buds become visible they should be removed.

How are peonies disbudded? A peony stem usually has from 3 to

7 buds. The main or terminal one produces the largest and most perfect flower. All of the buds except the terminal one should be picked off, leaving but 1 on each stem.

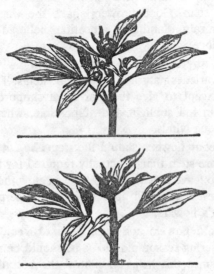

Disbudding peonies.

Should the flower buds of newly planted or transplanted peonies be removed the first year? Some growers do this to help the plants recover from shock, but it is not absolutely necessary. Most gardeners allow their plants to bloom even though the flowers are not so large and perfect as they will be later.

Do peonies need to be cultivated? Very little cultivation is necessary except to remove weeds. The best time to destroy weeds is very early in the spring before the plants have made much growth, or late in the fall after the tops have been cut off. During summer the top 2 ins. of soil should be kept loose by shallow hoeing.

Do peonies require much moisture? A moderately moist soil is suitable. In spring when the flowers are developing, if the natural rainfall is not abundant, thorough watering increases the size and quality of the flowers.

Does irrigating peonies when in bud bring the flowers on sooner, or does it hold them back? It tends to hasten flowering. If the soil is very dry, irrigation also greatly improves the size and quality of the blooms.

How can I keep the stems of peonies from falling over? Support with special, circular wire "peony stakes," or use individual stakes to each stem. Good growers shake the water out of peony heads after each rain. Planting in a location sheltered from wind helps to prevent damage.

Is there any way to make the stems of peonies stronger? Some otherwise fine varieties naturally have weak stems. There is little that can be done except to give them artificial support. It is also well to plant them in full sunlight and, if possible, where they are protected from strong winds.

In picking peony flowers, should the stems be cut at ground level? Do not take more stem than is actually required for the arrangement. It is advisable to leave at least 2 or 3 leaves below the point where the stem is cut. These leaves will produce food for the production of the succeeding year's flowers.

Should the old flowers and seed pods of peonies be removed? During the flowering season old blossoms should be picked off before the petals fall since this helps to control the botrytis blight disease. Seed pods compete with the roots for the food produced in the leaves. Do not remove leaves when picking off the old flowers and seed pods.

Should the foliage on peonies be cut back after the blooming season? No. The foliage should not be cut until it has been killed by hard frosts. The food manufactured in the foliage is stored in the roots, and thus helps produce flowers the following year. If the foliage is cut back shortly after blooming, the plants are deprived of their next year's food supply.

Should the dried foliage of peonies be cut off to the ground in the fall, or left on until spring? In fall. Its removal helps to prevent the spread of disease.

When is the proper time to cut down a peony? After the foliage has been killed by frost. The autumn coloring of peony foliage is usually quite attractive.

Should peonies be protected in winter? Peonies should be mulched the first year after planting to prevent heaving. After they are well established, no protection is necessary.

Will peonies do well in warm climates such as Florida? No, they require low temperatures to complete their rest period.

Are peonies hardy in cold climates? They are among the hardiest of garden flowers.

Why do peonies, several years old, fail to bloom? The following conditions may prevent blooming: too deep planting; too shady a situation; poor drainage; plants need dividing; disease, especially of the roots; botrytis blight disease; roots infested with nematodes; lack of fertilizer; lack of moisture; lack of sunlight; injury to buds due to late frosts.

I have peonies, about 12 years old, that only have a blossom or two a year. The soil is black, sandy loam. They are not planted too deep. Are they too old, or what can be the trouble? An application of complete fertilizer at the rate of 4 lbs. per 100 sq. ft. can correct the trouble. Nematodes also can cause failure to bloom. If infested with nematodes, the best thing to do is to discard roots.

Is there any way to tell the color of peonies from the roots or from the buds on the roots? No. Experienced growers can recognize certain varieties by root and bud coloring, but there is no general rule to follow.

What would you do with peonies that have been in the ground for many years and are not doing well? Dig and divide them during October. Replant them in well-prepared soil in a good sunny location.

What can I do to make peonies bloom as they did for the first 5 years? They were divided 4 years ago and are growing in a sunny situation in well-drained clay soil. Try fertilizing them each spring with a mixed commercial fertilizer.

I have some very old peonies. Last summer the flowers were almost single, and many did not bloom well. Why? Old plants often fail to produce perfect flowers. They should be dug, divided, and replanted in well-prepared soil.

When should peony flowers be cut for use indoors? Preferably in the early morning. Select, for cutting, buds that have just started to open.

How are peonies scored or rated? On a scale of 10. A rating of 10 represents the highest possible excellence, or absolute perfection, in both plant and bloom. Varieties rated at 9 or above are very high in quality. Between 8 and 9 they are considered good. Few varieties are grown that rate less than 7.5.

Can peony roots be divided in spring with as much success as in fall? No, *early* fall is the best time.

How are peony plants divided? Dig the clumps carefully so as not to injure or bruise the roots. Wash off all soil. With a heavy, sharp knife cut each clump, through the crown, into several pieces. Each division should have several plump buds, which in the fall are approximately ½ in. long. Roots without such buds rarely produce plants.

Would it be advisable to separate a peony root with a spade, leaving part in the ground and removing part? This method can be used and has the advantage of not interrupting the bloom of the portion that is left in place. However, it is usually better to dig the entire plant and divide it carefully. Before replanting there is an opportunity to prepare the soil to improve growing conditions.

Can peonies be raised from seeds? Yes, but this method is used only for the production of new varieties; it is slow and tedious.

How should seeds of peonies be sown? Collect when ripe. Keep in damp moss until November. Sow in a cold frame or protected bed. Cover the seeds to their own depth, and mulch with peat moss the following spring. Keep the bed shaded and reasonably moist. They usually take 2 years to germinate.

How long does it take peonies to bloom from seeds? They ordinarily germinate 2 years after sowing. After 3 years' growth, a few flowers can be expected. This means 5 or more years from seed-sowing to bloom.

What can I do to control ants that are eating the flower buds of my peonies? Ants do not eat peony buds; they feed on the sweet, syrupy material secreted by the developing buds. They do no harm to the peonies except, possibly, to spread botrytis blight disease.

Why do peony buds dry up without developing into blossoms? The plant seems disease-free. The leaves do not dry nor is there any sign of bud rot. Probably botrytis blight. This can be prevented by carefully cleaning the bed in the fall and by keeping it clean of dead leaves all seasons. Spraying with zineb or Benlate every 10 days from the time the leaves show until the flowers open is a good control measure.

Late frosts in spring can also kill buds, but disease is the more likely culprit.

Is there something lacking in the soil when peony leaves turn brown at the edges early in July? Usually this is the result of drought, or of infection with some root disease.

What are the names of the different types of peony flowers? The most distinct are single, Japanese, anemone, and double.

What is the difference between single peonies and the Japanese type? Singles have 5, or possibly a few more, true petals around a center of showy, fertile stamens. Japanese types have a single row of large petals, but the center consists of much enlarged stamens which bear very little, or no, pollen.

What is the anemone type of peony? It somewhat resembles the Japanese but the centers of the flowers are composed of much enlarged, petal-like stamens which bear no pollen whatever. These center petals are long and narrow, more or less incurved, and imbricated.

What varieties of anemone-flowered peonies are desirable? There are many fine varieties, but here are three: 'Nippon Parade', red; 'Nippon Gold', pink and yellow; 'Prairie Afire', fiery pink.

What are a few good single peonies? 'Krinkled White', pure white; 'Sea Shell', pink; 'Arcturus' and 'President Lincoln', red.

Which are some popular varieties of the Japanese type? 'Mikado', red; 'Nippon Brilliant', bright red; 'Amo-No-Sode', bright pink; 'Carrara', white; 'Nippon Gold', dark pink.

Which are a few of the best double peonies? 'A. B. Franklin', white; 'Baroness Schroeder', white; 'Festiva Maxima', white; 'Hansina Brand', pink; 'Karl Rosenfield', red-crimson; 'La France', light pink; 'Reine Hortense', rose; 'Sarah Bernhardt', deep rose; 'Therese', pale rose; and 'Walter Faxon', pink.

Which peony flowers 2 weeks before the common herbaceous ones? The fern-leaf peony (*Paeonia tenuifolia*) is a very early-flowering species with delicate, finely cut leaves and single or double red flowers. In general the tree peonies flower before the herbaceous peonies.

Is there a yellow herbaceous peony? Yes. Look for 'Oriental Gold', a double lemon yellow. Among the species there is *P. mlokosewitschii*.

TREE PEONIES

What is the difference between Japanese, European, and lutea hybrid tree peonies? The European and Japanese are developed from the same *Paeonia suffruticosa*. The European tree peonies are usually fully double with thickly petaled flowers, and the foliage is broad. The Japanese type have single or semi-double flowers, often with crinkled petals, and most have a lovely circle of yellow stamens; leaves are finer than in the Japanese. The lutea hybrids are crosses of *P. suffruticosa* by *P. lutea*. They are notable for their colors, ranging through many shades of yellow to orange, to orange tints and combinations of red and yellow.

What is the proper type of soil for tree peonies? A friable rich soil is necessary. Incorporate well-rotted manure, compost, or leafmold. The optimum pH value is between 5.5 and 6.5.

How deep should tree peonies be planted? The crowns or eyes should be set from 4 to 7 ins. deep.

Are tree peonies completely hardy? They have been known to survive 20° to 30° F. below zero.

How should the soil be prepared for tree peonies? By spading as deeply as possible. Mix in some organic material, such as well-rotted manure, peat moss, leafmold, or the like. The addition of a complete commercial fertilizer is also desirable. If a 5–10–5 or some similar grade is available, use it at the rate of 4 lbs. per 100 sq. ft.

Can tree peonies be planted in spring? While October is the best season, success can be had from *very* early-spring planting.

How old do tree peonies need to be before they will flower? Tree peonies are often slow to begin blooming. Normally, however, they produce a few blooms the second or third year after planting.

How can I propagate tree peonies? The usual method is by grafting in August or September. The scion should have at least 2 eyes. Its base is cut wedge-shaped and is inserted in a piece of root about ½ in. in diameter, and 3 or 4 ins. long, taken from an herbaceous peony plant. The scion is held in place with raffia or with a rubber band. The grafted roots are placed in good soil, in a cold frame, where they can be protected during winter. If a cold greenhouse is available, the grafts can be placed in a deep pot and kept indoors over winter. One of the eyes of the scion should be below soil surface. Tree peonies can also be propagated by layering, division, and by seeds.

Which are some of the best tree-peony varieties? 'Carolina d'Italie', flesh-pink; 'Madame Stuart-Low', salmon-red; 'Fuji No Akebono', bright scarlet; 'Reine Elizabeth', salmon and copper; 'Osirus', chestnut-brown; 'Akashi Gata', peach-pink; 'Hanadayin', purple; 'Alice Harding', yellow.

PERENNIAL PEA (LATHYRUS LATIFOLIUS)

How do you start what is called "wild sweet pea"? I have tried planting seeds and roots without success. The perennial pea (*Lathyrus latifolius*) is best started from seeds sown in autumn, preferably where they are to grow permanently. The plant has long, fleshy roots and resents disturbance.

What is the best way to plant and care for everlasting peas? If by "everlasting" peas you mean the perennial kind, they rarely need special soil preparation or care. A sunny location and average garden soil are about all they require.

I have a well-established perennial sweet pea, which failed to bloom last year. What can I do to it to produce bloom? The perennial pea usually flowers freely when established, even in poor soil. Try mixing superphosphate with the soil, 6 oz. per square yard.

Should hardy sweet peas be cut back in the fall? How far? They can be cut back to just above the ground level any time after the tops have dried up.

Is the perennial pea a good plant for a large lattice fence? Yes, if the slats are not too large for the tendrils to grasp. It will grow to a height of about 8 ft.

PHLOX (SUMMER OR GARDEN)

How is soil prepared for phlox (Phlox paniculata)? Soil should be dug to a depth of 1 ft. to 18 ins. and mixed with a 3-in. layer of rotted manure, leafmold, or mixture of peat moss and compost.

When is the best time to plant garden phlox? Either in early fall or early spring. Plants in containers can be planted even in mid-summer. If fall planting is practiced, the plants should be mulched with a 3-in. layer of rough litter, hay or straw, to prevent possible heaving as a result of freezing.

What is the best exposure for phlox? They thrive in full sun, but will grow in partial shade. A minimum of 3 to 4 hours of full sunshine is desirable.

What are some good varieties of garden phlox? *White:* 'Mount Fujiyama', 'White Admiral', 'World Peace', 'Snowball'; *Lilac:* 'Lilac Time'; *Red:* 'Starfire'; *Orange-Red:* 'Orange Perfection', 'Prince of Orange'; *Salmon Pink:* 'Roland Smith', 'Salmon Beauty', 'Sir John Falstaff'; *Dark Red:* 'Leo Schlagater'; *Pink:* 'Dodo Hanbury Forbes'; *Soft Pink:* 'Dresden China'; *Purple:* 'Excelsior', 'Purple Heart'.

Are there any dwarf varieties of garden phlox? Yes, there are several. 'Juliet', a pale heliotrope-pink, is only 2 ft. tall, and 'Pinafore Pink' is 6 ins. tall with large flower heads. 'Norah Leigh', pale lilac, is 15 ins. tall with variegated foliage.

What is the earliest blooming phlox? The earliest are probably 'Miss Lingard' and 'Reine du Jour', both white, and 'Rosalinde', pink.

How far apart should phlox be planted? Set them 15 ins. apart and allow 3 or 4 shoots to grow from each plant.

Do phlox require much water? They need plenty of water during the growing season, but the soil must be well drained.

Do phlox require summer feeding? If the bed was well prepared by deep digging and the incorporation of manure, it may not be necessary; but they do respond to side dressings of fertilizer or to applications of liquid manure when flower buds are about to form.

How can I handle phlox to get more perfectly shaped heads of blossoms? They now grow ill shaped. Probably your plants are old and need lifting, dividing, and replanting. Good trusses are obtained by thinning out the shoots that appear in spring, leaving several inches between those left. Give liquid fertilizer weekly. Perhaps you have a poor variety.

Would appreciate some tips on raising phlox. Is it advisable to reset plants, and how? Phlox grow best in a well-drained rich soil; need a fair amount of water. Lift, divide, and replant about every 3 years. Cut off old flowers. They are subject to mildew; spray or dust regularly.

In transplanting phlox, how deep should they be set? Phlox should not be planted deeper than 1 to 2 ins.

Do you spread out the roots when planting phlox, or leave them straight? Phlox roots should be planted straight down, so dig the holes deep and give them plenty of space.

My yard is on a slope. I have trouble with hardy phlox. They don't seem to bloom as they should. Is the soil the cause? May be. Phlox need a rich, moist, but well-drained soil. It might be the variety—some are poor bloomers. Disease or a pest like red spider may be responsible. It might be due to drying out of the roots, which are close to the surface.

Why don't my phlox thrive? Foliage is sometimes whitish looking, turning to brown, lower leaves drop off, and blooms are poor. (New York City.) Phlox are subject to red spider mite infestation, which causes a whitish appearance at first, then leaves turn brown; also mildew and a disease which causes the lower leaves to drop. Deep, rich, moist, but well-drained soil and periodic dusting with sulfur or spraying with Karathane will help. Phlox is extremely difficult to grow in the city.

Do phlox "run out"? Yes. Phlox will deteriorate if not lifted, split up, and replanted in good soil every 3 or 4 years.

Should phlox be pinched back, thus preventing top-heavy plants while in bloom? Pinching would induce branching, resulting in smaller heads of flowers.

Could I plant hardy phlox at the base of poplar trees to follow tulips? It depends on what kind of phlox. *Phlox divaricata* and the arendsii hybrids, which would flower with the tulips, grow very well in part shade. The regular summer phlox will have too much competition from the tree roots and probably too much shade.

What is the procedure in propagating perennial phlox by cutting up the roots into small sections? When is best time to do this? The plants are dug in September, and the roots cut into lengths of 1 to 2 ins. They are scattered in a cold frame and covered, ½ in. deep, with a half-and-half mixture of sand and soil. The young growths are kept in the frame until spring, and are then planted out in nursery-bed rows.

How should I start the better varieties of phlox? Mine always die.

Phlox is propagated by lifting and dividing in the fall. Choose the new divisions from the outer edge of the clump, and discard the old center, which is too woody for good growth.

Why did my phlox change color? Many plants which were white, salmon, or deep red, are now a sickly magenta. You probably allowed seeds to ripen and self-sow. Unfortunately, self-seeded phlox tend to revert to their ancestral purplish color; and, as they are usually exceptionally vigorous, they crowd out the desirable but less sturdy varieties. Weed out seedlings and do not permit plants to go to seed.

Should the seed heads be cut off the new hardy phlox? Yes, because that will help the plant conserve its energies and also prevent seedlings from self-sown seeds, which can smother the original plants.

I have been told that unless phlox seed heads are kept cut off they will revert back to the original lavender. Is it possible for roots of any plant to change like that? The reason for the so-called reversion is self-seeding. The seedlings are always different in color, are very vigorous, and in time will displace the original variety. The original roots normally do not change. Cut off faded flowers to prevent reseeding.

Does dwarf phlox reseed itself? Please name a few kinds. Yes, some of the dwarf phlox seed themselves but will probably not be the same color as the original plant. _Phlox subulata_ with many varieties; _P. stolonifera, P. divaricata,_ and _P. d. laphamii._

PLATYCODON

Do platycodons need a rich soil? No; any garden soil will suit them in the open. It must be well drained.

When should platycodon plants be set out? In the spring.

How deep should platycodon be planted? The crown should be only barely covered with soil.

How do you keep platycodon in bloom? Keeping the old flowers pinched off to prevent seed formation will help.

Should platycodon be pinched back? It is not necessary, but permissible if a more bushy plant is desired. It must be done when the plants are about 6 ins. tall.

How tall does platycodon grow? Most varieties grow about 2 ft.

tall, but there is a lower-growing variety that grows only 10 ins. tall—platycodon variety *mariesii*.

Does platycodon come in any color but blue? Yes. There is a shell pink and a white.

Are platycodons difficult to transplant? Yes. They do have long, fleshy roots so you must take care when digging not to break them. Old plants often go down 18 ins. or more. Young plants are easier to move.

Do platycodons need winter protection? They are perfectly hardy and need no protection.

How is platycodon propagated? By careful division, in spring; or by seed, sown in fall or spring. Division is not as simple as for most fibrous-rooted perennials. Cut off outer sections of the thickened crown so that both buds and roots are present on each division. Dust cuts with fungicide to prevent infection. Fortunately, platycodon needs infrequent division.

I have been told that platycodon is slow to appear in spring. Is this so? Yes, it is one of the last perennials to appear above ground. Therefore, it's best to mark the location in fall so as to avoid injuring the plants in spring before they emerge.

PLUMBAGO (LEADWORT)

What perennial of easy culture has bright blue flowers late in the season? *Ceratostigma plumbaginoides*. It is tolerant of city conditions, thrives in sun or partial shade, and blooms until frost.

POPPY

What fertilizer for perennial poppies? Any balanced one will give good results. Take your pick of the several special garden fertilizers such as 5–10–5 or similar formula.

Will you give full planting instructions and care of Oriental poppies? Should be planted out in August or September, making the hole big enough so that the fleshy roots are not broken or twisted upward; water well if weather is dry. A few weeks after planting, a crown of leaves will appear. In relatively mild climates these can remain green for part of the winter. Protect in winter with marsh hay or dry leaves to prevent crown rot.

How shall I care for Oriental poppies? (Maryland.) They don't need much attention. Cut off flowers as they wither. In the spring, work in side dressings of balanced fertilizer.

After flowering the leaves of my poppies start to turn yellow and then die. Is this normal? Yes, poppies will lose their leaves but they will reappear in the fall. If you find them unsightly, plant something like day-lilies near-by to hide them after they bloom.

My Oriental poppies come up and grow well, but never bloom. They get afternoon sun. Should they be in a different place? Transplant in April or August into a sunnier spot.

When is the best time to plant or transplant Oriental poppies? In August, after the leaves have withered, and early in spring before growth commences. They dislike being transplanted, so injure the roots as little as possible; don't keep them out of the ground long, and water in thoroughly. If you grow them from seed, transfer the seedlings from flowerpots with the ball of soil intact.

When is the best time to thin out plants such as Oriental poppies? Thin out seedlings whenever the young plants tend to crowd. In growing practically all plants, thin out so carefully and continually that seedlings do not touch each other. If you mean dividing the roots of large plants, August is the time.

Will Oriental poppies planted in the spring bloom the same year? Yes, but you should buy large established plants. Plant them in March or early April, give them good care, and you are quite likely to get some flowers.

Can I sow Oriental poppy seed in May, to bloom next year? Yes, if the plants are given good care. Transplant seedlings into individual pots to avoid root disturbance when they are planted in their flowering positions.

How do you protect Oriental poppies in winter? I have lost 3 different settings. They can be set out in very early spring, but the best time is in August, when they are dormant. Is the soil well drained or waterlogged in winter? They resent the latter. Little protection is needed. A light covering of marsh hay or coarse ashes over the crown will suffice.

Is it necessary in this section to mulch fall-planted Oriental poppy before December? (South Dakota.) Tuck excelsior around the crown beneath the leaves; then mulch them with rotted manure or compost after the soil freezes.

Is there any danger of Oriental poppy plants mixing if they are planted close together? Occasionally parent plants will mix, and after a few seasons, you can hardly help having in your group of plants some which are self-sown from seed dropped from the parents. These will be mixed.

Do poppies come in any color besides orange? Indeed they do. In white there is 'Barr's White'; pink: 'Helen Elizabeth' and 'Salome'; flesh pink: 'Lighthouse', 'Spring Morn'; salmon: 'Victoria Dreyfus', salmon with silver edge; mahogany: 'Mahogany'.

Is there a double poppy? 'Crimson Pompon' is a fine blood-red double; and 'Salmon Glow', salmon-orange double.

PRIMROSE

What kind of soil do primroses need? A fairly rich and moist, but well-drained, soil; the addition of leafmold or peat moss mixed with rich compost is good. Should be planted in partial shade. Some, such as *P. japonica* and *P. rosea,* will grow in full sun where the soil is constantly wet.

Do primroses need fertilizer? Yes, they need a fairly rich soil. Well-rotted or dehydrated cow manure is probably the best.

What do you advise as a fertilizer for cowslips (Primula veris)? (Virginia.) Well-rotted or dehydrated cow manure. Maintain the soil near neutral point by applications of pulverized limestone, if necessary.

What summer care and winter protection do primroses need? (Virginia.) Should be given shade and not allowed to dry out in summer. They are hardy and should not require any winter protection in Virginia.

What time of year is best for splitting up primroses? After they have finished flowering in late spring.

Are primroses easily raised from seed? When is seed sown? Primroses come readily from seed. It's best to sow the seed as soon as ripe, which is in early summer. Spring-sown seed should be subjected to alternate freezing and thawing in the ice cube tray of the refrigerator. Freeze and thaw several times for a week. Always refreeze immediately after thawing. Sow seed immediately after the final thawing. Seeds can also be sown early in the year in a greenhouse or under fluorescent lights. Some growers sow in late fall in a protected frame where seeds are subjected to natural freezing and thawing. They then germinate in the spring and sometimes through summer. Protect the seedlings from hot summer sunshine.

PYRETHRUM (CHRYSANTHEMUM COCCINEUM)

How do you separate pyrethrums? Should be divided after they have finished flowering. The clumps are dug up and pulled apart, or pried apart with two spading forks.

ROSE-MALLOW (HIBISCUS)

How shall I treat hibiscus (mallow) before and after flowering? In spring dig in rotted leafmold and bone meal or superphosphate. Cut off faded flowers, and prune back to the ground in the fall after frost.

Should rose-mallow be left in ground all winter? Yes; the roots are perfectly hardy.

How can hibiscus (mallow) be grown successfully from seeds— how many years before plant will be large enough to bloom? Hibiscus seeds are best sown, 2 in a pot, and then planted out from the pot in permanent position. Will take about 3 years to bloom. However, a fairly new hibiscus, an F₁ hybrid called 'Southern Belle', will bloom the first year if seed is started early indoors. Plants grow 4 ft. tall and have blooms 10 ins. across. Colors include rose, pink, and white with a red eye.

Rose-mallows are beautiful plants, but attract Japanese beetles in droves. Are there any means of keeping the beetles off them? Use a spray such as Sevin.

SALVIA

What extra care would you advise for Salvia pitcheri? *Salvia pitcheri* grows well in good garden soil with a reasonable amount of moisture, and in full sun. Lift and divide the plants about every 3 or 4 years. The plants usually require staking.

Are there any perennial salvias? Yes; there are many. The ones usually found in gardens are *Salvia farinacea, S. officinalis, S. pitcheri,*

S. pratensis, S. jurisicii, and *S.* x *superba. S. farinacea* is often treated as an annual in northern gardens. In addition there are a few fine hybrids. For example, 'East Friesland' with intense violet-purple flowers on spikes 18 ins. long. They appear all summer.

SCABIOSA

When and how do I divide my scabiosa roots, grown from seed planted last spring? Your plants would hardly have grown enough from seed last spring to be divided now; plants 2 or 3 years old can be divided by cutting or pulling the plants apart in early spring and replanting.

FLOWERING SPURGE (EUPHORBIA)

When should flowering spurge (Euphorbia corollata) be planted? Spring or fall? Best in spring.

What is the full name of the euphorbia that blooms at the same time as tulips? It is *Euphorbia epithymoides,* sometimes commonly called cushion euphorbia. It is showy because of its very bright yellow bracts just below the inconspicuous flowers. It is an excellent non-spreading subject (although it will self-sow to some extent) for the spring garden among other perennials. It is especially effective with tulips, as you mention, but the plants remain neat all summer.

SHASTA DAISY (CHRYSANTHEMUM MAXIMUM)

What is the best way to protect Shasta daisy plants in the winter? Cover with marsh hay after ground is well frozen, and gradually uncover in spring.

How should Shasta daisies be divided? By digging up, in early spring, the outside rooted shoots either singly or in clumps. Shasta daisies are usually short-lived in the North and should be divided every year or two.

Can Shasta daisies be grown from seed? Yes, there are strains of both single and double forms that can readily be grown from seed. There is also an excellent dwarf—'Little Miss Muffet'—that is only 15 ins. high.

TRADESCANTIA

What is the botanical name of "widows' tears"? *Tradescantia virginiana.* It is also known as common spiderwort and snake-grass.

Are there any improved forms of tradescantia? Look for 'Iris Pritchard', white flushed with blue; 'Pauline', pale pink; 'Purple Dome', bright purple; 'J. C. Weguelin', pale blue; and 'Snow Cap', white.

What growing conditions does tradescantia require? It will grow well in any ordinary garden soil in sun or partial shade. Plants are very hardy. Although the flowers are pretty, the plants tend to be sprawly and invasive.

TRITOMA (KNIPHOFIA)

Can you grow tritomas from seed in the winter and transplant in the spring? Yes; transplant the seedlings into 2½-in. pots, and plant out in early May.

Should tritoma be cut down to the ground after blooming? Just the flowering stems should be cut away after blooming. The foliage usually persists through the winter and affords some protection to the crown.

How do you prepare tritomas for winter along the north Jersey coast? When is the best time to separate tritomas? Give winter protection with marsh hay or some other suitable material; do not cut off their leaves until spring. Separate tritomas in spring only.

Is it possible to divide tritomas? How should it be done? Divide them in spring only. It can be done by division of the roots, but much easier to dig up the offsets which come on the side of the main crown. See that these have roots.

VERONICA

The crowns of my veronica are rising above the surface. Can I remedy this? Veronicas tend to raise their crowns if left in the same spot for some time. Lift and replant every 2 or 3 years.

Why does my veronica, variety 'Blue Spires', sprawl instead of growing upright as the spicata and subsessilis varieties do? I have it from 3 different nurseries and all plants do it. It is characteristic of this variety to have weak stems. Little can be done to overcome this, other than to support the stems. This is best done by sticking twigs in the soil around the plants before the shoots begin to sprawl. Try variety 'Blue Champion'.

VIOLA

Are violas just small versions of the familiar pansy? For all practical purposes, yes. Both are botanically *Viola* and those commonly referred to as viola were developed largely by hybridizing *V. cornuta* with the pansy (*V. tricolor hortensis*). In general, violas have smaller flowers than pansies and bloom over a longer period. Many violas are hardy and live over winter in cold climates for years—others behave like pansies and die the winter after the first year's bloom.

What is the proper time to plant viola seed for spring bloom? In latter part of summer.

Will you discuss culture of violas? I planted good plants last year, but blossoms didn't form till frost. Nearly all violas need cool conditions, moisture, and partial shade. Hot, exposed locations are not conducive to good results. Provide a moist soil containing plenty of leafmold and the above conditions.

Does Viola pedata, the birdsfoot violet, prefer sun or shade? Grows naturally in full sun and in an acid, sandy soil. It's difficult to retain under cultivation.

VIOLETS

Are the so-called sweet, wood, and Russian violets related to violas and pansies? Yes, they are all separate species and varieties of the genus *Viola* to which both the pansy and viola belong.

Is the wood violet a perennial? I grow it as a house plant. It is difficult to say which violet you have, as several are known in different regions as the wood violet. All of these are perennials.

I am very much interested in growing sweet violets. Have a cold frame, and yet don't seem to have any success; had good roots and thrifty leaves; flowers very small and few. Will you give me some information? Remove sash, and shade the frame with lath screens in summer to keep plants cool; cut off all runners as they appear; feed and water to build up vigorous plants for late fall. Ventilate freely in fall, winter, and spring whenever temperature is above 35° to 40° F.

Should the runners be clipped off violet plants? Why do the plants grow up out of the soil instead of staying in it? How may large blooms and long stems be secured? In commercial culture the runners are cut off as fast as they appear in order to build up the plants for flowering. The plants root at the surface, with the crown above; as they develop, the crown rises still higher above the soil. Young plants give the best bloom, hence a number of these must be kept coming along. Long stems and good flowers are produced on young, well-developed plants in a rich but well-drained soil. Thin out old plants in spring.

My sweet violets produce seeds, but I never see any blooms; or maybe they bloom without petals, for they never come out of the ground like a flower, but develop into seed pods. Can you explain? Violets produce cleistogamous flowers, which are mostly on or under the ground. These are small, self-fertilizing flowers which never open.

YUCCA

How old must a yucca plant (from seed) be to blossom? Will it bloom frequently? About 4 to 5 years old; then the clump should bloom every year or at least every second year after that.

Is it necessary to mulch a yucca plant? No; the common yucca is very hardy and prefers a dry, sandy soil.

What is the preferred time for moving yuccas? Best done in early spring, when plant is dormant.

Have several yucca plants that were on the place when we moved here 5 years ago; why don't they bloom? Probably planted in shade, or too heavy a soil. They prefer a light, sandy soil, good drainage, and full sun.

When can I separate yucca? Detach young suckers in early spring; or divide old clumps immediately after flowering, or in the spring.

8
Annuals and Biennials

ANNUALS OFFER the gardener the means—when it comes to beautifying his or her new home with flowers—of getting the fastest and the mostest, for the leastest.

By no means, however, should annuals be considered merely as stopgap plants, to be used for temporary results until one can obtain something better. For many purposes, and for many special effects, there *is* nothing better. Many of the famous gardens of England make lavish use of annuals to obtain the breath-taking color displays for which they are noted.

While most annuals are so easily grown that they present no great challenge to the gardener's skill as a grower, they do test his skill—and offer him endless opportunities—in the employment of color and design in ways that will give his or her place individuality as well as beauty. And they do possess the great advantage of *flexibility*. Shrubs and perennials, once established, become more or less permanent fixtures. Annuals, used to supplement them, make it possible to shift the emphasis as one wishes, from year to year, or even during one season, and thus to obtain a series of interesting focal points not otherwise possible.

The flower arranger, too, will find that some annuals are almost indispensable to maintain a really constant supply of blooms for cutting and for supplementary foliage.

For pots, tubs, window boxes, and planters, annuals are the perfect answer. In fact a fabulous display can be assembled by using a multitude of pots and tubs of various sizes—some raised on props to give an allusion of height. Many city gardens are made up entirely with plants so displayed.

—*F. F. Rockwell, Esther C. Grayson and Margaret C. Ohlander*

 Annuals and Plants
Commonly Treated As Such

What is an annual?   An annual is a plant that lives but one season from seed sowing to flowering, setting of seed, and death.

What is meant by a hardy annual? A half-hardy annual? A tender annual?   Hardy annuals are those the seeds of which can be planted in fall or very early spring. Half-hardy annuals are cold resistant, and seeds of these can be planted early in spring. Tender annuals are easily injured by frost and must be planted only after the ground has warmed up and all danger of frost is past. There are several plants treated as annuals that are really tender perennials. Examples are wax begonia and snapdragon.

WHAT TO GROW

Can you give me a list of a few annuals that will stand early planting in the spring? (Vermont.)   Sweet-alyssum, scabiosa, candytuft, sweet peas, cosmos, cornflowers, larkspur, Shirley poppy, prickly-poppy (*Argemone*).

Will you give list of annuals requiring least care for home gardens?   Marigold, verbena, gaillardia, cosmos, spider-flower (*Cleome*), calliopsis, petunia, zinnia, salvia, scabiosa, annual phlox, sweet-alyssum, impatiens.

What annual flower would you recommend for planting in a completely shaded area?   There are no annual flowers that will grow well in *total* shade. A perennial ground cover such as *Pachysandra terminalis,* English ivy, *Ajuga reptans,* and periwinkle (*Vinca minor*) would be more suitable for such conditions. Your best choices, if you want to try annuals, would be cleome, lobelia, nicotiana, wishbone-flower (*Torenia fournieri*), and impatiens.

Which annual flowers are best for flower beds—along sidewalks

and on side of house? Ageratum (dwarf forms); *Begonia semper-florens* (wax begonia) varieties; dusty-miller (*Centaurea cineraria*); *Lobelia erinus;* marigolds (*Tagetes*) dwarf varieties; petunia (dwarf varieties); sweet-alyssum.

What annual would you suggest that I plant in the borders around my terrace? The area is partially shaded. Impatiens should do very well. There is a wide color range to choose from, heights from 6 ins. to 1½ ft., and you can count on the plants remaining in good condition all summer.

How do I go about planting an annual garden from seed sown in place? The garden is about 4 ft. wide and 15 ft. long and receives sun all day. What annuals would be the most reliable to sow? After raking the soil as smooth as possible, use lime to outline the various sections or rectangles where the seed is to be planted—as though you were making a giant plan on paper. For the easiest annuals to sow directly in place (you can broadcast the seeds), select sweet-alyssum as an edging, then nasturtium, and several varieties of marigolds and zinnias of medium height, and finally cleome and tall African marigolds and zinnias for background. Once the seeds germinate, you can transplant or thin, but in a display of this sort, a certain amount of crowding is permissible and even desirable. If one kind of seed doesn't germinate, spread out those from other sections to fill in its space.

Which are the easiest annuals to grow in a sunken garden? Fragrant kinds preferred. Ageratum, sweet-alyssum, calendula, centaurea, dianthus, iberis, lobelia, dwarf marigold, matthiola, mirabilis, nicotiana, petunia, phlox, portulaca, torenia, nasturtium, viola, dwarf zinnias, if low-growing plants are desired, otherwise any variety.

Will you give me the names of a few unusual annuals, their heights, and uses? Bells-of-Ireland (*Molucella laevis*), green, 24 ins.; flower arrangements. Nemesia, various (except blues), 18 ins.; edging, bedding. Nierembergia, lavender-blue, 12 ins.; window boxes, edging. Nigella (love-in-a-mist), blue or white, 12 ins.; bedding.

INDOOR PROPAGATION

What are the basic requirements for starting seeds indoors? A sterile starting medium, adequate sunlight or fluorescent light, steady moisture, good air circulation, and suitable temperature.

What are the various methods of starting seeds indoors? Traditionally seeds have always been started in flats or pots. However, today many other specially designed units are sold for the purpose to help simplify the process, especially for beginners. All are really just modifications of the traditional system. One such unit consists of a small plastic tray sold filled with a sterile planting medium (usually vermiculite and nutrients) plus seeds that adhere to the plastic cover. To activate the tray all one does is to punch holes in special indentations in the cover to release the seeds and then add the specified quantity of water. Such a unit eliminates the handling of seeds, provides a sterile starting medium, spaces the seeds a reasonable distance apart, and helps to avoid the danger of over- or underwatering.

Other trays contain 6 or more compressed blocks of a special peat-based growing mixture in which one or two seeds per block are either pre-sown or sown by the gardener. The unit is then watered.

Still another popular variant is the Jiffy-7, a flat peat moss wafer when dry; but when moistened it expands to form a small, filled pot in which a seed or seeds are sown. The wafers are usually placed side by side in a flat or other container. Large seeds can be sown one to a wafer and the plants that result left to grow until ready to transplant outdoors. Small seeds are usually sown several to a pot and transplanted once before being set outdoors.

Is one seed disinfectant satisfactory for use on all seeds? No. There are special disinfectants for certain seeds. For annual seeds use Semesan.

What is a flat? A shallow, topless box (usually about 3 ins. deep) with slits in the bottom to allow for drainage of water from soil. It is used for sowing seeds, inserting cuttings, etc. Shallower flats, usually of plastic, can be used without drainage holes if particular care is taken not to overwater. One disadvantage of a shallow flat is that it dries out quite quickly, but this size is better for window culture. Various discarded kitchen containers, such as temporary aluminum foil pans, can also be used. Drainage holes can easily be punched in the bottom.

Is there any rule about the dimensions of flats? There is great variety in flat sizes. Usually they should be not less than 2½ ins., nor more than 4 ins. deep. If more than 14 × 20 ins., they are likely to be too heavy to carry with comfort.

What soil mixture is preferable for seeds sown indoors? One part good garden loam, 1 part leafmold or peat moss, and 1 part sand, screened through ¼-in. mesh screen; or half sand and half peat moss; or pure fine sand, vermiculite, or sphagnum moss watered with nutrient solution. The most convenient material is a prepared mix sold for this purpose and containing sufficient nutrients to carry seedlings through until transplanting time.

What is the procedure in raising seedlings in sand, with the aid of nutrient solutions? Take a flat 3 to 4 ins. deep, with provision for drainage. Place a piece of burlap or sphagnum moss over the holes and fill with clean sand. Soak it with water, then with the nutrient solution (liquid fertilizer) diluted 1 part to 5 parts water. Sow seeds thinly; cover with sand; firm well. Keep the sand moist with the dilute solution. When the seedlings have made true leaves, use equal parts nutrient solution and water.

How do I go about sowing seeds of annuals indoors in a flat? Cover drainage holes in containers with moss or pieces of broken flowerpot; follow with an inch of "rough stuff"—flaky leafmold, moss, or screenings; fill with screened soil mixture (¼-in. mesh); press down level, and sow seeds. If you prefer, use a prepared mix sold for this purpose.

How deep should seeds be planted in flats and pots indoors? How deep in rows outdoors? Indoors, very small seeds are merely firmly pressed into soil with a tamper, or covered with a dusting of fine soil, sand, or vermiculite; medium-sized seeds covered ⅛ to ¼ in.; large seeds about 3 times their diameter. Outdoors, seeds are customarily covered a little deeper—half as much again.

What is a tamper? An oblong piece of board with a handle attached (similar to a mason's float) for tamping soil firm in flats. For use in pots or bulb pans the base of a tumbler or flowerpot can be used.

Is it better to scatter the seeds, or to sow them in rows? When flats are used, it is preferable to sow in rows. You can judge germination better, cultivate lightly without danger of harming seedlings, and transplant with more ease. When pots are used, seeds are generally scattered evenly and thinly.

How can very small seeds be sown evenly? Mix thoroughly with sand before sowing. Hold seed packet between thumb and forefinger and tap gently with forefinger to distribute seed.

When starting seeds in the house in the winter, what do you put in the soil, so that the plants will be short and stocky and not tall and spindly? No treatment of the soil will prevent this. Good light, moderate temperature, and avoidance of overcrowding are the preventives. Turn pots daily to keep the plants from "drawing" to the light. If your windows supply insufficient light, use fluorescent lights.

When would seeds for annuals be planted in seed flats in spring? Mid-March usually is soon enough, in the North especially, if raised under space limitations. Allow from 6 to 8 weeks before it is safe to plant the seedlings outside.

What fluorescent unit is best for starting seeds under fluorescent lights? The most commonly sold unit consists of two 40-watt fluorescent tubes 4 ft. long. This will usually grow most seedlings satisfactorily until they reach a sufficient size for planting outdoors. However, for superior results and for flowering of many annuals and house plants indoors, more light is needed. The most popular setup is a unit consisting of four 40-watt fluorescent tubes 4 ft. long with six 25-watt incandescent bulbs spaced at intervals between the fluorescent tubes. The light unit should be adjustable so that it can be raised or lowered according to the needs of the plants. When plants are small the lights are set about 3 ins. above them and then gradually raised as the plants grow. If plants show signs of burning, lights should be raised.

Are there any good books giving detailed information on raising both indoor and outdoor plants under lights? There are several helpful books. They are *The Indoor Light Gardening Book,* by George A. Elbert (Crown Publishers, Inc., 1973); *Gardening Indoors Under Lights,* by Frederick H. and Jacqueline L. Kranz (The Viking Press, Inc., 1957); and *Gardening Under Artificial Light* (Brooklyn Botanic Garden, 1000 Washington Avenue, Brooklyn, New York 11225).

Are fluorescent lights left on constantly or should the plants have a dark period? For growing seedlings, the lights are generally left on for from 14 to 16 hours. This should be during the day. A time clock is a great convenience in turning the lights on and off.

What are the advantages of growing seedlings under fluorescent light as compared with growing them in a sunny window? The lights supply a steady supply of light at all seasons whereas in a window there will be cloudy days and in winter the light intensity is low and the duration of the light period is short. In addition, it will be found that the plants don't dry out as rapidly under fluorescent lights, which is a special advantage for anyone who can't keep an eye on the plants during the day. It is also usually easier to control temperature and humidity under lights.

How should seed flats be watered after the seed is sown? Water thoroughly after seeding with a fine overhead spray from watering can or bulb-type or mist sprinkler until soil is saturated. Subsequently, water when surface soil shows signs of dryness. Do not overwater, nor permit flat to dry out. (See following question.)

Can seed flats be watered by standing them in a vessel of water? Yes, if more convenient. Do not leave in water any longer than is necessary for moisture to show on the surface. Do not submerge flat; place in water about 1 in. deep. Many growers prefer this method to watering the surface, as there is less danger of washing out fine seeds.

I have tried starting annuals indoors but without much success. Is there some trick about watering, or soil, that I should know? I've always used ordinary wooden flats and bought good seeds. The soil for seeds should be porous. A mixture of equal parts loam, leafmold, and sand is good, but you might have better success with the prepared artificial soil mixes sold for this purpose. Keep the medium just moist, but not sodden. Sometimes poor germination comes from covering seeds too deeply. Sow them no deeper than twice their diameter.

Why do my seedlings, grown in the house, grow to about an inch, bend over, and die? Damping-off, a fungous disease. Prevent it by disinfecting seeds with Semesan or Rootone, thin seeding, not overwatering, and giving seedlings fresh air without drafts. In severe cases, disinfecting soil or sand is advisable.

The seedlings in my seed flat get very tall and leggy, and very light in color. Why? Seedlings in this condition are said to be "drawn." The causes are insufficient light and too-high temperature. Overcrowding may result in insufficient light. Grow them under fluorescent lights.

What is the best germinating temperature for annual nicotiana and annual gaillardias? I have planted both late in the spring with dubious results. Must they have a cooler temperature to start? Indoors in

April a night temperature between 50° and 55° F. is suitable. Annual gaillardia germinates well outside in late May or early June. Self-sown nicotianas often germinate in early June, but are a bit late for best effect.

What is proper time to plant indoors seeds of pansy, petunia, and other annuals, that should be started early, but not too soon, as we often have frost here in May? (New Hampshire.) Pansy can be sown inside in January, but the best plants for spring display come from seed sown in August. The pansy can stand some frost; March or April is a good time to sow petunias for good plants to set out as soon as the weather is warm enough.

How can I start seedlings indoors so as to prevent too-rapid growth and decay? When shall I plant outdoors? Too-high temperatures and too early a start often account for conditions described. Few plants need starting indoors around New York before late March. Most of these are ready for planting outdoors in late April or early in May.

How do you make new plants blossom early in spring? There is not much that can be done to make them bloom early unless they are forced in a greenhouse. Most plants have to reach a certain age before they will flower.

Among annuals and plants treated as annuals, which ones take the longest time to come into flower in the North and therefore should be started indoors under fluorescent lights? Ageratum, wax begonia (*Begonia semperflorens*), snapdragon, petunia, lobelia, impatiens, nicotiana, salpiglossis, blue and red salvia, verbena, *Vinca rosea,* coleus, torenia, tithonia.

OUTDOOR PROPAGATION

What should the temperature be before planting annuals in the garden? (New York.) There can be no set temperature figure. Hardy annuals can be seeded as soon as the ground is ready to work; half-hardy annuals about 4 weeks later; tender ones when all danger of frost is past for the region. In and about New York this is usually during the second week in May.

How early can annuals be planted in the Philadelphia, Pennsylvania, area? Hardy annuals late March to April 1; half-hardy kinds mid-April to end; tender kinds from first week in May to end of month.

What does this mean: "Sow seeds when the maple leaves are expanding"? The unfolding of the maple leaves in the spring indicates that the season has sufficiently advanced for the gardener to sow certain of his hardier seeds outdoors.

How does one sow seeds for annuals in patches outdoors? Rake surface soil to break lumps and remove large stones. If seeds are small (sweet-alyssum, petunia, portulaca), scatter evenly, and pat down soil. For medium-sized seeds, rake soil again lightly *after* sowing, and pat down. For seeds which have to be covered ¼ in. or more, scrape off soil to required depth, sow seeds, and return soil removed or cover rows with fine vermiculite.

English sparrows take dust baths in my newly planted seed patches. How can I prevent this? Lay pieces of burlap or of fine brush over the seeded areas. Remove when seeds have germinated. Keep seed bed constantly moist.

What is the best method of insuring germination of small flower seeds in heavy clay soil, which consists mostly of subsoil, due to excavation for house? It grows plants very well once they get started. Hoe out rows 2 ins. wide and deep, fill with good screened compost, and sow the seeds in that. Before sowing work in a generous amount of peat moss, sifted compost, or rotted manure, if possible, to improve the general texture of the soil.

Which annual seeds are suitable for autumn planting? Larkspur, poppy, gilia, sweet pea, portulaca, nicotiana, salvia, celosia, cleome, sweet-alyssum, centaurea, petunia, coreopsis, kochia, euphorbia, cosmos, candytuft. They must be sown sufficiently late, so they will *not* germinate before freezing weather.

Which seeds can be sown out of doors, not later than November, to germinate next spring? (Ohio.) Annual poppies, balsam, California-poppies, cornflower, portulaca, larkspur.

Can larkspur, centaurea, and other seeds which are recommended for planting in the fall, be planted in February? (Maryland.) Seeds of these plants can be sown outdoors just as soon as the soil is dry enough to work in the spring. For a broad naturalistic effect the seed could be scattered in February even if the ground was not fit to rake.

Is it advisable to sow seeds of annuals, such as cosmos, zinnias,

and marigolds, in late autumn, so that they can germinate the first warm days of spring?   Cosmos is the only one of these likely to come up if sown outdoors in autumn, and there is nothing to be gained by this for early flowering, if seed can be sown in a cold frame in April.

How late is "late" when we are told to plant seed in late autumn? Usually about the average time of killing frost for your locality. Some seeds (sweet peas and other hardy annuals) can be sown after frost, provided the ground is not frozen.

Is it necessary to prepare the soil for seed planted in the fall? Yes. Soil should be just as carefully dug, fertilized, raked, and graded for fall planting as for spring planting.

Which flower seeds should be sown where they are to grow because of difficulty in transplanting?   Poppy, annual larkspur, calendula, California-poppy, nasturtium, dwarf lupine, portulaca, mignonette, Virginia stocks.

If such plants as petunia, phlox, etc., are permitted to self-seed, is there a true-to-original-color reproduction?   Not usually.

CUTTINGS

How are plants like snapdragon, petunia, verbena, and other annuals started as slips from the original plant?   These may be rooted if short side shoots, 3 to 4 ins. long, are placed in sand in a closed container, in July and August. If the slips have flower buds, these should be pinched off. (See Cuttings.)

Cutting of patience-plant, with leaves trimmed from base, ready for insertion in rooting medium. Cutting of tradescantia.

Why does coleus wilt so badly when I try to start new cuttings in soil? The air about the cuttings is too dry. Cover them with a pre-serving jar or polyethylene bag until they have formed roots. Trim large leaves back one half.

How are geranium slips rooted? Geranium slips may be rooted in sand or a Jiffy-7 pot at almost any time of year indoors during cold weather. The cuttings should be about 4 ins. long, and about ⅓ of the stem should be inserted in medium. Make the basal cut ¼ in. below leaf attachment. They can be rooted readily out of doors in September. Keep medium moist but not soggy.

What is the best method of handling lantana cuttings—our cuttings this year rooted well and got off to a good start after potting, but after a short time wilted and died. We kept them on the dry side, and shaded. After potting them, water thoroughly and keep in a closed, shaded propagating case for a week or two. Then gradually admit more air and remove the shade.

TRANSPLANTING

When should flat-raised seedlings be transplanted? How many times? First transplanting should be done when seedlings have formed their first true leaves. Many plants benefit from a second transplanting, when 2 or 3 ins. high, to individual pots, before they are moved outdoors. However, if seedlings are grown in Punch 'N' Grow units they can be thinned and the remaining plants allowed to grow in original tray until ready to go outdoors.

What is the best mixture of soil for transplanting seedlings from flats to pots, or to the cold frame? Sandy loam mixed with ¼ well-rotted manure (or dried manure or rich compost), and 4-in. potful of a complete fertilizer to a wheelbarrowful. Or use one of the arti-ficial soil mixes, such as Jiffy-Mix or Jiffy-Soil, which can be pur-chased at local garden centers.

What annuals do you recommend as foliage plants for use in ar-rangements? Castor-bean; sideritis, gray; coleus, variegated; prickly-poppy, white-veined foliage; *Amaranthus tricolor,* variegated.

What are the best tall annuals for background planting? Celosia, cleome, cosmos, datura, hollyhock, larkspur, marigolds (tall varie-ties), salvia, tithonia, snapdragons (tall varieties), zinnias (tall varie-ties).

I have difficulty in removing annuals from flats without ruining their root systems. Any pointers?   Water thoroughly a few hours before transplanting. With an old knife, or a small mason's trowel, cut soil into squares, each with a plant in the center. The plants can easily be removed with root system almost intact. Annuals that have been grown individually in peat pots can be left in pot when planting so pot and plant are set out as one unit. However, it is advisable to break the pot in a few places to help roots penetrate into soil more readily. Be sure to set the top edge of pot below soil level or it will act as a sponge, drawing water from the soil which will quickly evaporate; plant can suffer. Water thoroughly after planting and as necessary thereafter until plant roots have penetrated through pot into soil.

What is the right technique in setting out annual plants?   Remove plants from flats with as little root disturbance as possible. Stab trowel in soil, pull toward you, set plant in hole, remove trowel, push soil around roots, *press soil* firmly, and leave a slight depression around stem to facilitate watering.

How does one "thin out" seedlings?   Choose cloudy weather when soil is moist, and spread operation over 2 or 3 weeks or as necessary as plants develop. Pull up weakest seedlings before they crowd each other, leaving 2 to 6 ins. between those remaining, according to their ultimate size. When those left begin to touch, again remove the weakest, leaving the remainder standing at the required distance apart.

How much space should be given annuals, when thinning them, or planting them out?   Distance varies according to variety and habit of growth. A rough rule is a distance equal to ½ their mature height. Swan-river-daisy, Virginia stock, and similar weak growers, 4 ins.; marigold, Shirley poppy, etc., 1 ft.; strong growers, such as spider-flower and sunflower, 2 to 3 ft.

When can seedlings raised indoors be transplanted into the open?   Hardy annuals, as soon as large enough. Tender annuals, when all danger of frost is past. First harden them off by placing them in a cold frame or protected spot for several days.

CULTURE

Is it wrong to plant the same kind of annuals in the same space, year after year?   So long as the soil is well dug each year and the humus content maintained, there is nothing wrong with the practice.

However, China-asters, snapdragons, and marigolds may well be changed each year.

What type of soil, and what fertilizing program, is best for annuals? Most annual flowers do best in a well-drained, rather light soil in full sun. Unless it is really run-down and deficient in plant nutrients, only a light annual application of rotted manure, peat moss, and compost, plus some standard commercial fertilizer, is advisable.

What is the best fertilizer for the annual and perennial flower beds? For most annuals and perennials a 4–12–4 or 5–10–5 fertilizer is recommended. For perennials with fleshy roots a 2–10–10 fertilizer can be substituted.

How deep should the soil be prepared for annuals? Nine ins. for good results. Some growers go twice this depth to assure maximum growth.

Do popular annuals have decided preferences for acid or alkaline soil? Most popular garden flowers tolerate either a slight acid or alkaline condition and thrive in a neutral soil.

My 3-year-old garden is on a slight slope, with sun all day. The first year, cosmos and pinks did fine. Now everything dwindles and dies. Even petunias won't grow. What can I do? Dig deeply and add 3-in. layer of well-rotted manure, leafmold, or peat moss. Set the plants as early as you can, depending upon your conditions. Sloping site and a hot sun are not conducive to good growth because of the moisture conditions. Get moisture down around the roots of the plants; keep a heavy mulch of partly decayed leaves, grass clippings or other material over the soil in summer.

How shall I top annuals to make them bushy? What does one do, pinch them or cut them with a knife or scissors? Pinch out no more than the growing point with thumbnail, if possible, so as to avoid wasted energy on the part of the plant.

Exactly what is meant by "pinching back"? Pinching back is the removal of the tip of a growing shoot to induce branching.

Which annuals, and at what stage, should be pinched back for better growth and more flowers? These annuals can be pinched to advantage when from 2 to 4 ins. high: ageratum, snapdragon, carnation, cosmos, nemesia, petunia, phlox, salvia, schizanthus, marigold, and verbena. Straggly plants of sweet-alyssum can be sheared back in midsummer for better growth and to induce flowering later in the season.

Is it true that if flowers are picked they bloom better?   On plants that continue to make flowering growth it is best to pick off flowers as soon as they fade, to prevent the formation of seed, which is a drain on the plant's energy.

What would cause annuals to grow well but come into bud so late in the summer they are of little use? Seed was planted late in April. Most annuals are blooming at midsummer from April-sown seed. Lobelia, scarlet sage, torenia, and tithonia are examples that should be sown indoors in March for good results. The late, older varieties of cosmos usually do not have time to flower in the North, even if sown early indoors.

Why do I have to stake so many plants—zinnia, marigold, and other common plants? They grow fine, bloom generously, yet if not tied, do not stay erect.   Insufficient phosphorus in soil; or perhaps they are exposed to too much wind; or heavy rains can have beaten them down. Full sun all day helps produce sturdy plants.

Most of our annuals pass out about August, leaving few flowers for fall. Is there any way we could renew our plantings so that flowers are available until late in the season?   There are numerous annuals which, sown in summer, will provide bloom right up to frost. These are *Browallia americana* and *speciosa,* calendula, celosia, the little fine-leaved marigold (*Tagetes signata pumila*), sweet-alyssum, *Torenia fournieri,* verbena, and all types of zinnias. The dates for sowing must be closely adhered to. These apply to the vicinity of New York City and would suit a rather large region. The date of the first killing frost in fall must be allowed for in the more northerly sections. With care, seeds can be sown outdoors and seedlings transplanted direct to their flowering quarters, or potted up and held over, and used as needed. The latter plan is better for torenia and browallia. Sow these the first week in June; transplant to 3-in. pots. At the same time sow celosia, nicotiana, dwarf scabiosa, and tall marigolds. Third week in June, sow California-poppy (sow where to bloom or in pots), globe-flower, candytuft, *Phlox drummondii,* and marigold. None of the above will grow to the size of spring-sown plants. Last week in June to first week in July sow calendulas, sweet-alyssum, and zinnias of all types. Sweet-alyssum, calendula, and verbena will survive light frosts.

How long from planting of seed to cutting of flowers on asters, stock, snapdragons? The length of time required will vary somewhat according to the type and variety, the time of year, and conditions under which grown. Early varieties of either might be ready in 14 to 16 weeks. Snapdragons will be bushier if pinched when about 3 ins. high, but pinching delays flowering.

How can I save the seed from annual flowers? Select healthy plants of the best type, allow the seeds to mature on the plant, but gather before they are shed, then dry in an airy, rainproof place safe from mice.

Will seed from hybrid annuals flower the following year; if so, will they come true? Seeds of the so-called annual hybrids saved one year should give flowers the next. Some may come pretty true, but variation may be expected.

I have looked and looked for the answer to this question and haven't found it yet. When different shades of the same flower are planted together, which ones may I save seeds from and have them come true to their parent? Which ones not? You have not much chance of getting seed which would come true from any of them.

Do the following come up without replanting? Bergamot, ageratum, four-o'clocks, sweet-alyssum, morning-glories, moonflowers. Of this group only bergamot is a perennial; this will come up each year. All the others are annuals. They come up from the seeds dropped from the plants the previous year. However, to be on the safe side it is best to sow seeds each spring.

Specific Annual Plants

AGERATUM

How is ageratum started for outdoor planting? Sow seeds indoors in March, or outdoors early in May when danger from frost is past. The best method is to sow them in seed pans or small pots of fine-screened soil or commercial seed starting mix. Sow on a level surface and press the seeds in. Set pan in water until moisture shows on the surface; cover with glass or polyethylene and shade; remove when germinated; transplant 2 ins. apart when first true leaves show and grow under fluorescent lights or in a sunny window.

What is the proper care of ageratums over the winter?   Young plants, started late in the season, may flower as house plants during late winter. Cuttings are taken from the young growth in September and rooted in sand.

ALYSSUM (SWEET-)

Why does white sweet-alyssum come up year after year when purple varieties don't?   The white alyssum reseeds itself prolifically, but the purple varieties are not as vigorous. Both of these are annuals.

ARCTOTIS

Would appreciate instructions for success with African-daisies (arctotis). Mine achieve the bud stage, but never blossom, falling off at that point. Can it be too much water, or are they perhaps potbound? (Kentucky.)   Dropping of buds can be caused by extremes. Too much moisture around the roots or their drying out; warm, humid conditions or a sudden chill. Use fine bone meal or superphosphate for fertilizer; have the soil open and well drained. Don't plant in very large pots.

ASTER (CHINA-ASTER)

How can I grow annual asters?   Select wilt-resistant seed. Plant indoors in flats or pots in late March or April; transplant into the open when danger of frost is past. Or sow seed outdoors in May. Select "early," "midseason," and "late" varieties for continuous bloom. If in a region where aster "yellows" (a virus disease) is prevalent, grow under cheesecloth screens.

What culture do asters require?   Prepare seed bed by forking over the soil and working in peat moss or leafmold. Make drills 2 to 3 ins. apart and ¼ in. deep; sow seeds 6 or 8 to the inch about mid-May. Cover with a half-soil, half-sand mixture, and water with a fine spray. A light covering with hay or strips of burlap will help retain moisture until germination; then remove *immediately*. Keep the seedlings watered. Transplant when seedlings have formed their first true leaves. Soak the soil a few hours before, lift seedlings with all roots, and keep them moist. If wanted for cut flowers, set in rows 18 ins. apart, the plants 9 to 12 ins. apart in the rows. Set the seedling in the soil so that the bottom leaves are resting on the surface. Give a good watering; keep soil cultivated until plants get large or apply a mulch. Enrich the soil prior to planting by digging in 3 ins. rotted manure; or use compost or peat moss mixed with dried cow or sheep manure—6 lbs. manure to 1 bu. of compost or peat moss. When flowers show, feed liquid fertilizer and manure weekly.

We have China-asters. Do they reseed themselves? (New York.) Yes, occasionally, especially the single-flowered kinds. However, it is better to raise new plants under controlled conditions annually.

Can't asters be planted in the same spot each year? Better not. They are subject to several diseases that collect in the soil, making it desirable to select a new site each year unless special precautions are taken. (See next question.) The ground, of course, can be used for other plants.

Is it true that asters cannot be planted in the same space a second year? No—not literally. Asters can be grown in the same spot by using disease-resistant strains, by disinfecting the seeds, by mixing tobacco powder with the soil to discourage root aphis, and by screening with cheesecloth to keep out leafhoppers which transmit the virus disease known as aster yellows.

What is the best procedure in disbudding asters? Should the top be pinched out when they are young to make them branch? Asters usually are self-branching, producing a number of branches, and do not need pinching. Each branch will bear a terminal flower, together with numerous other buds on small side shoots. All these must be removed, retaining the main bud only.

Do annual asters come true from seed collected from a flower bed? If several varieties were growing together, variation could be expected.

BALSAM (IMPATIENS BALSAMINA)

Is balsam worth growing? Yes, especially for positions in part shade. Try the camellia-flowered double strains on bushy, branching plants.

BELLS-OF-IRELAND

How are the seeds of bells-of-Ireland germinated? Mine don't come

up. Sow in a carefully prepared seed frame in May when soil has warmed up. Keep constantly moist until germination. Transplant to garden beds in late June.

My bells-of-Ireland don't look like the ones in the flower show arrangements. Why? Flowering stems are "groomed" by removing all the foliage, leaving only the bell-like bracts with the little flower "clappers" in the center of each.

BROWALLIA

When should browallia be sown for outdoor flowers? Which varieties should I use? For early flowering, sow in late March indoors, or in a cold frame after mid-April. Outdoor sowing can be done about mid-May. These dates apply in the vicinity of New York City; farther north it would be 7 to 12 days later and correspondingly earlier farther south. *Browallia americana* and *B. speciosa* are the best for summer.

What is the method of growing browallia for the house; and what is the best variety to choose for this? Sow seeds in August; transplant into 2½-in. pots; as the plants grow, shift to 4-in., then perhaps to 5-in. pots, but don't overpot; water sparingly after November. Sow again in January for early-spring bloom. Use *Browallia speciosa*.

CALCEOLARIA

Some years ago I saw a hardy annual about 6 ins. high, with lemon-yellow blossoms about the size of a fingernail, shaped like the calceolaria. Leaves were quite lacy and fernlike. What is its name? It may have been an annual calceolaria. The species *mexicana, scabiosaefolia,* and *profusa* all more or less agree with your description.

CAMPANULA

Are annual Canterbury bells easy to raise from seed? Yes, annual types bloom in less than six months from seed. Colors are the same as in biennial strains.

CANDYTUFT

My annual candytuft only bloomed a short time, then died. Why? Annual candytuft blooms very quickly from seed but only for a short time. Plant seeds at 2- or 3-week intervals for constant bloom during cool spring and fall weather. Candytuft does not do well in the heat of summer.

CASTOR-BEAN

I always grow a few castor-bean plants and am interested in them. Can you tell me more about them, their cultivation, and if there is a market for the bean? (Ohio.) Castor-bean plants grow best in a rich, well-drained loam soil. Seeds can be planted in May where they are to grow, or started earlier indoors and then set out later. There is a market for the seeds, of course, but it is well supplied by commercial growers. The commercial crop is produced in the South, where a long season allows for maximum production.

Is it advisable to plant castor-oil-bean seeds around the lawns to prevent molehills and mole runs? Castor-bean plants have very little, if any, effect on the mole population.

Is there anything poisonous about the castor-bean plant? The seeds contain a poisonous principle called ricin. They are best planted where children cannot get at and eat the beans. Fatalities have been reported from eating as few as three seeds.

CLEOME

I have seen lovely pink and white spider-plants. Are they something special? 'Pink Queen' is a fine variety which won a silver medal for excellence. 'Helen Campbell' is a pure white. If your plants self-seed, pull up all purplish-red volunteers.

COLEUS

Is it possible to raise coleus from seeds? If so, when should seeds be started? Coleus are easily started from seeds sown any time indoors. Germination is rapid (in about 1 week) and plants are ready for transplanting in another 2 weeks. For pot-plant use, look for one of the dwarfer growing types such as 'Carefree'.

Can coleus be rooted from cuttings? I have a favorite pink-leaved variety that I would like to increase. Coleus roots very readily. Stem cuttings 2 or 3 ins. long can be rooted in water, sand, vermiculite, or a regular rooting mixture.

CORNFLOWER (CENTAUREA)

Why do our bachelor-buttons or cornflowers show retarded growth, with feeble flower stalks? Sow the seeds on a finely prepared soil in the fall or as soon as you can work the soil in spring. Sow thinly; cover about ¼ in. Thin out the seedlings to 9 ins. apart when large enough. Yours probably were too crowded.

What treatment do you prescribe for bachelor-buttons for large blossoms and long period of bloom? If by bachelor-buttons you mean the annual cornflower (centaurea), you should get excellent results by giving them a moderately rich, well-drained soil and extra watering during dry weather. Keep faded flowers picked off. (See preceding answer.)

COSMOS

When should early cosmos be started from seeds? Sow in a cold frame in early April and transplant directly to the place to flower, or sow outdoors in late April.

I like and grow cosmos. Pink plant blossomed in early July—very unusual to me. Why should this happen? The rest of my plants blossomed in fall as usual. There are several forms of early-flowering cosmos, including pink varieties. The 'Sensation' type blooms in 8 weeks after the seed is sown. You probably have an early kind.

DAHLIA

Is it true that some dahlias flower the first year from seed? Yes, especially the dwarf bedding dahlias like 'Unwin Dwarfs' and 'Coltness Hybrids'. Many others are usually listed in seed catalogues.

DIANTHUS

What are the best annual pinks? Look for forms of *D. chinensis* such as 'China Doll', an All-America winner with double flowers in mixed colors; and 'Merry-Go-Round', a pure white single with scarlet center; *D. heddewigii* hybrids 'Bravo', a red single, 'Gaiety', fringed petals in mixed colors, 'Colorama', double in mixed colors, and 'Baby Doll', a dwarf single in mixed colors.

Dianthus 'Zing', although a perennial, starts to bloom a few weeks after sowing. Flowers are single in brilliant scarlet. It is a *Dianthus deltoides* hybrid.

DIMORPHOTHECA

How long can dimorphotheca be expected to stay in bloom? The plants I had last summer bloomed from about June 1 to July 15

and then died. Six weeks of bloom is about all you could expect, though the time might be lengthened somewhat by snipping off all withered blossoms to prevent seed formation. It is a good plan to make a second sowing of seed 4 to 6 weeks or so after the first, to provide blooming plants for the second half of the summer.

What are the requirements for African-daisy (dimorphotheca)? It just never comes up. Can it be planted early? I buy good seed. (Washington.) Sow the seed outdoors in spring when the ground has warmed up, or indoors 4 to 6 weeks earlier. Give the plants light, well-drained, and not specially enriched soil. Be sure they get plenty of sun.

EVERLASTINGS

I want to grow some everlastings for winter bouquets. What shall I select? Acroclinium; globe amaranth; helichrysum; statice; honesty; xeranthemum.

When should everlastings be cut for drying? Cut when the flowers have just started to open. Dry in a well-ventilated room and store away from any dampness.

FOUR-O'CLOCK (MIRABILIS)

I have been told you get larger bushes and a greater amount of flowers from four-o'clock roots the second season. Are they to be left in the ground, or dug up and dried like certain bulbs? (Missouri.) Mostly used as annuals; the roots would be very unlikely to live through winter outdoors in your region. The large, tuberous roots can be lifted before hard frost and stored indoors for the winter, like dahlias. It is the prevailing opinion that they will flower earlier and produce better bloom. Try it, but sow some seeds outdoors in May to be sure of a crop of flowers.

GODETIA

I have no luck with satin flower. Can you help me? These lovely, bushy, 18-in. annuals with their masses of hollyhock-like salmon, orange, pink, red and lavender flowers, prefer part shade and a cool, moist location. They thrive on Cape Cod and regions with cool nights in a well-watered garden but cannot stand areas where nights are hot and humid.

GOURDS (See Section 10, The Home Vegetable Garden)

IMPATIENS

How much shade will impatiens endure? Quite a bit and probably as much as any annual. Good light and a few hours of sun are needed for the best flowers, though.

KOCHIA

I have heard of an annual which can be used instead of a real hedge. What is it? Burning bush or kochia. The rounded plants, like sheared evergreens, grow 3 ft. tall. During hot weather the foliage is light green but in autumn it turns a rich red.

LARKSPUR

How early should larkspur be planted? (Virginia.) As early in the spring as the ground becomes workable, or in late fall about November.

What month is best to plant larkspur and ragged-robin? (Virginia.) Larkspur and ragged-robin (lychnis) can be sown in November for spring bloom, or as early in spring as possible.

Will larkspur do well if transplanted? It transplants very poorly; sow the seeds where the plants will flower, and thin out the seedlings to 9 ins.

When shall I transplant annual larkspur? Only when the seedlings are small—just large enough to handle; large plants do not transplant successfully. Better to sow where they are to bloom and thin them.

What is the secret for successful larkspur? Ours start well, but fade away before flowering. Sow seeds in well-drained, moderately fertile soil, in full sun or light shade. Thin seedlings to stand 9 ins. apart. (See preceding answers.)

LOBELIA

Will lobelia grow in part shade? Yes, the low-growing varieties are ideal for window and porch boxes or hanging baskets as well as for partly shaded edgings. Choose trailing 'Blue Cascade' for boxes and dwarf varieties for edgings.

MARIGOLD

What types of marigolds do you suggest for a garden of annuals? African tall, double including carnation-flowered, chrysanthemum-flowered, dahlia-flowered, peony-flowered; French Single; French Double; Dwarf Signet (*Tagetes signata pumila*).

What large-flowered, tall marigolds shall I grow for variety in color? 'Primrose Climax', pale yellow; 'Yellow Climax', bright yellow; 'Toreador', orange; 'Golden Climax', gold; 'Whitemost', near white.

Would you kindly tell me why my marigolds didn't blossom well last summer? Could it be the fault of the ground? It may have been any one, or several, of a number of reasons: too late sowing; too much rain; too-heavy or too-rich soil; insufficient sun; overfeeding or overwatering.

Are seeds good which have not been picked until after a killing frost, such as marigolds? The first killing frost would not be severe enough to harm the seeds.

NASTURTIUMS

What nasturtiums shall I grow to produce seeds for pickles and salads? What shall I do to keep them free of the little black bugs? The old-fashioned singles, either dwarf or tall. The much more beautiful and attractive sweet-scented doubles produce few seeds. Keep young plants sprayed with malathion to kill aphids.

NICOTIANA

I have seen flowering tobacco in mixed colors. What variety is this? The Affinis Hybrids or Sensation Mixed, about 32 ins. tall. 'Crimson Bedder' is deep red, 12 ins. tall. There is also a lime-green variety, 'Lime Sherbet', that grows 18 ins. tall. A dwarf red, 'Idol', only 8–10 ins. tall, looks well with 'White Bedder', 12 ins. tall. All are delightfully fragrant, and will grow in light shade.

NIEREMBERGIA

How shall I grow nierembergia from seed? Start indoors in March for early bloom. 'Purple Robe' is a fine violet-blue variety.

PERIWINKLE

How and where shall I plant the annual periwinkle? Periwinkle (*Vinca rosea*) is a native of the tropics and practically everblooming. Sow seeds in January in a warm temperature. The seeds are sometimes difficult to germinate, and at first the seedlings are slow of growth. Have the soil well drained and don't overwater. When these seedlings produce the first true leaves, transplant to 2¼-in. pots, later on to 3-in. pots. From these transplant to the open ground when all danger of cold weather is past. Provide a fairly rich soil. Once established they need little care beyond watering occasionally.

PETUNIA

Can petunias be grown successfully with only 4 hours of afternoon sun? Yes, provided other conditions are suitable.

How can I prepare seed bed for petunias? When shall I plant in St. Louis area? (Missouri.) Have the soil well drained, moderately rich, and very thoroughly cultivated, so that its texture is fine and light. Sow thinly in spring when soil is in good workable condition.

When is the best time to plant petunias? In what soil? (New York.) The new hybrid petunias are best started indoors in March in the vicinity of New York. See Propagation Indoors, this section.

When is the best time, and what is the best way, to plant petunia seed? (Alabama.) In your region, outdoor sowing of petunia seed is likely to be the most satisfactory. It can be done as soon as the soil has warmed up in spring. Have the soil finely prepared, and barely cover the seed.

Can petunias be sown in the fall? (Ohio.) Fall-planted petunia seed sometimes comes through the winter and germinates in the spring —this depends chiefly on climate, location, and the character of the winter. Spring sowing is preferable in middle and northern sections of the country.

How long does it take petunia seeds to germinate, and when should one transplant them? Good petunia seeds sown on prepared soil, only lightly covered, and kept at 65° to 70° F. temperature, should germinate in from 8 to 12 days. Transplant when the first *true* leaves appear. (The leaves that show at germination are only seed leaves.) This might be approximately 10 to 14 days after germination.

Should petunias always be transplanted, or will they bloom well where originally planted? If the soil and other conditions are favorable, they should do well where originally planted. But thin the seedlings to 6 ins. or so apart if they come up thickly.

I set out petunias in bed with partial shade when they had just begun to bloom; plants withered and died until 90 per cent were gone. Soil analysis said nothing was wrong. Gladiolus did well in same bed. What was wrong? Probably root injury when transplanting, plus too much water. Petunias will stand some shade but not too much.

I'd like a mass of petunias for borders but have no success growing from seed. How can this be done? How early to start, etc.? (Connecticut.) Petunia seed for a mass planting is best sown as soon as the soil has warmed up. Have the soil very thoroughly pulverized, and barely cover the seed. Keep watered, and thin out plants to 6 or 8 ins. apart when they are a couple of inches tall. For earlier bloom, start seed in flats indoors in March, and transplant outdoors early in May. If you have no success sowing your own seeds, try one of the pre-planted seed trays such as Punch 'N' Grow. Or buy plants at your local garden center.

Is there any way to prevent petunias growing lank during late summer? I keep seed pods picked off pretty well, still they look straggly by August. This tendency is hard to prevent in some varieties unless the flowers are cut quite often; prune back the longer stems to encourage stockiness. Use compact-growing kinds.

Why can't I raise petunias? They are the only plants I have a complete failure with. I buy good seed, but the plants that do grow just get tall (leggy), with very small bloom, if any. A hard question to answer without more information. The plants may be too crowded, or the soil may be too heavy and shaded. Try careful thinning and pinching back young plants.

Why can't I raise any petunias? They come up but die. Perhaps the soil is too heavy and claylike, or it may be too wet. A light, well-drained soil in practically full sun is best, and it should be only moderately rich.

What makes petunia plants turn yellow, especially if grown 2 years in succession in the same soil?   Petunias are subject to several virus diseases that discolor the leaves. The condition may also be due to a highly alkaline soil. Dig in peat or leafmold, change the location, and prepare the soil deeply.

Why do petunia plants grow large but have no blooms?   Soil probably too rich, thereby forcing excessive stem and leaf growth at the expense of blooms. Try them in another place where the soil is poorer. Don't overwater.

Can you explain just how to snip off a petunia plant (brought in from outdoors) so that it will have many blooms instead of spindly stems?   Cut back about half of the stems to 4 or 5 ins. When these have developed new growth, cut back the remaining stems in the same way.

How can I force petunia (giant and ruffle types) under average conditions as to light and heat found in a home?   Your chances of raising petunias under home conditions are slight. In greenhouses, cuttings are taken in September from summer plants, the young growths being used. These are rooted in sand and then potted up in small pots. They do not bloom much in the winter but begin about February. Seeds can be sown in January and February for early flowering. Petunias need plenty of light and a fairly even temperature—about 55° F. at night. You might try digging up old plants in fall, cutting them back, and planting in pots.

Will petunias reseed successfully? (Indiana.)   Sometimes they will; it depends on conditions. The more common kinds reseed freely, but the colors will be unsatisfactory. For good petunias secure good seed each year.

How can I root cuttings from double petunias?   If the plants are growing outdoors, take the cuttings in August or September. Select young growths about 2 ins. in length that grow from the older stems. Trim off the bottom leaves and insert them ½ to 1 in. deep in pure, moist sand in a cold frame in a warm atmosphere. Shade and keep the sash on for about a week. Give light when they are rooting; this will be indicated by the foliage remaining erect. Keep the sand moist.

How can I root petunia cuttings in winter?   About February take young side growths, trim off the lower leaves, and set them firmly in moist sand. (See previous question.)

Dwarf, compact-growing annuals, such as petunias, are useful for the foreground of mixed borders and for edgings along patios or walks.

Which kind of petunias shall I get to grow against a small white fence? Something not tall, but rather bushy. Choose your favorite colors in the multiflora and grandiflora classes.

What type of petunia is best for all summer beauty? The regular multiflora and grandiflora types are generally the most satisfactory.

POPPY

Do California-poppies (Eschscholtzia californica) and Shirley poppies reseed themselves? Yes, usually; but much digging of the soil in the spot where reseeding took place will bury the seed so deep it may not germinate.

When is best time to plant the (annual) peony-flowered poppy? Can it be successfully planted on top of the snow? (Kansas.) If in your region the poppy usually reseeds itself, and plants come voluntarily the following spring, you can very well sow on the snow. Otherwise sow the seed just as early as you can get on the soil.

When is the correct time to plant poppy seed? How is it best sown? Just as early as you can work the ground in spring. Rake the soil as fine as possible; make level and firm it slightly; scatter the seeds thinly, press them firmly into the soil but don't cover. Thin out the seedlings when 2 ins. high, spacing 3 ins. apart. Two weeks later thin again to 6 or 9 ins. apart.

PORTULACA

How can I make portulaca germinate and grow? Portulaca is usually easy to grow from seed sown outdoors in either October or early spring. It should have a well-drained, light, and not rich soil, in full sun.

*Garden centers and local nurseries offer
well-developed, often flowering, annual
plants in various kinds of pots and small
containers—ready for quick, easy planting
by the home gardener.*

**Does portulaca self-sow? Someone told me to let them go to seed
and I'd have plenty of plants next year.** They self-sow readily. Seedlings don't generally appear until fairly late in spring after soil has
warmed. If they are crowded they should be thinned or transplanted.

SALPIGLOSSIS

How can I grow large, healthy salpiglossis plants? (New Jersey.)
Sow seeds in a well-prepared bed in May. Work peat moss or leafmold
into the surface, sow the seeds thinly in rows 2 ins. apart. Cover
them not more than ⅛ in. deep. Transplant 12 ins. apart in soil
deeply dug and enriched with rotted manure or compost; or with
peat moss mixed with dried cow or sheep manure, 10 lbs. to a bushel
of peat, plus ½ lb. of ground limestone. Spread an inch deep and
dig in. Do not soak the soil until the plants are steadily growing and
have some size. Cultivate frequently. When flower stalks form, feed
with liquid fertilizer; or apply dehydrated manure. Hoe and water
in; repeat every 2 weeks during bloom.

SALVIA

How do you start red salvia seeds? (South Dakota.) The seed
should be sown indoors in a warm temperature, about the latter part
of March or beginning of April, in small pots or seed pans. Cover

seeds ⅛ in., and set pot or pan in water until moisture shows on surface. Cover with glass or polyethylene film and newspaper, but remove as soon as seed germinates.

Are there other colors of bedding salvia besides the red and blue? Yes, they can be had in white, salmon-pink, purple, mahogany, and lilac.

SCABIOSA

What is the best method of culture for scabiosa? (New Jersey.) Sow seeds outdoors about April 15 or indoors in March. Give the plants a sunny position where the soil is rather light in texture, moderately rich, and in full sun. Do not cover the seeds deeply; not more than ⅛ in. Transplant when the seedlings have made their first true leaves, setting them in the soil so that the lower leaves are resting on the surface. Set 9 ins. apart each way.

SNAPDRAGON (ANTIRRHINUM)

Do snapdragons require a rich, shady place? (Idaho.) No shade. They should have full sun and a light, well-drained soil that is only moderately enriched. Early planting is desirable for best bloom.

What is the best fertilizer for snapdragons? Rotted or dehydrated manure or leafmold when preparing the soil, which should be neutral or slightly alkaline. Feed with liquid fertilizer when coming into flower, or give a dressing of complete chemical fertilizer.

Can snapdragon be sown in the fall? (Kentucky.) Yes, in your part of the country, but it must be done sufficiently early to provide young plants which will be large enough to withstand the winter with protection. Sow in August.

When shall I plant snapdragons? (Wisconsin.) The best time to set young plants out is in the spring when the ground has begun to warm up. Seeds should be started indoors in March.

When is the best time to set out snapdragon plants? (North Carolina.) Early in spring, when the ground has really started to warm up.

Are snapdragons strictly annuals? Mine bloomed after several frosts and continued in leaf. (Virginia.) No; in the South they are often treated as biennials or even perennials. Generally speaking, they are handled as hardy annuals (more cold-resistant than most). Botanically they are perennials.

Must snapdragons be supported by stakes at planting time? Mine were all in curlicues, and staking them after 8 or 10 ins. tall didn't help at all. It is a good idea to put in the stakes at the time the young plants are set out, and start tying as soon as signs of flopping begin. A better plan is to use twiggy brush and insert pieces 18 ins. long among the plants. The growths will work up among the twigs. In an open situation, with proper care of soil, they ought not to need much support. Some varieties are base-branching and require less staking.

Can you tell me how to grow snapdragons? I buy the plants and they bloom a little while, then die. (Mississippi.) Perhaps the soil is too rich, too heavy and claylike, or poorly drained. Or there may be too much shade. Snapdragons like an open situation, light soil, and not too much feeding. They dislike a hot situation and bloom best in cool weather.

How can I attain many-flowered snapdragons in my summer garden? I get good plants but there are many stems and few blooms to a stem. Thin out weakest shoots, apply superphosphate and pulverized limestone to the soil at the rate of 8 oz. per square yard, and scratch into the surface. Full sunshine is necessary. Set out well-developed plants in early May.

Why can't I grow snapdragons from seed? They never come up. (Kentucky.) Sow in late April in well-drained place where the soil is light and only moderately rich and has been raked into fine texture, free of stones and lumps. Cover seed with sand not more than ⅛ in. deep, and do not pack hard. Cover with burlap, which remove as soon as seed shows germination. Water regularly in dry weather. Disinfect the seed with Semesan before sowing. It's easier to sow such fine seed indoors in pots or other containers.

Can snapdragons be carried over winter in a cold frame? (New York.) Yes, if they are less than 1 year old. Actually, these plants can be considered as biennials in the South, or in the North when frame protection can be given in the winter.

How shall I protect snapdragons outdoors to survive sub-zero winters? (Kentucky.) Attempts to bring snapdragons through such winter weather outdoors often fail, whatever precautions you take. Try mulching with 3 or 4 ins. of coarse straw or marsh meadow hay after ground freezes. A cold frame is about the only safe means of protection.

Are there such things as perennial snapdragons? No, from the practical gardening standpoint. Technically, they are all perennials, but in the North they are too tender to be treated as such.

What are the best snapdragons for the garden? I do not have good luck with "snaps" of late years. By all means get rust-resistant kinds. Select the colors you prefer from among the tall (3½ ft.), medium (15 ins.) and dwarf (7 ins.) varieties listed in seed catalogues.

STOCKS

What causes stocks to mature without blooming? May have been the common stock (*Matthiola incana*), which acts as a biennial and does not flower until the second year. 'Ten-weeks' stocks are annual, and flower the first year if conditions are to their liking. They require cool growing weather and should be started in early spring.

Of 100 'Ten-weeks' stock plants in our garden, 20 of the smallest, most puny ones bloomed. The other 80 grew into beautifully thrifty plants from early summer until a hard freeze came, but did not bloom. Why? 'Ten-weeks' stocks usually fail to bloom if subjected to constantly high temperature—60° F. and over. Yours were grown under border-line conditions, enabling a few individuals to bloom.

How can I make 'Ten-weeks' stocks bloom? (New Jersey.) By starting them indoors in March and setting them outside late in April. This enables them to make their growth before hot weather comes.

Can stocks be wintered through? (Kansas.) Yes, if you have the biennial kind, *Matthiola incana,* and a mild, dryish winter climate. For the average gardener, this type is not worth trying or bothering with.

SWEET PEAS

When is the best time to plant sweet peas? As early as the ground can be worked in the spring; or the seeds can be sown in a cold greenhouse or cold frame a month or more ahead of the time when frost can be expected to be out of the ground, and then transplanted. Sow one seed in an individual peat or Jiffy-7 pot for best results.

When and how shall I plant sweet peas to insure blooms? If you have a frost-free frame, you can sow the seed in September or October in a flat or in small pots, and in March transplant where they are to flower. Or if you have a coolish porch or window, temperature not above 45° to 50° F., you can sow in February, shift into pots, and, after hardening, plant out in late March. If there are no such facilities, sow where they are to flower as early in March as you can; prepare the ground the preceding fall. (See question on preparation.)

Can sweet pea seeds be sown in the fall, for earlier and stronger plants in the spring? If so, at what time, and how deep? Sweet peas can be planted in fall just before ground freezes, putting them 4 ins. deep and mulching lightly with straw or litter after hard freezing. It is doubtful, though, whether the plants would be appreciably earlier or finer than if spring-sown as soon as ground can be worked.

Can sweet peas be planted in very early spring if the ground softens to a depth of 2 ins.? No. Wait until all the frost is out; otherwise the soil will be too muddy to work.

What is the planting date for sweet peas in Oklahoma? Sow in November and give protection during the coldest part of winter; or sow in late winter, as soon as it is possible to work the soil.

In our mountain climate, what is the best time to plant sweet peas? When and how should I prepare the soil? (New York.) As early in the spring as it is possible to work the soil. If the soil could be prepared the previous fall, so much the better. (See previous and following answers.)

How shall I prepare ground for sweet peas for cut flowers? Dig a trench 1½ ft. wide and deep. Mix with the soil a 3- to 4-in. layer of rotted manure or peat moss and compost, and bone meal or superphosphate at rate of 1 lb. to 10 to 15 linear ft. If possible, do this in the fall so seeds can be planted without delay early in spring.

I want sweet peas in clumps in flower border. How do I go about it? Prepare soil as described in previous answer except that instead of a long trench you should make circular planting stations 2 to 3 ft. in diameter. Support the peas on brushwood or a cylinder of chicken-wire netting held up by 4 or 5 stakes. Or you can use a dwarf variety such as 'Little Sweetheart'.

Will you let us know something about the cultivating of sweet peas? How far apart should the plants be? Should they have commercial fertilizer? See preceding answers for soil preparation. The plants should not be closer together than 4 ins. Commercial fertilizers, used according to manufacturer's directions, are good for application along the sides of the row after the plants are 4 ins. high.

How deep should sweet pea seeds be planted? Usually about 2 ins. Some gardeners prefer to sow them in a trench 6 ins. deep, covering them at first with 2 ins. of soil. As the plants increase in stature, the trench is gradually filled in. This works well in sandy soils.

How early must I place the supports for sweet pea vines? When they are about 4 ins. high. If left until they topple over, they never seem to grow so well as they do when staked early. Twiggy branches stuck in on both sides of the row, or in among the plants if they are grown in clumps, make the best supports, but chicken-wire netting, or strings supported by a frame, will do.

How much sun for sweet peas? Soil? How to combat lice? General care? Full or nearly full sun is best; some shade is tolerated. Soil should be deep, well-drained, rich, and well supplied with humus material. Be sure it is neutral or somewhat alkaline—never acid. Spray with malathion for plant lice. Keep weeded and cultivated; water regularly; feed weekly with liquid fertilizer when buds begin to show.

I have never been successful with sweet peas, my favorite flower. I get about 3 bouquets, and then they die. Can you help me? I have used a number of methods with no success. (Oklahoma.) Maybe the summer sun is too much for them; try shading with cheesecloth as soon as really hot, dry weather starts. Water thoroughly and regularly. Try preparing the soil and sowing in November, or December, giving a little protection in cold weather. Spring-flowering type is somewhat heat-resistant.

Had very healthy-looking sweet pea vines, but no blossoms. Why? Soil may be deficient in phosphorous; or they may have been planted too late for buds to open before hot weather blasted them.

How can the blooming season of outdoor sweet peas be prolonged? By picking the flowers as fast as they mature and by shading from hot sun with cheesecloth or similar material, plus abundant, regular watering. Usually hot weather limits the season.

Sweet peas that are planted in November usually make some winter growth or early-spring growth. Will it be advisable to shear this top growth and let the base of the plant start new and tender growth?

(Virginia.) Yes, pinch the growth back to where the stem shows signs of sprouting at the base. This later growth produces better flowers.

Is there any way to keep birds from eating my sweet peas and ranunculus as they come up? (California.) Lay a few pieces of garden hose or rope alongside the rows; birds are afraid of snakes. Or cover with cheesecloth. Strings with white rags hanging from them may also help.

How can I successfully grow sweet peas in a greenhouse? (Texas.) For your region the seed should be sown in late August. These plants should give a crop the greater part of the winter. Try another sowing in late September. Prepare soil 18 ins. deep, with dehydrated manure ¼ the soil volume. Add 1 lb. ground limestone and ½ lb. super-phosphate per 20 sq. ft. Sow in rows 36 ins. apart, 1 ounce to 35 linear ft. Thin to 4 plants per linear ft. Support the vines by stretching a wire at ground level along the row, another at 10 to 12 ft. in height. Stretch strands of string between and train the vines up the string. Watering and feeding must be related to growth and flowering. In winter water only when moisture is low, as seen by examining the soil 1 to 2 ins. below the surface. After flowering begins, feed every 2 weeks with liquid fertilizer. Use only the greenhouse varieties.

Which varieties of sweet peas are the best for a hot, dry climate? What is best method of planting? (Kansas.) Sweet peas rarely succeed outdoors in a hot, dry climate unless sown very early. Your best chance is to plant in earliest spring, keep well watered, and shade with cheesecloth from direct sun. There are, so far as known, no varieties especially adapted to your conditions. The giant heat-resistant and spring-flowering types are quite heat-resistant but need abundant moisture.

TORENIA

What can I use instead of pansies in late summer? *Torenia fournieri,* an attractive little plant, very bushy with purple, lavender and gold flowers like miniature snapdragons. Foliage turns plum-colored in late autumn. Start the seeds in May in a seed bed as they are very tender. Grows well in sun or shade.

TITHONIA

My tithonia plants never bloom. Can you tell me why? This Mexican sunflower with its handsome, single, brilliant orange blooms, must be started early indoors to give generous bloom before frost. The variety 'Torch' grows only 4 ft. tall as against the type which reaches 6 ft. 'Torch' also blooms earlier. Use it at the back of the border or as a screen plant.

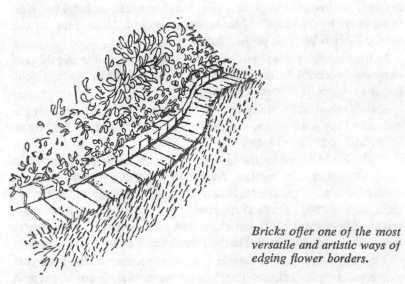

Bricks offer one of the most versatile and artistic ways of edging flower borders.

VERBENA

How can I raise verbenas? I have not much luck with them. (Kansas.) Verbenas are not easy unless you have facilities for raising them. The seed is variable in its germination. Requiring a long season, seeds must be sown about March 1 in a temperature of 60° F. at night and 70° to 75° F. during the day. The seedlings are transplanted into flats, after the first true leaf appears, using equal parts loam, sand, leafmold and rotted or dehydrated manure or compost. Keep in same temperature until established (10 days), then harden off the plants in a cold frame before planting outside. Set out in the ground when danger of frost is past.

When is the season to plant verbena? The plants should be set out when warm weather is established. Seeds are best sown indoors 2 months prior to setting out plants. (See previous question.)

ZINNIA

What soil is best for zinnias? Zinnias appreciate a fairly heavy, rich loam. Additions of rotted cow manure, compost, or peat moss and commercial fertilizer will produce sturdy plants.

We have been unable to grow zinnias. Our soil is rich and well drained. We are able to grow asters, but they attain no height or size. What could be the cause? Maybe soil is too acid. Have it tested, and if below pH 6 bring it up to neutral.

Is the middle of April too early to plant zinnia and marigold seed outdoors in central Pennsylvania? It might be suitable for marigold, but May 1 would be better for zinnia.

Should zinnias be transplanted? Zinnias are very easily transplanted. They can, if desired, however, be sown where they are to grow, and then thinned out.

How should I gather zinnia seeds? Select healthiest plants with the best flowers. During late August or early September allow the flowers to mature on the plant and when the seeds are quite dry and dark, harvest them. Spread on paper in a dry, airy place. When thoroughly dry, discard chaff and place best seeds in sealed envelopes or jars. Label and store until planting time. See also following question.

Why did seeds from a certain zinnia, when planted the next year, not come true to color? Because it was a variety not capable of transmitting its characteristics by seed, such as the new hybrids; or the flowers were fertilized with pollen from other plants of a different color.

Biennials

Biennials are plants which start their life cycle one year, pass the winter in a state of dormancy or "suspended animation," and then grow on to complete their lives in the following year. Pansies, best known of the biennials, and one of the easiest of all flowers to be grown from seed, are usually bought in spring as plants in full bloom, instead of being raised from seed—at a fraction of the cost of plants— by the gardener himself.

Biennial seed should be sown in May or early June—or, in the case of some of them, such as pansies and wallflower (*Cheiranthus cheiri*), as late as late July—and transplanted as soon as the true leaves develop. By mid-September or October the little plants are ready to be transferred to their allocated positions in the garden, or (in severe climates) carried over winter in a frame, under a protective covering of straw, rough compost or evergreen boughs, applied after the ground has frozen slightly. Covering with glass sash, except in *very* severe climates, is not necessary.

One of the great advantages of using some biennials in the garden scheme is that they provide very early color out of doors, weeks before spring-sown annuals will be in flower. They are unsurpassed for "filling in" wherever color can be lacking in the spring garden.

When is it best to sow seeds of most biennials? Late June and July are considered the best times. This gives a fairly long season to produce good-sized plants for blooming the following year. Hollyhocks, for extra-heavy plants, are best sown in June; but pansies and forget-me-nots are best sown in August, as very large plants of these may winterkill. Others fare very well from June sowings.

How are the so-called biennials best used in the garden? They are valuable in the mixed border for early-summer bloom. Solid plantings can be made of such kinds as foxgloves, with early lilies, such as madonna and *L. hansonii*. Combinations like Canterbury-bells in different colors, with sweet William, pansies, English daisies, and forget-me-not, are valuable as a ground cover for a bulb garden. The biennials must be followed with annuals to fill the bare spots left when the biennials die. In the mixed border they are best used in small groups near later-blooming perennials that will tend to cover the bare spots left. The later-blooming biennials (like hollyhock) can be given due prominence in a mixed planting.

Will you give a list of biennials, with their time of bloom? This will include many that are perennial but which in garden practice are grown as biennials. Canterbury-bells (*Campanula medium*), cup-and-saucer (*C. calycanthema*), steeple-bellflower (*C. pyramidalis*), June and July; English daisy (*Bellis perennis*), April and May; foxglove,

June–July; hollyhock, July; honesty (*Lunaria*), May; rose campion, May to June; pansy, April to June; Siberian wallflower (*Cheiranthus cheiri*), May to June; sweet William (*Dianthus barbatus*), June to July; forget-me-not (*Myosotis alpestris* and *M. sylvatica*), April to May.

Do any of the biennials self-sow? Yes, quite a few, such as foxglove, forget-me-not, rose campion, steeple-bellflower, and hollyhock. But if the soil is too assiduously cultivated, the seedlings may be killed.

Are biennials winter-hardy in northern gardens? The hardiest are the campions, foxglove, hollyhock, steeple-bellflower, honesty, sweet William, wallflower. Most other biennials (see list) need considerable protection, preferably a cold frame.

At what time of year should biennials be planted outdoors? Plants started the preceding year are set out in very early spring for blooming the same year.

Specific Biennial Plants

CANTERBURY-BELLS (CAMPANULA)

What is the best time of year to plant seed of Canterbury-bells and foxglove? June is a good time to sow seeds of these plants. If sown later, the plants may not be big enough to flower the next year.

Will Canterbury-bells grow well in upper New York State? When should the seed be sown? Yes, they will do very well but must have adequate winter protection. Do not stimulate growth by watering or feeding after mid-August. After a hard freeze, cover with brush over which spread a layer of marsh hay or similar covering. Sow seeds in June.

How can I grow Canterbury-bells and cup-and-saucer? The cup-and-saucer type (*calycanthema*) is a variety of the regular Canterbury-bell (*Campanula medium*). The cup-and-saucer requires the same culture and conditions as the regular Canterbury-bells.

What is the best winter mulch for Canterbury-bells? (Wisconsin.) Light, littery material that will not pack to a sodden mass over the leaves. Before covering, remove any bad basal leaves that might rot. Tuck the material in around the plants, and stick a few twigs among them to keep a light covering from lying directly on the leaves.

Why is it that Campanula medium sometimes does not blossom? This spring I had two dozen nice-looking plants, transplanted in fall last year; but none of them blossomed. Plants of Canterbury-bells, unless they reach a good size, can fail to bloom the first summer. Many, however, will persist through the second winter and set bloom the second summer. It usually means the seed wasn't sown early enough.

FOXGLOVES (DIGITALIS)

What do you do with foxgloves that do not bloom the second year? Will they bloom the third year if kept on? Yes, they probably will; foxgloves frequently behave in this way, especially when the seeds were not sown early enough.

Should we cover our foxglove plants heavily in winter? (Vermont.) In your region they will need adequate protection. Mulch soil with decayed leaves, lay cherry or birch branches over the crowns, and on top of this spread an inch or two of marsh hay or straw. If covering packs on top of the crowns it will cause rot, hence the branches. Evergreen boughs—not heavy ones—are also valuable. These are used alone.

Will foxglove, if separated in winter, bloom the following year? If you refer to the common foxglove, *Digitalis purpurea,* from seed sown the previous summer—probably no. The perennial kinds can be separated in spring.

What parts of foxglove are poisonous, if any? Probably all parts. The drug digitalis (poisonous in overdoses) is obtained from the second year's young leaves, so presumably the poisonous principle is most abundant in them.

What is the best method of gathering foxglove seed? Gather the lower seed capsules from the stem as soon as they show brown, but before they open to shed the seed. Select from the best type.

PANSY

What is the best location for pansies for good bloom? A cool, moist, well-drained soil, in a sunny location.

What is the best soil for pansies? Any soil which contains plenty of humus. Well-rotted manure, peat moss, or leafmold, mixed with the soil, will help. Neutral or slightly acid reaction is best.

When is pansy seed sown? (Minnesota.) In late July or August, to produce plants large enough, before cold weather, so they can be wintered in a covered cold frame.

What is the best method of growing pansies? (Iowa.) Plant seed in cold frames in August, transplanting 6 × 6 ins. when second set of leaves appear. When freezing weather arrives, cover plants with straw, and keep frames closed. About March 1 remove straw, but keep glass on, and ventilate freely. Remove glass about April 1, and set plants in permanent position between April 1 and May 15. Best soil is a good loam with plenty of humus and moisture.

What conditions are necessary to get pansy seed to germinate? (North Carolina.) First obtain *fresh,* plump seeds. For the seed bed use a mixture of 1 part each of soil, sand, and leafmold or peat moss, put through a ¼-in. mesh screen. Select as cool a spot as you can—a cold frame that can be heavily shaded is ideal. Level and lightly firm the soil. Broadcast the seed on the surface (or sow in rows 4 or 5 ins. apart), and cover with ⅛ in. of fine soil, press lightly, and shade, but leave space for ventilation. As soon as seeds have germinated remove the shading, except during the hottest part of the day. Give full sun when seedlings are well through.

Would pansy seed sown in the open in April come up and bloom by June 15? Pansy seed sown the first of April might possibly show a few flowers by June 15 if growing conditions were favorable. The finest spring display comes from seed sown in August.

Are pansy plants, from seeds sown outdoors in September, likely to survive the cold weather during winter and flower next summer? (New York.) No; the seed should be sown early in August. In vicinity of New York City young plants will live outdoors with light covering. Farther north they should be grown in cold frames.

Will you tell me when to transplant pansies? (Texas.) Presuming you mean pansy seedlings, you should plant them in their permanent locations (from seed beds, flats, or pots) in September or October for bloom during the following spring. Young plants, grown in cold frame or in open beds, may be transplanted in the early spring.

Is it better to purchase pansy plants for autumn planting, or for very early-spring planting, if one desires them for sale purposes around Mother's Day? Purchase seedling plants in September, and grow these on to blooming size.

Why don't pansy plants bloom and grow all summer when planted in spring in full bloom? Mine don't. They bloom best in the cool weather of spring and early summer. In an exposed place they deteriorate in the heat; also the earlier heavy bloom exhausts the plants.

What would be the cause of pansy plants growing long stems and very small flowers? Too much shade, or overcrowding. A good strain of seed, August sowing, winter protection, a good soil, and not too much shade are the prerequisites for success.

Why do blue pansies often have petals streaked blue and white? The seed strain is not good. Blue pansy seed that comes true to type is offered by reliable seedsmen.

When wintering pansies in a cold frame, should one wait until the soil in the frame has frozen, then close the frame and keep it covered with a mat or leaves until spring? No. Best plan is to give plants light, ventilate whenever frost on glass melts, and cover with mats only on coldest nights. Do not remove snow from frames.

What is considered a foolproof winter mulch for pansies? (Wyoming.) Branches of spruce, fir, or pine; straw or hay held down with chicken wire. If hungry mice or rabbits abound, spray pansies first with aluminum sulfate or commercial rabbit repellent.

When is the best time to apply winter protection for pansies? (Wyoming.) As soon as the surface inch or two of the ground freezes.

When is it safe to remove the winter covering on pansies? (Wyoming.) When severe freezing is past. It is well to remove this (and all such mulches) on a cloudy or rainy day. Sudden exposure to sun and wind is unkind to leaves and buds.

Last year's pansies did such a wonderful job of self-seeding for this season that the resulting plants are lovelier and stronger than the new ones we grew from seed with great care. Any particular reason? Probably due to some cross-pollenizing which developed strong, healthy plants. However, continuous intercrossing year after year will result in deterioration. To maintain the strain, weed out poor plants and poor colors as soon as flowers open.

ROSE CAMPION (LYCHNIS)

Will you please give botanical name of mullein pink or rose campion. *Lychnis coronaria,* of easy culture and hardy.

SWEET WILLIAM (DIANTHUS BARBATUS)

When shall I plant sweet William? What kind of soil is required? In a sunny spot, or in shade? (Missouri.) Set plants out as early in spring as the ground can be worked. They like a well-prepared soil with plenty of humus-forming material (like rotted manure, leafmold, or peat moss) in addition to a good dressing of dried sheep or cow manure. They prefer a sunny location.

Can seeds of Dianthus barbatus be planted in late fall or early winter? Will they bloom the following season? This is a biennial normally sown in summer for bloom the following year. There is an annual strain which would blossom the following season if planted under glass.

Sweet William will not live through the summer for me. Why? Sweet William is grown as a biennial. It usually dies after flowering.

Do foxglove and sweet William (Dianthus barbatus) come up a second year? The common foxglove (*Digitalis purpurea*) is a biennial. Sweet William is used as such. Rarely do they appear the second year except from self-sown seedlings. It is best to sow seeds of these kinds every year to insure a supply of plants.

WALLFLOWER

What is the difference between wallflower and Siberian wallflower? Wallflower (*Cheiranthus cheiri*), grows to a height of 2 ft. and produces yellow, mahogany, and brownish flowers in spring and again in autumn. Siberian wallflower (*Erysimum asperum*) is only about a foot tall and produces fragrant yellow flowers in early spring.

Can you tell me how to grow wallflowers? Both types of wallflowers require cool nights and moisture in the air during the growing season to thrive. They are supposedly lime-lovers but sometimes grow well in acid soil, as near the seashore, when other conditions suit them. *Cheiranthus cheiri* is quite tender inland, but grows well near the coast in New England. Wallflowers need full sun and a sandy soil. Both are usually grown as biennials.

9
Lawns and Turf Areas

THE FIRST "LAWNS" were probably little more than open ground around dwelling areas, "mowed" by grazing livestock. Some grassy swards were of importance enough during the Middle Ages to have been kept within bounds by scything; even today much mowing, particularly in the Tropics, is by hand with sickle or bushknife.

The first mechanical lawn mower was not invented until 1830 in England. During the century that followed, mowing the lawn became increasingly customary, although little other attention was given. Well-kept lawns were far from universal and most only a hobby of the well-to-do; working and rural people gave little heed to their lawns until about the time of World War II. Then with intensified migration to the suburbs, lawn-tending was destined never again to be a casual thing! The customary close-clipping of whatever vegetation volunteered (or arose from seeding with farm grasses and legumes), with little recognition of grass habits or requirements, gradually gave way to the more involved maintenance procedures used today. Remember, only a few decades ago very few people bothered even to fertilize a lawn, and what weeding was done was by hand digging or pulling!

The Modern Lawn

A "good" lawn typically consists of an overcrowded population of dwarfed grass plants, all so very much alike as to create an unblemished carpet. This provides a superlative backdrop for home landscaping, whether the emphasis is flower gardens or the form and texture effects created by trees and shrubs. Because of the crowding, often a thousand or more shoots to the square foot, individual grass plants are apt to be weak compared to what they might be if uncrowded and unmowed. If all are hereditarily alike (i.e., a monoculture), they are fair game for plagues which spread from one plant to another encountering no resistance. That is why lawn experts advise the planting of grass blends or mixtures, so that there is likelihood some resistant grass will confront whatever disease or other pest chances on the lawn.

This dense, perpetually defoliated carpet is expected to be constantly solid underfoot, to keep pets and people walking over it "out of the mud" at all seasons. It must not only look good, even if given inexpert attention, but it must refresh the air, cool the environs in summer, insulate the ground in winter, prevent soil wash, endure deicing salts, be a playfield and a picnic ground, and whatever else is demanded. The grass family almost alone provides the rather few candidates able to meet these requirements. Such plants have their growing points close to the soil (only the elongating leafs are mowed); the foliage exhibits basal rather than tip growth; most spread by underground stems (rhizomes) or surface runners (stolons). This pattern of growth equips the plants to survive under constant low mowing.

Only about a dozen grass species find much service for lawns, a few each for the northern ("cool season") and southern ("warm season") regions. The growth habits of these few grasses (and their multitudinous cultivars or "varieties") must be understood for intelligent lawn maintenance. It is not only a case of doing the right thing, but of doing it at the right time as well.

The Basic Needs of Lawn Grass

Although growth influences vary due to environmental differences, these principles prevail in general:

Southern grasses, typically planted from Tennessee southward, grow best at relatively warm temperatures, above 80° F. They are exuberant in spring and summer, and should receive major attention then. Northern grasses, however, grow best when temperatures don't exceed 80° F. (at least at night); they husband resources best in autumn, winter and spring. By and large they benefit most from attention in autumn, and are weakest during the heat of summer. It is thus evident that July fertilization of Bermuda grass in the South may help it compete with weeds then, while in the North summer feeding could help weeds such as crab grass more than the perennial bluegrass!

All lawns are mowed, and height of mowing can have considerable influence. Of course some grasses are better adapted to low-mowing than are others (bent grasses and Bermuda grasses, for example; newer low-growing cultivars of bluegrass as contrasted to the old-fashioned types). But in general, reasonably high mowing benefits the grass, probably because more green leaf is retained (the food-making resource for the plant). Disease is less severe and weeds are fewer in a tall-mowed turf than in a short-clipped one. Roots below ground correspond to top growth above ground, and are usually about 40 per cent dry weight of the tops. Taller-mowed grass thus roots more deeply, with the consequent benefits of reaching a greater soil mass for moisture and nutrients.

The water needs of a well-kept lawn do not vary greatly from grass species to species, although certain grasses are more able to endure prolonged drought than are others (for example buffalo grass, though not making a good sod, does survive unirrigated in the arid High Plains). At peak season, any flourishing lawn will transpire about an inch of water per week, which must be provided from stored moisture in the soil, by irrigation, or by rainfall, if the lawn is to be kept attractive. Of course location has a tremendous influence on water need. Sunny, windy spots in the southwestern deserts will lose far more moisture than will a protected northern lawn, especially if it is in a cloudy upland location where nightly dews are prevalent. In regions where water demands are great, and rainfall insufficient, irrigation is essential for lawn survival.

Soil is quite influential. A heavy (clay type) soil can hold 3 ins. of moisture in its top foot, whereas a Coastal Plain sandy soil perhaps only half an inch. Obviously, watering must be more frequent on such sand than on clay. On the other hand, relatively brief watering is all that is required on a sand (because it will hold only the half inch or so of water anyway), and water will soak in readily; clay, however, may be almost impervious to water penetration, and usually requires a slow watering for a prolonged time until 2 or 3 ins. of water have reached the rootzone.

Obviously, natural fertility, mowing history (have certain nutrients become unbalanced?), acidity-alkalinity, organic content, and so on will influence not only maintenance procedures (liming, fertilization, etc.) but the kind of grass most suited to the situation. In general, clays poor in organic content are much more difficult to handle than are loams or even sands. They are cultivatable only a few times during the year, when moisture content is just right for tilling without clodding. Wet clays tend to compact from being walked upon, or having equipment run over them. On the other hand, loam soils (rich in organic matter), and especially sandy soils, are little injured by tillage, traffic, or abuse at almost any season.

Homeowner preferences vary. Some people insist upon mowing the lawn very low, whether or not the kind of grass is adapted to such treatment. Others insist upon watering, whether needed or not (thus bringing in water-loving weeds). Many will overfertilize ("if a little is good, a lot is better"), and some will apply "remedies" unrelated to the problem at hand.

Actually, no lawn-keeping program need be burdensome or unduly expensive if the homeowner takes time to learn about his grass-growth requirements. He can then work with the lawn's natural needs rather than against them. Because tastes vary, assess your preferences, willingness to provide care, and budget that will be available, before choosing your grass (avoid high-maintenance cultivars such as are used for golf greens, unless you are willing to provide the intense care that they require). One pays a price in increased upkeep the greater his demands are for special luxuriance.

The Lawn Grasses

The box on pages 697 and 698 gives major fine turf species for lawns in the United States. The chart on page 698 names some of the many cultivars that had reached commercial status in the early years of the 1970s. More new cultivars have been bred for the seeded northern grasses than for the vegetatively propagated southern ones. Apomictic Kentucky bluegrasses have been especially profuse, because a newly created genotype can be perpetuated more easily than with a highly sexual grass species. Kentucky bluegrass in large measure produces seed on the mother plant without fusion of a male gamete (apomixis). Some sexuality occurs in bluegrass, but strains that are strongly apomictic can be maintained "pure" rather easily by roguing the few viable offtypes that occasionally occur. A high level of sexuality in southern species, such as Bermuda and zoysia, has mitigated against true-breeding cultivars from seed. As was noted, most southern grasses are vegetatively propagated, as are many golf-green creeping bent grasses and zoysias recommended in the North.

LAWN GRASSES

Southern

GRASS	GROWTH-APPEARANCE	SPECIAL CHARACTERISTICS
Bahia Grass	Perennial; fairly open, coarse; spreads by runners; seedheads unattractive.	One of the easiest southern turf grasses to plant and to care for; often used in mixture.
Bermuda Grass	Perennial; fast-growing, aggressive, spreading by runners. Attractive texture and deep color if well tended.	Sun only; so vigorous as to require frequent care (a pest in borders); will thatch. Dormant near freezing, doubtfully hardy north of Tennessee.
Centipede	Perennial; medium texture; spreads by runners.	Low-maintenance grass, resenting heavy fertility; turns chlorotic unless soils are acid (needs iron).
St. Augustine	Perennial; coarse but not unattractive; spreads by runners; few seedheads; usually dark green.	Very tolerant of shade. Recently subject to severe chinch bug attack and several diseases, hence not a carefree grass; will thatch.
Zoysia	Perennial; spreads by runners; growth is slow; dense and among most attractive of southern grasses.	Slowness a disadvantage on planting, but reduces mowing demand later. Does not require a great deal of attention. Billbugs serious in Florida.

Northern

Bent Grass	Perennial; low, trailing or semi-trailing; small leaf blades with excellent texture.	"Show" grasses for well-tended turfs (fertilized, watered, frequently mowed). Prone to diseases in hot, muggy weather and to snowmold under cool, damp conditions (recommend fungicidal protection).
Bluegrass	Perennial, gracefully aristocratic, deep green, gracefully arching shoots, spreading by rhizomes.	Among world's best sod formers. Fairly open, rhizomes instead of stolons limit thatching. Strongly recuperative, widely adaptable; one of best all-around grasses; easily cared for.
Fescue, Fine	Perennial. Slowly spreading, attractively fine-textured, beautifully dark green, rather stiff and "wind-swept" in appearance.	Rugged, adapting well to poor conditions. Widely adaptable; one of best shade grasses in the north, persisting on poorish soils in dry locations. Attractive under minimum fertility.
Rye Grass	Perennial. Attractive shiny green leaves, less coarse than annual type.	Quick to sprout and reasonably attractive; though perennial under proper care, not as enduring or tight a sod as Kentucky bluegrass.

IMPROVED LAWN GRASS VARIETIES

Kentucky Bluegrasses: Sow 2 to 3 lb./1,000 sq. ft. for a fairly dense stand giving fine texture and reasonably dwarfed plants. Fertilize to provide 3 lb. or more nitrogen per 1,000 sq. ft. annually for good color.

ADELPHI—dark green hybrid from Rutgers, with medium texture and all-around excellence

ARBORETUM—an old-fashioned bluegrass with built-in durability

ARISTA—bright European selection of medium texture and attractive habit

BARON—dark-green selection from Holland with bold texture and low profile

BONNIEBLUE—like Adelphi

FYLKING—a leading newcomer from Sweden, of soft-green color and elegant recumbent texture

GALAXY—like Adelphi

MERION—the original standard of excellence, dark green, of fairly bold texture but increasingly prone to disease in certain areas

NUGGET—unusually attractive Alaskan discovery, very dense, dark green with a fine texture like Fylking but more erect (like carpet pile)

PENNSTAR—performance-proven at Pennsylvania State University from European stock, with characteristics much like Fylking

PRATO—European cultivar of sparkling color and fine texture, an excellent companion grass

SODCO—Purdue University's multi-line development, unusually low and slow-growing, dark and bold-textured

SYDSPORT—an outstanding north European cultivar of brilliant color and medium texture for a well-tended turf

Perennial Rye Grasses: Newly-bred, fine-leaved varieties have gained quick acceptance, although not of bluegrass quality for long-term turf. Very fast starting. Used alone, sow 6 lb. per 1,000 sq. ft. and handle as for bluegrass.

COMPAS—a European introduction, medium green and of acceptable hardiness

MANHATTAN—a multi-line Rutgers triumph mainly from Central Park sources, dark green and low

NK-100—a hardy cultivar giving outstanding performance in the East (Long Island, N.Y.)

NK-200—a denser, finer-textured improvement on NK-100, widely adapted

PELO—European introduction, darker green with winter hardiness second only to Manhattan and Pennfine

PENNFINE—a Penn-State release of unusually fine texture, good hardiness, mowing more neatly than many rye grasses

Fine Fescues: Used alone, sow about 4 lb./1,000 sq. ft., especially for shade and dry sites. Fertilizing more lightly than bluegrass is satisfactory. Otherwise, handle the same as bluegrass.

HIGHLIGHT—a dense Chewings-type from Holland of outstanding beauty

JAMESTOWN—an exceptionally low-growing, dark-green Chewings cultivar from the University of Rhode Island

PENNLAWN—a Penn-State multi-line variety, the standard of comparison newer varieties must meet

RUBY—a European creeping-red fescue introduction of particular usefulness in blends

Bent Grasses: Best suited to pampered turfs in humid locations. Should be mowed frequently (Colonial, ¾ to 1 in.; Velvet and Creeping, ¼ to ½ in.). Sow 1 to 2 lb./1,000 sq. ft.

EXETER—a Colonial bent grass from the University of Rhode Island of excellent uniformity

HIGHLAND—an attractive Oregon ecotype of Colonial habit, open-growing, bluish-green

HOLFIOR—a dark green Colonial selection from Europe, more uniform than Highland

KINGSTOWN—the ultimate in fine texture. A velvet bent grass bred at the University of Rhode Island. For a well-tended turf on neutral or acid soils

PENNCROSS—a history-making multi-line creeping bent grass from Pennsylvania State University. Of outstanding vigor

Soil Is All-Important

While most lawn grasses are widely adaptable—grow in soils having a range of nutrient qualities, pH differences (acidity-alkalinity), and so on—their culture is simpler and their performance generally better if the soil is good. Once a lawn is established, not much can be done for the rootzone; fertilizers and other treatments can only be applied at the surface. So, before a lawn is planted improve the soil in which the grass will grow as much as possible. Especially, if the soil is low in phosphorus, mix superphosphate into the rootzone before seeding or sodding. Phosphorus is fixed on soil particles, and moves downward only very slowly from the surface.

It has been customary for lawn experts to give elaborate instructions for preparing the soil prior to seeding. Deep cultivation; mixing in organic materials abundantly; fertilization with fertilizers compounded according to soil tests; indeed even a fallowing-cultivation sequence (to reduce weeds); or the growing of a green manure (plowing the residues into the soil) are the recommendations often made. All of them can be helpful, of course. But in the real world few are attempted and rarely well accomplished. The truth is that soil adequate for growing a good lawn can generally be had from nothing more than shallow cultivation (disking, rotary tilling) and mixing in fertilizer 2 or 3 ins. deep. With infertile soils, use double the normal rate recommended on the bag of a phosphatic fertilizer. The level of soil fertility—and whether it is unduly acid or alkaline—can be determined by a soil test, but it is generally known to gardeners and agriculturists in the area (you can consult your county agent).

A caution against cultivating heavy soils when they are wet has been noted earlier. Each lawn soil will have some virtues and some liabilities. Since we cannot foresee particular happenstances, the best advice to be given is "to use common sense." Procedures will vary from soil to soil, from region to region. The objective is to loosen compact soil so air and fertility can reach the rootzone, and accomplish this at times and in ways which will not be detrimental to soil structure. As a general rule, soil preparation is easier in late summer for an autumn planting than in spring, when weather and soil conditions are less favorable.

Common sense should also guide you in grading. Avoid depressions that will accumulate water, or mounds and ridges that will be scalped in mowing. Where low pockets are inevitable perhaps a drainage system will be needed (tiles laid a foot or so deep are conventional, but slit-trench drains—narrow cuts into the soil filled with loose rock—are often an economical substitute). Any drainage system should be accurately laid to slope gently away from the moist pocket into a free-flowing channel.

During home construction, piles of soil often accumulate from foundation diggings. These should be spread in a gentle contour to slope away from the house. If possible, have the richer topsoil bulldozed aside before construction, and replaced on the surface in the finished contour. However, lack of topsoil does not ordinarily necessitate its purchase; bought topsoil is often of poor quality and generally quite weedy. Good lawns can be grown even on subsoil if adequately fertilized. In fact subsoils typically have one bonus—fewer weed seeds. As grass grows, their structure will improve due to roots adding organic material throughout the rootzone.

Seeding and Sodding

The lawn area should be prepared just as thoroughly for sodding as for seeding. After final grading, any compacted spots or crusted soil should be broken up and raked level. With many soils it is well to await a rain or to irrigate the lawn before seeding or sodding, to note any uneven settling. Rake level again, breaking up surface crust so that seeds may settle into chinks and roots penetrate easily. A "pebbled" surface, with soil chunks ranging from pea to grape size, makes a better seed bed than one pulverized to dust; seeds will sift into the crevices readily, and water will soak in for a longer time before "melting" the surface into relative imperviousness.

Most sod is professionally laid, but if you do buy your own at a garden center use common sense in laying it in tierlike pattern if it is in squares (similar to the way bricks are placed in making a wall or path). Roll new sod after placement, and if soil or compost is available, sift it into cracks between the fittings.

Seed is most accurately sown with one of the modern spreaders, although it is possible to cast it by hand if carefully done. It may be wise to extend small, expensive seeds with an equal quantity of a like-size material, say cornmeal, to provide more bulk for casting. With either hand or spreader sowing, it is wise to spread half the seed in one direction, the other half at right angles, thus better insuring against voids. If the seed bed is friable, probably no rolling will be needed; watering will settle the soil comfortably about the seed for good sprouting. Some seed beds, however, may be fluffy, and will profit from light rolling (not sufficiently weighty to compact the soil, but enough to restore capillarity). Generally, a rolled surface accepts water less satisfactorily than one left loose.

Whether the new lawn is seeded or sodded, it should be kept moist continuously until the grass is well established. This may require light sprinkling—daily in hot or windy weather. Watering can become less frequent (but more prolonged) as the grass roots grow deeper. Let a new seeding dry out a bit before its first mowing, so that the mower will not rut the surface nor tear the very lush growth. Mowing ordinarily begins when the new grass reaches half again to twice what its customary mowing height will be.

Permanent Turf

Once the lawn is established it should receive continuing reasonable care. Mowing is inevitable, and since it will be the most time-consuming task encountered in lawn tending, top-quality equipment is worth its cost. Make mowing relaxing and pleasurable rather than dreaded! Mowing should be frequent enough so that no more than half of the green foliage is removed at any one cutting. Mow at a height suited to the particular grass and owner preference.

Equally important is sensible fertilization. As was noted earlier, northern grasses benefit especially from autumn feedings as cool weather approaches. But the newer, disease-resistant cultivars have been selected for response to reasonable feeding year round. Suggested lawn fertilizer rates generally provide about 1 lb. of elemental nitrogen to each 1,000 sq. ft. (say 5 lbs. of a 20–5–10—these figures indicating the respective percentages of nitrogen, phosphorus, and potassium). A real boon for the amateur has been the development of the controlled-release, non-burning lawn fertilizers, most of them based upon ureaform (UF) nitrogen.

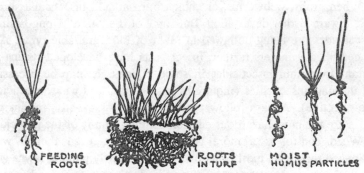

FEEDING ROOTS   ROOTS IN TURF   MOIST HUMUS PARTICLES

A square foot of turf contains some 400 individual grass plants, each of which must be well fed. An abundance of humus in the surface soil is especially important in maintaining the moisture supply.

Less necessary generally, but often important locally, are irrigation, pest control, and bolster seeding. Earlier discussion pointed out that irrigation should match climatic needs, and amplify rainfall for a total of about an inch of water weekly. In most cases (depending upon soil) watering at infrequent intervals is best, so the soil dries out a bit and drains thoroughly between waterings. Inexpensive home-lawn irrigation systems (some can be installed by handy homeowners) can be established underground with plastic pipe. A few are set up to operate automatically. Even in regions of adequate average rainfall, there can be temporary droughts that cause lawns to go off color unless they are watered.

Pest control has become quite complicated, not only because problems vary greatly from place to place, but because availability of pesticides has been restricted due to environmental concern. Some states prohibit the sale of certain chemicals, or permit their application only by licensed services.

The need for fungicides should diminish with the introduction of newer turf-grass cultivars bred for disease resistance. When fungicidal protection is required, the new breed of systemic fungicides (picked up by the grass sap stream) gives promise of long-lasting effectiveness and less bother. Fortunately, change of weather stalls most disease, and in most cases the homeowner can assist by being careful not to overwater or overfertilize.

When grubs, webworms, or chinch bugs attack, insecticidal sprayings thwart further devastation. But some of the "hard" (long-lasting) insecticides are being outlawed in favor of biodegradable types. And to complicate matters further, insect pests have developed strains resistant to certain insecticides in some regions. It may be necessary to alternate insecticides (inquire of local authorities what insecticides are effective). Always follow product directions exactly, for insecticides are the most hazardous environmentally of any of the pesticides.

Weed control is a more general necessity, even though well-managed turf fights most of its own battles. Newly planted lawns generally have a fair abundance of weeds, but these tend to disappear because of mowing and crowding by the grass as the seedlings grow older and become more aggressive. Broadleaf weeds, such as dandelions, plantains, and chickweed, are no longer the problem they once were because of ready availability of phenoxy weedkillers. The herbicide, 2, 4-D, perhaps in combination with Silvex or Dicamba and applied at an appropriate season, takes care of most dicotyledonous (broadleaf) pests. Crab grass is controlled by several excellent pre-emergent chemicals, or after it has sprouted with arsonate sprays. No really good selective herbicides exist for taking perennial weed grasses out of perennial turf grass, but several chemicals are effective for killing all vegetation and then allowing reseeding or sodding with a wanted grass. Certain herbicides scorch all vegetation encountered, but are inactivated in the soil; these prove useful for edging plant beds, and for control of grass around base of trees to facilitate mowing.

Lawn renovation without the cumbersome plowing of the old sod has become feasible with the advent of specialized scarifying equipment ("power rakes," thinners, dethatchers, aerifiers). When used in combination with a knockdown herbicide, the seed bed can be made receptive to a bolstering with improved strains of grass. Even without chemical knockdown, occasional bolster seedings at an appropriate season may help thicken thin turf, and can perhaps upgrade quality by introducing preferred cultivars.

—*Robert W. Schery*

Grading

How should a lawn be graded? What operations are involved? Grading first depends upon the particular site and whether paths or driveways are to be laid out. Existing trees and areas for planting must also be considered. Outline the paths and drives with stakes. Remove the topsoil from these and spread it over the lawn area. If the dwelling is much higher than the street, slope the grade gradually down to meet the lower level. Do not terrace unless the situation demands it. If the dwelling is on a level area, give the lawn a slight pitch from the house to the street.

How much pitch must be given a lawn, and how is the pitch determined? A pitch of 1 ft. in 20 ft., or even 30 ft., unless the soil is heavy clay, is sufficient to give surface drainage. The grade can be established by using a line and a line level, and thus determining the difference, in height, between the high and the low points.

If there is much unevenness in the ground, should it be dug or plowed before grading? The soil, of course, will have to be loosened to move it. The practical thing to do is to remove all the topsoil, loosen the subsoil, and do the grading; then finish the grade with the topsoil. This insures an even depth of good soil over the entire area.

Our house sits quite a way back from the street and several feet above it. How should the front lawn be graded? A low, sloping terrace will tend to lower its profile. Work the soil down to a gradual slope from the bottom of the terrace to the street.

How is the soil leveled to make it even for seeding? In most cases basic grade and leveling is completed with big equipment, such as a bulldozer or backhoe. If the soil becomes compacted, loosen by disking or rotary tilling. A tractor with a York rake attachment or a chainlink mat drag can level off high spots and fill depressions quickly. More tedious is hand raking. Final touch-up and removal of debris (stones, small boards, etc.) must be done by hand with a rake or broomrake. If doubtful about uniform firmness of the soil, soak the lawn (and after it dries sufficiently, rake again), or roll lightly and re-rake to fill depressions.

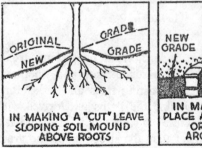 

Grading around an established tree to obtain a properly sloped lawn surface.

We need to fill in to get a good slope for a lawn, but there are large trees in the way. Will the grading injure them? If the grade is to be carried much over the existing level, some protection must be given the trees. It may be necessary to build a dry well of stone around the trunks to allow air and moisture to reach the roots, although this is no guarantee of survival. One must weigh the value of the tree against cost (and uncertainty) of preservation measures.

How high can the soil be raised around a tree without injuring it? This depends somewhat on the kind of tree. In general, however, where the soil is light and well drained, the grade may be raised around trees a foot or two without appreciable injury. If the soil is heavy and not well drained, raising the grade as little as 6 ins. may cause injury.

How large should a tree well be? Generally speaking, the diameter of a tree well should be at least four times the diameter of the tree. Deep wells should be provided with tile drains running out laterally from the bottom. They should not be narrowed in at the top, since it may be necessary to get down into them to clean out leaves.

Preparations for Sowing

When is the best time to prepare the soil for a lawn? Over most of the country, late summer or early autumn. The soil is easier to cultivate then, having dried out through summer (usually heavy soils are soggy in spring). Preparing the soil for seeding is usually done a week or so before the desired seeding time. This allows for any settling to show, and debris or vegetation clumps can be noticed and removed. If chemical soil sterilization is practiced, follow instructions for the sterilant used; many chemicals require days, some even weeks, to dissipate.

How thoroughly should the soil be cultivated? Work the soil sufficiently so that clods are broken up into chunks no larger than your thumbnail, but avoid pulverizing the soil (which breaks down its structure). See discussion in Introduction. Needs will vary locally. Seed bed cultivation has these objectives: destruction of unwanted vegetation; mixing fertilizer into the soil; loosening the soil enough so air exchange occurs well beneath the surface (permitting deeper root growth); loosening the soil for easier leveling; and creating a pebbled surface that accepts seed well and allows for water penetration.

What about planting a lawn on sandy soil? Sandy soils have the advantage of not compacting easily and needing little cultivation. On the other hand, they do not hold moisture or fertilizer nutrients well. The latter deficiency can be helped by *thoroughly* mixing in about an inch of clay, or, more practically, organic residues (such as weed-free peat moss, compost, and so on). Even without special modifications, a sandy soil can be made to support grass by practicing frequent, light fertilization and watering.

How about starting a lawn on heavy soil? The problems with a heavy soil are just the opposite from those with a sandy one. Clays become compacted easily, especially when wet, and can be cultivated well only when slightly damp. If compacted, they should be loosened at least 2 or 3 ins. deep, care being taken to cultivate when moisture content is such that the soil will crumble rather than form clods (which become like rocks when they dry). As with sandy soil, organic material is a good leavener, helping to loosen heavy soils; but adding sand is useless (for the sand will "set-up" in the clay as it does in concrete). However, heavy soils do have the advantage of being relatively retentive of soil nutrients and moisture.

What about thin soils and stony ground? If there is sufficient soil to support grass roots and the drainage is adequate, a stony soil can be made into a good lawn, although any obtrusive stones that materially interfere with the level (and the use of equipment) should be removed. Of course rocky outcrops are very difficult, tending to hold moisture in rainy periods and to dry out quickly during dry weather; in such instances there are two possibilities: to purchase enough good soil to provide at least 4 ins. of rooting area over the indifferent base before sowing seed, or to forget about a lawn here and instead treat the area as a semi-rock garden with appropriate plantings.

Must the soil for a lawn be fertilized? There are very few soils that will not benefit from fertilization. A soil test will provide a clue to fertility level. Even with fertile soils, additional fertilization at no more than twice the rate called for on established lawns will cause no harm and should contribute to the nutrient "bank account." As noted in the Introduction, it is especially important to mix phosphorus-rich fertilizer into the soil before planting the lawn. With infertile soils needing rather heavy fertilization, it might be wise to choose a fertilizer having a low "salt index," i.e., in which there is the minimum of soluble salts and a proportionally higher percentage of "water insoluble" nutrients (noted, for nitrogen, as WIN percentage on the bag).

Is the bringing in of topsoil advisable? This will depend on how adequate the residual soil is. If the soil is very thin, perhaps topsoil will be needed. But in most instances, the residual soil can be improved sufficiently to make a good seed bed much more economically than additional topsoil can be purchased. Moreover, topsoil is often of poor quality, not necessarily fertile, and almost invariably full of weed seeds (unless it has been expensively sterilized).

Should the seed bed be rolled? See the discussion under grading. Unless needed for pointing up irregularities, or for re-establishing capillarity on fluffy soils, rolling is probably not needed, and with heavy soils can be more harmful than a help.

Can steps be taken to prevent future problems? Yes, as, for example, through the buildup of nutrient reserves in the soil. If pests are apt to become a problem, measures can be taken against them, too. Seed beds can be "grub-proofed" by mixing in insecticides such as chlordane; residual weed seeds, disease-causing fungi, or even eelworms (nematodes) can be curtailed. Except for the mixing of an insecticide, most of these procedures are fairly complicated and expensive; unless you feel the problem is really serious, it may be more sensible to forego elaborate treatments at this stage.

Can't the seed bed be sterilized? Yes, indeed it can, but completing the operation thoroughly, safely, and efficiently usually calls for professional help. Widely used is gaseous fumigation with methylbromide—applied to a loosened seed bed under a tarpaulin, something few homeowners are equipped to handle. However, sterilant drenches such as DMTT, SMDC, or Vorlex usually can be applied by a homeowner with a sprinkling can; but the cost, hard work, and potential hazard to ornamental plantings (through their roots) must be weighed against the possible benefits. Sterilization is temporary; sooner or later pests reinvade, although by then the grass should be established and in position to check most weeds.

Will it be necessary to till the ground in order to sow grass seed? Soil cultivation makes the best seed bed, but it is possible to renovate an old lawn or sow a new one if grading is satisfactory. Powered scarifying machines can be purchased or rented which chop surface vegetation and scratch the soil, making a reasonably receptive seed bed. If old vegetation is first killed chemically to forestall competition with the new seeding, surface scarification has an even better chance of being effective.

What about a temporary lawn?   If home construction is finished at a season inopportune for planting the permanent lawn, certain temporary plantings can keep you "out of the mud." It is best to sow cover that will not compete later with the permanent grass, or if it does persist will not be an eyesore. Examples: Korean lespedeza, a hot-weather annual which gives way gracefully to bluegrass in northern lawns; fine-textured rye grass, which in the South makes a pleasing autumn-winter cover before spring planting of lawns.

How quickly does newly sowed lawn seed sprout?   How fast seed will germinate depends both upon the kind of grass and the weather. Rye grass is fastest, fescues slightly slower, bluegrasses and bent grasses still a bit slower. Under ideal conditions, rye grass sprouts in just a few days, while bluegrass may take two weeks. Seed must be kept moist and warm for fast sprouting; germination is most rapid when daytime temperatures get into the seventies (F.). Also, seed that has been properly produced and handled will be more vigorous than that which has been mishandled. Seed can lie dormant in the soil during freezing weather, and will sprout only very slowly at temperatures below 50° F. Still, for spring sowings, it is best to seed the lawn as early as possible, letting the seed imbibe water and begin the sprouting process even though much "action" won't be seen until temperature warms later in spring.

Lawn Grasses

What is the best lawn grass?   "Best" will vary with the climate, local conditions, and your own preference. Bluegrass is the species most widely utilized in the northern two thirds of the country, Bermuda grass in the upper South, perhaps St. Augustine in the Deep South, but where conditions are suitable, bent grasses, fine fescues, and even perennial rye grasses are equally attractive in the North; zoysias in the South, and centipede or even bahia for the Deep South. Except for the special needs of the Deep South, almost all of the preferred lawn grasses are "fine-textured," i.e., have relatively narrow foliage that does not give a coarse appearance. They are also long-lasting (perennial), and in most cases spread by runners or rhizomes.

What grass seed do you suggest to make a lawn under maple trees? Grass is not successful under maple trees. Maples are surface-rooting trees, and grass could not compete with the large roots for food and moisture. By midsummer the grass usually disappears.

There are so many new varieties (cultivars) now, that I am confused. How can I choose intelligently? It is helpful to realize that all bluegrasses behave somewhat alike, all fine fescues like fescues, and so on. The difference between individual cultivars is mostly a matter of preferred color, texture, growth habit, or such, and not too much of a consideration so far as care is concerned. Seed firms provide helpful information concerning their proprietary cultivars, and responsible houses will utilize quality components in their seed mixtures which you can accept on faith. The new cultivars would not have been brought to market had they not exhibited at least some superior characteristics. They are chosen for reasonable resistance to the usual lawn diseases, for comparatively low rather than tall growth, and for attractive appearance. Examples of typical improved cultivars are given in the chart on page 698.

How can I avoid confusing good lawn grasses with poor ones? Unfortunately, some uncertainty occurs with common names, and the botanical names seldom appear in component listings or are misunderstood by the uninitiated. "Bluegrass" generally refers to the valuable Kentucky bluegrass species (*Poa pratensis*), while "annual" bluegrass is a weed and other bluegrasses (such as 'Canada' or "woods") are of lesser quality. But 'Kentucky-31' is the legal name for a coarse fescue, not to be confused with Kentucky bluegrass. Indeed, the unwanted coarse fescues (*Festuca arundinacea,* in such cultivars as the 'Kentucky-31', 'Alta') should not be mistaken for the red fescue group (*Festuca rubra*), generally termed fine or lawn fescues, including the desirable 'Chewings' and creeping-red varieties. These are perhaps the major cases causing confusion, but one must become sufficiently acquainted with lawn grasses to recognize their names on the required component listings of the seed box to feel entirely confident.

Why are mixtures of several kinds of seed advocated? This was discussed at some length in the Introduction. In brief, it is an effort to introduce enough variability into the lawn so that not all grass will be susceptible to the same affliction; though a certain disease may attack one cultivar, another is likely to be resistant. Some grass suited to the many micro-habitats (shade-sun, south-north slope, poor-good soil pockets, high-low ground, etc.) is apt to be found in a mixture, whereas a single cultivar might not be adapted to all of these situations. Bluegrass-fescue combinations, with perhaps a touch of perennial rye grass for quick cover, is a typical mixture; the bluegrasses are great for open areas, but fescues usually survive better in the shade and on dry-infertile soil under trees. Even where an all-bluegrass lawn is wanted, blends of cultivars are advocated to better "spread the risk."

What is meant by "nurse grass"? A nurse grass makes a stand quickly, until the permanent turf (generally slower in getting started) can take over. Unfortunately, the nurse grass competes for space and nutrients, slowing the permanent grass or even preventing its establishment. Ordinarily, a nurse grass should not constitute more than about 20 per cent of a mixture on a seed-count basis. A nurse grass is expected to protect the new seeding, then gradually give way to better grasses. The concept is rather outmoded these days, what with modern planting techniques and mulches, and reasonably fast-sprouting permanent cultivars. In a sense fine fescue in a bluegrass blend serves as a nurse grass, and is useful if it persists. More often perennial rye grass would be used. Annual rye grass and redtop were formerly much used, but annual rye grass is overly aggressive and redtop often carries a few unwanted species (such as timothy) with it.

Are timothy and other farm grass species suitable for lawns? Where the better lawn grasses can be grown, "hay grasses" are best left to the pasture; in the lawn they become coarse and clumpy. An exception would be for very difficult sites where survival of the finer grasses is questionable. Such sites are often seeded to tall fescue, the only turf possible without a great deal of maintenance.

What grasslike ground covers other than grass are used? A number of creeping broadleaf species make excellent ground cover, but only dichondra (in the morning-glory family) is handled in the same fashion as are lawn grasses (seeding, mowing, etc.). Dichondra use is pretty well confined to southern California. Creeping legumes, such as white clover, are acceptable for warm weather cover, but are generally not favored because of their contrasting appearance in turf.

What grasses are recommended for shade? Essentially the same species are planted for shade as for sun, although the proportion of shade-tolerant types may be increased. Grasses perform better in the shade if helped by tall mowing and more frequent fertilization and watering. Rough bluegrass (*Poa trivialis*), an attractive but shallow-rooting grass that does not wear well, adapts well to moist shade. Fine fescues are good for dry shade. All southern grasses except Bermuda stand shade reasonably well.

What are some good but economical grasses for large lawns that can't be pampered? Some of the "old-fashioned" self-reliant cultivars so well adapted to the casual care of yesteryear might fill the bill. Among the Kentucky bluegrasses are 'Arboretum' (Missouri) and 'Kenblue' (Kentucky) strains for the southern portions of the bluegrass belt, 'Park' (Minnesota) for northern and western zones. These and similar varieties can withstand reasonable neglect, but should be mowed fairly tall (at least at a 2-in. clipping height).

What are the advantages and disadvantages of white clover in the lawn? White clover is an excellent companion to Kentucky bluegrass, having microbial nodules on its roots that trap nitrogen from the air; thus clover enhances soil fertility. However, clover is patchy in the lawn, especially disruptive when white flower heads form. The flowers attract bees. Clover foliage is "soft" compared to grass, may be slippery underfoot, and is likely to stain clothing more readily than would grass. Clover leaves die down in winter and are not as good cover as cool-season grass foliage.

What grasses are best for winter color? Southern lawn grasses turn dormant and brown near freezing. So do the native American prairie grasses. Lawns must depend almost entirely on introduced grasses from Europe, such as the bluegrasses, fescues, bent grasses, and rye grasses, for persistent green in winter. Sow rye grass or a mixture of these cool-season species for a green lawn in the South. In the North, the same grasses remain green much of the winter, turn brown only when exposed to drying winds or bitter cold. Lawns adequately (but not excessively) fertilized show better late color. Green dyes are sold for spraying dormant southern grasses in the upper South. Dyeing is especially appropriate for zoysia, a grass typically too dense for good winter-grass overseeding, and, unlike Bermuda, with persistent enough foliage to stand winter wear.

What are the advantages—and the disadvantages—of establishing a zoysia lawn in the North? The chief advantages to zoysia are its competitiveness against weeds in hot weather, and good density without a lot of mowing. Chief disadvantage is an abbreviated growing season in the North; seldom is zoysia attractive before May, and it turns off color again at frost. Zoysia lawns in the North typically take several years to fill in from plugs or sprigs.

What selections of zoysia would you recommend for vegetative planting in the North? I have admired my neighbor's lawn which was planted from seed of Zoysia japonica, but he has advised me to seek one of the selected zoysia grasses, as he says they are less coarse. The 'Meyer' strain of Z. *japonica* is most frequently offered for northern lawns, being quite hardy; the finer-textured *matrella* strains usually don't perform as well in cool climates as does the 'Meyer' strain. 'Meyer' zoysia is not so coarse as would be the variable population resulting from sowing Z. *japonica* seed (because of sexual crossing, zoysia seed does not come true-to-type).

How far north can Zoysia japonica and its selections be expected to grow without winter injury or kill? 'Meyer' zoysia should be hardy through the northeastern states except perhaps at higher elevations and particularly exposed situations. Hardiness is perhaps less a concern than is its unattractive color where the summer is short and coolish.

I understand that there are green plant dyes used in the South on winter lawns. Would these dyes be practical in the North? (Although we try to take care of our lawn, it usually turns quite brownish in the winter. If our snow cover would last, the look of the lawn in winter wouldn't matter, but in recent years, the snow has melted!) We also have a section of zoysia lawn in the back of the house which, of course, always turns very brown. Could we dye that, too? Lawn colorants can be used on discolored grasses having dead foliage that is resistant to withering and wear, as with zoysia. Application of dye is difficult in winter weather. With northern grasses (which normally stay reasonably attractive until Christmas, maybe all winter under snow), natural color is probably more attractive than dyed turf.

Sowing Seed

Would it be O.K. to sow lawn seed in winter if the ground is clear of snow? In winter, it is good practice to seed while there is a *little* snow on the ground. On slopes, where the seed might wash in a thaw, it is better to wait until the ground is clear.

Is spring or fall better for lawn seeding? (Illinois.) The best possible time for lawn seeding is in the fall, early September generally. Grass seed germinates well in this period with cold nights and sufficient moisture. Fall-sown grass becomes firmly rooted. There is no weed competition, and the grass has an early start in spring. In spring sowing the danger is that the young grass will not be strong enough to withstand summer tribulations.

When is the best time to sow grass seed? In the section of the country extending from southern New York west to Omaha the first half of September is the best. Farther southward somewhat later; farther north somewhat earlier.

How early in spring can lawns on Long Island be seeded? As early as the soil can be worked; early March if possible.

Is it best to wait until warm weather to sow grass seed? No, grass thrives best during the cool, moist periods of very early spring and early fall.

What methods insure sowing seed evenly? Best is to use a mechanical seed spreader, sowing half in one direction, half at right angles. For hand sowing, see suggestions in the Introduction.

Why are there differences in seeding rates? Whether the grass plants are large or tiny, customarily crowded or spread out, will have some influence. But mainly, it is a question of seed size. Bent grass seed runs about 8,000,000 seeds to the pound; fescues over 500,000; Kentucky bluegrass 2,000,000 and rye grass about 250,000. The more seeds per pound, the less poundage needed. Most mixtures are sowed about 3 lbs. to 1,000 sq. ft.

Is a spreader which casts or throws seed, or one which drops it from the hopper, preferable?   Both the cyclone-type seeder (which throws seed from a whirling disc) or the kind that lets seed drop from regulated apertures at the bottom of a hopper will do an excellent sowing job if in good working condition. The casting spreaders complete seeding quickly, since they cover a band up to 10 ft. wide in a single pass. They will not, however, define a course as accurately as will a gravity spreader. When operating the gravity spreader, more passes are needed, and one must be careful to overlap wheel tracks in order to avoid missing strips. With either type more assured coverage can be obtained by sowing half the seed in one direction, the other half crossways.

Does a new grass seeding need protection?   Protection is essential only in special cases, such as on strongly sloping ground or a poorly prepared seed bed that leaves the seed perched quite at the surface. Most grass seed is too small to tempt birds, and it sifts into soil crevices where it is hidden. However, any seeding will *benefit* from a protective mulch.

What is mulching?   A surface blanket of any inert material that is open enough to let sprouts emerge (and rain soak into the seed bed) can serve as a mulch. Straw—a few straws deep—has been widely used, but it is difficult to procure in urban areas. Excelsior, chopped twigs, grass clippings, sphagnum peat moss, woven nettings, Fiberglas mats, and similar materials can be used. The most procurable material for most homeowners today is peat moss, usually available in 6-cubic-ft. bales.

Why is a mulch helpful?   A mulch helps prevent soil wash, serving as a barrier that breaks the force of rain. This is especially important on slopes. But perhaps even more important generally, a mulch acts as a partial barrier in retarding the drying out of the seed bed. Seed will sprout quickly only if kept continuously damp. A mulched seeding requires less frequent watering than one exposed directly to air and sunlight, and usually makes a stand more quickly.

What mulch is best?   Mulches thick enough to retard evaporation but loose enough not to interfere with water penetration or seedling emergence work best. Mulches which will not blow easily in wind and which decay naturally (not requiring later removal) have advantages. On the whole nothing has proved much more satisfactory than straw, if material free from weeds can be procured. Most of the time a straw mulch stays in place if walked upon to press it down; in especially windy spots it can be held down with string tied between stakes. Excelsior is another excellent mulch.

Is mulching a large area feasible?   Machines have been developed for mulching large areas, such as newly seeded roadsides. Some blow straw along with an asphalt "tack" that binds the straw. Other hydraulic seeders pump a slurry, typically containing woodpulp fibers as the mulch. These machines can cover acres per hour. Many landscaping services have smaller versions which can be engaged for custom service.

What mulch is good for lawn repairs or important small seedings? Perhaps the most effective "mulch" for bringing a new seeding up rapidly is a clear polyethylene cover fastened at the margins by large nails or wire wickets pushed into the soil. This is not unlike a greenhouse. If the seeding is watered initially, the polyethylene not only prevents evaporation but condensation drips back and no additional watering is needed for days. In sunny weather warmth is trapped; the soil temperature rises enough to speed sprouting early in the season. However, unless carefully watched, the temperature under the polyethylene can reach lethal levels quickly on a sunny day; sprouting seed and young seedlings will not survive temperatures much above 100° F.

How should a new seeding be watered?   New seedings are best watered with a fine spray, frequently applied. Forceful watering, es-

Underground sprinkler systems are a major aid in modern lawn maintenance.

pecially on an unmulched seed bed, disperses soil, preventing water penetration. Consequent rilling washes soil and seed away. Sprinkle lightly, frequently enough to keep the seed bed moist without surface runoff.

What about sprinkler systems for new lawn seedings? Most convenient would be underground piping activated by a time clock set for brief waterings at frequent intervals. Installations using plastic components (which do not require plumbing talent for installation) are now available. Or above-ground sprinklers can be set to cover sectors of a circle; these can be placed at the edge of the seeded area to prevent walking in the soft ground. Heavy or cumbersome above-ground sprinklers—apt to tear a seed bed—are to be avoided, as are ones that apply water more rapidly than the particular area can absorb it.

What assistance other than mulching and watering can be given a newly seeded lawn? Seedling grass derives its nourishment from stored reserves in the seed, and will not need fertilization for some time. Seedlings are tender, susceptible to chemical injury. The grass must mature at least until it has been mowed a few times before applying any weedkiller. An exception is bromoxynil, which, at the recommended rate, can be safely applied to most seedling turf for elimination of broadleaf weeds.

When should a new lawn be mowed first? Seedlings need a fair root system before mowing, in order not to be torn out of the ground. But don't let the grass grow so long that it flops over. It is generally wise to begin mowing before the grass has reached twice again what will be its customary mowing height. By then the grass should be rooted deeply enough so that the soil can be allowed to dry out sufficiently to prevent foot-printing and mower rutting. Obviously, new grass should be dry for its first mowings.

Are there special precautions for seeding slopes with grass seed? Because of the obvious danger from erosion and the inconvenience of operating on steep slopes, consider sodding rather than seeding. Even a strip or two of sod across the slope helps control wash. A seeded slope should receive all the protective measures that have been discussed, including a nurse grass in the seed mixture and a good mulch. Of course, in the case of a really steep slope, grass may not be the solution at all. Rather, consider the planting of ground covers, such as creeping junipers, English ivy, myrtle.

Planting Lawns Vegetatively

What is sod?   Sod consists of a community of mature grass plants started elsewhere, delivered as flat squares or "rolls," like carpets, for laying to make an "instant lawn." In effect you pay a sod farm, the "nursery," to oversee the seeding through the tedious seedling stages. Only grasses having spreading stems make sod able to hold together during lifting and replanting. Bluegrass is one of the best sod grasses.

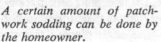

A certain amount of patch-work sodding can be done by the homeowner.

Is sodding worth while?   Having your lawn sodded is certainly more expensive than seeding it, but you gain cover instantly. Professionally grown sod should provide just as good a grass in your lawn as if you had planted it yourself.

Does sodding make seed bed preparation less necessary?   Sod planted on poorly prepared soil will perform no better in the long haul than would a seeding given inadequate seed bed preparation. Before laying sod, prepare the soil the same as for seeding, i.e., mix in fertilizer, add lime if needed, loosen the rootzone soil, remove debris, level, etc.

Are special pains needed with a newly sodded lawn?   It takes several weeks for sod to reroot, and during this interval, it should be watered regularly. Firm newly laid sod into the soil by light rolling with a roller, and, if possible, topdress (with sterilized soil) where the sod blocks meet or where depressions are noted. Fertilize later as you would an established lawn.

Can I save costs by sodding my own lawn?   Yes, sod can be purchased from a garden center and laid at home. It is more difficult
to do a smooth job from lifting your own sod from another part of
the lawn; sod growers use machines that cut sod squares to exact
thickness, something not possible with ordinary garden tools. However, a certain amount of patchwork sodding can be successfully done
by the homeowner.

Is there anything to be wary about in purchasing sod?   Buy sod
from reputable sources which identify the grasses. Look for weeds
or offtype grasses. Ask for assurance that there are no pests in the
sod, such as crab-grass seed, harmful insects, and so on. Sod cut
about ¾ in. thick roots most rapidly, but it also dries out more readily
than does thicker sod; before accepting delivery, be certain the sod is
fresh and has not dried out (is not yellowing).

Are there less expensive alternatives to sodding?   Yes, small bis-
cuits of sod (called plugs) or stem fragments (called sprigs) can be
planted. Either will spread into a tight turf in time. Southern lawns
—for which no seed is available—are often planted this way. Sprigs
will give more coverage than an equivalent weight of plugs, but sprigs
dry out readily and require immediate planting. Zoysia sprigs spread
a bit more quickly than do plugs. Even so, zoysia is so slow growing
that a year or more is required to make a solid stand. On the other
hand, Bermuda grass makes a stand in just a few weeks. Other
southern grasses fall between these extremes.

Can grass fragments be used to start a lawn?   With certain grasses,
yes, particularly creeping bent grasses and Bermuda grasses. Sod is
shredded—or stem clippings cut—to make what is called "stolons," and
these are scattered over a prepared seed bed just as with grass seed.
Because these stolons dry out quickly, they should be topdressed
immediately with ¼ in. or so of soil (or at least be firmly pressed
into the ground). The new stolons must be watered without fail until
roots develop at the joints and new growth appears. This is more a
practice for the professional than for the homeowner.

**Are sodded lawns or lawns planted from sprigs or plugs preferable
to seeding?**   The only advantages to sodding are quickness in providing mature turf, or perpetuation of cultivars (in sprigging or sodding) that don't come true from seed. Sod may forestall weed
appearance, but the potential for weeds is still in the soil if the sod

fails. Such vegetative planting risks the introduction of pests and diseases more than does direct seeding, and some experts feel seeded grasses—rooting directly in "home soil"—do better than grass that is transplanted.

What grasses are most used for vegetative plantings? While all lawn grasses can be transplanted vegetatively, the extra effort or expense (compared to seeding) makes quality sod or select cultivars the best investment. 'Floratine' and 'Floratam' St. Augustine grasses are becoming commercially available in Florida, the 'Tift' series ('Tifgreen', 'Tifway', etc.) and 'Santa Ana' Bermuda grasses throughout the South and California. 'Emerald' and local zoysia cultivars are had in the South, 'Meyer' zoysia for the North; the bluegrass and fescue cultivars cited on page 698, alone or in mixture, are used for northern sod.

Would you recommend vegetative strains of greens-type bent grass? An excellent creeping bent grass from seed, 'Penncross', is now available, and for lawns "like a golf green" this would be recommended either as seed or sod. Seed of 'Kingstown' velvet bent grass, the ultimate in fine-textured turf, is also on the market. However, should one want a particular golf course clone (such as 'Cohansey', 'Evansville', 'Toronto', and so on), live starts must be procured from a nursery and be planted vegetatively, since these cultivars do not come true-to-type from seed and no seed supplies are available. However started, a lawn of creeping or velvet bent requires more attention than would bluegrass-fescue, and especially more frequent and precise mowing.

Must colonial bent grasses be started vegetatively? No, colonial bents such as 'Exeter', 'Highland', and 'Holfior' are available as pureline seed. Colonial bents do not require the intensive care that the lower-growing creeping bent grasses do, and would be the cultivars used for mixture with other grasses, such as low-growing bluegrasses. Colonial bent sods are best mowed at a ¾- to 1-in. clipping height.

Tending the Established Lawn

What are the main lawn-care needs? Mowing is inevitable, of course. With few exceptions, fertilization is needed (the exact program will vary with kind of grass and climate). In most cases, watering will be required, and, alas, when things go wrong, such necessary procedures as weed, pest, and disease control must be resorted to.

Do maintenance programs differ for differing kinds of lawns? Yes, indeed. Obviously timing will differ for northern grasses compared to southern ones (see Introduction). Some grasses require more attention than do others, especially the "heavy feeders" such as Bermuda and bent. Fast-growing types, such as Bermuda, require more of just about everything (especially mowing and fertilization) than will a "poor man's grass" such as centipede (which actually suffers if fertilization is generous). Some grasses, such as fine fescues and zoysia, can get by with little attention, but look better when well cared for. Zoysia is slow-growing and stands infrequent mowing, but looks more attractive if clipped each week or so.

What attention can an "average" lawn be expected to need, say in bluegrass country? Weekly mowing (perhaps each five days at height of spring growth, maybe each ten days during summer "slowdown"), a few fertilizations annually (particularly in autumn for bluegrass), probably a 2, 4-D treatment for broadleaf weeds (the weeds are most noticed in spring–summer, but autumn weed control helps prevent spring occurrence), perhaps watering during dry periods, and occasional chemical treatments to combat specific afflictions if they threaten.

What makes a lawn "look good"? Good looks are due mainly to density, uniformity, and rich color. Planting of improved cultivars helps greatly, but you still must mow regularly, eliminate discordant weeds, and fertilize (both for deep color, and to keep the grass vigorously contesting weeds).

What are the main lawn problems to be expected? Probably most noticeable will be weeds, although after a while these should lessen, succumbing to vigorously growing grass and occasional chemical treatments. Selective herbicides exist for broadleaf weeds, such as dandelions and plantains, and for annual grasses such as crab grass, but not for perennial grass weeds. Disease can be troublesome seasonally, although this has become less of a problem with the newer disease-resistant cultivars.

Should clippings be collected? This is a matter of preference, and to an extent depends upon the kind of grass. Bent and Bermuda cultivars probably should have the clippings collected, since their density prevents the clippings from sifting down near the soil where decay is rapid. Clippings of most grasses, if regularly mowed, are short enough to work into the sod and not be noticeable. Some pathologists feel that a mass of clippings constitutes a reservoir for disease inoculum. Clippings left on the lawn do have fertility value. Clippings collection is a bother, and in general they are removed only on the highly manicured turfs.

What is lawn thatch? Thatch is the accumulation of incompletely decayed tissues and other debris at the base of sod. It consists mainly of ligneous grass roots, stems, and lower leaf sheaths. Thatch is continuously decomposing at the bottom, while additions accrue above. Clippings, being succulent and easily decayed, contribute rather little to thatch buildup.

Is thatch harmful? If not excessive, say up to ½ in. thick, it is normal and probably a useful recycling of vegetative remains and an aid to soil aggregation. Thatch may harbor certain pests, however. If excessive, it can insulate the soil so thoroughly that fertilizer or other surface applications will not penetrate to the rootzone, at least evenly. Zoysia thatch is so indestructible that some zoysia lawns shed water —as if shingled—rather than letting it soak through to the soil.

On a trip through northern New England in the spring, I saw farmers burning pastures and fields. (I used to see this as a child, but had thought it might now be outmoded.) Is this still a good practice? I know the new grass growth after the burning is very green, but aren't nutrients lost in the process? And would you recommend this as a practice in the spring on our very large zoysia lawn, which is choked with thatch (although it performs quite well once it turns green)? We have plenty of hoses and good water pressure so there would be no fire hazard. With restrictions on air pollution, burning, whether of field or lawn, is indeed "outmoded." Burning is an effective way to remove accumulated duff, especially pronounced with zoysia; burning dormant turf will not kill the grass, and may have a rejuvenating effect. But a burnt-over lawn is messy and an eyesore until new growth occurs. Nutrient loss is not consequential, and can easily be compensated for through fertilization.

I plan to rent a dethatching machine. Should I use it in spring or fall? I suppose I should apply fertilizer after I use it? It is generally best to dethatch just prior to a season favorable for grass growth (which will vary with kind of grass and climate); that way fresh grass rather than weeds fills in the scars. Fertilize your lawn according to its needs (see discussion of fertilization), whether or not the lawn is dethatched. For efficiency's sake it would be more sensible to apply fertilizer after rather than before thatch removal.

Why is thatch more of a problem now than formerly? Modern standards call for vigorous, dense cultivars, which are made to grow profusely by fertilization, watering, etc. Tissue decomposition can't keep up with production, especially on stoloniferous turfs where the thatch hardly contacts soil—needed to speed decay. Pesticides can sometimes inhibit thatch decomposition, too. When earthworms are eliminated, as with chlordane treatments, thatching generally increases.

How can thatch be controlled? Try to keep natural processes in balance so decomposition is rapid. (Speedy decay requires moisture, moderate pH, some nitrogen, and reasonable aerification.) The most effective means for reducing thatch is to topdress lightly with weed-free soil, something more practical for a golf course than for a home lawn. Thatch can be reduced for a growing season by mechanical removal; powered equipment variously termed "vertical mower," "dethatcher," "thinner," "power rakes," and so on can be rented. These slice into the thatch, kick it to the surface for pickup. Aerification machines, which can also be rented, punch holes through the thatch into the soil and should help, especially if the soil cores are then scattered back over the thatch layer.

What is the nutrient value of grass clippings? Nutrients equivalent to one or two fertilizations at normal rates are contained in a year's clippings. Most of the nutrients are recycled as the clippings decay.

How can lawns be contained, that is, the grass restrained at bor-

ders? This requires persistent attention. The problem is most pronounced with grasses having vigorous runners and rhizomes, such as Bermuda and zoysia. If only surface runners are involved, edging tools and powered edgers can trim the runners. If spread is by underground stems, metal or plastic barriers driven several inches into the soil may help. Sometimes it may be possible to toxify soil strips, though this is hazardous because the chemical may leach elsewhere. Chemical edging is also possible with a contact foliage spray of such substances as paraquat, cacodylic acid, or even petroleum derivatives. This is a useful approach for driveways and walks, and to create a grass-free mowing zone around trees.

What causes earth mounds on my lawn? Moles and gophers are usually responsible for tunnelings and soil piles at a burrow entrance. Other mammals may dig or scratch. Large earthworms ("night crawlers") leave castings that are noticeable on low-clipped swards such as bent grass. Mole cricket mounds are found on sandy soils of the Deep South, and those of crayfish on soils with a high water table.

How can damage from moles, gophers, or larger burrowing animals be checked? Poison baits and traps are helpful, although seldom completely successful. A more general approach is to remove the food that attracts these animals, in most cases soil insects. A "grub-proofing" of the soil with a long-lasting insecticide such as chlordane may be the best solution.

What about earthworm castings? Insecticides make the soil unattractive to earthworms, which retreat to lower levels or move elsewhere (doubtless the population is also reduced by the insecticide). Remember, however, before eliminating earthworms that their burrows are beneficial where soil aerification is needed, and the worms do consume thatch.

Should a lawn be rolled to make it level? Rolling can flatten mole runs, or reset sod plugs and grass clumps heaved by winter's alternate freezing and thawing. It will squash, but not eliminate, soil mounds. Instead, scatter mounded soil by raking. It is usually preferable to level a lawn surface by filling in depressions with additional soil than to crush high spots. Rolling compacts soil, and undoes the benefit of cultivation (whether mechanical or due to freezing).

Is lawn liming necessary? As a regular procedure similar to fertilization, no. The chief value from liming is to make acid soils "sweeter" (more alkaline). If soil is near neutral, within a pH range of 6–8, lime is probably not needed. Very acid soils, some with a pH so low as 4, should benefit from liming, especially if planted with such grasses as bluegrass or Bermuda, which "prefer" a higher pH. The only sure indication of the need for lime is to have a pH soil test made.

What is the action of lime on lawn? If the soil is heavy, lime will help to keep it porous, permitting air and moisture to penetrate. Because of many decayed roots, lawns tend to become acid. Lime will correct this tendency and will release plant-food materials for the grasses.

Both gypsum and ground limestone have been recommended to "break up" the very heavy clay on which our lawn grasses are struggling—without much success. Now I realize we should have applied the limestone or gypsum before sowing the seed, but since there is grass cover, though sparse, I'd like to save it. Which material now would work faster—the gypsum or limestone? The clay soil is acid, as it came from a potato field. Both materials are effective for aggregating soil where the calcium ion is needed (as in substituting for sodium in soils that slake readily). Gypsum is the more soluble, and in that sense the more "immediately" effective. But other factors, such as acidity, may be a more important consideration. Gypsum would probably be preferable on alkaline soils in the West, while limestone would probably be preferable on acid soils in humid climates.

If lime is needed, what kind do I use? The best is crushed limestone, preferably the dolomitic type (containing magnesium). Spread 50–100 lbs. per 1,000 sq. ft., as you would fertilizer, each few years if need be until pH tests to at least 6. In northern climates a good time to lime is in the winter or fall.

Is it necessary to acidify alkaline lawns? The need is less frequent than for liming, but may be required in arid regions. Ten to 50 lbs. of sulfur per 1,000 sq. ft. may be needed, depending upon the degree of alkalinity; however, the problem is often one of sodium excess rather than alkalinity alone, in which case gypsum (calcium sulfate) would prove a better corrective than sulfur.

What are the causes of lawn blemishes? This is sometimes hard to determine. Try a process of elimination: what about—soil adequacy (buried debris or spilled contaminants); pattern relating to dog urination; the possibility of spilled salt, fertilizer, etc.; insects associated with the damage (such as grubs in the soil, chewing off roots; web-worms burrowing deep in the sod, chewing off foliage; tiny chinch bugs, sucking juices from the foliage); possibility of physical damage, such as from scuffing or the repeated passage of equipment; past treatments, which with overusage may have accumulated to toxic levels (say of arsenic, or of crab-grass preventer). If none of these seem to fit, probably disease is the culprit, of which there are many kinds not easily identifiable. Your county agent may help and be aware of local problems causing the trouble.

How can I most easily repair a lawn blemish? Injury is generally quite localized, and the spot can be reseeded, sodded, or planted to plugs and sprigs, just as with a new lawn. If soil is at fault, remove obstructions, and replace toxic soil with fresh. An inexpensive hollow-tube plug lifter can cut plugs where turf is thick for replacement in voids. As the plugs exit from the top of the tube simply drop them in holes that the plugger makes in the repair area, and firm them in place with the foot.

Is spiking a lawn helpful? Spiking may loosen thatch with attendant advantages, but it is generally not worth the trouble for improving soil. Indentations forced into the soil are more likely to intensify compaction than to relieve it. Better would be aerifying machines which remove cores of soil.

Will tree leaves injure the lawn? Anything that obstructs light from reaching green leaf will reduce the grasses' food-making ability; but no toxicants occur in tree leaves that will appreciably inhibit the growth of familiar lawn grasses. The problem, thus, is mainly a mechanical one, not a chemical one. Tree *roots,* however, may reduce grass growth by competing strongly for fertilizer and moisture. Small leaves, or larger ones shredded by a mower, should cause no difficulty in the typical lawn (of bluegrass-fescue or other open-textured turf) if not more than an inch or two thick. The leaf fragments will settle into the grass foliage, which will soon overgrow them. Where fallen leaves are so abundant as to smother the grass, they should, of course, be gathered for the compost pile.

Mowers and Mowing

Of what value to the lawn is mowing?   Except that mowing is harder on most weed plants than on the grass, mowing does little to benefit the lawn other than to improve appearance. We all strive for a level grass carpet, and to achieve this, mowing becomes necessary. Foliage lost as clippings is a physiological drain on the grass, for each green leaf is productive food-making tissue. Mowing *does* stimulate side branching, causing the lawn to become denser, though the individual plants become stunted and more shallowly rooted. Lawns left unmowed form seed, become patchy, and gradually weeds and brush overwhelm the grass.

Does disease enter through the sheared tips of grass blades?   Some diseases are thought to, but in most instances, if conditions are right for a disease, it will find ways of infecting grass, mowed or not. But unmowed (and tall-mowed) grass has some advantage in resisting disease, probably mostly due to the extra food-making power of additional green leaf.

How frequently should the lawn be mowed?   This, of course, will vary with the growth rate. Well-kept lawns, at peak seasons, may have to be mowed every few days. This is especially true with luxurious turfs such as a golf green, which are usually mowed every other day. A good rule of thumb is to mow any time that the grass gains an additional 50–100 per cent of its customary mowing height.

What if I can't "keep up" with the mowing, due to rain or other cause?   If the grass gets excessively tall, cut it back a little at a time, gradually reducing the height. If a grass plant is suddenly bereft of most of its green leaf (is "scalped"), it will certainly be weakened; roots can fail to grow for many weeks. This is especially damaging in spring, when stored food has been used to make fresh leaves; eliminating this growth then may kill the plant.

Our house has a field of grass on which we look out. We enjoy the daisies and first stand of young grass. After that, when should it be cut, and how often per year, to keep it attractive? It is now

full of red bunch grass. Cut the first grass before the seed ripens in the heads. Two more cuttings at monthly intervals during the summer should keep it orderly.

What mowing equipment should I get? This will depend upon preference, kind of grass and its ideal mowing height, and funds available. Since mowing represents most of the time people spend on their lawn, it should be made as pleasant a preoccupation as possible; top-quality equipment, with capacity to get the job done quickly and conveniently, is strongly recommended.

What are the advantages of reel mowers? Reel mowers cut with a scissors-like action of rotating reel against a fixed bedknife. If in good repair, this is the most precise mowing instrument available. Reel mowers are especially recommended for low-mowed turfs that are well tended. Reel mowers are somewhat safer than other types.

What are the disadvantages of a reel mower? Reel mowers are rather hard to adjust and sharpen. They are also somewhat more expensive. Because their wheels protrude beyond the cutting edge, adjacent mowing passes must overlap, and the machine cannot get very close to barriers. Riding on two wheels only, a reel mower maintains a constant cutting height above the soil, and thus reflects any unevenness occurring in the lawn's surface.

What are the strong points of a rotary mower? Rotaries are less expensive and easier to maintain than reels. They are also more versatile, get close to obstructions, and are especially useful for mowing tall, floppy grass which is "sucked up" into the cutting chamber (a reel "blows down" lanky foliage ahead of the bedknife).

And the disadvantages of rotary mowers? They can be hazardous, sometimes flinging with the speed of a bullet metal fragments or rocks that are struck. Cutting by the impact of a speeding blade, rotary mowers tend to bruise and fray leaf tips more than do reels, especially when dull. Rotary cutting is generally not so "neat" or precise as is a reel cutting, but far more popular.

Are there other types of mowers for home use? None widely used. A hammerknife design, in which loose-hanging blades are extended from a rotating reel by centrifugal force, has found some favor; it is safer than the typical rotary, but not so easily maintained. A few garden tractors still have sickle-bar attachments, the farmer's familiar hay-cutting tool; a sickle-bar is not very suitable for low-cut home lawns, and may be hazardous for inexperienced users.

How soon after rain can I mow?   Use common sense. Wet grass clippings tend to wad and disperse poorly, but sometimes wet weather is so persistent that getting the mowing job done at all outweighs performing it well.

What about electric mowers?   Now that battery-powered models are available, electric mowers may become more versatile. The inconvenience of dragging a cord makes mowing a large lawn, especially if there are trees, cumbersome with an electric mower using a power outlet. Electric power is superior for quietness, easy starting, and low maintenance. Corded electric mowers should not be used on wet turf.

Is occasional lawn scalping of benefit?   Removal of foliage scorched brown by winter weather may let sunlight reach the soil and grass crowns more abundantly and speed spring revival. There is little disadvantage to the grass then, since this foliage no longer has much food-making capacity and will soon be replaced by new leaves. Such a scalping is permissible only in late winter before new foliage grows. Low mowing of a weedy lawn is sometimes practiced in summer, on the theory that seeds of crab grass and similar weeds are thus removed; probably there will be plenty of weed seeds anyway, and the setback from low mowing to whatever good grass exists probably more than offsets any weed reduction benefits. A *slight* reduction in mowing height may stimulate new growth, help "tidy up" a lawn when done shortly before some special occasion.

What mowing pattern should I follow?   Efficient mowing varies with the contours of the land, but in general should minimize the need for turning and backing, and have obstructions (such as flower and shrub areas) oriented in the direction of mowing for easy skirting. Try to alternate or vary the direction of mowing—to avoid "grain" due to continuous sweep of the mower in one direction.

What is a suggested mowing height for northern grasses?   Velvet and creeping bent grasses are typically mowed quite low, no taller than ½ in.; colonial bent grasses are generally mowed ¾ to 1 in. The newer low-growing bluegrass cultivars, such as 'Fylking' or 'Baron', do well at 1 in., but most bluegrasses are better mowed at 1½ ins. or taller. Fescues and rye grasses should be handled the same as is bluegrass, although 'Jamestown' fescue is quite low-growing.

The suggested mowing height for southern species? Improved Bermuda grasses are generally mowed quite low, from ¼ in. with golf-green types such as 'Tifdwarf', to 1 in. or taller with common Bermuda. Zoysia and centipede are generally mowed at an intermediate height, between 1 and 2 ins. Bahia and St. Augustine are mowed fairly tall, typically 1½ to 2½ ins.

No matter how sharp I try to keep the blades of my rotary mower, they seem to "tear" rather than clean-cut my grass (Zoysia japonica). The result is that the tips look ragged and usually turn brown soon after mowing. A neighbor has suggested I use a reel-type mower. Do you think this would help? Zoysia tissue is unusually tough. Heavy-duty mowers are recommended, and a well-adjusted reel mower should mow more neatly than might a rotary (see discussion of lawn mowing).

How early in spring should mowing start? Mow just as soon as there is appreciable growth, weather permitting; before the grass has doubled its usual mowing height.

How late should mowing continue in autumn? As long as there is appreciable new growth. However, bluegrass lawns develop much shorter recumbent foliage in autumn than in spring, tending to thicken then rather than grow tall; mowing is not nearly so burdensome in autumn as in spring.

Need the lawn be clipped short for winter? No. Continue at customary mowing height through autumn so that the grass gains full advantage of ample green leaf.

Are collected clippings of any value? Yes, they make an excellent mulch, or a fine addition to the compost pile. Fresh clippings mold rather quickly unless spread out. Scattered about the garden they can be a valuable soil additive, both for nutrient value and for the humus they provide.

Lawn Irrigation

Is watering the lawn essential?   Only in arid climates, or during prolonged drought. The ability to resist drying varies with the kind of turf grass, but east from Kansas seldom is drought bad enough to kill the usual lawn grasses even though they may brown temporarily.

Would a covering of peat moss over the grass in summer help to hold the moisture and do away with watering?   In actual practice this does not result. If the peat moss becomes dry, it will absorb the moisture from the soil. It would be better to incorporate the peat moss *in the soil* at the time it is prepared for seeding. Peat moss does much to retain moisture as it holds sixteen times its own weight in water.

What is the advantage of lawn irrigation in humid climates?   Mainly an assured supply of moisture whenever it is needed. This is especially important for newly seeded lawns, and for keeping the lawn attractive when rainfall fails.

What is the best irrigation system?   See discussions in the Introduction, and for new seedings. Any system that supplies an adequate amount of water, uniformly, at a rate such that it soaks into the soil rather than runs off, should prove excellent.

Is it good to water the lawn frequently?   This will partly depend upon kind of grass and its use (low-clipped, shallow-rooting turfs, such as bent grass, will benefit from more frequent watering than a bluegrass lawn would need). It is usually best to water the average home lawn only frequently enough to prevent drought discoloration, letting the soil surface dry between waterings. Intermittent drying-out above the rootzone helps control disease and weeds.

Can lawn irrigation cause difficulties?   Watering is not a cure for any problem other than drought, and, indeed, it can intensify disease. Overwatering can result in more problems than no watering at all; it especially encourages unwanted wet-habitat vegetation (annual bluegrass, volunteer bent grass, nut sedge, *Poa trivialis,* etc.) at the expense of the lawn grass.

How heavily should I water? Enough to soak the rootzone, in most cases to percolate a foot deep or deeper. An application of less than an inch of water may suffice with a sandy soil, but a clay may need 3 ins. for a good soaking. Apply water only as rapidly as it can soak into the soil. Sandy soils may accept an inch of water in rather few minutes, but a clay may have to be watered at light rate for hours to achieve a 3-in. penetration.

Are there ways to improve water penetration? Growing grass itself helps, through organic additions that aggregate tight soils. Wetting agent sprays, such as Aqua-Gro, reduce surface tension, often enabling water to seep through thatch and into tight soils more readily. In preparing a new seed bed, amendments such as ground limestone and gypsum can be included to loosen tight or slaking soils.

Can the lawn be watered at any time of day? Watering in the heat of the day can waste water through evaporation, but the cooling effect should benefit the grass. There is no truth to the idea that water droplets act as magnifying lenses, causing burn. Watering late in the day is efficient, but some custodians have aversion to leaving a lawn "wet" through the night for fear of encouraging disease (much of the time dew wets the grass anyway!). This leaves early morning as perhaps very slightly favored for watering the lawn.

Is treated water all right for grass? Any water suitable for general home use will not injure grass, even if heavily chlorinated. Muddy water from ponds, even treated sewage effluent, is satisfactory for irrigation. In arid regions, where the soil is already quite salty, highly saline water from wells could worsen soil structure, especially if not applied heavily enough to leach completely through the rootzone.

Lawn Fertilization

Why should lawns be fertilized? Fertilizer is perhaps the most helpful tool for achieving the objective of a dense, attractive stand of grass, but it is essential to "bolster" a plant that is constantly being depleted of new growth. Lawn grass fertilized at the proper stages of the growing cycle is in a much better position to make a tight cover and to overpower weeds than is "weaker" unfertilized turf. Balanced fertilization also gives the grass a deeper color.

What is a complete fertilizer?   A complete fertilizer contains all three of the major nutrients: nitrogen, phosphorus, and potassium; they are listed by percentage in that order in the analysis (20–8–12 means 20 per cent nitrogen, 8 per cent phosphorus, and 12 per cent potassium).

Do I need to worry about secondary nutrients in my lawn fertilizer? In most cases, no, unless soil tests or experience indicates that they are particularly deficient. Calcium and sulfur are typical secondary elements; much of the time they are included as unlisted ingredients in a complete fertilizer, and often reach the lawn in small quantity in rainfall or dust.

What about minor nutrients?   Minor or trace nutrients are required in only very small proportions. Their lack causes the so-called "deficiency diseases," more often the result of the minor element being tied up by soil imbalance than because of complete absence. The only trace deficiency that occurs with any frequency in lawn grass is iron, often immobilized in alkaline soils of semi-arid climates such as the High Plains. Centipede grass is very sensitive to iron deficiency, and may turn chlorotic with only a slight rise of pH or due merely to fertility imbalance. Application of iron sulfate or iron chelates corrects iron chlorosis, but often a better solution is to acidify alkaline soils, making the iron tied up in the soil available. Copper, zinc, manganese, molybdenum, and a few other trace elements occasionally restrict crop growth but seem not to be a problem with lawns.

Don't lawns recycle their nutrients more than do agricultural crops? Yes, especially if clippings are left on the lawn. However, additional nitrogen will almost always be needed, since nitrogen compounds are readily volatilized and leached. Potassium may leach or be removed in clippings. Phosphorus, secondary, and trace nutrients are often supplied sufficiently by decaying vegetation and soil reserves.

What is the most important nutrient for lawn grass?   Nitrogen. Its addition gives the greatest growth response. The value of a lawn fertilizer is viewed chiefly on the basis of nitrogen content, and application rates are usually set to provide about 1 lb. of elemental nitrogen to each 1,000 sq. ft. regardless of other nutrient percentages.

What are the chief sources of nitrogen in lawn fertilizer? There are three general classes of nitrogen-yielding components: 1) soluble or inorganic chemicals such as nitrate or ammonium salts, 2) natural organic materials such as sewerage sludge, tankage, or processing residues, 3) tailor-made synthetic organics such as ureaform and IBDU.

What are the features of soluble fertilizer materials? Dissolving readily in water, they are immediately and abundantly available. This may be advantageous for quick spruce-up, especially in cold weather, but it can also cause overstimulation followed by debilitating letdown. Soluble fertilizer salts easily desiccate or "burn" foliage upon contact, and they may temporarily increase the salt concentration in the soil to deleterious levels. Soluble fertilizers are relatively inexpensive and can be effective when skillfully and carefully used.

What about organic fertilizers for the lawn? Organics are quite safe, but also quite expensive in terms of nutrient value. Upon decay organic substances release the whole gamut of nutrients found in tissue, and should contribute a balance of minor nutrients as well as major ones. Manures were once widely available, but are expensive and difficult to procure today. Their nutrient content varies with kind and handling, and they often contain weed seeds. Agricultural by-products such as cottonseed or soybean meal have become expensive for fertilizer. Tankage, leather scraps, seaweed materials, and other less valuable by-products vary in quality and usefulness. Processing sewage to acceptable form is expensive; in some instances sewerage may carry unwanted heavy metal components from industrial wastes. However, most of these materials are excellent sources of humus, and when available locally, can be mixed with the soil before seed is sown. (See Introduction to Soils, Section 1.)

And what about synthetic organic nitrogen sources? These are especially tailored for lawn usage, their composition regulated to provide limited immediate effect, but long-lasting release as the more complex polymers are broken down by soil processes. Most used is a co-polymer of urea and formaldehyde called ureaform or UF, frequently a component of mixed lawn fertilizers. The synthetic organics are non-burning and long-lasting.

Do you suggest the use of farm manure for a grass lawn? Only in the preparation of a new lawn when it could be incorporated in the soil to supply organic matter.

I live near a riding academy and can get all the horse manure I want. Should my lawn be covered with it in the fall? No. It is sure to bring in weeds, and may injure the grass. It also makes a spotty lawn. However, it can be mixed with soil to make a new lawn.

Would you advise using well-rotted cow or horse manure in preparing a lawn? How much on 1,500 sq. ft. of area? Because of its beneficial action on the soil and grass, rotted cow manure would be an excellent material to use in preparing soil for a lawn. If the soil is poor, apply a coating 2 to 3 ins. deep.

How is cow manure best applied? Spread over the ground and dug into the soil.

Is mushroom manure good for lawns? Mushroom manure, although not too rich in nutrients, is a splendid source of humus for lawns. It gives maximum results when worked into the soil at the time of preparation.

Are there other controlled-release lawn fertilizers? Yes, prills of soluble fertilizer coated with resin or sulfur to retard release of nutrients. Effectiveness will depend on the uniformity of the coating, whether it has been cracked during handling, and how resistant it is to soil decomposition.

Should a complete fertilizer be used on the lawn, or nitrogen alone? Nitrogen alone is satisfactory if a soil test indicates ample other nutrients. It is often no more costly to utilize a mass-marketed complete fertilizer rich in nitrogen than nitrogen alone, thus assuring that other nutrients will not be in short supply. As a general rule use a complete fertilizer at least once a year.

What is a good lawn fertilizer analysis? No single analysis fits all soils, depending upon which nutrients are abundant or lacking. It can be assumed that nitrogen will be needed by any lawn, and that this nutrient should predominate (be 2 or 3 times as abundant as other components). Humid climates generally need potassium more than do arid ones. A good lawn fertilizer analysis for lawns in the eastern United States might be 23–5–8 or something similar.

Is an analysis such as mentioned in the previous question equally suited to young and old turf? Yes, except that in mixing fertilizer into a seed bed more phosphorus should be included (the phosphorus equaling or exceeding the other nutrients).

At what rate should I apply lawn fertilizer? Authorities suggest about 1 lb. of elemental nitrogen to each 1,000 sq. ft. (i.e., 5 lbs. of a 20 per cent nitrogen fertilizer such as 20–6–6). Follow recommendations on the bag. Lawn fertilizer directions usually indicate appropriate spreader settings.

How is lawn fertilizer best applied? If at all possible, use a spreader; it is very difficult to apply fertilizer uniformly by hand casting. See discussions under seed spreading, and use the same techniques. Follow product directions.

Is there any advantage to one chemical form or nutrient compared to another? The grass doesn't "care" just so long as the nutrient becomes available to its root system. Ammonium nitrogen is held by soil particles better than nitrate (or urea) nitrogen, but soil microorganisms are continuously oxidizing ammonium so that it becomes about equally soluble in warm weather (and may volatilize more). UF nitrogen is very stable. The sulfate of potassium rather than the usual chloride may have some advantages, sulfur typically being useful and chloride unneeded; the sulfate has a slightly lower salt index, too.

The soil of our lawn is composed of sand covered thinly with black soil. This has hardened. Would an application of fertilizer this spring help to open it up? Lime would open it up better than fertilizer. Use 60 lbs. ground limestone per 1,000 sq. ft. Follow some time later with fertilizer. Loosen soil with a spiked tamper, or tines of a fork, before application.

When is the best time to fertilize lawns? Adjust to the seasonal needs of the grass (see introductory discussion). Some species are "heavier feeders" than others, such as creeping bent grasses and 'Merion' bluegrass in the North, Bermuda grasses and some St. Augustines in the South. Six or more pounds of elemental nitrogen may be required annually for intensively managed turfs, applied no more than 1 lb. at a time (except when controlled-release fertilizer is used). Pace fertilization throughout the growing season, keeping in mind that fertility is not lost from heavy soils when cold (below about 50° F. nitrogen mostly becomes fixed; you can advantageously feed northern lawns in cold weather).

Does fertilizer have to be "watered in" after application? Not with most modern formulations; even soluble forms are generally prilled (not dusty) and roll off grass foliage to the soil, hardly risking burn. There is no risk with organic or ureaform types of nitrogen, but other salts of a complete fertilizer may adhere to damp foliage; then a sprinkling will insure against burn. Used on dry turf, few present-day lawn fertilizers need immediate watering-in. Of course, when rain fails to appear, you will want to water your lawn to speed action by the fertilizer.

I bought some black material which I was told was a good lawn food, but it did no good. Was this a fertilizer? No, it probably was not fertilizer. A lot of dark materials can be sold as lawn food. Most of them are waste from manufacturing plants or virtually worthless organic matter in an advanced stage of decay. Lawn food materials should be purchased only from reliable firms.

Should shaded grass be fertilized differently from that in the sun? Conflicting forces are at play here. Many of the shade-tolerant species do not require high fertility, but on the other hand tree roots will be grabbing a good bit of the sustenance. As a general rule it is probably helpful for grass in the shade of trees to be fertilized more frequently rather than more heavily, thus taking care of the needs of both tree and grass. Of course, controlled-release fertilizer can be applied more heavily without overstimulating the grass and intensifying disease (often the *coup de grâce* for turf in the shade).

What influence do the individual fertilizer nutrients have on grass? Nitrogen stimulates growth, especially of foliage, and a deep green color. Phosphorus is necessary for general balance and good root development, and may reduce succulence that makes grass prone to disease. Potassium contributes to "tone," sturdier foliage, and winter hardiness. Insufficient minor nutrients generally cause chlorosis (blanched foliage).

Will lawn fertilization help the trees? Yes, indeed. A tree on a fertilized lawn will probably grow twice as fast as its counterpart unfertilized. Some gardeners prefer to place fertilizer more deeply in holes in the soil around the periphery of a tree. Fertilizer compressed into spikes which can be driven into the soil with a hammer has become available, eliminating the need to bore holes.

Are hardwood ashes good or not good for lawns? Hardwood

ashes promote growth and hardness of grass stems. Applied as a top-dressing, 5 to 10 lbs. per 100 sq. ft., it is a good grass fertilizer.

When should lime and wood ashes be put on the lawn? It would not be necessary to put both on at the same time. Wood ashes contain a high percentage of lime as well as potash. Apply the lime—if needed —in late fall and the wood ashes in April from the fireplace. (See preceding question for suggested rate of application.)

Is it possible to renew an old lawn by adding fertilizer and some seed? Provided the turf has not deteriorated too seriously, a program of this sort coupled with weed eradication consistently kept up would go far to restore an old lawn. Annual dressings of compost would still further improve it.

Lawn Weed and Pest Control

What are the chief kinds of pests apt to bother a lawn? Perhaps most obvious will be weeds. Diseases are ubiquitous but more subtle, and insects are infrequently serious.

Are pests a major lawn-keeping concern? Fortunately, most lawns, if at all thrifty, endure pest attack without permanent damage and revive again seasonally. However, if *your* lawn is under fire, you will probably want to take corrective action in order to minimize damage.

Is it difficult to control pests? Yes and no! Yes, in the sense that some type of pest is always around ready to attack any time lawn resistance weakens. No, because for most pests effective controls are readily available these days.

What kind of lawn pests are most apt to give a homeowner difficulty? Probably diseases, because inoculum is ever-present and because the causal fungi are obscure; disease is usually little evident until too late. Weeds and insects are more conspicuous, and more handily controlled upon first notice by direct attack with herbicides and insecticides.

What pesticides should I stock for my lawn? This will vary with the local conditions, but almost certainly should include a phenoxy broadleaf weedkiller (usually 2, 4-D in combination with Silvex or Dicamba); an approved (biodegradable) insecticide such as malathion, carbaryl, or dursban, for emergencies; possibly a fungicide, if your lawn is prone to seasonal disease attack of serious proportions.

Can such pesticides be readily procured?   Compounds mentioned are available at retail as this is written, but new restrictions are being considered in some states making uncertain what pesticides will be available on a continuing basis. Check local informational sources.

Why is it difficult to procure useful lawn pesticides?   Environmental concern has given pesticides a "bad press"; harmless products are often considered environmental pollutants, along with harmful ones, even though only a few pesticides have been proved deleterious under *normal* usage.

How are lawn pesticides best applied?   This varies with the pest and the product. Many pesticides are impregnated on granular materials and can be applied to the lawn with a seeder-spreader. Crabgrass preventers, weed-and-feed products, some broadleaf herbicides, a few fungicides and insecticides are examples. As a rule, however, sprays coat vegetation more fully and economically than will granulars. Most weedkillers (as contrasted to preventers operating in soil) and the great majority of fungicides and insecticides are more efficient as sprays. A good pressure sprayer is about as essential around the home as is a seeder-spreader. Pesticide dusts are little used on the lawn because of their tendency to drift. Granular materials often depend upon volatilization to protect foliage not directly contacted; for more certain foliage coverage, spray materials (wettable powders and liquids) are usually preferred.

Will pesticides toxify the soil?   Most pesticides are inactivated in soil or are broken down by soil microorganisms in short order. A few, especially if containing heavy metals, can build up to toxic levels with repeated use. Some organic types are fairly slow to break down or dissipate, perhaps requiring a year or more before their influence is no longer felt. Most soils are highly buffered and subject to great insult before their biological balance is upset. The majority of pesticides cause only temporary soil toxicity or none at all. Always observe cautions on the label before using any pesticide.

WEEDS

What are the most frequent weed pests?   These will vary from region to region. They are apt to be more diverse in the South, more abundant (as a particular species) in the North. Several broadleaf weeds (particularly dandelion, plantain, chickweed, knotweed, clover) are widespread in lawns, but are readily controlled with phenoxy chemicals. Annual grasses, such as crab grass and foxtail, are abundant, too, but are controllable with preventers and post-emergent sprays. The perennial grasses, such as tall fescues and other forage species, are perhaps not so prevalent, but nonetheless are really the worst lawn weeds (because they are difficult to control selectively). Ordinarily a general herbicide that kills back all vegetation must be used to stop perennial grasses, and be followed by replanting.

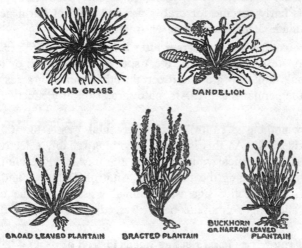

CRAB GRASS   DANDELION

BROAD LEAVED PLANTAIN   BRACTED PLANTAIN   BUCKHORN OR NARROW LEAVED PLANTAIN

SOME COMMON LAWN WEEDS

What is the herbicide for broadleaf weeds?   Phenoxy compounds, of which 2, 4-D is the most familiar and most economical; some broadleaf (dicotyledonous) weeds are resistant to 2, 4-D, but succumb if a bit of Silvex, Dicamba, or something similar is combined with the 2, 4-D.

When are dandelions, plantains, and similar broadleaf weeds best treated?   Weeds are more susceptible to weedkillers when young or when vigorously growing; 2, 4-D (but not Dicamba) is apt to be more efficient in reasonably warm weather. Thus, for summer weeds, treatment in spring might be most efficient, although hazards to budding ornamentals are greater then than later. Winter weeds, like cresses, are best treated in autumn. If weeding is needed at a less opportune season, increase the herbicide strength.

What about crab-grass prevention?   A number of very effective crab-grass preventers are on the market, applied in spring before crab-grass seed sprouts (crab grass germinates when soil temperature rises above 50° F.). The materials must be used exactly as directed, be spread uniformly to blanket the soil (since they affect only sprouting seed, not growing plants). Most preventers are 90 per cent effective or better; examples include bensulide, benefin, DCPA, siduron, terbutol, and others. Overapplication sometimes retards rooting of the permanent grass, so be judicious about repeated application. Siduron is fairly specific for crab grass and will not harm new lawn seedings made at the same time as treatment.

Is there control for crab grass after it has sprouted?   Yes, two or three arsonate (AMA, DSMA, etc.) sprays made a week or ten days apart should kill crab grass and certain other annual grasses without injuring the permanent turf. Arsonates are also fairly effective against nut sedge.

Is there nothing to control weedy perennial grasses like tall fescue and quackgrass?   As this is written, nothing reliably selective. That is, there is no chemical which will kill the unwanted perennial grass without also damaging the turf grass. Amitrol, Dalapon, and similar herbicides are effective against perennial grasses, but the chemical must be allowed to dissipate before reseeding or planting the lawn grass.

Would you advise hand digging weeds instead of using a herbicide?   For a few weeds—yes. Also, hand digging is obviously appropriate for weeds for which there is no selective herbicidal control, such as clumps of tall fescue, nimble Will, or small patches of any unwanted perennial.

Are herbicides hazardous to animal life?   Scarcely, although of course they shouldn't be ingested or carelessly handled. Herbicides are probably the least likely of the pesticides to harm animals, or to cause irreversible ecological change.

Is there a specific weedkiller for wild garlic (or wild onion— I don't know which) which comes up in clumps in my lawn? I've tried hand digging, but can't keep up with it. Each spring there seem to be more clumps. Repeat treatments with 2, 4-D and/or Dicamba will eliminate onion or garlic (both are *Allium*) if made in early spring (and perhaps again in autumn, if the weeds persist).

I am tired of my zoysia lawn and would like to start over fresh with a 'Merion' bluegrass-fescue mixture. But how can I get rid of the zoysia? It appears to be indestructible. Probably best would be to have the sod removed. The zoysia could be killed chemically (see renovation), but dense sod left in place, even if dead, is difficult to seed into. In bluegrass climates zoysia is ordinarily not so aggressive as to become a troublesome weed.

Aren't there natural controls for weeds? Letting the lawn dry out occasionally (rather than keeping it continuously moist) helps restrain water-loving weeds; some years favor certain weeds over others (we experience good and bad nimble Will years, for example, and see appreciable tall fescue killed some winters). Many weeds in a new lawn will surely be squeezed out as the grass matures, a transition aided by proper fertilization. But nature dislikes monoculture and leans toward diversification, so some weeds are inevitable.

DISEASES

Are lawn diseases particularly a problem? They are ubiquitous, especially in lawns not planted with disease-resistant cultivars. Most of the time, however, diseases weaken turf rather than killing it outright, and the grass snaps back as weather conditions change. Disease prevention is burdensome (usually repeated fungicide application is required to keep new foliage covered), costly, and difficult for an inexperienced person to time properly (by the time damage is obvious, the disease has probably run its course).

What brings on a disease attack? Several conditions favorable to the disease must coincide. The weather and season must be appropriate, the lawn must be physiologically susceptible, and the pathogen must be present and in an active phase. Most fungi are quite particular! Disease is generally favored by monoculture, generous fertilization, wet weather (some diseases like it hot, some cool), and, of course, by a handy source of inoculum.

How is lawn disease best checked?   Fortunately, changes from moist to dry weather, or in temperature, or in seasonal rhythm of the pathogen, do much to end attack. The gardener, of course, can help check diseases. He can apply a fungicide *before* the disease has made serious inroads (it is necessary to anticipate on the basis of weather and past experience when a disease is likely to attack). He can also withhold water and reduce fertilization (especially soluble nitrogen).

What particular diseases should be looked out for?   Hundreds of diseases can attack turf, and you should consult a book or pamphlet picturing different diseases and detailing measures for their control for specific information. Bluegrass lawns often suffer leafspot in the cool weather of spring (this may change to crown-rot in summer), and depending upon cultivar may suffer a serious attack of stripe smut or *Fusarium* patch in summer. Bent grasses often come down with brownpatch in warm weather, snowmold in winter. Rust often attacks rye grass and other species, especially in autumn; and mildew, almost any grass in the shade. Fine fescues often die in patches in hot weather (especially if the soil is wet) and this is often attributed to "disease." Diseases attacking southern grasses are even more profligate than in the North. Check with local authorities, such as a county agent.

Can I identify diseases in the lawn?   Some symptoms, such as those of leafspot, are quite evident; consulting books in which diseases are pictured (Extension Publication No. 12, *Lawn Diseases in the Midwest,* University of Nebraska; or similar publications from other states, and from commercial companies) should help. But even the experts are uncertain about many diseases, short of isolating the fungus in a laboratory and reinoculating with it.

What do I do if my lawn is diseased?   General control measures have already been mentioned. If not too late, apply a fungicide, and in most cases reduce watering and fertilization (fertilization helps control dollarspot). If you *know* that disease is the problem, put the lawn on lean rather than generous fare, even though the latter is the normal reaction to a declining turf. If disease is chronic, consider introducing new disease-resistant cultivars into the lawn.

INSECT PESTS

Do insects often damage the lawn?   Not often, but when attacking in force they can devastate a turf almost overnight.

What are the most serious insect problems? Although there are many pests of localized importance, soil grubs (the larvae of such species as June and Japanese beetles), sod webworms (the larval stage of the lawnmoth), and chinch bugs (both juveniles and adults) are probably the three most serious lawn insects nationally.

What do I do about soil grubs? Grubs eat grass roots, and can often be identified by pulling up a section of sod (if it lifts easily like a carpet, most of its roots have been severed). An insecticide soaked into the soil is the obvious answer, but in many states restrictions prevent the sale of long-lasting insecticides such as chlordane (which has proven effective for up to ten years). A slow-acting but eventually effective cure for grubs is inoculating them with the milky spore disease.

How do we defend against sod webworms? Webworms live in silk-lined burrows deep in the sod and are seldom seen because they feed at night (they chew off the grass near soil level, leaving frass and chaff). An insecticide soaked deeply into the soil is usually the answer. However, some strains of webworm have developed resistance to insecticides used repeatedly. If so, alternate insecticides. Webworms are the larvae of lawnmoths, which are frequently seen flitting over the lawn about twilight laying eggs. Cycle from egg to moth is about one month, so that drenching the lawn with insecticide about 10 days after lawnmoths are abundant should catch most of the young webworms. Webworms are seldom prevalent enough in the first generation to be a bother, but become damaging as populations build up later in summer.

How do I check chinch bugs? Grass attacked by chinch bugs turns off color, and eventually browns in irregular patches; active insects are most abundant in adjacent green grass. They can be discovered by shaking grass over white paper, and looking for white and black (some with red spots) insects not much bigger than a pinhead. Chinch bugs suck the sap from grass culms, debilitating and eventually killing the above-ground parts. Spray insecticide well into the undamaged turf.

Are there other kinds of lawn pests besides weeds, diseases, and insects? There is no end to pests, but fortunately few others are serious. Eelworms (nematodes) are widespread, and often quite troublesome in Florida. Drenching the soil with a nematocide helps, at least for a while. Arthropods such as chiggers are often nuisances, as might be slime molds, algae, and other lower organisms.

With all of the lawn pests, it would seem that prospects for having a good lawn are not cheery.   Reciting the many troubles a lawn can have may overemphasize the negative. There are numerous things going for success, too! The favorite lawn grasses have proven themselves; they wouldn't be around if their progenitors hadn't had the stuff to fight most of their own battles. We may seduce them with soft living, but inherent toughness and the balance that nature imposes usually end blights and predations without disaster. Most lawns recover quickly from calamity, especially if aided by intelligent maintenance. It should prove possible for anyone to have an acceptable lawn in almost any location without lawn care becoming burdensome!

Moss Lawns

What is the name of the "moss" that is used for planting lawns? Will it grow anywhere?   Its botanical name is *Sagina subulata*, commonly called pearlwort. It is used extensively in the Pacific coast states. It will grow almost anywhere in the United States except the Rio Grande Valley and the region south of Fort Pierce, Florida. In extreme northern latitudes, it usually winterkills. It is not a true moss.

Does the "moss" used for lawns need a good soil?   It thrives best on a fertile soil, but it has grown well on the adobe soils south of San Francisco. Having a shallow root system, it can be surface fed like bent grass.

Is the "moss" that is used in lawns grown from seed? How is it planted?   Pearlwort is planted from divisions. Two-in. squares are planted 6 ins. apart. A quicker effect can be had by planting them 3 or 4 ins. apart. In planting the roots are well covered and firmed, and the crown (sprig) kept above the surface. However, pearlwort is most commonly used between steppingstones on a terrace or walk.

How many years can I expect a "moss" lawn (pearlwort) to last?   In a climate where no great winter cold occurs, it can last for several years.

Would the fact that "moss" has flowers add to its value in the lawn? True, it blooms very prolifically in early summer with tiny flowers on 1-in. stems and it is very pretty. The flowers, however, do not last long.

Index